IN PRAISE OF SCRIBES

In Praise of Scribes

Manuscripts and their Makers in Seventeenth-Century England

PETER BEAL

The Lyell Lectures, Oxford 1995–1996

CLARENDON PRESS · OXFORD
1998

Oxford University Press, Great Clarendon Street, Oxford OX2 6DP

Oxford New York

Athens Auckland Bangkok Bogotá Buenos Aires Calcutta
Cape Town Chennai Dar es Salaam Delhi Florence Hong Kong
Istanbul Karachi Kuala Lumpur Madrid Melbourne Mexico City
Mumbai Nairobi Paris São Paolo Singapore Taipei Tokyo Toronto Warsaw
and associated companies in
Berlin Ibadan

Oxford is a registered trade mark of Oxford University Press

Published in the United States
by Oxford University Press Inc., New York

British Library Cataloguing in Publication Data
Data available

Library of Congress Cataloging in Publication Data
Beal, Peter.
In praise of scribes: manuscripts and their makers in seventeenth
century England / Peter Beal.
(The Lyell lectures, Oxford; 1995–1996)
Includes bibliographical references and index.
1. English literature—Early modern, 1500–1700—Criticism, Textual.
2. English literature—Early modern, 1500–1700—Manuscripts.
3. Literature publishing—England—History—17th century.
4. Authors and readers—England—History—17th century.
5. Manuscripts, English—History—17th century.
6. Scriptoria—England—History—17th century.
7. Manuscripts, English—Editing.   8. Transmission of texts.
9. Scribes—England.   I. Title.
II. Series: Lyell lectures; 1995–1996.
PR438.T42B43   1998   820.9'003—dc21   97–44266
ISBN 0–19–818471–9

1 3 5 7 9 10 8 6 4 2

Typeset by Jayvee, Trivandrum, India
Printed in Great Britain
on acid-free paper by
Bookcraft Ltd,
Midsomer Norton, Somerset

Preface

Although my title, *In praise of scribes*, may be interpreted ironically—given the considerable attention paid here to the case for the prosecution—my concern *is* to establish the importance of scribes in the early modern period: to recognize them as figures at the centre of civilized life, as men to be reckoned with, and as key agents in the process of written communication and literary transmission—as men every bit as vitally productive as printers and publishers, rather than the anonymous, shadowy, marginal figures who have traditionally been ignored. Paradoxically the very notoriety of scriveners in their own time—scribes who developed a special role in the world of finance and law—argues for their significance: they were men whom their contemporaries did *not* ignore.

The five subjects chosen for discussion arise out of an interest in the manuscript culture of late sixteenth- and seventeenth-century England and in some of its sociological ramifications. For as long as I have been preoccupied with manuscripts—some twenty-three years or more—my concern has always been to consider them first and foremost as physical artefacts which have their own peculiar nature and mode of being. That is to say, a manuscript text is not simply a verbal record which happens to have been made by hand rather than by other means. Inspired by a detective's inquisitiveness, the questions I have learned always to ask are: What is this manuscript trying to tell us? Why is it constituted the way it is? What can we understand from it about the circumstances of, and reasons for, its production? And how should we be dealing with this evidence? From the manuscripts themselves, and the texts they bear, arises a natural curiosity about the people who wrote them—in some cases, spending their lives writing them— and about the people who read them: the society in and for which they were written, and the function they played there. It is inevitable, too, that one should wonder about the relationship manuscript culture had to print culture. Our world—at least until the development of current electronic systems—has been so dominated by *printed* text that it was not so very long ago that editors could seriously wonder why it was that, after the invention of movable type in the mid-fifteenth century and the manifest advantages of printed publication, anyone should want to bother copying by hand anything of any consequence at all. Although, with the growth in recent years of manuscript studies in the early modern period, scholars are now less likely to treat its manuscripts as a curious anachronism, the task of standing traditional assumptions on their heads, and of imagining a world where manuscripts were a *normal* mode of literary communication rather than an occasional exception or aberration, has far to go.

It is probably fair, too, to recognize that a traditional impediment to the study of manuscript texts is not only the potential difficulty of reading unfamiliar earlier forms of handwriting—a situation which either more widespread tuition in palaeography, or (as in my case) simple exposure to a large range of manuscript materials and consequent learning by experience, must palliate—but also the very anomalous nature of the subject itself. The problem for scholars is partly a search for form. Besides the relatively uncharted immensity and disparateness of the surviving corpus of manuscript sources—with English manuscripts of this period being scattered throughout the world in hundreds of repositories, both public and private, not all accessible, and not all permanent—there is not even a consensus as to how they should be treated. With many, perhaps the majority of manuscripts uncatalogued, or inadequately so, and with no equivalent on the horizon of an STC or Wing to bring them all into a useful perspective, it is symptomatic that even citations of manuscripts sound invariably awkward and cumbersome—each repository, moreover, imposing a classification or call system of its own, ranging from the simplest numerical reference (MS 1, MS 2, etc.) to a heterogeneous and Byzantine amalgam of symbols denoting conditions of acquisition, location, size, date, binding, and other details more suited to catalogue descriptions, designed to serve the convenience of the library rather than its readers. This situation is not helped by the occasional decision that has been made, even by major repositories, to change for their own purposes their entire system of reference.

All things conspire, in fact, to reinforce a sense of the uniqueness of manuscript texts. Unlike printed books, which exist in multiple, wholly or virtually identical, duplicates, each manuscript is peculiar: it is physically and ontologically unique. Even multiple scribal copies of the same work, perhaps made by the same individual, are each a separate edition of that work, each one subject to contingent circumstances of production, readings and interpretation, decisions of presentation within given traditions, and the influence of contemporary readers. And when we turn to physical evidence itself—to matters of paper, ink, and its application, as well as handwritings—we become even more aware that, ultimately, for all the usefulness of modern technology, there is no substitute for the original: in the last analysis, we must handle the materials themselves—microfilms and electronic reproductions will not do. This fact makes the current drive of certain major repositories—in the interests of 'conservation' and because reproductions are mistakenly deemed to be adequate substitutes (when they should be leading readers *towards* the originals, not *away* from them)—especially unfortunate. Just when manuscript studies in the early modern period are 'up and running', it threatens to produce a generation of people who, though endowed with five senses, will never learn, or be encouraged to learn, to recognize inherent clues to interpretation or dimensions of understanding of material texts other than what is instantly transmissible on a screen.

From a concern primarily with physical and empirical evidence, abetted by a natural

suspicion of generalizations, especially theoretical ones, and by a sense of the importance of the agents of transmission in affecting the meaning and function of texts, as well
as from a fundamental interest in the wider issue of manuscript culture *vis-à-vis* print
culture, arise my topics.

In the first chapter I look briefly at the scribe—and his development in the form of
the 'scrivener'—as a figure in society, at the reputation he acquired and the reasons for
it, at evidence of the physical environment in which he lived and plied his craft, and at
aspects of his activity which distinguish him from the makers of printed books. I conclude with an account, based on fresh evidence, of 'Captain' Julian, the most notorious
purveyor of manuscripts of all, whose career towards the end of the seventeenth century may be symptomatic of what tipped the balance in favour of print rather than
manuscript as the dominant mode of literary communication.

In the second chapter I turn to a major poet, devotional writer, and maker of manuscripts, John Donne, and to his great but problematical prose treatise *Biathanatos*. I
consider his ambivalent attitude towards the media options which confronted him,
and, in light of this and a new source, examine the surviving texts of the discourse in an
attempt to discern their possible relationship, to determine the circumstances which
may have given rise to them, to speculate on the extant texts' possible witness to
Donne's original manuscript and conception of the work, and to suggest some of the
implications these considerations may have for modern editors. In this story, too,
scribes play their part.

In the third chapter I provide a case study of one particular scribe: an anonymous,
highly prolific, professional London copyist of the 1620s–1630s, whom I have christened the 'Feathery Scribe'. Besides considering him as in some measure a craftsman
in his own right, I examine the evidence for his career, for his mode of operations, and
for the nature and circle of his associates and clientele, and I argue for the importance
of his scriptorium—which was, in my view, as significant as any publishing house of the
century—in the context of the bustling ferment of ideas and their dissemination in the
years leading up to the Civil War.

In the fourth chapter I pursue this same scribe by establishing the notable part he
played in the history of one particular text: Sidney's *Letter to Queen Elizabeth* on the
proposed Alençon marriage. Sir Philip Sidney himself provides a classic example of a
major Elizabethan writer who confined himself exclusively to manuscript circulation.
His *Letter* was politically the most important work he ever wrote and the one most
extensively disseminated in manuscript form. By examining in some detail extant
examples, I seek to qualify and complement modern editorial assumptions about this
text and its transmissional complexities, to throw light both on the practical circumstances of its original production and on its variegated history—a history marked
by response to changing readership, in which form and meaning are essentially

interrelated, and which is also in many ways paradigmatic of the nature, treatment, and evolution of texts themselves in a scribal culture.

Finally, in the fifth chapter, taking advantage of recently discovered sources, chiefly manuscript, I look beyond the role of professional agents of transmission to the career of one other writer who has traditionally been regarded as a 'manuscript poet'— Katherine Philips—and I consider her attitudes towards the media options which confronted *her*. As a writer circumscribed by her social status perhaps even more than by the fact that she was a woman, and one acutely conscious of her 'virtue' and 'honour', she would find in manuscript culture, with its selective social bonding, her principal medium of literary transmission. While she ostensibly despised 'descending' to the public medium of print as much as did Sidney and Donne, her ambitions effectively vied, however, with the restraints imposed by manuscript culture. The resulting forms which her works adopted, especially after her death—in the media not only of manuscripts but also of print and the theatre—offer what, I believe, is a fascinating perspective from which to view her career, her own constructions of authorship, and her life's achievements.

To a multitude of friends and informants I am indebted for help and support of various kinds. Among those who have been most generous in their advice I must mention especially Kathy King (not least for her patient care and perceptiveness in reading my early drafts) and Hilton Kelliher (who, among other things, led me to many of the Feathery Scribe's manuscripts in the British Library). Henry Woudhuysen also kindly passed on to me some Feathery discoveries of his own. Paul Quarrie originally brought the Derby Manuscript of Restoration poems to my attention and gave me the benefit of his knowledge of bindings. Nigel Ramsay generously shared with me his discovery of the Canterbury Manuscript of *Biathanatos*, and I have also received the benefit of spirited discussions on this subject with I. A. Shapiro, now in his 93rd year, whose healthy scepticism and scrupulous scholarship have diminished not a jot. Other scholars who have kindly supplied points of information or made other contributions include Betty Hageman (whose opinions on Katherine Philips matters are invariably perceptive and welcome), Colin Tite (for relevant material on Cotton manuscripts and for leading me to some of Sir Thomas Wilson's papers), Ernest Sullivan (for comments on Donne and for drawing to my attention the notable Orinda folio in Dublin), Steven May (for checking for me some manuscripts at Harvard), Richard Hardin (for the same service in Kansas), Peter Selley (for a similar service in Dublin), James Collett-White (for searching records in Bedford on the Revd John Morris), Laetitia Yeandle (for informative comments on Folger materials), Patricia Basing (for helpful comments on Robert Beale matters), Shirley Bury (for her expert information about the Crown Jewels), and Andrew Thorol of the History of Parliament (for information about

Sir Robert Oxenbridge). For sundry other kindnesses and points of information I must express my gratitude to Peter Lindenbaum, Harold Love, Germaine Greer, Don McKenzie, John Baker, Warren Chernaik, and K. J. Höltgen.

My debt to various curators, librarians, and archivists in Britain, Ireland, and North America, as well as to certain private collectors, who answered my enquiries, supplied copies of relevant materials, or allowed me access to their holdings, is paramount. I am also, of course, greatly obliged for permission granted by respective collections for the reproduction of so many of the illustrations used in this book.

To two other persons I owe special debts. One is Mary Hobbs, whose wonderful knowledge and enthusiasm about manuscript verse miscellanies of the 1630s were such a major boost to my own engagement with literary manuscripts of this period in the mid-1970s. The other is Wayne Williams, who undertook much of the photography used for this volume and whose patience and care, in sometimes less than ideal conditions, were exemplary.

Having said all this, and written at such length on scribal matters, feathery and otherwise, I can express to the courteous reader only a hope that my treatment will be found no more exhausting than it is exhaustive. Partly with this in mind, I have endeavoured to retain here something of the oral, and occasionally colloquial, quality of the original Lyell Lectures (delivered between 14 and 28 May 1996) upon which this book is based, even though, of course, elaborating the more formal aspects of scholarly exposition where necessary. As Dick Hardin reminds me, if my presentation is too ponderous the reader will feel like the 1930s Hollywood film producer Louis B. Mayer, who became heartily tired of the vogue for historical costume dramas. 'I don't want no more scripts', he said, 'where there's a guy with a feather.'

P.B.

May 1997

Contents

List of plates xii

List of figures xxi

List of abbreviations xxii

1. In praise of scribes 1

2. 'It shall not therefore kill itself; that is, not bury itself': Donne's *Biathanatos* and its text 31

3. The Feathery Scribe 58

4. 'Hoping they shall only come to your merciful eyes': Sidney's *Letter to Queen Elizabeth* and its transmission 109

5. 'The virtuous Mrs Philips' and 'that whore Castlemaine': Orinda and her apotheosis, 1664–1668 147

Appendices

I. Seventeenth-century characters of clerks and scriveners 192

II. Manuscripts by the Feathery Scribe 211

III. Catalogue of papers in Ralph Starkey's study 269

IV. Manuscript texts of Sidney's *Letter to Queen Elizabeth* 274

V. Katherine Philips's letter to Lady Fletcher 281

VI. John Taylor's verse satire on Katherine Philips 282

Index of manuscripts cited 285

Bibliography 292

General index 307

List of plates

Plate 1. A German scriptorium shown in a woodcut in Francesco Petrarca, *Hülff Trost und Rath in allemanligen der Menschen* (Frankfurt, 1559), p. xlii   12

Plate 2. Depiction of a scribe at his desk with a client, a detail (here enlarged) in the additional engraved title-page of *The compleat clark, and scriveners guide* (London, 1655)   14

Plate 3. Title-page of the first printed edition of William Lambarde's *Archeion* (here spelt *Archion*), 4to, 1635   16

Plate 4. Title-page of a folio manuscript copy of William Lambarde's *Archeion*, *c.*1620s–1630s. Reproduced by courtesy of Professor J. H. Baker, St Catharine's College, Cambridge   17

Plate 5. Flyleaf of the Derby Manuscript of poems on affairs of state, showing inscriptions by the ninth and tenth Earls of Derby (in a private collection). Reproduced by permission. Copyright reserved   21

Plate 6. Knowsley Hall, Lancashire, as shown in a mid-seventeenth- century print reproduced in *Private devotions and miscellanies of James seventh Earl of Derby, K.G.*, ed. Revd F. R. Raines, volume i (Chetham Society 66, 1867), after p. clx   22

Plate 7. An opening of the Derby Manuscript (pp. 108–9) showing the end of 'Nobilitas sola atq[ue] unica virtus' and the beginning of Andrew Marvell's 'On the Statue in the Stock's Markett' (in a private collection). Reproduced by permission. Copyright reserved   22

Plate 8. The contemporary binding on the Derby Manuscript (in a private collection). Reproduced by permission. Copyright reserved   23

Plate 9. Pages 100–1 in the Derby Manuscript, showing verses on Charles II and the CABAL added in the hand of the ninth Earl of Derby (in a private collection). Reproduced by permission. Copyright reserved   24

Plate 10. Page 120 in the Derby Manuscript, showing annotations to the Earl of Dorset's poem 'The Game att Chess' made by the ninth and tenth Earls of Derby (in a private collection). Reproduced by permission. Copyright reserved   26

Plate 11. Pages 178–9 in the Derby Manuscript, showing the last page of the main text in the hand of the original scribe and one page in the hand of a second scribe (in a private collection). Reproduced by permission. Copyright reserved   27

Plate 12. Pages 186–7 in the Derby Manuscript, showing the beginning of the last poem written in the hand of a third scribe (in a private collection). Reproduced by permission. Copyright reserved   27

Plate 13. The last two pages of the 'Index' at the end of the Derby Manuscript, showing additions made by the ninth and tenth Earls of Derby, as well as by the second scribe (in a private collection). Reproduced by permission. Copyright reserved 28

Plate 14. Autograph letter of presentation signed by Donne to Edward Herbert opposite the title-page of the Herbert Manuscript of *Biathanatos* which is in the hand of an amanuensis (Bodleian Library, Oxford, MS e. Mus. 131, pp. x–xi). Reproduced by permission of the Bodleian Library 33

Plate 15. Two facing pages in the Herbert Manuscript of *Biathanatos* (Bodleian Library, Oxford, MS e. Mus. 131, pp. 214–15). Reproduced by permission of the Bodleian Library 36

Plate 16. Two facing pages in the Canterbury Manuscript of *Biathanatos* (Canterbury Cathedral, U210/2/2, pp. 158–9). Reproduced by permission of the Dean and Chapter of Canterbury 39

Plate 17. A page of the preliminaries in the Canterbury Manuscript of *Biathanatos* (Canterbury Cathedral, U210/2/2, p. [iii]). Reproduced by permission of the Dean and Chapter of Canterbury 41

Plate 18. Page 89 of the Quarto edition of *Biathanatos* [1647], shown with one paragraph boxed off by the present editor 42

Plate 19. Page 64 of the Canterbury Manuscript of *Biathanatos*, shown with the same paragraph boxed off by the present editor (Canterbury Cathedral, U210/2/2, p. 64). Reproduced by permission of the Dean and Chapter of Canterbury 43

Plate 20. A page of the preliminaries in the Canterbury Manuscript of *Biathanatos* (Canterbury Cathedral, U210/2/2, p. 3). Reproduced by permission of the Dean and Chapter of Canterbury 46

Plate 21. A page of the preliminaries in the Canterbury Manuscript of *Biathanatos* (Canterbury Cathedral, U210/2/2, p. [viii]). Reproduced by permission of the Dean and Chapter of Canterbury 48

Plate 22. Page 28 of the Quarto edition of *Biathanatos* [1647] 50

Plate 23. Page 10 of the Canterbury Manuscript of *Biathanatos* (Canterbury Cathedral, U210/2/2, p. 10). Reproduced by permission of the Dean and Chapter of Canterbury 51

Plate 24. Flyleaf inscribed by Sir Robert Harry Inglis opposite the title-page of the Canterbury Manuscript of *Biathanatos* (Canterbury Cathedral, U210/2/2). Reproduced by permission of the Dean and Chapter of Canterbury 56

Plate 25. Part of a page in the Feathery Scribe's copy of *A Breiffe Discours off: the Lowe Countryes* (Collection of Dr Peter Beal, London, MS 2, f. [4r]) 59

Plate 26. First page of Feathery's copy of *A Breiffe Discours off: the Lowe Countryes* (Collection of Dr Peter Beal, London, MS 2, f. [1r]) 61

Plate 27. Feathery's title-page in a copy of the Earl of Northampton's *An: Aunswere, to, the, Coppye of a Rayleinge Invectyve (against, the Regyment of woemen in*

generall) (Cambridge University Library, Add. MS 9276, No. 7). Reproduced by
permission of the Syndics of Cambridge University Library   64

Plate 28. Last page of Feathery's copy of Sir Walter Ralegh's *A: Discours: Touchinge
a Marryage, Betwene Prince Henrye of England, And, a Daughter of Savoye*
(Cambridge University Library, Add. MS 9276, No. 15). Reproduced by
permission of the Syndics of Cambridge University Library   65

Plate 29. A page showing the date at the end of Feathery's copy of *The Three Greate
Kingdoms of England, ffraunce, and Spayne* (National Library of Wales, Aberystwyth,
Castell Gorfod MS 1, f. 32v). Reproduced by permission of The National Library
of Wales   65

Plate 30. Last page of Feathery's copy of Sir Edward Littleton's *Argum^te:
Concerning the personall Libtye of the Subiecte beffore the Lordes & Comons in the
Painted Chamber And Reported . . . the 19. of Aprill 1628* (British Library, London,
Harley MS 161, f. 195r). Reproduced by permission of the British Library Board   66

Plate 31. First page of Feathery's copy of George Puttenham's *Discourse* on the
execution of Mary Queen of Scots (Bodleian Library, Oxford, MS Tanner 108,
f. 1r). Reproduced by permission of the Bodleian Library   68

Plate 32. Last page of Feathery's copy of Samuel Daniel's *A: Breuiarye, of the,
Historie, of, Englande* (Folger Shakespeare Library, Washington, DC, MS G. b. 9,
f. 205r). Reproduced by permission of the Folger Shakespeare Library   69

Plate 33. Last page of Feathery's copy of *The, Life, and, manner, of, Death: of . . .
John: ffisher, Bishop of, Rochester* (Bodleian Library, Oxford, MS Tanner 108,
f. 181r). Reproduced by permission of the Bodleian Library   70

Plate 34. First page of Feathery's copy of *Certayne Replyes and: Obiections,
Aunswered: by Willm Lord Burleigh, Att the Councell: Table* (Collection of Dr Peter
Beal, London, MS 1, f. [2r])   71

Plate 35. Feathery's note on payments received on a leaf attached to his copy of
Sir Robert Cotton's *An: Aunswere, made: by Comaund of prince Henreye, to Certayne
proposicons, of Warre; and peace* (Yale University, New Haven, Osborn Collection,
b 180). Reproduced by permission of the James Marshall and Marie-Louise Osborn
Collection, Beinecke Book and Manuscript Library, Yale University   71

Plate 36. Overall view of an indenture written chiefly by Feathery and signed by
Robert Tichborne and Thomas Grinsell, 30 June 1635 (William Salt Library,
Stafford, M 527). Original size *c.*442 × 524 mm. Reproduced by permission of the
Trustees of the William Salt Library, Stafford   73

Plate 37. Portion of the 1635 indenture showing the change of hand at the bottom
right (William Salt Library, Stafford, M 527). Reproduced by permission of the
Trustees of the William Salt Library, Stafford   73

Plate 38. Portion of the 1635 indenture showing the signatures of the witnesses, including Izaak Walton (William Salt Library, Stafford, M 527). Reproduced by permission of the Trustees of the William Salt Library, Stafford 74

Plate 39. A page in Feathery's copy of *Leicester's commonwealth* with contemporary marginal scribbling (Pierpont Morgan Library, New York, MS with MA 1475, p. 10). Reproduced by permission of the Pierpont Morgan Library 75

Plate 40. End-leaf of Feathery's copy of *Leicester's commonwealth* with contemporary scribbling (Pierpont Morgan Library, New York, MS with MA 1475, p. 231). Reproduced by permission of the Pierpont Morgan Library 76

Plate 41. Drawing of pillars watermark as it appears in Feathery's copy of Sir Charles Cornwallis's *The manner Off the: sicknes, and death of Prince Henrye* in Cambridge University Library MS Ee. 2. 32, ff. 1r–11v. Reproduced by courtesy of Hilton Kelliher 78

Plate 42. Pillars watermark, No. 3494, in Edward Heawood's *Watermarks mainly of the 17th and 18th centuries* (Hilversum, 1950), plate 476. Reproduced by courtesy of the Paper Publications Society, Hilversum, The Netherlands 78

Plate 43. Quatrefoils within circle watermark in Feathery's copy of *A Breiffe Discours off: the Lowe Countryes* (Collection of Dr Peter Beal, London, MS 2) 78

Plate 44. Bunch of grapes watermark in Feathery's copy of *Certayne Replyes and obiections Aunswered by Willm Lord Burleigh, Att the Councell Table* (Collection of Dr Peter Beal, London, MS 1) 78

Plate 45. A page in a copy of *A Councell of Warre: the xxvij° Nouembris 1587* showing a mid-sentence transfer of hands in the eleventh line from an anonymous scribe to Feathery (British Library, London, Harley MS 444, f. 111v). Reproduced by permission of the British Library Board 80

Plate 46. A page in a copy of Sir Francis Bacon's *Opinyon Touchinge the imployem^te of M^r: Suttons Charritye* showing the mid-sentence transfer of hands in the eighth line from Feathery to another scribe (British Library, London, Stowe MS 151, f. 46r). Reproduced by permission of the British Library Board 81

Plate 47. First page of a table of contents in a volume of tracts, the heading by an anonymous scribe (Feathery's 'master'), the text in Feathery's hand (British Library, London, Stowe MS 145, f. 1r). Reproduced by permission of the British Library Board 83

Plate 48. Feathery's title-page in a copy of *Obseruations Politticall: And, Civill; Wrytten, by: S^r. ffrauncis Bacon knight, &c* (Cambridge University Library, Add. MS 9276, No. 12). Reproduced by permission of the Syndics of Cambridge University Library 84

Plate 49. First page of the table of contents in a copy of *Obseruations Politticall: And, Civill; Wrytten, by: S^r. ffrauncis Bacon knight, &c*, the heading in Feathery's hand, the text by another scribe (his 'imitator') (Cambridge University Library,

Add. MS 9276, No. 12). Reproduced by permission of the Syndics of Cambridge
University Library   85

Plate 50. A page in a copy of *Obseruations Politticall: And, Civill; Wrytten, by:
Sʳ. ffrauncis Bacon knight, &c* in the hand of an anonymous scribe (Feathery's
'imitator') (Cambridge University Library, Add. MS 9276, No. 12, f. 14v).
Reproduced by permission of the Syndics of Cambridge University Library   86

Plate 51. A page in a copy of *The obiections of the kinges Councell against the
declaracon of the Comons . . . the .16.ᵗʰ of May. 1628* chiefly in the hand of Ralph
Starkey, the last twenty-seven words in Feathery's hand (British Library, London,
Harley MS 161, f. 214r). Reproduced by permission of the British Library Board   87

Plate 52. First page of a copy of *Mʳ Mason of Lincolnes Inne his speache vppon the Bill
pʳsented to the Lower Howse toucheinge the Libtye of the Subiecte the < > daye of Maye:
1628*, the heading in Feathery's hand, the text in Ralph Starkey's hand (British
Library, London, Harley MS 37, f. 275r). Reproduced by permission of the British
Library Board   93

Plate 53. Last page of a copy of *The Substance of the obiections made by mʳ Atturney
generall before a Comittie of bothe Howses . . . And the Answers . . . by mʳ Seldon the < >
of Maye 1628*, the first twelve words in Ralph Starkey's hand, the remainder in
Feathery's hand (British Library, London, Harley MS 37, f. 254v). Reproduced by
permission of the British Library Board   95

Plate 54. A page in Feathery's copy of Sir Robert Cotton's *Speech . . . att the
Councell Table the < > daye of September, 1626: Touchinge debaseinge of Coyne:* with a
contemporary reader's annotations (University of Chicago, MS 878, f. [117v]).
Reproduced by permission of the University of Chicago Library   97

Plate 55. A page in Feathery's copy of John Selden's *Englands Epinomis* with
annotations by Sir William Dugdale (Bodleian Library, Oxford, MS Dugdale 28,
f. 178r). Reproduced by permission of the Bodleian Library   98

Plate 56. A page in Feathery's copy of John Selden's *Englands Epinomis* with
marginal annotations by an unidentified contemporary reader (Bodleian Library,
Oxford, MS Dugdale 28, f. 145v). Reproduced by permission of the Bodleian
Library   99

Plate 57. A page in Feathery's compilation on the Court of Chancery showing a
late-seventeenth-century reader's extensive annotations addressed to a Lord
Chancellor (Harvard Law School Library, Cambridge, Massachusetts, MS 1034,
f. 32v). Reproduced by permission of the Law School Library, Harvard University   100

Plate 58. Feathery's copy of Henry King's poem 'The Farwell' (Bodleian Library,
Oxford, MS Rawl. D. 692, f. 111v). Reproduced by permission of the Bodleian
Library   101

Plates 59 and 60. Two facing pages in Feathery's hundred-page miscellany of
poems, including a satirical epitaph and elegy by John Donne (Bodleian Library,

Oxford, MS Rawl. poet. 31, ff. 21v–22r). Reproduced by permission of the
Bodleian Library   102–3

Plate 61. The stemma giving 'a general picture of the relationship of the texts' of
Sidney's *Letter to Queen Elizabeth* in *Miscellaneous prose of Sir Philip Sidney*,
ed. Katherine Duncan-Jones and Jan Van Dorsten (Clarendon Press: Oxford,
1973), 39. Reproduced by permission of the Delegates of the Clarendon Press   112

Plate 62. A page in Sidney's autograph manuscript of his *Defence of the Earl of
Leicester*, *c*.1585 (Pierpont Morgan Library, MA 1475, f. 6r). Reproduced by
permission of the Pierpont Morgan Library   114

Plate 63: A page in Sidney's autograph manuscript of his *Discourse on Irish
Affairs*, *c*.1577 (British Library, London, Cotton MS Titus B. XII, f. 564r).
Reproduced by permission of the British Library Board   115

Plate 64. First page of the Colbert Manuscript of Sidney's *Letter to Queen
Elizabeth*, *c*.1580s (Bibliothèque Nationale, Paris, Cinq cents de Colbert n° 466,
f. 89r). Reproduced by permission of the Bibliothèque Nationale de France   117

Plate 65. First page of the Colbert Manuscript of Sidney's *Defence of the Earl of
Leicester*, *c*.1580s (Bibliothèque Nationale, Paris, Cinq cents de Colbert n° 466,
f. 111r). Reproduced by permission of the Bibliothèque Nationale de France   118

Plate 66. First page of the Beale Manuscript of Sidney's *Letter to Queen
Elizabeth*, *c*.1580–3 (British Library, London, Add. MS 48027 [Yelverton
MS 31], f. 230r). Reproduced by permission of the British Library Board   120

Plate 67. First page of the Harington Manuscript of Sidney's *Letter to Queen
Elizabeth*, *c*.1580s (British Library, London, Add. MS 46366, f. 100r).
Reproduced by permission of the British Library Board   123

Plate 68. A page in a manuscript of Sidney's *Letter to Queen Elizabeth* in the hand
of an associate of the Feathery Scribe, *c*.1630, with an unidentified contemporary
reader's annotations (Folger Shakespeare Library, Washington, DC, MS X. d.
210, f. 3r). Reproduced by permission of the Folger Shakespeare Library   124

Plate 69. A page in a précis of Sidney's *Letter to Queen Elizabeth* among papers
probably belonging to Lord Burghley, *c*.1580 (British Library, London,
Lansdowne MS 94, f. 54r). Reproduced by permission of the British Library
Board   126

Plate 70. Title-page of a manuscript of Sidney's *Letter to Queen Elizabeth* in the
hand of the Feathery Scribe, *c*.1630 (Trinity College, Dublin, MS 732, f. 33r).
Reproduced by permission of the Board of Trinity College Dublin   133

Plate 71. First page of a manuscript of Sidney's *Letter to Queen Elizabeth* in the
hand of Ralph Starkey, *c*.1620s (British Library, London, Cotton MS Caligula
E. XII, f. 25r). Reproduced by permission of the British Library Board   135

Plate 72. Last page of a manuscript of Sidney's *Letter to Queen Elizabeth* in the

hand of the Feathery Scribe, *c.*1630 (Trinity College, Dublin, MS 732, f. 45r).
Reproduced by permission of the Board of Trinity College Dublin   137

Plate 73. A page in a manuscript of Sidney's *Letter to Queen Elizabeth* in the hand
of the Feathery Scribe, *c.*1630s (Trinity College, Dublin, MS 588, f. 10v).
Reproduced by permission of the Board of Trinity College Dublin   138

Plates 74 and 75. Two facing pages in a manuscript of Sidney's *Letter to Queen
Elizabeth* in the hand of the Feathery Scribe, *c.*1630s (British Library, London,
Harley MS 1323, ff. 54v–55r). Reproduced by permission of the British Library
Board   140–1

Plates 76 and 77. Two facing pages in a manuscript of Sidney's *Letter to Queen
Elizabeth* in the hand of the Feathery Scribe, *c.*1630s (Somerset Record Office,
Taunton, DD/AH/51/1/3, ff. 51v–52r). Reproduced by permission of the
Somerset Record Office   144–5

Plates 78 and 79. Contemporary transcript of John Taylor's satirical poem 'To
M[rs] K: P:' (University College London, MS Ogden 42, pp. 225–6). Reproduced
by permission of University College London   152–3

Plate 80. The first two commendatory poems, by Katherine Philips and the
Earl of Monmouth, in *Comedies tragi-comedies, with other poems, by M[r] William
Cartwright* (London, for Humphrey Moseley: 1651)   156

Plate 81. Henry Lawes's setting of a poem by Katherine Philips in his *Ayres and
dialogues, the second book* (London, for John Playford: 1655)   157

Plate 82. Printed broadside of Katherine Philips's poem on the arrival of
Catherine of Braganza (London, for Henry Herringman: 1662) (Worcester
College, Oxford). Reproduced by permission of the Provost and Fellows of
Worcester College, Oxford   158

Plate 83. Title-page of *Poems, by several persons* (Dublin, 1663) (Folger
Shakespeare Library, Washington, DC, C6681.5). Reproduced by permission
of the Folger Shakespeare Library   159

Plate 84. Last page of the Index in *Poems, by several persons* (Dublin, 1663)
(Folger Shakespeare Library, Washington, DC, C6681.5). Reproduced by
permission of the Folger Shakespeare Library   160

Plate 85. First page of Lord Orrery's poem 'To Orinda' in *Poems, by several
persons* (Dublin, 1663) (Folger Shakespeare Library, Washington, DC,
C6681.5). Reproduced by permission of the Folger Shakespeare Library   161

Plate 86. Title-page and imprimatur leaf of Marriott's unauthorized *Poems by
the incomparable, Mrs. K.P.*, 1664 (Huntington Library, San Marino, California,
RB 147220). Reproduced by permission of the Huntington Library   162

Plate 87. The tomb of Margaret Cavendish, Duchess of Newcastle, and her
husband William, Duke of Newcastle, in the north transept of Westminster Abbey   166

Plate 88. The effigy of Margaret Cavendish on her tomb in Westminster Abbey   167

Plate 89. A side panel on the tomb of the Duke and Duchess of Newcastle in
Westminster Abbey   168

Plates 90 and 91. First and last pages of Polexander's three-page dedication in
the Rosania Manuscript (National Library of Wales, Aberystwyth, NLW
MS 776B, pp. 5, 7). Reproduced by permission of The National Library of Wales   170–1

Plate 92. Black morocco sombre binding on the Rosania Manuscript (National
Library of Wales, Aberystwyth, NLW MS 776B). Reproduced by permission of
The National Library of Wales   172

Plate 93. A characteristic page of text, showing the beginning of 'Rosania
shaddowed', in the Rosania Manuscript (National Library of Wales,
Aberystwyth, NLW MS 776B, p. 274). Reproduced by permission of The
National Library of Wales   173

Plate 94. Title-page of Herringman's folio edition of Katherine Philips's *Poems*,
1667   174

Plate 95. Frontispiece, engraved by William Faithorne, in Herringman's folio
edition of Katherine Philips's *Poems*, 1667   176

Plate 96. Frontispiece depicting Margaret Cavendish, Duchess of Newcastle, by
Abraham van Diepenbeke, engraved by Peter van Schuppen, in her *The worlds
olio* (London, 1655)   177

Plate 97. Contemporary red morocco gilt binding on a copy of Herringman's
folio edition of Katherine Philips's *Poems*, 1667 (Huntington Library, San
Marino, California, RB 144857). Reproduced by permission of the Huntington
Library   179

Plate 98. Sir Peter Lely's portrait of Lady Castlemaine as the goddess Minerva
(Collection of Her Majesty the Queen, Hampton Court). Reproduced by
permission of The Royal Collection (c) 1998 Her Majesty Queen Elizabeth II   181

Plate 99. Cast-list of *Horace* written by the second Earl of Bridgewater in a copy
of Herringman's folio edition of Katherine Philips's *Poems*, 1667 (Harvard
University, Cambridge, Massachusetts, Houghton Library, fEC65.P5397.667p).
Reproduced by permission of the Houghton Library, Harvard University   183

Plate 100. Cast-list of *Horace* written in a copy of Herringman's folio edition of
Katherine Philips's *Poems*, 1667 (Trinity College, Dublin, Old Library, V.ee.4,
sig. Aaaaᵛ). Reproduced by permission of the Board of Trinity College Dublin   183

Plate 101. Prologue to *Horace* written in a copy of Herringman's folio edition of
Katherine Philips's *Poems*, 1667 (Trinity College, Dublin, Old Library, V.ee.4,
after p. 112 at end). Reproduced by permission of the Board of Trinity College
Dublin   186

Plate 102. Epilogue to *Horace* written in a copy of Herringman's folio edition of

Katherine Philips's *Poems*, 1667 (Victoria & Albert Museum, London, National Art Library, Dyce Collection, Dyce Catalogue No. 7416; Pressmark D.23.A.33 Folio). Reproduced by courtesy of the Board of Trustees of the Victoria & Albert Museum   189

Plate 103. Epilogue to *Horace* written in a copy of Herringman's folio edition of Katherine Philips's *Poems*, 1667 (Trinity College, Dublin, Old Library, V.ee.4, after p. 112 at end). Reproduced by permission of the Board of Trinity College Dublin   189

List of figures

1. Watermark in the Canterbury Manuscript of *Biathanatos*   41
2. Hypothetical stemma of texts of *Biathanatos*   54
3. Typical spellings by the Feathery Scribe   63
4. 'Ship's pilot' passage in Sidney's *Letter to Queen Elizabeth*   112
5. 'Ivy knot' passage in Sidney's *Letter to Queen Elizabeth*   127
6. Stemma of selected texts of Sidney's *Letter to Queen Elizabeth* 134

List of abbreviations

Baker, *CUL*	J. H. Baker, with J. S. Ringrose, *A catalogue of English legal manuscripts in Cambridge University Library* (Woodbridge, 1996)
Baker, *USA*, ii	J. H. Baker, *English legal manuscripts in the United States of America: A descriptive list, part ii: Early modern and modern periods (1558–1902)* (London, 1990)
Bald	R. C. Bald, *John Donne: A life* (Oxford, 1970)
BC	*Book Collector*
Berry	*John Stubbs's Gaping gulf with letters and other relevant documents*, ed. Lloyd E. Berry (Charlottesville, Va., 1968)
BIHR	*Bulletin of the Institute of Historical Research*
BL	The British Library
BLJ	*British Library Journal*
BMQ	*British Museum Quarterly*
Boswell	Eleanore Boswell, *The Restoration court stage (1660–1702)* (London, 1932; reprinted 1966)
Braunmuller	A. R. Braunmuller, *A seventeenth-century letter-book: A facsimile edition of Folger MS. V.a.321* (Newark, NJ, 1983)
Briquet	C. M. Briquet, *Les filigranes*: The New Briquet. Jubilee Edition. General Editor J. S. G. Simmons. A facsimile of the 1907 edition with supplementary material contributed by a number of scholars, ed. Allan Stevenson, 4 vols. (Amsterdam, 1968)
Churchill	W. A. Churchill, *Watermarks in paper in Holland, England, France, etc. in the XVII and XVIII centuries and their interconnection* (Amsterdam, 1935)
Commons debates 1621	*Commons debates 1621*, ed. Wallace Notestein, Frances Helen Relf, and Hartley Simpson, 7 vols. (New Haven, 1935)
Commons debates 1626	*Proceedings in Parliament 1626*, ed. William B. Bidwell and Maija Jansson, 4 vols. (New Haven, 1991–6)
Commons debates 1628	*Commons debates 1628*, ed. Robert C. Johnson, Maija JanssonCole, Mary Frear Keeler, and William B. Bidwell, 6 vols. (New Haven, 1977–83) [last two volumes of the series retitled *Proceedings in Parliament 1628*]
Commons debates 1629	*Commons debates for 1629*, ed. Wallace Notestein and Frances Helen Relf (Minneapolis, 1921)
Cottoni posthuma	J[ames] H[owell], *Cottoni posthuma: Divers choice pieces of that renowned antiquary Sir Robert Cotton, knight and baronet* (London, 1651)
Crum	*First-line index of English poetry 1500–1800 in manuscripts of the Bodleian Library Oxford*, ed. Margaret Crum, 2 vols. (Oxford, 1969)
CSPD	Calendar of State Papers Domestic (in the Public Record Office)

CUL	Cambridge University Library
DNB	*Dictionary of national biography*
Donne, *Letters* (1651)	John Donne, *Letters to severall persons of honour* (London, 1651)
Draper	Peter Draper, *The house of Stanley* (Ormskirk, 1864)
Duncan-Jones, *Sidney*	Katherine Duncan-Jones, *Sir Philip Sidney: Courtier poet* (New Haven, 1991)
Duncan-Jones & Van Dorsten	*Miscellaneous prose of Sir Philip Sidney*, ed. Katherine Duncan-Jones and Jan Van Dorsten (Oxford, 1973)
E&S	*Essays & Studies*
ELN	*English Language Notes*
ELR	*English Literary Renaissance*
EMS	*English Manuscript Studies 1100–1700*
Evelyn	*The diary of John Evelyn*, ed. E. S. De Beer, 6 vols. (Oxford, 1955)
Feuillerat	*The prose works of Sir Philip Sidney*, ed. Albert Feuillerat, 4 vols. (Cambridge, 1912; reprinted 1968)
Fontes Harleiani	*Fontes Harleiani*, ed. Cyril Ernest Wright (London, 1972)
Gaudriault	Raymond Gaudriault, *Filigranes et autres caractéristiques des papiers fabriqués en France aux XVIIe et XVIIIe siècles* (Paris, 1995)
GM	*Gentleman's Magazine*
Grant	Douglas Grant, *Margaret the first* (London, 1957)
Gutch	[John Gutch], *Collectanea curiosa; or Miscellaneous tracts, relating to the history and antiquities of England and Ireland*, 2 vols. (Oxford, 1781)
Harrison	G. B. Harrison (ed.), *The Letters of Queen Elizabeth* (London, 1935)
Hearne	Thomas Hearne, *A collection of curious discourses written by eminent antiquaries upon several heads in our English antiquities*, 2nd edn., 2 vols. (London, 1771)
Heawood	Edward Heawood, *Watermarks mainly of the 17th and 18th centuries* (Hilversum, 1950; reprinted 1969)
HJ	*Historical Journal*
HLB	*Harvard Library Bulletin*
HLQ	*Huntington Library Quarterly*
HMC	Historical Manuscripts Commission (i.e. Reports of the Royal Commission on Historical Manuscripts)
Index	Peter Beal, *Index of English literary manuscripts*, vol. i: *1450–1625*, parts 1 and 2 (London, 1980); vol. ii: *1625–1700*, parts 1 (1987) and 2 (1993)
JSA	*Journal of the Society of Archivists*
Kissing the rod	*Kissing the rod: An anthology of seventeenth-century women's verse*, ed. Germaine Greer, Susan Hastings, Jeslyn Medoff, and Melinda Sansone (London, 1988)
LCUTA	*Library Chronicle of the University of Texas at Austin*

Love	Harold Love, *Scribal publication in seventeenth-century England* (Oxford, 1993)
LS	*The London stage 1660–1800*, part 1: *1660–1700*, ed. William Van Lennep (Carbondale, Ill., 1965)
MLR	*Modern Language Review*
MS(S)	Manuscript(s)
Murphy	Gwendolen Murphy, *A bibliography of English character books 1608–1700* (Bibliographical Society, 1925)
Murphy, *Cabinet*	Gwendolen Murphy, *A cabinet of characters* (London, 1925)
N&Q	*Notes & Queries*
Notaries public in England	C. W. Brooks, R. H. Helmholz, and P. G. Stein, *Notaries public in England since the Reformation* (London, 1991)
OED	*Oxford English dictionary*
Parliamentary history	*The parliamentary history of England from the earliest period to the year 1803*, vol. i: *1066–1625* (London, 1806) and vol. ii: *1625–1642* (London, 1807)
PBA	*Proceedings of the British Academy*
PBSA	*Papers of the Bibliographical Society of America*
Pepys	*The diary of Samuel Pepys*, ed. Robert Latham and William Matthews, 11 vols. (London, 1970–83)
Phillipps MS	Manuscript from the collection of Sir Thomas Phillipps (1792–1872), of Middle Hill, Broadway, Worcestershire
POAS, i	*Poems on affairs of state*, vol. i, ed. George deF. Lord (New Haven, 1963)
POAS, ii	*Poems on affairs of state*, vol. ii, ed. Elias F. Mengel, Jr (New Haven, 1965)
POAS, v	*Poems on affairs of state*, vol. v, ed. William J. Cameron (New Haven, 1971)
PQ	*Philological Quarterly*
PRO	Public Record Office, Kew
Rudick & Battin	John Donne, *Biathanatos*, A modern-spelling edition, with introduction and commentary, by Michael Rudick and M. Pabst Battin (New York, 1982)
Rushworth	John Rushworth, *Historical collections*, 7 vols. (London, 1659–1701)
SB	*Studies in Bibliography*
SC	*A summary catalogue of western manuscripts in the Bodleian Library at Oxford*
SEL	*Studies in English Literature 1500–1900*
Sharpe	Kevin Sharpe, *Sir Robert Cotton 1588–1631: History and politics in early modern England* (Oxford, 1979)
Somers	*A collection of scarce and valuable tracts, on the most interesting and entertaining subjects . . . particularly that of the late Lord Somers. The second edition revised . . . by Walter Scott*, 13 vols. (London, 1809–15)
SP	*Studies in Philology*

Spedding	*The works of Francis Bacon*, ed. James Spedding, Robert Leslie Ellis, and Douglas Denon Heath, 14 vols. (London, 1857–74)
SQ	*Shakespeare Quarterly*
Starkey	'Catologue of Papers in Mr Starkys study' (see Appendix III below)
	State trials Cobbett's complete collection of state trials, [compiled by T. B. Howell and T. J. Howell], 33 vols. [and general index by David Jardine] (London, 1809–28)
STC	*A short-title catalogue of books printed in England, Scotland, & Ireland and of English books printed abroad 1475–1640*, first compiled by A. W. Pollard and G. R. Redgrave, 2nd edn. revised, begun by W. A. Jackson and F. S. Ferguson, completed by Katharine F. Pantzer, 3 vols. (London, 1976–91)
Steer, *Company of Scriveners*	Francis W. Steer, *A history of the Worshipful Company of Scriveners of London* (London, 1973)
Sullivan	*Biathanatos by John Donne*, ed. Ernest W. Sullivan II (Newark, NJ, 1984)
Thomas	*The collected works of Katherine Philips the matchless Orinda*, ed. Patrick Thomas, Germaine Greer, and R. Little, 3 vols. (Stump Cross, 1990–3)
Tite, *MS library of Cotton*	Colin G. C. Tite, *The manuscript library of Sir Robert Cotton* (London, 1994)
TLS	*Times Literary Supplement*
TN	*Theatre Notebook*
Trithemius	Johannes Trithemius, *In praise of scribes (De laude scriptorum)*, trans. Elizabeth Bryson Bongie, ed. Michael S. Batts (Alcuin Society: Vancouver, 1977)
TSWL	*Tulsa Studies in Women's Literature*
Watson	Andrew G. Watson, *The library of Sir Simonds D'Ewes* (London, 1966)
Welsby	Paul A. Welsby, *George Abbot: The unwanted archbishop 1562–1633* (London, 1962)
Wilson, *Court satires*	*Court satires of the Restoration*, ed. John Harold Wilson (Columbus, Oh., 1976)
Wing	*Short-title catalogue of books printed in England, Scotland, Ireland, Wales, and British America and of English books printed in other countries 1641–1700*, compiled by Donald Wing, 2nd edn. revised, 3 vols. (New York, 1982–94)
Worden	Blair Worden, *The sound of virtue: Philip Sidney's Arcadia and Elizabethan politics* (New Haven, 1996)
Woudhuysen	H. R. Woudhuysen, *Sir Philip Sidney and the circulation of manuscripts 1558–1640* (Oxford, 1996)
YES	*Yearbook of English Studies*

1

In praise of scribes

IN 1978, addressing some American students, the novelist Kurt Vonnegut Jr talked about what he called 'clarking' (*sic*). 'Clarking, a wholly human enterprise', he said, 'is sacred . . . Clarking is the most profound and effective form of meditation practiced on this planet . . . Why? Because clarks, by reading well, can think the thoughts of the wisest and most interesting human minds throughout all history. When clarks meditate, even if they themselves have only mediocre intellects, they do it with the thoughts of angels. What could be more sacred than that?'[1]

By 'clarks', I take it, Vonnegut means *scribes*—people, both clerics and laymen, who physically *write* or *copy* things for a living, at even the most humble, mechanical level. Though he stops short of saying that it is clerks rather than poets who are the unacknowledged legislators of the world, Vonnegut sees these lowly artisans as the people who have channelled and supported literacy in society and effectively preserved the great ideas of mankind.

Vonnegut's exalted view would have received some measure of support from the late fifteenth-century German abbot Johannes Trithemius (1462–1516). His tract *De laude scriptorum* (*In praise of scribes*) was written in the auspicious year of 1492 and (somewhat ironically) *published* in 1494.[2] 'What can I say which is praise worthy enough for a scribe?', he writes. 'Whatever I shall say does not suffice for their glory since my limited inspiration will fail before words to fit their honour are exhausted . . . A scribe distinguished by piety is the herald of God.'[3] Trithemius was reacting to the advent of the printing press, and putting up a rearguard defence of the values—both aesthetic and spiritual—of the traditional methods of copying texts by hand. He was, of course, primarily concerned with the Scriptures—and there is a constant, no doubt deliberate ambiguity in his tract in the word 'scriptura', meaning both 'writing' and 'Scriptures' in the biblical sense—although he supported the copying of secular texts too if they were morally sound. Besides arguing that it is manuscripts (on parchment or

---

[1] Kurt Vonnegut, 'Funnier on paper than most people' (address to Fredonia College, Fredonia, New York, 20 May 1978), in *Palm Sunday* (New York, 1981), 180.

[2] *De laude scriptorum* was printed in 1494 for Peter Friedberg at Mainz. The small quarto volume is printed in black letter and rubricated by hand.

[3] Johannes Trithemius, *In praise of scribes (De laude scriptorum)*, trans. Elizabeth Bryson Bongie, ed. Michael S. Batts (Alcuin Society: Vancouver, 1977), 5. All quotations from Trithemius henceforth are from this edition. The work is also published in a scholarly edition by Klaus Arnold, in a translation by Roland Behrendt, OSB (Lawrence, Kan., 1974).

vellum) rather than printed books (on paper) which will preserve texts for posterity—printing on paper, he said, was purely ephemeral—and in addition to his animated encomia on the traditional scribal skills of embellishing books—'For printed books', he says, 'are never so made that they may be considered the equal of manuscripts'[4]—Trithemius was concerned, like Vonnegut, with the psychology of copying—with its laudable effect both on civilized society and on the scribe himself. To his mind, the scribe is not performing a purely mechanical task. He has a special relationship with his texts and their meaning—a deep and incalculably beneficial engagement with them—which cannot be reproduced in any other process. 'Sitting in peace and solitude', he says, the scribe 'is gradually led thereby to an understanding of [their] mysteries, then inwardly in his heart he is greatly enlightened. For those things that we copy we impress more deeply in the mind.'[5] The words of Scripture and the process of copying become, in effect, one and the same thing: a spiritual exercise in which there is no dissociation of functions. Trithemius' scribe, like Vonnegut's clerk, is inspired with the thoughts of angels.

Unfortunately for Trithemius, his monks at Sponheim disagreed with him. After over a decade of reluctantly acquiescing in his regime, they found the task of constant copying both irksome and pointless. The monks finally rebelled against him in 1505, and he was obliged to leave the monastery.

And so followed the much-vaunted, so-called '*triumph* of the printing press' throughout Europe—which, as one eulogist of printers wrote in 1663, put 'Books into every mans hand', and compared with which the *pen* was 'but as a Rush-candle to a Torch'.[6] In fact, an awful lot of rush-candles did continue to burn—for over two centuries—and the age of the scribe was nowhere near over. Nevertheless, the expulsion of Trithemius, a matter of no great significance in itself, signals a notable development. The age of the pious monastic copyist *was* over. The secular scribe, the professional scribe, the scribe who stepped down from the sanctity of the cloisters into the hurly-burly of the market-place—his was the future.[7]

---

[4] Trithemius, 21.   [5] Ibid. 19.

[6] *A brief discourse concerning printing and printers* (London, 1663) [Wing B4578], 22–3.

[7] The generalized picture of the 'scribe' I present in this overview obviously simplifies the complex details of historical development of the clerk/scrivener in his various professional roles and functions—at Court, in government administration, in the service of particular noblemen, or of stationers, notaries, lawyers, usurers, or independent entrepreneurs—from humble copyist (of the 'Court letter' or 'text letter') to legal conveyancer and financial broker, precursor of the modern stockbroker and banker. Among relevant studies of aspects of this history might be noted Sir William Holdsworth, *A history of English law*, 16 vols. (London, 1924), vi. 446–8; H. C. Gutteridge, 'The origin and historical development of the profession of notaries public in England', in *Cambridge legal essays written in honour of . . . Doctor Bond, Professor Buckland and Professor Kenny* (Cambridge, 1926), 123–37; R. D. Richards, *The early history of banking in England* (London, 1929), 14–18; D. C. Coleman, 'London scriveners and the estate market in the later seventeenth century', *Economic History Review*, 2nd ser. 4 (1951–2), 221–30 ('The scrivener . . . to-day, is stockbroker, estate agent, banker, solicitor, accountant, clerk'); Frank T. Melton, *Sir Robert Clayton and the origins of English deposit banking, 1658–1685* (Cambridge, 1986); Eric Kerridge, *Trade and banking in early modern England* (Manchester, 1988); Norman Jones, *God and the moneylenders: Usury and law in early modern England* (Oxford, 1989), ch. 7, 175–98 (charting the steps by which usury came reluctantly to be accepted for practical reasons, and regulated, in 1604–24); Nigel Ramsay, 'Forgery and the rise of the London Scriveners' Company', in Robin Myers and Michael Harris (eds.), *Fakes and frauds* (Winchester, 1989), 99–108 (con-

Not least notable in his progress was the multiplicity, overlapping, and blurring of his functions. The word 'scribe' is perhaps the nearest we are going to get to a neutral term denoting someone who simply writes or copies something by hand, for whatever purpose. Every other term carries with it a parcel of associations—'clerk', 'secretary', 'scrivener', and so on.[8] This is because the scribe no longer *was* neutral. As he entered the world of business—most especially that of the law and finance—he came to be *identified* with that world: he might even come, unexpectedly, to play a crucial role in it.

For at the centre of it all—in what is still, essentially, a manuscript culture, for all the growth of the printing press—is a sense of the power, the potential importance and consequentiality of manuscripts themselves, and therefore of their makers, in civilized society.[9]

It was by means of *manuscripts* that you corresponded with your fellow human beings at long distance and conducted business and administration—local, civic, or national; ecclesiastical, military, and all matters of state—as well as personal, private communications. It was with carefully drawn up documents that you sealed legal agreements, bought, sold, rented, leased, and entailed land and property: establishing the very bases of practical security. It was with a document that you made known and secured the enactment of your wishes and bequests after death. In the most dramatic of cases, it might even be a simple document which *determined* death: the execution warrant. 'Look, with a spot I damn him,' says Mark Antony in *Julius Caesar* (IV. i. 6), when he,

sidering the need for regulation which gave rise to the Scriveners' Company in the 14th century, their development as money brokers signalling the extent to which the profession was trusted); Peter Earle, *The making of the English middle classes: Business, society and family life in London, 1660–1730* (London, 1989), 48–9; C. W. Brooks, R. H. Helmholz, and P. G. Stein, *Notaries public in England since the Reformation* (London, 1991); and Woudhuysen, 52–66; as well as Francis W. Steer, *A history of the Worshipful Company of Scriveners of London* (London, 1973), and his *Scriveners' Company Common Paper 1357–1628* (London Record Society, 1968).

[8] Besides the specific equation of the Latin 'scriptor' with the English 'scrivener' (found, for instance, in deeds of 1692 involving the London scrivener Humphrey Bowyer: Suffolk Record Office, Ipswich, HA 93/2/3174), the flexibility and changing meanings of terms defining or applied to the scribe and his role(s) are encountered in numerous instances. One example is the definition of a 'Bibliographer' in Thomas Blount's *Glossographia* (London, 1656), as 'a writer of books, a Scrivener'. Another is the 'scrivener' who appears in the early manuscript of the Duke of Newcastle's play *The country captain* (BL Harley MS 7650, p. 40), who, in the 1649 printed version (p. 8), has been transmogrified into a 'solicitor'. When James I was considering new methods of raising money from the rental of lands, Sir Robert Flood was twitted by Sir John Bennet for wanting to 'make the kinge a scryvener' (*Commons debates 1621*, v. 291). One later satirist symptomatically referred to 'this Scrivener, Pettifogger or what other name you will call him by (for you cannot call him bad enough)': Richard Head, *Proteus redivivus* (London, 1675), 281. While, like a traditional but essentially conservative trade union, the Company of Scriveners in this period strove to maintain control over both the role and professional conduct of scriveners, it is likely that the vast majority of the scribes encountered in surviving documents had no connection with this guild.

[9] For a historical account of, *inter alia*, the means by which writing (i.e. literacy) becomes an instrument of domination in society, see especially Henri-Jean Martin, *The history and power of writing* [1988], trans. Lydia G. Cochrane (Chicago, 1994). A somewhat less lucid, 'Derridaean' investigation of the potency and ideology of writing (by hand) in the Renaissance period, based chiefly on a selective study of printed writing manuals, is offered in Jonathan Goldberg, *Writing matter: From the hands of the English Renaissance* (Stanford, Calif., 1990).

One might profitably make a study of the use of writing and associated terms in literature of the period: e.g. the employment of specific writing metaphors (of pens, letters, ink, and other physical materials) in so much poetry. There is a notable recourse to such metaphors in descriptions of momentous events: e.g. Gerrard Winstanley's comment on the new order after the execution of Charles I: 'the old world . . . is running up like parchment in the fire': *The true levellers standard advanced* (1649), reprinted in Winstanley, *The law of freedom and other writings*, ed. Christopher Hill (Cambridge, 1983), 78–9.

Octavius, and Lepidus are mulling over their list of men 'prick'd' to die. That is all it took: a name, a spot of ink, a tick, or a signature.

Could anything illustrate more the power and import of documents than the execution warrant of Mary Queen of Scots?[10] Recall Queen Elizabeth's interminable agonizing over this warrant: a single membrane of vellum, the text prepared by Lord Burghley, authorizing the relevant agents 'to cause by y*ou*r comaundeme*n*t execuc̄on to be don vppon her p*er*son in the presence of y*ou*r selues . . . in suche manner and forme . . . as . . . shalbe thought by y*ou*r discrecons co*n*venient, not*w*ithstandinge anie lawe, Statute, or ordinance to the contrarie';[11] the warrant engrossed at his request by her secretary William Davison; lacking only her signature and the consequently authorized seal for enactment; the weeks of procrastination; the charades that had to be played, her prolonged twisting and turning to avoid the actual step of signing her name; and then finally, of course, the failure of nerve, the attempted retraction of responsibility symbolized so unmistakably in that prominent, bold, flourished signature: the blaming of Davison for dispatching it (even though signed) before she had expressly ordered him to do so. With the destruction of a life, a career, and (perhaps) a royal conscience—quite apart from the huge political and military consequences—there could be no illusion about the potential, extraordinary, even terrifying significance of a simple document.

At the more mundane, everyday level of business transactions it is hardly less surprising that the key importance of documents—and the crucial factors of correct phrasing and preparation—gained ever wider recognition. The cliché of the power of the pen, 'mightier than the sword', is echoed by many seventeenth-century commentators, but has a quite specific application: meaning not necessarily the outpourings of the great Miltonic poets and polemicists of the world, but the products of the humble clerk and scrivener. And along with this power went the possibility of enormous negative consequences. 'A dash alone of his pen ruin'd many,' says one epigrammatist of the scrivener.[12]

Sir Walter Ralegh provides a case in point. For Ralegh had his entire manor of Sherborne Castle confiscated by the Crown in 1609 because the rather complicated indenture of 1602, whereby, with apparently prudent foresight, he conveyed the manor to his

---

[10] For the fullest documented account of the proceedings against Mary Queen of Scots, see Nicholas Harris Nicolas, *Life of William Davison, secretary of state and privy counsellor to Queen Elizabeth* (London, 1823).

[11] The actual execution warrant of 1 February 1586/7 is not known to have survived, although various contemporary transcripts are preserved. The text quoted here is from a scribal copy annotated by Robert Beale, the Clerk of the Queen's Council who carried the warrant to Fotheringay Castle and read the text aloud before the execution; this was offered at Sotheby's, 16 December 1996, lot 42 (and is now in a private collection). Another scribal copy is among Beale's papers in BL Add. MS 48027 [Yelverton MS 31], ff. 645r–646r, and bears Beale's annotation: 'Her M*ajesty*s hand was also in the Coppie.' These copies were obviously preserved as a record of the authorization by which the commissioners of the execution did what they did and as evidence of the Queen's responsibility in the matter.

[12] 'On a Scriuener', line 12 (Appendix I below, No. 16). Cf. Robert Lenton: 'Hee is one who will doe more with a gray Goose wing, than euer *Robin Hood* could doe, and is very dangerous, if once hee puts his hand to't' (Appendix I, No. 13).

wife and family, was deemed faulty in the phrasing and therefore pronounced invalid. According to Sir Edward Coke, the essential, binding words were 'omitted in the deed', for, at a particular point, it ought to have contained ten words relating to the trustees: that they '*shall and will from henceforth stand and be thereof seised*'. The crucial omission was made, Coke thought, by 'the clerk in the engrossing' of the deed.[13]

Poor Ralegh!—ruined by a negligent clerk. Indeed, if we are to credit John Chamberlain, there was almost contemporary disbelief that such consequences *could* stem from so humble an agent. 'The error or oversight is said to be so grosse', he says, 'that men do meerly ascribe yt to Gods owne hand that blinded him [Ralegh] and his counsaile.'[14] An interesting implicit image is here of God's intervening, putting his hand over Ralegh's eyes and deliberately using the engrossing clerk as his agent to write, or seal, Ralegh's fate. 'And those that have cursed the Invention of the *Press* for *others* sakes,' says one writer about the legal scrivener, 'may more justly do the same to that of the *Pen* for *his*.'[15]

No wonder that wise counsel always stressed (and no doubt still does) the importance of careful scrutiny of potentially consequential documents. Lord Strange's tutor, Dr Thomas Wilson (1663–1755), once dropped some painfully burning sealing wax on his young pupil's fingers when he was about to sign something he had not read: in order, it is recorded, 'to impress a lasting remembrance on his mind never to sign or seal any paper he had not first read and attentively examined'.[16]

No wonder too that the integrity and competence (or otherwise) of the scribe himself, the producer of such manuscripts, came to be seen as so crucial. And no wonder—considering the possible disastrous consequences when documents were not drawn up properly, or when they had implications unsuspected by their commissioners or recipients, let alone when they were used deliberately to entrap and exploit—that the activities of clerks and scriveners would come to provide a frequent subject for *satire*.

And satire they did provide—a rich vein of it—from prose 'characters' to verse 'epitaphs', and many allusions in plays and elsewhere. In almost all of it what we encounter is anything *but* 'harmless drudges', least of all figures of exemplary moral or spiritual rectitude. In fact, looking at both the extent and ferocity of this satire, we might be forgiven for suspecting that Trithemius' 'heralds of God'—Vonnegut's bastions of literacy inspired with the thoughts of angels—had evolved universally into knaves, villains, and scoundrels—or, at best, snivelling panders to masters who were themselves so: especially those most hated figures, lawyers and moneylenders.

---

[13] Edward Edwards, *The life of Sir Walter Ralegh*, 2 vols. (London, 1868), i. 468–9, 473–4.

[14] John Chamberlain to Dudley Carleton, 10 January 1608/9 (PRO SP 14/43/14), printed in *The letters of John Chamberlain*, ed. Norman Egbert McClure, 2 vols. (Philadelphia, 1939), i. 280–1; cited in Edwards, *Life of Ralegh*, i. 474.

[15] Jeremiah Wells, 'A London Scrivener' (Appendix I, No. 21).

[16] Peter Draper, *The house of Stanley* (Ormskirk, 1864), 254–5.

'*A Scrivener*', we are told, 'Is a Christian Canniball that devoures men alive. He sits behinde a deske like a Spider in a Cobweb to watch what flies will fall into his net.'[17] He is a '*Devil*' who 'walks up and down seeking whom he may devour'; 'a *Devil* that comes to *torment* men *before* their *time*. While the *Divine prepares* you for *Death*; and the *Physitian hastens* it, he does *both*. Like the *Hangman*, he first *disrobes* you of your *outer garments*, and then *kills* you.' He is a torturer or inquisitor, who 'stretches' his victim 'upon the *Wrack*, writing down his *Confession*, out of all which he draws up a *Sentence*, miscalled a *Bond* or *Conveyance*'[18] (the indenture itself thus becoming a death warrant).

He is a trickster or conjuror, who uses the legal formulae, ambiguous abbreviations, and even archaic script and language of his documents as a means to confuse and deceive;[19] a criminal, who deserves to lose his ears; a thief; a forger or perjurer; a disease or plague; a monster; a viper, wolf, beast of prey, rat, vermin, or pariah; a leech, worm, louse, or other parasite which ultimately destroys what it feeds on—gnawing 'their *Livelyhood* out of the *bowells* of those they hang upon'.[20]

In his professional relationship with usurers and other associates, he is seen not only as a colluder or enforcer of his master's deceptions—the usurer's clerk is 'the *Vulcan*, that forges [t]he Bonds and Shackels which he imposes on other men';[21] or the *jackal* to the *lion*—who '*divide* the *Prey*; the *Usurer gnaws off* all the *flesh*, and the *Scrivener picks the bones*'[22]—but also, significantly, as a kind of *prostitute* or a prostitute's *pimp*. If it is the usurer who 'puts his money to the vnnaturall Act of generation'[23]—who, 'like a common whore . . . lets her out to trading'[24]—it is 'his *Scriuener*' who 'is the superuisor Bawd to't'.[25] 'He is the usurer's pimp, that *procures* statute, bond, and mortgage to satisfy his insatiable desire of getting.'[26] 'Sometimes', says another, he himself 'playes the *Baud*, prostitutes the same *Title* to all commers'.[27] In a satire by Donne, it is lamented that the only 'City trades' now flourishing are those of the 'Bawd, Tavern-keeper, Whore and Scrivener'.[28] And the sense of scrivener as pimp or bawd extends not only to the service he occasionally supplied of finding rich widows for his clients, but even

---

[17] Wye Saltonstall, 'A Scrivener' (Appendix I, No. 15).

[18] Wells, 'A London Scrivener'. In 'A Covetous Griping Usurer and Extortioner', in *The character of a Whig* (London, 1700), 113–15, the Usurer is described as '(in some sort) worse than the *Devil*, he never *Gives* but *sells* his Days of *Payments*, *Bloods* you by Degrees, till the *Spirits* of your Estates are insensibly exhausted, and then makes *Dice* of your *Bones* to play at *Size-Ace* with his *Scrivener*'.

[19] See, for example, Head, *Proteus redivivus*, ch. IX (p. 274): 'Some of them have the snatch of a Scholar, and yet use Latin very hardly, and lest it should accuse them, cut it off in the midst, and will not let it speak out; and fearing that his Hand-Writing should prove Traitor to his actions, it is as difficult to be understood as his countenance.'

[20] Wells, 'A London Scrivener'.

[21] Wye Saltonstall, 'An Vsurer', in *Picturae loquentes* (London, 1631), No. 13, sigs. D6ᵛ–8ʳ.

[22] Wells, 'A London Scrivener'.   [23] 'A Diuellish Usurer' (Appendix I, No. 7).

[24] Saltonstall, 'An Vsurer'.

[25] 'A Diuellish Usurer'. In the recast version published in *The character of a Whig* (1700), 113–15, this passage reads: 'his Scrivener is the Supervisor Cock Baud to it.'

[26] Samuel Butler, 'A Scrivener' (Appendix I, No. 20).   [27] Wells, 'A London Scrivener'.

[28] 'A tale of a citizen and his wife', lines 45–6: *The poems of John Donne*, ed. Herbert J. C. Grierson, 2 vols. (Oxford, 1912; reprinted 1968), i. 107.

to insinuations about his own domestic *ménage*. A scrivener's wife, we are told, was likely to be 'the Daughter of som ritch Vseror' or else the cast-off mistress of 'some ritch Batchelo',[29] and one jaunty little musical ditty ironically celebrates the scrivener as a contented cuckold who, in effect, profits from his wife's infidelities with clients.[30]

Nor are satirists slow in drawing analogies between scriveners and the Scribes and Pharisees so unflatteringly portrayed in the New Testament. The Scribes and Pharisees were meticulous and rigorous interpreters of the Law; they strictly enforced payments (in the form of tithes) and could be seen as extortioners (Matthew 23: 23–5; Luke 11: 42–6); they could be condemned as greedy and covetous men, who effectively worshipped both God and Mammon (Luke 16: 13–15); as a brood of vipers (Matthew 3: 7, 12: 34, 23: 33); as whited sepulchres (Matthew 23: 27); and, most of all, as hypocrites (Matthew 23; Luke 11: 44, 12: 1, 18: 9–14). As viewed by satirists, Scribes, Pharisees, and scriveners alike were self-serving hypocrites who, in strict observance of the letter rather than the spirit, perverted the words of Scripture, 'Gods own wordes',[31] if not also the Law, to their own ungodly ends, even to the point of 'devour[ing]' (foreclosing on, or taking possession of) 'widdowes houses' in satisfaction of outstanding debts.[32]

Indeed, in making their pens lethal weapons, their bonds and indentures diabolical instruments of ensnarement and perdition, it is almost as if scriveners had assumed and accentuated all the negative functions, aspects, and implications of writing itself: thereby representing, in a sense, the ultimate stage of Man's damnation on earth through false covenants. There are shades here, perhaps, of that old tradition by which, in effect, writing itself could be seen as both a consequence and a token of the Fall, for Man had no need of writing in Paradise where there was perfect (oral) discourse. One tradition even held the first 'covenant' to have been between Man and Satan, who was himself sometimes represented as a scribe who kept a perpetual record of human sins; Adam was usually seen as the first scribe on earth; and St Augustine saw the very materials of writing, parchment made from the skins of dead animals (like the garments with which God clothed Adam and Eve's nakedness after their loss of innocence), as

---

[29] 'A Charector of a London Scriuenor' (Appendix I, No. 12).

[30] 'The Scriueners seruants Song of Holborne' (Appendix I, No. 3). Cf. also 'A Charector of a London Scriuenor' (Appendix I, No. 12): 'His Wife to ad perfection to hyr husbands Profession putts all to vse too and hyr Husband is noe loser by it'; and the later characterization of the extremely wealthy scrivener Sir Robert Clayton as a 'Scrivener Cuckold' (Appendix I, No. 24). By contrast, a broadside verse lampoon of 1681, *The Protestant cuckold: A new ballad. Being a full and perfect relation how B[enjamin] H[arris] the Protestant-news-forger, caught his beloved wife Ruth in ill circumstances* (copy in CUL Sel.2.116[53]), celebrates how a well-known publisher (with 'no Ink in your Pen') was cuckolded ('your Spouse has furnish't you with an *Ink-horn*') by '*Timothy Dash the Scriveners Apprentice*'.

[31] 'A Charector of a London Scriuenor'.

[32] 'He is a Scribe by profession, for he devoures widdowes houses, and a Pharisee in his religion, for though he doe no good, yet he loves good deedes in Parchment' (Saltonstall); 'And he makes your *Will* like a *Pharisees long prayer*, with a *house* at the *end* of it' (Wells): Appendix I, Nos. 15 and 21. Cf. Matthew 23: 14; Mark 38: 40; Luke 20: 46–7.

symbolic of Man's state of sinfulness.[33] Thus it is that one satirist, for instance, could declare:

had *God* made *Scriveners*, he would never have pronounced of the seven days work, that all was *good*. Had *Scriveners* bin in the *old World*, it had saved the *Deluge*, and accursed Mankind had destroyed one another. A *surreptitious* race of men, not of *Gods Creation*, but born (like *Vermin*) out of the *corruption* of several *Ages*.[34]

It is this inherent sense of how far writing, and the very act of writing, had developed—or rather degenerated—in the hands of mortal scriveners that gives resonance to a little poem called 'The pens prosopopeia to the Scrivener'.[35] Through analogies between writing instruments and materials (penknife, ink, etc.) and the tokens of Christ's Passion (wounding, blood, etc.), it seeks to turn the situation around, as it were, converting a secular process of writing into a religious meditation. Through enlightenment, the essentially sinful preoccupation of the scrivener is psychologically or spiritually transformed into an act of repentance and redemption.

Ah, how far removed all this is from the sanctified sphere of writing operations blessed by Trithemius! And, at a more mundane level, how different too from the relatively innocent 'Adam scriveyn' depicted with such good-humoured exasperation by Chaucer—his careless, plodding copyist, with his 'long lokkes', whose only fault lay in his 'negligence' in not writing 'trewe' and in making his master have 'to rubbe and scrape' to 'correcte' him.[36]

Not the least significant aspect in satirists' derision was the clerk or scrivener's social level. He is constantly mocked for his lowly origins and inadequate education. 'Hee is a farmers sonne, and his Fathers vtmost ambition is to make him an *Atturney*,' says one commentator.[37] Though, says another, 'His father thought it too chargable to

---

[33] For a discussion of the traditions summarized here, see Eric Jager, 'Did Eve invent writing? Script and the Fall in "The Adam Books" ', *SP* 93 (1996), 229–50 (especially pp. 232–6). For a characteristic analogy between writing and sinfulness, see Francis Raworth, *Jacobs ladder, or the protectorship of Sion* (London, 1655), 22: 'God when he comes, finds . . . not a *rasa tabula*, a milk *white Paper*, but he finds the Devil to have been *scribling*, and the World to have been *scribling*.'

[34] Wells, 'A London Scrivener'. In the adaptation of Wells, 'A Wheedling Cheating Scrivener', published in *The character of a Whig* (1700), 115–21, this passage is rendered: 'Had *Scriveners* been in the Antedeliuvian World, the *Deluge* might have been *spared*, for Mankind would have *destroyed* one another, without any other help than theirs; and therefore we must not look upon them as part of the *Creation*, which was wholly good; but as a *Surreptitious* Race of Men, bred out of the *Corruption* of several Ages.'

[35] Appendix I, No. 17.

[36] 'Chaucers wordes unto Adam, his owne scriveyn', in *The works of Geoffrey Chaucer*, ed. F. N. Robinson, 2nd edn. (Boston, 1961), 534 (commentary on p. 859). As for Adam's 'long lokkes', if there was any particular hair fashion associated with scriveners and their apprentices by the 17th century, it would seem, curiously enough, to have been not long but short cropped hair, implied by the word 'notched' (see *OED*). Thus Dryden refers to 'notch'd prentices' who write 'whole sermons' (Prologue to *The Spanish fryar*, 1681), and a writer prefacing an anonymous satire in 1692 calls 'the scrivener that writ it' [i.e. copied it] a 'notched rogue' (*POAS*, v. 534). A portrait found in a 1607 Bible, reproduced in a Phillips's sale catalogue on 8 September 1994 (lot 80), shows a man signing his will on his deathbed, the attendant lawyer, notary, or scrivener characterized by short cut-back hair, a cropped style also evident in a self-portrait (1593) by the draper and scrivener Thomas Fella (illustrated in J. L. Nevinson, 'Lively drawings of a Suffolk scrivener', *Country Life Annual* (1964), 156–8). In a satire probably written in the 1620s, an 'Extortioner' (at whose feast 'Scriveners' serve, as it were, as 'Cookes') has hair 'short as his eye-browes': Anon., *The Wandering-Jew, telling fortvnes to English-men* (London, 1640), 35–6 [Murphy, 121–2].

[37] 'A Puny-Clarke' (Appendix I, No. 6).

keepe him at Schoole til he could read *Harry Stottle*, and therefore preferd him to a man of Law'.[38] 'Hee may pretend *Schollership*', says another,[39] but 'He is noe greate Scholler', says yet another, 'yet trades much in Lattine'[40]—and scriveners' imperfect (if not fraudulent) knowledge of Latin becomes a standard joke. As for his grasp of the law itself: 'His utmost knowledge is the names of the Courts and their severall offices, and [he] begins after a while like a [Mag]Pie that has his tongue slit, to chatter out some tearmes of Law, with more *audacity* than knowledge.'[41]

'No Gentleman, nor yet no Clown',[42] the clerk or scrivener is generally represented as being pretty well on a par with city apprentices—fit company for 'Coster-mongers, Porters, and Tripewiues, Chaundlers, and ffidlers'[43]—and also, perhaps (for all the prejudice against lawyers in general), to be clearly distinguished from the truly respectable dignitaries of the legal profession at Westminster.[44] At the same time, he is the kind of *saucy* apprentice who had social pretensions. 'At a new play hee'le be sure to be seene in the threepeny Roome . . . When hee heares some *stale jest* (which he best apprehends) he fils the house with an ignorant laughter.'[45] And Face in Jonson's *The Alchemist* (i. ii) characterizes a 'fine clarke' as one that 'knowes the law, and writes you six faire hands', is 'heire to fortie markes a yeere', and 'Consorts with the small poets of the time'.[46] He might even 'itch towards a poet' himself[47]—though, if so (satirists never let us forget), such an ambition would be an aberration from his main concern, which was purely mercenary.

Of course, *all* satire is exaggerated, and subject to the conventions of genre; more-over, in the recurrence of certain motifs and terminology in these attacks there is undoubtedly some element of derivativeness. Even so, besides the evidence of actual cases of nefarious malpractice by particular scriveners,[48] one suspects that the sheer vehemence and persistency of this satire touches on a nerve of strong popular feeling and prejudice. It may even articulate a deep and widespread social anxiety.

[38] Saltonstall, 'A Lawyers Clearke' (Appendix I, No. 14).

[39] John Stephens, 'A Lawyers Clarke' (Appendix I, No. 4).

[40] 'A Charector of a London Scriuenor'.   [41] Saltonstall, 'A Lawyers Clearke'.

[42] Robert Dixon, *Canidia* (Appendix I, No. 23).

[43] 'A Coppie [o]f a Letter to George Wither in answere [t]o a late Pamphlet partly Imp[rin]ted by George Wood', BL Add. MS 18648, ff. 17–22; printed in Allan Pritchard, 'George Wither's quarrel with the Stationers: An anonymous reply to *The schollers purgatory*', *SB* 16 (1963), 27–42 (p. 40). It may be added that in parliamentary Acts and debates in 1621 'Scriveners' are put on a par with 'Brokers, Chaundlers, Tapsters, Ostlers', 'Ale-house-keepers . . . Bakers, and such like' who buy licences for 'Carrs' to make a profit 'att unreasonable Rates': *Commons debates 1621*, vii. 93, 96, 99.

[44] See, for example, Head, *Proteus redivivus*, ch. IX, 'The Countrey-Attorney . . . and other Law Hangers-on' (pp. 278, 294): 'I do not in any ways reflect or throw disgrace upon the glorious Profession of the Law, which hath in all Ages raised so many emi-nent Persons . . . it is the Ignorant Knavish Countrey-Attorney that I have had a fling at.'

[45] Saltonstall, 'A Lawyers Clearke'.

[46] *The workes of Benjamin Jonson 1616*, facsimile edition by The Scolar Press (London, 1976), 612.

[47] 'A Puny-Clarke'.

[48] e.g. the case brought against the scrivener Lawrence Edwards, who fraudulently got William Hanbie's nephew to sign a bond for £300 to promote his suit for a young woman: *Notaries public in England* (1991), 99. Such examples advanced the devel-opment of the 'unfavourable reputation for devious and usurious dealings from which [scriveners] were never entirely able to escape'.

If all people who wield power inevitably attract suspicion and enmity—and with them their agents and minions by association—how much more so if they themselves are so personally and socially unprepossessing, and their influence seems so disproportionate to their humble status: that, indeed, it may seem even a blatant infringement of the social order itself.[49]

I think we can detect an awareness that there was a kind of protean, sliding scale operating for people who earned their living in any way by the pen, and that it extended from the humblest of 'clerks', through 'scriveners', to 'secretaries' and, at the highest level, to 'secretaries of state'. Thus, when it suited them, satirists—smarting at the inequity of what they saw as intrinsically unimportant creatures wielding power—would see fit to remind even the highest on this scale that they were no more than mere mercenary mechanics. So, for instance, in the 1660s, when the Lord Chancellor, Clarendon, was accused of wanting to feather his nest by getting his daughter Anne to marry the future James II, there was a ready means to cut him down to size:

> Then the *Fat Scrivener* doth begin to think
> 'Twas time to mix the Royal blood with *ink*.[50]

Added to all this, we should mention, is the great play satirists make of the physical materials used by scribes, the tools of their trade. Here were opportunities aplenty for an abundant repertoire of puns—puns on hands and instruments, on parchment and sheepskin, sheets, ink (including its constituents gall and copperas), inkhorns, seals, wax, impressions, pens, penknives and (goose) quills, blotting or pin-dust, labels (strips of supplementary text affixed to indentures), rulers, and so on—as well as scriveners' lettering, engrossing, grammar (points, periods, capitals, dashes, abbreviations, and contractions), wordiness (to draw out the length of their documents), and favourite set phrases (*Noverint universi*: 'Know all men', etc.), besides *kinds* of document (deeds, covenants, bonds, copies . . . and the rest). Certain poems are constructed as virtual catalogues of such things.[51]

The typical scrivener himself is variously depicted sitting behind his desk looking 'so thinne that a man may picke a good stomacke out of his face';[52] sitting, by one account, 'in all his *Formalities*, his furr'd *Cap* and *Gown*, his *Pen* to *one Ear* . . . composing his *Countenance* after the gravest Mode, *dreadfully ridiculous*, and most *Majestically sim-*

---

[49] One suspects, besides, not only contemporary resentment concerning scriveners' 'central position in the great expansion of credit transactions' in this period (ibid. 99), but also suspicion of people who did not stick to one clearly defined trade; an urge to debunk and demystify the practitioners of legal writing in general (which led to the 22 November 1650 parliamentary Act that 'all Proceedings whatsoever in any Courts of Justice . . . shall be in the English Tongue only, and not in Latin or French . . . And that the same . . . shall be written in an ordinary, usual and legible Hand and Character, and not in any Hand commonly called *Court-hand*' [Wing E1137]; and, perhaps, even fear about the social disruptions of capitalism itself—in addition, of course, to the traditional religious prejudice against any kind of usury.

[50] Satire quoted in Christopher Falkus, *The life and times of Charles II* (London, 1972), 80.

[51] See, for example, the epitaph 'On a Scriuener' in Appendix I, No. 16.   [52] Saltonstall, 'A Scrivener'.

ple';[53] or, alternatively, dressed in a '*Gown* . . . curs'd to a perpetual *Autumn* . . . ever bare', with 'as little *woo'l* upon it, as if at next remove it were to be made *Parchment*';[54] and wearing 'cutfingerd dogskin gloves, for his ease, or [as if] the desire of bribes makes his hands grow itchy'.[55] When not commenting on the cloakbag or buckram bag which legal clerks were obliged to carry for their masters—as if this were a comical token of their lowly station as mere servants and dogsbodies,[56]—satirists also like to remind us that the scrivener generally worked in 'his *Shopp* . . . the Gentlemans house of Correction',[57] sitting, perhaps, 'nigh the dore to give accesse to strangers, and at their going forth [give] them a legge in expectation'.[58] And like other common businesses in the street, the scrivener's 'shop' evidently sported some kind of trade sign hanging outside. 'Hee has no signe but a few tottering Labells', says one commentator, 'which are *hang'd* there to shew their masters *desert*.'[59] Unless it is to be taken literally, and refers to indentures hanging about the scrivener's shop like the manuscripts seen in the German scriptorium illustrated below in Plate 1, this comment would tend to support the implication of a remark made by Nashe, complaining of the unauthorized manuscript proliferation of one of his own texts: 'That Coppie progressed from one scriueners shop to another, & at length grew so common, that it was readie to bee hung out for one of their signes, like a paire of indentures.'[60] So if the scrivener did have a trade sign, it may, on occasions perhaps, have been a couple of indentures, complete with their 'labels'; though if so, we have no specific record of such a sign, and one evident alternative— used at least by certain members of the Company of Scriveners itself—would have been a spread eagle.[61] It seems, from other references, that it would not generally have been a hand holding a pen unless the proprietor were also offering the services of a writing master.

Such comments as these on the physical world of clerks and scriveners are useful—even in a satirical context—because, frankly, our knowledge of scribes and scriptoria in this period *is* so relatively scant. Where might we go, for instance, for a graphic illustration

[53] Wells, 'A London Scrivener'.　　[54] Ibid.　　[55] Saltonstall, 'A Lawyers Clearke'.

[56] See, for example, the references in Appendix I, Nos. 4, 6, 13, and 14.

[57] 'A Charector of a London Scriuenor'.　　[58] Saltonstall, 'A Lawyers Clearke'.

[59] Saltonstall, 'A Scrivener'.

[60] Thomas Nashe, dedication to Elizabeth Carey of *The terrors of the night* (1594), reprinted in *The works of Thomas Nashe*, ed. R. B. McKerrow, rev. F. P. Wilson, 5 vols. (Oxford, 1958–66), i. 341 (and for other contemptuous remarks by Nashe about scriveners, see iv. 450).

[61] The spread eagle seems to have been a common sign not only for scriveners but also for printers, booksellers, and stationers, as well as for certain other professions: see Bryant Lillywhite, *London signs: A reference book of London signs from earliest times to about the mid-nineteenth century* (London, 1972), especially pp. 508–10. An 'Eagle volant . . . holding in his mouth a Penner and Ink-horne . . . standing upon a Booke' was incorporated in the arms of the Company of Scriveners: see Steer, *Company of Scriveners*, frontispiece, plate II facing p. 7, and pp. 47–8. It was certainly the sign (and arms) of Milton's father, John Milton (1563?–1647), registered scrivener, of Bread Street, Cheapside: see William Riley Parker, *Milton: A biography*, 2 vols. (Oxford, 1968), i. 5. The home of the dramatist John Lyly's father Peter Lyly, who in 1551 became registrar of the Canterbury Consistory Court, also bore the sign of a 'Splayed Eagle': William Urry, *Christopher Marlowe and Canterbury* (London, 1988), 10.

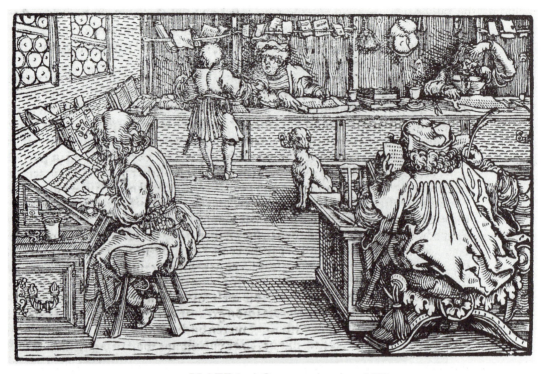

PLATE 1: A German scriptorium, 1559

to show us what a Renaissance scriptorium actually looked like—*any* kind of scriptorium? We can find plenty of pictorial representations of individual writers sitting at their desks—as there are in medieval times—but I know of only one illustration showing scribes in their place of work—and even this comes from an earlier Continental source: that reproduced in Plate 1. This is a woodcut in a German edition of Petrarch, first published in 1532.[62] It shows some kind of stationer's shop, one where maybe printed materials also were offered. The sheets hanging up on belts nailed behind the counter and on the wall to the left, whether to dry, or for storage, or for display, recall a feature seen in contemporary illustrations of Renaissance printing shops. Nevertheless, the impression here is that the main service offered is on-the-spot scribal copying. All four men working in the shop are engaged in manuscript production: one of them (at the front right) seen actually writing; the man top left behind the counter interrupted in his writing (of some sort of indenture), and the other two (one with a pen in his mouth) apparently checking over documents already written. We might recall some of the details mentioned by later satirists when we note that two of the scribes wear hats and cloaks, or gowns—presumably denoting their superior status—

---

[62] Plate 1 shows the woodcut as it appeared in an edition of Petrarch published in Frankfurt, 1559. The woodcut (measuring 98 × 154mm) first appeared in Francesco Petrarca, *De remediis utriusque fortunae* (Augsburg, 1532), whence it is reproduced in Sigfred Taubert, *Bibliopola . . . pictures and texts about the book trade*, 2 vols. (London, 1966), ii. 17.

including the rather portly-looking scribe who is serving the customer and who is maybe the 'master' or proprietor. The ungainly scribe at the top right ostentatiously scratching his head—an 'Adam scriveyn' figure perhaps—might be a junior clerk or apprentice. The scribes work either at sloping desks—perhaps the main site for extensive professional copying—or else on the flat surface of the counter. And, so far as we can see, they sit on stools without backs so that they lean *into* the work, as it were. The scribe at the front right, who seems to be sitting on a more expensive and comfortable seat with a cushion, has an hour glass, which suggests both that he is acting as time keeper—and timing would have affected the pricing of items—and that copying proceeded as, perhaps, a series of one-hour stints. A penknife and pair of scissors are in evidence at the top right, while the little cups by the side of each scribe are what were known in England as 'pounce-pots' or 'sanders', containing the fine sand or 'pin-dust' which was used before the development of blotting paper. That some of their manuscripts might finish up as bound volumes is suggested by the one near the head of the scribe on the left, which is obviously a volume sewn up in decorated boards. The only other detail we should mention is the figure of the dog in the centre of the shop. Professor K. J. Höltgen kindly informs me that in Germany dogs traditionally symbolized vigilance and sagacity: the implication here being that this shop is a well-run, orderly one.

What resemblance this sixteenth-century German scriptorium bore to British examples, either contemporary or some decades later, I do not know, though I suspect there were basic affinities. It is possible to find evidence for one additional feature, however, in the arrangement for scribes' exemplars, the German scriptorium showing no clear sign of any exemplars being copied. In his description of ancient methods of tacking sheets together to form a scroll, John Evelyn writes of 'the *Scribs* or *Librarii* hanging [them] ouer a convenient frame before their Deskes, perhaps not vnlike what our *Scriveners* and Lawyers Clearks now vse'.[63] While the exact form of such a 'frame' remains unclear, something of the sort is indicated in an engraving which appears in *The compleat clark, and scriveners guide* (London, 1655 [Wing C5633]), where a scribe is seen writing at his desk before a client (Plate 2). His exemplar is a deed, complete with two pendent seals, propped up by some means at the top of the raised panel at the back of his desk, where it might readily be copied by the scribe on his sloped writing surface.

All the same, if we consider the relative wealth of surviving evidence illustrating the printing shop, in all its manifold activities and operations, the single depiction of a scriptorium in Plate 1 stands in striking contrast. It is a situation somewhat paradigmatic of the relatively sparse attention traditionally paid by scholars to the world of

---

[63] 'Of manuscripts' in *Memoirs, illustrative of the life and writings of John Evelyn*, ed. William Bray, 2 vols. (London, 1818), ii/1. 333–48 (p. 345).

PLATE 2: A scribe at his desk with a client, 1655

scribal production in general, as compared to the vast industry devoted to every aspect of the history, technology, and commercialization of the printed book in this period.[64]

There is also that curious impediment to the study of scribal publication which constitutes one of the great paradoxes of manuscript culture: namely, the extent to which professionally created manuscript texts tend to be produced anonymously.[65] It is

---

[64] Happily, and especially following the attention drawn to this field in my *Index of English literary manuscripts* (1980-93), some major pioneering steps towards a coordinated study of manuscript culture in this period have been made. In the forefront earlier was Mary Hobbs's unpublished doctoral dissertation 'An edition of the Stoughton Manuscript . . . connected with Henry King . . . seen in relation to other contemporary poetry and song collections' (University of London, 1973), which was later adapted for her *Early seventeenth-century verse miscellany manuscripts* (Aldershot, 1992). Other notable studies of scribal culture are Harold Love's *Scribal publication in seventeenth-century England* (1993), and H. R. Woudhuysen's *Sir Philip Sidney and the circulation of manuscripts 1558–1640* (1996). In addition, particular aspects of manuscript circulation are surveyed in Margaret J. M. Ezell's *The patriarch's wife* (Chapel Hill, NC, 1987) (especially ch. 3, pp. 62–100: 'Women Writers: Patterns of Manuscript Circulation and Publication'), and in Arthur F. Marotti's *Manuscript, print, and the English Renaissance lyric* (Ithaca, NY, 1995). These writers would surely concur in stressing how much more needs to be done. Would that we had, for instance, a dictionary of scribes, secretaries, and scriveners, comparable to those we have of printers, publishers, stationers, and booksellers!

[65] This phenomenon is so universal that I cannot resist citing a rare exception which proves the rule: a copy of Cardinal Wolsey's negotiations, made *c*.1630 and among the Trumbull MSS now in the BL (provisionally Add. MS 72466), where the scribe goes (only) so far as to state at the end 'Transcript per H: P.' The most notable exception, of course, is Esther Inglis, who, over a period of three and a half decades, produced a series of meticulous and exquisitely crafted manuscripts, some of minuscule proportions, various of them containing prefaces extolling the virtues of her art. Nearly sixty of them are known today, every one signed, and some even containing portraits of herself: see, especially, A. H. Scott-Elliot and Elspeth Yeo, 'Calligraphic manuscripts of Esther Inglis (1571–1624): A catalogue', *PBSA* 84 (1990), 11–86; also Phillips's sale catalogue for 11 November 1993, lot 599; Sotheby's sale catalogue for 13 December 1994, lot 21; and Thomas Lange, 'A rediscovered Esther Inglis calligraphic manuscript in the Huntington Library', *PBSA* 89 (1995), 339–42. Esther Inglis's calligraphic skills are basically an extension in the field of manuscripts of the traditional feminine handicraft of needlework, the aesthetic of which is to some extent reflected in the decorative patterns, borders, and layout she employs in her copying (with characteristic motifs of coiling foliage, honeysuckle, gillyflowers, peapods, butterflies, caterpillars, etc.), as well as in the heavily embroidered bindings she sometimes supplies. Although she might be described as in some sense a 'professional scribe', she was not simply an agent: the motivation for her industry is that of an author. Since her artefacts—in which for the most part fairly standard religious texts are used as occasions for demonstrations of dazzling virtuoso finesse and ingenuity of penmanship—were all designed for presentation to eminent public figures, from whom she expected reward and patronage, self-advertisement—clear identification of their maker—was obviously essential.

printed books—that most mechanized form of literary production—which usually have title-pages and imprimaturs, giving precise details of the persons responsible for them.

From one logical perspective, wouldn't we expect to see manuscripts giving every bit as much detail of their production? After all, as commentators on the history of literacy have long been telling us, is it not manuscripts which represent the more personalized mode of literary communication? They are not mass-produced by machines, their letters stamped out by metal, but written by hand, by individual human beings—in their personal, cursive, living script, on a one for one basis. And, as Walter Ong would argue,[66] is it not handwritten texts, rather than printed ones, which contain residual traces of the voice and presence of the individual author or story-teller? It would seem to be but a simple, logical concomitant that the manuscript should personalize itself, as it were, by openly identifying itself as the handiwork of specific, named human beings.

Even today, when we buy a piece of handicraft, we set a premium on personalized work. We would value more highly a vase or pot hand-made by a local craftsman than an example of mechanized factory-production. And the shop which sells the pot to us is hardly likely to be slow in signalling its status and setting its price accordingly—the tagging of the item with name and particulars of the individual craftsman responsible being deemed essential.

In the case of manuscripts, even Trithemius, in 1492, had no objection to scribes' identifying themselves and their handiwork. 'Your memory . . . will be handed down to posterity with glory from the books that you write,' he said. And though the desire for 'empty fame' should not be the *prime* motive for copying, nevertheless, he says, 'If . . . you should wish to put your name on the manuscripts copied by you, this should be done with the intention of inciting those who come after to intercession for you or to imitation. With such an intent you may safely and properly subscribe your full names on manuscripts that you write.'[67]

To illustrate what, by contrast, we find in the seventeenth century, let us take a specific example. In Plate 3 we have the title-page of the first edition of William Lambarde's treatise *Archeion*, printed in 1635, half a century or more after the work was actually composed. So we see here the title—spelt out in full. The name of the author—in full: *William Lambard*—together with a clear indication of his character and status—*of Lincolns-Inne, Gent[leman]*. Then—after a conventional printer's ornament—the place of publication: *London*—followed by the names of the printer and the publisher—in this case the printer and publisher are one and the same: *Daniel Frere*. Then details of precisely where copies of the book may be purchased—at Frere's *shop in little Brittaine,*

---

[66] See, especially, Walter J. Ong, *Orality and literacy: The technologizing of the word* (1982; reprinted London, 1990). A valuable contribution to this subject is also made by D. F. McKenzie in 'Speech-manuscript-print', *LCUTA* 20 (1990), 87–109.

[67] Trithemius, 40.

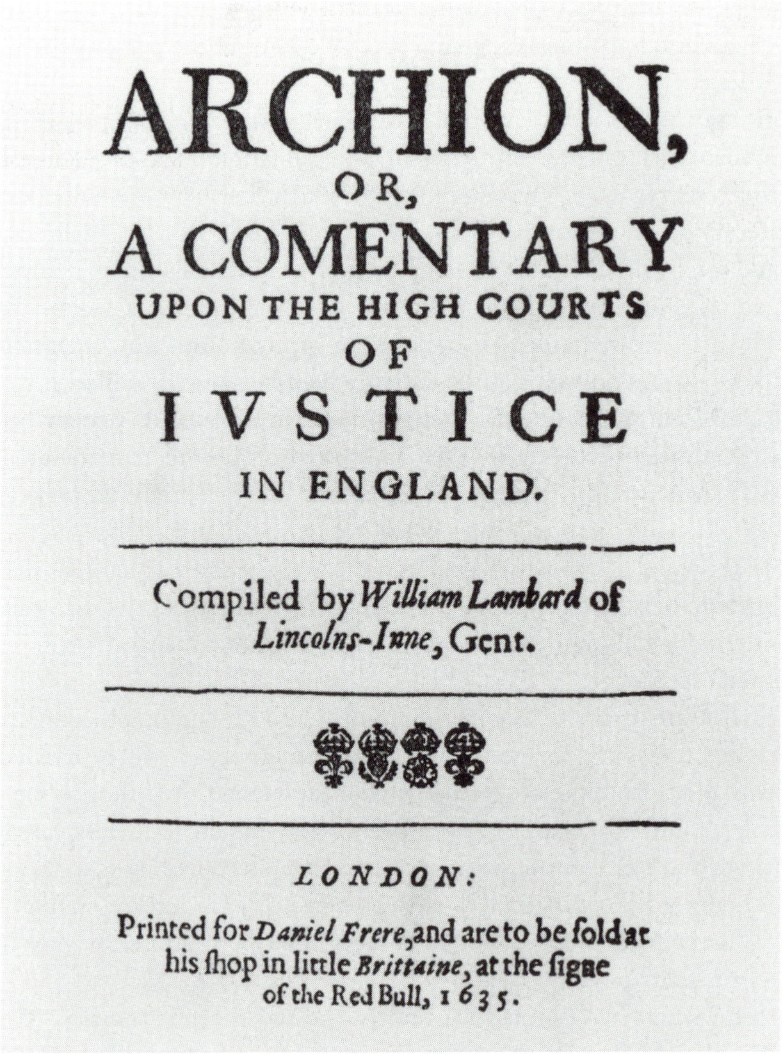

ARCHION,
OR,
A COMENTARY
UPON THE HIGH COURTS
OF
IVSTICE
IN ENGLAND.

Compiled by *William Lambard* of
Lincolns-Inne, Gent.

LONDON:

Printed for *Daniel Frere*, and are to be fold at
his fhop in little *Brittaine*, at the figne
of the Red Bull, 1 6 3 5.

PLATE 3: Title-page of William Lambarde's *Archion*, 1635

at the signe of the Red Bull—with, finally, the date of the edition: *1635*. I count here seven elements of information (eight if printer-publisher is seen as two)—setting aside the printer's ornament.[68]

By comparison, we have in Plate 4 the title-page of one of the many scribal copies of this work produced during the decades before its publication—an example, somewhat appropriately, still in private ownership. Instead of all the detailed information of the

---

[68] The second edition of *Archeion*, published in the same year by Henry Seile, has a title-page containing even more elements of information, since it claims superior status for its copy-text ('Newly Corrected, and enlarged according to the *Authors* Copie'), as well as mentioning both publisher and printer ('*E.P.*') and quoting an apposite Latin aphorism by Cicero.

PLATE 4: Title-page of a manuscript copy of Lambarde's *Archeion* (private collection)

printed edition, we see on its title-page but two elements of information. First, identification of the author, though not by his full name—let alone status—simply as *Lambert*. Secondly, the title of the work—almost the same except in slightly abbreviated form. The scribe himself does assert his presence in the text—but only by a spiral flourish—equivalent, perhaps, to a printer's device—together with a little indulgence in calligraphic ornamentation of the main lettering (with loops and cross-hatching)—a range of personal expression denied to the compositor. The scribe remains, none the less, a nameless agent of transmission—albeit one who hints at his status as a craftsman. Least of all is there any indication where or when the artefact was produced, or under whose auspices, or where further *exempla* might be *for sale*.

So—if we compare printed with manuscript text—we have a kind of paradoxical inversion. The wider the audience or market for the product, and the more mechanized the technology of production, the more detailed and personalized the information given about its production. Correspondingly, the narrower the audience, the more specifically targeted it is, and the more personalized both the means of production and mode of distribution . . . the less need be said about it.

So (and this I take to be purely symptomatic) the select clientele for the scribal copy of *Archeion* do not need to be told who William Lambarde was—they know already. And incidentally, bearing in mind Ong's dictum that handwriting preserves vestiges of orality—that manuscripts are closer to speech, more likely to register sound, than printed text—it is interesting to see the name here spelt *Lambert* rather than *Lambard*. 'Lambert' is obviously how the name was then pronounced—how it *sounded* to the scribe.

Thus: the manuscript—private and personalized both in its means of production and in the nature of its social function—eschews announcing itself; whereas the printed book needs, in a sense, publicly to create its own context, its own social justification, its own clientele, by displaying itself in every particular. Which is what, essentially, a printed title-page is: a trade advertisement.[69]

We could go on to say that scribes wished to be seen as anything *but* tradesmen. It is as if in the social hierarchy—and for all the actual commercial basis of their activities—they knew their place—or seemed to. They discreetly downplayed their personal contribution; avoided the faintest suggestion—at least in their texts—that there was a *shop* where duplicates of their product could easily be *purchased* by all and sundry (though satirists, of course, liked to remind us of that fact); and, tacitly, scribes maximized the sense of the specialness, even exclusivity, as well as 'authority',[70] of their product in the eyes of its users. And the fiction of exclusivity was sustained even when, in practice, scriptoria might be working to full capacity to produce multiple copies of particular

---

[69] In using *Archeion* as an example—as paradigmatic of the difference between manuscript and print cultures—I am not, of course, claiming that *all* printed books of the period 'advertise themselves' in exactly the same clear-cut way. For a salutary discussion, for instance, of the conventions of anonymity and their uses, which in part demonstrates this point, see Marcy North, 'Ignoto in the age of print: The manipulation of anonymity in early modern England', *SP* 91 (1994), 390–416; and see also D. F. McKenzie, 'The London book trade in 1644', in John Horden (ed.), *Bibliographia* (Leeds, 1992), 131–51.

[70] Besides benefiting from an implicit sense of privilege in MS copies (vividly exemplified in Jonson's remark that news only remained news so long as it was 'written', not printed: see Love, 10), scribes would scarcely neglect to incorporate implicit tokens of the authority of their texts if they were at hand: for instance, clear attribution (sometimes misattribution) to well-known writers like Sidney, Bacon, or Ralegh, or subscriptions or colophons legitimizing their copy. A good example of the latter is found in MSS of the Vere–Northumberland quarrel of 1602 (see Appendix II below, No. 11): 'Examined, wth the Coppye, wch. S^r: ffrauncis Veere; sent vnto mee, Att, the very ffirst daye; taken fforth of it, wch was even vppon his departure, out of London, ffor the Lowe Countryes, Soe; went, all the waye by Land, ffrom London, to Thames, wheere hee tooke shippinge; M^r: White, his Man; brought it vnto mee.' The effectiveness of this subscription in one copy (Appendix II, No. 41.9) is demonstrated by the assumption of one modern commentator, John W. Shirley in *Thomas Harriot: A biography* (Oxford, 1983), 207–8—being unaware of the recurrence of the same statement in many MS copies over a period of three decades—that this particular MS 'should, therefore, be a true and accurate copy'. Nevertheless, it is publishers, in a competitive market, who bring claims to authenticity to the fore on their title-pages, the second edition of *Archeion* (see n. 68 above) being a case in point.

discourses currently in demand. Even the *price* of the manuscript—the ultimate token of commercialism—conspired in its favour: higher price, greater prestige. The reader who got hold of an expensive handwritten text felt in some measure that he was privy to coveted and restricted access to the work in question; he was an 'insider', part of some unclearly defined coterie, or privileged network, of select readers of that kind of literature. Had manuscripts advertised themselves and their circumstances of production as shamelessly as printed books, that special dimension would have been obviated; *manuscripts themselves would have been devalued.*

I suspect that, in a sense, and despite the retention of scribal anonymity, that *is* what finally happened.

The last great flourishing of manuscript literary culture in England was the proliferation of so-called *Poems on affairs of state* in the late Restoration period. It was, in some measure, fuelled by the enforcement of Government anti-libel laws, which threatened to consign 'Makers, Printers, Sellers, or Publishers' of any kind of 'libels . . . Whatsoever . . . to prison'[71] and tended (at least to some extent) to drive satire 'underground': to encourage the circulation of potentially dangerous satires in manuscripts—which were technically outside the licensing system—rather than in printed texts. Though fully aware that purveyors of any kind of 'transgressive' texts in this period needed to remain politically circumspect,[72] I would part company, however, with those who would see censorship *per se* as being the dominant, indeed determining force behind this culture.[73] Manuscript circulation was a medium already well established and available; it was not simply a reaction to print, nor to Government attempts to control printing.[74] If manuscript lampoons flourished in the 1670s, 1680s, and 1690s, it was not because manuscripts were necessarily 'safer' than print—their producers too could be tracked down and prosecuted if the Government and its agents and spies really wanted to. It was because, for a complex of social reasons, manuscript circulation provided an especially immediate and congenial culture in which such risqué, topical, and

[71] The King's 'Proclamation for the suppressing of seditious and treasonable books and pamphlets', 31 October 1679 (copy in CUL Sel.2.118⁴²).

[72] Fairly vivid examples of the prevalence of an element of circumspection at a time of political uncertainty or crisis appear in one of the letterbooks of Sir William Boothby (1637–1707), when he finds himself, in late 1688 and 1689, being denied 'private' and 'secrett papers' by booksellers who evidently see him as an 'outsider' and do not altogether 'trust' him: see my article ' "My books are the great joy of my life": Sir William Boothby, seventeenth-century bibliophile', *BC*, 46/3 (Autumn 1997), 350–78.

[73] e.g. Paul Hammond, in 'Censorship in the manuscript transmission of Restoration poetry', *E&S* NS 46 (1993), 39–62, argues that 'scribes produced copies of the latest political and erotic poems which no printer would risk handling' and that 'The scribal culture was in effect produced by the government's attempts to control printing.' I would, however, endorse his argument that 'manuscript circulation unlocked the creativity of readers by removing ['securing' *I would say*] poetry from the fixity and dignity of print, with its claims for definitive authority', etc.

[74] Neither is it certain, despite the recorded instances of Government prosecutions of offending publishers, whether the anti-libel laws had any real suppressive effect whatsoever. In August 1680, for instance, one broadside writer could comment on how 'Since that intolerable yoak of Licensing hath been broke . . . people may freely scribble what they think, and . . . Print what they scribble', the relative freedom and safety of circulation being assisted by 'the Ingenious undertaking of the Penny-Post': *Will with a whisp to Robbin Goodfellow* [Wing W2259] (copy in CUL Sel.2.118¹⁹²).

selectively communal material could most effectively flourish: when the interreaction between author, text, and reader of such things was at its liveliest, most coordinated, and most appropriate.

Anyone at all familiar with this body of literature will have come across references to *Julian*: namely, 'Captain' Robert Julian. After working as a naval secretary in the 1660s, Julian flourished as an independent entrepreneur from sometime in the 1670s to the late 1680s.[75] His particular contribution was to become, so far as we can tell, the principal purveyor of manuscript verse in this period. Facetiously dubbed the 'Secretary of the Muses', Julian is reported to have hired at least two scribes to copy out current verse satires and defamatory material on public figures, affairs of state, and other social goings-on. And then he is reported to have carried these handwritten lampoons around the town in his large coat pockets, hawking them about for ready money in taverns, coffee-houses, and other resorts. By so doing he became the butt of a host of lampoons himself. Mocked as a lumpish, ignorant, dull-witted, ulcerous, sottish man, over-fond of wine and brandy—he became a useful symbol, and occasional facetious mouthpiece, in satirical literature of the period as the archetypal 'scandal-carrier'. He offended too for political reasons, incurring the wrath of the Duke of Buckingham's anti-Court faction, for instance, by indiscriminately purveying Tory propaganda as well as Whig, besides antagonizing the Court itself. One lampoon on Charles II that he was caught selling ('Old Rowley') cost him a spell in prison and on the pillory, in November 1684, where, if some satirists are to be believed, he lost one or both of his ears.[76]

Here I can claim some satisfaction in being able to show what one of Julian's products looked like. We know from contemporary references that Julian produced not only single copies (or 'separates') of lampoons but also—and perhaps as his great speciality—what are described as 'books': 'books | Of scandal'.[77] Yet though it is assumed that some of his products *must* be among the numerous manuscripts of Restoration poems which still survive, no one has ever been able to identify a single one of them—again, precisely because the scribes carefully maintain their anonymity, leaving no attestation of provenance. The sole exception now arises in the case of a privately owned and hitherto unknown manuscript—because its provenance has been recorded on the flyleaf by its original owner (Plate 5):

I bought this booke of Julian not so much for my own use as to prevent others reading of it.

---

[75] For accounts of Julian's career, see the sources summarized in the section on Rochester in my *Index*, ii/2. 229–30, to which may be added Love, *passim* (especially pp. 249–59). The latest reference to Julian as a more or less current, if not positively active, figure would appear to occur in the Prologue to Dryden's *Amphitryon* in October 1690, where it is alleged 'Still *Julian's* interloping Trade goes on'. Thereafter references to him are clearly retrospective.

[76] It was actually for *forgery* that the harsh penalty of cutting off both ears, slitting the nostrils, and searing with a hot iron was imposed in the 17th century: see *Notaries public in England*, 101. It seems highly unlikely that Julian would have suffered this punishment by the 1680s. Nevertheless, besides indicating the degree to which Julian became a kind of legend or stereotype, rather than an individual known to satirists personally, the allegation reflects a commonplace of earlier satires on scriveners in general: see, for instance, references to loss of ears in Appendix I, Nos. 10, 20, and 21.

[77] 'Satire to Julian' (1682), printed in Wilson, *Court satires*, 86.

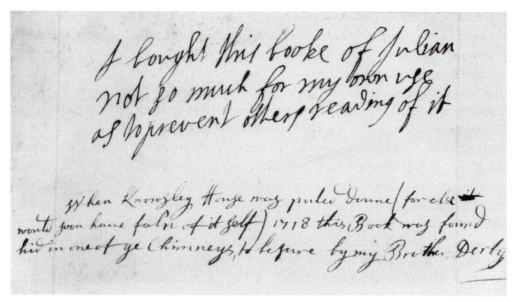

PLATE 5: Flyleaf of the Derby Manuscript (private collection)

That early owners of potentially sensitive material might be apt to treat it with a degree of circumspection, and even of guilty furtiveness, we know already from Pepys, who hid his 'collection' of Rochester's poems in a drawer as being 'written . . . in a style I thought unfit', he says, 'to mix with my other books'.[78] Here—in the second, later inscription found on this flyleaf—we have recorded an even more extreme instance of secretion:

When Knowsley House was puled doune (for else it would soon haue faln of it self) 1718 this Book was found hid in one of yᵉ Chimneys, to be sure by my Brother Derby.

In other words, the manuscript was bought directly from Julian by William Stanley, ninth Earl of Derby (*c.*1655–1702), who wrote in his own hand the first inscription here. This would most likely have been in 1682, to which the latest original contents of the manuscript can be dated. Then, sometime later, Derby hid the manuscript away at one of his country estates, at Knowsley House in Lancashire—perhaps in one of the very chimneys seen in the contemporary print shown in Plate 6. This was done before the ninth Earl's death in 1702, when he was succeeded by his brother James, tenth Earl of Derby (1664–1736), who found the manuscript in 1718 and added the second inscription recording the fact.[79]

---

[78] Pepys to William Hewer, 2 November 1680, printed in *Letters and the second diary of Samuel Pepys*, ed. R. G. Howarth (London, 1932), 104–5.

[79] This discovery would have been made twelve years after the tenth Earl had sold off his brother's library of some 2,900 volumes, in September 1706, to the Lichfield bookseller Michael Johnson (father of Dr Samuel Johnson): see Aleyn Lyell Reade, 'Michael Johnson and Lord Derby's library', *TLS* 27 July 1940, pp. 363, 365.

PLATE 6: Knowsley Hall, Lancashire

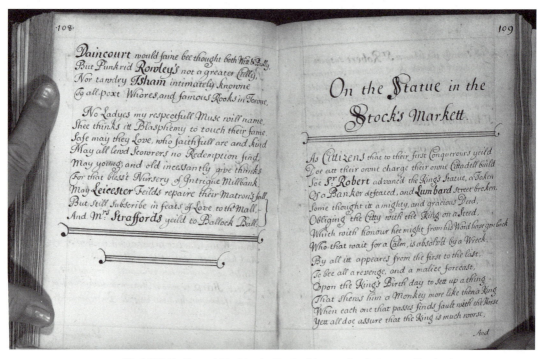

PLATE 7: Pages 108–9 in the Derby Manuscript (private collection)

PLATE 8: The contemporary binding on the Derby Manuscript (private collection)

As may be seen from a typical opening of the manuscript shown in Plate 7, the text is neatly, almost calligraphically set out in a thoroughly professional manner, on even, regularly spaced lines, complete with highlighting of certain words, engrossed or in bold for emphasis, and a little select ornamentation of majuscules; with the use of catchwords, pagination, and ruled margins; all set out with generous spacing—there is no attempt here to cram material on the page. And the scribe's accomplished, but conventional, flourished script would scarcely be distinguishable from that of any professional copyist of the period except for one or two little idiosyncrasies: such as his triple rules under titles and at the end of poems, with that distinctive C-shaped, or inverted C-shaped, curl at each end.

There is no gainsaying the quality of production here, its de luxe appearance: its overt look of expensiveness. The manuscript is a sturdy quarto volume with some 170 of its original pages covered in writing, containing an anthology of thirty poems and one prose satire; and it is handsomely bound in black goatskin—in the slightly coarser-grained type of morocco known as Turkey leather—elaborately tooled in gilt by a contemporary London craftsman (Plate 8).[80]

[80] The black Turkey leather is gold tooled with panels on the covers, corner and side pieces, and at the centre a coronet, the outer corners of the panel decorated with the same motif as the sides, but reversed, with bunches of grapes pendent from the edges,

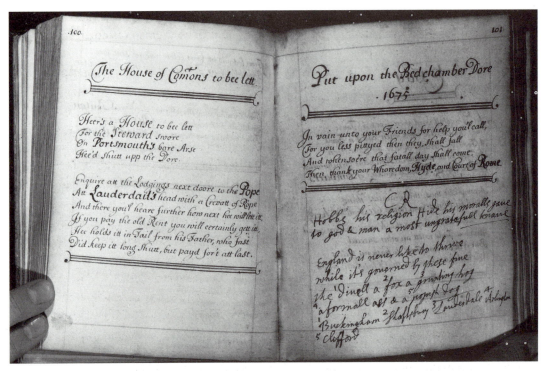

PLATE 9: Pages 100–1 in the Derby Manuscript (private collection)

All in all, the volume has the look of a *commissioned* product. And yet this is belied—as being but an illusion—by Derby's inscription, which implies that the book was there already, when he bought it to prevent anyone else's reading it. In other words, it was one of Julian's stock items—perhaps (though this is uncertain) even complete with binding—something that could be bought from him ready-made, off the peg, so to speak.

At the same time, there are features of this volume which remind us of essential differences between manuscript and print culture. *Bound* it might be, all the pages gilt-edged too, but *bounded* it is not. It is not a fixed, finalized, unchangeable production: a closed system, determined and circumscribed by its 'publisher', or even, in any sense, 'authorized'. The 170 pages of original writing are complemented by no fewer than eighty blank pages: in other words, the owner is invited to continue the anthology, to make additions—or have further poems professionally entered to order from time to time—just as if it were his private verse miscellany or commonplace book, *he* being the person who determined and controlled the texts. So it is not just the scriptoria who had a kind of 'rolling stock' of materials to purvey: their clients are invited to develop their

and surmounted by a vase of flowers; the spine in six compartments, one lettered 'PASQUI' (i.e. Pasquils), three with an 'arc and arrowhead' design (exemplified in Pepys's style H on his copy of Robert Boyle's *Sceptical chymist*, 1680, illustrated in Howard M. Nixon, *Catalogue of the Pepys Library at Magdalene College Cambridge*, volume vi: *Bindings* (Cambridge, 1984), plate 16*b*).

own rolling stock. The manuscript books, and even their texts, are open; still fluid and living, as it were; their clients encouraged to participate, to be themselves engaged in the process of collecting, even writing, as well as reading.

And this is exactly what Lord Derby did. So, for instance, on page 101 (Plate 9), we see the ninth Earl adding in his ungainly but unmistakable hand some verses on Charles II and on the CABAL in one of the blank spaces left by the original scribe.[81] And again, on page 120 (Plate 10), in the middle of a satire by the Earl of Dorset, we see the ninth Earl sufficiently engaged in the text to insert his own comments. 'Ashley was crafty', he says, and he adds a few names too to the next stanza, at the bottom of the page. It is also interesting to see here, in the word 'pedantick' on the sixth line, an addition written in the hand of the tenth Earl—entered maybe after he retrieved the book, but much more likely added earlier, when the poem was more topical and the volume perhaps subject to shared readership by the two brothers: another reminder of the select communal audience to which this kind of manuscript material might be subject. We see too how Derby has subsequently had two other professional scribes add poems dating up to November 1683 on some of the blank pages, chiefly at the end (Plates 11 and 12), bringing the total number of entries to 37.[82] And, finally, the ninth Earl has taken the trouble to update the original table of contents at the end—adding headings for the additions on pages 101 and 118, while the second professional scribe adds at the end (before deleting the one recorded already) the titles of *his* three contributions (Plate 13).

As for the contents of the volume, there was ample reason for Lord Derby to be interested in acquiring such a thing. Granted the occasionally forthright scatological or sexual language common to lampoons of the period, this is not a collection of salacious or pornographic materials—the kind of thing which probably accounted for Pepys's nervousness. It is essentially a collection of political, indeed predominantly Whig, satires attacking Charles II, his behaviour, his policies, and his Court.[83] We know that the ninth Earl of Derby—and especially his more politically active brother, the tenth Earl, soldier and staunch adherent of William III—were Whig supporters. And we know that the Derbys had a long-standing grudge against Charles II, who they believed had treated them shabbily after the Restoration.[84] So there was no ostensible reason for

---

[81] The ninth Earl's distinctive hand is found elsewhere in various surviving letters by him, as well as in some family books annotated by him, and I can identify one other poem copied by him—a text of the second Duke of Buckingham's elegy on Lord Fairfax ('Beneath this Place doth Lye')—at the University of Nottingham (Portland MS Pw V 424).

[82] A second scribe is responsible for adding three poems on pp. 118, 179–85, and a third scribe for the final poem on pp.186-8. The latest datable poem (pp. 183–5) is Robert Gould's elegy 'To ye Memory of Mr John Oldham', who died in November 1683.

[83] The thirty-one items in the hand of the original scribe include satires by Andrew Marvell, John Ayloffe, Henry Savile, and the Earl of Dorset, as well as by various anonymous writers.

[84] The tenth Earl even had an inscription mounted on the south front of his rebuilt Knowsley Hall in 1732 referring to Charles II's refusing [in 1672] 'a Bill passed unanimously by both Houses of Parliament, for restoring to the Family the Estate lost by his [i.e. James, the seventh Earl, executed by Parliament 15 October 1651] loyalty to him': Draper, 250, 252–3, 257–9, 306.

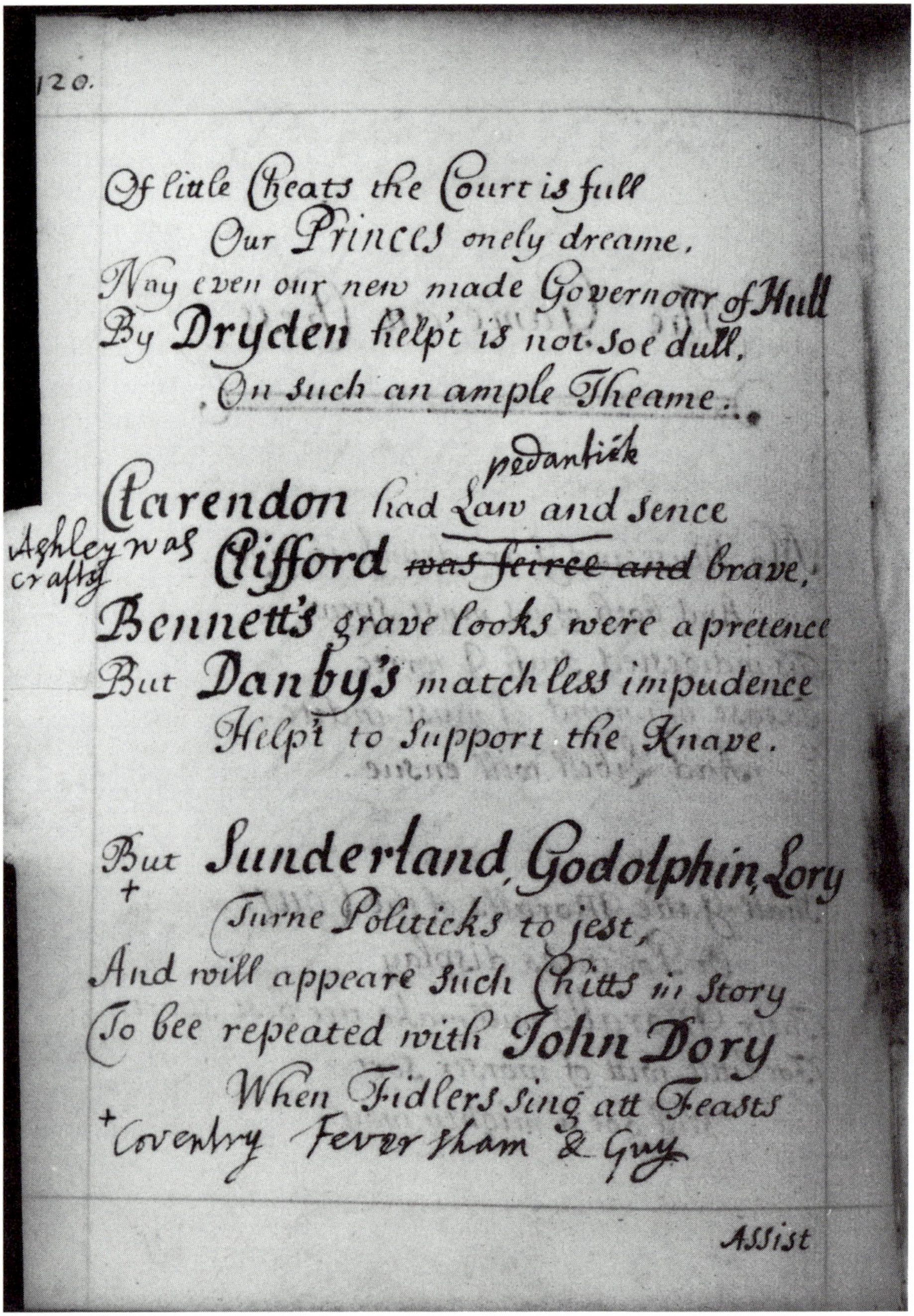
120.

Of little Cheats the Court is full
Our Princes onely dreame,
Nay even our new made Governour of Hull
By Dryden help't is not soe dull,
On such an ample Theame.

Clarendon had pedantick Law and sence
Ashley was crafty Clifford ~~was feirce and~~ brave;
Bennett's grave looks were a pretence
But Danby's matchless impudence
Help't to Support the Knave.

But Sunderland, Godolphin, Lory
\+ Turne Politicks to jest,
And will appeare such Chitts in Story
To bee repeated with John Dory
When Fidlers sing att Feasts
\+ Coventry Fevershham & Guy

Assist

PLATE 10: Page 120 in the Derby Manuscript (private collection)

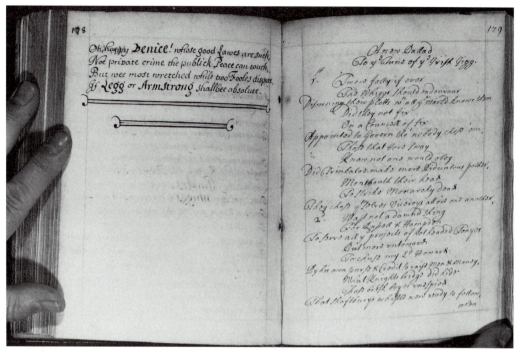

PLATE 11: Pages 178–9 in the Derby Manuscript (private collection)

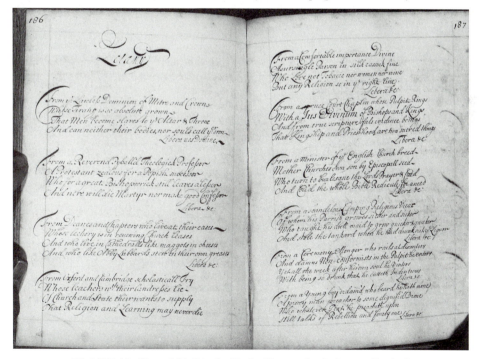

PLATE 12: Pages 186–7 in the Derby Manuscript (private collection)

	Page
Marvile's Ghost	75
Nostredamus, a Prophecy	79
St Martin	83
A Ballad	87
The Dr of Br's Lettany	95
The House of Commons to bee lett	100
Putt upon the Bedchamber Doore never likeh thine 1675	101 +
The Rabble hate &c	103
Nobilitas sola atq unica virtus A Satyr	105
On the Statue in the Stocks markett	109
The Queen's Ballad	113
Karacter of E M	116
Recipe	117
The Game att Chess	119
Peyton's Fall	123

	Page
A Dialogue between the two Horses &c	127
The Fancy	141
Quem Natura &c A Satyr	155
The Whores Address	169
my Opinion	173
The Commons Petition	110
A New Ballad	179
Elegy on Mr Oldham	103

PLATE 13: Last two pages of the 'Index' in the Derby Manuscript (private collection)

disapproval of the manuscript's contents, although, of course, they may have wished to exercise political caution in not displaying these satires openly and, in some symbolic way, of distancing themselves from the offending texts.

Nevertheless, in Derby's inscription, for all its ambiguity, we can, I believe, glimpse *inter alia* that all-telling, ambivalent attitude towards the man who had made and purveyed the very artefact which Derby might have been expected to enjoy. For despite all the sense of privilege and exclusivity which such a manuscript invites its owner to feel, I cannot help sensing in the terms of opprobrium which satirists in general heaped on Julian's head an underlying accusation: that, besides all else he had to answer for, Julian had effectively cheapened manuscript culture itself. He had appropriated it for ignoble uses. Instead of being a discreet servant, to whom a gentleman applied for a private and respectable service, Julian actively paraded himself around town searching out customers: he effectively brought manuscripts out of the relatively 'private' and socially elevated sphere of gentlemanly circulation on to the streets, as if they were chapbooks. A totally undiscriminating purveyor, who would transcribe anything for anybody for money, *and* hawk it around to all and sundry, Julian was—in the words of one harsh satirist—but the

> common shore of this poetic town,
> Where all our excrements of wit are thrown

and Julian himself, he accuses, 'Dost from this dung thy well-pick'd guineas gather'.[85] We see shades too of that old tradition we noted earlier—of the scrivener as prostitute. Julian was 'a Scribe . . . known | To ev'ry Bawd, Whore, Pimp . . . in Town';[86] 'Like a Bawd' he trafficked 'up and down' and procured 'for halfe the towne',[87] the brothels as much a venue of his trade as the coffee-houses.[88] He was effectively 'pimping' for his bread[89]—and, we may surmise, manuscripts themselves were debased by the association.

In fact, if we consider Lord Derby's inscription again, what *is* he saying? 'I bought this booke of Julian not so much for my own use as to prevent others reading of it.' Even if we interpret these words ironically, as some kind of flippant joke (though I do not think they are), we can detect clear unease, if not embarrassment: the need to find some kind of excuse for his purchase, the need to exonerate himself from culpability if anyone happened to find this manuscript in his possession, and as if it had been bought against his better judgement. We cannot exclude political considerations concerning its contents, of course. Nevertheless, read another way, this is not a neutral record of provenance: it is an indictment. It is a declaration of contempt for this book. Handsomely turned out as the volume is, superficially fit to occupy a proud place in a nobleman's library, its dress and appearance are meretricious. The book is, besides all else, invisibly but palpably *stigmatized*. It carries the mark of *Julian*. It is effectively condemned as prostituted wares, not fit to be in circulation: reviled, and shamefully hidden away.

Alas, the progression we have traced! From the sphere of angels we have descended to a chimney—and worse: to the gutter, and the sewer. Leaving the hallowed cloisters of the monastery and entering the practical, grubby world of business, finance, and law, the scribe lost his innocence—he became a 'scrivener' and all that that meant. His products—his deeds and bonds—occupying a place at the heart of the everyday transactions of society, he himself is condemned for becoming contaminated by commerce; indeed for his intimate association with the very instruments of commerce, and for his disproportionate and seemingly undeserved power. Nevertheless, by judicious methods of presentation, the manuscript culture which the scribe supports manages to some extent to remain aloof from the vulgarity of the market-place—at least in the sphere of 'literature'—'literature' in the narrow sense. Manuscripts of poems, dialogues, political,

---

[85] George Villiers, second Duke of Buckingham, 'A Familiar Epistle to Mr. Julian, Secretary to the Muses' (1677), reprinted in *POAS*, i. 387–91.

[86] Anon., 'Epitaph on the Secretary to the Muses', in Jane Barker, *Poeticall recreations, part II* (London, 1688), 65–6.

[87] Anon., 'A Rambling Satyr' (Lincolnshire Archives Office, Anc 15/B/4, 104–5).

[88] 'A letter to *Julian* in prison' (1684/5), in the Duke of Buckingham, *Works*, 2 vols. (London, 1703), ii, sig. Bb5ᵛ.

[89] 'Satyr Unmuzzled' (1680), in *POAS*, ii. 209, and 'Julian's Farewell to the Muses' (1685), in Wilson, *Court satires*, 138–9.

philosophical, legal, and antiquarian discourses and compilations remain largely the prerogative of cultivated gentlemen (and just occasionally of ladies as well)[90]—and are demonstrably more valued than printed books. And then, finally, 'literature' too shares the infection; it too becomes tainted. Just as authors themselves shake off the pretence of gentlemanly amateurism; as *they* descend to the market-place and write for money; and as the relentless democratization of literature leads to an ever-increasing sense of its degeneracy;[91] the pretence of manuscript texts to be in any way élite, to be above the common level of the market-place, is no longer sustainable. Those special qualities of manuscript culture which seemed to enhance literature are finally seen as being themselves but a commercial ploy and a deceit. Its dress is worn threadbare; its essential monetary basis no longer hidden; its prestige and distinction eroded; its hollowness exposed.

Julian himself—the most vilified purveyor of literary manuscripts of his century, and indeed the first such purveyor ever to be singled out for such sustained individual abuse—seems to appropriate all the denigration ever meted out to scribes and scriveners in general. *He* becomes emblematic of the larger changes. *He* becomes the incarnation of contemporary anxieties about where literature is heading. *He* becomes the whipping boy for what is perceived to be the commercial debasement and prostitution of literature itself.

Within a few years of the turn of the century, publishers have learned to capitalize on a public demand substantially created by lampoons disseminated by scribes, and most of the *Poems on affairs of state* have been printed. Manuscripts have finally descended to print. Julian's ultimate successors and heirs are not further scribes—the likes of Warcup and Somerton.[92] They are the likes of John Dunton, Edmund Curll, and the denizens of Grub Street.

[90] See, for example, the verse-collecting activities of Dame Sarah Cowper (1644–1720), mentioned (besides elsewhere) in Love, 201–2. An interesting, hitherto unrecorded case is that of Princess Mary (the future Queen Mary II), who writes from Holland in the 1680s to her friend Carey Frazier, Viscountess Mordaunt, commenting disparagingly on the latest 'verses' and 'lampoons' (in manuscript, perhaps) encountered or sent to her, but lamenting on one occasion the lack of 'New ones' ('I hope that wont grow out of fashion or change like othere things') (West Sussex Record Office, Chichester, Goodwood MS 1431/23, 29–30).

[91] Contempt for the hordes of indiscriminate 'scribblers' who 'invade' the press and cheapen literature is a commonplace of late-Restoration lampoons. In a characteristic example, *The character of wit's squint-ey'd maid, pasquil-makers* (London, 1681: copy in CUL Sel.2.123[139]), the satirist laments how

> The Curat poor Soul now goes to the Streets,
> His *Bibliotheque* buyes in their loose sheets.
> Nothing of volums *in Folio* are sold,
> The Stationers books moth eaten and old

and how

> This World is full of prepost'rous chat,
> Our *English* writers all are Transmigrate,
> In Pamphlet pennes, and diurnal *Scribes*,
> Wanton Comedians, and foul *Gypsy* Tribes

fulminating against the flourishing of 'Pedling, Petty, Sawcy Scribblers . . . crop-ear'd, circumcised, antique slave[s]', etc.

[92] From allusions in satires it is clear that Julian's immediate 'successors' as purveyors of MS lampoons in the late 1680s were Captain Lenthal Warcup (d. 1692), of the 1st Regiment of Foot Guards, and one John Somerton (*Index*, ii/2. 230); but their activities appear to have been very short-lived.

2

'It shall not therefore kill itself; that is, not bury itself': Donne's *Biathanatos* and its text

IN a well-known, often-quoted letter of 1619, John Donne entrusted a manuscript to Sir Robert Ker, later Earl of Ancrum (1578–1654). He declared: 'I only forbid it the Presse, and the Fire: publish it not, but yet burn it not; and between those, do what you will with it.'[1]

This has been regarded as one of Donne's key statements about his own texts. Indeed it has been seen as encapsulating Donne's whole attitude towards his unpublished works in general—as showing, in effect, his wholehearted support of the coterie manuscript culture to which they belonged.[2] This may be so. Nevertheless, I think we must also recognize that Donne is applying very specific instructions to one very specific work: *Biathanatos*, his huge, elaborately argued, copiously documented treatise on suicide, or self-homicide, as he calls it. This is his first major prose discourse, so far as we know, and, with the sole exception of the 430-page *Pseudo-Martyr* which followed shortly afterwards (1610), it is by far the longest single work in the Donne canon.

It would be easy to speculate at length on why Donne felt so demonstratively cautious, if not nervous, about this work. There is its subject for a start. Suicide is hardly the safest or least challenging of subjects in the field of Christian ethics. There is, moreover, Donne's own personal, and potentially vulnerable situation at this time, in these years before he entered the Church—one which impelled caution, to say the least, about his pronouncements on doctrinal matters. Not to mention the fact that theological controversy, even in the best of circumstances, was like entering a minefield. 'Contemplative and bookish men', he says, in what must surely be understatement, 'must of necessitie be more quarrelsome then others'.[3] Most especially, as he tells Ker, the discourse was capable of inviting unfortunate interpretations: it was, he says, 'upon a misinterpretable subject', and he had had negative reactions from 'some particular friends

---

[1] John Donne, *Letters to severall persons of honour* (London, 1651), 22.

[2] e.g. Richard B. Wollman, 'The "press and the fire": Print and manuscript culture in Donne's circle', *SEL* 33 (1993), 85–97.

[3] John Donne, *Biathanatos: A declaration of that paradoxe, or thesis, that selfe-homicide is not so naturally sinne, that it may never be otherwise* (London, [1647]), Preface, p. 20. (This edition is henceforth cited as *Quarto*.)

in both Universities'. They had detected—rightly or wrongly, perhaps—'a false thread in it,' he says, though 'not easily found'.[4]

We might sense the sort of thing that Donne feared when we read, for instance, what that great connoisseur of arcane learning and heresy Jorge Luis Borges (1899–1986) had to say about it. He once suggested that the central idea behind *Biathanatos* is the notion that God created the world in order to construct his own scaffold.[5] The devout Anglican Dame Helen Gardner is reported (in hearsay) to have been taken aback by the suggestion that Donne's comments on the Crucifixion seemed to imply that Christ, in effect, committed suicide. And yet Donne is perfectly clear on this point. He discusses it at some length: 'nor was there any other then his own will, the cause of his dying at that time', he says.[6]

Moreover, Donne's comments *might* be interpreted as a confession that he was simply not confident of the work's success *as* a treatise: that—for all its serious and elaborate argument and learning—he was not sure it actually measured up to the magnitude of its theme, or proved wholly convincing. After all, if properly handled, its subject might *not* have been 'misinterpretable'.

Are we really meant to take seriously Donne's comment to Ker that 'it is a Book written by *Jack Donne*, and not by D[r]. *Donne*'?[7] Are we really supposed to think that *Biathanatos*, written in his mid-thirties, a work of immense labour, clearly meant to be taken very seriously indeed, was no more than an effort by the author of 'On his mistress going to bed', or the *Satyres*, or 'The character of a Scot', and the like? Yes, there are other ways of reading this remark: such as that 'Jack Donne', the private man, did not have the kind of responsibility of 'Dr. Donne', the public man,[8] or that 'Jack Donne' the layman might have certain freedoms not appropriate to a Christian cleric, and so on. Nevertheless, it is at least possible to wonder whether he might not have been expressing some anxiety: a considered view that, in relation to its pretensions, the treatise was immature—no more than a kind of student exercise—or a sort of embryonic doctoral dissertation (or *thesis*, as indeed it is called in its subtitle) that did not quite make the grade: something not *worthy* of 'Dr. Donne'.

This brings us to the situation Donne found himself in when he allowed a copy of his work to be made and given to someone else—to his friend Sir Edward Herbert. In his presentation letter to Herbert (Plate 14) Donne is found—having finished the work—wondering, in a sense, what he should do with it. He recognizes fully the irony of his position, the paradox—that he should be concerned about the preservation of a trea-

---

[4] Donne, *Letters* (1651), 21–2.

[5] J. L. Borges, 'The *Biathanatos*', in *Other inquisitions 1937–1952*, trans. Ruth L. C. Simms (London, 1973), 89–92 (p. 92).

[6] *Biathanatos*, III. iv. 5: 1647 *Quarto*, 189; John Donne, *Biathanatos*, A modern-spelling edition, with Introduction and Commentary, by Michael Rudick and M. Pabst Battin (New York, 1982), 171; *Biathanatos by John Donne*, ed. Ernest W. Sullivan II (Newark, NJ, 1984), 129.

[7] Donne, *Letters* (1651), 22.   [8] Rudick & Battin, pp. xv–xvi.

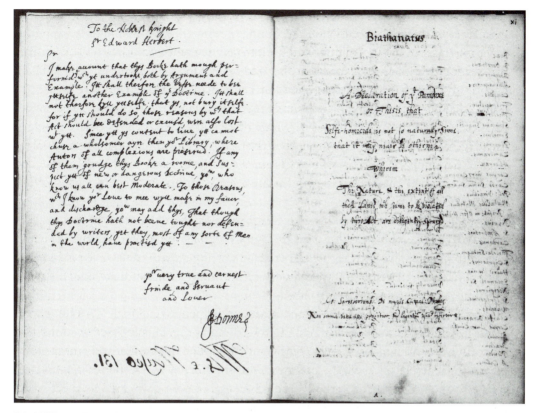

PLATE 14: Donne's autograph letter to Edward Herbert opposite the title-page of the Herbert Manuscript (Bodleian Library MS e. Mus. 131, pp. x–xi)

tise about self-destruction—compounded by a possible awareness that there is no fully satisfactory medium in which it can survive. In a kind of limbo, he finally decides: 'It shall not, therefore, kill itself; that is, not bury itself.' While himself retaining the original manuscript, his decision is effectively to entrust the preservation of the work (though, incidentally, he never says its *exclusive* preservation) to a manuscript copy, consigned to the wholesome air of Herbert's library, with Herbert himself acting as its custodian and, as he puts it, his 'moderator' ('yow, who know us all, can best Moderate', he says). We might recall that in the universities a 'moderator' was the don who had the final say (or 'determination') on subjects treated by disputants for an academic degree.

If we ask, then, who got the chance to read *Biathanatos* in Donne's own lifetime, the scant and inconclusive evidence available to us suggests that the numbers may have been pretty small. From comments made by Donne himself in 1619, we know that 'some particular friends in both Universities' had read it;[9] though whether that means

---

[9] Donne, *Letters* (1651), 21.

at about the time it was written—that is, probably in 1608—or later, during the next decade, is uncertain. John Donne the Younger, who (despite his father's expressed wishes to the contrary) took it upon himself to *publish* the work in the 1640s, identifies two readers who had had access to the treatise before then when he tells William Cavendish (1592–76), Marquess and later Duke of Newcastle: 'you were pleased to looke vpon this Booke, when it was in an imperfect Manuscript, (manie yeares since) in the hands of Sr Ieruaise Clifton'[10]—Sir Gervase Clifton, Bt. (1587–1666), if indeed this is the particular 'Sir Gervase Clifton' referred to, being a Nottinghamshire neighbour of Cavendish's. At least one of Donne's editors assumes that these aristocratic gentlemen would qualify as two of Donne's early university friends, and that the 'imperfect Manuscript' made available to them was nothing less than Donne's holograph.[11] In 1607/8 both Cavendish and Clifton were students, between 15 and 20 years old: Clifton at St John's College, Oxford, until 1612; Cavendish at St John's College, Cambridge, and apparently receiving his MA incorporated at Oxford on 8 July 1608.[12] But is it likely that Donne would be showing his work to undergraduates half his age—soliciting *their* advice, deferring to *their* judgement—effectively using *them* as his university moderators, instead of men much more academically qualified? The suggestion seems implausible, to say the least. It might be thought more likely that Cavendish and Clifton were among a few select gentlemen who were shown Herbert's 'imperfect' manuscript copy later. As for the precise identity of the 'particular friends in both Universities' whom Donne consulted and who *were* early readers, we can only speculate.[13]

Even Donne's old friend Sir Henry Goodyer (1571–1627) was denied a copy—at least initially so. Writing probably in 1608, Donne mentions 'the copy of my Book' that he has had made in London, 'of which', he says, 'it is impossible for me to give you a copy so soon, for it is not of much lesse then 300 pages', and he goes on to assure Goodyer that he has 'not appointed it upon any person, nor ever purposed to print it'.[14] Again we are left to wonder whether this 'copy' is that he subsequently gave to Herbert. Certainly the approximate number of pages tallies, as we shall see.

The rather ambiguous sentence in which his reference to 'the copy of my Book' appears has, I think, misled certain scholars into adding one other name to the brief list of early readers—that of his friend Sir Edward Conway, first Viscount Conway (*c*.1564–1631). It has even been argued that Donne sent an autograph copy to Conway

---

[10] Presentation inscription by John Donne Jr (1604–62), 10 May 1648, in a copy of *Biathanatos* (London, [1647]) at Harvard University (EC.D7187.644b (C)); printed in Sullivan, p. xlvii.

[11] Sullivan, pp. xxxv–xxxvi.   [12] Ibid., pp. xxxv–xxxvi, lxviii–lxix.

[13] In a private communication I. A. Shapiro has suggested to me that these 'particular friends' are likely to have been distinguished academics whom Donne met while working as assistant to Thomas Morton (1564–1659) in his preparation of anti-Catholic polemics from about 1605 to 1607 and perhaps afterwards: see Bald, 202–12. 'Bald', Shapiro observes, 'is sceptical about Jessopp's statements about this employment, but my researches have amply justified them.' Shapiro also notes that most of the authors cited by Donne in *Biathanatos* are those cited in Morton's *Apologiae Catholicae* (London, 1605–6) [STC 18173.5, 18175.5].

[14] Donne, *Letters* (1651), 34–5.

in the Netherlands.[15] For he begins the sentence: 'The day before I lay down, I was at *London*, where I delivered your Letter for Sr *Ed. Conway*, and received another for you, with the copy of my Book [etc.].' Besides what seems to me to be the inherent unlikelihood of Donne's sending a manuscript to Conway in the Netherlands, his sentence contains, I think, two or three quite separate and unrelated statements. The dominant idea is not what is going on in relation to *Conway*, but what Donne is doing in *London*. So I would interpret Donne's slightly convoluted sentence as saying: 'The day before I became ill, I was at London, where I delivered your letter for Sir Edward Conway, and where I received another letter for you, and where I also collected the copy of my book'. So, no, I do not think that Conway did necessarily ever see the work.

Otherwise *Biathanatos* is known for sure only to have been seen by Herbert and Ker. And on both occasions Donne is effectively solving his problem of what to do with it by putting a manuscript into the hands of a trusted confidant and arbiter—or, if you will, custodian and librarian—one who will (*a*) preserve it, and (*b*) decide for him who should see it and who not (Herbert being entrusted to 'moderate', Ker to 'do what you will with it'). In Ker's case, the two likely consequences seem to be either that (as Ernest Sullivan believes) Donne retrieved his manuscript sometime after his return from Germany in January 1619/20,[16] or else (as I. A. Shapiro believes) the manuscript was retrieved later from Ker by the younger Donne to use as his copy-text in the 1640s.[17] In Herbert's case, there was a kind of limited posthumous 'publication' of sorts, in so far as, in 1642, eleven years after Donne's death, Herbert made the decision to deposit his manuscript copy in the Bodleian Library, where it still remains.[18] The full 'publication' of the work in print was the younger John Donne's Quarto edition, entered in the Stationers' Register on 25 September 1646 and almost certainly put out in 1647.

Since the Herbert Manuscript is the first copy known to have been made—and actually survives—it is worth further consideration.

The Herbert Manuscript is a small folio, 287 pages long, written for the most part in a neat, careful, scribal hand, and was clearly produced at Donne's instigation, for Donne himself has gone through it adding in his own hand scores of marginal citations. Some of them can be seen in Plate 15. On page 215 Donne has inserted in the margin

---

[15] Paul R. Sellin, *So doth, so is religion: John Donne and diplomatic contexts in the Reformed Netherlands, 1619–1620* (Columbia, Mo., 1988), 17–21.

[16] Sullivan, p. xli.

[17] Private communication by I. A. Shapiro, who notes that both Donne Jr and Ker were living in London in the 1640s; that Ker himself was in a state of 'infirmity' in these years, as well as in a precarious financial situation; and that Donne Jr probably retrieved from Ker at the same time a number of his father's letters to Ker which he afterwards printed in the 1651 *Letters*.

[18] This would, of course, be another reason why Donne Jr did not use Herbert's MS as his copy-text, since he had no exclusive access to it. Textual variants between the holograph of Donne's presentation letter to Herbert and that printed in *Letters* (1651), 20–1, suggest, moreover, that Donne Jr was printing in the latter from a MS copy rather than from Herbert's original: see Ernest W. Sullivan II, 'The problem of text in Familiar Letters', *PBSA* 75 (1981), 115–26 (pp. 118–20). Certainly Donne Jr was very aware of his father's comments in this letter, as echoes and paraphrases of them occur repeatedly in his dedications and presentation inscriptions in the Quarto *Biathanatos*: see Sullivan, pp. xliii–xlvii, 249–50.

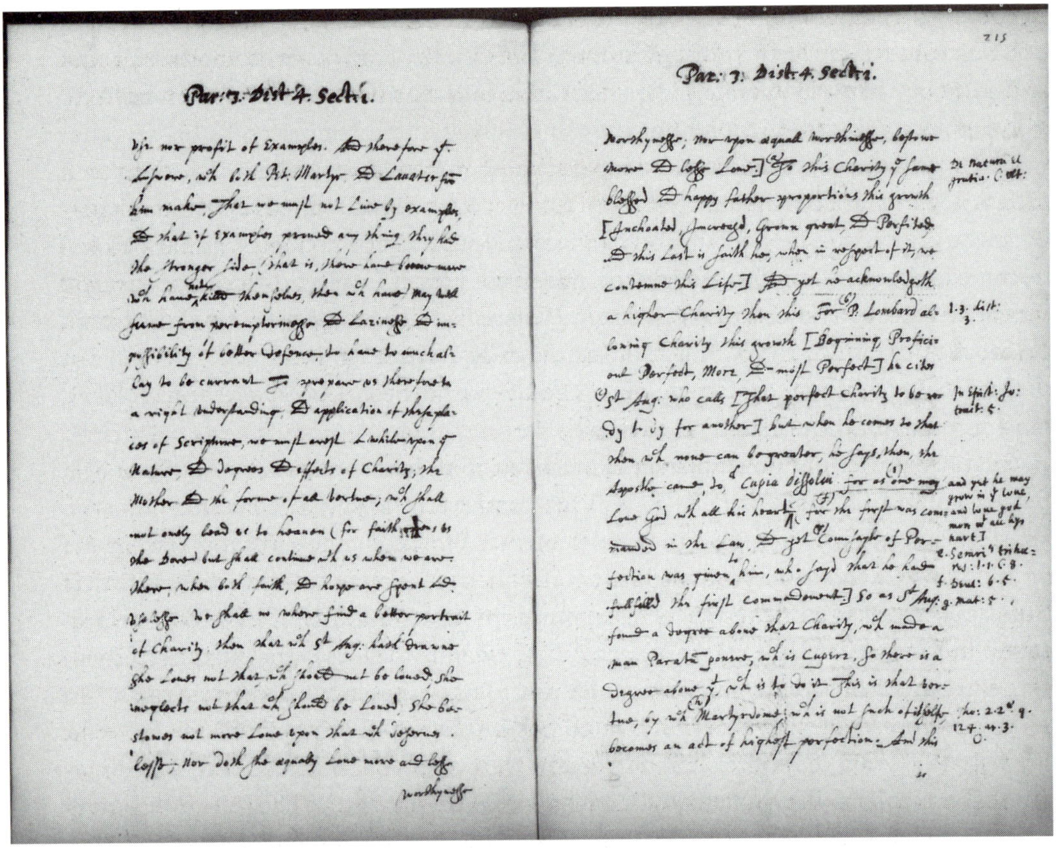

PLATE 15: Two facing pages in the Herbert Manuscript (Bodleian Library MS e. Mus. 131, pp. 214–15)

a sixteen-word addition, probably to fill in a lacuna left by his amanuensis as a result of eyeskip. The passage here, above three autograph citations on the right, completes the sense of a sentence about loving God: 'For as one may loue God with all his heart *and yet he may grow in y^t loue, and loue god more w^t all hys hart.*' There are also, in the main body of the text in this manuscript, a few other corrections in Donne's hand. Nevertheless, although the overall impression is that the manuscript was pretty carefully prepared, and though Donne picked up and corrected a few errors here and there that he happened to spot, it is quite clear that he made no systematic attempt to check every word of this copy, and, in fact, many errors certainly remain uncorrected.

There are two schools of thought on the dating of this manuscript. One, the traditional one, since the time of Evelyn Simpson, is that it was prepared not long after the completion of the work itself in 1608, or at least within a year or two.[19] The other,

---

[19] Evelyn M. Simpson, *A study of the prose works of John Donne* (Oxford, 1924; 2nd edn., 1948), 162. Incidentally, Donne Jr refers, in 1647, to the work's having 'lyen still' [i.e. lain hidden from sight] 'these fiftie last years' (Sullivan, p. xlv). Donne Jr was notoriously vague and unreliable in factual details of this kind (50 sermons get cited by him as '60' sermons, and so on).

Ernest Sullivan's view, is that it dates probably from the late 1620s. Professor Sullivan finds corroboration for this dating from the watermark in the paper, comprising a staff and pennant, one which he has also discovered in letters of 1628 and 1629 written to and from the Earl of Pembroke.[20]

For my part, I side with the traditionalists. I believe that watermark evidence is inconclusive—stocks of paper could be used over a period of years and watermark patterns are not unknown to recur.[21] I think, too, that the style of address in Donne's letter to Herbert is compelling evidence. He signs himself 'yo*r* uery true and earnest frinde, and Seruant and Louer J: Donne'. This is the kind of address he uses in letters before his ordination in 1615, and in fact from his Mitcham period before 1612, not thereafter. In later years, and certainly in the 1620s, he tends to subscribe letters: 'Your poor servant in Chr[ist] Jesus' and the like.[22]

Furthermore, and more importantly, it seems to me that the whole tenor of Donne's presentation letter to Herbert is that of a man still essentially engaged with the work— the text is still warm and living, as it were, and Donne is ostensibly addressing the notion of whether or not to kill and bury it. This is quite distinct from the import of his letter to Ker—written in March 1619, and, as *I* think, a decade later—which shows an essential distancing between him and the work. *Biathanatos* is a treatise which has then, as it were, become cold: something worthy of being preserved, if *not* resurrected, but only as a sort of monument to the 'Jack Donne' of years ago. When Donne tells Ker in 1619 that no copy of the work has ever been made—'no hand hath passed upon it to copy it', he says—I would not discount here a degree of rhetorical licence, or exaggeration, or indeed diplomatic strategy. This was, I suspect, the result of Donne's state of mind at this time, when he was, in all seriousness, tidying up his affairs in case he did not come back alive from his trip to Germany with Viscount Doncaster. Besides his having to explain his renewed attention to the treatise—something he does not have to do when he writes to Herbert—it suits his case to stress to Ker how unique his manuscript of *Biathanatos* is, to make Ker look after it the more carefully and earnestly. It would have been less than tactful to mention that there might have been at least one other copy in existence.

At this point I would like to consider briefly the text of *Biathanatos* and what editors have hitherto assumed about it.

Michael Rudick and M. Pabst Battin, whose edition appeared in 1982, and Ernest Sullivan, whose edition appeared in 1984, seem to be agreed that a single exemplar lies behind both *Herbert* and the 1647 *Quarto*—albeit representing the work in different

---

[20] Sullivan, p. xxxviii.

[21] In a private communication, I. A. Shapiro concurs: 'This watermark is common from ca 1606 in my experience.'

[22] Rudick & Battin, p. xcviii.

states of revision or 'completeness'. Rudick and Battin inform us (p. c) that there are some 825 substantive variants between the two texts—many of which are undoubtedly transmissional errors to which the printed *Quarto* would seem to be even more subject than *Herbert*. The editors part company in that Sullivan assumes (p. xli) that the common exemplar is Donne's autograph manuscript, or holograph, while Rudick and Battin postulate (pp. c–ci) that the copy-text for *Quarto* could well have been a scribal transcript that itself perpetuated the kind of errors found in *Herbert*.

As for what the two sources tell us about the evolution of the work, Sullivan postulates (pp. xxxvii, xxxix–xl) that Donne probably added the citations to his own retained manuscript at about the time that he did so to *Herbert*, and that he then went on to add in his own manuscript (as an afterthought, perhaps) a passage not found in *Herbert*, as well as various other corrections and minor revisions.

However, what Sullivan rejects as the work of Donne is the many scores of numbered sidenotes in the *Quarto* which provide paragraph-summaries of the text. After Donne's death, he says (p. xl), 'The hundreds of marginal glosses and Distinction and Section headings . . . may have been added to the holograph by Donne's son', a step taken, he suggests, in anticipation of publication, 'to widen the possible audience of the work'. Partly for this reason Sullivan chooses as his copy-text *Herbert*, which, for all its shortcomings, he considers the more demonstrably authoritative of the two (p. lviii). Rudick and Battin, on the other hand, accept *Quarto*—also despite its *own* crop of errors and corruptions—as being the more reliable witness to Donne's complete text (pp. ci–cii, cix). Nevertheless, they too neglect to print the summary-sidenotes, which they, like Sullivan, regard as an unnecessary addition (p. cv). We shall return to this question of the sidenotes, for I think it is of some significance in the light of new evidence.

One statement made by Sullivan in his introduction may now flatly be refuted. 'No evidence', he says (p. xxxix), 'supports the existence at any time of manuscript copies other than the holograph and M [*Herbert*].' In fact, we do have another surviving manuscript of *Biathanatos*—a third surviving witness to Donne's text—which I would now like to introduce.

It would be appropriate if a new manuscript had turned up in the library of Donne's own (albeit rebuilt) church, St Paul's Cathedral. It is perhaps only slightly less appropriate that one should have come to light in a collection now kept in that other great shrine of the Anglican Church, Canterbury Cathedral. For this reason I shall call it the Canterbury Manuscript—or *Canterbury* for short.

The manuscript—of which a characteristic opening is shown in Plate 16—is a small quarto volume, made up of quires of irregular size,[23] altogether 245 pages long.

---

[23] Collation: 1^{20}, 2–7^{16}, 8^{12}; 2 separate leaves on upper pastedown; final leaf of last quire forming the lower pastedown, with a further single leaf pasted over it.

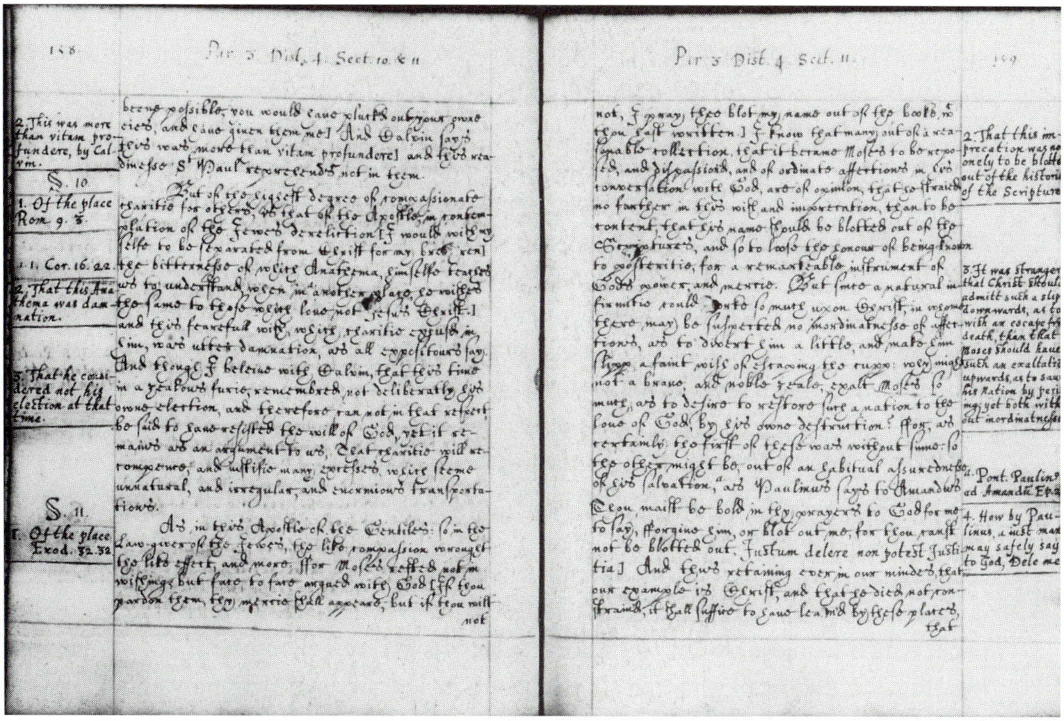

PLATE 16: Two facing pages in the Canterbury Manuscript (Canterbury Cathedral U210/2/2, pp. 158–9)

Biathanatos is the only text in the volume, occupying 210 pages, with the 35 pages after it left blank. It was certainly bound after the writing was completed, and almost certainly it retains its original binding: plain vellum boards with green silk ties. One interesting, if incidental, detail is that on the inside of the lower cover someone has inscribed in ink two Greek words: Πείθεσθε ἡγουμεύοις (peithesthe hegoumenois). This is a quotation from the Greek New Testament, from St Paul's Epistle to the Hebrews (13: 17), which is translated in the Authorized Version as 'Obey them that have the rule over you'. It recalls Donne's own, somewhat controversial attitude to the King's prerogative, which he describes in this very work as 'incomprehensible' (meaning 'illimitable') and which, he says, 'overflowes and transcends all law'.[24]

The manuscript also contains on a flyleaf some later scribbling, but I shall say more about that later.

Canterbury is written throughout in a single hand: a fairly neat, professional-looking, Secretary script. The text is methodically laid out, with ruled margins and running heads, and the pages are closely written—the scribe does not believe in wasting space. It may be seen in Plate 16 how, for instance, he relegates section headings to the side—Sections 10 and 11, or just 'S10' and 'S11', as he has it—instead of centring headings

---

[24] *Biathanatos*, I. ii. 2: *Canterbury*, 29; *Quarto*, 48.

with plenty of surrounding space, as the *Quarto* does—while all the sidenotes and citations are closely packed into the margins. The hand (which I have not come across anywhere else) is obviously quite different from that of the amanuensis employed by Donne for *Herbert*. It is safe to say that *Canterbury* shows no sign of having been produced under Donne's supervision, or, for that matter, of having any direct connection with the author himself. We cannot prove that Donne did not commission the manuscript, but there is no trace of his hand in it—or, indeed, of any hand in the text other than the copyist's. There are no corrections, and everything about the manuscript—both its appearance and the variable quality of its text—suggests that this was a purely professional copy, made for someone by a hired scribe, completed perhaps as quickly and efficiently as he could, but as a purely routine job without any specially careful attempt to check the accuracy of his transcript.

Whoever commissioned the manuscript, it is worth considering that it contains something like 75,000 words, and that it would probably have taken at least a good week's work—maybe two weeks' work—to produce. As an experiment, I have tried copying out pages of this manuscript myself and timing myself: depending on the degree of haste adopted, it varied from less than seventeen to fully twenty minutes per page, which would amount to the best part of sixty or seventy hours of copying altogether.[25] If the scribe charged somewhere between a penny-ha'penny and twopence a page—which seems to have been about the average rate, so far as we can tell, although (especially for more complicated copy, as this is) some accounts for scribes go as high as fivepence a page[26]—the cost of producing this manuscript, including paper and binding, is very unlikely to have been under a pound and might have been considerably more. In other words, the total cost of *Canterbury* may well have amounted to more than the retail price of the 1623 First Folio of Shakespeare.

As for dating, the evidence is suggestive, but inconclusive.

The watermark in the paper (Figure 1) comprises a coat of arms in the form of a shield, with a horizontal band of stars (a *fess* of *estoilles*, to use the proper heraldic terms), and with some not entirely clear lettering at the base. I find nothing in Briquet, Heawood, Churchill, or Gaudriault remotely like it. It might, possibly, represent the municipal arms of some town, perhaps in France, but there seems to be nothing at present to date it precisely within the first half of the seventeenth century.

---

[25] An interesting witness to the sheer tedium and laboriousness of scribal production is found in the journal of William Thomas Statham (1694–1738), who records in 1737, between 19 September and 15 October, simply ruling lines and margins on 288 leaves: 'I reckon I was about sixty hours in finishing the whole' (Sotheby's sale catalogue, 7 December 1984, lot 351). Other records exist of long periods spent in transcribing, though without specific counts of man hours. For instance, Sir Thomas Wilson, Keeper of the Records, mentions on 30 July 1623 that the copies of relevant papers made by him and his two clerks in preparation for Edward Lord Herbert's embassy to France (1619–24) 'cost at least 2 or 3 munthes labour in writeing' (PRO, SP 45/20, f. 91r), and the scribe responsible for University of London MS 285, a folio volume of 428 leaves 'bound vpp the 25th of Aprill 1637', records copying it in Mostyn Hall from books belonging to Sir Roger Mostyn's son-in-law, Richard Grosvenor, 'at my being there from Christmas to May' (and cf. Appendix II below, No. 82).

[26] See below, Ch. 3 n. 12.

FIGURE 1

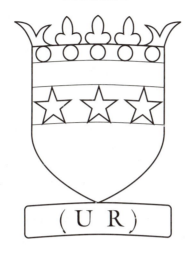

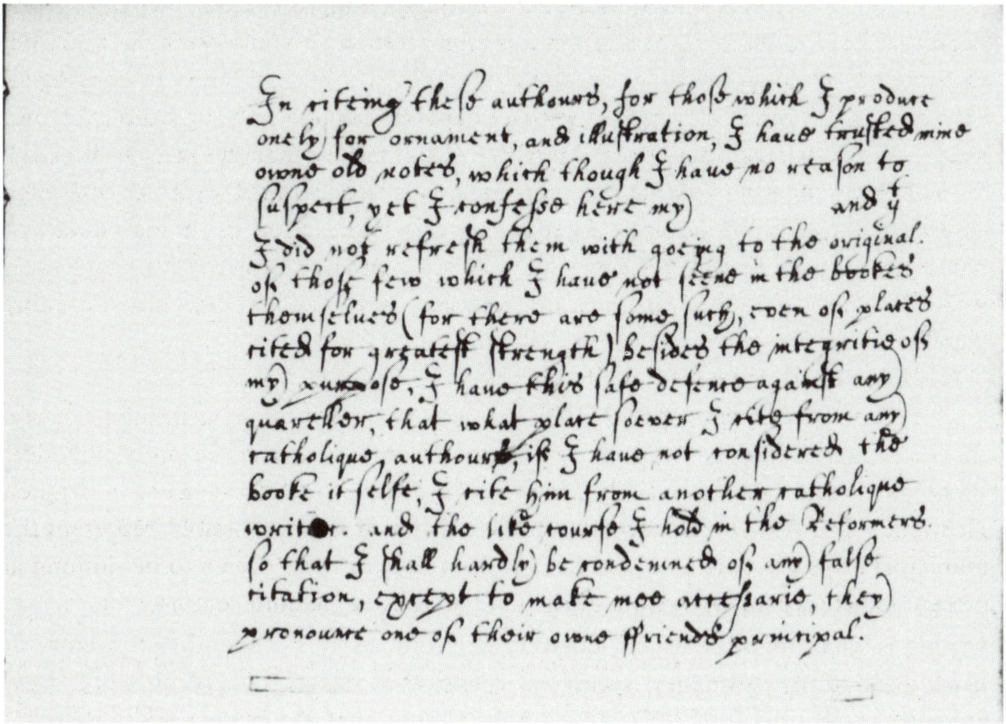

In citing these authours, for those which I produce
onely for ornament, and illustration, I have trusted mine
owne old notes, which though I have no reason to
suspect, yet I confesse here my   and yt
I did not refresh them with going to the originall.
of those few which I have not seene in the bookes
themselves (for there are some such, even of places
cited for greatest strength) besides the integritie of
my purpose, I have this safe defence against any
quarreller, that what place soever I cite from any
catholique authour, if I have not considered the
booke it selfe, I cite him from another catholique
writer. and the like course I hold in the Reformers.
so that I shall hardly be condemned of any false
citation, except to make mee accessario, they
pronounce one of their owne ffriends principal.

PLATE 17: A page of the preliminaries in the Canterbury Manuscript (Canterbury Cathedral U210/2/2, p. [iii])

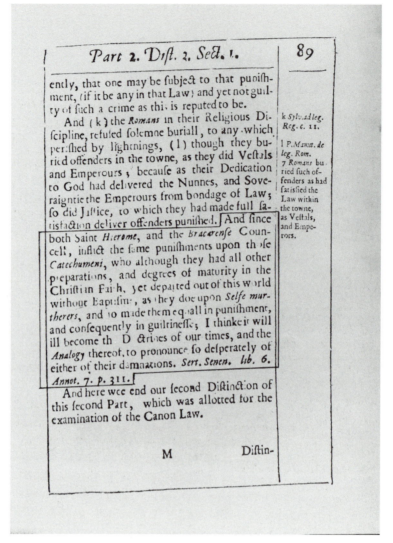

PLATE 18: Page 89 of the Quarto edition, [1647] (with paragraph here boxed off)

The parameters of the handwriting can be set scarcely more closely. The handwriting is what might be called, not very helpfully, early 17th-century Secretary. It bears none of the distinctive features of rounded or mixed Italic script which were creeping into handwriting style in the 1620s–1630s—no fashionable, innovative mannerisms such as clubbed descenders, and the like—but, then, much work by professional scribes was not influenced by such things. It is a script that could have been produced at any time between the early 1600s and, just possibly, as late as the 1640s.

As for the nature of its text, *Canterbury* is independent of both *Herbert* and the

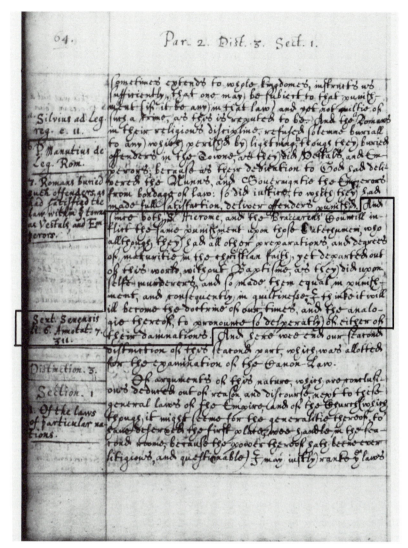

PLATE 19: A page of the Canterbury Manuscript (with paragraph here boxed off) (Canterbury Cathedral U210/2/2, p. 64)

Quarto. We can state categorically that none of these three texts was copied from either of the others.

As if there could be any doubt about the matter, *Canterbury* was certainly copied from a manuscript. As can be seen in Plate 17, showing Donne's 'apology' after the preliminary list of authors cited, in line 4 from the top there is a space for a word the scribe (or else the scribe responsible for his exemplar) could not decipher: the word 'laziness' ('yet I confesse here my *laziness*').

Canterbury contains the complete text, as printed in the *Quarto*, including all its additional sidenotes and the substantive revisions which do not appear in *Herbert*. Most notable among these additions is the passage (in II. ii. 3) on page 89 of the *Quarto*—nearly 90 words, extending Donne's argument about the *Catechumeni*, a body of early Christian novitiates (see Plate 18, where I have taken the liberty of boxing off the relevant passage). As Sullivan notes in his edition (p. xl), it is interesting to see the way the citation is printed (at the bottom of the boxed section). What is printed as 'Sert. Senen.' etc.—a reference to the sixteenth-century Jewish Dominican, Sextus Senensis—should appear in the margin, but it appears here directly after the passage as if part of the main text. Sullivan conjectures that this arises probably because this additional passage was written by Donne in the margin of his manuscript, and the compositor later failed to discriminate between the main-text addition and the citation which was supposed to stay in the margin. This mistake was not made by the *Canterbury* scribe, as may be seen in Plate 19 (with the relevant passage again boxed off). The citation is relegated correctly to the margin—though without any key letter—and, incidentally, with the citation more correctly rendered as 'Sext. Senensis', instead of 'Sert. Senen[sis]'.

So, then, in light of all this: Do we have here a third, independent, and direct witness to Donne's original manuscript?

I cannot give an exact count, but *Canterbury* contains several hundred substantive variants from the *Quarto* edition—the text which it most closely approximates. Many of the variants are peculiar to *Canterbury*; others support *Herbert* over against *Quarto*, and just occasionally *Canterbury* will even support a reading found in *Quarto* over against *Herbert*. I can best summarize, I think, by considering the work as a series of sections, or even layers—an approach which Donne's own elaborate arrangement in this treatise, of multiple Parts, Distinctions, and Sections, would seem to encourage.

First of all, there is what we may call the main body of text—the text beginning with Part I, after all the preliminaries—but, for the moment, excluding all the sidenotes. Here the pattern which seems to emerge is that the vast majority of the variants in *Canterbury* can be explained by simple mechanical errors, misreadings of a common source. We find pretty well all the usual kinds of errors and corruptions associated with scribal transmission: words omitted through eyeskip; words and phrases needlessly repeated (because they get lodged, as it were, in the scribe's mind); verbal misreadings resulting from inadequate attention to meaning—the *Canterbury* scribe will write, for instance, 'afford' instead of 'offend', 'included' instead of 'violated', 'courage the Beasts' instead of 'corrupt the Beasts', and so on; and then, on the other hand, changes which come about precisely because the scribe is interpreting meaning rather than the letter of his exemplar—so he will say 'manner' instead of 'fashion'; 'written in the heart' instead of 'written in hearts'; or else he will vary the syntax, such as saying 'deadly wounded' instead of 'wounded deadly', or 'sinful and wicked' instead of 'wicked and sinful', and the like. And we could go on explaining a host of other variant readings palaeographically: *u*s and *v*s inverted; a *y*ᵗ (*y* superscript *t*) in the exemplar which might be read either as *yt* (it) or as an abbreviation for *that*; an extended Italic terminal *e* in the exemplar which might be read as an *e* but which was perhaps intended to be an abbreviation for *es*; and so on.

Altogether one has a strong impression that the *Canterbury* scribe is no more accurate than *Quarto*, and in many cases less so, though the two texts are subject to independent sets of errors. The *Canterbury* text reminds us of W. J. Cameron's inescapable truism that '*all* texts are in fact conflated texts—a conflation of the exemplar and a structure of linguistic expectations that is present in the mind of the scribe'.[27]

Can we deduce from his vagaries whether the *Canterbury* scribe is copying Donne's original manuscript directly, or whether he is duplicating another scribal copy, one which itself contains errors that *Canterbury* is perhaps augmenting? At this point, I would suggest, the jury is still out. Given his qualities and habits as a scribe, his exemplar is not yet determinable.

The same conclusion applies to Donne's list of authors among the preliminaries. If we had any doubts about the 'mechanical' nature of the *Canterbury* scribe, they are certainly dispelled here. When it comes to this list of 173 authors, most of whom would obviously have been unknown to him, the scribe mechanically and unhesitatingly copies out what he thinks is the name and spelling of each, producing a whole series of misreadings and, in effect, creating new authors. Thus Alcuinus becomes Alevinus; Gregorius becomes Georgius; Sansovinus becomes Sanschinus; Sextus Senensis becomes Sectus Sencasis, and so on. The scribe here is simply wrong. But again it is not hard to see how the misreadings occur (*c*s mistaken for *e*s, *u*s for *v*s, etc.); so the status of his exemplar is no clearer.

Proceeding further in the preliminaries, what about Donne's Preface? At last *Canterbury* offers us interesting readings which *might* suggest differences of exemplar.

Of these, the most significant is the unique reading we find when Donne quotes a study of the Pharisees, Sadducees, and Essenes by the Jesuit Nicolaus Serarius (Plate 20). He gives a quotation introduced in *Herbert* by the words 'the Pharises stilled'.[28] In *Quarto* (p. 19) this is exactly the same except that 'stiled' is spelt with one *l*. In fact—as we may see in Plate 20, in the middle of line 10 from the top—only *Canterbury* (p. 3) provides us with what is undoubtedly the correct reading at this point: 'the Pharisee Hillel'. This is an accurate reference to the Rabbi Hillel, the founder of rabbinical hermeneutics, who lived from about 70 BC to AD 10 and many of whose teachings resemble those of Jesus Christ. It is easy to see how the unfamiliar word 'Hillel' in Donne's manuscript could be misread by a copyist as 'stilled', the capital *H* being taken as a long *s* followed by a *t* and the terminal *l* as a *d*.

This is a telling variant for it means one of two things. Either, on the one hand, all

²⁷ William J. Cameron (ed.), *POAS*, v. 529.   ²⁸ Sullivan, 30.

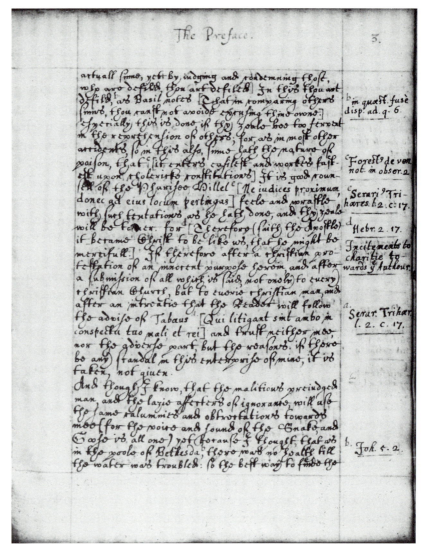

PLATE 20: A page of the preliminaries in the Canterbury Manuscript (Canterbury Cathedral U210/2/2, p. 3)

three copyists or compositors are using Donne's holograph, two of them misreading a word written in his cursive script, while one of them reads it correctly; or, alternatively, *Canterbury* is using a different exemplar from that used by the other two. What is *not* possible is that all three could be using a scribal transcript in which the word 'stilled' appears—a word which, by some extraordinary logic, *Canterbury* is capable of converting back to the word 'Hillel'.[29]

---

[29] This point helps, I believe, to negate the argument in Rudick & Battin (pp. c–ci) that the exemplar for both *Herbert* and the *Quarto* was probably a scribal transcript. Incidentally, one of the three textual errors which, as supporting evidence, they cite

But now—moving to the very beginning of the preliminaries—we come to the lengthy List of Contents—the 'Distribution of this Booke into Parts, Distinctions and Sections', which takes up between 22 and 24 pages in each of the three sources. It is here that things start diverging. For example, for I. iii. 2 both *Herbert* and *Quarto* have 18 headings. *Canterbury* has a total of 19 headings—though, as may be seen (Plate 21), there is some confusion because No. 16 is at first omitted and then added at the bottom out of sequence. *Canterbury*, in fact, incorporates in the list, as his No. 17, 'Ignatius solicitation for it'. The next two items, which are Nos. 17 and 18 in *Herbert* and *Quarto*, thus become Nos. 18 and 19 in *Canterbury*. Furthermore, *Canterbury* is right. If we check the main-body text to which these paragraph-summaries relate, there is indeed reference to St Ignatius—and in *Quarto* (p. 64), as well as in *Canterbury* (p. 44), 'Ignatius solicitation for it' appears as a sidenote, numbered '17'. There is no way our mechanical scribe has invented this heading in his Contents-list, and he is unlikely to have taken the trouble to check it against the main text. The heading is there in his exemplar; however, one might wonder whether it is in the exemplar used by the compositor of *Quarto*, let alone by the *Herbert* amanuensis. Moreover, the correct numbering of the sidenotes in *Canterbury* (pp. 43–5) suggests that some amendment and shuffling up is taking place. The note 'Cyprians professors . . .' is here numbered 14 after another number (?13) has been heavily deleted; the number for 'Enforcers . . .' is 15 overwritten on the number 14; and 'Examples . . .' has the number 16 overwritten on the number 15. Since these changes for the better fail to bring all the various numbers in the three texts into alignment, we must wonder whether there was a single manuscript behind all three in which the numbers ever were all clearly and correctly set out. And the same query arises when we see other differences in both numbering and wording in the List of Contents, which could be elaborated.[30]

This leads us at last to the sidenotes throughout the work. We might recall that there are two kinds of sidenote—both illustrated in our various Plates. One kind, usually keyed by letters (lower-case *a*, *b*, *c*, etc.), is citations (sometimes inaccurately called 'glosses' by editors), which perform the function of footnotes, to indicate sources cited. That Donne himself originally provided all these notes is beyond question. Most are added to *Herbert* in Donne's own hand, and at the end of his list of 'Authors cited in this Booke' he apologizes for 'citing these *Authors*' from his 'owne old notes' without

---

(p. 15) as being especially characteristic of a copyist rather than the author—namely 'externall' instead of 'eternall' in I. i. 5—is correctly rendered in *Canterbury* (p. 15) as 'eternall'.

³⁰ e.g. the continuous and erroneous numbering for I. vi. 3–4 in the *Quarto* Contents-list against the correct numbering in both *Herbert* and *Canterbury*; 'Of Beza[e]s answer[e] to Ochius Polygamy' for III. i. 1 in both *Herbert* and *Quarto* becomes 'Of Beza his answere to Ochin his booke of Poligamie' in *Canterbury*; and 'yet Kings of England, Fran[ce] and Spaine doe it' for the Conclusion in both *Herbert* and *Quarto* becomes 'yet Kings of England, Scotland, france and Spaine doe it' in *Canterbury*. These are in addition to occasional scribal muddling, such as (in the Contents-list for I. iii. 2: see Plate 21) *Canterbury*'s 'Eternall honour of Martyrs' and 'In times when they exceeded in discreet disposings of themselues' instead of the other two's 'Externall honors to Martyrs' and 'In tymes, when they exceeded in indiscreete exposings of themselues' respectively.

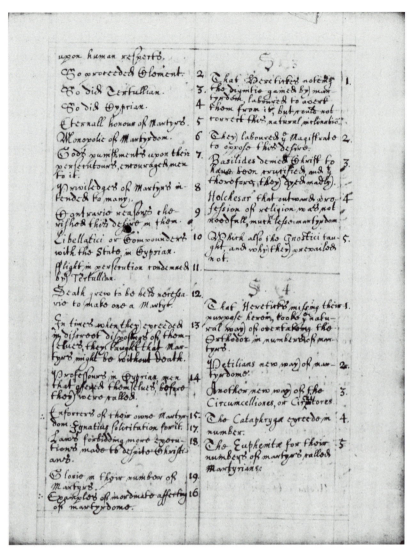

PLATE 21: A page of the preliminaries in the Canterbury Manuscript (Canterbury Cathedral U210/2/2, p. [viii])

recourse to 'the Originall' books.[31] Moreover, they are the kind of notes he provides also in *Pseudo-Martyr* (1610) and in *Ignatius his conclave* (1611), as well as in his later Sermons and Devotions. There are variants in the precise form of these citations, in that *Herbert* will tend to give the longest form (for example, 'De Somnior. Significat.'), *Canterbury* a slightly abbreviated form ('De Somn. significat'), and *Quarto* an even more reduced form ('De som. sign.'); although occasional exceptions are encountered

---

[31] Sullivan, 5.

when, for example, *Canterbury* provides the longest form (such as 'ad Usorij historiam' against *Herbert*'s 'ad Osorij Histor.' and *Quarto*'s 'ad Osor. Hist.'). Nevertheless, there is nothing in their actual text to suggest that they could not all have derived from Donne's holograph, variants arising simply from the habits of each particular scribe or compositor and the need to fit the citations into the space available.

The second kind of sidenotes, keyed numerically, is the many scores of side-headings, summarizing paragraphs of the text, which serve as signposts: as a guide, reference or finding system for the reader. It is these which were omitted from *Herbert* and which Sullivan thinks were added by the younger John Donne for publication purposes.

What becomes increasingly apparent, as we compare both kinds of sidenote and, in particular, their positioning in *Canterbury* with those in *Quarto*, is that—as in the List of Contents—we have here elements of confusion. To take a single instance among many, Plates 22 and 23 show page 28 of *Quarto* against page 10 of *Canterbury*. If we ignore the top two sidenotes on the left, and compare the next two or three notes with the notes at the top of the manuscript page, we see how both texts are juggling with two sidenotes that refer to the same passage, concerning a form of involuntary sin. *Canterbury* has the citation ('Perer. Exod. [etc.]') before the paragraph-summary ('When it is poena peccati [etc.]'); *Quarto* has it the other way round. While *Quarto* (as also, incidentally, *Herbert*) then goes on to have a citation (Plate 22: 'Can. 17' at the bottom left keyed to the letter *c* in the text, against 'penitential Cannons'), *Canterbury* (Plate 23) omits both this citation and its key-letter, which should appear in line 7, altogether.

There are, I would suggest, two possible explanations for this instability. One is that the sidenotes were all there in *Canterbury*'s exemplar, but that the *Canterbury* scribe was guilty of carelessness and lack of foresight in duplicating and arranging them properly. The other is that, for some reason, both the *Canterbury* scribe and the *Quarto* compositors were presented with a choice. The fact that the notes, as well as their numbering, get jumbled up at times, and even prompt further errors, might even suggest that instead of being written on the same physical page as the main text, they—or some of them at any rate—were written on separate sheets, or interleaves, and possibly not even in completed form or fully keyed or numbered. In this case it would be up to the copyist or compositor to make the best collation he could—putting, in effect, two sets on sidenotes on to the same physical page—with varying results, as we see.

If we go one step further and ask what the actual mechanics of adding paragraph-summaries to Donne's manuscript might have been—whoever it was who performed that task—we can see a link with the List of Contents: because the summary-sidenotes against the main text and the headings set out in the List of Contents are, in fact, simply repetitions or paraphrases of one another. We cannot determine for certain which set was originally written first. Were the sidenotes written in Donne's manuscript and

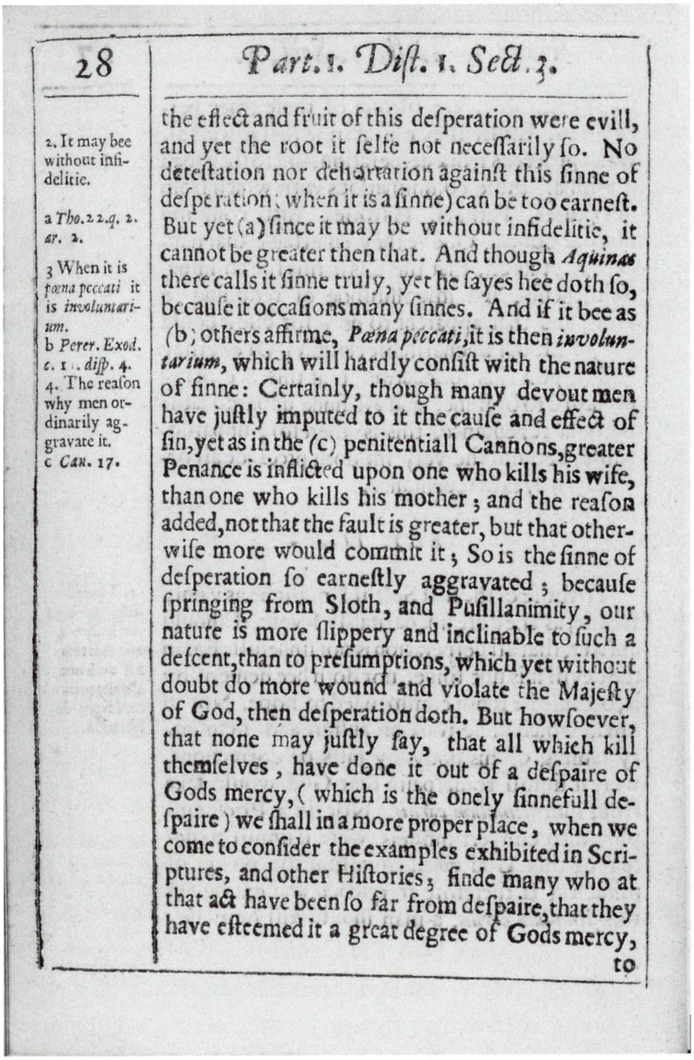

28	*Part.* 1. *Dift.* 1. *Sect.* 3.
2. It may bee without infidelitie.	the effect and fruit of this defperation were evill, and yet the root it felfe not neceffarily fo. No deteftation nor dehortation againft this finne of defperation; when it is a finne) can be too earneft. But yet (a) fince it may be without infidelitie, it cannot be greater then that. And though *Aquinas* there calls it finne truly, yet he fayes hee doth fo, becaufe it occafions many finnes. And if it bee as (b) others affirme, *Pæna peccati*, it is then *involun-tarium*, which will hardly confift with the nature of finne: Certainly, though many devout men have juftly imputed to it the caufe and effect of fin, yet as in the (c) penitentiall Cannons, greater Penance is inflicted upon one who kills his wife, than one who kills his mother; and the reafon added, not that the fault is greater, but that other-wife more would commit it; So is the finne of defperation fo earneftly aggravated; becaufe fpringing from Sloth, and Pufillanimity, our nature is more flippery and inclinable to fuch a defcent, than to prefumptions, which yet without doubt do more wound and violate the Majefty of God, then defperation doth. But howfoever, that none may juftly fay, that all which kill themfelves, have done it out of a defpaire of Gods mercy, (which is the onely finnefull de-fpaire) we fhall in a more proper place, when we come to confider the examples exhibited in Scri-ptures, and other Hiftories; finde many who at that act have been fo far from defpaire, that they have efteemed it a great degree of Gods mercy,
a *Tho.* 2 2. *q.* 2. *ar.* 2.	
3 When it is *pæna peccati* it is *involuntari-um*.	
b *Perer. Exod. c.* 11. *difp.* 4.	
4. The reafon why men or-dinarily ag-gravate it.	
c *Can.* 17.	

to

PLATE 22: Page 28 of the Quarto edition, [1647]

then an amended list of them produced for the preliminaries, or was it the other way round? If we pursue the second of these options for a moment, we might speculate that the sequence would be, first, the decision as to the *positioning* of the summary-sidenotes; then a drawing-up of the full text of them (as given as headings in the Contents-list); and, finally, the actual insertion of abbreviated forms of these headings in the margins of the main text itself. In this case, whoever was performing the task would need directly in front of him a copy of the Contents-list to work from—a Contents-list which, however, does not correspond precisely in the three known texts.

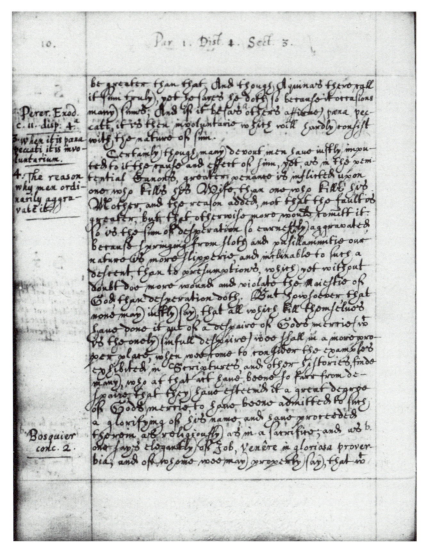

PLATE 23: A page of the Canterbury Manuscript (Canterbury Cathedral U210/2/2, p. 10)

Indeed, the most likely occasion for changes to be made to the original Contents-list would be when it came to the task of adding the summary-sidenotes, because then some of the omissions and misnumbering would be noticed and the Contents-list amended accordingly.

Does that mean, then, that modern editors are right in supposing that the summary-sidenotes were added—in what was very probably a quite separate operation—by someone other than the author himself?

It is possible, but not, in my view, very likely. Rudick and Battin are wrong, for a start, in conjecturing (p. cx) that these sidenotes were compositorial—the existence of *Canterbury* itself disproves that theory. Then, turning to Sullivan's theory, if Donne Jr is adding the sidenotes, why does his edition not include a more correct, more complete, and properly numbered Contents-list instead of the often inaccurate one that it does? The fact that a more accurate list was not reproduced by his printer might suggest that it was not, by the 1640s, available, let alone produced or used by Junior himself to prepare the work for the press. And then, granted the consensus that Donne Jr was not always the most reliable of editors—he could certainly take liberties with a text when it suited him, as we see in the 1651 edition of his father's letters (where he allows dates and names of correspondents to be altered to make the selection of letters seem more widely representative)—nevertheless, why *should* Junior take the trouble to add all these sidenotes a generation later—a labour of many hours? What purpose could this serve at this stage? His father had not thought this kind of sidenote—or, indeed, for that matter, an elaborate List of Contents—necessary for the 1610 edition of *Pseudo-Martyr*, for instance. Instead of the twenty-four-page Contents-list of *Biathanatos*, *Pseudo-Martyr* has a two-page list (sig. A4^{r-v}). Instead of the scores of elaborate Parts, Distinctions, and Sections of *Biathanatos*, *Pseudo-Martyr* has simply twenty chapters, with numbered paragraphs—and, as I have said, it dispenses with paragraph-summaries altogether. It seems to me that, by 1610, Donne had learned, like his modern editors, that this kind of elaborate apparatus was redundant. Least of all did he, or his son, have to feel it necessary to introduce such an innovation *after* that date.

I think that other arguments could be adduced in favour of the authenticity of the summary-sidenotes—including the fact that the paragraph-summaries are drawn up with some degree of intelligence, rather than being a mechanical scribal task—but I shall summarize by saying just this: that, in my view, the overall arrangement, division, presentation, and layout of *Biathanatos*, as we now have it in both the *Quarto* and *Canterbury*, represent not a later editorial construct, but, on the contrary, an elaborate, rather cumbersome, highly *academic*, and also somewhat archaic mode of presentation, which Donne himself adopted, in this his first major prose discourse, but then quickly learned (or was maybe persuaded) to abandon—to simplify and streamline—when it came to the publication of his new theological treatise, *Pseudo-Martyr*, a year or so later.

So far as Donne Jr's role in the matter in the 1640s is concerned, I would submit that he was doing precisely what he claimed he was doing: first, making available to the public a work which had been seen hitherto only by a few close friends of his father many years before; second, publishing a text composed entirely and solely by his father ('soe entirely from the Authors owne Penn'), with no substantive additions by anyone else; third, establishing it irrefutably as a work by his father so that no one else could plagiarize it; fourth, offering the complete text of a work which had generally (though maybe not exclusively) been seen in 'imperfect' form (imperfect even in the manuscript given to

Herbert); and, fifth—and perhaps ironically (this being his excuse for publishing given to Cavendish)—he was trying to 'defende it from the mistakes of carelesse transcribers'.[32]

Whether the Canterbury Manuscript will prove a boon or a bane to future editors of *Biathanatos* I shall leave them to decide. Certainly I think there is now evidence for thinking that the history of transmission of the text of this remarkably ambitious discourse is a little more complicated than editors have generally supposed.

Whatever conclusions they may ultimately reach about the status of each witness, I wonder whether we might not get the tiniest glimpse of Donne's own manuscript, not only by the occasional vestige in subsequent texts of what may have been original (perhaps deleted) readings, but also by certain tantalizing cross-references. Thus we have, uniquely, in *Quarto* (II. v. 2, p. 115) the sidenote: 'Infra fol. 249.' Alluding to a point made by Aristotle about the cowardliness of suicide, one supported by St Augustine, this note refers to a discussion which appears towards the end of the treatise, in III. v. 9 (*Quarto*, p. 211; *Canterbury*, p. 175), and which indeed occurs in *Herbert* on p. 249. For its own part, *Quarto* (p. 211) refers back to the exposition of Aristotle's point with the sidenote 'Supra fo.130'—and indeed the passage in question occurs in *Herbert* on p. 131—while *Canterbury* (p. 175) has the sidenote 'Supra. pag: 103', which might conceivably be a mistranscription of the same page reference, 130 (the passage in question appears in *Canterbury* on pp. 83–4 and in *Quarto* on p. 115). Then on the next page in *Quarto* (p. 212), we find an incomplete sidenote saying simply 'Supra' against a reference to Donne's earlier discussion of [Attilius] Regulus, a sidenote which appears in *Canterbury* (p. 176) as 'Supra. pag. 31.'—and this reference tallies correctly with page 31 of both *Herbert* and *Canterbury* (in I. ii. 3). Yet again, in I. iii. 2, the *Quarto* (p. 66) has as sidenote *h* 'Supra fo. 66.', which *Herbert* omits and which *Canterbury* (p. 45) gives as simply 'Supra pag.', the reference being to a passage on *Herbert*, 66 (*Quarto*, 65; *Canterbury*, 44). And finally, in *Canterbury* (p. 17, in I. i. 7), at the end of the sidenote (which appears also in *Quarto*, 36), 'To doe against nature makes us not guiltie of a greater sinn but more inexcusable', there is added (uniquely in *Canterbury*) the note: 'vide fol. 3.' It is tempting to suggest that this reference may be to the discussion of 'the sinn of desperation so earnestly aggravated, because springeing from sloth and pusillanimitie [of] our nature' in I. i. 3, which (although appearing in *Canterbury* on p. 10 (*Quarto*, 28)) actually appears there on the third page of the main text itself, discounting the seven-page Preface. Were it not for the discrepancies at present under discussion, these cross-references would tend to support the view that all three texts known to us relate closely to Donne's original manuscript.

So how can we account for the discrepancies found in the preliminaries and sidenotes?

---

[32] Sullivan, pp. xliii–xlvii, 249–50.

One hypothesis—the more complicated one—would be that *Canterbury* derives from an intermediate text, this providing the occasion whereby amendments were made to the Contents-list and related paragraph summaries.

FIGURE 2

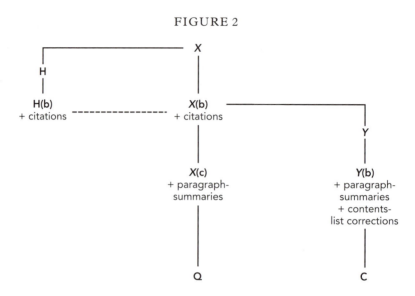

In this case, we might postulate the hypothetical stemma shown in Figure 2. *X* at the top is Donne's lost original manuscript, which I shall join Sullivan in assuming was substantially, if not totally, autograph, was the manuscript which passed down to the author's son (maybe via Ancrum), and was the copy-text for the 1647 *Quarto* (Q). *Y* is a hypothetical lost intermediate scribal copy standing between Donne's own manuscript (*X*) and *Canterbury* (C).

So what we have here is this. Whatever notes and working drafts lie behind it, Donne substantially completes a manuscript of *Biathanatos*: X. An amanuensis commissioned by him makes a copy for Herbert: H. This includes the text of the Contents-list as it appears in *X*. Donne himself then adds citations to H. This—we might speculate with Sullivan—is the occasion for Donne's tidying up or copying more fully and neatly, if not adding *ab initio*, the same citations (which may not have been in a fit state to be copied by the *Herbert* scribe) to his own manuscript, *X*. *X*, at this stage, also having been very slightly revised, is then at some point copied by an amanuensis to *Y*. This, we shall speculate, is the occasion for Donne to complete his work by adding the paragraph-summaries to *Y*, at the same time correcting the Contents-list in *Y*. He then follows the same procedure as with the citations earlier by having these sidenotes tidied up and/or copied in his own manuscript, *X*. For some reason, however, the changes made in the Contents-list in *Y* are overlooked and the Contents-list in *X* stays just as it was when it was copied for H. *Y, including* all the sidenotes, *including* the amended Contents-list, is subsequently copied by another scribe, outside Donne's sphere, to C: the Canterbury Manuscript. Finally, some fifteen years after Donne's death, *X, including* all the side-notes, but *without* the changes to the Contents-list, provides his son with the copy-text for the 1647 *Quarto*.

Since we have now ventured into the realms of speculation, we might suggest that if an intermediate text, *Y*, existed, the most likely person for whom it would have been prepared is Donne's perennial, if not always discreet, literary friend Sir Henry Goodyer. We know, from Donne's letter on the subject, that Goodyer was clamouring for a copy—no doubt to go with all the other manuscript copies of works by Donne that we know he had, whether congenial to his personal literary interests or otherwise. If only for fear of offending him, Donne might have felt obliged to supply him with one sooner or later, albeit with reluctance. In this case, Donne would have been repeating the same pattern as with Herbert and, later, Ker: that is, not actively 'circulating' the work himself, but effectively entrusting it to a close friend to look after it and decide for him who else might see it—or even, in this instance, copy it, out of his sight.

The alternative to this scenario is simply that *Canterbury*, like *Herbert* and *Quarto*, was copied directly from Donne's own manuscript, *X*. This option has the advantage of being the simplest explanation and is the one which we assumed to be the case at the very beginning of this investigation. As already stated, there appear to be no substantive differences between the main texts of *Canterbury* and *Quarto* which cannot be explained in terms of scribal/compositorial errors. The more puzzling variants are those in the preliminaries and sidenotes. If both were copied directly from Donne's holograph, we would have to explain how differences especially in numbering occur and how it is that corrections appear in *Canterbury* which do not appear in *Quarto*.

Finally, do we know who might have commissioned or owned the Canterbury Manuscript? I can offer one slim clue for speculation.

There are some pencil notes in the manuscript, on the flyleaf opposite the title-page (Plate 24). These can be identified as having been written in 1810 by Sir Robert Harry Inglis, second Baronet (1786–1855), who became a barrister, MP, editor, member of the Record Commission, Trustee of the British Museum, and Professor of Antiquity at the Royal Academy. He records here that, previous to him, the manuscript had been owned by the Revd John Morris, who died (at the age of 71) in May 1798. Morris's library turns out to have been sold at Sotheby's on 6 and 7 June 1799. No mention of *Biathanatos* is made in the sale catalogue, but Inglis's reference to the manuscript's coming with 'a Lot of Copy Books' suggests that it might perhaps correspond to lot 275, described as 'MANUSCRIPT SERMONS, 24 dozen & two, (Original ones)', sold for £2 14*s.* to 'Tibbets'.

Now from 1766 to 1798 John Morris was rector of Milton Bryant, his library

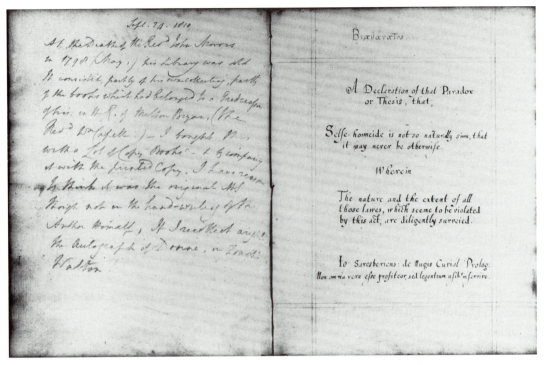

PLATE 24: Flyleaf inscribed by Sir Robert Harry Inglis opposite the title-page of the Canterbury Manuscript (Canterbury Cathedral U210/2/2)

consisting, says Inglis, 'partly of his own collecting, partly of the books which had belonged to a Predecessor of his, in the R[ectorship] of Milton Bryant, (the Rev^d W[illia]m Capell)' (that is to say, William Capel, who was rector of Milton Bryant from 1710 to 1763). Milton Bryant (or Bryan) is a little village in rural Bedfordshire, in the middle of nowhere except that it is situated on the very edge of the Woburn Abbey estate.[33] Since the seventeenth century, Woburn Abbey has been the main seat of the Russell family, Earls and later Dukes of Bedford. Moreover, before becoming a rector, John Morris was curate of Woburn and, in 1762–3, he was chaplain to the statesman John Russell, fourth Duke of Bedford (1710–71), when he was Ambassador in Paris. Morris, who is posthumously described in his Parish Register as a 'pious, learned, good hearted man & much respected',[34] certainly had access to the Woburn library over a period of many years.

Is it possible that he could have borrowed, or even have been given, one of the library's manuscripts that interested him—especially, perhaps, during a period when

[33] The manor of Milton Bryant, owned by Woburn Abbey, came into the possession of the Inglis family in 1785 when Catherine Johnson settled it upon her husband, Sir Hugh Inglis, first Baronet (d. 1820), father of Sir Robert Harry Inglis: see *The Victoria history of the county of Bedford*, vol. iii, ed. William Page (London, 1912), 417–19.

[34] For this, and other information about Morris and Capel derived from parish records, I am indebted to Mr James Collett-White of the Bedfordshire Record Office.

Woburn itself, including the library, was undergoing severe disruptions through extensive rebuilding?[35] We cannot know for certain. But if there is one family, outside Donne's 'university' friends, who would assuredly have been interested in acquiring a copy of Donne's treatise given the chance, it is the Russells. Lucy, Countess of Bedford—who died in 1627, in the same year as her husband Edward, the third Earl—was one of Donne's most celebrated friends and correspondents, as well as his erstwhile patroness—the addressee of some of his best-known verse epistles.[36] She was especially so in 1608 at around the time *Biathanatos* was written, and when she was godmother to his daughter Lucy (1608–27), who was named after her. We know, too, that her husband's cousin, Francis Russell (1593–1641), who succeeded in 1627 as fourth Earl of Bedford, was interested in Donne, at least in the 1620s, because his commonplace book, still in the Woburn muniments, contains extracts from Donne's poems and sermons.[37] It might be added that the Countess of Bedford is known to have been a confidante at Court of Sir Henry Goodyer (who, curiously enough, also died in 1627).[38]

In any event, I think we can conclude by saying that, although Donne was both cautious and ambivalent about the circulation of *Biathanatos*, he certainly did not *kill* it, nor did he *bury* it quite as deeply as we once thought.

---

[35] The old library in the south-west angle at Woburn was extensively refurbished by Sir William Chambers for the fourth Duke of Bedford around 1770 and again by Henry Holland for the fifth Duke after 1788: see, for instance, the illustrated account of Woburn by Dorothy Stroud in *Country Life* (8 July 1965).

[36] For discussions of Donne's relationship with the Countess, which declined after 1613, see references cited in Joan Faust, 'John Donne's verse letters to the Countess of Bedford: Mediators in a poet–patroness relationship', *JDJ* 12 (1993), 79–99.

[37] Woburn Abbey, Duke of Bedford, MSS HMC No. 26. See my 'More Donne manuscripts', *JDJ* 6/2 (1987), 213–18 (p. 213).

[38] In a private communication, I. A. Shapiro notes having collected a substantial file of materials on the relations between Goodyer and Lady Bedford, which 'were close and confidential about some court affairs of Lady Bedford in June 1605 and which had evidently been so for a few years'.

3

The Feathery Scribe

IN my first chapter, *In praise of scribes*, I spoke about knaves, as well as drudges, in the world of seventeenth-century clerks and scriveners. I now want to introduce one particular scribe—a drudge, perhaps. But whether harmless or not I shall leave an open question.

A case history of one particular scribe is not, I would suggest, unseasonable. For, as I have said before, while we have a mountain of information about seventeenth-century printers, stationers, and publishers—and even about some compositors—we know little, if anything, about individual *scribes*—and even those who have attracted some attention (Ralph Crane, for instance) have done so only because they happen to be associated with particular literary or dramatic interests, not because their work is felt to deserve bibliographical study in its own right.

The anonymous but extremely distinctive and prolific scribe I am now focusing on flourished in the 1620s and 1630s. He is a scribe whom I christened many years ago the 'Feathery Scribe'.[1] The reason for this epithet will, I hope, become apparent from illustrated examples of his work. Plate 25, for instance, shows a few lines in one of two manuscripts by him I own myself. He writes in a script quite unmistakable in its really quite sophisticated sense of style. In his own way, this scribe is as much a conscious, professional craftsman, with pen, ink, and paper, as a cabinet-maker is with wood and cutting-tools, and I would invite you to consider his work (at least to some extent) in this light.[2] While few bibliographers would regard the seventeenth century as an age of fine printing, there is at least a case for judging its scribes from a different perspective.

This man's style is distinguished, among other things, by the very light, fine-nibbed ornamentation of the lettering: the wispy, trailing strokes to which he is prone. His is a busy, sometimes swirling, fluttery style, marked by a characteristic lightness of touch.

---

[1] The epithet was originally suggested to me by the late P. J. Croft, on the steps of the British Museum, at about the time I recorded some of Feathery's manuscripts in the first volume of my *Index* (1980). My interest in this scribe has been shared by Hilton Kelliher, who independently kept notes on examples of his work in BL MSS, and by Henry Woudhuysen, who has incorporated some information about him in his *Sidney and the circulation of manuscripts* (1996), especially pp. 185–9. A plate illustrating the first page of one of my own Feathery MSS appeared in Harold Love's *Scribal publication* (1993), 112 (and see p. 111), and the term incidentally achieved some prominence when Love's full-page review of Woudhuysen's book in *TLS* 23 August 1996, p. 11, was headed 'The Feathery Scribe'.

[2] The quality, studied formality, and professionalism of Feathery's script become more evident if it is compared, for instance, with the mass of hurried, untidy, and often inaccurate 'separates' of parliamentary speeches dashed off in haste by some other scribes of the period.

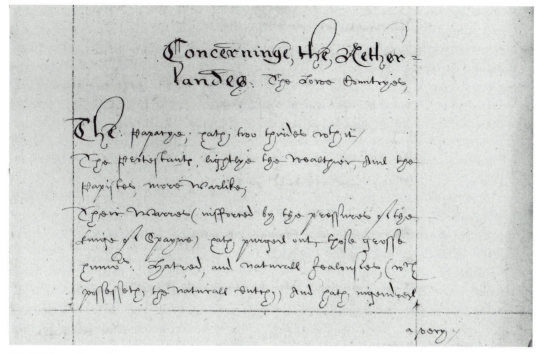

PLATE 25: Part of a page in Feathery's copy of *A Breiffe Discours off: the Lowe Countryes* (Peter Beal MS 2, f. [4r])

I shall look a little more closely at some of his idiosyncrasies in a moment. For convenience's sake, I shall refer to him henceforth as simply 'Feathery'.

First, just how prolific was Feathery? To give some basic statistics: I have found Feathery's hand in well over a hundred separate physical manuscripts, or manuscript volumes, some of which actually comprise a quantity of separates bound together (for a complete listing, see Appendix II below). These manuscripts are now located in some two dozen libraries, record offices, and private collections in Britain, Ireland, and the United States, from London to California. A rough count of pages in his hand comes to well over 11,000. With (judging by a few random samples) the number of words varying from as few as 140 to as many as 225 per standard page, the total count of words in his hand discovered so far would probably amount to a figure in the region of two million. This is not including those words written by other scribes associated with Feathery, or who have contributed to manuscripts only partly in his hand, the total figure for which would be almost incalculable. It might indeed be said of Feathery, as one epigrammatist said of the scrivener in general, that he 'hath writ more then many men haue read'.[3]

The works copied wholly or partly by Feathery range from state papers, parliamentary

---

[3] 'On a Scriuener' (Appendix I, No. 16).

journals, political tracts, proposals on trade and economic matters, through legal and antiquarian treatises, to religious discourses, biographical accounts, and poetry, by a wide variety of authors, including some of the best-known writers of the Elizabethan and early Stuart periods. It is difficult to quantify titles, since 'works' copied range from a single-page poem, letter, or Exchequer list to a legal compilation of over 1,100 pages. If I say that I have listed about 300 'titles', it should be noted that some of these represent anthologies of perhaps scores of 'works' each. So even in the light of present, no doubt extremely imperfect evidence, we are confronted here with a highly industrious copyist. Heaven only knows what the full scope of his work would have been.

Now, what we see illustrated in Plates 25 and 26 is Feathery's 'normal', most often encountered, 'mature' script. I say 'mature' because this is the script found in the great majority of his known manuscripts, including his latest ones: that is to say, including those which date from between 1628 and 1641.

Although, like any scribe of the period, Feathery will occasionally adopt Italic forms for special effect—for words in Latin and for certain names, for instance, as well as for some headings—his normal script is almost pure Secretary, with only the slightest admixture of Italic forms (such as the *e*s, for instance, in the second word in Plate 26: 'Breiffe'). Elizabethan Secretary forms otherwise predominate: the *e* in the word 'Lowe' on the second line, for instance; the capital *C* in the next word, 'Countryes', the elongated *f* in 'of' on the third line, the *r* in 'Albertus' on the fourth line—and so we could go on, noting his characteristic Secretary *d*s, terminal and double-*ss*, his *p*, *h*, *k*, *sh*, and so on. In abbreviations, we see his use of the macron or tilde—of which there are several examples here—such as, in 'condicons' in the sidenote on the right. Strictly speaking the macron should be over just the terminal 'con' in this word. Characteristically, this knight of the swirling tilde uses this as an opportunity for flamboyant ornamentation and flourishing—looping across from the terminal *s* over the last five letters. Then, of course, we see similar kinds of ornamentation elsewhere: the flicked tail and flourishing in the word 'Secondlye' at the beginning of the second line from the end, for instance, or—in the heading—the little flicked inverted apostrophe marks after the *f*s and *ss* in 'Breiffe Discours Off'. This first line of the heading is characteristically highlighted by him, with engrossed lettering and heavy inking for a bold effect, as are the very first word of the main text, 'The', and the first word of the paragraph at the bottom, 'Secondlye'.

In his layout, Feathery is generous in his spacing, he leaves wide margins—which might well have been even wider originally, before the binder trimmed them. He incorporates sidenotes as occasion demands, uses the margin for strategic numbering of sections, arguments, etc., and he invariably leaves a catchword at the bottom of the page—a professional habit he shares with any printer of the period. Generally he main-

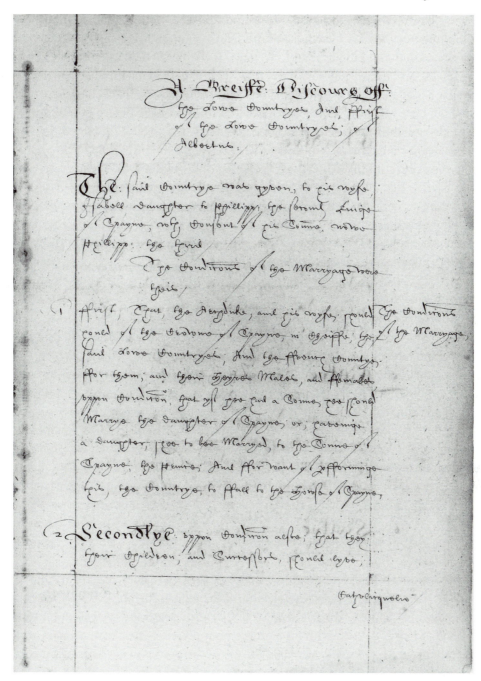

PLATE 26: First page of Feathery's copy of *A Breiffe Discours off: the Lowe Countryes* (Peter Beal MS 2, f. [1r])

tains regular proportions in his attention to centred headings or sub-headings, para-graphs, and indentations. He tends to justify the lines as best he can—rather than leave blank spaces at the end of lines he often resorts to elaborate tildes, or else a brief row of *x*s, as fillers. And he is also pretty regular in the evenness of his lines, considering that the paper is not ruled horizontally. As for the marginal ruling, which tends to be con-sistently in light red ink, I am not sure whether this was done before or after the writ-ing. Logic would dictate that it was done before the writing, as a guide to the scribe. Nevertheless, the degree of untidiness, hastiness, and inconsistency in the marginal ruling sometimes found in Feathery's manuscripts suggests that it may have been rather indifferently added by someone afterwards (conceivably—judging by the light-ness, fuzziness, and accidental doubling-up of some rules—with the occasional use of some kind of ruling frame or taut ink-soaked string as a faster alternative to ruler and quill) in order to square the manuscripts with an expected 'house-style'. A number of Feathery's manuscripts also retain vertical fold marks, at approximately two-inch inter-vals, which, if produced at a preliminary stage (though I think this unlikely), he may have used as a guide to margins and proportions.

Yet another extremely distinctive feature of Feathery's work is his peculiar, indeed highly idiosyncratic, sense of punctuation. We might take the heading in Plate 26 as an example. It reads *A*—full stop—*Breiffe*—colon—*Discours Off*—colon—*the Lowe Coun-tryes*—comma—*And*—comma—*ffirst of the Lowe Countryes*—semicolon—*of Albertus*—colon—virgule or slash. By Feathery's standards, the punctuation here is restrained. When the fit is upon him he bursts into a riot of commas, semicolons, colons, full stops, and virgules, with no discernible regard whatsoever for any grammatical function such elements are supposed to perform. Any attempt to identify some inherent logic to his punctuation *as* punctuation is dashed by its sheer inconsistency—for he is capable of punctuating the same texts, in multiple copies, in quite different ways—on what seems to be a purely arbitrary, whimsical basis: as the mood takes him. In other words, his punctuation is simply an extension of his decorative tendencies—used as yet another form of stylistic flourishing and ornamentation—for visual effect, not for its grammat-ical significance.

More could be said of other features such as Feathery's characteristic orthography. Figure 3 gives a very brief selection of some of his typical spellings, as well as a few of his normal abbreviations. We have a pretty liberal attitude towards vowels, for instance: 'also' and 'who' both spelt with an *e* on the end, 'hereby' spelt with three *e*s, *i*s and *y*s interchangeable, and so on, as well as the use of two vowels instead of one for certain diphthongs—*au* in 'aunswered', or *ou* in 'oulde', which are, I take it, a phonetic reflection of contemporary pronunciation. These spellings are not peculiar to Feathery, nor particularly eccentric, though they do have an element of luxuriance somewhat reminiscent of the kinds of spelling in which William Henry Ireland

FIGURE 3

alsoe	disswadeinge	observaç$\overline{ons}$
aucthoritye	dyvers	offerr
auncyent	eccliall [= ecclesiastical]	offyce
aunswere	ffruyteffull	oulde
authenticque	gouernm^{te} [= government]	Parliam^t [= Parliament]
beniffitt	greiveaunce	p^{r}fferringe
beyounde	heereby	psons [= persons]
breiffe	highnes	rayleinge
Brittayne	hir	receyve
butt	houldinge	remarckeable
cittie	honno^{ble} [= honourable]	Ro$\overline{bt}$e [= Robert]
conscerninge	howse	sub^{te} [= subject]
contynueinge	inffinyte	Touchinge
coppye	libtye [= liberty]	Trayterous
co^{rte} [= court]	l$\overline{re}$ [= letter]	veiwe
demaund	lyked	whoe
devided	Matie [= Majesty]	Will$\overline{m}$ [= William]
discours	nobillitye	woemen

indulged in his Shakespearian forgeries. Neither is Feathery always completely consistent—he can write 'written' or 'wrytten', 'conserninge' or 'conscerninge', 'marriage' or 'marryage', and so on—and especially when he is confronted with an unusual or foreign word: he is never, for instance, quite sure how to spell 'Monsieur', which is apt to come out as 'Mounsieur', 'Mownsieur', or 'Monsuer'. The only general observation I would make is that these spellings are essentially Elizabethan: the kind of spelling which survives in the early Stuart period, to be sure, but which comes increasingly to be seen as archaic, as, indeed, does the pure Secretary script itself. It may well reflect a certain resistance to change which was perhaps a tendency of clerks and scriveners in general.

One further very characteristic feature of Feathery's work is his frequent (though not invariable) use of title-pages, which take the form exemplified in Plate 27. The title, with the top line engrossed in bold, is centred on the page, and enclosed within two sets of heavily inked double rules terminating in sinuous, leaf-shaped flourishes at each end, the rules both surmounted and subscribed by circular, spiralling flourishes. The counterpart to this feature is the way Feathery usually finishes each work—with, as may be seen in Plate 28, a bold, engrossed 'ffinis:', followed by a double rule with the same terminal leaf-patterns as on the title-page, and similar spiralling beneath. In both main-text headings and endings there is one additional feature which occasionally occurs. This is the way he sometimes sets out the date of a work—as can be seen in Plate 29. Thus 'Anno, D[omi]ni: 1623' is underlined, the rule transected by two sets of little curls (rather like pairs of alternating commas and inverted commas), concluding with a somewhat diamond-shaped flourish of convoluted loops. This device, which at times is varied by the rule's having an introductory flourish looking like the figure *2*, is an

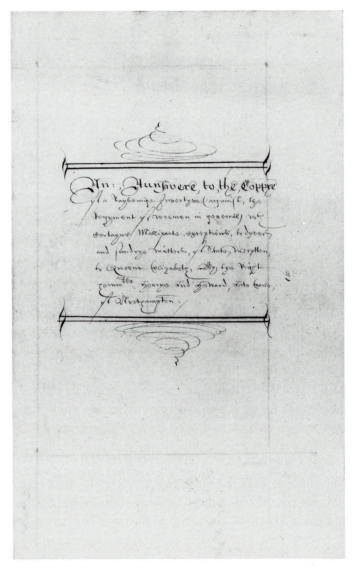

PLATE 27: Feathery's title-page in a copy of Northampton's
Aunswere, to, the ... Invectyve (against, the Regyment of woemen)
(CUL Add. MS 9276, No. 7)

occasional rather than consistent feature of Feathery's headings; one suspects that it
was a habit which tended to fall away in his later work. At any rate, it is his version of a
device which can be found elsewhere in formal documents written by legal clerks of the
Elizabethan period[4] and it is yet further evidence that Feathery was a trained profes-

---

[4] The device is common, but to give a single example to hand: one occurs in an indenture signed in 1576 by Robert Dudley,
Earl of Leicester, now in the Denbighshire Record Office (DD/WY/2020).

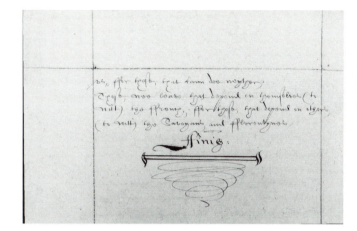

PLATE 28: Last page of Feathery's copy of Ralegh's *Discours: Touchinge a Marryage, Betwene Prince Henrye . . . And, a Daughter of Savoye* (CUL Add. MS 9276, No. 15)

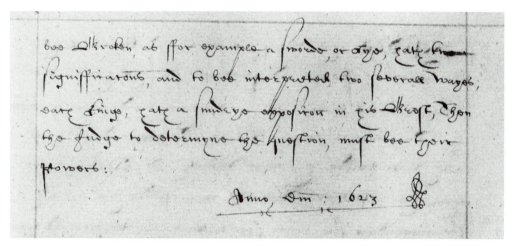

PLATE 29: Part of a page in Feathery's copy of *The Three Greate Kingdoms of England, ffraunce, and Spayne* (National Library of Wales Castell Gorfod MS 1, f. 32v)

sional scribe, even if—like most practising scribes of the period—he was not, so far as we can tell, an enrolled member of the Company of Scriveners.[5]

Now the examples shown so far are of Feathery's 'mature', controlled script. Do we ever catch him off guard, in less formal mode? Perhaps such an instance is seen in a page in one of the Harley manuscripts, dating from 1628 (Plate 30). Here, right at the end of an account of some arguments in Parliament, he adds—as an afterthought, it

[5] I have searched in vain for any trace of Feathery in the Common Paper of the Scriveners' Company (Guildhall Library MS 5370), which members inscribed with their professional paraphs. This register extends to 1628. If, perchance, Feathery became a member of the Company after that date (which seems unlikely, since he was a well-established practitioner before then), he would have been enrolled in a continuation of the Common Paper which no longer exists, though a transcript of it (useless for purposes of identifying handwriting) is preserved in Bodleian Library MS Rawl. D. 51: see *Scriveners' Company Common Paper 1357–1628 with a continuation to 1678*, ed. Francis W. Steer (London, 1968).

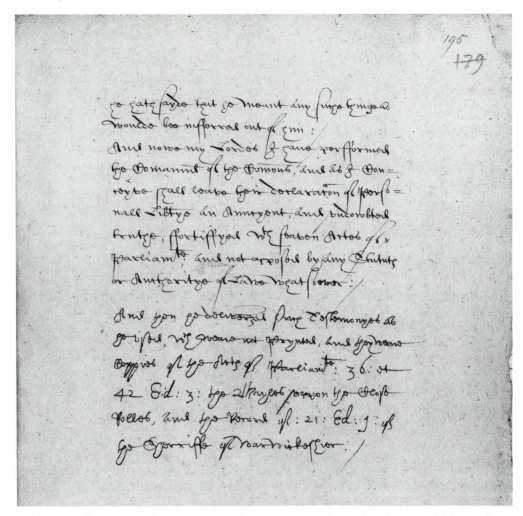

PLATE 30: Last page of Feathery's copy of Littleton's *Argum^te: Concerninge the personall Libtye of the Subiecte ... 1628* (BL Harley MS 161, f. 195r)

seems—a final paragraph in different ink ('And then he delivered such Testemonyes as he vsed, wch weare not Prynted; and they weare Coppies of the Acts of Parliam^te [etc.].'). Relatively speaking, we see here a somewhat liberated, cursive version of his hand—it has a rather hurried, dashed-off look about it, with even more than his customary eccentricity of spelling (his 'delivered', for instance, comes out looking more like 'deliverzed'). Yet there is no question but that this is one and the same scribe.

Nor, I think, is there any question about the identity of Feathery in the relatively few examples I have found of what seems to be an early, or 'immature' version of his hand. Particularly in five volumes of tracts, perhaps copied in the 1620s, we find the kind of script seen in Plate 31, from a volume now in the Bodleian. Without indulging in a blow-by-blow comparison of the various letter-forms shared by this script and Feathery's 'mature' script—though there *is* an accumulation of similarities, including Feathery's peculiar punctuation habits—I shall summarize by saying that this script represents a more constrained, more tightly regulated, and relatively subdued version of his hand. It has all his professional competence, but less of the stylistic and decorative exuberance that can be seen in his very latest work. In these early volumes there is no sign of any title-page, but he concludes his texts with an alternative version of his later 'ffinis': see Plate 32 for an example in the Folger Shakespeare Library. He has the word 'ffinis' (though here in Italic and not engrossed) followed by a single heavily inked rule encased in a kind of looped envelope—a little bit reminiscent of the shape of a pen. I have not found this particular pattern used by any other scribe.

One incidental feature of this early group of manuscripts is the occurrence of what looks, at first sight, to be a possible clue to Feathery's identity. At the end of one long work in the Bodleian (Plate 33), we find this sequence: an ascription to one 'J. C.'; followed by Feathery's 'ffinis'; a peculiar cluster of dots; his rule in its 'envelope'; and then (apart from a contemporary reader's approving comment on the work at the bottom right) we have a kind of paraph, or monogram, formed by the letters 'J J' transected by a wave-shaped line, pointed in the middle. Could this, by any chance, be Feathery's scribal paraph—with *his* initials, 'J. J.'? If it were, I may say, it would be interesting for more reasons than one, because this particular tract is a mid-sixteenth-century hagiography of John Fisher, the Catholic martyr executed by Henry VIII.[6] It would not be the safest kind of text for a scribe to be conspicuously associated with, in either the Elizabethan *or* Stuart periods.[7]

In fact, though, if we consider more closely, we find that the scribe has not signed or identified himself at all. We find a similar 'J J' formation elsewhere—for instance, in the seventh line illustrated in Plate 34, near the end of the heading: 'whether it maye stand with: good pollicye ffor hir Ma[jes]tie to ioyne w[i]th J. J. in their Enterprise of :#:'. In other words, like the hatch-mark at the end, 'J J' is meaningless—it is a symbol denoting something unspecified—rather like *X* today, or *AB* or *NN* which are sometimes found performing this function elsewhere in this period.[8] I am afraid that our Feathery Scribe—wisely, perhaps—remains as deliberately anonymous as ever.

---

[6] Appendix II below, No. 97.2. In his edition of *Vie du bienheureux martyr Jean Fisher* (Brussels, 1893), 4–7, Fr Van Ortroy, SJ, records this and ten other manuscripts of this Life (chiefly in the BL; others at St John's and Gonville and Caius Colleges, Cambridge, and Stonyhurst College), one of which (Harley MS 250, ff. 1–94) is bound with material in the hand of Ralph Starkey (see below).

[7] An earlier example of an antiquary who fell foul of the authorities, in 1569, for possessing 'unlawfulle bookes' which showed him to be 'a great favourer of papistrye' is John Stow (1525?–1605): see *A survey of London by John Stow*, ed. Charles Lethbridge Kingsford, 2 vols. (Oxford, 1908), i, pp. xvi–xvii.

[8] As an alternative explanation for the motto at the end of the Life of Fisher, it has been suggested to me that, given the religious context of the treatise, 'J J' might stand for '*J[esu] J[uva]*' (meaning 'O Jesus, help'). This epigraph is found, for instance, at the beginning of autograph scores by J. S. Bach (e.g. the openings of the autograph cantatas illustrated in Sotheby's sale catalogues of 22 November 1989, p. 11, and 15 May 1996, p. 60).

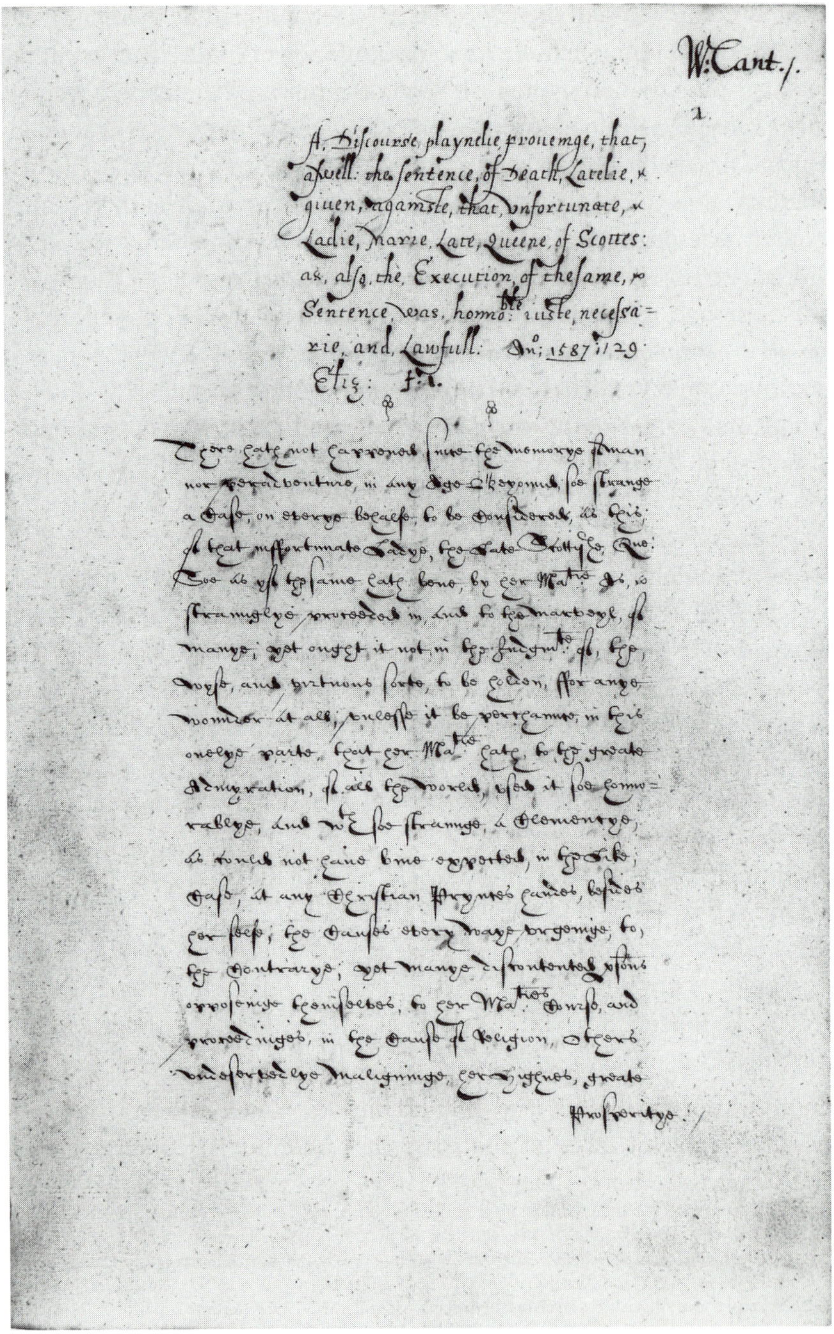

W: Cant. /

A, Discourse, playnelie, prouenge, that,
aswell: the, sentence, of, death, Latelie, ×
giuen, agaynste, that, unfortunate, ×
Ladie, Marie, Late, Queene, of, Scottes:
as, alsq. the, Execution, of, the same, ×
Sentence, was, homō: iuste, necessa=
rie, and, Lawfull: Anᵒ; 1587 1/29
Eliz: Ra.

PLATE 31: First page of Feathery's copy of Puttenham's *Discourse* on the execution of Mary Queen of Scots (Bodleian Library MS Tanner 108, f. 1r)

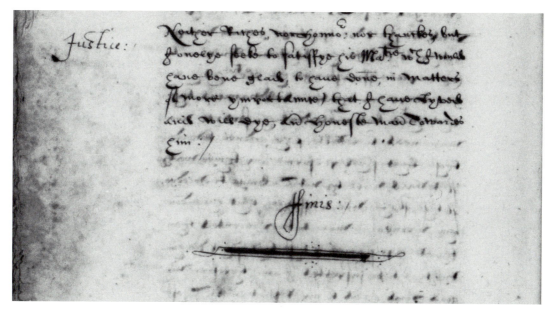

PLATE 32: Last page of Feathery's copy of Daniel's *Breuiarye, of the, Historie, of, Englande* (Folger Shakespeare Library MS G. b. 9, f. 205r)

That Feathery was a professional scribe scarcely needs demonstrating. But we *can* find confirmation in the form of a brief note by him jotted on a blank cropped page attached to his copy of a tract by Sir Robert Cotton, now at Yale (Plate 35). He records receiving 5 shillings for 'this, Essex his Arraignm[en]te And Mountgomerye vppon the Navye Royall'. This is a slightly frustrating record, because it supplies not quite enough information for us to calculate his charge per page with certainty. John Montgomery's treatise on the Navy, completed in 1588, would occupy probably no more than twenty folio pages,[9] but unfortunately accounts of Essex's arraignment in 1601 can range from less than half a dozen pages[10] to nearly fifty pages,[11] depending on how detailed they are. Thus, depending on the length of the Essex piece, Feathery's charge would work out at either three-quarters of a penny (three farthings) or else one and a half pennies (three ha'pence) a page. If I find the latter a more attractive proposition, it is because an average of three ha'pence a page would not be altogether inconsistent with other records we have of scribes' charges.[12] In this case, I might add—for the

---

[9] Decorated presentation copies of the full text of *A treatise co[n]cerning the nauie of England written in anno 1570 by I° Montgomery with an addicion there to made by the saide author in an° 1588* are in the BL, Add. MS 20042 (64 small quarto pages) and Arundel MS 22 (37 large quarto pages), and another decorated copy is in the Pepys Library, Magdalene College, Cambridge, No. 1774 (41 small quarto pages). A copy in BL Lansdowne MS 1225, ff. 23r–32r, occupies 19 folio pages.

[10] e.g. BL Add. MS 4155, ff. 94r–97r.

[11] e.g. BL Harley MS 4289, ff. 17r–40r (47 folio pages). What is probably Humphrey Dyson's copy in Bodleian Library MS Willis 58, ff. 175r–184r, occupies 19 folio pages; it is unfortunately not one of the items in this volume which is priced.

[12] Records of clerks' and scriveners' charges are variable and inconclusive, and depend much upon circumstances of production. Among the household accounts of Lady Elizabeth Kytson *c*.1587, for instance, among the Hengrave Hall MSS (82 (4)–83

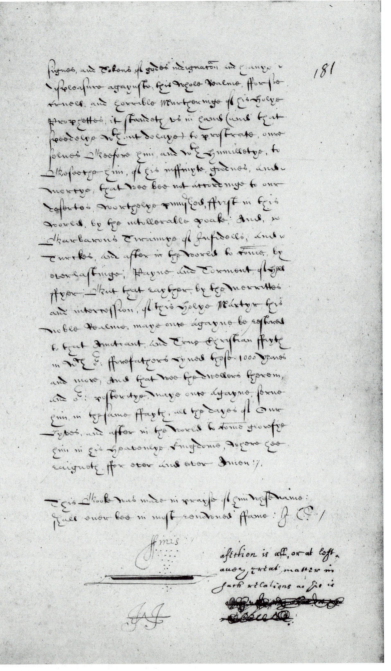

PLATE 33: Last page of Feathery's copy of *The, Life, and, manner, of, Death: of . . .
John: ffisher* (Bodleian Library MS Tanner 108, f. 181r)

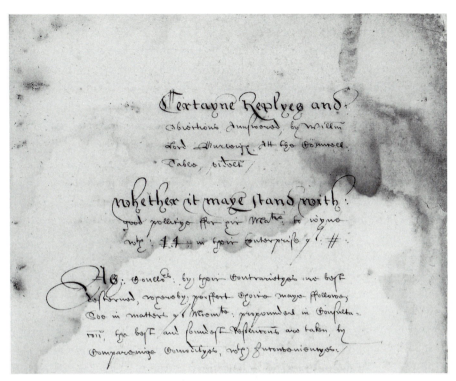

PLATE 34: First page of Feathery's copy of *Certayne Replyes and: Obiections, Aunswered: by Willm Lord Burleigh* (Peter Beal MS 1, f. [2r])

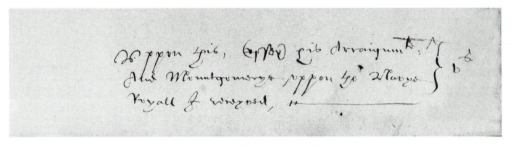

PLATE 35: Feathery's note on receipts attached to his copy of Cotton's *Aunswere . . . to Certayne proposicons, of Warre; and peace* (Yale Osborn Collection b 180)

(1)) in CUL, the Attorney-General Sir John Popham's 'man' is given 5*s.* 'for the wryting' of a petition and 20*s.* 'for wrighting and engrossing' a 'Ch[arte]r warrant', while 'a scrivener' is paid 8*d.* each for a series of bonds. The fees suggested (but subsequently debated) in December 1620 for Sir Robert Flood, as clerk of the office for engrossing wills and inventories, were 'for every skin of parchment having at least 40 lines each, 20 inches long, 10*s.*, for engrossing transcripts of wills 18*d* for every press of parchment 24 inches long and 5 inches wide', whereas 'th'ordinary fee was until this patent about 5*s.* nowe at 10*s.*', although on occasions 'Proctours, Attorneys, and Skriveners' had formerly charged £5 or more 'for provinge a will that hath not exceeded one skinne of parchment' (*Commons debates 1621*, vii. 470–1, 507). On the evidence of notes in Inner Temple Library MS Petyt 538, vol. 18, ff. 19r and 46r (printed, incidentally, in *Commons debates 1629*, pp. xxxiii–xxxiv), Baker (*CUL*, pp. xliii, 135) records retail prices as high as 8*s.* per twelve-leaf quire (= 4*d.* per page) for the much sought-after 1628 parliamentary debates on the liberty of the subject (cf Appendix III below, No. 83 n.), while a legal work bought by Lincoln's Inn in 1615 cost 15*d.* a leaf (= 7½*d.* per page). For statistical record—Feathery's total earnings for all the manuscripts which at present we know he wrote would probably be something in the region of £70.

We can also establish that, at least sometime in his life, Feathery was a law clerk. Quite apart from the considerable amount of material copied by him devoted to legal matters, we find clear evidence of his legal role in the form of an indenture, now in the William Salt Library in Stafford (Plates 36–8). Feathery is responsible for all the main-body text, down to 'In wyttnes whereof', and another hand, perhaps that of a senior scrivener or lawyer, has then completed the details in the last line or so, before the relevant parties and witnesses step forward to sign. The indenture is dated 30 June 1635, and the only reason it has attracted any attention hitherto is the identity of the first witness: none other than Izaak Walton.[13] Although the document relates to property in Stafford, it was clearly drawn up in London—and indeed the deceased party, Dame Margaret Temple, as well as her two executors, Walton's brother-in-law Thomas Grinsell and Robert Tichborne, are all described as citizens of London. One wonders, indeed, whether the office in which this deed was drawn up was not in Walton's own neighbourhood—on the north side of the Inns of Court, on or near Fleet Street, where Walton's church of St Dunstan in the West stands, or else on Chancery Lane just around the corner, where Walton is known to have lived and to have owned property.[14] This is the only actual legal instrument which I have come across in Feathery's hand, though, for all we know to the contrary, legal scrivening may even have been his main livelihood.

Moving on from there, we can establish beyond doubt that Feathery belonged to some kind of professional scriptorium, legal or otherwise. Although it is conceivable that he worked at times in a loosely organized consortium of independent entrepreneurs, the likelihood that he and his associates generally worked in a particular physical establishment would seem more compelling. At the risk of flippancy, I might even

an unbound folio tract by Cotton, Edward Lord Herbert of Cherbury paid £1 5s., which, at 147 pages of writing, works out at just under 2d. a page (National Library of Wales, Powis 1959 deposit, series II, bundle XVI, No. 4). An example of a specific and fairly detailed charge made in 1640, which might serve as a provisional benchmark, is found in a 975-page folio volume among the Yelverton Manuscripts (BL Add. MS 48186): 'In this Booke there is 10: quire of paper wch cost writing vizt the 2. first quires 16^s: a quire. in all 1^{li}–12^s–0 and the other 8 quires 1^{li}–12^s–0 a quire in all. 12^{li}–16^s–0. the paper. 10^s: the binding 3^s–6^d the totall of all wch somes are—15^{li}–1^s–6^d.' The variation of charges here between the first two quires and the rest would seem to be explained by the fact that the writing on the first two quires averages about 450 words per page (= just under 2d. per page) as opposed to about 660 words per page for the rest (= just under 4d. a page). The prices for MSS recorded in the notary Humphrey Dyson's catalogues (All Souls College, Oxford, MS 117) range from just over 1d. to just over 1½d. per page (cf. Appendix II, Nos. 77.2–3, 97.1, and 105.3). Some other examples of prices for various MSS (ranging from about 1½d. to 5d. per page) are cited in Woudhuysen, 176 *et passim*. It should also be noted that in one of his satirical characters in 1631 Francis Lenton speaks of the lawyer's clerk's charging 'Foure pence a sheet' when flourishing and 'a halfe-penny a sheet' when down on his luck (Appendix I, No. 13).

[13] *Index*, ii/2 (1993), 622 (No. iii).

[14] Walton possessed 'half a shop' two doors west of Chancery Lane in Fleet Street as early as 1614; he is recorded as living at the very bottom of Chancery Lane in 1638 (T. C. Dale, *The inhabitants of London in 1638*, Society of Genealogists (London, 1931), i. 233); he was a vestryman at St Dunstan's in the West at least in 1641 when he signed the parish records; and he bequeathed 'a house in Chancery-lane' in his will of 1683. Chancery Lane itself had been the location for at least one scrivener: George Symcotts, who identified himself as such and signed an indenture, also signed by Richard, Earl of Dorset, on 16 February 1623/4 (Suffolk Record Office, Ipswich, HA 93/10/125).

PLATE 36: Overall view of an indenture written chiefly by Feathery, 30 June 1635 (William Salt Library M 527)

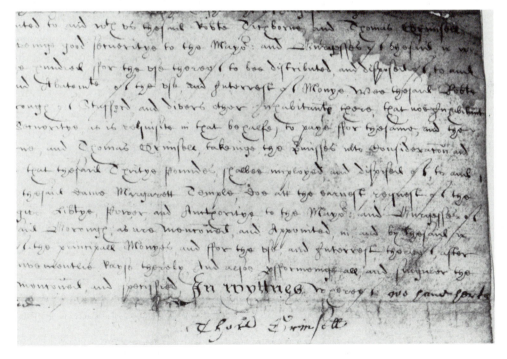

PLATE 37: Portion of the 1635 indenture, towards the bottom right (William Salt Library M 527)

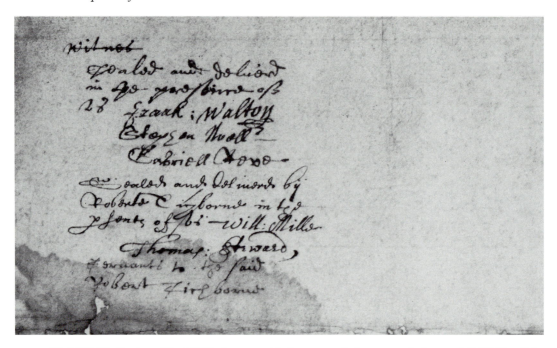

PLATE 38: Portion of the 1635 indenture, with signatures of witnesses at the bottom left (William Salt Library M 527)

describe it, as Earles did an attorney's office, as where 'though but pen-featherd, he hath now nested for himself'.[15] It is just possible that Feathery may even have been involved in the scrivener's business of moneylending. A clue to this possibility is found in a copy of the notorious libel *Leicester's commonwealth*, now in the Pierpont Morgan Library. Except for the first sixteen pages (which look as if they have been hastily copied by someone to replace lost pages), the text of this manuscript is in Feathery's hand. In the margins of one page (Plate 39) are some heavily deleted annotations in other hands, which seem to refer to a 'Mr Peake . . . ouer against St [?] Church in Smithe Alley' and to 'M^{ris} Nicholes' who 'liues att the Sign . . . in ye Strand oue^r against ye ffountaine'. At the end of the manuscript (Plate 40) more partly deleted scribbling records a variety of names and addresses in London, as well as in some cases outstanding debts. They include 'George Hard at ye Angell and Star in Birchinlane | M^r. Cornewall lodges att M^{rs}. Collords house over ag^t. the suger Loafe in Red lyon Court Right ag^t serjont . . . Inn ffleetestreete . . . Ben Walker att the Nagges head Inn in James streete in Covent Garden | . . . and the rest to be paid at xix[?] shillings a weeke till ye debt be paid . . . Mr Cosgraue [who] lodgeth hard by the dog tauerne in pallace yard Westminster', and so on. Of course, some independent owners of the manuscript might have added this scribbling. Nevertheless, it is a distinct possibility that this somewhat defective manu-

---

[15] John Earle[s], *The autograph manuscript of Microcosmographie: A Scolar Press facsimile* (Leeds, 1966), 30.

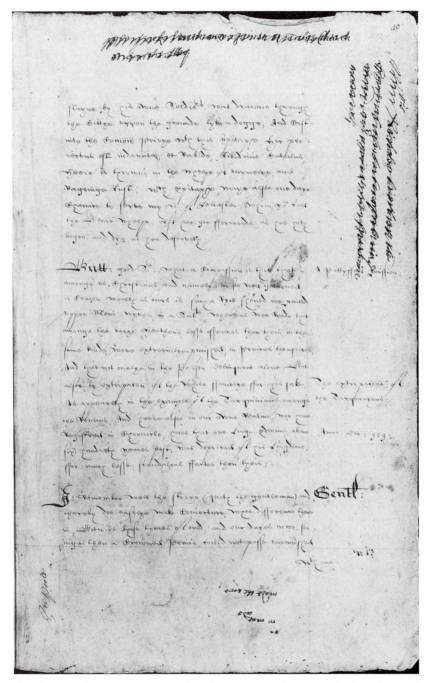

PLATE 39: A page in Feathery's copy of *Leicester's commonwealth* with marginal scribbling (Pierpont Morgan Library MS with MA 1475, p. 10)

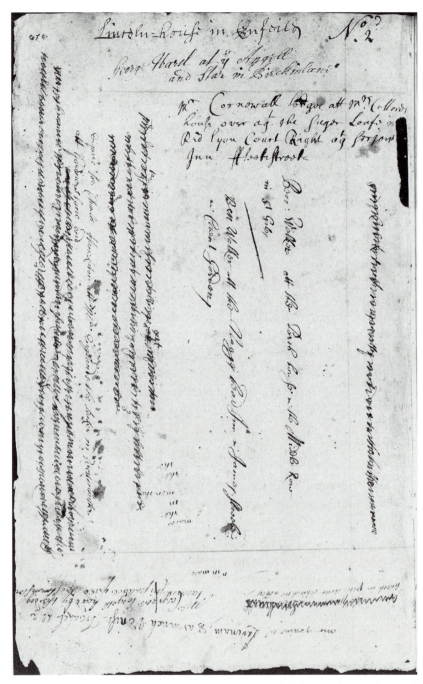

PLATE 40: End-leaf of Feathery's copy of *Leicester's commonwealth* with scribbling (Pierpont Morgan Library MS with MA 1475, p. 231)

script was retained in the scriptorium as a kind of general-purpose 'in-house' copy (if not exemplar) and that the jottings record some of their clients—who, as we can see, were scattered throughout the commercial, as well as fashionably residential, areas of London north of the Thames—chiefly from the area of Fleet Street and the Inns of Court westwards to Covent Garden and the Strand and down to Westminster, though also over to the City and even, in one instance, up as far as Enfield in Middlesex.[16]

With the establishment of a scriptorium, other features of Feathery's work start to fall into line. For instance, we can note the almost total consistency in the paper format he uses: almost always gatherings in folio. Indeed I have come across only two instances when he uses anything else: small-quarto formats for copies of tracts by Sir Charles Cornwallis and George Ashley now at Harvard and Lambeth Palace.[17] Over a career of at least one and a half decades, we could not expect to see Feathery using a single stock of paper. Indeed, we find examples of his writing on paper with a variety of watermarks, including urns or pots, crowns, croziers, fleurs-de-lis, and other patterns. Nevertheless, certain watermarks do occur in his work with striking regularity. The commonest is a kind of H-shaped pair of posts or pillars, surmounted by a bunch of grapes, with a cross-bar often bearing lettering, the most regular being 'RDP' (Plate 41). This is a slightly more elaborate version of Heawood 3494 (see Plate 42), a watermark Heawood dates 1633.[18] Other fairly recurrent watermarks include a wheel-shaped device comprising quatrefoils within a double circle (Plate 43) and, in variant forms, a bunch of grapes (a characteristic example, with the lettering 'IVG', is seen in Plate 44, conforming to Heawood's 2179, which he dates 1638).

By far the most obvious indication that Feathery was associated with one or more scriptoria, however, is the presence in his manuscripts of multiple hands. Of the 300 so-called 'titles' I referred to, over fifty show shared responsibility for copying—with perhaps as many as a dozen other scribes making fairly regular appearances in the manuscript volumes in which Feathery's hand occurs. As for their *modus operandi*—their working routine—what we find is a kind of pragmatic fluidity, with scribes taking over from one another at almost any point in a text as occasions for breaking off arise. Most commonly, when changes occur, one scribe will simply stop at the end of a page, usually with the catchword, and the next scribe will take over at the top of the next page. But there are plenty of examples of changes of hand on an irregular basis—when, for whatever reason, another scribe will pick up in the middle of a page, even in the middle

---

[16] This kind of recording of names and addresses, suggesting scriptorium clients, is found elsewhere, including a notable verse miscellany of the 1680s (Bodleian Library MS Firth c. 16), which appears to be written partly in the hand of Aphra Behn (1640–89). It is evidence that, at least towards the end of her life (if not earlier, for she knew how to draw up a formal petition apparently by 1668), this writer worked as a professional scribe: see *Index*, ii/1. 2 (No. 12), 3; Mary Ann O'Donnell, 'A verse miscellany of Aphra Behn: Bodleian Library MS Firth c.16', *EMS* 2 (1990), 189–227 (addresses illustrated on p. 191); Janet Todd, *The secret life of Aphra Behn* (London, 1996), 353–6.

[17] Appendix II, Nos. 9 and 75.

[18] Edward Heawood, *Watermarks mainly of the 17th and 18th centuries* (Hilversum, 1950), 142 and plate 476.

PLATE 41: Drawing of pillars watermark in one of Feathery's manuscripts

PLATE 42: Pillars watermark: Heawood No. 3494

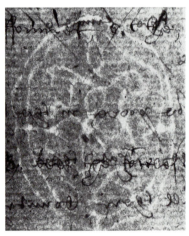

PLATE 43: Quatrefoils within circle watermark in one of Feathery's manuscripts

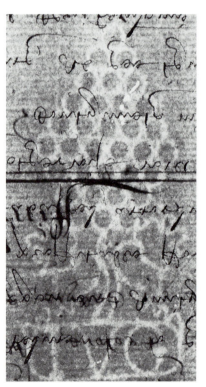

PLATE 44: Bunch of grapes watermark in one of Feathery's manuscripts

of a sentence. An example of this may be seen in the Harley manuscript shown in Plate 45. The first scribe breaks off about half-way down the page, two words into a line, having just started a new sentence—'For the'—and Feathery continues: 'manner, howe to ffight wth the Enemye [etc.]'. Another example, in a Stowe manuscript, may be seen in Plate 46. Feathery starts the page off, goes down as far as the middle of the eighth line— 'The | Morrall whereof (Besides the'—and breaks off (again, like the end of *Finnegans wake*, with a dangling definite article) before a second scribe takes over to complete the sense: 'Ceremonie) may be that God is not pleased [etc.]'. So, besides all else, the procedures employed—the mechanics of rostering—have precious little to do with the meaning or organization of the *text*. In a professional operation to produce a continuous stream of copy on a practical basis, no special care is taken to transfer at the end of chapters, sections, or distinct textual units—such considerations are largely irrelevant.

Thus the scribes seem to work to some extent as a team, almost certainly in one location, and to share the text piecemeal, but evidently—for the most part—*not* according to the medieval *pecia* system.[19] Generally speaking, we see little evidence, I think, of any regulated system of copying by multiple scribes according to apportioned quires, or units, of a given work: little indication that it was customary for portions of a single exemplar to be distributed to different scribes for simultaneous copying and then reassembled when all the parts were complete. Nor, from the examples I have encountered of multiple copies of the same work, is there any clear evidence that scribes had allocated to them particular sections of a work to copy over and over again—as if familiarity would speed up the copying process. No, the transition to other hands in such multiple copies fails to recur in the same place. In brief, the Feathery scriptorium would appear customarily to preserve the exemplars intact, each scribe working on one at a time, the transition from one scribe to the next occurring apparently because of interruption or as their respective stints come to an end—the changes being thus made on an *ad hoc* basis, not according to a pre-determined division dictated by some kind of assembly-line system.

Having said this—as if to demonstrate that it is the exception which illustrates the rule, as well as to show the potential flexibility of the copying process—I have come across only two instances in which anything like a *pecia* system seems to have operated. One occurs in Feathery's copy of one of the arguments in the Ship Money debate in 1638, now in Cambridge University Library (MS Dd. 9. 22),[20] where we find his copy ending on f. 150v 'hath been att a great', followed by a 2½-inch space and then the catchwords 'att a great' before the next page (f. 151r) starts 'att a greate Charge besides': an indication that this text was not copied consecutively but pieced together by Feathery for some reason. Even more telling is a 900-page transcript of diplomatic

---

[19] The system associated particularly with the official stationers of the University of Paris in the 13th century, whereby separate quires of unbound master copies were hired out for copying, the separate units of the resulting copies then being united to produce a complete duplicate text.

[20] Appendix II, No. 5.4.

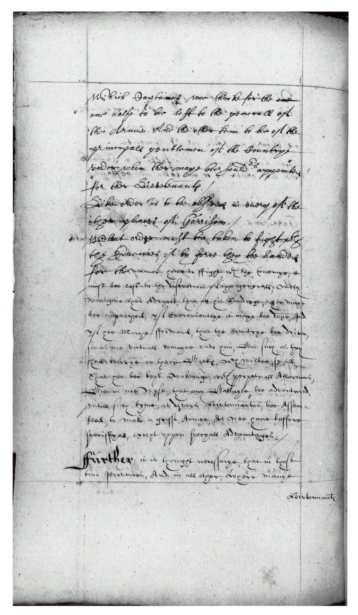

PLATE 45: A page in a copy of *A Councell of Warre ... 1587* showing a transfer of scribal hands (BL Harley MS 444, f. 111v)

correspondence of 1570–3 concerning the proposed Alençon marriage, now among the Harley manuscripts (Harley MS 260).[21] Several scribes were employed on this

---

[21] Appendix II, No. 49. Humfrey Wanley (1672–1726) noticed the speed and errors of transcription in this volume, observing the signs that 'several Writers were employed about the writing it, at the same time': *A catalogue of the Harleian Manuscripts in the British Museum*, 4 vols. (London, 1808–12), i. 100.

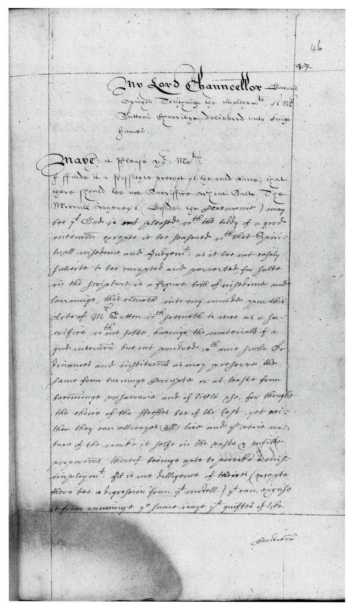

PLATE 46: A page in a copy of Bacon's *Opinyon Touchinge ... Suttons Charritye* showing a transfer of scribal hands (BL Stowe MS 151, f. 46r)

lengthy transcript, but there are plenty of signs that it was, at least in part, a piecemeal rather than sequential operation. Clear indications that scribes were allocated distinct textual units, which were subsequently amalgamated, come in the form of incomplete lines and then spaces left at the end of various verso pages (thinly disguised by spiral flourishes), or even miscalculated sufficiently to leave a whole verso page blank, before another (or occasionally the same) scribe takes over on the next recto page, sometimes adding catchwords to the previous page (characteristic examples occur on ff. 10v–11r, 340v–341r, 394v–395r, 419v–420r, 443v–444r). It seems, indeed, that for some reason this manuscript was a particularly hasty production, scarcely marked by seamless coordination. It serves to throw into relief the vast number of other Feathery-related manuscripts which were *not* so produced.[22]

Can we infer from Feathery's particular contributions to this operation what his relative position was in the pecking order—in the hierarchy—of things? I think we *can* discern certain developments over a period. For instance, if we take the example shown in Plate 47, we can see what I think is a master–servant relationship, or at least relationship between a superior and a subordinate—one which occurs in a number of these manuscripts. Here what I shall provisionally call Feathery's 'master' takes responsibility for starting off a very substantial volume of state letters and tracts—by himself writing the heading: 'A Table of all the severall Tracts and Treatices Written in this Booke Followinge videlicet'. He writes it, moreover, with a considerable degree of elaboration, engrossing in bold the first couple of lines and ornamenting the initial letter with flourishes, foliage, and cross-hatching in the tradition of the writing masters of the period—so there is no mistaking *his* professional status. He then, as it were, hands the pen over to Feathery to do the donkey work: to write the actual text. The dominance of this 'master' is also apparent in various instances where he is seen checking over the copy—perhaps when the whole volume is finished—making a few corrections here and there, adding a few omitted catchwords for the sake of consistency, and even adding the 'Finis' at the end: in other words, acting as the overall supervisor under whom Feathery and his colleagues are evidently subordinates.[23]

In later manuscripts we see this role reversed when Feathery graduates to becoming himself a supervisor of others. In various manuscripts he is responsible for little more than the title-page—conceivably added to a body of text already prepared, but perhaps more usually written to set off another scribe. So in Plates 48 and 49 we have Feathery writing not only the title-page for a set of essays (wrongly) attributed to Bacon,[24] but also the heading of the next leaf—'The: Table:, Off: the: severall Heades, Conteyned, in this Booke; vizt:'—before handing over to another scribe the task of writing the

---

[22] One other possible example of a *pecia* operation that I have come across was produced by Feathery's associate Ralph Starkey, who is discussed below. What may have been retained as a rough, cobbled-together 'reference' copy is a folio MS (signed 'Ra: Starkey') of 'Sʳ Walter Ralegh his Appollogy touching his Jurney to Guyana delyuedd the Kynge the 5 of August .1618. at Salesbury' in the Essex Record Office, Colchester (D/DRg 3/3). It shows clear signs of piecemeal assembly, with pages written to fit pre-allocated space. Starkey writes the first six pages, but crams his last few lines on p. 6 down the margin to make them fit the paper. Other scribes copy pp. 7–18 (pp. 17–18 being a single leaf glued to the stub adjoining p. 8, as if a replacement); Starkey resumes on p. 19 (which is conjugate with p. 6) and ends on p. 20 with a ½-inch gap before the catchword, which is followed by a ¾-inch space; leaving page 21 (marked at the top 'Last') in the hand of another scribe; the 25 pages of this copy (including blank end-leaves) being sewn within wrappers formed from a MS broadsheet which was once f. 5 of a draft legal agreement.

[23] Among other examples, this 'master's' hand is found in Trinity College Dublin MSS 732, 802, and 845, BL Add. MS 73087 and Harley MS 444, and Folger Shakespeare Library MS V. b. 50 (Appendix II, Nos. 18, 20, 21, 35, 53, and 109).

[24] Appendix II, No. 3.2.

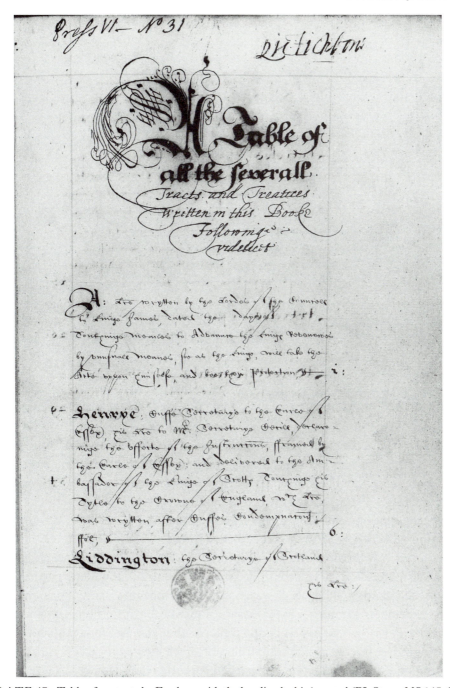

PLATE 47: Table of contents by Feathery with the heading by his 'master' (BL Stowe MS 145, f. 1r)

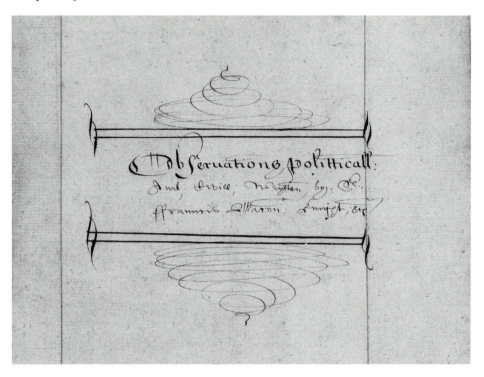

PLATE 48: Feathery's title-page in a copy of *Obseruations Politticall: And, Civill … by: S*ʳ*. ffrauncis Bacon* (CUL Add. MS 9276, No. 12)

actual text. And Feathery's 'dominance' here—and elsewhere in the late 1630s—is reinforced by the occasional corrections we see him making in the text of other scribes, where it is clear that he is the one checking over their copy, and sometimes also adding the foliation, occasional headings or omitted catchwords, and even the last couple of lines or a 'Finis'—to top and tail the text, as it were.

Supplementing the indications that Feathery attained some kind of standing or seniority in the scriptorium there is even evidence that he had an imitator. By 'imitator' I mean the scribe who takes over from Feathery in Plate 49 and who is seen again later in the same manuscript, in less controlled mode, in Plate 50. If we look particularly at his engrossed words—'The:', 'Off: Councells, in Democaties', and 'Nurinburghe'— we can see Feathery's influence in the way the junior scribe forms his letters and decorates them with wispy, feathery loops and trailers—though never for a moment does he here achieve the finesse and accomplishment of Feathery himself, compared with whose work his relatively uneven, unbalanced lettering seems clumsy.[25]

[25] Other examples of this 'imitator's' work occur elsewhere: for instance, in National Library of Wales Wynnstay MS 44, BL Add. MS 11308, Harley MSS 1323 and 1853, and Trinity College Dublin MS 731 (Appendix II, Nos. 2, 17A.1, 28, and 57). Sometimes this scribe even goes so far as to imitate Feathery's distinctive title-page format of two sets of double rules with leaf-like terminal flourishes and spiralling, a feature which helped to mislead even the eagle-eyed Henry Woudhuysen into classifying Harley MS 7021, ff. 65r–122r, as a work by Feathery himself (Woudhuysen, 185 n. 40).

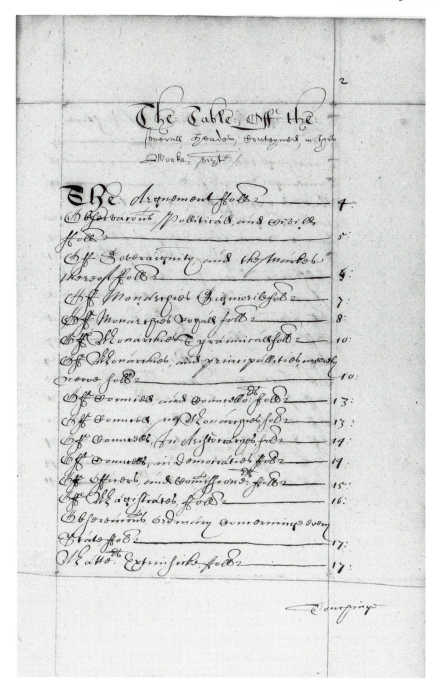

PLATE 49: Table of contents in *Obseruations Politticall: And, Civill … by: S'. ffrauncis Bacon* with heading by Feathery and text by his 'imitator' (CUL Add. MS 9276, No. 12)

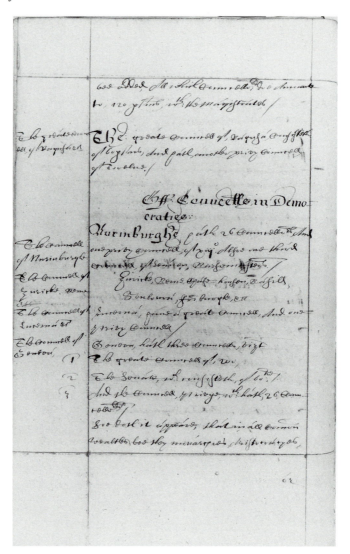

PLATE 50: A page in the main text of *Obseruations Politticall: And, Civill … S^r. ffrauncis Bacon* by Feathery's 'imitator' (CUL Add. MS 9276, No. 12, f. 14v)

In this world of anonymity—of what, depending on the charitableness of our disposition, we might call either faceless hacks or scribal craftsmen—is it possible to identify any of Feathery's employers, colleagues, or associates?

In one important case the answer is 'yes'. In a number of manuscripts now among the Harley Collection in the British Library we find Feathery working in close collaboration with the particular scribe whose work may be seen illustrated in Plate 51. Before we see Feathery assuming the pen towards the foot of this page—in the last word of the fifth line from the bottom, mid-sentence, after '*Inter Recorda domini Regis Caroli in*'—

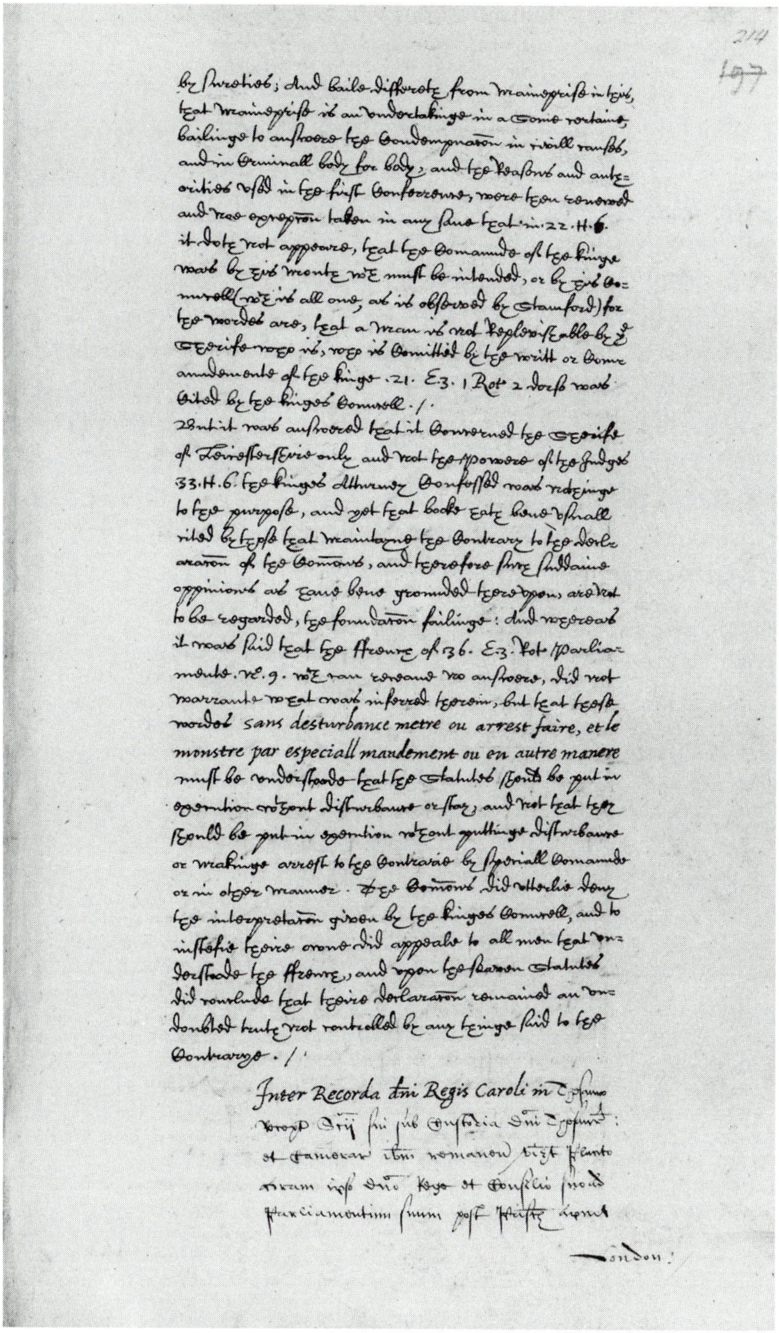
214

197

by Sureties; And baile differeth from Mainprise in this, that Mainprise is an undertakinge in a some certaine, bailinge to answere the Condempnation in civill causes, and in Criminall body for body; and the Reasons and authorities used in the first Conference, were then renewed and noe exception taken in any save that in 22. H. 6. it doth not appeare, that the Comaunde of the Kinge was by his mouth which must be intended, or by his Councell (which is all one, as is observed by Stanford) for the wordes are, that a man is not Replevisable by the Sheriffe who is, who is Comitted by the writt or Commaundemente of the kinge. 21. E3. 1 Rot 2 dorso was cited by the kinges Councell./

But it was answered that it concerned the Sheriffe of Worcestershire only and not the power of the Judges 33. H. 6. the kinges Attorney confessed was nothinge to the purpose, and yet that booke hath bene usuall cited by those that maintayne the contrary to the declaration of the Comons, and therefore theire suddaine oppinions as have bene grounded thereupon, are not to be regarded, the foundation failinge: And whereas it was said that the Statute of 36. E3. Rot Parliament. no. 9. which can receave noe answere, did not warrante what was inferred therein, but that those wordes *sans desturbance metre ou arrest faire, et le monstre par especiall maundement ou en autre manere* must be understoode that the Statutes should be put in execution without disturbance or stay, and not that they should be put in execution without puttinge disturbance or makinge arrest to the contrarie by speciall Comaunde or in other manner. The Comons did utterlie deny the interpretation given by the kinges Councell, and to iustifie theire owne did appeale to all men that understande the Statute, and upon the same Reason Statutes did conclude that theire declaration remained an undoubted truth not controlled by any thinge said to the contrarye./

Inter Recorda dni Regis Caroli in Thesauro Recepte Scij sui sub Custodia Dni Thesaurarii et Camerar ibm remanen viz. Placita coram ipso Dno Rege et Consilio suo ad Parliamentum suum post Pasche tent London.

PLATE 51: A page in a copy of *The obiections of the kinges Councell against … the Comons … 1628* by Ralph Starkey and Feathery (BL Harley MS 161, f. 214r) the neat, regular, self-contained, predominantly Secretary script responsible for this page can be identified as that of Ralph Starkey.

Ralph Starkey, who came originally from Cheshire, and flourished between 1595 and 1628, was a London merchant and an enthusiastic antiquary and copyist.[26] That rather humourless and puritanical lawyer, antiquary, and parliamentarian Sir Simonds D'Ewes (1602–50) described him, somewhat dismissively, as 'an ignorant, mercenarie indigent man'—terms suggesting, perhaps, D'Ewes's sense of Starkey's 'amateurism', lack of formal education, and ungentlemanly station in life as a tradesman. But this did not stand in the way of D'Ewes's respect for Starkey's *collections*. 'Hee had gathered together manye olde deedes and some old Manuscripts & coines', he says, 'But hee had great plentie of new written collections, & diuers originall lettres of great moment, & other autographs of later time, besides diuers olde parchments & other particulars.'[27] For this reason D'Ewes jumped in to purchase whatever he could of Starkey's collections after Starkey's death in October 1628. D'Ewes's own collections were later sold by his grandson to Sir Robert Harley, first Earl of Oxford (1661–1724), which is why the Harley Manuscripts are a particularly rich source for Starkey's papers.[28]

---

[26] Brief accounts of Starkey, or informative references to him, are given in the *DNB*; Andrew G. Watson, *The library of Sir Simonds D'Ewes* (London, 1966), 24–6, 85; Kevin Sharpe, *Sir Robert Cotton 1588–1631* (Oxford, 1979), *passim* (where he is described as a 'little-known, but important collector'); Colin G. C. Tite, ' "Lost or stolen or strayed": A survey of manuscripts formerly in the Cotton Library', *BLJ* 18 (1992), 107–47; Tite, *MS library of Cotton* (1994), 52, 58 (where he is described as 'a professional copyist'); and Woudhuysen, *passim*. Besides references cited in the present account, other sources which throw biographical light on Starkey include his elaborate 'Booke off Coppies of Euidence . . . Deuised and p[er]formed by mee Raphe Starkey of London marchante second sonne of John Starkey of Oltone in the Countie of Chestore Esquire in An° 1595' (BL Add. MS 39851, with entries to 1612, his sources, among them various heralds and lawyers, including John Lacy, Francis Thynne, Mr Drury, Robert Barneres, Mr Denham, John Coats, James Strangmant, Randolph Crew, and Sir Robert Cotton); a statement in BL Harley MS 537, f. 98r, recording the ages of his sons by his wife Winifred Poynter: John (b. 29 January 1601/2) and James (b. 18 June 1604), both baptized at St Michael's, Wood Street, Cheapside, with particulars of their godfathers and godmothers, including 'John Lacye, Clotheworkere', 'Sebastion Harvy, Ironmonger', 'Dr James Medowes', and 'Francis Mosley one of Sr Nicholas Mosle[y]'s sonnes', and also (f. 81*v) his postal address ('at the gardeners howse there at a corner entring into Bloo[m]sebury'); the Starkey family pedigree in Cheshire Record Office DDX 255 (Phillipps MS 12235), p. 64 (showing two further sons, Samuel and Thomas, who died in early infancy, and his daughters Elizabeth and Jane); and his prolonged legal battle to secure his rights in properties in Cheshire worth about £500 p.a. left by his father and possessed by his younger brother Henry, a matter which resulted not only in his litigious pleas (such as that docketed and retained by Sir Julius Caesar, Master of the Rolls, on 19 October 1619, in BL Lansdowne MS 163, ff. 8v–10v), but also in Starkey's unsuccessfully petitioning Parliament in 1624, 1626, and 1628, and even in his printing off a broadside bill setting out his claim (STC 23235.5: exemplum in BL Cotton MS Titus B. III, ff. 61v–62r): see especially *Commons debates 1628*, v. 146–9, 564–8 (3 April and 30 May 1628), and vi. 25; and *Commons debates 1626*, i. 53, 57, 270, and iv. 105; as well as his miscellaneous notes on the Starkey family from medieval times to 1626 (BL Harley MSS 306, f. 100v; 506, ff. 66r, 105v, 180r, 185v–186r; 537, f. 95r; and 2012, f. 46r).

[27] BL Harley MS 646, f. 115v, cited in Watson, 24; also in *The autobiography and correspondence of Sir Simonds D'Ewes, Bart.*, ed. James Orchard Halliwell, 2 vols. (London, 1845), i. 391–2. Cf. also D'Ewes's comment elsewhere on Starkey as 'a most extreme ignorant man' (Watson, 105), and his annoyance at finding out in the middle of copying one of Cotton's manuscripts that 'one Ralph Starkie had made the copies of that book common by his base nundination or sale of them' (Woudhuysen, 128). This remark indicates D'Ewes's additional grievance that (like Julian later) Starkey was debasing MSS themselves by trading them as merchandise.

[28] For a listing and discussion of D'Ewes's manuscripts (with comments on those from Starkey) among the Harley MSS, see Watson, and also Cyril Ernest Wright, *Fontes Harleiani* (London, 1972), 131–7, 314. Other examples of Starkey's hand are found in collections elsewhere: for instance, in Bodleian Library MSS Ashmole 840 (ff. 73r–91v), Perrott 4, Tanner 72 (f. 117r), and Tanner 103 (ff. 196r–198v); BL Add. MSS 4149 and 39851; Lansdowne MS 163; CUL MSS Dd. 3. 86 and Ii. 5. 9; University of Chicago MS 878; Essex Record Office, Colchester, D/DRg 3/3 (cf. n. 22 above) and 3/4, items 5 and 12; Folger Shakespeare Library MSS V.b.184, V.b. 276, and X.d. 236; and Inner Temple Library Petyt MS 538, vol. 50; as well as in the BL Cotton MSS

Another notable record of his activities comes in the form of an order issued by the Privy Council on 10 August 1619. This makes it clear that Starkey's collecting had been getting a little too adventurous for comfort. 'Whereas wee are informed', the order states, 'that one Rafe Starky gent. and others have gotten into his and ther hands diuers papers and matters of State, w^ch: belonge vnto his Ma^ty as namely those which in tymes past were in the custody of Mr Secretary Davison and others which he and they have Collected & gathered vpp in diuers places and doe detaine them to their priuate vse . . . '; and the order goes on to authorize Sir Thomas Wilson, Keeper of His Majesty's Papers and Records, 'to repayre vnto the lodging of the said Rafe Starky and such others as you shall know to have any of the said papers and to sease into your hands all such papers of any quality whatsoeuer which eyther ought to belong vnto his Matie, or may otherwyse conduce to his service and to bringe the same vnto the office of his Ma^ts papers for buisinesse of State to be kept and conserved for his Ma^ts: service'. Four days later, on 14 August, Wilson himself signed and inscribed his copy of the warrant, saying: 'I have receyud to his Maties vse a sack full of papers to the number of 45 paquetts wch wer in m^r S[e]c[re]t[ar]y Davisons & wch m^r starky saith he had fro[m] W Duncomb'[29]—the lawyer William Duncombe, incidentally, being Davison's son-in-law.[30]

This warrant is of interest, among other things, because it shows where Starkey was getting some of his best materials from—from the family of Queen Elizabeth's ill-fated secretary William Davison (1541?–1608), who had drawn up the execution warrant of Mary Queen of Scots in 1586–7. And here we have what, in a broad perspective, seems to be one of those periodic, but erratic, episodes when the monarch and his Council were suddenly alerted to taking an interest in retrieving, and re-exercising control over, papers of state business and of possible political sensitivity, before lapsing into their usual neglect and indifference to such matters, before the *next* alarm occurred. All the same, it marks one of the limited successes of that indefatigable Keeper of the Records Sir Thomas Wilson (1560?–1629), who, struggling against all the odds of indifference, neglect, inadequate accommodation, under-staffing, and under-funding (in 'this pore

(cf. n. 36 below). Other MSS in the Bodleian, BL and elsewhere were owned by Starkey or in part copied from his materials (some are mentioned in Woudhuysen, 128 n. 78). Several of the Harley MSS recorded by Watson contain items written or used before Starkey by the antiquary John Stow: see also Stow's *Survey of London*, ed. Kingsford, i, pp. xxii, lxxxvi.

[29] BL Harley MS 286, f. 286r (the copy inscribed by Wilson and apparently left with Starkey by way of authorized receipt for the papers seized). Wilson recorded this seizure, with some satisfaction, in the report on his services signed by him on 30 July 1623: 'whereas I haue of late found out where the old papers of *Secretary Dauisons* time were concealed and kept and were offered to be sold away, I haue by a warrant from his Matie: vnder his hand ceazed vpon them, and brought them into the office for the buisnes of *Scotland* of those times and other partes of *Christendome*, and am nowe putting [them] into there heads and binding [them] into bookes with the rest' (PRO SP 45/20, f. 100r). What would seem to be a chance stray from the Davison papers retained by Starkey is among a group of Sir Simonds D'Ewes's papers in the Essex Record Office, Colchester (D/DRg 3/4, f. 1): namely, a letter by Queen Elizabeth to Davison in the Netherlands, 1 June 1578, actually signed by her, but evidently kept as Davison's file copy (a note by D'Ewes, also witnessed by Thomas Cooke, records comparing it with 'the autograh' [*sic*] on 26 February 1637/8).

[30] William Duncombe was admitted to Gray's Inn on 21 February 1617/18. He married William Davison's daughter Catherine. *Inter alia*, he is found as witness to an indenture of 29 January 1630/1 signed by John Selden while prisoner in the Gate House Prison, now in the Inner Temple Library (Misc. MS 199).

and painfull office wherin I serue yor: Ma^{ty}'),[31] actually made the 1620s and (by his example) the 1630s a period when state papers, and copies thereof, were at last, in some measure, being taken seriously by the authorities.[32]

Starkey made some bid for intellectual respectability—not only by writing his own *Discourse of the high court of parliament*[33] (though this too might have been construed by the civil authorities as impertinent), but also, earlier, by presenting to the Lord Chancellor, Baron Ellesmere, a carefully prepared transcript of a legal treatise by Arthur Agard—describing himself in the dedication as 'haveinge bene for manie yeares a gleaner in other mens harvests of this kinde'. This semi-calligraphic volume, of nineteen quarto leaves (plus blanks) bound in vellum, is among the Ellesmere Papers in the Huntington Library, California.[34]

Besides having dealings with the wax chandler, scrivener, and public notary Humphrey Dyson (d. 1632/3),[35] Starkey was involved with the ubiquitous antiquary, politician, and collector Sir Robert Cotton (1571–1631). Besides the sheer number of manuscript materials in Starkey's hand among Cotton's collection,[36] there are three letters by him addressed to Cotton directly. One, undated but evidently written

[31] PRO SP 45/20, f. 91r.

[32] Wilson's zeal in the office of Keeper of the Records after 1610 led to the custody or seizure of papers of, *inter alia*, Secretaries of State Sir Thomas Lake, Naunton, Morton, Calvert, and Sir Edward Coke, as well as to a monitoring of collections of papers of Lord Dorchester, John Wright, Lord Conway, John Selden, William Prynne, and others: see Wilson's papers in the PRO (especially SP 45/20), discussed and summarized in *The thirtieth annual report of the Deputy Keeper of the Public Records* (1869), appendix 7, pp. 212–93 (especially pp. 212–14, 217–40). Wilson's contribution to bringing 'order out of chaos' is touched on in R. B. Wernham, 'The public records in the sixteenth and seventeenth centuries', in Levi Fox (ed.), *English historical scholarship in the sixteenth and seventeenth centuries* (London, 1956), 11–30 (especially pp. 22–4); but his career awaits full recognition.

[33] In Starkey's own copy (though it is not in his hand) in Harley MS 37, ff. 36r–60v, the work is dedicated to Prince Charles (after 20 November 1620 and before 27 March 1625). It is, says Starkey, on 'a Subiect of great Consequence and a worke of worth if it were labored by one whose Learning could illustrate soe pretious a Jewell'. The discourse was later printed anonymously as *The priuilege and practice of Parliament* (London, 1628) [STC 7749]. For Feathery's copies of the work, see Appendix II, Nos. 6.2 and 74. There are many other contemporary copies of it (in its slightly shorter earlier version): see Baker, *CUL* 193 (and also BL Add. MS 48159; House of Lords Record Office, Braye MS 5, [pp. 193–234], and House of Commons Library MS 6).

[34] Huntington Library EL 35.B.60. The entry on Starkey in the *DNB* attributes to him one other literary work—a 581-stanza verse 'Life of Edward the second kynge of Englande' by 'Infortunio', copied chiefly in his hand in BL Harley MS 558—but this poem (comprising 664 stanzas in the full version) is, in fact, by Sir Francis Hubert (1568/9–1629), and, besides printed editions from 1628 onwards, it survives in various other MS copies: see *GM* 94 (1824), 19–22, and *The poems of Sir Francis Hubert*, ed. Bernard Mellor (Hong Kong, 1961).

[35] The will of Dyson—who in at least one document is actually referred to as a scrivener—was proved on 28 February 1632/3: see R. L. Steele, 'Humphrey Dyson', *Library*, 3rd ser. 1 (1910), 144–51, and William A. Jackson, 'Humphrey Dyson and his collections of Elizabethan proclamations', *HLB* 1 (1947), 76–89 (p. 77). Woudhuysen (pp. 178–80) draws attention to Dyson's catalogues of historical works (All Souls College, Oxford, MS 117) and observes that 'Against many of the prices for the items listed . . . up to the end of Queen Elizabeth's reign are the initials RS or just S' which suggest that Starkey was their 'purchaser'. He admits, however, that this evidence 'may be complicated and capable of different interpretation'. I myself would go so far as to suggest that, given their prominence and recurrence, these initials are likely to indicate some kind of special arrangement between Starkey and Dyson in connection with particular texts, though whether Starkey was acting as Dyson's supplier, purchaser, or distributor is unclear.

[36] The innumerable examples of Starkey's hand among the Cotton MSS in the BL include various items in Caligula C. IX, D. I, and E. XII; Cleopatra E. IV, F. I, and F. II; Faustina E. I and E. VII (f. 15v); Otho E. VII and E. X; Titus B. IV, B. V, B. XII, C. I, C. IV, F. I, F. III, and F. IV; Vespasian C. I (illustrated in Tite, *MS library of Cotton*, 58), C. II, C. III, C. VII, C. VIII, C. XII, C. XIII, and C. XIV; and Vitellius C. XVI, as well as BL Add. MS 46410 (formerly Claudius B. VIII). For a number of these references I am indebted to Colin Tite.

between May 1608 and June 1609 when Cotton was a commissioner for the investigation of abuses in the Navy, establishes that Starkey was, in fact, a timber merchant, for, addressing Cotton as 'my fauorabell frynd', he advances an elaborate argument to show why he should be made the King's supplier of wood, most especially ships' masts (offering a cut price of 21s. per 'palme' for 'Magdeburgh dealles' and the best and most durable German timber for other works).[37] More to the point, a second letter by him, also undated, makes it clear that Starkey was one of Cotton's suppliers of historical manuscripts, as well as one of his borrowers.[38] The third and longest letter, however, gives a particularly vivid account of the effects of the plague on Cotton's London household in September of 1625—from which it is evident that Starkey was then acting as Cotton's steward, he and at least one of his two daughters looking after Cotton's London house while Cotton retreated to the more salubrious air of his Connington estate in Huntingdonshire.[39]

Whether it was through Starkey that Feathery came to supply Cotton with manuscripts we do not know, but among the surviving Cotton manuscripts there is at least one item produced by Feathery, and, indeed, it is his longest known piece of work: his two-volume, 1,500-page transcript of the diplomatic letterbooks of Sir Charles Cornwallis, English Ambassador in Spain, for the period 1607–11.[40] The unusual stock of paper used in these volumes (with a spread-eagle watermark) reinforces one's impression that they were produced by special commission on a single occasion, and were not characteristic products of Feathery's scriptorium. The nature of the script also suggests a somewhat early dating—perhaps from the mid-1620s.

Some lists of manuscripts and notes of provenance still among Starkey's papers— partly written by both William Davison's son Francis and Starkey himself—add to our knowledge of the legal and antiquarian circles in which the kind of material he collected and copied was passed around at this time—including various specified lawyers,

---

[37] BL Cotton MS Otho E. VII, ff. 159r–160r.

[38] BL Cotton MS Julius C. III, f. 362r. Starkey sends Cotton all his papers 'of the Lowe Countreys . . . from 1590 to 1600' and seeks to borrow a 'booke of Goewarantes [?Charter warrants ?Covenants] of E[dward] the .1. first or other tymes after'. Starkey's role as a supplier is confirmed by a list in his hand of speeches by Sir Nicholas Bacon, Queen Elizabeth, and Sir Walter Mildmay, which Cotton has marked up, adding a note: 'All thes that I have marked I desier to se and Examine by my book and the shalbe safly returned you with many thanks. Your assurd frend Robert Cotton' (BL Harley MS 6846, f. 45r). 'Mr Starky' is also mentioned as one of Cotton's borrowers—of, among other things, medieval deeds, Tudor 'pattents', a French romance, certain 'Cronicon[s]' ('for wᶜʰ he is to gett me Mʳ Standsby old booke'), and a tract by Lord Northampton, in the 'Catalogus Librorum Manuscriptorum in Bibliotheca Roberti Cottoni 1621 [and later]' in BL Harley MS 6018, ff. 150r and 173v. On f. 155v MSS lent to Lord Northampton (1540–1614) include 'A book in 4ᵗᵒ bound that was Mʳ Starkeys of Armory'.

[39] BL Cotton MS Julius C. III, ff. 360r–361v. The letter is dated 18 September 1625. Among much other news, it mentions that 'mʳ [Humphrey] dysone the Scrivenor hath had the Sicknes but is vpon recouery'. Incidentally, neither this nor any other letter cited supports the notion that Starkey was Cotton's 'secretary', mentioned in Simon Adams, 'The papers of Robert Dudley, Earl of Leicester: II. The Atye–Cotton collection', *Archives*, 20/90 (October 1993), 131–44 (pp. 138–9), where (in an otherwise valuable study) a somewhat speculative argument is advanced that Starkey was 'the central figure in the dispersal' of the papers of Sir Arthur Atye (c.1540–1604), principal secretary of Robert Dudley, Earl of Leicester.

[40] Appendix II, Nos. 37 and 38. It may be noted that 'A bundle of lres from Sʳ: Charles Cornewallis from Madrid to my Mʳ: from 1606 till 1609' is recorded as item 9 in 'A Register of my Mʳˢ: [i.e. Sir Thomas Wilson's] papers at home in his study' in PRO SP 45/20, ff. 122r–123r. The likelihood is, however, that the transcript by Feathery was made later from a formal letterbook rather than from the original letters.

gentlemen, and dignitaries such as the Privy Counsellor Edward, Lord Zouche (1556–1625), Sir Francis Bacon's brother-in-law and literary co-executor Sir John Constable, and the Bishop of Oxford (presumably John Howson, 1557?–1632, Bishop of Oxford 1619–28).[41] They also include a certain 'Mr Stanesby', who might have been the printer and bookseller William Stansby (*fl.*1590–1639), one of whose publications provoked the Council (in 1623?) to nail up his printing house and break down his presses.[42] More likely, it is Starkey's fellow-sufferer John Stanesby, who would petition Parliament on 24 February 1640/1 in an attempt to retrieve the 'sundry manuscripts, journals, and other passages of Parliament, with divers other notes and papers . . . to the number of about 300 quires of paper' which Stanesby had 'collected, with much expense of time and labour' and which Thomas Meautys, one of the Clerks of the Council, confiscated in November 1629.[43] The lists in Starkey's papers even mention some of the *literary* works which were currently sought after in manuscript: 'John Duns Satyres', for instance, which were lent to Christopher Davison, and copies of which (Francis Davison suggests) might be got from the law-student Eleazor Hodgson or else from Ben Jonson.[44]

So far as Feathery is concerned, there is no evidence that he was associated with Starkey before 1619, when the Davison papers were carted away. But there is ample evidence that he was working for Starkey at least by the late 1620s—when Starkey's collecting and copying activities were obviously being pursued as vigorously as ever. In many of the Harley manuscripts, in the copying of political and historical tracts, the hands of Starkey and Feathery alternate—and they alternate, interestingly enough, on an almost equal basis, as if genuinely complementing one another: completing, correcting, and annotating each other's copy—even though, presumably, Starkey is Feathery's employer. So, for instance, it is Feathery who adds (though not quite complete)

---

[41] Lists in Francis Davison's hand are in BL Harley MS 298, ff. 158r–160r. These are transcribed in *Davison's Poetical rhapsody*, ed. A. H. Bullen, 2 vols. (London, 1890), i. li–lv. Lists in Starkey's hand are in BL Harley MS 292, f. 139r–v (itemizing his 'paperes' chiefly 'touchinge Scotlande', especially relating to Mary Queen of Scots); and Harley MS 298, ff. 153r–v, 156r–157r, 158v (listing Tudor and Stuart state papers and tracts with Messrs Waight, Davison, Kinestone, and others, Sir Robert Cotton, and 'Mr Lathame the Duke of Lynneuxe [Ludovick Stuart, second Duke of Lennox (1574–1624), Deputy Earl Marshal and Steward of the Royal Household, whose rooms in the Tower adjoined the State Paper Office] his Secretarye', his notes on f. 158v enclosing those by Davison); Harley MS 537, ff. 80r–86r, 91r–v, 107r (chiefly itemized lists of similar materials, including items *temp.* Mary I and Edward VI, 76 items *temp.* Elizabeth, and 12 *temp.* James I, and a list dated 1614, including 'Richard the Third his deathe by the Lord Standley'; f. 91r–v being a list of titles of political tracts, etc. against folio numbers from 'fo. 304' to 'fo. 344'). A list in another hand in Harley MS 537, ff. 77r–79r, is docketed in Starkey's hand 'Contractes of marryages wth other Princes'. Further lists in other hands are in Harley MS 298, ff. 154r–155v, 161r–165v.

[42] W. W. Greg, *A companion to Arber* (Oxford, 1967), 61–2, 66–7, 210–11.

[43] HMC, 4th Report (1874), appendix, part I, p. 54; also cited in *Commons debates 1629*, p. xxxv.

[44] Apropos of Donne (whom, according to Drummond of Hawthornden, Ben Jonson esteemed 'the first poet jn the World jn some things', and who was on friendly terms with Sir Robert Cotton), it may be noted that an unrecorded copy of his brief epigram 'A lame begger' in Starkey's hand occurs in BL Harley MS 306, f. 100v. In Harley MS 364, a volume containing other material in Starkey's hand, there is a bound-in leaf (f. 45**v) inscribed 'Doctor Dunnes Sermon farewell the Lo. of Bridgwaters sermo[n], left here b[y] Mr Thomas J- 7. Dec. 1619', presumably a note which once accompanied a MS copy of Donne's *A sermon of valediction at my going into Germany, at Lincoln's Inn, April 18, 1619* (cf *Index*, i/1. 556: DnJ 4009–13). The 'Mr Thomas J' mentioned might conceivably be Thomas James (1573?–1629), Bodley's librarian.

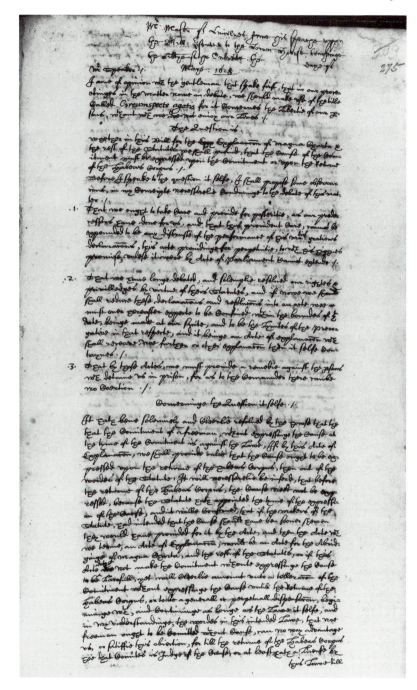

PLATE 52: First page of a copy of *M* Mason ... *his speache ... toucheinge the Libtye of the Subiecte . . . 1628* with heading by Feathery and text by Starkey (BL Harley MS 37, f. 275r)

the heading at the top of Starkey's transcript of a parliamentary speech of May 1628 (Plate 52). It is Feathery who finishes off yet another speech in the same manuscript (Plate 53), adding the final ten and a half lines after Starkey breaks off in the middle of the second line. Feathery also goes through the whole text, making other occasional corrections and insertions.

Indeed, it seems likely that Starkey and Feathery were working together at about, or just before, the time of Starkey's death, since they are found copying together parliamentary speeches dated as late as the end of June 1628[45]—and we know from D'Ewes that Starkey was dead by October of that year. We can add an especially important piece of evidence about the closeness of their collaboration at this time in the form of a three-page 'Catologue of Papers' found in 'Mr Starkys study'—and since the titles include (No. 73) a parliamentary journal for 1627 and 1628 it is evident that the list relates to manuscripts found in his study after his death. This 'Catologue' is now among the Ellesmere Papers in the Huntington Library (see Appendix III below). It is significant that of the eighty-nine titles or volumes listed here, easily two-thirds can be found represented among the known manuscripts by or associated with Feathery.

After Starkey we have no information so concrete about any of Feathery's other employers, or his scriptorium's clients, although we know the names of at least some of the early—if not original—*owners* of his manuscripts. Predominantly English, occasionally Welsh, Scottish, or Irish, their social position is likely to be indicative of the nature of Feathery's market and clientele. For instance, one early owner was the staunch Protestant parliamentarian and Sheriff of Cheshire Sir Richard Grosvenor, Bt. (1585–1645),[46] who once exhorted a local election committee, in 1624, to exercise complete freedom and independence of conscience. 'Freedome of voyce is your inheritance and one of the greatest prerogatives of the subject', he said, 'which ought by all meanes to bee kept inviolate and cannot be taken from you by any commaund whatsoever.'[47] Another was the somewhat inactive MP Sir Robert Oxenbridge (1595–1638),

---

[45] Appendix II, No. 47.12.

[46] Grosvenor's list of 'manuscripts . . . bound up in severall volumes', dated 18 February 1634[/5], is among the muniments of the Duke of Westminster at the Eaton Estate Office, Eccleston (Personal Papers 2/25), and has been printed in *The papers of Sir Richard Grosvenor, 1st Bart. (1585–1645)*, ed. Richard Cust (Record Society of Lancashire and Cheshire, vol. 134, 1996), 43–51. Of the nine volumes calendared in this list, three (*Libri* 3, 4, and 9) contain materials in Feathery's hand, as well as a further one owned by Grosvenor and not on the list (Appendix II, Nos. 12, 79, 81 and 82; also Ch. 2 above, n. 25). For the record it may be noted that of the other *Libri* recorded, No. 2 is still at Eaton (Miscellaneous 13), No. 5 at Yale University (Osborn Collection fb 178), No. 6 at the University of Kansas (MS D 153), No. 7 at Harvard (fMS Eng 1266, vol. 2), and No. 8 at the House of Lords Record Office (Historical Collections No. 53). *Liber* 1 remains untraced (and was not recorded in the 1872 HMC report on the Eaton MSS [HMC, 3rd Report, appendix, pp. 210–16]). Other manuscripts owned by Grosvenor—some (such as Yale Osborn Collection b 50) also associated with the Feathery scriptorium and containing tracts copied by him elsewhere—are widely dispersed (see especially Sotheby's sales on 19 July 1966 and 20 February 1967), and his parliamentary diaries for 1626 and 1628–9 are at Trinity College, Dublin (MSS 611–12: see *Commons debates 1628*, i. 23–6, *et passim*; *Commons debates 1629*, 173–244). Familiar titles are also recorded as 'Manuscripts in folio' in Grosvenor's list of 'Deeds and writings sent to mee by [Thomas] Booth from my Sonn: [6] Nov: 1637' (Eaton Estate Office, Personal Papers 2/26).

[47] Richard Cust and Peter G. Lake, 'Sir Richard Grosvenor and the rhetoric of magistracy', *BIHR* 54/129 (May 1981), 40–53 (p. 50).

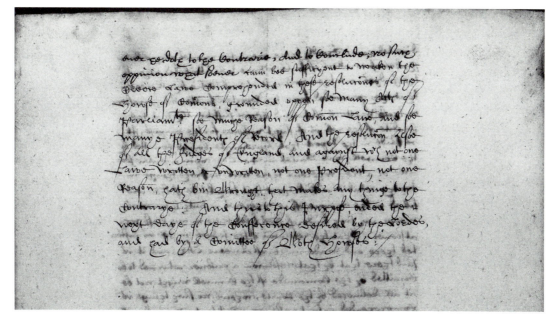

PLATE 53: Last page of a copy of *The . . . obiections ... by m^r Atturney generall ... 1628* by Starkey and Feathery (BL Harley MS 37, f. 254v)

of Hurstbourne Priors, Hampshire;[48] another probably the Hampshire MP and Royalist Sir Richard Tichborne (*c.*1578–1652), who became Gentleman of the Bedchamber to Charles I and was sent as Ambassador to the Queen of Bohemia;[49] yet another William Howard, just possibly the antiquary, bibliophile, and friend of Cotton Lord William Howard (1563–1640) of Naworth;[50] and so we could go on speculating about the possible contemporary members of many other old and titled families among whose muniments Feathery's manuscripts survive—the Acland-Hood, Betenson, Finch-Hatton, Petty, Mostyn, Gordon, Parker (Macclesfield), and Yelverton families, among others. Besides clear indications of ownership and use by various lawyers, including Sir Jerome Alexander (*c.*1600–70), Justice of the Irish Common Pleas,[51] and Sir John Trevor (1637–1717), Master of the Rolls,[52] we find contemporary and slightly later owners in the seventeenth century among scholarly clerics, such as Thomas Barlow (1607–91), Bishop of Lincoln; Edward Stillingfleet (1635–99), Bishop of

[48] Appendix II, Nos. 90, and 95–7. Information about Oxenbridge, who was MP for Whitchurch or Hampshire between 1621 and 1626, is supplied by the History of Parliament, and see also Pauline Croft, 'Annual Parliaments and the Long Parliament', *BIHR* 59 (1986), 155–71, and Woudhuysen, 186–8.

[49] Appendix II, Nos. 35 and 71.

[50] Appendix II, No. 92. The signature here cannot be identified for certain. The MS would seem to correspond to none of the MS items on the list of Lord William's books and MSS printed in *Selections from the household books of the Lord William Howard of Naworth Castle* (Surtees Society 68, 1878), 469–87. The greater part of his surviving library (including autograph notebooks of his uncle, the Earl of Northampton) was sold at Sotheby's, 15 December 1992, lot 171, and is now at the University of Durham.

[51] Appendix II, Nos. 17A, 18, 19, 22, and 23.   [52] Appendix II, No. 13. See also below.

Worcester; John Moore (1646–1714), Bishop of Ely (whose library was bought for Cambridge University by George I); Thomas Tanner (1674–1735), Bishop of St Asaph; Archbishops Ussher (1581–1656) (whose library was bought for Trinity College Dublin by Cromwell's soldiers in Ireland), Sancroft (1617–93), and Tenison (1636–1715); as well as collectors and antiquaries such as John Evelyn (1620–1706), William Petyt (1641?–1707), John Anstis (1669–1744), and Peter Le Neve (1661–1729)—not to mention numerous well-known eighteenth-century collectors (one of whom even lent a Feathery manuscript to Queen Anne),[53] nor the host of anonymous early owners who have inscribed their shelfmarks, to denote locations in what were evidently substantial private libraries.

To all of this may be added clear evidence that Feathery's manuscripts (or a number of them, at any rate) were actually *read*: a consideration which traditional literary historians have not *always* taken into account. The manuscripts were commissioned or bought, paid for at higher prices than printed works of comparable length—and they were read—sometimes closely, if readers' annotations are anything to go by. So, for instance, in Feathery's copy of a 1626 speech by Sir Robert Cotton 'Touchinge debaseinge of Coyne'—a manuscript now in Chicago (Plate 54)—we find a very ungainly hand correcting and scribbling in the margins throughout, one highly engaged with the text and even adding critical remarks. The same hand is found elsewhere in the volume commenting, for instance, on an account of Henri IV of France: 'It is conceiued that all the present designes of 1644 (which apeare wonderfull) worke vppon yᵉ principles and foundations layed by this prince.'[54]

Another example that may be cited is a manuscript in the Bodleian where we find a scrupulous scholar and antiquary at work—in this case, Sir William Dugdale (1605–86), Garter King-of-Arms, protégé of Lord Hatton, and erstwhile custodian of Sir Robert Cotton's manuscript collection.[55] In one example (Plate 55) he is seen carefully correcting Feathery's faulty Latin, as well as underlining both Latin text and proper names and amplifying the documentary citations and sidenotes. This annotation occurs in Feathery's 100-page copy of John Selden's history of English law, *Englands epinomis*. Characteristically, Dugdale's is not the only reader's hand present—the manuscript passed through several hands—one of which may be seen in Plate 56, adding side-headings on matters relating to marriage, as a reading guide or *aide-mémoire*.

One final example which I cannot resist mentioning is one of Feathery's most ambitious tomes: his 1,100-page transcript of a massive compilation of historical materials relating to the Court of Chancery, now at the Harvard Law School.[56] Among the various

---

[53] Appendix II, No. 45.   [54] Chicago MS 878, f. 48r (Appendix II, No. 16).
[55] For Dugdale's involvement in sorting and annotating the Cotton MSS, see Tite, *MS library of Cotton*, 64–70.
[56] Appendix II, No. 13.

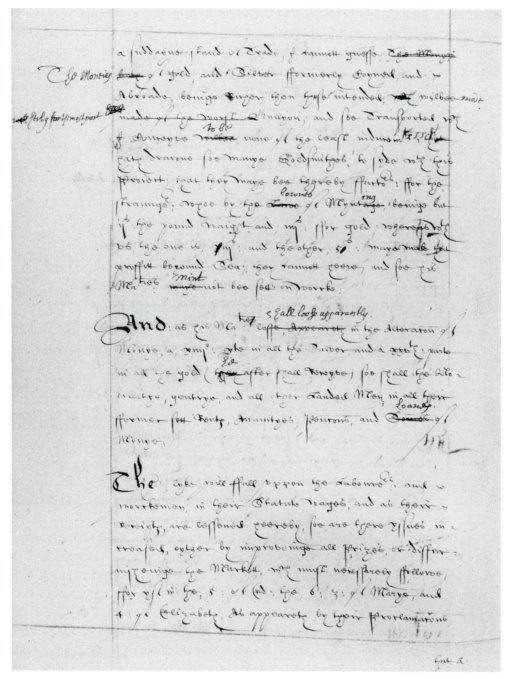

PLATE 54: A page in Feathery's copy of Cotton's *Speech ... 1626: Touchinge debaseinge of Coyne* with a reader's annotations (University of Chicago MS 878, f. [117v])

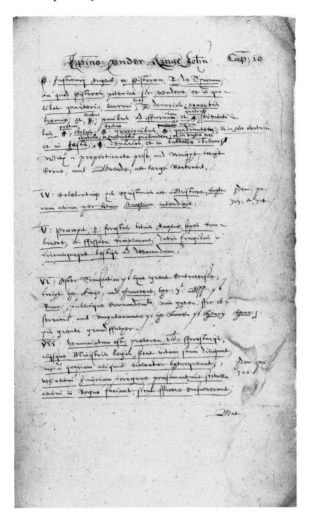

PLATE 55: A page in Feathery's copy of Selden's *Englands epinomis* with annotations by Sir William Dugdale (Bodleian Library MS Dugdale 28, f. 178r)

readers (presumably members of the legal profession) who have used and annotated this compendium over the years is one whose imposing and stylish hand can be seen in Plate 57. Dating from the late seventeenth century, this hand appears in a section concerning 'The errection of the IX°: Clarkes of the Enrollem^te in the Chauncery'. Presumably in response to a question, the annotator would seem to be drawing various clauses concerning the Lord Chancellor's position in relation to the appointment of deputies to the attention of the Lord Chancellor himself. Given the fact that an early owner of this volume was almost certainly Sir John Trevor, Master of the Rolls, it is highly likely that the addressee here was none other than his cousin and patron, the notorious Judge Jeffreys. George, first Baron Jeffreys of Wem (1648–89), was successively Lord Chief Justice and Lord Chancellor in 1683–9, and his energetic attempts,

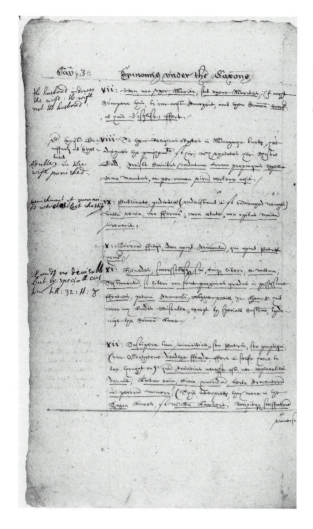

PLATE 56: A page in Feathery's copy of Selden's *Englands epinomis* with a reader's annotations (Bodleian Library MS Dugdale 28, f. 145v)

partly abetted by Trevor, to root out irregularities in the Court of Chancery were not the least of his preoccupations in these years.[57]

So, finally, what of the texts themselves? What kind of materials did Feathery copy so industriously, which people so wanted to possess and to read?

His range was certainly wide, as I have said. It even included 'literature' in the traditional, narrow sense. One wonders, for instance, what the *raison d'être* is behind Feathery's copying a single amatory poem by Henry King at the end of a pamphlet—on the somewhat soiled and exposed outer leaf seen in Plate 58.[58] Was Feathery using a

---

[57] See G. W. Keeton, *Lord Chancellor Jeffreys and the Stuart cause* (London, 1965), 377 *et passim*. It is possible that the hand responsible for the annotations in question is that of Trevor himself (cf. the remarkably similar script in autograph letters by him, dated 1677–8, in BL Egerton MSS 3330, f. 97, and 3331, f. 86), but the identification is not certain.

[58] Appendix II, No. 92.13.

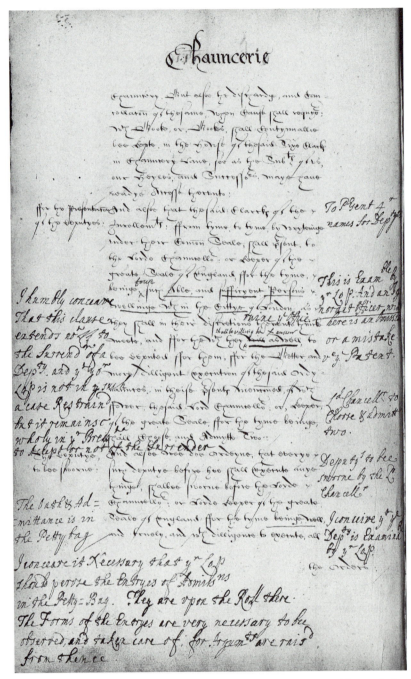

PLATE 57: A page in Feathery's compilation on the Court of Chancery with a reader's annotations for a Lord Chancellor (Harvard Law School Library MS 1034, f. 32v)

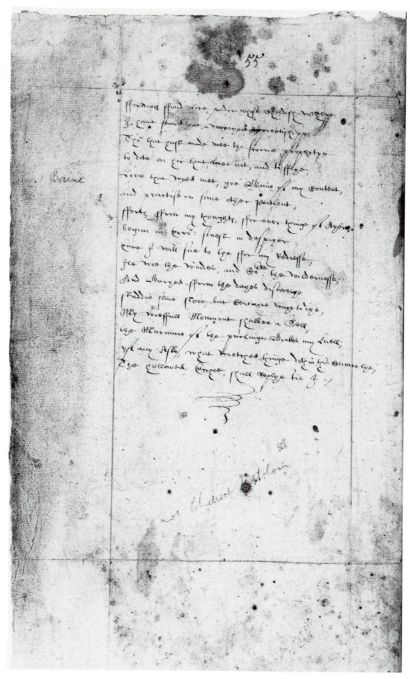

PLATE 58: Feathery's copy of Henry King's poem 'The Farwell' (Bodleian Library MS Rawl. D. 692, f. 111v)

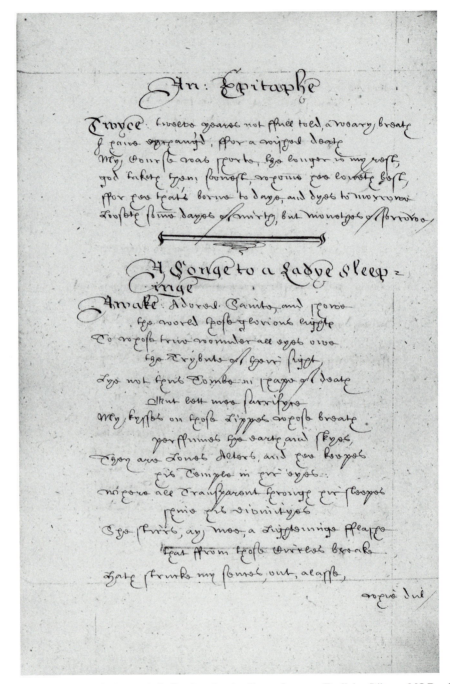

PLATES 59–60: Two facing pages in Feathery's miscellany of poems (Bodleian Library MS Rawl. poet. 31, ff. 21v–22r)

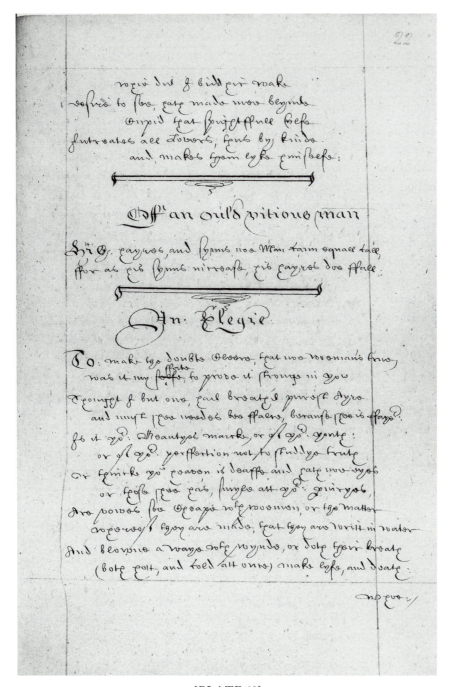

[PLATE 60]

currently popular lyric which happened to be at hand simply as a filler, or even, per-haps, copying it for his own reference or amusement? Certainly it bears no relation to the pamphlet itself, which contains state letters and speeches from 1586 to 1630 and is written in a slightly variant style of Feathery's hand, on less than regularly even lines, suggesting that it was a retained earlier piece of work to which the poem was added at a subsequent date in his 'normal' script.

Perhaps this is a reminder of Francis Davison's quest for poems in manuscript men-tioned earlier, and supports the evidence that there was a flourishing circulation of verse in the Inns of Court and related circles in this period. Feathery's most ambitious contribution to this vogue that we know of is what must surely have been a commis-sioned anthology of some seventy-six Elizabethan and Stuart poems, now among the Rawlinson manuscripts in the Bodleian: a 100-page miscellany of poems by the likes of John Donne, Ben Jonson, and many other well-known poets.[59] We see two characteris-tic facing pages in Plates 59 and 60—including the opening of an elegy by Donne[60]— and, incidentally, if I am right in my conjectures about Feathery's location, this might well have been copied within yards of St Dunstan in the West, where Donne was vicar, and occasionally preached, after 1624. Still in what is almost certainly its original vel-lum binding, this volume is up to Feathery's highest professional standards: his stylish Secretary script in confident form, the text expertly centred and spaced, uncluttered, on faultlessly even lines, with wide margins. This is Feathery in full showcase mode.

There are other examples of verse in Feathery's hand, including, interestingly enough, what must have been one of his very latest products—his copy of the so-called 'A' version of Sir John Denham's *Cooper's hill*, of 1640, among the Harley manu-scripts.[61]

Nevertheless, verse was one of Feathery's relatively subsidiary lines. As we survey the vast array of political, parliamentary, historical, legal, religious, and antiquarian dis-courses, as well as other state letters and records, which comprise the huge bulk of Feathery's output in these two decades, there can be no mistaking where the epicentre of his activities lies. Many of his texts are precisely the kind of state papers which the Government seized from his associate Ralph Starkey in 1619, specifically to take them out of circulation and bring them under official control. It is scarcely coincidental that a sense of the secrecy (and hence desirability) of such material was stressed by later publishers of collections of state papers, with titles and sub-titles such as *Cabala* (a Hebrew word denoting secret knowledge or modes of interpretation) and *Mysteries of*

---

[59] Appendix II, No. 94.

[60] The second page shown here includes one of Donne's epigrams, 'Off an ould vitious man', and the opening of his elegy 'The Expostulation': see *The poems of John Donne*, ed. H. J. C. Grierson, 2 vols. (Oxford, 1912), i. 77, 108–10 (and cf. *Index*, i/1. DnJ 1888 and 1232). The anonymous 'Epitaphe' on the first page shown is on the death of Mr Lewis 'of the Temple' (Crum T3434) and tends to support the likely association of this miscellany with the Inns of Court.

[61] Appendix II, No. 56.1.

state (meaning both the business of state and its 'mysteries' in the modern sense), the repositories of these 'mysteries' (the books themselves) being *Scrinia sacra* (literally, sacred chests) or 'cabinets'.[62]

Nor is it coincidental that Feathery flourished especially between 1629 and 1640—that eleven-year period in which Charles I dismissed Parliament and ruled alone. Not that the earlier 1620s were much less controversial: the period which could see James I tearing 'manu sua propria' from the Journal of the House of Commons itself the pages containing a Protestation which he found offensive and thus declared 'to be invalid, annulled, void, and of no effect'—a symbolic act already denoting the monarch's reluctance to engage in public debate and his closing of those channels of communication.[63] We hardly need reminding that in such a context virtually everything is politicized.

So was Feathery contributing to the literature of political dissent and subversion? Is *that* why his scriptorium was kept in business, feeding a clandestine, underground market for material which it would have been dangerous for any printer to attempt to publish?

Certainly we shall find among his products a fair sprinkling of tracts questioning, even blatantly attacking, royal policy. Neither can it be seen as purely accidental that so many of the authors whose tracts are represented in Feathery's work fell foul of the monarch or Privy Council for political reasons at one time or another in their careers, suffering spells of imprisonment or the indignity of having their papers seized—Ralegh, Cotton, Cornwallis, Coke, Selden, and others, as well as radical parliamentarians such as Pym and Marten. But I think it would be a distortion to see overtly oppositional material as dominating Feathery's output. What we see in the huge corpus of his work is rather an ubiquitous spirit of inquiry—of considering, defining, questioning, and testing basic tenets of the established structures of authority in society, and their underlying principles. Most of all, perhaps, we see a looking back to the past and establishing of *precedents* for how things had been, and therefore perhaps might or should be, done.

This preoccupation extends to almost everything Feathery copies. We see it in the Elizabethan and Stuart histories of the great legal institutions of the realm—in far-ranging works by Lambarde, William Bird, Selden, and others; as well as in a variety of treatises on the proceedings of the Chancery and other courts, including the Star Chamber: that most unpopular and least open of the King's Courts, against which there was no appeal; not to mention the texts of heated contemporary debates on the individual rights and liberties of the King's subjects. To this, of course, can be added a

---

[62] See, for instance, *Cabala: sive Scrinia sacra. Mysteries of state & government* (London, 1654) [Wing C184]; (new edn. London, 1663) [Wing C185]; *Scrinia sacra; Secrets of empire* (London, 1654) [Wing S2110]; *Scrinia Caeciliana: Mysteries of state & government* (London, 1663) [Wing S2109]; and, among various 'cabinets' devoted to political discussions, *The cabinet-council: Containing the cheif arts of empire* [wrongly attributed to Ralegh] (London, 1658) [Wing R156]; new edn. *The arts of empire and mysteries of state* (London, 1692) [Wing R155].

[63] Rushworth, i. 54 (30 December 1621); Annabel Patterson, *Censorship and interpretation* (Madison, 1984), 76–7.

host of considerations of the nature, structures, and authority of various offices of Government, such as the Exchequer, and of Parliament itself, as well as forthright discussions of the King's prerogative, of the management of his revenues, and of his historical right to impose taxation—a not surprising reflection of current debates over forced loans and Ship Money.

The copying of historical records—including some very substantial and detailed parliamentary journals of Queen Elizabeth's time—made for a body of precedents and examples of how, in fact, people in the past had dealt with *their* monarch—of how they had attempted (successfully or otherwise) to advise, petition, or persuade *them*.

The constant re-examination of former proceedings, especially controversial ones, extends to negotiations and alliances with foreign powers—including England's dealings with France, Spain, the Low Countries, and the Palatinate, and proposed marriage alliances with Roman Catholics. It incorporates accounts of inglorious military and naval adventures—such as those against France and Spain in the 1620s—in which England's commanders were found singularly wanting. It extends, even more significantly, to the rights and wrongs of former rebellions, acts of treason, and monarchs' justification in ordering executions.

To all of this we can add a host of discourses which, at first sight, might seem to be purely *antiquarian*—such as those by members of the Society of Antiquaries (Camden, Cotton, Tate, Dodderidge, and others),[64] which busy themselves with such matters as the history of various heraldic offices, the justification for lawful combats, the privileges of towns and boroughs, or the privileges and rights of precedency of the nobility as a class. In fact, there are few aspects of national life which do *not* seem to be touched on in these discourses—whether it be medieval laws regulating brothels, or formalities of which nobleman had the right to walk before another in a procession. And lest we might think that antiquarian and heraldic matters were regarded as purely academic—that antiquaries were no more than the rather grubby, absurd, and eccentric figures whom John Earles caricatures in his *Microcosmographie*[65]—we might recall that the Earl of Essex employed a researcher to establish his rights as Earl Marshal of England as one of the steps in his play for power in Elizabeth's time; that the Duke of Buckingham ordered the production of a 'booke of all thinges belonging to the office of Earle Marshall when it was thought that his Lo*p*: should haue had that place';[66] and that in 1622 Sir Robert Cotton's researches into the offices of Earl Marshal and Constable of Eng-

---

[64] For a list of members of the Society, with brief biographies, see Hearne, ii. 421–49.

[65] Earles, 'An Antiquarie', in *Microcosmographie*, 26–30 ('Printed Bookes he contemnes, as a nouelty of this latter age, but a Manu = script he pores on euerlastingly, especially if the couer be all Moth = eaten, and the dust make a Parenthesis betwixt euerie Syllable'). This attitude is shared by other satirists, but sometimes with an uneasy sense that antiquaries are potentially subversive disturbers: e.g. John Cleveland, in *The character of a London-diurnall* (London, 1647), who comments, *inter alia*, that 'Selden intends to combate Antiquity'; and the author of 'The Character of an Antiquarian' in Samuel Austin's *Naps upon Parnassus* (London, 1658, sigs. F2*v*–4*r*), who sees them as vexing, unlettered vermin.

[66] Sir Thomas Wilson, in an account of his services, 30 July 1623 (PRO SP 45/20, ff. 99r–100r).

land helped to augment the power of his patron, Thomas Howard, second Earl of Arundel (1585–1646), who was thereby enabled virtually to deputize for the King.[67] If there was power in the research of such offices, even more significant is the fact that the Society of Antiquaries, a body of scholars and enthusiasts independent of the Crown, lapsed after 1607 in no small part for political reasons, 'lest . . . they should be prosecuted as a Cabal against the Government'.[68] It was all very well antiquaries writing learned treatises, but there was a whiff of danger about them—they could poke and pry too much into the foundations of things and raise too many questions.

This, it seems, was precisely what Feathery's clients wanted. They wanted not only the texts of current parliamentary and legal debates, but also historical materials covering the previous hundred years or more—materials which could provide the basis for a consideration of those same issues in a detailed historical context, which would help to illuminate the relevant principles and arguments, and which might, indeed, provide parallels or analogies to what was currently going on. They might even provide arguments to be cited in parliamentary debates themselves.[69]

So, yes, Feathery was operating on the fringes of what was acceptable to the political 'Establishment'. But if we ask whether he was positively fuelling the fire of radicalism, I would be inclined to say, 'not consciously so'—if only because he copies such a variety of materials, representing differing points of view. He is no single party hack, but is catering to what is probably a substantial group of educated, professional, sometimes aristocratic men, involved in public life, who are certainly scrutinizing the system of things, but who have not yet, perhaps, made up their minds—and might, indeed, even come to different conclusions. It is in this sense, and in this context, that Feathery's work loses or retains its innocence, depending on one's point of view.

Indeed the extraordinary range and nature of these surviving products of Feathery and his scriptorium enable us to perceive, clearly and at first hand, not only the sheer vitality of a particular manuscript culture, but also that remarkable ferment of ideas which preoccupied the educated classes of the 1620s and 1630s—his centre of production being probably, and significantly, the vicinity of the Inns of Court, the training ground not only of so many common lawyers but also of many of the most eminent politicians and political activists of the day, whose mode of debate was more than a

---

[67] Sharpe, 137–8; Appendix II below, No. 88.

[68] 'Life of the author' [by Pierre Des Maizeaux] in Richard Carew, *The survey of Cornwall*, revised edn. (London, 1723), p. xiv; cited in Sharpe, 28–9. Sir Henry Spelman attributed failure to revive the Society in 1614 to the fact that 'His Majesty took a little mislike' of it, 'not being enform'd, that we had resolv'd to decline all matters of State': *Reliquiae Spelmannianae: The posthumous works of Sir Henry Spelman Kt.*, [ed. Edmund Gibson] (Oxford, 1698), 69–70. For other accounts of the Society of Antiquaries, see especially Linda Van Norden, 'Sir Henry Spelman on the chronology of the Elizabethan College of Antiquaries', *HLQ* 13 (1949–50), 131–60; Philip Styles, 'Politics and historical research in the early seventeenth century', in Levi Fox (ed.), *English historical scholarship in the sixteenth and seventeenth centuries* (London, 1956), 49–72; C. E. Wright, 'The Elizabethan Society of Antiquaries and the formation of the Cottonian Library', in Francis Wormald and C. E. Wright (eds.), *The English library before 1700* (London 1958), 176–212; and F. Smith Füssner, *The historical revolution: English historical thought 1580–1640* (New York, 1962; reprinted Westport, Conn., 1962), 92–106.

[69] e.g. Appendix II, No. 2.

little coloured by the principles and legalistic thinking they had learned there. If Feathery's career, apparently, comes to an end by 1641—for I find nothing by him which can positively be dated later than December of 1640,[70] a month after the opening of the Long Parliament—then it is hardly a matter of coincidence. While the significance of the House of Commons's long-awaited abolition of the Star Chamber in July 1641 *vis-à-vis* an end to press 'censorship' may have been more symbolic than real and effective,[71] the King's attempted stifling of intellectual debate was hastening to an end speedily enough. That debate was less and less confined to private manuscript circulation among a limited, albeit influential, coterie, and the period soon witnesses that phenomenal output by the printing presses with which historians and bibliographers are by now justly familiar.[72]

By 1641, though, the scriptoria had largely done their work. In our anonymous Feathery Scribe, with his seemingly anachronistic Secretary script—in him as much as in any publisher of the century—we have one of the small but vital players in this most consequential era of our history: as, in effect, an agent for the vigorous, persistent, organized dissemination of those very materials and ideas which would challenge authority and lead slowly, but inexorably, to that great, national upheaval which we call the English Civil War.

[70] Appendix II, No. 78.3.

[71] Discussed notably in D. F. McKenzie's lecture on censorship in his 1987–8 Lyell Lectures ('Bibliography and history: Seventeenth-century England'), incorporated in part in his 'The London book trade in 1644', in John Horden (ed.), *Bibliographia* (Leeds, 1992), 131–51.

[72] The fact that a fair number of discourses represented in MSS by the Feathery Scribe listed in Appendix II below were printed—often in poor texts, but in obviously much cheaper editions—in the 1640s is scarcely coincidental. It indicates at the very least a widening at this time of the public for these discourses: a demand which the circulation of MSS had effectively created and which printers now felt both politically and economically able to satisfy.

4

'Hoping they shall only come to your merciful eyes': Sidney's *Letter to Queen Elizabeth* and its transmission

During the course of the year 1579 one of the crucial episodes in the life of Queen Eliza-beth I came to a head. This was the proposal that she should marry François, Duc d'Alençon (who was by now also Duc d'Anjou), brother of Henri III of France. He was the Frenchman she affectionately called her 'little frog', and who *may* be the one immortalized in the nursery rhyme 'A frog he would a-wooing go'.[1] The proposal, first mooted in 1572, had been rumbling along for seven years; but negotiations took a sig-nificant new turn in 1579 when Alençon's agent, Jean de Simier, was sent over to plead his cause to the Queen with more than customary ardour and eloquence; when the 46-year-old Virgin Queen gave unexpected indications that she was at last taking him ser-iously, even consulting physicians for advice on whether a woman of her age could still safely bear children; and when her Council realized, with alarm, if not horror, that the next heir to the English throne might well be a Frenchman and a Papist.[2]

As we know, the scheme eventually evaporated. It has often been said that of all her nominal suitors—and despite the likely persistence until 1578 of Leicester's ambition to marry the Queen—Alençon was, in a sense, the only serious candidate for a husband Elizabeth ever had, and that she knew it. With his departure, and the fizzling-out of negotiations, the possibility of her marrying and bearing children was closed for ever.

While the threat was perceived to be real, there was immense public concern and a deep division of opinion. Supporting the alliance was, most notably, the Queen's trusted Secretary of State Lord Burghley, as well as the Earl of Sussex. Strongly against the match was a larger faction headed by the Queen's old favourite Robert Dudley, Earl of Leicester, together with, notably, Sir Francis Walsingham, supported by Henry, Earl

---

[1] Katherine Duncan-Jones, *Sir Philip Sidney: Courtier poet* (New Haven, 1991), 161. The possible connection with Alençon is not recorded in *The Oxford dictionary of nursery rhymes*, ed. Iona and Peter Opie (Oxford, 1951; reprinted 1983), 177–81, where the earliest recorded version of the song is given as that in Thomas Ravenscroft's *Melismata* (1611).

[2] For an account of the Alençon marriage proceedings and of the earnest and complex political circumstances which gave rise to them, see especially Blair Worden, *The sound of virtue: Philip Sidney's Arcadia and Elizabethan politics* (New Haven, 1996), 71–124.

of Pembroke, Sir Christopher Hatton, and a nucleus of leading churchmen. Leicester's case was not advanced, however, when Alençon's agent found out in July that Leicester had been secretly married for more than six months to Lettice Knollys—a revelation which Simier correctly calculated would send the Queen into a rage. Meanwhile, the rituals of courtship between her and her 'little frog' proceeded apace.

Thus was the stage set for the particular contribution to the debate made by Leicester's nephew, the 24-year-old Philip Sidney. Motivated in part, no doubt, by his own family interests, he penned a 4,300-word discourse addressed to the Queen, setting out a thoughtful, organized series of arguments against the marriage—enumerating the dangers which Alençon would present both to the State and to the Queen's own person, and encouraging her, instead, to stand alone and rely for her strength on the unswerving loyalty of her subjects.

We can be quite sure that Sidney took this task seriously. This was no *Arcadia*, which he could pretend to pass off as 'but a trifle, and that triflingly handled'.[3] He was effectively appointed spokesman for the faction of his temporarily disgraced uncle—Sidney's correspondent Hubert Languet refers to Sidney's being 'ordered to write . . . by those whom you were bound to obey'.[4] And he was writing in a climate of opinion so dynamically charged that one printed tract opposing the marriage, written by the courageous but intemperate Puritan John Stubbs,[5] so infuriated the Queen—even though she thought that he and his associates were only 'the secretaries of men more wicked than they'[6]—that, in November of 1579, it cost Stubbs and his publisher William Page, MP, their right hands on a public scaffold at Westminster.[7] Sidney, who shows awareness in his very opening sentence that he was perpetrating an act of 'boldness' which might be thought 'amiss', was effectively involved in the single most politically sensitive and most potentially dangerous literary undertaking of his life.[8]

My present concern is not so much with Sidney's arguments as with his text and its

---

[3] 'To My Dear Lady and Sister the Countess of Pembroke', in *The Countess of Pembroke's Arcadia (The Old Arcadia)*, ed. Jean Robertson (Oxford, 1973), 3 (lines 14–15). The Alençon marriage crisis and Sidney's views thereon are, incidentally, reflected in *Arcadia*, as is explained in Worden.

[4] Hubert Languet to Sidney, 22 October 1580; cited in Duncan-Jones & Van Dorsten, 33.

[5] John Stubbs, *The discouerie of a gaping gulf whereinto England is like to be swallowed by an other French mariage* (London, 1579) [STC 23400]; ed. Lloyd E. Berry, *John Stubbs's Gaping gulf with letters and other relevant documents* (Charlottesville, Va., 1968). Written by 4 August 1579, Stubbs's pamphlet was published, with a print-run of 1,000 copies, by 27 September, when it was banned by the Government (Proclamation: STC 8114). Copies were urgently sought after and seized upon—a circumstance which explains why some texts of the pamphlet survive in MS transcripts (see Woudhuysen, 147).

[6] Worden, 112.

[7] For further comment on this 'remarkable publishing event', see, *inter alia*, Patrick Collinson, 'The Elizabethan exclusion crisis and the Elizabethan polity', *PBA* 84 (Oxford, 1994), 51–92 (pp. 76–7), as well as Berry and Worden (especially pp. 110–11). It has usually been supposed (e.g. by Duncan-Jones & Van Dorsten, 33–4) that Sidney's *Letter* followed on the heels of Stubbs's tract, and was probably composed in November–December 1579. Worden (pp. 112–13) argues plausibly, however, for a date of composition in the late summer of that year *before* Stubbs's work appeared.

[8] Sidney hints that the excuse for his boldness is that he is simply setting out in more detail 'words' which have 'already delivered to your gracious ears what is the general sum of my travelling thoughts therein': implying that he has already expressed his general views to the Queen by word of mouth. While taking encouragement from this fact, however, he does not imply that the Queen encouraged him to write further at large, otherwise he might be expected to remind her of it directly.

history. Given the proliferation of manuscript copies, which offer a profusion of variant readings, it is hardly surprising that the *Letter* has presented its modern editors with a considerable headache—the most heroic effort to tackle the problem being made in 1973 by Katherine Duncan-Jones and the late Jan Van Dorsten.[9] If I am here inviting a reconsideration of the transmission of this text, it is not because I can pull out the answers, or any definitive authorial text, like a rabbit from a hat. I propose only to draw attention to certain aspects of its history to see what they might have to tell us. In addition (the special interest I declare here) the story involves the scribe I introduced in my last chapter: my so-called Feathery Scribe.

Sidney penned the discourse as, ostensibly, a private letter to the Queen. 'I will in simple and direct terms', he says, '(as hoping they shall only come to your merciful eyes) set down the overflowing of my mind in this most important matter' (1973, p. 46). Nor is there any reason to think that he did not actually send it to the Queen, *as a personal communication*,[10] even if the alleged privacy of the discourse *was* a fiction.[11] The Leicester–Walsingham faction was hardly going to let it remain private.[12] Neither the letter actually sent, nor any manuscript in Sidney's own hand, survives, so far as we know. Instead we have more than three dozen extant manuscript copies or versions of the work (many, incidentally, not known at the time to the 1973 editors)[13]—in addition to some later printings from 1663 onwards.[14] We cannot really begin to guess how many manuscript texts may actually once have existed.

How do these copies come about? And what do we know about their relationship to one another?

Any editor's assertion about an author's text presupposes an initial hypothesis. That of the 1973 editors, encapsulated in their stemma (Plate 61), is that all the manuscript copies seem to derive 'from Sidney's holograph or a fair copy of it (O) through one of two intermediaries . . . X and Y' or, on occasions, through 'a poor relation of X conflated with Y' (p. 40). In any event, the archetype was, they imply, a single, finalized, authorial text.

To take the first assumption first. Was the archetype—the supposed common

---

[9] *Miscellaneous prose of Sir Philip Sidney*, ed. Katherine Duncan-Jones and Jan Van Dorsten (Oxford, 1973), 33–57, 181–5. Quotations from *A letter to Queen Elizabeth* hereafter derive from this edition (cited henceforth as 1973) unless otherwise stated.

[10] He presumably delivered the *Letter* by means of a trusted courier, not in person—though the latter is not impossible. When the disgraced Leicester delivered some unspecified arguments against the match in November 1579 by means of a chaplain, the Queen reportedly had the chaplain imprisoned (Worden, 112).

[11] Sidney may, in some measure, have been following the same course as Lord Henry Howard, who, in his subsequent answer to Stubbs's tract, made sure to distinguish his treatise from the 'sundry libels and pamphlets thrown abroad and published to the view of the world' (appendix II in Berry, 155).

[12] In October 1580 Hubert Languet thanked Sidney for his account of 'how your letter about the Duke of Anjou has come to the knowledge of so many persons' (Worden, 113). Would that Sidney's letter giving this account had survived!

[13] While recognizing that other manuscript texts 'may well appear', they assume, somewhat rashly, that 'it is unlikely that fresh manuscripts will materially alter the present picture of the text' (p. 38).

[14] The *Letter* was first published in *Scrinia Caeciliana: Mysteries of state & government . . . being a further additional supplement of the Cabala* (London, 1663) [Wing S2109], 201–9, and also in *Cabala: sive Scrinia sacra* (London, 1663) [Wing C185], 363–7. A brief descriptive catalogue of most of the surviving manuscripts was offered in my *Index*, i/2 (1980), 485–8. This can be updated in the fresh account of the MSS given below in Appendix IV (Nos. 1–37), cited henceforth according to the respective 'No.'

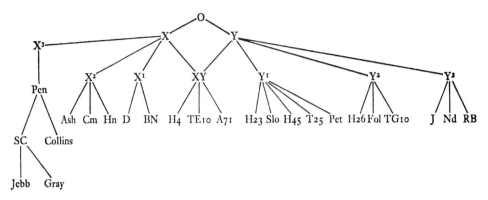

PLATE 61: Stemma of the texts of Sidney's *Letter to Queen Elizabeth* given in the 1973 edition

ancestor—of all the copies a single working holograph or was it a fair copy? And if there *was* a single archetype, why are there so many variant readings—scores and scores of them—among the manuscripts supposedly descended from it?

Just to show an example of the kind of variants we are talking about, Figure 4 sets out a few lines with variants found in a selection of manuscript texts. If, for the sake of argument, and following the 1973 edition (p. 55), we take the readings in bold on the bottom line as base text, the superscribed readings are those found elsewhere. Square brackets enclose those words which some texts omit. While the overall sense of this passage is reasonably

FIGURE 4

```
                                              time present
                                              time
        So [as] that if your subjects [do] at this [present]
                for         other change
                at   every after  change
        but look to  [any]   after chance [it is] but as [the]
                                          the
                       his              this boat
        pilot [doth] [to]  the ship[s] boat [But] if his ship
                                       of        bottom
        should perish [driven by [the] extremity to the one]      but
        so carefully            like
        so living              with
        as long     [as he can] [as]   his life tendering the
                if they do [it]
                if they will
                if they can
        other and this I say      not only [love you] for the
        lovely                             yet
        lively         that    are         only
        good  parts  which be  in you [but even] for their own
                                 needs must     see
        sakes [so will they do it] since they must need[s]  foresee
                                         s
        what [the] tempest[s] sorely threaten[eth] them
```

clear, I think—Sidney is comparing the naturally cautious, self-protective attitude of the Queen's subjects to that of a ship's pilot, who wisely bears in mind the ship's boat even though he would not dream of abandoning his ship for it except as a last resort—nevertheless, there is considerable diversity in the way different scribes thread their way through Sidney's prose here. Whether this is because they are disentangling an unclear exemplar, or pointing themselves what they take to be his meaning, is the issue in question.

Suggesting one explanation for the existence of variants, the 1973 editors observe (p. 40): 'Some readings vary so widely that one suspects a cluster of attempts to make out a baffling orthographical configuration.' If this is the case, are we likely to be dealing with an authorial fair copy, in which 'baffling orthographical configurations' should have been largely resolved? The alternative is a working holograph—one, perhaps, written in Sidney's least attractive, and far from uniformly legible, script.

A sense of what that script *might* have been like can be gauged from the surviving holograph of another of Sidney's polemical works, his *Defence of the Earl of Leicester*, now in the Pierpont Morgan Library (Plate 62). This draft, with its *currente calamo* revisions, is written in Sidney's most characteristically cursive hand: a free, sinuous, somewhat careless and variable Italic. His awareness that his hand was hardly of exemplary clarity is shown clearly enough by his (just) complaint to his brother Robert in 1580: 'I would by the way your worship would learne a better hand, yow write worse than I, and I write evell enough.'[15] It might not be so bad, perhaps, if it did not all look quite so rushed and so cramped, with so much squeezed on to the page. As for the deletions and interlinear insertions, it would hardly be cause for surprise if a copyist misunderstood some of these: for instance, in Plate 62, the position of that long boxed passage five lines down—a passage which is evidently supposed to be transposed to the end of line 14, but which one copyist at any rate misunderstood and simply transcribed as it stands.[16]

For the record, we might point out that not all of Sidney's manuscripts would necessarily have looked quite like this. Besides a number of his letters, we have one other surviving holograph discourse by Sidney: a four-page fragment, among the Cotton Manuscripts, of a brief *Discourse on Irish affairs* sent probably in 1577 to his father, Sir Henry Sidney (Plate 63). As may be seen from the example illustrated, Sidney produces for his father a text written in a somewhat less hurried Italic, the words more clearly and legibly shaped—the lettering more upright and better spaced—even though he still makes occasional changes, deletions, and additions. Even that marginal note on the left may be deliberate: an afterthought, perhaps, but one which does not quite fit into the formal design of his fifth section and which he has chosen to add as a piece of supplementary sidenote commentary.

The point is that there are far more potentially 'baffling orthographical configurations' in the kind of working manuscript seen in Plate 62 than there are in the

---

[15] Philip Sidney to Robert Sidney, 18 October 1580: *The prose works of Sir Philip Sidney*, ed. Albert Feuillerat, 4 vols. (Cambridge, 1912; reprinted 1968), iii. 133.

[16] See further comments on the Colbert MS of this work below; also the relevant collation in Feuillerat, iii. 332–4.

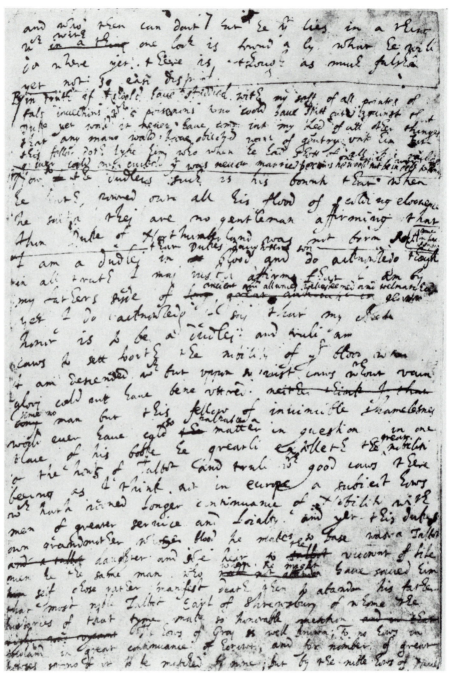

PLATE 62: A page in Sidney's autograph *Defence of the Earl of Leicester* (Pierpont Morgan Library MA 1475, f. 6r)

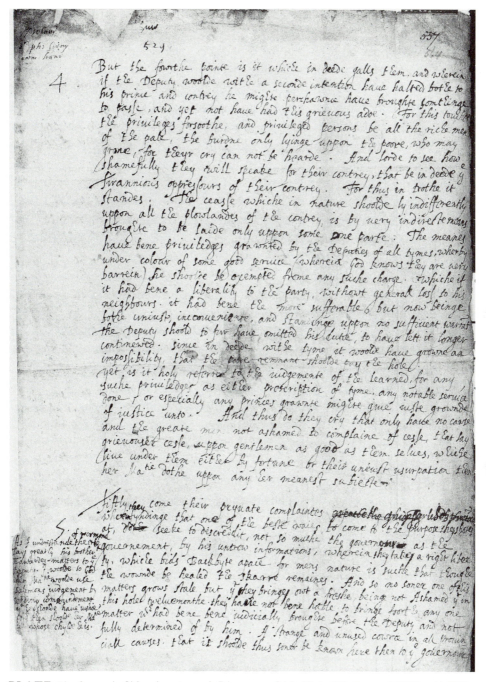

authorial 'fair copy' seen in Plate 63, and hence greater possibilities for subsequent mistranscription.

The process would be even more complicated if scribes got to work copying the author's holograph while composition was still in progress. This presents a second possible element of confusion, although, interestingly enough, it is one the 1973 editors dismiss. 'There is nothing', they insist, 'to suggest that Sidney revised his *Letter*, and given its occasional character,' they say, 'it would be very surprising if he had done so' (p. 40). I should say that, to my mind, it would be very surprising if, within a limited period of time, he, or his immediate circle, had *not* done so.

Or then again, is the accumulation of variants due simply to what the editors call 'a process of constant deterioration . . . in the transmission of the text' (p. 39)? In other words, do changes multiply as a result of scribal carelessness, or of unwarranted sophistication, as successive copies get made from one another over a long period? I suspect that the answer is 'yes', but that this is only part of the explanation.

So which are the earliest texts that survive?

If the pickings are slim, it may, paradoxically, be not because copies were so few but because the *Letter* was indeed well circulated and that the manuscripts suffered the wear and tear of active use. If the earliest texts we can find seem to be preserved in official or semi-official 'state papers', it may be precisely because such 'file copies' were spared the fate of mainstream copies, which were handled, passed about, and then discarded when their current interest was exhausted.

The first I shall mention—one traditionally known to editors—is what may be called the Colbert Manuscript. It is preserved among the Colbert Papers in the Bibliothèque Nationale (Plate 64). It is written in a cursive, predominantly Italic hand, but the hand is certainly English, marked by the occasional Secretary form. The heading—'A discours of Syr Ph. S.'—dates the manuscript *after* January 1583, when Sidney was knighted; but how much later is uncertain. Although little more than this can be adduced in the way of concrete evidence to support any claim to special status, it is worth noting that the Colbert volume in which this text is bound also contains a transcript of Sidney's *Defence* of his uncle, Leicester (Plate 65).[17] In fact, this is the only contemporary transcript of the *Defence* known to exist and, almost certainly, was made directly from Sidney's holograph (now in the Pierpont Morgan Library), a manuscript which is known not to have left the family papers at Penshurst before the eighteenth century.[18] The association between the two Colbert transcripts in question would be even closer were they (as I once believed)

[17] Sidney's *Defence* dates from 1585 (Duncan-Jones & Van Dorsten, 123). The Colbert scribe's superscription, 'Apologie par le feu ren[n]omé Chevaleir Ph. Sidney p[ou]r le Co[m]te de Leycester so[n] oncle'—referring to Sidney as 'the late renowned knight' (though the date at the side is incorrectly given as '1582')—would seem to date the transcript after Sidney's death in 1586; however, the somewhat squeezed-in nature of this French docketing in the upper margin and top corner suggests the possibility that it was added sometime later than the transcript itself.

[18] The only other known transcript of the *Defence* was made at Penshurst by Arthur Collins (1682?–1760). This is now in the Centre for Kentish Studies, Maidstone (U 1475 Z3): *Index*, i/2, SiP 174.

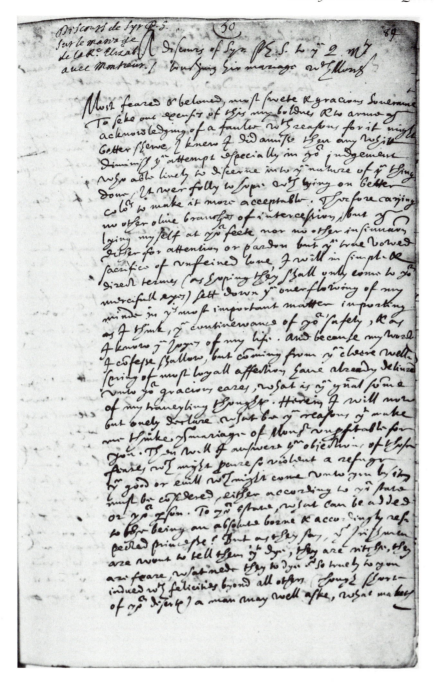

PLATE 64: First page of the Colbert Manuscript of Sidney's *Letter to Queen Elizabeth* (Bibliothèque Nationale Cinq cents de Colbert n° 466, f. 89r)

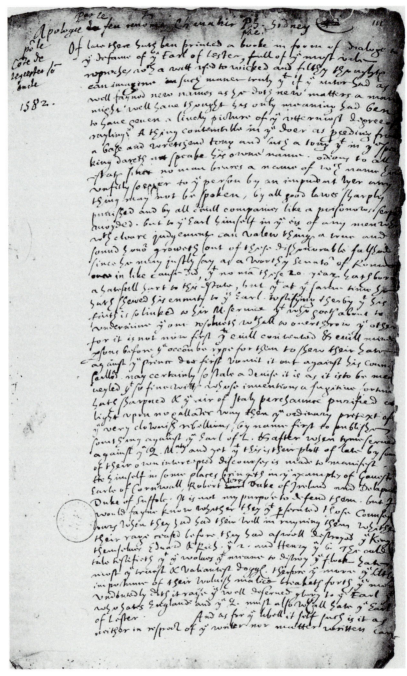

PLATE 65: First page of the Colbert Manuscript of Sidney's *Defence of the Earl of Leicester* (Biblio-thèque Nationale Cinq cents de Colbert n° 466, f. 111r)

in the hand of the same scribe; but, although sharing many of the same generic characteristics, the two scripts cannot positively be identified as being written in one and the same hand.[19] Nevertheless, faced in this volume—a set of contemporary French state papers in an official French source—with two somewhat similar transcripts of two separate works by Sidney, at least one of which was copied (almost certainly) from his holograph, we cannot altogether help wondering whether copyists who had access to one holograph might not have had access to another as well. Would that we knew more about those scribes and their French connections or employers.

The circumstantial case for taking the Colbert Manuscript of the *Letter* seriously is supported by the apparent quality of its text. Editors have considered it a self-evidently 'good' text—in the sense that it lacks a proliferation of obvious absurdities and garbling. Nevertheless, to turn once again to the *Defence* by way of comparison, it is a salutary exercise to see just how many errors and changes are liable to occur even when the exemplar is the author's holograph. In the Colbert *Defence* the scribe is capable of dating the Dudley family's pedigree as 'four thousand' years old instead of 'four hundred', for instance, and there is an accumulation of other minor errors and inconsistencies besides: 'defame' instead of 'defaming', 'thereby' instead of 'herebi', and so on. Besides this, the transcript of the *Defence*—in which the scribe usually ignores Sidney's spelling and (admittedly sparse) punctuation—reminds us that we can virtually abandon hope of recovering the author's accidentals in any text of which his original manuscript no longer exists. This is because scribes simply did not reproduce them, but—like printers—felt free to follow their own habits and conventions: this was their recognized prerogative. Thus it is that, but for the chance survival of the holograph, we would not know from the Colbert *Defence* (short of conjecturing from other examples of Sidney's writing) that in this treatise the author used peculiar combinations of vowels: for instance, *i* instead of *y* in *may* ('mai') or *nay* ('nai'), as well as in *Italy* ('Itali'), and the vowels in such words as *like* ('lyke'), *sound* ('sownd'), *resolves* and *imagine* without the terminal *e*, and so on, as well as such spellings as 'trewe' for *true*, 'spokne' for *spoken*, 'cace' for *cause* or *case*, 'cownceilours' for *counsellors*, and many others.[20] And if not in a transcript of the *Defence*, why should a transcript of the *Letter* be any different?

Before we say more about the *X* tradition which the Colbert Manuscript represents, let me mention another early manuscript—one not widely known (Plate 66). It is in one of the Yelverton Manuscripts in the British Library, among the state papers collected by Robert Beale (1541–1601), Clerk of the Queen's Council. Beale—who, incidentally, was known to Sidney[21]—had a close professional and personal association with Sidney's

---

[19] I am here correcting the misassumption which informed the references to these two MSS in my *Index*, i/2, SiP 173 and 184.

[20] For a list of some of Sidney's 'typical spellings' in general, see *The poems of Sir Philip Sidney*, ed. William A. Ringler, Jr (Oxford, 1962), p. lxiv.

[21] See the respectful references to Beale ('Belus') in Sidney's letters to Languet (Feuillerat, iii. 117, 119, 121). Like Sidney, Beale was apparently a witness to the St Bartholomew's Day massacre in Paris on 24 August 1572.

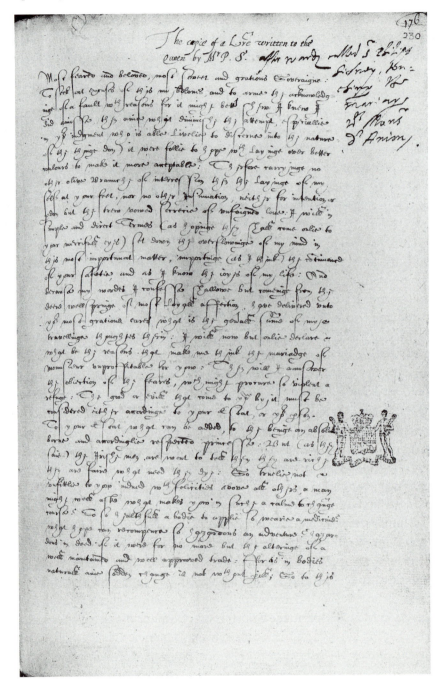

PLATE 66: First page of the Beale Manuscript of Sidney's *Letter* (BL Add. MS 48027, f. 230r)

father-in-law Walsingham,[22] had little sympathy for a Catholic succession, and may be expected to have been sympathetic towards the Leicester–Walsingham faction in this matter. He would have wanted to get hold of a copy of Sidney's *Letter* on Alençon as soon as possible, if only because of his special interest in the subject of state marriages.[23]

Since Beale's copy of the *Letter* is headed by the scribe 'The copie of a Lre written to the Queen by Mr P. S.', its exemplar at least can be dated before 13 January 1582/3, when Sidney was knighted. The transcript itself may well date from the 1580s in any event.[24] Sometime before his death in 1601 Beale himself added the note at the top right of the first page of the *Letter*: 'after wards called Sr Philipp Sidney, touching the mariage wth Monsr d' Aniou'.

However, if we look to this evidently early Beale Manuscript to supply us with a reliable witness to Sidney's original text, we may be a little disappointed. According to Beale's scribe, for instance, Sidney offers the Queen not 'the true vowed sacrifice of unfeigned love' but the 'true vowed secrecie of unfeigned love'. The hearts of the Queen's subjects will be 'glad' not 'galled' when she marries a Frenchman and a Papist. The Papists are 'indeed not rightly to be called a faction' instead of 'most rightly indeed to be called a faction'. There is a universal doubt about the French race's (or perhaps French ruling family's) 'unfaithfulness' rather than 'unhealthfulness' (a change which neatly eradicates Sidney's hint that the whole lot of them were syphilitic). In evil princes 'abuse' here 'revives' rather than 'ruins' itself. Uncertain good here brings 'content' to certain good rather than 'contempt', and 'the bliss of children' here becomes 'the blaze of children' (a strikingly luminous image). Alençon's ultimate defence would not be 'like Ajax' shield, which weighed down rather than defended those that bore it'; it would be 'like a wax shield'. And (my favourite reading) Rome was not a popular state 'where indeed men were to rise or fall'; it was a state 'wherein dead men were to rise or fall'.

In short (and these readings are by no means atypical) Beale's scribe manages repeatedly to change meanings virtually to the opposite of what the logic of the argument dictates. His work is careless and undiscerning.

On the other hand, it has to be said that it is not hard to guess how most of the errors occur, and to perceive what lies behind them. So, for instance, 'ruins' might easily be

---

[22] Beale was Walsingham's secretary in the 1570s, married the sister of Walsingham's second wife, and lived mainly at Barn Elms near Walsingham's house.

[23] For accounts of Beale and of his literary, diplomatic, antiquarian, and scholarly interests and activities, see his entry in the *DNB*; also B. Schofield, 'The Yelverton Manuscripts', *BMQ* 19 (1954), 3–9; P. W. Hasler (ed.), *The House of Commons, 1558–1603* (in The History of Parliament series), i (London, 1981), 411–14; and *The British Library catalogue of additions to the manuscripts: The Yelverton Manuscripts*, 2 vols. (London, 1994), i, pp. ix–xviii, *et passim*; also the informative letter by Beale offered in Sotheby's sale catalogue of 17 December 1996, lot 44 (of which Beale's retained copy is BL Add. MS 48039, ff. 74r–75v).

[24] Although not always easy to distinguish from the general 'house style' of Beale's secretariat, this scribe's hand seems to appear frequently among Beale's papers: e.g. in his correspondence dating up to October 1584 in BL Add. MS 48039 (Yelverton MS 44), ff. 42r–61v. He is also apparently responsible for the copy in Add. MS 48027 (ff. 197r–215r) of Lord Henry Howard's discourse in support of the Alençon marriage. Mrs Patricia Basing of the BL informs me that she regards this scribe as 'Beale's clerk' and believes that examples of his script can be found among the Yelverton MSS throughout the 1580s and 1590s and even as late as 1621: see *The Yelverton MSS* (1994), i, pp. xx–xxi.

read as 'revives' if the original spelling were 'rewines'; and so on. So this rather mechanical scribe's incompetence does not altogether invalidate his witness to what must be one of the very early texts which circulated at Court, or at least among the Privy Council.

Textually too the Beale Manuscript supports, for the most part, the *X* tradition to which the Colbert Manuscript belongs. In fact, if these two manuscripts of Sidney's *Letter* were the only ones to survive, editors might feel justified in assuming that they had here sufficient basis to establish a reasonably accurate text.

So how does a 'rival' *Y* tradition arise?

For what may be an early glimpse of it let me mention another manuscript not used by the 1973 editors, one I shall call the Harington Manuscript (Plate 67). This is among the papers of the Harington family, in the British Library: among those belonging to the Queen's godson Sir John Harington of Kelston (1560-1612), the poet and translator, and a collector who had access to other early manuscripts of works by Sidney.[25] More specifically, however, it is copied in a manuscript volume which had belonged to his father, John Harington of Stepney (1520?–82). John Harington the Elder was a cultivated gentleman and politician and, incidentally, a good friend of William Cecil, Lord Burghley.[26]

If we ask whether the text here conforms to the *X* tradition of *Colbert*, we can establish a connection—with *Colbert* specifically, since both *Harington* and *Colbert* lack one particular sentence which, at some point in the chain of transmission, was omitted obviously through eyeskip (it reads 'As I take it, you imagine two natural causes thereof, and two effects you think you find thereof', and it occurs in a passage containing a plethora of *thereof*s). While it is not impossible that two scribes might have made this simple mistake independently, the fact that it seems not to occur elsewhere and that both scribes pick up at the same *thereof* (out of a choice of them) would seem to indicate fairly clearly that *Colbert* and *Harington* are linked in some way.

Nevertheless, *Harington* is not simply an *X* party-member. He has somehow been wooed, or at least influenced, by a rival party or parties. This may be illustrated by one or two examples.

At one point (1973, p. 51) Sidney summarizes the Queen's two alleged political motives for the marriage with Alençon: 'the fear of standing alone in respect of foreign dealings, and in home respects doubts to be condemned.' 'Doubts to be condemned'? What does that mean? This is the reading in the Colbert Manuscript (and *X* tradition).[27] *Harington* (agreeing with the mainstream *Y* tradition) supplies us with the reading: 'doubt of contempt'. Sidney is referring—as he says later—to 'contempt in

---

[25] Extant manuscripts of *Arcadia*, Sidney's *Psalms*, and parts of *Certain sonnets* and *Astrophil and Stella* are in Harington's hand or in compilations made by him (*Index*, i/2, SIP 5, 15, 23, 24, 53, 54, 74, 94), and yet other Sidney sources can be found quoted in his works: see the discussion of Harington in Woudhuysen, *passim*.

[26] Ruth Hughey, *John Harington of Stepney, Tudor gentleman: His life and works* (Columbus, Oh., 1971), 53, 67, *et passim*.

[27] *Beale*, however, omits sixteen words at this point, including this phrase.

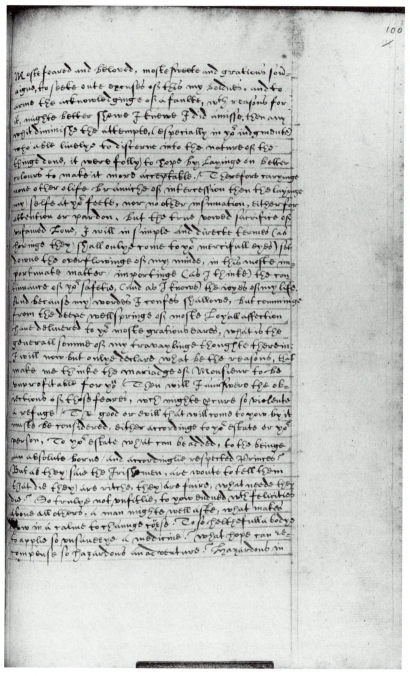

PLATE 67: First page of the Harington Manuscript of Sidney's *Letter* (BL Add. MS 46366, f. 100r)

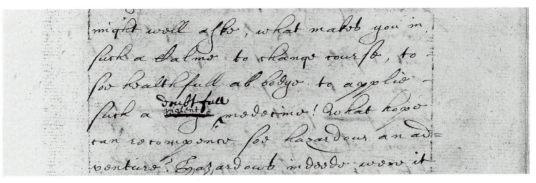

PLATE 68: A page in a manuscript copy of Sidney's *Letter* by a scribe associated with Feathery and with a reader's annotations (Folger Shakespeare Library MS X.d.210, f. 3r)

your subjects': to the possibility of the Queen's alienation from her subjects' affection. 'Doubt of contempt' in this period could mean not just uncertainty but, as Spenser used it,[28] 'danger', 'apprehension', 'fear', or even 'dread', of being held in contempt. Indeed this is precisely how Sidney uses the term elsewhere in the *Letter*, when, for instance, he speaks of 'discontented persons' who are 'so much the more to be doubted'. And it is how Elizabeth herself used the word in one of her own poems, which begins 'The doubt of future foes exiles my present joy'—a poem which goes on to lament how 'falsehood now doth flow and subjects' faith doth ebb'.[29]

At another point (1973, p. 47), where Sidney is rhetorically asking what the purpose of this marriage is, he says (according to *Colbert, Beale*, and the *X* tradition): 'To so healthful a body to apply such a weary medicine?'[30] A '*weary*' medicine? If it were 'weary' it might not really matter whether the Queen applied it or not. Sidney's point is surely that it was not only an unnecessary but a dangerous medicine. Indeed, if we look ahead for a moment to the manuscript tradition in general, we can see that copyists sensed that something was wrong here. Certain copyists miss out the adjective altogether, even leaving a space rather than guessing wrongly.[31] There is one later manuscript, now in the Folger Shakespeare Library (Plate 68), where we find a reader editing this line for himself: crossing out 'weary', writing over it boldly in black ink his emendation, 'doubtfull', and then perhaps thinking again, and writing underneath in less confident lettering, 'violent'.[32] It is an interesting example of a seventeenth-century reader's engagement with the text—where, one suspects, he is vaguely moving along

[28] *OED*, citing *The Faerie Queene*, v. xi. 47.

[29] *The poems of Queen Elizabeth I*, ed. Leicester Bradner (Providence, RI, 1964), 4.

[30] *Beale* has a slightly variant reading here: 'To so healthful a body, to apply so weary a medicine?'

[31] e.g. the Cheshire MS (Appendix IV, No. 21) and University of London MS 308 (No. 30). The Juel-Jensen MS (No. 26) has 'so needless a medicine'.

[32] The order of emendation here may be the other way round, of course, though it would be more normal to write an alteration *above* the word and only *below* it when space no longer permitted a superscript. Alternatively, the reader could be recording collations in other sources. Kansas MS 4A:1 (Appendix IV, No. 28) has 'violent' instead of 'weary', and Kansas MS E205 (No. 27) has the reading 'so violent and unsavoury a medicine'.

the right lines—but also an indication of how some spurious readings were liable to get started.

Harington's reading here is 'so unsavoury a medicine'—which at least shows awareness that some degree of emphasis is required. This reading is interesting too because it links *Harington* to the fourth, and only other, early manuscript text of Sidney's *Letter* that we know—one now among the Lansdowne Manuscripts in the British Library. This text has limited value to editors because, as may be seen (Plate 69), it is only a précis of the *Letter*—a six-page series of notes summarizing Sidney's arguments. Nevertheless, if we look at line 19 on the page illustrated we find the clear reading: 'To so healthfull a bodie to apply so unsavoury a medicine.' Thus the précisist was using as his exemplar not a clear-cut *X* tradition manuscript, like *Colbert* or even *Beale*, but one like *Harington*.

The Lansdowne précis is certainly early. It is docketed in a contemporary hand with the note '1579: Notes out of m^r Phillip Sidneys l[ett]re to ye Q[ueen] touching hir mariage wth. Monsieur'—again *Mr*, not *Sir* Philip Sidney; and, incidentally, the watermark in the paper is almost identical to that in the Harington Manuscript—a type of pot watermark current from the mid-sixteenth century onwards.[33] Moreover, we can be reasonably confident that this précis derives from the papers of Harington's friend Lord Burghley—an archive which, despite its haphazard binding many years ago, occupies much of the Lansdowne collection.[34] The chances are that this was a précis produced in the secretariat of Lord Burghley himself—who, we may recall, was the leader of the rival faction in the Privy Council which *supported* the Alençon marriage. Certainly Burghley had every reason to acquire and digest arguments opposing his position.

So, to summarize, I think we can find evidence that, virtually from the start—let alone decades later—there was a divergence of textual traditions in the copies made available to contemporary courtiers and officials. Moreover, there are indications that the alternative mainstream tradition which we see emerging (*Y*)—one seen in *Harington* as, so to speak, an early contaminating influence, but represented in later manuscripts in full force—does not merely *coexist* with *X*: it *challenges* it.

To pursue the 'weary medicine' crux for one more moment: the reading found in several *Y*-tradition texts—including, incidentally, the 1973 editors' copy-text, although they ignore it and adopt the *X*-reading—is the simple word 'very': a word which, if hastily written, *might* perhaps be misread as 'weary' (or even, preceded by 'such a', as 'unsavoury'). Etymologically linked to the Latin *veritas* (= 'verity', 'truth'), the word 'very'—in 'such a very medicine'—would mean such a 'true', 'genuine', or even 'strong' medicine—which would arguably fit the context better than 'weary'.

---

[33] Briquet No. 12802: see Appendix IV, Nos. 18 and 10.

[34] See *A catalogue of the Lansdowne Manuscripts in the British Museum* [ed. Henry Ellis and Francis Douce] (London, 1819), p. ix. The Burghley Papers comprise MSS 1–122 of the collection. MS 94 itself contains numerous other documents written or signed by, or else relating to, Lord Burghley.

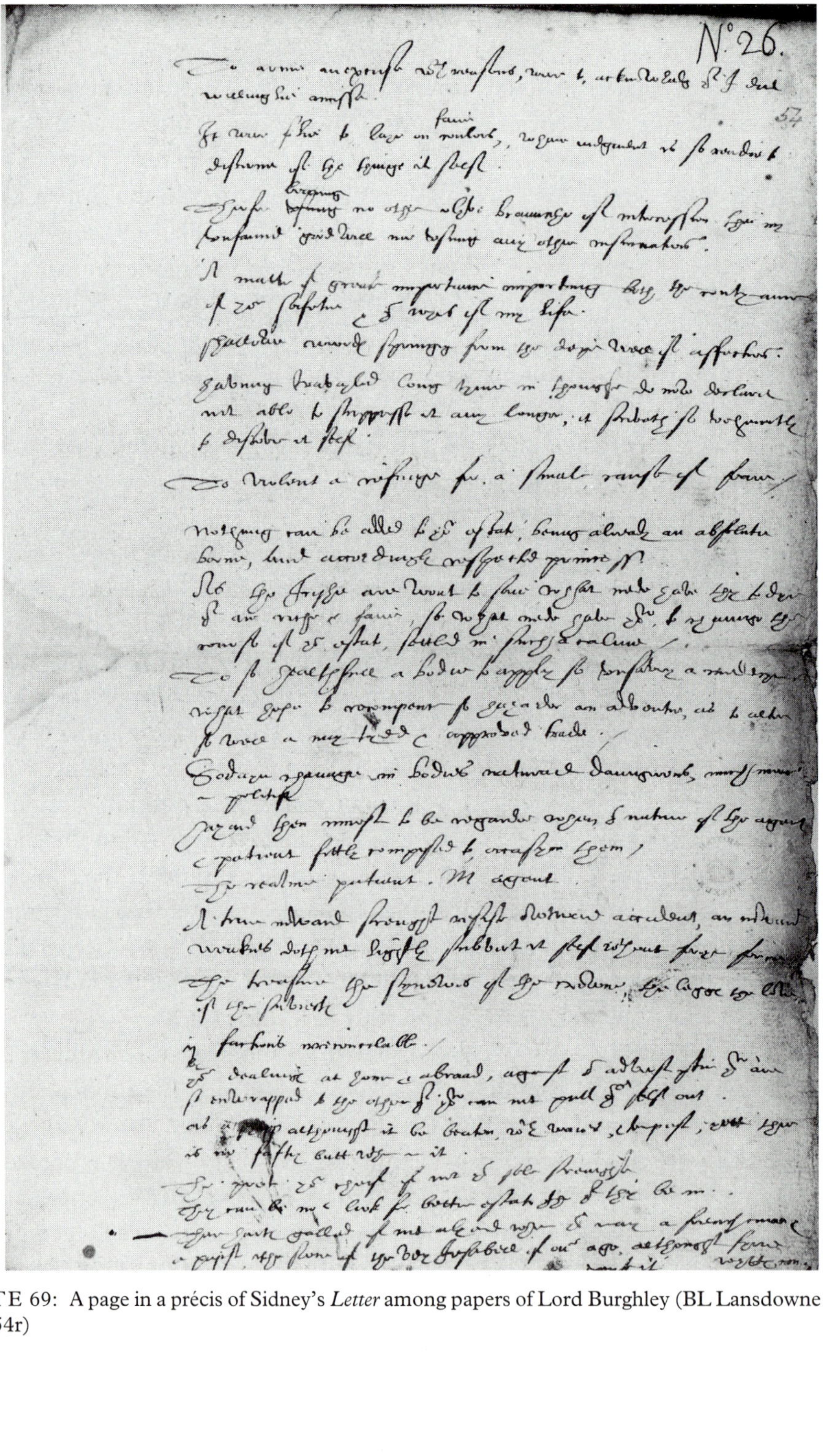

PLATE 69: A page in a précis of Sidney's *Letter* among papers of Lord Burghley (BL Lansdowne MS 94, f. 54r)

Having mentioned the word 'very', I cannot resist joining the debate about the most celebrated crux in this work—in the passage set out in Figure 5, where—at least as rendered by the 1973 editors (p. 53, lines 3–6)—Sidney says of Alençon:

So that if neither fear nor desire be such in him as are to bind any public fastness, it may be said that the only fortress of this your marriage is of his private affection, a thing too incident to your person without laying it up in such ivy knots.

FIGURE 5

```
                            desire nor fear    but
        So that if [neither]  fear nor desire  be such

                                        safety
        on                  build       safeness
        in him as [are] to bind any public fastness [upon]

        it may be said that [the] only fortress of

        this your marriage is of his [owne] private affection

                    coincident[al]
                    evident          the         which
        a thing too  incident        [un]to your person without

                                < >
                                vin
                                Gordian
                                indissoluble
                                unkindly
                                a
                                eight
                                high
                                keighe
                                keye
                                sleight
        tying        on some slight
        laying it up in such  [ivy]        knot[s]
```

There is, as may be seen, some confusion here: for instance, about the word 'fastness', which *Colbert* reads (not very plausibly, I think) as 'safeness', and the phrase 'laying it up' (which, with knots in mind, *Colbert* reads as 'tying it up').[35] But this is as nothing compared to 'ivy knots' at the end. It is a nice image, but what does *ivy* have to do with it? We could almost construct a guide to the scribal ingenuity of the period from this crux alone and from the repeated attempts to resolve it. 'Ivy' is very much a *Y*-tradition reading. *Colbert* and *Beale* supply the synonymous readings 'slight' and 'sleight' respectively, which have the advantage of making sense if we interpret Sidney's point here as stressing how *unreliable* are the knots by which the Queen seeks to bind 'public fastness' in Alençon. *Harington* reads the word as 'keighe'—a reading which should certainly not be dismissed out of hand[36]—while other, later, manuscripts offer us the possibly related

---

[35] As the 1973 editors point out (p. 43), the term 'laying' has a relevant connotation in that it is used in rope-making to mean 'twisting yarn to form a strand'.

[36] Unless it be a complete misreading, the word 'keighe' might be related to 'key' (in the sense of that which locks up) or, alter-

'high', or even 'eight' (which at least presents a nice image, of 8-shaped knots). Yet other scribes abandon this path altogether and supply instead 'such a knot', 'unkindly knots', 'an indissoluble knot' (again, stressing the strength rather than weakness of the knot),[37] or, in one remote tradition (where the scribe is at least prompted to recall what other knots he may have heard of), 'Gordian knots'.

While we need not worry about some of the more outlandish sophistications here, we may, nevertheless, assume that the fairly consistent *Y*-tradition, which insists on the word 'ivy', is based on *something*. And one possibility, first mooted by Henry Woudhuysen,[38] is that 'ivy' is a misreading for, yet again, the word 'very'—a word which, incidentally, Sidney would have spelt 'veri' (and it is interesting to see how two scribes fumble over readings that come out looking like 'vni knots' and 'vinknotts' respectively).[39] 'Very' here again means 'true'—as indeed Sidney himself uses the term in *Arcadia*, where Euarchus refers to 'the prince's person being in all monarchal governments the very knot of the people's welfare'.[40] So perhaps in this passage Sidney is playing paradoxically with the opposition of weakness and strength: implying that it is bad enough that the Queen should be dependent solely upon the personal affection of Alençon without confirming this weakness by such firm—meaning inextricable—knots.

Whatever the solution of this crux, it is well to bear in mind how even the slightest change, by even the subtlest shift of tone or emphasis, can alter the meaning of the text significantly. A signal example is the passage in which Sidney turns to the vexed question of the Queen's successor. As the 1973 editors see it (p. 54, lines 13–16), this passage begins as follows:

As for the uncertainty of succession, although for mine own part I know where I have cast the uttermost anchor of my hope, yet for England's sake I would not say anything against any such determination.

They then devote a paragraph in their generally admirable commentary (p. 184) to speculating on '*where*' Sidney had cast 'the uttermost anchor' of his 'hope': that is, which candidate he was implicitly nominating or supporting as Elizabeth's successor—finally deciding it was the young King James of Scotland.

However, the word 'where' in this sentence is imported by the editors from the *X* tradition. In their copy-text—and generally in the *Y* tradition at large—the word appears not as 'where' but as 'well'. Thus Sidney says: 'I know well I have cast the uttermost anchor of my hope.' In other words, it is not the *location* which is at issue here, but

natively, to the obsolete word 'keigne' (meaning chain or chained, an image which reinforces the sense of the binding power of the knot, as well as the knot-like 8-shape of two links in a chain).

[37] In a reader's emendation comparable to those noted earlier in a Folger MS, 'an Indissoluble' is added in a different hand to the space left at this point by the original scribe in the Huntington MS (Appendix IV, No. 24). Similarly, the Inner Temple MS (No. 25) has the reading 'tyeing' above 'laying', indicating possible conflation.

[38] H. R. Woudhuysen, 'A crux in the text of Sidney's *A letter to Queen Elizabeth*', *N&Q* 229 (June 1984), 172–3.

[39] Cambridge MS Kk. 1.3 (Appendix IV, No. 20) and Kansas MS 4A:1 (No. 28).

[40] *Arcadia*, ed. Robertson (1973), book V, p. 383 (lines 12–14); cited in Woudhuysen, 'A crux in the text'.

the strength of the commitment. He is complimenting the Queen herself: *that* is where his 'uttermost . . . hope' lies. He is echoing a sentiment already used earlier where he refers to the Queen's Council as being 'renowned over all Christendom . . . having set the uttermost of their ambition in your favour'. Indeed, if Sidney *were* telling the Queen that he knew whom *he* was tipping for her successor, it would have been the most astonishing act of tactlessness, given her well-known sensitivity to this matter. And in fact, if we follow his argument carefully, he is doing exactly the opposite. He is supporting precisely her own policy, which was not to have *any* declared successor—going so far as to argue, as yet another reason for her not marrying, that even having children was potentially dangerous ('many princes have lost their crowns', he says, 'whose own children were manifest successors; and some . . . had their own children used as instruments of their ruin'). His clear implication is that it is far safer to leave the succession undetermined.

The 1973 editors conclude from their overall collations that there is nothing to choose between the relative merits of the two apparent divergent traditions, *X* and *Y*: neither is better or worse than the other, they say (p. 43). They decide—as they admit, almost arbitrarily—to choose a representative of the *Y* tradition for their basic copy-text, but do not hesitate to import emendations from the *X* tradition as they see fit.

As the examples given may suggest, I think their view may be questioned. Time and time again, a qualitative difference between the traditions does seem to emerge. We might give two or three characteristic examples. At one point (1973, p. 51) *Colbert* has Alençon separating himself with 'further discontentment of heart than ever before'. *Y*, supported by both *Beale* and *Harington*, has him separating himself with 'further disuniting of heart than ever before'. *Y*'s choice of noun here is to accentuate the sense of conflict, of the strong contradictory impulses and interests to which Alençon is liable to be a prey: he is not simply going to be passively 'discontented'. At another point (1973, p. 54) *Colbert* speaks of 'very common reason', which 'would teach us to hold that jewel dear'. *Y*, again supported by both *Beale* and *Harington*, speaks here instead of 'very common profit'. *Y* thereby reinforces the dominant image here: shifting the emphasis from general common sense, as it were, to positive commercial advantage, or 'profit', in safeguarding a 'jewel'. Then (1973, p. 52), addressing the question of whether Alençon is in any way motivated by 'fear', *Colbert* has Sidney declaring: 'fear hath a little show of reasonable cause to match you together.' The *Y* tradition, virtually without exception, says: 'fear hath as little show of reasonable appearance to match you together.'[41] I say 'appearance', but if we look more closely, we see that in both *Beale* and *Harington* the word is actually 'apparance'. In fact, the *OED* informs us that the now obsolete term 'apparance' (or 'apparaunce', as the word may in any case have been pronounced) had a specific meaning in this period: it meant 'a making ready', a

---

[41] Signs of scribal unease with this reading occur in Bodleian Library MS Eng. hist. f. 8 (Appendix IV, No. 6), which reads 'of outward appearance as reason', and in Yelverton MS 49 (No. 12), which reads 'or reasonable apparance'.

'preparation' (the *OED* cites nicely a quotation by Langley in 1546: 'The night is a time of counselling & apparaunce'). This sense is arguably appropriate here. Instead of the apparent tautology of a 'show' of 'appearance' (in the modern sense), the *Y* text means that fear is no justification for this match, in the sense that fear is unable to demonstrate, as it were, a just readiness for it.

In short, in each of these instances we see *Colbert* using a perfectly logical and acceptable word, but one which is relatively 'obvious' compared to the alternative represented in the *Y* tradition. And in determining whether or not there is anything to choose between the two traditions I am inclined to think that we might go just one step further.

In one passage (1973, p. 47), for instance, Sidney speaks of the Queen as 'endued with felicities above all others'. This is then qualified in *Colbert* by the phrase 'though short of your deserts': a plausible enough compliment, but this phrase is omitted in *Beale*, in *Harington*, and in the whole *Y* tradition. So we must believe either that the Colbert scribe (or his prototype) invented it; or that it was in Sidney's original but was overlooked, or deliberately omitted, by other scribes; *or* that it was in the author's manuscript when (perhaps) the Colbert scribe copied it, but not there (having been deleted) when other scribes copied it. In other words, it represents a revision or emendation: whether an addition or a deletion as the case may be. The difference of emphasis between the two is that *X* is laying the compliment on rather thick; *Y* is being slightly more restrained.

Similarly, Sidney comments on the English Catholics (1973, p. 48) that—to quote both *Colbert* and *Beale*—they were 'all grieved at the burdenous weight of their consciences'. The *Y* tradition, supported by *Harington*, reads here simply: 'all burdened with the weight of their consciences.' In other words, there is slightly less emphasis: not laying it on quite so thick again. Having the Catholics 'grieving' at the 'burdenous weight' of their 'consciences' *might* be considered just a trifle too sympathetic towards them.[42]

And finally: exemplifying Alençon's unreliability (1973, p. 49), Sidney says—according to both *Colbert* and *Beale*—these 'are evident testimonies of a light mind carried with every wind of hope'. By contrast the *Y* tradition, supported again by *Harington*, says simply: they 'are evident testimonies he is carried away with every wind of hope'. Once again, the effect in *Y* is a toning down: the avoidance in this case of a positive insult, that Alençon had 'a light mind'.

So something *is* going on here, as readings typical of one tradition are substituted for those of another. They are *not* quite Tweedledum and Tweedledee, or arbitrary beyond distinction. There is a just perceptible shift of emphasis: some political fine tuning. If we ask whether it is that relatively 'mild' phrasing is being strengthened, or

---

[42] In the Juel-Jensen MS (Appendix IV, No. 26), in the *Y3* tradition, it is interesting to note further signs of unease at this point, since the following line ('of great riches, because the affairs of state have not lain upon them') is heavily deleted.

'strong' phrases are being tactfully toned down—well, the answer to this question would determine precisely what use both Sidney and his contemporaries were making of his text.

In brief, whatever allowances we make for the elements of both scribal corruption and sophistication which must inevitably enter into so prolonged a history of manuscript transmission, there are, I think, sufficient indications of an element of early instability in the text of Sidney's *Letter* to bring into question whether there ever was a single, fixed, unrevised archetype behind all the texts which now survive.

If we indulge, for a moment, in speculation, Katherine Duncan-Jones has suggested that Sidney may have been galvanized into writing this discourse under the pressure of a considerable sense of urgency: perhaps writing it, she says, 'in white heat', even, maybe, within 'a single day'.[43] Whether written in a single day or not (and the considerable degree of what Duncan-Jones herself calls the 'diplomatic as well as rhetorical finesse' with which Sidney marshals his arguments[44] would induce me to question this), we have already suggested what Sidney's original draft may have looked like—though unlike his *Defence of Leicester*, which never progressed beyond a draft, the *Letter* was worked through to completion. Moreover, its political importance demanded thorough consideration and not a little circumspection. So is it likely that Sidney would keep the *Letter* to himself, rather than consult other interested parties who had a considerable stake in the matter, before it was actually sent to the Queen?[45] In this case, did other scribes have access to his manuscript—to make copies for his uncle—before Sidney had finished working over it? Or did he decide to recopy his text after receiving reactions from confidential readers? And so we could go on, speculating about what *might* have happened to complicate the processes of both composition and transmission.

Then at last—when Sidney *and* his consultants were satisfied with the formulation of his arguments—the text had to be copied fair for the actual letter sent to the Queen herself. Of this version one thing can, I think, safely be assumed. As a letter by an aristocratic gentleman purporting to be a strictly private communication, intended *solely* for *her* 'merciful eyes' and no other's—added to the well-established considerations of social decorum at this time (the hand and the heart being one, as it were)—the letter *had* to be written in Sidney's own hand, and clearly and legibly so at that, *not* by a secretary. That process too would have provided the occasion for further, final thoughts about presentation—which he might or might not have taken the trouble to incorporate in a retained manuscript.

---

[43] Duncan-Jones, *Sidney*, 164.   [44] Ibid. 162.

[45] The impetus for the *Letter* may even have arisen when Leicester returned to London in mid-August 1579 and presided over some sort of conference at Baynard's Castle, the London home of Sidney's brother-in-law the Earl of Pembroke, which probably both Sidney and his father Sir Henry Sidney attended (Duncan-Jones, *Sidney*, 162; Worden, 112). It is also interesting to note that the poet Edmund Spenser, whom Sidney befriended, was very likely a member of Leicester's household at this time at Leicester House in the Strand.

In other words, however we look at it, there are reasons to suppose that there were several stages in the evolution of the text—a text which, one suspects, rarely stood still, let alone constituted the epitome of stability—and there seems to be a distinct possibility that more than one manuscript copy was made at one or another of these progressive stages. (This would be a state of affairs, we might add, not altogether dissimilar to what later happened to *Arcadia*.)[46] And that is all before we come to the stage when, as the 1973 editors note (pp. 38–9), 'contemporary copies were made of the work for use as propaganda by the Leicester–Walsingham party'.

We might pause to wonder whether we are even right to assume that the text of the *Letter* put into 'propaganda' circulation and the text as actually sent to the Queen herself were necessarily identical. In the most literal sense, their readership was different—which meant that the different texts might play different roles. A private letter to a sovereign might not be the same thing necessarily as a polemic circulated to ministers of state—any more than a modern cabinet member's private letter to a prime minister is necessarily identical to the press statement he may choose to issue at the same time. Readership, perhaps, dictated all.[47]

This brings us, at last, to my Feathery Scribe (Plate 70). Where does *he* come into all this?

Bringing Feathery into the equation is not without irony. In their discussion of the available texts, the 1973 editors draw attention to a particular group of three manuscripts which they describe as 'uniform in format and title, and perhaps in handwriting' (p. 41). These three manuscripts—variously in the British Library and Trinity College Dublin—are seen on their stemma (Plate 61 above), in their *Y1* configuration, denoted by the sigla *H23*, *Slo*, and *T25*. These, they say, 'may well be some of the original scribal copies made for circulation at Court' (p. 41). Partly for this reason, they choose one of them, *H23* (Harley MS 1323), as copy-text for their edition. In fact, all three of these texts are entirely in the hand of our Feathery Scribe. Far from being contemporary copies circulated at Court around 1580, they date from half a century later—probably from well into the 1630s.

The extent of Feathery's contribution may be shown even more graphically by my amended version of the editors' stemma (Figure 6)—which incorporates additional manuscripts not known to them at the time (see Appendix IV for details). In fact, we can now identify no fewer than nine manuscripts as being either wholly or partly in Feathery's hand—signalled in this stemma in bold. In addition, in the mixed *XY* trad-

---

[46] See the extensive discussions of the textual history of *Arcadia* by its editors, notably Ringler (1962) and Jean Robertson (1973); also in Woudhuysen (1996).

[47] Or, in Don McKenzie's now celebrated dictum: 'New readers make new texts and their new meanings are a function of their new forms': D. F. McKenzie, *Bibliography and the sociology of texts: The Panizzi Lectures 1985* (London, 1986), 20; cited to notable effect in Roger Chartier, *The order of books* (Stanford, Calif., 1994), 5–6 *et passim*.

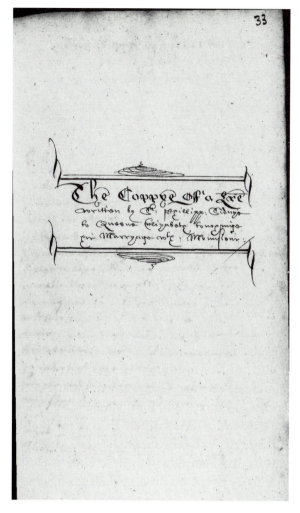

PLATE 70: Title-page of a manuscript copy of Sidney's *Letter* by the Feathery Scribe (Trinity College Dublin MS 732, f. 33r)

ition seen on the left, we have two related manuscripts, signalled by Italic. One, *H4* (Harley MS 444), is not by Feathery himself, but is in the hand of a scribe found associated with him and evidently in the same scriptorium.[48] The other, *Cot*—a Cotton manuscript which did not remain unscathed by the fire of 1731 (Plate 71)—is in the familiar hand of the antiquary Ralph Starkey, who, as noted in my last chapter, was one of Feathery's principal associates (and among whose papers a copy of Sidney's *Letter* was found after Starkey's death in 1628).[49] So these two manuscripts too are part of the equation.[50]

[48] Harley 444 contains numerous pages in Feathery's hand, and the same scribe also appears, for instance, in BL Stowe MS 151: Appendix II below, Nos. 53 and 72.

[49] Appendix III below, No. 39.

[50] In fact, yet another MS (Kansas MS E205: Appendix IV, No. 27) is in a professional hand occasionally found associated with Feathery. This hand is found also in various MSS in Sir Robert Cotton's collection, as well as in association with Ralph

FIGURE 6

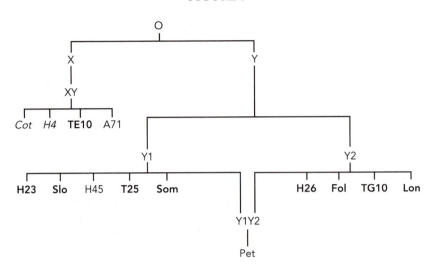

Sidney's *Letter* turns out to be the work which Feathery copied most often, at least according to our present knowledge,[51] while these eleven Feathery-related copies in turn account for nearly a third of all the known manuscript texts of the *Letter*.

Moreover, if there was a surge of recopying and recirculating of Sidney's *Letter* in the late 1620s and 1630s, it is not difficult to guess why—given public concern over the question of a royal marriage with a Continental Roman Catholic—a concern which had persisted ever since 1623, with the disastrous proposal for the Spanish match of Prince Charles. It was even more fuelled by Charles's marriage in 1625 to the French Catholic Henrietta Maria, daughter of Henri IV and Marie de Médicis (1573–1642). Distantly, but unpropitiously, related to the notorious Catherine de Médicis (1519–89), Sidney's 'Jezebel of our age' (1973, p. 48) who was responsible for the St Bartholomew's Day massacre in 1572, Henrietta Maria's perceived influence at Court—seen, moreover, in conjunction with the High Church leanings of the King and Bishop Laud (Archbishop by 1633)—did nothing to diminish the general escalation of anti-Catholic feeling in the 1630s. Sidney's fifty-year-old discourse served, in effect, as a classic warning about the dangers of such an alliance—or at least as a historical precedent for such considerations. Prominence was given to Sidney's name on all the title-pages or headings in this period (see Plate 70, for instance)—and even in a later printing of 1663, the publisher took pains to remind readers of how the great Prot-

Starkey, who, for instance, annotates this scribe's copy in BL Harley MS 293, ff. 19r–26v, and whose work is interspersed with his in Cotton MS Titus F. IV. He is also copyist of many of the same tracts and letters copied by Feathery (e.g. a 346-leaf folio in Inner Temple Library, Petyt MS 538, vol. 36, and items in Bodleian Library MS Willis 58, which is at least in part associated with Humphrey Dyson. For an illustration of this scribe's hand, see *EMS* 6 (1997), 143. His text of Sidney's *Letter* is, however, a somewhat sophisticated one distinct from the traditions associated with Feathery.

[51] The nearest comparison is the so-called 'Speech without doors' of 1627, of which seven copies by Feathery are known: Appendix II, Nos. 1.11, 40.1, 61, 78.2, 83.3, 106.5, 112.

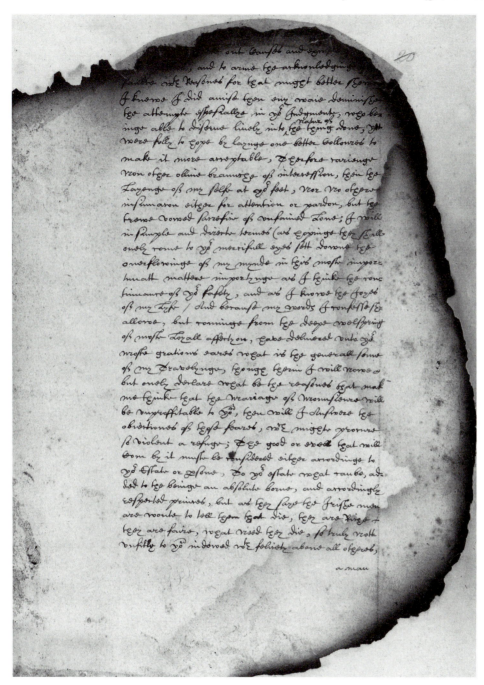

PLATE 71: First page of a manuscript copy of Sidney's *Letter* by Ralph Starkey (BL Cotton MS Caligula E. XII, f. 25r)

estant Sidney was 'that choice Darling of the *Muses* . . . in whom *England*, *Netherland*, the Heavens, and the Arts, the Souldiers and the World, did emulate a share'.[52] This is a clear reminder that his name still had tremendous cachet: his authorship validated the discourse.

So what does Feathery, who seems to have played so significant a part in this revival, *do* with the text?

We are obliged to say, for a start, that he does not produce faultless copy. He too on occasions can write 'Henry VIII' instead of 'Henry V', or 'Philip, that Good Duke of Burgundy' instead of 'Philip the Good, Duke of Burgundy'. Parallel lines which 'can never join' in certain copies 'can never wynne' in others; while with people who 'have in the beginning contrary principles', for them to 'bring forth one doctrine' would generally need 'some miracle', it might alternatively require 'some Oracle'. One striking improvement by Feathery: some of Alençon's followers have not 'defiled their hands in odious murders'; they have 'distilled their hands in odious murders' (trying to improve on the perfumes of Arabia, perhaps?). And Feathery is not alone in getting his French mixed up in Sidney's anecdote about Charles V. The Emperor's reply to someone who told him 'Les Hollandois parlent mal' was 'Mais ils payent bien': meaning 'never mind what they say, so long as they pay'. Feathery sometimes has the Emperor's answer repeating the same verb—'Mais ils parlent bien' instead of 'payent bien'—thereby completely missing the point of the anecdote.

So, no, Feathery is not infallible, any more than his predecessors, contemporaries, or successors are. Moreover, it is clear that he and his scriptorium are *not* working consistently from a single exemplar—a point illustrated, apart from other collation evidence, by the different directions his work follows in our stemma. Not only do certain of his copies mix the *X* and *Y* traditions, but he seems even to have initiated one subsidiary tradition himself: that designated in Figure 6 as the *Y2* tradition. The four manuscripts represented here (*H26*, *Fol*, *TG10*, *Lon*)—as also, conceivably, the linked manuscript shown at the bottom, *Pet*, which has a slightly more complex history—may well have been produced as a series at a particular time. Unlike all Feathery's contributions to the *Y1* tradition, which are written wholly in his hand, these four *Y2* manuscripts are written only partly in his hand. In each case he writes, or adds, the title-page himself, letting another scribe start off the main text, before returning (at a different point in each text) to finish off the work in his own hand. Moreover, in three of the four texts the second scribe involved is one and the same: the hand seen earlier in Plate 68 (*Fol*).

What these *Y2* texts principally have in common is that they all break off three sentences before the end: an example, from *TG10*, is shown in Plate 72. As may be seen,

---

[52] 'The Stationer to the Reader', *Scrinia Ceciliana* (1663), sig. [A4ᵛ], these terms being adapted from a contemporary epitaph on Sidney (Crum E67). The publishers go on to describe the *Letter* as being 'fortified with many pressing and effectual Reasons against that match; and penned with a Politick and Ingenuous Stile'.

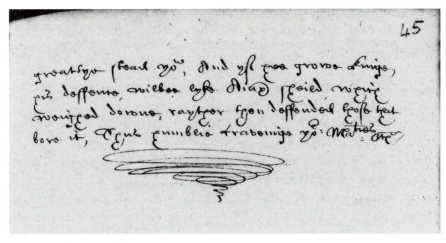

PLATE 72: Last page of a manuscript of Sidney's *Letter* by Feathery (Trinity College Dublin MS 732, f. 45r)

the *Letter* here comes to an abrupt halt, ending on a paragraph which encourages the Queen to rely on her religion and its supporters as surety against her 'mightiest enemies', and then trailing off with a conventional valedictory subscription: 'Thus humbly craving your Majesty's etc.' A fuller form of this valediction is found in *Pet*, where it reads:

And soe humbly craueing yor Maties.
graceous favour & Pardon I
Rest/ Yo^r most obedient
and duetifull subiect
and Servant
& &
&
./
Phillipp Sydney.

Whether derived from an authentic source, or subsequently added to emphasize the polemic's character as a letter, this formulaic coda stands in place of Sidney's highly rhetorical peroration, urging the Queen to adopt policy which would confirm her status as 'the example of princes, the ornament of this age, the comfort of the afflicted, the delight of your people, the most excellent fruit of all your progenitors, and the perfect mirror to your posterity'.

If this resounding finale is dropped, we may wonder whether it is, as the 1973 editors suggest (p. 41), because the manuscripts derive from 'a defective common ancestor', or whether the text has not rather been deliberately curtailed. Could Sidney's conclusion—with its overwhelmingly Royalist ideology, its encouragement of the monarch to trust

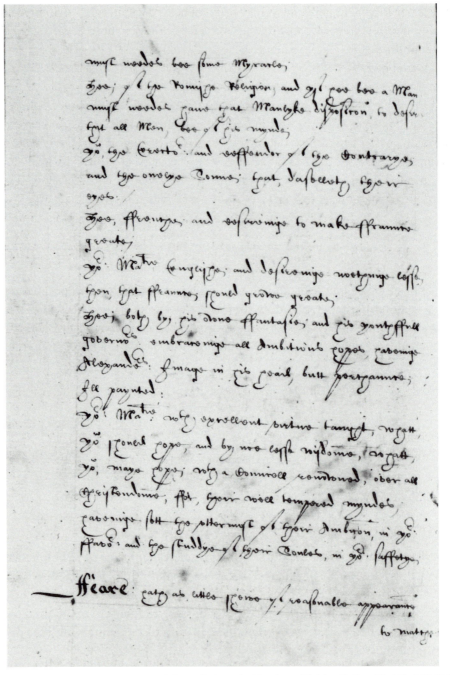

PLATE 73: A page in a manuscript of Sidney's *Letter* by Feathery (Trinity College Dublin MS 588, f. 10v)

implicitly her Privy Council, and to be worthy of her 'progenitors'—be deemed some-what less than relevant or useful by the time of Charles I (whose Stuart progenitors counted for little in England, let alone those of his Medici wife)? It seems that at least in one particular batch of copies, it was felt to be redundant and could safely be discarded.

Thus does Feathery become, in effect, Sidney's editor. And, in practice, he adopts this role in *all* his copies—apart from all else, by the very physical layout he chooses.

If we recall the early manuscripts illustrated in Plates 64, 66, and 67, Sidney's text is written as a single, continuous, very lightly punctuated block of text, completely with-out paragraphs, breaks, or indentation.[53] Feathery does exactly the opposite. Just as he automatically adopts a kind of professional 'house style' when he lays the text out within defined margins, with catchwords, and also with a separate title-page, so also does he think in terms of introducing spaces to relieve a dense mass of continuous prose, and of engrossing certain words to break up the monotony of uniform-sized let-tering. At this point we see him responding to the rhetorical structure of the work. By this I mean the sort of thing we see in Plate 73 (*T25*).

Here Sidney is comparing and contrasting, point by point, the differences in policy between Alençon and the Queen. The scribe is even given a hint as to how he might set out the arguments—as a series of antithetical parallels, as it were—by Sidney himself:

Monsieur's desires and yours, how they should meet in public matters I think no oracle can tell: for as the geometricians say that parallels, because they maintain diverse lines, can never join, so truly, who have in the beginning contrary principles, to bring forth one doctrine, must be some miracle. (p. 52, lines 9–13)

He goes on to enumerate examples in a kind of list. The Feathery Scribe seizes on this feature and isolates each point, as a kind of semi-paragraph, by ranging each one to the left on a separate line. Thus:

He of the Romish religion [etc.]

Next line:

you the erector and defender of the contrary [etc.]

New line:

he French, and desiring to make France great:

New line again:

your Majesty English, and desiring nothing less than that France should grow great;

And so on: accentuating the contrast between 'his' (Alençon's) interests on the one hand and 'your' (the Queen's) interests on the other by the layout on the page.

[53] The most we get to this effect is the occasional half-hearted virgule in the Harington MS.

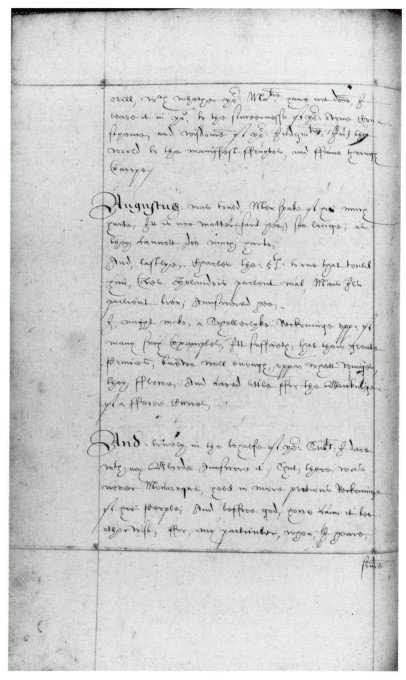

PLATES 74–5: Two facing pages in a manuscript of Sidney's *Letter* by Feathery (BL Harley MS 1323, ff. 54v–55r)

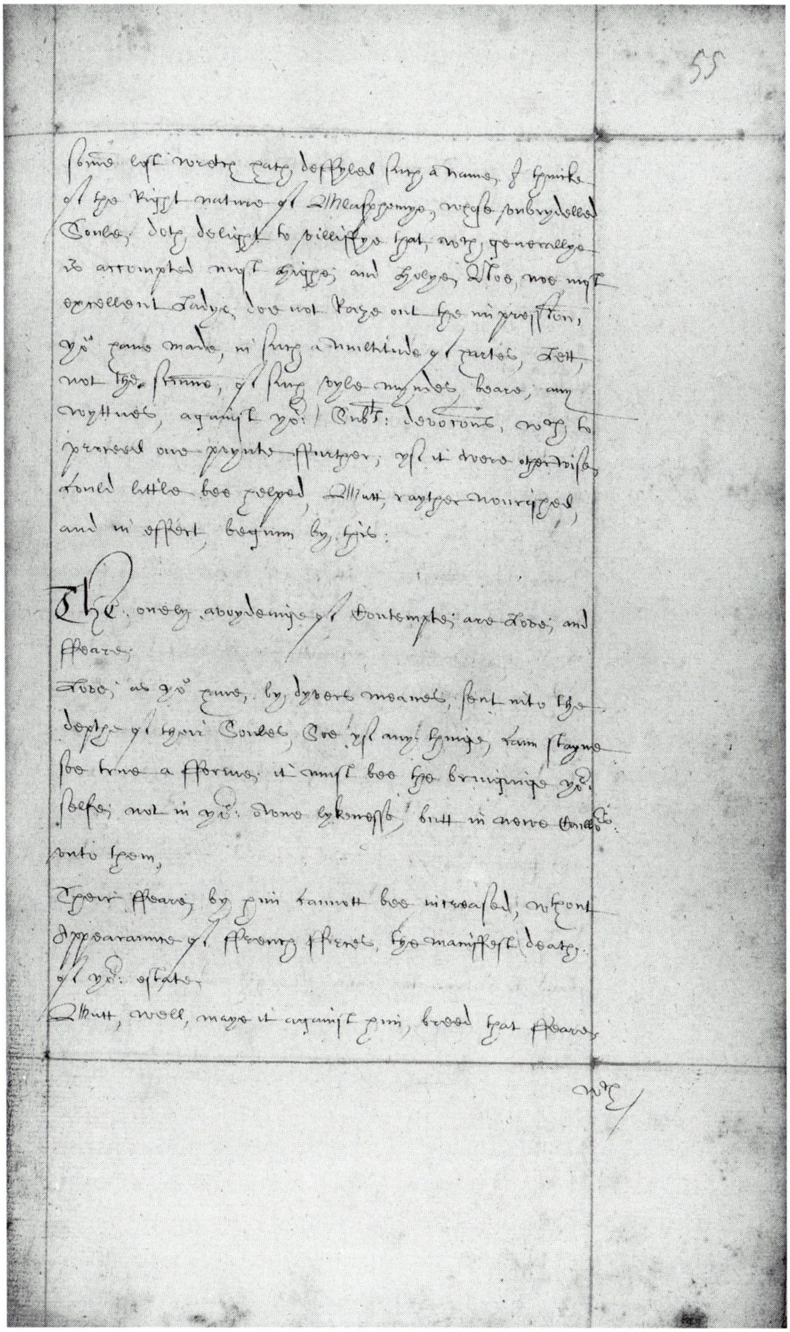

55

[PLATE 75]

This aptitude of Feathery to pick up on rhetorical patterns extends even to slightly less obvious structures. So, to take another example, if we consulted the 1973 editors' copy-text (*H23*: Harley MS 1323, ff. 45v–46r) for a series of arguments about the condition and likely reactions of the Queen's faithful Protestant subjects, a series they set out, with a single paragraph break, on their pp. 47–8, we might observe how Feathery picks up on the word 'Theis', which he engrosses in bold at the beginning of a fresh paragraph. Each repetition of the word then signals a new sub-paragraph, as it were, as he relegates each to a fresh line. So:

These, therefore, as their souls live by your happy government, so are they your chief, if not your sole, strength.

New line:

These, howsoever the necessity of human life make them look, yet can they not look for better conditions than presently they enjoy.

Next line:

These, how their hearts will be galled . . .

And so on, the construction continuing with the word 'That', signalling a break: 'That his brother made oblation of his own sister's marriage [etc.]'; 'That he himself, contrary to his promise [etc.]'. Then he starts a new paragraph for the word 'This'—'This, I say . . .'—before he introduces a space to denote a section break, picking up immediately in his new paragraph on the word 'The', which he engrosses—'**The** other faction [etc.]'. Thus the scribe's layout—his spacing and selective emphasis on particular repeated words—visually reinforces the inherent rhetorical rhythms, the accumulative drive of Sidney's argumentation, and the polemical structure of his prose at this point.

Other examples could be cited of Feathery's visual manipulation of verbal patterns. All of these the 1973 editors were, of course, justified in ignoring for their edition—except that, ironically, they themselves were partly guided by Feathery in introducing paragraph divisions to produce their modernized reading-text. In Plates 74 and 75, for instance, we see an opening of their copy-text. Like Feathery, they start a new paragraph in the middle of the second page: 'The only avoiding of contempt' [etc.]. But they ignore all Feathery's previous breaks—which is fine so long as we realize that this too subtly affects the meaning and effect of Sidney's arguments. In constructing a lengthy paragraph, which begins on the page previous to those illustrated here (on pp. 55–6 of their edition), they discern, quite rightly, a certain logical unity in Sidney's treatment of malicious remarks made by ill-disposed subjects against their sovereigns, all concluding with his exhortation that she should avoid doing anything which would give 'such vile minds' any kind of excuse for their slanders. However, by dividing this unit in the way *he* does, partly to pause and emphasize the effect of specific examples (of Augustus, etc.) cited along the way, Feathery not only allows certain other 'conclusions' within this unit to stand on their own, but points the antithesis between one set of conclusions and the other: one being that 'these great princes knew well enough upon what wings they flew, and cared little for the barking of a few curs'; the other being that Elizabeth, on the contrary, is held in 'precious reckoning of her people' and her strength lies precisely in what people think of her—thus she is vulnerable to slander in a way that Augustus and Charles V were not. By the arrangement of his spacing, divisions, and a little selective calligraphic highlighting, the point is set up and reinforced by Feathery in a way which is not quite so clear when all this is run on together as one long unbroken paragraph.

So to summarize: what we see Feathery doing in all these copies is preparing and presenting Sidney's text for a contemporary readership—setting it out as clearly as he can and in such a way as to facilitate a seventeenth-century reader's grasp of the rhetorical structure of the discourse. This process reaches its apogee, perhaps, in a manuscript now in the Somerset Record Office (*Som*), illustrated in Plates 76 and 77. Here we find not only a series of paragraph breaks, with more than generous spacing, but also the addition of side-headings, signposting the subject of each 'paragraph' for ready reference: 'The saying of Caesar', 'Otho's mind', and so on. It is as if he is going out of his way to make the text as lucid, as digestible, and even as useful, as possible. This may well be the latest and most genuinely sophisticated text of the *Letter* produced by Feathery. Its almost exemplary layout is also, as I see it, a further indication that his copies of this famous letter of advice to a monarch *were* meant to be read: they were produced to meet a positive demand and were not just routine shelf copies.

Whether these various considerations take us much closer to Sidney's original text I shall not speculate. I never promised editorial solutions.

As I see it, there is evidence for supposing that Sidney's text was unstable and even 'open'—that it was subject to some degree of reworking right from the start—and was not a single, fixed archetype. I would also leave open the possibility that the *Y* tradition represents, for the most part, a slightly but consciously revised version—though whether made preparatory to the version sent to the Queen or for a version put into wider circulation afterwards is not clear. There is evidence of a process of cross-fertilization of divergent traditions at a very early stage—maybe even within the very first wave of manuscript circulation. And once launched into a relatively 'public' domain, the *Letter* took its natural course—as an autonomous, but in a sense living, and therefore inevitably changing, organism; as a piece of communal property independent of its author—whose prestigious name: that of one of the most celebrated Protestant champions of a recent golden age—could nevertheless be invoked to perform a useful propagandist function; and as a text subject to the influences of changing readership.

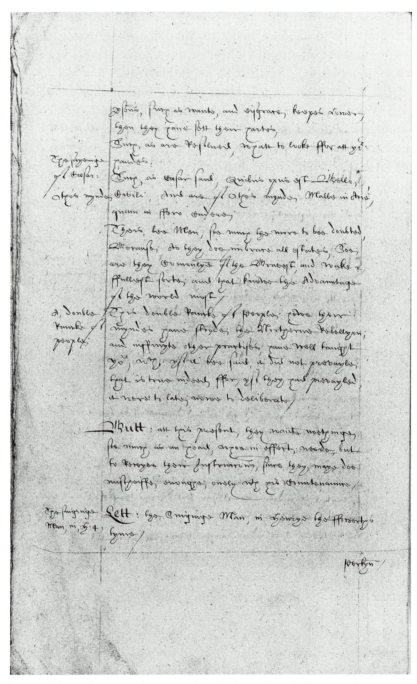

PLATES 76–7: Two facing pages in a manuscript of Sidney's *Letter* by Feathery (Somerset Record Office DD/AH/51/1/3, ff. 51v–52r)

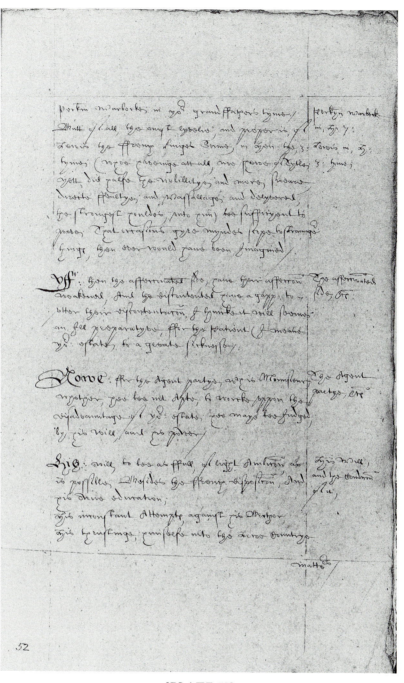

[PLATE 77]

Certainly, with a text such as this, there are no thoroughbreds—only hybrids and mongrels.

We see too how the initial process of copying and circulation—which extended sporadically to the 1590s and early 1600s—repeated itself vigorously in the mid-1620s and 1630s, when the text was subject to a quite fresh recycling, with priority now given chiefly to the *Y* tradition, but with, once again, a measure of cross-fertilization, the professional scriptorium of our Feathery Scribe playing the key role: effectively exercising the function of editors and, in response to the interests and demands of its own clientele, establishing the mode of presentation which would dominate a whole generation.

Finally, in a sense, we see the same—or at least an equivalent—process happening again in our own century, as, in a fully conscientious pursuit of what they themselves recognize to be an elusive will-o'-the-wisp, the author's original text, editors decide to modernize and standardize spelling and punctuation, introduce new paragraphing and layout, and construct a new, subtly conflated, composite text, to meet the needs, uses, and expectations of modern readers. And in this they are guided, though unwittingly, by the practices of seventeenth-, not sixteenth-century, *scribes*.

As for the one text which, did it still exist, might offer us a fulcrum of stability—the letter actually written by Sidney and sent to the Queen herself—the text which might have been expected to provide the clear, legible master-copy behind all the scribal copies, but which the diversity of extant readings suggests may not have been the case—I cannot help wondering whether that letter ever did serve as an exemplar at all. Perhaps, in the most literal sense, Sidney's *Letter*—the actual physical document which he penned in his own hand and delivered to the Queen—perhaps that *was* produced for her eyes only.

5

'The virtuous Mrs Philips' and 'that whore Castlemaine': Orinda and her apotheosis, 1664–1668

IN Delarivière Manley's comedy *The lost lover*, of 1696, there is a character named Orinda, who is described as 'an Affected Poetess'. Orinda appears in the play as a conceited, snobbish, socially obsequious 'poetess', who pretends to suffer from a glut of 'Addresses' made to her. In a characteristic speech, she says:

Lard, *Marina*, I finish't a Copy of Verses last night, which I have sent to half a score of my Friends for their approbation, I bestow'd the last upon admirable Sir *Amorous Courtal*, but I'le send you one of them.[1]

Does this stage caricature bear any relation to the real Orinda, who had died eight years before Mrs Manley was born?[2]

I mean Katherine Philips, the 'Matchless Orinda', who, in the 1650s and 1660s, occupied the centre of a genteel literary coterie of both women and men, her so-called 'Society of Friendship', and who engaged in the writing, copying, and disseminating of manuscripts of her own works, in England, Wales, and Ireland, during the greater part of her short life. A 'scribe' in the narrow sense she may not have been, but a 'maker of manuscripts' she certainly was. Indeed, even if Katherine Philips had no other claim to attention, she would have a special place in literary history as the foremost woman writer of the seventeenth century to flourish in the context of a manuscript culture.[3]

Whereas Katherine Philips is supposed to have written only for a highly select coterie, however, the stage Orinda is seen busily turning out multiple manuscript copies of her poems to send to 'Friends' (and a sense of indiscriminate circulation is implied by the reference to 'half a score' and more); furthermore she does all this primarily to secure 'approbation'. So what of this?

---

[1] Mrs [Delarivière] Manley, *The lost lover; or, The jealous husband* (London, 1696), 23.

[2] For an entertaining account of the life of Delarivière Manley (1671?–1724), see Fidelis Morgan, *A woman of no character: An autobiography of Mrs Manley* (London, 1986). Manley's adventurous life included, as it happens, a six-month period in 1694 living as protégé, and in lodgings, of Lady Castlemaine (pp. 49–59).

[3] For an account of the extant MSS of her work, see my *Index*, ii/2.125–81. Further MS texts are still coming to light.

We might consider a hitherto unpublished letter by Katherine Philips (signed 'Orinda'), which is found in a manuscript miscellany of Royalist verse copied in the mid-1650s, now at University College London (see Appendix V below). Addressed 'To the noble Parthenia The Lady Fletcher', the letter begins:

Madam, | Ther were no excuse for such a presumption as this from a person so vnworthy & so vnknowne, were it possible for me to be a stranger, where ever my dearest Rosamia hath an Interest or for any one to want some kind of worth where she will recomend.

In other words, Philips is unknown to Lady Fletcher and is introducing herself by virtue of their common friend 'Rosania' (Mary Aubrey). The wholly unacquainted Lady Fletcher also has bestowed upon her the sobriquet 'Parthenia'.[4] Entreating her as 'your servant, though at so great a distance' and 'your votary', and pleading 'Now since my devotion is as impossible to be concealed as supprest', Philips begs her to 'be pleased to accept an Offering': and this refers to an accompanying ninety-line poem headed 'Orinda, To Parthenia: A Shaddow of Rosamia'. It is a poem, she implies perhaps ruefully, written in the 'barren . . . Rocks & Mountaynes' of Wales.[5]

We do not know what response this unsolicited poem evoked in the mysterious Lady Fletcher. What we *can* say is that in only one other known contemporary manuscript text of the poem—also in a 1650s miscellany of Royalist verse—is there any mention of 'Parthenia'.[6] In neither this nor in any of the five other recorded manuscripts of this poem—including the version in Philips's own autograph book of verse, the Tutin Manuscript at Aberystwyth, where she initially dated this poem 19 September 1651,[7] or in any 'authorized' manuscripts relating thereto[8]—is there any trace of the name 'Lady Fletcher'.

We can detect here, I think, two things. First, we have an instance of relative authorial control over the 'history' of a particular text so long as it remained in manuscript form and within a circumscribed 'society'. For any, shall we say, 'official' version of a poem, which she chose to distribute, she could amend the record and eliminate, for all intents and purposes, unwanted traces of its original context and history.[9] At least,

---

[4] Parthenia is a character is Sidney's *Arcadia*, who was captured and horribly disfigured by Demagoras before being miraculously restored to her constant Argalus. It is also a name associated with a virgin (hence the related terms 'partheniad' and 'parthenogenesis').

[5] University of London MS Ogden 42, p. 221 (the letter); pp. 217–20 (the poem). The MS, formerly Phillipps MS 4001, is a 264-page folio miscellany of poems and songs (some 220 of them), predominantly by Royalist writers, copied apparently in a single hand. One of the latest that can be dated is by Katherine Philips herself: her elegy on the death of her son Hector (who died 2 May 1655), which appears on p. 215. This MS is that recorded in my *Index* (ii/2. 135–6) as having last been seen in 1946, but which I managed to track down in 1994.

[6] A shorter, 46-line version of the poem, headed 'To Parthenia', and with 'Parthenia' substituted for 'Rosania' in the text, is found in a quarto miscellany associated with William Godolphin and Henry Savile in CUL MS Dd. 6. 43, f. 20r–v. For drawing my attention to this text I am indebted to Germaine Greer.

[7] National Library of Wales, NLW MS 775B, pp. 19, 21, 23; printed in *The collected works of Katherine Philips the matchless Orinda*, ed. Patrick Thomas, Germaine Greer, and R. Little, 3 vols. (Stump Cross, 1990–3), i. 117–20.

[8] *Index*, ii/2. 161: PsK 314–18.

[9] That Philips was inclined to change names or sobriquets in poems when occasion demanded is seen also in 'Lucasia' (beginning 'Not to obleige Lucasia by my voice': Thomas, i. 103–5), found in Balliol College, Oxford, MS 336, ff. 7v–8v, with the name

these traces would not have spread too far—nothing compared to the permanence, in the public sphere, of a printed record.[10] Secondly, in this attempt by the middle-class, 19-year-old poet to extend her literary 'Society'—to 'target' a selected, socially distinguished candidate for invited membership, so to speak—we see a clear manifestation of Philips's keen sense of social ambition right from the start.

Might she also have realized just yet that manuscript culture itself not only entailed certain social advantages of privileged exclusivity, but also imposed upon the poet inhibiting restrictions? It was a mixed blessing. On the one hand, manuscript circulation within a private group of cultured and sympathetically minded people was safe; on the other hand, her audience was then essentially limited. It alone would not necessarily allow her to make the transition from a 'private' to an acceptably 'public' sphere: to achieve the wider, meaningful recognition by that élite society whose general approbation she might seek.

If Katherine Philips worked in the sphere of manuscript circulation, it was both because that was what was available to her and because it had genuine protective advantages—it was a sanctioned sphere of operations for a woman of her class. Nevertheless, we have reason to believe that she was a woman who felt herself to be something of an outsider—both socially and even physically (isolated and exiled, as she largely was, among the 'barren . . . Rocks & Mountaynes' of Wales)—and who struggled against *de facto* exclusion from the literary world of her time. Thus she was not a 'manuscript poet' in the way that, say, Sir Philip Sidney had been. Her manuscripts were not tokens of an incidental, aristocratic, leisurely pursuit (though she might sometimes pretend they were). For her, despite their limitations, they had a social, even political purpose: they were a means of access to the *beau monde* itself.

At the same time it would be an over-simplification to conclude that in Katherine Philips the 'manuscript poet' was a 'print poet' trying to break out. That is because it

---

'Syndaenia' throughout instead of 'Lucasia': see Elizabeth H. Hageman and Andrea Sununu, '"More copies of it abroad than I could have imagin'd": Further manuscript texts of Katherine Philips, "the matchless Orinda"', *EMS* 5 (1995), 127–69 (pp. 132–5), and also Patricia M. Sant and James N. Brown, 'Two unpublished poems by Katherine Philips', *ELR* 24 (1994), 211–25.

[10] While stressing the point about the permanence of print, one must concede that a certain infringement of privacy was endemic even to the dynamic of manuscript culture, which in some ways operated rather like gossip. There was an initial deliberately controlled and targeted circulation of things one *wanted* to remain 'private', but their very exclusivity set a premium on them and, in practice, invited an expansion of the audience to include more and more supposedly privileged 'insiders'. Thus the complaints about indiscretion occasionally encountered. For instance, Lord Middleton was annoyed at Dryden's allowing unvetted and attributed copies of unbuttoned verse epistles which passed between them and Etherege for their private amusement to be spread around in 1686. As reported by Owen Wynne to Etherege: 'How farre your Verses were Censured I know not; sure I am Mr Dryden & his Son [Charles] (who Copied the father's answer to yow) were, for suffering Copyes of ym to steal abroad, with my Lord's name in the Title-page' (Wynne to Etherege, 17 December 1686, in Bischöfliches Zentralarchiv, Regensburg, Germany, BZA/Sch. F. XVII, Fasz. 4, No. 19). Etherege himself is reprimanded for exposing 'to publick View' private and 'unfinisht' drafts in Wycherley's poem 'To Sir George Etheridge, on his shewing his Verses imperfect': *The complete works of William Wycherley*, ed. Montague Summers, 4 vols. (London, 1924), iv. 227.

was not just a 'print poet' that was trying to break out: it was a would-be dramatist, Court favourite, Poet Laureate,[11] and literary icon trying to break out as well.

Her obstacles were formidable. Behind the somewhat nervously constructed mask she presented—of a humble, modest gentlewoman who wrote only for the amusement of herself and a few friends—was a woman extremely anxious about the possibility of *exposing* herself to precisely the kind of public ridicule which Mrs Manley so obligingly supplied some decades later. Indeed we do not have to look so far ahead to find such denigration. In the same 1650s Royalist miscellany in which her letter to Lady Fletcher appears occurs another unpublished piece: a remarkably truculent attack on her—by none other than John Taylor, the plebeian 'Water Poet' (see Plates 78 and 79, and Appendix VI below).[12] 'You dame of Corinth', it begins—implying a showy, meretricious, even harlot-like woman:

> Comitt no Rape.
> Vpon the Muses be not bold.
> To make them scold

And he continues:

> But Bedlam ffuries, native hate.
> Only create,
> The fetterd follies of thy Rhymes
> Like ill tun'd chymes.
> The Jangling of bells backward rung
> So is thy tongue.
> Snatcht from Vipers dryd' in Hell
> Alecto's Cell
> Ownes thee, the mistresse of her Schoole . . .

And so it goes on for fifty-two lines, in a torrent of poetic abuse. Near the end, Taylor declares:

> May you a second Sapho prove
> To write in Love;
> And if like her you doe not die
> Then soone will I,
> Iambick you Lycambes ffate.

---

[11] Abraham Cowley, 'On the death of Mrs Katherine Philips', lines 38–40:

> But if Apollo should design
> A Woman Laureat to make,
> Without dispute he would Orinda take.

[12] The poem appears in University College London MS Ogden 42, pp. 225–6. Judging by its style and tone, it is not written by the Royalist song-writer John Taylor (*fl.*1637–45), the lyrics for one of whose songs appear elsewhere in this MS (pp. 115–16), but by John Taylor (1578–1653), who published a collected folio edition of his own *Workes* in 1630. It is not recorded in, for instance, the bibliography of Taylor's works supplied in Bernard Capp, *The world of John Taylor the water poet 1578–1653* (Oxford, 1994).

So, in effect, he invites her to *hang* herself, as Lycambes did as a result of a poet's satire on *him*.

This remarkable piece of invective, with all its sexist stereotypes, would appear to disprove *one* general assumption: that—apart from what appears to have been a single politically motivated 'libell' on her by a certain J. Jones (a libel she scornfully refutes in one of her poems to Lucasia)[13]—there was no serious male attack on Katherine Philips's reputation in her own lifetime, or indeed until 1712, with the malicious and unsavoury diatribe against her published by Thomas Newcomb.[14] Whenever it was Taylor wrote his attack, it cannot have been later than December 1653, when the old misogynist died.[15]

No wonder that Katherine Philips was afraid of publication. If we consider how few of her poems could have been known to Taylor before 1653, how much more fuel would he have had for his furious onslaught had he had access to her complete works.[16]

Although she never says as much directly, I suspect that one of Philips's main underlying fears was that she might ever put herself in a position to invite direct comparison with that other great female literary figure of her time, Margaret Cavendish, Duchess of Newcastle. For all the public eulogies she attracted, we have ample evidence that Cavendish—who published, at her own expense, a series of her own works from 1653 onwards—was privately regarded in polite society as a figure of ridicule, if not as downright mad. There were 'many soberer People in Bedlam', said Dorothy Osborne dismissively.[17]

Indeed, I think we can imagine the mixed feelings Philips would have had over the implicit comparison between them made by the almanack writer Sarah Jinner in *An almanack or prognostication for the year of our Lord 1658*. In her spirited address 'To the

---

[13] Thomas, i. 114–16: 'To (the truly competent Judge of Honour) Lucasia, upon a scandalous libell made by J. Jones' (and see also pp. 116–17, 346–8).Taylor's satire may well have been related to this issue, however: see pp. 282–4 below.

[14] [The Revd Thomas Newcomb], *Bibliotheca: A poem. Occasion'd by the sight of a modern library* (London, 1712): see Roger D. Lund, '*Bibliotheca* [*sic*] and "the British dames": An early critique of the female wits of the Restoration', *Restoration*, 12 (1988), 96–105, and Paula Loscocco, '"Manly sweetness": Katherine Philips among the neoclassicals', *HLQ* 56/3 (Summer 1993), 259–79 (especially pp. 273–5).

[15] For an account of Taylor's work, including his habitual tendency to depict women as coarse, sensual, and promiscuous, and to rail against their insubordinate usurping of male authority, see Capp, *The world of John Taylor* (especially pp. 34, 113–20). Taylor's characteristic attitudes were not sweetened in his later years by the relative poverty in which he was obliged to live after 1645 (pp. 153–62). It may be noted that Taylor visited Cardigan Bay, Katherine Philips's area of Wales, in the summer of 1652, as also, on 17 August, Golden Grove in Carmarthenshire, seat of the Earl of Carbery and his recently married Countess, to whom Orinda had just addressed a poem (Thomas, i. 84–5, 331–2): see Capp, *The world of John Taylor*, 159–60, and Taylor's *A short relation of a long iourney made round or ovall by encompassing the Principalitie of Wales* [London, 1653] [Wing T512].

[16] The fury of Taylor's assault might, nevertheless, suggest that Philips had begun to have some measure of reputation already.

[17] Dorothy Osborne to William Temple, Letter 20 [7 or 8 May 1653], in Dorothy Osborne, *Letters to Sir William Temple*, ed. Kenneth Parker (London, 1987), 79 (and for other remarks that she 'is a litle distracted', 'Extravagant', and 'ridiculous', see p. 75). For accounts of Margaret Cavendish, see, *inter alia*, Douglas Grant, *Margaret the first* (London, 1957); Jean Gagen, 'Honor and fame in the works of the Duchess of Newcastle', *SP* 56 (1959), 519–38; Kathleen Jones, *A glorious fame* (London, 1988); James Fitzmaurice, 'Fancy and the family: Self-characterizations of Margaret Cavendish', *HLQ* 53 (1990), 199–209; and Sandra Sherman, 'Trembling texts: Margaret Cavendish and the dialectic of authorship', *ELR* 24 (1994), 184–210. Grant (pp. 216–17) mistakenly thinks that Cavendish was a member of Orinda's 'Society', Policrite, confusing her with Mary Butler, Lady Cavendish (cf. n. 76 below). For one reference to Margaret Cavendish by Philips herself (citing Edmund Waller's effective dismissal of Cavendish's poem 'The hunting of the stag'), see Thomas, ii. 119.

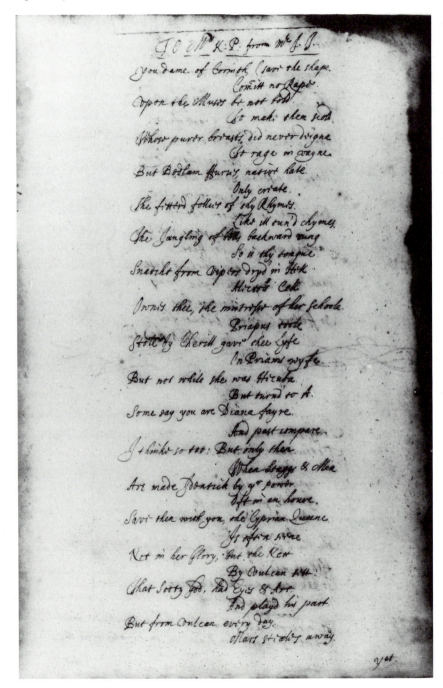

PLATE 78: Contemporary transcript of John Taylor's poem 'To M^rs K: P:' (University College London MS Ogden 42, p. 225)

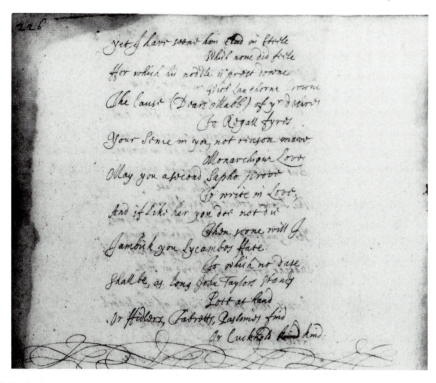

PLATE 79: End of contemporary transcript of John Taylor's poem 'To M^rs K: P:' (University College London MS Ogden 42, p. 226)

Reader' Jinner explicity defends the right of women to appear in print: 'You may wonder to see one of our Sex in print especially in the Celestial Sciences,' she says. In the middle of a catalogue of women who have equalled or excelled men in various fields, she observes:

What rare Poets of our sex were of old: and now of late the Countess of Newcastle. And, I pray you, what a rare Poem hath one Mistres Katherine Philips near Cardigan writ, it is printed before Cartwrightes Poems, who, if her modesty would permit, her wit would put down many mens in a Masculine strain.[18]

This is an especially notable contemporary tribute to Philips since it seems to be based on acquaintance with but a single poem by her, and also apparently on hearsay knowledge, both that the 'K. P.' who signed this poem was Katherine Philips and that she lived in Cardigan.

For all Jinner's intended compliment, I think it is safe to assume that Philips herself would have been much more comfortable with the kind of view represented, for instance, by some later remarks of Mary Evelyn, who was not alone in 1667 in being

[18] Sarah Jinner, *An almanack or prognostication for the year of our Lord 1658* (London, [1657/8; Wing A1844]), 'To the Reader', sig. B.

scandalized by the visit to London of the 'amasingly vain and ambitious' Margaret Cavendish. 'What contrary miracles dos this Age produce', she wrote, 'This Lady and Mrs Phelips, the one transporded with the shadow of reason the other possessed of the substance and insensible of her treasure, and yet men who passe for learned and wise not only put them both in iquall balance but make the greatnesse of the one wheigh downe the certaine and reall worth of the other'.[19]

Yes, a comparison between the two women writers was unthinkable—unthinkable, but also, it would seem, inevitable. This is because they were both striving for recognition—even if by different means, determined, in part, by their very different social positions.

The one, Margaret Cavendish—with the privilege of her eminent aristocratic status—could be bold, open, almost brazenly self-promoting. She made no bones about her burning desire for validation as a writer—her craving for fame and for immortality.[20] She wanted her books to make 'so loud a Report', she declared, 'that all the World shall hear it'.[21] Without her writing, she wrote with disarming frankness, people would not remember her name after her death—they would not even recall which of her illustrious husband's wives she was.[22] It was, in effect, only in the form of writing, *as* text, that Cavendish could survive—and text not in manuscript (especially given, as she admits, her appalling handwriting), but as printed text: it is this which would remain as a fixed *monument* to her.[23] And in this ambition—for all her detractors—she had the privilege of rank. Cavendish reminds us not only of the Renaissance humanistic ideals of 'fame' and 'honour', as outward expressions of inward virtues and merits,[24] but also of that tradition which Jürgen Habermas has traced back as far as Aristotle: that sense that virtues lay essentially in the public, rather than private, sphere; that only those of a certain social status could be defined or represented, or in a sense exist, as real people in public terms.[25]

So it is this, as much as anything, that the disadvantaged Katherine Philips was up against: Philips—an essentially bourgeois gentlewoman, powerless in herself, and

---

[19] Mary Evelyn to 'Mr Bohune Fellow of New Coll' (i.e. to Dr Ralph Bohun, author of a 'Character' of Mary Evelyn in 1695), among the Evelyn Papers now in the BL (uncatalogued: 'Mrs E Box 3'; copies are in two further quarto letterbooks of Mary Evelyn, in Evelyn Papers 9 and in a folder of fragile 'Mrs E' material). Mary Evelyn's respect for Katherine Philips is also evinced in another undated letter by her, to James Tyrrell ('Mr Terryll': probably Philips's 'Musidorus') in Ireland, in which she wonders what charms Ireland can have to detain 'persons of so much witt and merit' as 'Mrs Philips or Mr Terryll . . . souls so much raised aboue the Vulgar' (Evelyn Papers 9, f. [9]).

[20] 'for I am very ambitious, yet t'is neither for Beauty, Wit, Titles, Wealth or Power, but as they are steps to raise me to Fames Tower, which is to live by remembrance in after-ages': Cavendish, 'A true relation of my birth, breeding, and life', appended to *Natures pictures drawn by fancies pencil to the life* (London, 1656), 389.

[21] 'A dedication *to Fortune*', in *The world's olio* (London, 1655), sig. A1^v.

[22] 'for my Lord having had two Wives, I might easily have been mistaken, especially if I should dye, and my Lord Marry again': Cavendish, 'A true relation of my life', 391.

[23] Sherman, 'Trembling texts', 198, 206.   [24] Gagen, 'Honor and fame', 521–2 *et passim*.

[25] Jürgen Habermas, *The structural transformation of the public sphere: An inquiry into a category of bourgeois society*, trans. Thomas Burger with the assistance of Frederick Lawrence (Cambridge, Mass., 1991), 4: 'The virtues, whose catalogue was codified by Aristotle, were ones whose text lies in the public sphere and there alone receive recognition,' and 7: 'Words like excellence, highness, majesty, fame, dignity, and honor seek to characterize this peculiarity of a being that is capable of representation.'

dependent upon the support of her social superiors—careful and discreet; eschewing public self-promotion—which in her eyes meant 'exposing' herself to the censure of the vulgar rabble and of the malicious—but nevertheless craving the approval of the discerning élite of her society.

Thus motivated, what we see Katherine Philips doing throughout her brief life is exploiting to the full the opportunities which each of her available media afforded her—yet essentially without transgressing their social boundaries.

Despite her chief preoccupation with manuscript circulation—to which the large quantity of surviving manuscript texts bears witness—she broke into print on at least five occasions. In Plate 80 we see the poem Sarah Jinner mentioned, Philips's tribute to William Cartwright printed in Humphrey Moseley's octavo edition of Cartwright's works in 1651—her first publication.[26] Standing as the first of fifty-four commendatory poems (all the rest being by men, arranged by descending order of rank), it is modestly signed 'K. P.' Then in 1655 we have two contributions by her to John Playford's folio edition of Henry Lawes's *Ayres and dialogues, the second book*: her prefatory poem in commendation of Lawes, boldly signed 'Katharine Philips', and later (Plate 81) one of her Lucasia poems in Lawes's setting, a poem not signed on this page but clearly designated in the contents list as by 'Mrs. Catherine Philips'.[27] Seven years later, in 1662, we have a broadside published by Moseley's successor, Henry Herringman, of Philips's poem celebrating the arrival in England of Queen Catherine of Braganza. This broadside (Wing T1598A) has only recently been identified by Elizabeth Hageman and it apparently survives in but two known copies.[28] As can be seen from Plate 82, it was published anonymously. Then, a year later appears in Dublin the quarto miscellany *Poems, by several persons*. This is known from the apparently unique surviving copy now in the Folger Shakespeare Library (Plate 83). The volume contains no fewer than three of her poems—all designated in the index at the end as 'By a Lady' (Plate 84). And finally, published shortly before this miscellany by the same Dublin printer, John Crooke, is the edition of her play *Pompey*, translated from Corneille. The title-page gives no indication of authorship, but references to 'a Lady', and then to 'the incomparable Lady Mrs. *Phillips*', were used by Crooke in subsequent advertisements.[29] And

---

[26] Thomas, i. 143.   [27] Ibid. 87–8, 90–1.

[28] Elizabeth H. Hageman, 'The "false printed" broadside of Katherine Philips's "To the Queens Majesty on her happy arrival"', *Library*, 6th ser. 17/4 (December 1995), 321–6. Hageman reproduces (p. 323) the copy at Harvard University. The poem is printed from another source in Thomas, i. 74–5. Four MS texts of the poem are recorded in my *Index*, ii/2.173, to which may be added copies in the Berkshire Record Office (a single folio leaf in D/EBtZ37) and BL Add. MS 28758, f. 123r–v (among a group of her political poems in a miscellany).

[29] 'There is now published that excellent *Tragedy of Pompey*': advertisement by Crooke in *Mercurius Hibernicus* No. 10, for 17–24 March 1662/3 (cited in Hageman, 'The "false printed" broadside', 325 n. 10), and he advertised *Pompey* as 'a Tragedy, often acted in the New Theatre in *Dublin*, and written by a Lady' in a list of books printed by him appended to his edition of Jeremy Taylor, *Chrisis Teleiotike: A discourse of confirmation* (Dublin, 1663). Philips herself told Cotterell on 15 April, 'But should I once own it publickly, I think I should never be able to shew my Face again' (Thomas, ii. 79–81).

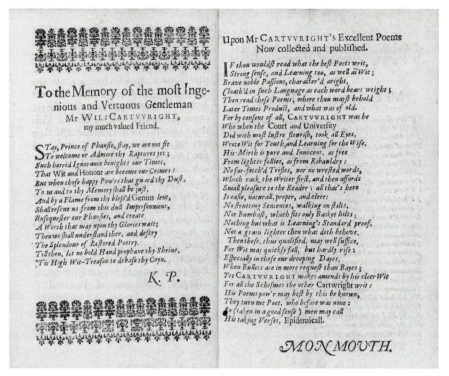

PLATE 80: The first two commendatory poems in *Comedies tragi-comedies, with other poems, by Mʳ William Cartwright*, 1651

this edition, which allegedly had a printing-run of 500 copies,[30] and was therefore by contemporary standards a best-seller, was reprinted by Crooke in London later in 1663, despite attempts by Herringman to secure the rights to it.[31]

These various publications did not altogether escape comment—and Philips herself was not averse to making discreet and politic disavowals of responsibility for them. But in fact what they have in common is that, in every case, she is essentially safe and protected. She was not 'exposed'—that great fear which echoes repeatedly, even obsessively, throughout her correspondence with Sir Charles Cotterell[32]—because these printings were adequately sanctioned. Moseley's edition of Cartwright and Playford's edition of Lawes were anthologies of coterie Royalist verse in which Philips was comfortably secured, along with various other members of her 'Society', including Sir

---

[30] Thomas, ii. 79–81.

[31] Crooke's London edition was advertised in *Mercurius Publicus* for 25 June to 2 July 1663 as '*Pompey*: A Tragedy. Written Originally in French by the exquisite Pen of *P. Corneille*, and now Rendered into English by the incomparable Lady Mrs. *Phillips*' (Hageman, 'The "false printed" broadside', 325 n. 10). Philips's letter of 15 April (Thomas, ii. 79–81) shows that she seriously considered authorizing Herringman to reprint the play in London, appointing her brother-in-law Hector Philips 'to treat with him about it', though, as it turned out, Crooke held on to his prerogative and reprinted the play in London himself.

[32] The word 'expose' and its cognates occur repeatedly in her letters to Cotterell: e.g. Thomas, ii. 66, 75, 80, 117, 118, 126 (twice), 128, 129, and 130; also 142 (twice, in her letter to Dorothy Osborne).

Mutuall Affection betweene *Orinda* and *Lucatia*.

Come, my *Lucatia*, since wee see that miracles mens faith do move by wonder and by prodi‑gy: to the fierce ang‑‑ry world let's prove, there's a Religi‑‑on in our Love.

(2)
For though we were defign'd t'agree,
That Fate no liberty deftroyes,
But our Election is as free
As Angels, who with greedy choice
Are yet determin'd to their joyes.

(3)
Our hearts are doubled by their loffe,
Heer mixture is addition grown,
We both defuse, and both ingroffe,
And we whofe minds are fo much one,
Never, yet ever are alone.

(4)
We court our owne captivity,
Then Thrones more great and innocent,
T'were banifhment to be fet free,
When we wear fetters whofe intent
Not bondage is, but ornament.

(5)
Divided joyes are tedious found,
And griefs united eafier grow:
We are our felves but by rebound,
And all our titles fhuffl'd fo,
Both Princes, and both Subjects too.

(6)
Our hearts are mutuall victims layd,
Which they (fuch pow'r in friendfhip lies)
Are Altars, Priefts, and Offrings made,
And each heart which thus kindly dies,
Graces deathleffe by the facrifice.

Difdaine.

Ake heed faire *Chloris*, how you tame (with your difdain) *Amintor's* flame. A noble

PLATE 81: Henry Lawes's setting of a poem by Katherine Philips in *Ayres and dialogues, the second book*, 1655

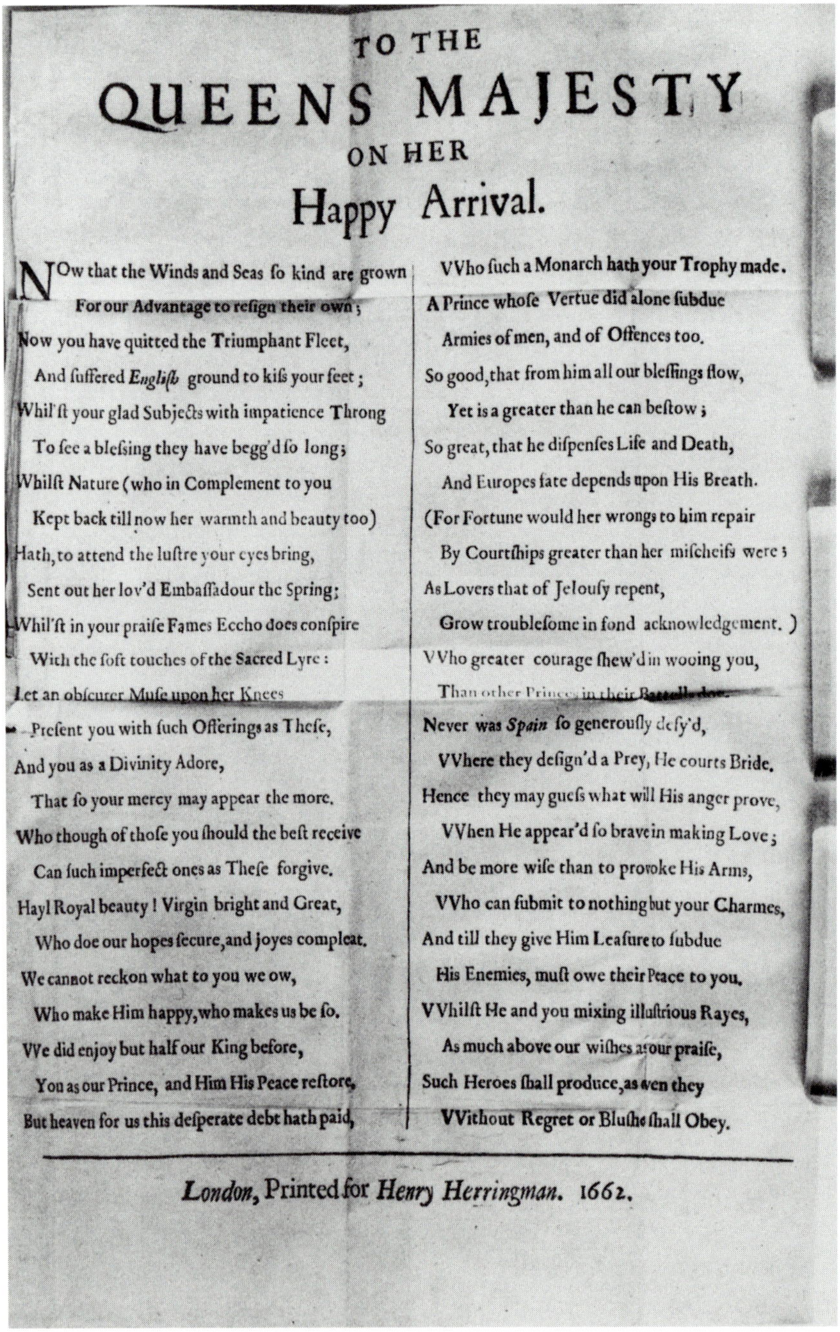

TO THE
QUEENS MAJESTY
ON HER
Happy Arrival.

Now that the Winds and Seas so kind are grown
For our Advantage to resign their own;
Now you have quitted the Triumphant Fleet,
And suffered *English* ground to kiss your feet;
Whil'st your glad Subjects with impatience Throng
To see a blessing they have begg'd so long;
Whilst Nature (who in Complement to you
Kept back till now her warmth and beauty too)
Hath, to attend the lustre your eyes bring,
Sent out her lov'd Embassadour the Spring;
Whil'st in your praise Fames Eccho does conspire
With the soft touches of the Sacred Lyre:
Let an obscurer Muse upon her Knees
Present you with such Offerings as These,
And you as a Divinity Adore,
That so your mercy may appear the more.
Who though of those you should the best receive
Can such imperfect ones as These forgive.
Hayl Royal beauty ! Virgin bright and Great,
Who doe our hopes secure, and joyes compleat.
We cannot reckon what to you we ow,
Who make Him happy, who makes us be so.
We did enjoy but half our King before,
You as our Prince, and Him His Peace restore,
But heaven for us this desperate debt hath paid,

Who such a Monarch hath your Trophy made.
A Prince whose Vertue did alone subdue
Armies of men, and of Offences too.
So good, that from him all our blessings flow,
Yet is a greater than he can bestow;
So great, that he dispenses Life and Death,
And Europes fate depends upon His Breath.
(For Fortune would her wrongs to him repair
By Courtships greater than her mischeifs were;
As Lovers that of Jelousy repent,
Grow troublesome in fond acknowledgement.)
VVho greater courage shew'd in wooing you,
Than other Princes in their Battells do:
Never was *Spain* so generously defy'd,
VVhere they design'd a Prey, He courts Bride.
Hence they may guess what will His anger prove,
VVhen He appear'd so brave in making Love;
And be more wise than to provoke His Arms,
VVho can submit to nothing but your Charmes,
And till they give Him Leasure to subdue
His Enemies, must owe their Peace to you.
VVhilst He and you mixing illustrious Rayes,
As much above our wishes as our praise,
Such Heroes shall produce, as even they
VVithout Regret or Blushe shall Obey.

London, Printed for *Henry Herringman.* 1662.

PLATE 82: Printed broadside of Katherine Philips's poem on the arrival of Catherine of Braganza, 1662 (Worcester College, Oxford)

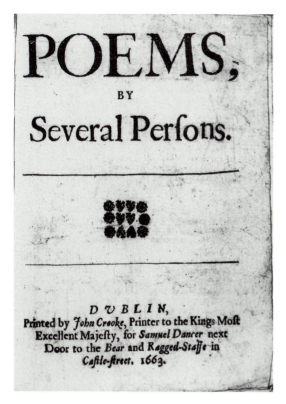

PLATE 83: Title-page of *Poems, by several persons*, 1663 (Folger Shakespeare Library C6681.5)

Edward Dering and his wife, her schoolfriend Mary Harvey, who was the dedicatee of the Lawes volume. Even the anonymous broadside on Queen Catherine was on pretty safe ground—politically—though she complained that it was badly printed.[33] As for the Dublin miscellany—although Philips made sure to complain to Cotterell that the three poems had been 'stolen' from her and printed without her 'Consent or Privity',[34] methinks the lady did not protest *too* much. Why? Because the offending printer was no less than 'John Crooke, Printer to the Kings Most Excellent Majesty'; the book was sold in Castle Street, just outside Dublin Castle, the seat of the Lord Lieutenant of Ireland himself; and the company she keeps in the miscellany comprises the likes of the powerful Irish politician Lord Orrery ('him who had so lately commanded a Kingdom', as Philips describes him)[35]—including his eulogy 'To Orinda' (Plate 85)—as well as the most celebrated poet of his day, Abraham Cowley, with, among other things, his complimentary ode 'On Orinda's Poems'. The miscellany represents, in fact, the very essence of a coterie circulation of verse connected with the Dublin Court, much of it inspired by 'Orinda' herself. And if the likes of Lord Orrery were not complaining about it, Philips had the sense not to make too much fuss herself. While, as for *Pompey*,

---

[33] Thomas, ii. 79. [34] Ibid. 88. [35] Ibid. 47.

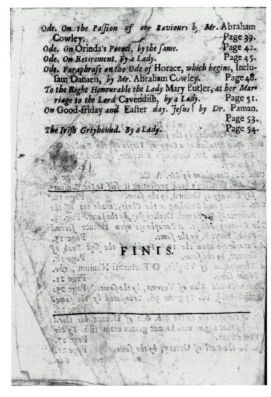

Ode. On the Passion of our Saviour, by Mr. Abraham Cowley.   Page 39.

Ode. On Orinda's Poems, by the same.   Page 42.

Ode. On Retirement. By a Lady.   Page 45.

Ode. Paraphrase on the Ode of Horace, *which begins,* Inclu- fam Danaen, *by Mr. Abraham Cowley.*   Page 48.

To the Right Honourable the Lady Mary Butler, *at her Marriage to the Lord* Cavendish, *by a Lady.*   Page 51.

On Good-friday and Easter *day.* Jesus! *by Dr.* Paman.   Page 53.

The Irish Greyhound. By a Lady.   Page 54.

PLATE 84: Last page of the Index in *Poems, by several persons*, 1663 (Folger Shakespeare Library C6681.5)

this was from start to finish produced under the auspices of Lord Orrery, who chose (for his own political reasons) to encourage and patronize her in this venture, as well as personally to finance costumes for the production.[36] In none of these instances did Katherine Philips's reputation—her 'Vertue and Honour'[37]—ever risk seriously being compromised by the bold step of venturing into print.

Pompey also provides the occasion for Philips's greatest lifetime achievement in her third medium: the theatre. With its opening performance by John Ogilby's company at the new Smock Alley Theatre, less than a couple of hundred steps away from Dublin Castle itself, on the afternoon of Wednesday, 18 February 1662/3,[38] attended by the cream of Dublin society—including the Duke of Ormonde, the Lord Lieutenant of Ireland, to whom the Prologue was addressed; Lord Orrery; his brother, the Earl of Cork,

---

[36] Philips told Cotterell that Orrery had 'advanc'd a hundred Pounds towards the Expence' of the costumes (ibid. 75). Neither Orrery's political motivation for his involvement here, nor the overall political dimension of *Pompey*—a play concerned with the problematical nature of kingship and republicanism after a civil war—have yet, I think, been fully explicated by scholars, although a notable recent contribution to the subject is made in Andrew Shifflett, ' "How many virtues must I hate?": Katherine Philips and the politics of clemency', *SP* 94 (1997), 103–35.

[37] Thomas, ii. 129.

[38] '18 [February 1662/3] Joined this day with my L[or]d duke [of Ormonde] and in the afternoone wee went to hear Pompey': entry in the autograph diary of Richard Boyle, Earl of Cork, in the Library of the Duke of Devonshire, Chatsworth House; this MS is mentioned in Kathleen M. Lynch, *Roger Boyle first Earl of Orrery* (Knoxville, Tenn., 1965), 117, 265.

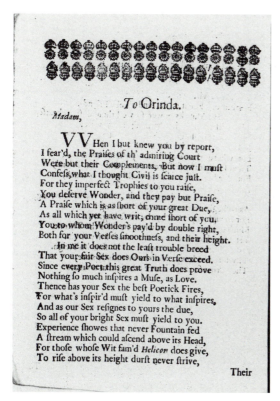

PLATE 85: First page of Lord Orrery's poem 'To Orinda' in *Poems, by several persons*, 1663 (Folger Shakespeare Library C6681.5)

and various other members of the Boyle and Butler families; no doubt Lord Roscommon, who wrote the Prologue, and Philips's good friend Sir Edward Dering, who wrote the Epilogue, as well as many other notables—this was a production in every way encouraged and protected by distinguished society. Only in the context of these safeguards could *Pompey* become, so far as we know, the first play by any woman to be produced on any public stage in Great Britain. In effect, *Pompey* represents the crowning literary and social triumph of Philips's life: the point at which she came the closest to general recognition by her peers and satisfactory public validation as a writer.

But then, right at the end of the same year, 1663, came the bombshell: the publication in London, by Richard Marriott, of the octavo edition of *Poems by the incomparable, Mrs. K. P.*—the innocuous-looking title-page of which can be seen in Plate 86.[39] The printer's device in the middle even offers the poet a laurel wreath of honour, and the edition is prefaced by two commendatory poems on Orinda by Cowley and by one 'H. A.' Philips's response, to what she clamorously insisted was a totally unauthorized,

---

[39] Nathan P. Tinker has recently identified the printer of this volume as John Grismond: see 'John Grismond', *ELN* 34/1 (1996), 30–5. It is curious, incidentally, to note that this problematical edition was published at Marriott's 'Shop under S. *Dunstans* Church in Fleet-street': i.e. in the putative earlier vicinity of our Feathery Scribe!

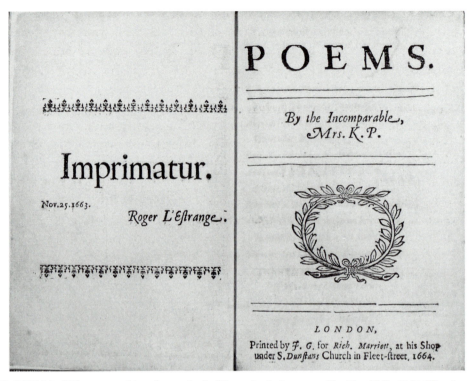

PLATE 86: Title-page and imprimatur leaf of *Poems by the incomparable, Mrs. K.P.*, 1664 (Huntington Library RB 147220)

'wretched Artifice',[40] was a wail of unhappiness, in consequence of which she had influential friends in London, Sir Charles Cotterell and John Jeffreys, successfully prevail upon Marriott to suppress the edition and withdraw copies from circulation. At least that is the picture of events that has traditionally been painted.

An interesting argument has recently been put forward by Germaine Greer postulating that Katherine Philips was in fact responsible for this publication herself after all. Greer argues, in brief, that, alarmed by the personal nature of some of the poems, which were not always disguised by the use of sobriquets, it was Cotterell and Jeffreys who initiated suppression of the edition, not her; they alerted her to the damage this publication could inflict on her reputation, and a belated realization of this prompted her urgent backtracking and determined attempt to distance herself from 'the whole ill-advised enterprise'. Greer sees corroboration for this interpretation of events in the fact that the text of the 1664 edition, far from being hopelessly corrupt, was a good one—evidently derived from an authentic source—and that the publisher himself, Richard Marriott, far from being a 'knave' scrambling 'to get a groat', as Philips contemptu-

---

[40] Thomas, ii. 129.

ously described him, was highly respectable and was clearly under the impression that he was publishing the poems in good faith, as he put it himself, with 'that ingenious lady's allowance to have them printed'. Moreover, Greer sees a reason for this publication—a financial one. The Philipses were in financial difficulty in 1663. An author's payment for this edition would not have come amiss.[41]

This is an interesting, even in some ways an attractive thesis. But I don't buy it.

To take the question of payment for a start. What would an author have received from a publisher for a work like this? Peter Lindenbaum has shown that the notorious payment to Milton in 1667 of £20, in instalments, for three editions of *Paradise Lost*, far from being derisory, could be considered, by contemporary standards, a reasonable deal.[42] And Warren Chernaik reminds us that later, in 1684, Aphra Behn was obliged to haggle with Jacob Tonson for £25 for her Poems (though 'I shou'd really have thought 'em worth thirty pound', she says).[43] So Philips might, at most, have got £25 or £30 for her Poems: much more likely £10, if that—hardly a bonanza to salvage the Philipses' declining fortunes even by contemporary currency standards.

As for Marriott's reaction, yes, he thought he was authorized to publish, but it is clear from his printed notice of withdrawal (on 18 January 1663/4) that he had not dealt directly with the author herself.[44] He had simply been misinformed—by the supplier of his copy—which was evidently derived from one of those collections which were produced within Philips's circle, probably while she was in Dublin in 1662–3.[45] It was, moreover, an unvetted copy, in which certain sobriquets were identified—exactly the kind of thing which would *not* have happened had Philips herself prepared it for viewing outside their circle.

Having said this, my real reluctance to accept the notion that she consciously conspired to publish in 1664 is that this would run totally against the grain of all other evidence we have for the nature of her psychology, ambition, and demonstrable

[41] Germaine Greer, *Slip-shod sibyls: Recognition, rejection and the woman poet* (London, 1995), ch. 5: 'The rewriting of Katherine Philips', 147–72.

[42] Peter Lindenbaum: 'Milton's contract', *Cardozo Arts & Entertainment Law Journal*, 10/2 (1992), 439–54; 'The poet in the marketplace: Milton and Samuel Simmons', in P. G. Stanwood (ed.), *Of poetry and politics: New essays on Milton and his world* (Binghamton, NY, 1994), 249–62; 'Authors and publishers in the late seventeenth century: New evidence on their relations', *Library*, 6th ser. 17/3 (September 1995), 250–69.

[43] Aphra Behn to Jacob Tonson, [1684], printed in *GM* NS 5 (May 1836), 481–2; cited in Warren Chernaik, *Sexual freedom in Restoration literature* (Cambridge, 1995), 161; and cf. my *Index*, ii/1. 2 (No. 16).

[44] Thomas, i. 20.

[45] The Dering MS (at Texas), Clarke MS (at Worcester College), and 1664 edition are all closely related, for the greater part of their contents, to Philips's own autograph notebook, the Tutin MS at Aberystwyth (cf. *Index*, ii/2. 128–30). It seems highly likely that the Dering MS was produced during Dering's stay in Dublin as one of the Commissioners for the Settlement of Ireland, from July 1662 to July 1663, while the Clarke MS probably passed to George Clarke from his father, the politician Sir William Clarke (1623?–66), who appeared as a witness at the trial of Katherine Philips's husband James Philips in June–July 1661 (BL Egerton MS 2979, ff. 108r–127r: Thomas, ii. 160). *Inter alia*, Sir William had business connections with Ireland in the 1660s involving his licence for selling wine there: see CSPD Ireland, 1660–2, pp. 92, 203, and CSPD Ireland, 1663–5, pp. 225, 235, 248, 276, 278–9. Perhaps significantly, the Clarke collection at Worcester College contains (MS 120: Plays 9.19) the only currently known MS of Orrery's heroic play *Altamira*, performed privately in Dublin on 18 October 1662 (publicly there on 26 February 1662/3), and not brought to London (in a revised version retitled *The Generall*) until September 1664.

sense of political diplomacy. Katherine Philips was not reckless—indeed her acute sense of vulnerability, her nervous caution about anything that might be construed as compromising her reputation, 'honour', and social position, suggest quite the opposite tendency. During the last year of her life, in 1663–4, especially inspired by the success of *Pompey*, she was more socially ambitious than ever—producing occasional verse for a variety of aristocratic friends and patrons, even sending a poem to the Archbishop of Canterbury, and, most of all, maximizing Cotterell's influence at Court on her behalf, sending presentation copies to the Duchess of York and even to the King himself. No, her aspirations were running in quite a different direction from what she clearly recognized, throughout her life, to be the great problem associated with print in any context other than under the sanction of patronage which I have suggested. By reaching an untargeted, indiscriminate, 'vulgar' audience, the publication of a body of verse which celebrated the feelings, activities, and relationships of a 'private' circle of genteel friends could only lower, not enhance, her prestige in the eyes of that social class whose approbation alone she sought. Least of all did she need Cotterell or Jeffreys to warn her of the dangers.

The features which stand out most, I think, in her letter to Cotterell of 29 January 1663/4, reacting to Marriott's publication, are its passionate sincerity and transparency.[46] The letter amounts virtually to an official *apologia*: indeed Cotterell was encouraged to show it around as such, and thus it eventually came to be printed in 1667.[47] As in any polemical self-vindication, there is a rhetorical tidying-up of the facts, to be sure. We might choose to take with a pinch of salt, for instance, her disclaimers to her ever having sought 'applause', or having written for anything more than her 'own amusement in a retir'd life', or her assertion that she 'never writ any line in [her] life with an intention to have it printed' (the Cartwright poem at least would seem to contradict that). But there is a world of difference between exaggeration, as I think this is, and outright falsehood. Philips goes on to declare, pointedly and emphatically, that she would not have accepted £1,000 to allow Marriott's edition to be published. If, in fact, by Greer's reckoning, she *had* contracted for the publication and expected payment for it, she must now be exposed as a downright liar. It is not a difference of *degree* that is involved here; it is a difference of *kind*. I am not prepared to accept that she made that transition.

There is genuine indignation, as well as anxiety and self-reproach, in this *apologia*, I would suggest, for two principal reasons. One, because her social ambitions were threateningly exposed. Second, because she recognized that she had seriously underestimated the extent to which even manuscript circulation entailed loss of authorial control when it was no longer regulated within proper safeguards. She had been

---

[46] The letter is cited at some length in Greer, *Slip-shod sibyls*, 157–9, and is printed in full in Thomas, ii. 128–31.

[47] Philips instructed Cotterell to show it, if he wished, 'to any body that suspects my Ignorance and Innocence of that false Edition': Thomas, ii. 125.

beguiled, or 'seduc'd', into allowing what she calls 'fugitive Papers' to escape her hands and into permitting friends to make 'Copies for their divertisement'. In a curious way, for all her attempted excuses, I suspect that she would have accepted, with some remorse, Mrs Manley's chief judgement on her in the stage caricature of Orinda.[48] She was a 'poetess' whose desire for 'approbation' had led her to allow numbers of manuscript copies of her works to be made and circulated indiscriminately—almost as if, in a sense, *they were print.*

Within little more than six months of Marriott's unwelcome edition, Katherine Philips was dead—from smallpox, in London, on 22 June 1664. Nor was there any great marble monument erected to her memory, which would endure the ravages of time and perpetuate her memory. She was buried in a relatively modest church—at St Benet Sherehog in the City, 'at the end of Syth's lane', as Aubrey records, 'in the north ayle under the great stone with the brasen monyment'.[49] Whatever this 'monyment' was it did not survive the Fire of London two years later.[50]

By contrast, Cowley, dying three years afterwards, in 1667, would be buried with full honours in Westminster Abbey, near Chaucer, Beaumont—eventually Dryden and Prior—and some sixteen steps away from Spenser and Jonson. Margaret Cavendish, Duchess of Newcastle, dying nine years later, in 1673, would, as befitted her station, have the grandest monument of all: an elaborate and ornate rectangular tomb, with pillars and canopied backdrop, in white, black, and yellow marble, shared with her distinguished husband (Plate 87).[51] Attributed to Evelyn's protégé Grinling Gibbons (1648–1721),[52] this tomb stands in the north transept of Westminster Abbey. While the mortal prowess of the Royalist commander-in-chief Newcastle himself is represented by his baton and in the panelling by traditional martial images of armour and weapons, Margaret Cavendish's effigy is adorned with literary symbolism. She can be seen holding a book, with pendent inkhorn (for a close-up of this taken from her feet, see Plate 88), and she is, in effect, reading—with the implication of also writing—into

---

[48] I may be engaged in a circular argument here, but I suspect that Mrs Manley's caricature is, in fact, a reading of this very *apologia.*

[49] Bodleian Library MS Aubrey 8, f. 38r–v; John Aubrey, *Brief lives*, ed. Andrew Clark, 2 vols. (Oxford, 1898), ii. 153; cited in Thomas, i. 21.

[50] The site of St Benet Sherehog—where also Katherine Philips's ten-day-old son Hector was buried in 1655 (Thomas, i. 205, 220, 379)—is shown as being on St Pancras Lane opposite the end of St Size Lane on page 26 (H12) of John Ogilby's and William Morgan's City of London Map of 1676 reproduced in *The A to Z of Restoration London*, ed. Ralph Hyde, with John Fisher and Roger Cline (Lympne Castle, 1992), 53. The site in EC4, opposite Bucklersbury, the street where her father John Fowler had lived, is today buried under a huge construction development.

[51] An engraving of this tomb appears in Arthur Collins, *Historical collections of the noble families of Cavendishe, Holles, Vere, Hartley, and Ogle* (London, 1752), after p. 44, where it is described as 'a Noble Monument of white Marble, adorned with two Columns (of black Marble) and an Entablature of the *Corinthian* Order, with their Graces Portraitures, in full Proportion'. The tomb is also noted in Grant, 237–9 (and plate 9 opposite p. 236), and in Graham Parry, 'Cavendish memorials', *Seventeenth Century*, 9/2 (Autumn 1994), 275–87 (p. 285).

[52] It is so attributed, upon what authority I cannot say, in an official guidebook to Westminster Abbey, although no mention is made of it in standard books on Gibbons himself, such as Geoffrey Beard, *The work of Grinling Gibbons* (London, 1989).

PLATE 87: The tomb of Margaret Cavendish, Duchess of Newcastle, and her husband William, Duke of Newcastle, in Westminster Abbey

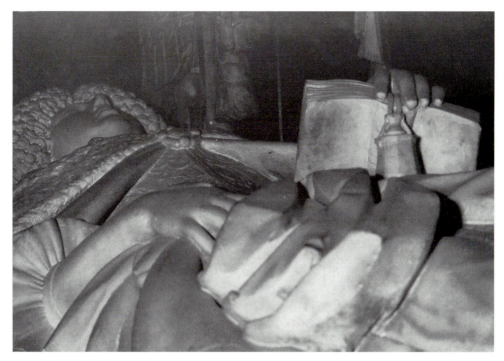

PLATE 88: The effigy of Margaret Cavendish on her tomb in Westminster Abbey

eternity.[53] On a side panel on the south side, centred beneath the couple's feet, is the piece of carving seen in Plate 89. It depicts yet more books, nine in all, variously upright and lying flat, partly with their spines outwards, partly with fore-edges and ties out-wards: a piece of symmetrical patterning which conveys a sense of ordered bookshelves, and—just a hint, perhaps—of ladders: a symbol we shall encounter again in a moment. A carved inscription at the front of the tomb (penned presumably by the Duke) praises the Duchess, not only as 'a most Virtuous & a Loueing & carefull wife', but also as 'a wise wittie & learned Lady, which her many Bookes do well testifie'. Thus the monu-ment symbolizes publicly, and resoundingly, her principal virtues, and represents her immortality through writing—exactly, we may suppose, as she would have wished.[54]

Yet if Katherine Philips was denied such auspicious representation as this, she did

[53] This iconography is not altogether unique to Margaret Cavendish. For instance, on her tomb in the Abbey of Fontevrault, Queen Eleanor of Aquitaine (d. 1204) is depicted lying down and reading a book: see Alberto Manguel, *A history of reading* (Lon-don, 1996), 150. In the Newcastle tomb, however, an additional dimension is introduced and symbolized by the inkhorn (with its cords suggesting attachment to a penner on the other side of the book). Especially since they are portable and used *in transit* (as opposed to a static inkwell), these writing instruments effectively suggest Cavendish's readiness for, and continuation of, writing, as well as reading, on her journey into eternity.

[54] The Duke of Newcastle was effectively counteracting his wife's expressed fear:

My *Bookes*, and I, all in a *Grave* lye dead.
No *Memory* will build a *Monument*

(Margaret Cavendish, '*A* Dialogue *between* the Body, *and the* Minde', in *Philosophicall fancies* (London, 1653), 78.)

PLATE 89: A side panel on the Newcastle tomb in Westminster Abbey

have her own monuments of a different kind. Ironically, it *was* only her death which could create the right circumstances for her virtues to be made public without compromising her honour; only then that she could achieve full and unreserved public recognition. Death made it possible too for her to achieve an apotheosis, an ascension to immortality, of sorts—moreover, in each of her three chosen fields of communication: in manuscript, in print, *and* in the theatre.

In the sphere of *manuscripts* there exists a remarkable monument to Orinda in the form of the 'Rosania Manuscript'.[55] This is a 400-page quarto volume containing a collection of Philips's works written for presentation to her friend 'Rosania': namely, Mary Aubrey, wife of Sir William Montagu, the Queen's Attorney-General. Presented—as may be seen in Plates 90 and 91, showing the first and last pages of his high-flown dedication—by someone using the sobriquet 'Polexander',[56] the manuscript is written almost throughout in a somewhat carefully formed and spaced, rounded Italic hand:

[55] National Library of Wales, NLW MS 776B: *Index*, ii/2. 129.

[56] Polexander is a sobriquet likely to be derived from the romance *Polexandre* by Marin le Roy, Sieur du Parc et de Gomberville (first published in Paris, 1632–8, translated into English by William Browne, 1647)—a work which, incidentally, also provided source material for Dryden's *The Indian Queen* and *The Indian Emperour*. However, see also Hageman and Sununu, ' "More copies of it abroad" ', 148, for the name's association with 'Declaration'. Polexander's dedication is printed, with some discussion, in Thomas, iii, pp. xii–xiii (and see also ii. 177–8).

the neat but slightly hesitant, variable, and probably non-professional script of an amanuensis, who might, just possibly, be a woman.[57]

This handsome and elaborate volume is conceived not simply—as the dedication says—'as a sad Monument' to Orinda—though its funereal character *is* heightened by its black, sombre morocco binding (Plate 92), not to mention by its arrangement: concluding in a series of poems of religious consolation on the theme of Death. It is a highly wrought artefact, which seems to draw attention to itself both as a piece of material text *and* as a transcendent symbol. It is presented almost as the manuscript equivalent of a kind of private Baroque chapel to Orinda, in which she is immortalized, in which her triumph over death is celebrated, and in which she is actually empowered to communicate with her beloved friend from Heaven. 'Orinda, though withdrawn, is not from you', he says. 'In lines so full of Spirit sure she lives; and to be with you, is that only spell, can share her with yᵉ bright Abodes; your Eyes, her heaven on Earth.' Orinda is presented as almost literally in a state of apotheosis: in Paradise, in 'those Glorious Mansions', in a state of 'beatitude'. And he seems to imply that the manuscript verse text itself, which enables communion, is a living thing. 'These clear Streams' of verse are a 'rich veine', he says: the ink flows, as it were, on the handwritten pages like blood in the veins of living people.

And if this conceit were not High Baroque enough, he introduces what is, I think, the implicit concept of Jacob's ladder: the vision dreamed by Jacob in Genesis 28: 12, wherein he saw 'a ladder set up on the earth, and the top of it reached to heaven: and behold the angels of God ascending and descending on it'. Thus Polexander declares: 'Here is a beatifick converse! Angels, thus, are still ascending & descending.'[58] Even the very layout of regularly spaced and even lines of verse on each page (see, for example, Plate 93) might be construed as a series of rungs. Indeed, the manuscript itself becomes, in a sense, that ladder. It becomes analogous to a kind of prayer (and prayer *was* described by one contemporary writer as 'the Jacob's Ladder of the soul').[59] It

---

[57] One poem ('Rosania's private marriage') is added in a second hand, on pp. 358–9.

[58] Polexander does not mention Jacob's ladder directly, but—in what may be a subconscious verbal echo—he does mention Jacob's staff, a kind of navigational instrument ('Thus, will her Raptures be to your harmonious Soull, a Jacobs=staff, to leuell at her Gloryes'). The image of Jacob's ladder is found elsewhere in artefacts from medieval times onwards: for example, one vivid depiction, begun by Oliver King (d. 1503), Bishop of Bath and Wells, is on the turrets of the west front of Bath Abbey: see the illustration in R. W. M. Wright, *The pictorial history of Bath Abbey* (Stockport, 1962), 4. A notable depiction is found in the MS of a 1640s Latin poem addressed to James Butler, Marquess of Ormonde, in which Ormonde is himself described as the 'Scala Jacobi' which conveys heavenly gifts and prayers between Heaven and Earth, and the ladder is represented in watercolour in the margin: see the illustration on the back cover of Sotheby's sale catalogue of 19 July 1994 (and lot 276). The image is frequently cited (and even occasionally echoed in the typographical layout of 'The seuerall steppes and degrees' involved) in 16th- and 17th-century religious literature: e.g. tracts and sermons entitled *Jacob's ladder* by Henry Smith (1595), Thomas Wilson (1611), John Wall (1626), (Cardinal) Roberto Bellarmino (1637, the dedication by H.I[saacson?], the title-page depicting two ladders), Francis Raworth (1655), and John Hall (1672), as well as Henry Vane's *A pilgrimage into the land of promise, by the light of the vision of Jacobs ladder and faith* (1664) [STC 22677, 25795, 24988, 1839.5; Wing R373, H387A, V73].

[59] 'Prayer is the Jacob's Ladder of yᵉ soul whereon it goes up & down to God & confers with him': quotation in a miscellany also including extracts from Katherine Philips's poems and apparently belonging to the family of Anne Owen ('Lucasia'), Viscountess Dungannon (Yale University, Osborn Collection, b 118, p. 185).

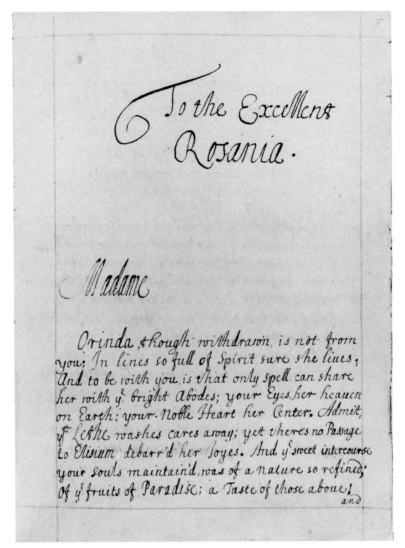

PLATE 90: First page of the dedication in the Rosania Manuscript (National Library of Wales NLW MS 776B, p. 5)

unites Heaven and Earth, enabling the souls of the dead poet and the reader (Rosania) to ascend and descend, and have communion, in the very act of reading these lines.

The only note of ambiguity arises when Polexander says:

To appear in print, how un:enclined she was? (I confess an Edition now, would gratify her Admirers, and 'twere but a just remeriting that value which (in hers, & in their own Right) was yᵉ Universall consent).

Is Polexander hinting that it is Rosania's responsibility—as her High Priestess, as her

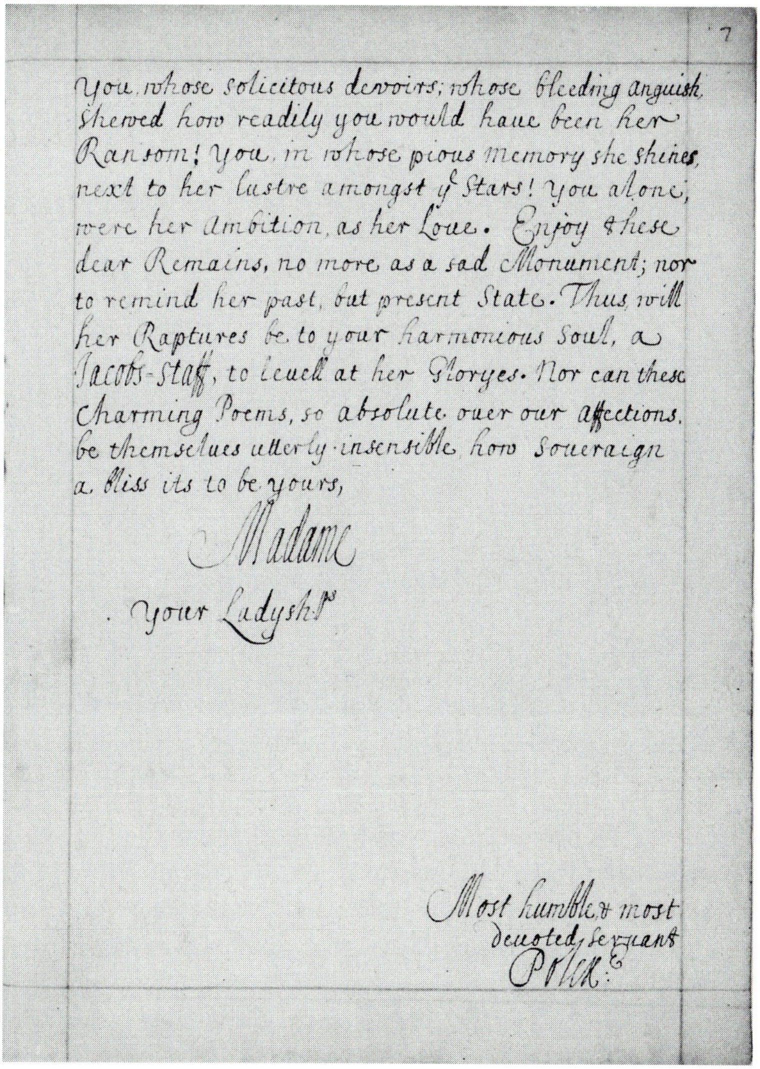

You, whose solicitous devoirs; whose bleeding anguish, shewed how readily you would haue been her Ransom! You, in whose pious memory she shines, next to her lustre amongst y Stars! You alone, were her ambition, as her Loue. Enjoy these dear Remains, no more as a sad Monument; nor to remind her past, but present State. Thus will her Raptures be to your harmonious Soul, a Jacobs-Staff, to leuell at her Gloryes. Nor can these Charming Poems, so absolute ouer our affections, be themselues utterly insensible, how Soueraign a Bliss its to be yours,

Madame

Your Ladysh͞p

Most humble & most deuoted seruant Ph͞il:

PLATE 91: Last page of the dedication in the Rosania Manuscript (National Library of Wales NLW MS 776B, p. 7)

guardian of the flame, as it were—to see that Orinda's works do now get fully published? that it is now universally agreed by her 'Admirers' that the time has come for such an edition? and that this very manuscript provides the basis for it? The paradox here is striking: that in this, the most sophisticated manuscript collection of Katherine Philips's works ever produced, and an essentially *private* offering made on a personal basis by a particular admirer to a particular lady—presented, moreover, as almost a sacred object—there is a perception that the limits of communication in this form have been reached. For Orinda to become fully realized, in *public* representation, the next step *is* print.

PLATE 92: Black morocco sombre binding on the Rosania Manuscript (National Library of Wales NLW MS 776B)

And print there was—though there is no evidence that Rosania had anything to do with it, or that her manuscript was at all consulted.

The result is well known to editors and scholars. Even so, one wonders whether the full measure of its importance, as one of the great milestones in the history of women's literature, has yet been generally appreciated.[60] I mean the folio edition of Philips's works finally brought out by Henry Herringman in late August or early September of 1667,[61] its title-page proudly proclaiming itself '*POEMS By the most deservedly Admired M*[rs.] *Katherine Philips The matchless ORINDA*' (Plate 94).

Avoiding precisely what Humphrey Moseley had been obliged to apologize for in his 1651 octavo edition of Cartwright—'so scant a Volume', he calls it, where the contents were 'crowded' to keep the price down to a third of what it would have cost in folio—

[60] A somewhat ironic reinforcement of my argument here is that the facsimile edition of the 1667 *Poems* published (with an introduction by Travis Dupriest) by Scholars' Facsimiles & Reprints (Delmar, NY, 1992) is reduced virtually to an octavo-size format and omits the frontispiece as well as the plays!

[61] Herringman bought out the rights of Marriott's unauthorized edition of 1664: this was witnessed by the Stationers' Company on 21 January 1666/7. Pepys heard that the edition was forthcoming when he visited Herringman's bookshop on 10 August, it was licensed by Roger L'Estrange on 28 August (imprimatur on sig. g[2ᵛ]), and Pepys was reading it by 16 September 1667: see Pepys, viii. 380, 439.

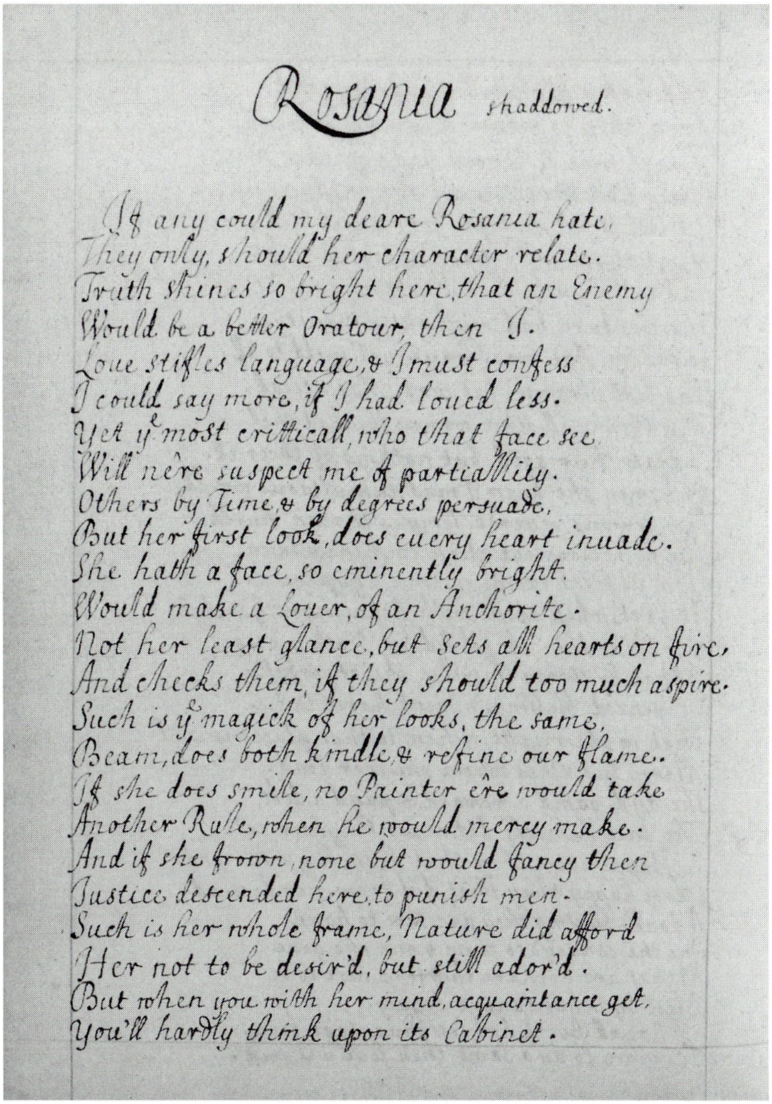

Rosania shaddowed.

If any could my deare Rosania hate,
They only, should her character relate.
Truth shines so bright here, that an Enemy
Would be a better Oratour, then I.
Loue stifles language, & I must confess
I could say more, if I had loued less.
Yet ye most critticall, who that face see
Will ne're suspect me of partiallity.
Others by Time, & by degrees persuade,
But her first look, does euery heart inuade.
She hath a face, so eminently bright,
Would make a Louer, of an Anchorite.
Not her least glance, but sets all hearts on fire,
And checks them, if they should too much aspire.
Such is ye magick of her looks, the same,
Beam, does both kindle, & refine our flame.
If she does smile, no Painter e're would take
Another Rule, when he would mercy make.
And if she frown, none but would fancy then
Justice descended here, to punish men.
Such is her whole frame, Nature did afford
Her not to be desir'd, but still ador'd.
But when you with her mind, acquaintance get,
You'll hardly think upon its Cabinet.

PLATE 93: A characteristic page of text in the Rosania Manuscript (National Library of Wales NLW MS 776B, p. 274)

his successor, the enterprising Herringman,[62] produced a handsome, high-prestige, 353-page volume in comfortable folio format. It comprises 121 poems by Philips, arranged with a fanfare of public, celebratory, or occasional pieces involving royal, aristocratic, or distinguished figures coming first, before the more intimate, coterie verse about friendship and other miscellaneous items appear—followed by five translations,

[62] For some account of Herringman and his professional status, see C. William Miller, 'Henry Herringman, Restoration bookseller-publisher', *PBSA* 42 (1948), 292–306.

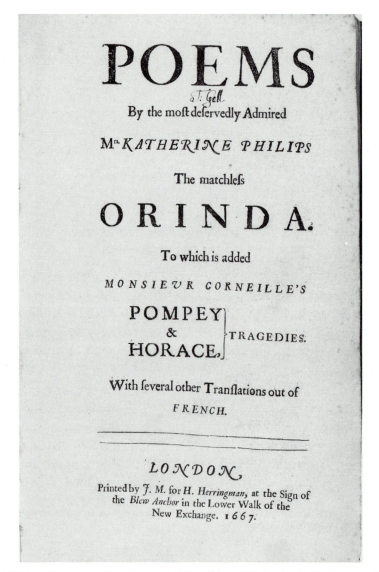

POEMS

By the moſt deſervedly Admired

Mrs *KATHERINE PHILIPS*

The matchleſs

ORINDA.

To which is added

MONSIEVR CORNEILLE'S

POMPEY
&
HORACE,
} TRAGEDIES.

With ſeveral other Tranſlations out of

FRENCH.

LONDON,

Printed by *J. M.* for *H. Herringman,* at the Sign of
the *Blew Anchor* in the Lower Walk of the
New Exchange. 1667.

PLATE 94: Title-page of Herringman's folio edition of Katherine Philips's *Poems*, 1667

and then, each with its own title-page, by two plays, *Pompey* and *Horace*.[63] The collection is prefaced by an anonymous address to the reader, presumably by the self-justifying publisher, condemning the 1664 'false Edition of these Poems' (which, of course, the present more worthy edition replaces) and discussing the changes 'Orinda'

[63] For some discussion of the arrangement of the contents of the 1667 folio—described as presenting us 'with an utterly conventional, a socially impeccable, fervently pro-Stuart Orinda who is also an unsurpassed translator of poetry . . . a paragon of womanhood', see Ellen Moody, 'Orinda, Rosania, Lucasia *et aliae* [*sic*]: Towards a new edition of the works of Katherine Philips', *PQ* 66 (1987), 325–54. In a letter to Tonson in 1684, Aphra Behn refers to 'Mrs. Philips her plays' coming last in an edition because they occupy 'the largest volume': see n. 43 above.

might have made had she lived to correct this edition herself—but, in effect, implicitly equating her works with this edition as if they were one and the same thing. 'This Monument which she erected for her self, will for ever make her to be honoured as the honour of her Sex, the emulation of ours, and the admiration of both,' he says. Seven commendatory poems on Orinda which occupy the next twenty pages—including eulogies by Orrery, Roscommon, and Cowley—all reinforce the sense of her immortality by virtue of her writings.

And the whole thing is preceded by a frontispiece (Plate 95), engraved by the most prominent portrait engraver of the period, William Faithorne (1616–91). The Preface virtually apologizes for this:

here is only a poor paper shadow of a Statue made after a Picture not very like her, to accompany that she has drawn of her self in these Poems, and which represents the beauties of her mind with a far truer resemblance, than that does the liniaments of her Face.

So—reiterating a commonplace found notably in Ben Jonson's epigram in the 1623 Shakespeare Folio ('Reader, looke | Not on his Picture, but his Booke')—Herringman stresses the inadequacy of physical representation for such a poet, as opposed to her 'true' beauty represented in her verse. As if to underline, somewhat crudely, his point, the only contemporary reaction to this portrait I have been able to find is that of the Italian traveller Lorenzo Magalotti, who remarked, unchivalrously, in 1668 on the 'Signora Filippa Poetessa': 'Ell' era pero brutissima di corpo' ('physically, however, she was extremely ugly').[64]

In fact, Faithorne's unflattering engraving adds to the monumental character of the edition. In one of only six portrait engravings ever produced by Faithorne in this mode—and the others are chiefly writers as well[65]—he presents Orinda as, quite literally, on a pedestal: as a bust, raised on a plinth, set within a rounded niche. The very gown draped around her shoulders has a classical look, and implicit in the image of a

---

[64] Anna Mario Crinò (ed.), *I letterati della restaurazione nell' relazione magalottiana del 1668* (Florence, 1956), 20. For a later malicious view of Faithorne's portrait we might note Thomas Newcomb's comments in 1712:

> She warbles with so ill a Grace,
> Thy Airs are coarser than thy Face
> And will be found (believe me) still
> To frighten ten, for one they Kill

(*Bibliotheca.*) For the general iconography of Katherine Philips, see Philip Webster Souers, *The matchless Orinda* (Cambridge, Mass., 1931), 249–50 (and frontispiece), wherein are also quoted Aubrey's unflattering comments on her 'read pumpled' and 'reddish' face as described to him by his cousin Mary Aubrey ('Rosania') and one Mrs Blackett. For an amusing 19th-century depiction of her, based on the Knole portrait, where she is praised for her amiable, feminine placidity ('and her bosom is like a rose full-blown'), see Brian W. Procter, *Effigies poeticae, or The portraits of the British poets*, 2 vols. (London, 1824), i, No. 45. For a modern depiction of her as the stuff of Restoration comedy, see the cover of R. T. Jenkins's Welsh novel *Orinda* (Caerdydd, Hughes a'i Fab, 1943) [BL pressmark: 874. n. 67].

[65] Louis Fagan, *A descriptive catalogue of the engraved works of William Faithorne* (London, 1888), especially pp. 19, 43, 47, 54, 59, 62. Depicted on pedestals in Faithorne's engravings are the antiquary Elias Ashmole (1652), the lawyer and future President of the Royal Society Sir John Hoskins (n.d.), the ancient Greek writer Lucian (1664), the French poet Paul Scarron (n.d.), and (full-length on a pedestal, in a print perhaps partly by White) the devotional writer Jeremy Taylor (1663). Most of Faithorne's many other portraits, from royalty downwards (and, incidentally, including Lady Castlemaine in 1668), are presented in oval frames; a few (such as Cowley) in octagonal frames; and just a few in full-length scenes.

PLATE 95: Faithorne's frontispiece in Herringman's folio edition of Katherine Philips's *Poems*, 1667

niche is the idea of a classical pantheon of fame, in which all the most distinguished personages of history take their immortal place.

The point of this simple, one might almost say severe, portrayal becomes evident if we compare it with the way Margaret Cavendish chose to be portrayed in the most widely distributed engraving of herself in 1655 (Plate 96).[66] She is seen as a statue in a similar niche, but posing full-length in a fur-lined toga, wearing a tilted coronet on her head, and flanked by the figures of Minerva and Apollo, representing heroic virtues and

[66] Frontispiece by Abraham van Diepenbeke, engraved by Peter van Schuppen, bound in various works by Margaret Cavendish, including *The worlds olio* (1655). It is also reproduced in Grant, after p. 154; in Antonia Fraser, *The weaker vessel* (New

PLATE 96: Frontispiece
depicting Margaret Cavendish,
Duchess of Newcastle, in her *The
worlds olio*, 1655

divine patronage for the arts. Philips, of course, could claim no aristocratic sanction for
such a representation herself, and her friends could only hint at a comparison.[67]

York, 1984), after p. 112; in Fitzmaurice, 'Fancy and the Family', facing p. 199; and elsewhere. The frontispiece was used again
in the folio of Cavendish's *Plays, never before printed* which (perhaps partly in response to the Herringman folio) Anne Maxwell
printed in 1668: an illustration of this appears in *SQ* 47 (1996), 390–1.

[67] One might indeed ask how many—or rather, how few—frontispieces representing women authors there were in England
before 1667. Apart from Cavendish, one recalls at present those of Vital d'Audiguier (*c.*1569–1624) in her *Love and valor or The
diuers affections of Minerva*, trans. W.B. (1638); Sarah Jinner in her *An almanack or prognostication for the year of our Lord 1658*; and
the two portraits (aged 22 innocent and 38 experienced) of the impostor Mary Carleton in her self-vindication *The case of Madam
Mary Carleton* (1663): see Mihoko Suzuki, 'The case of Mary Carleton: Representing the female subject, 1663–73', *TSWL* 12/1
(Spring 1993), 61–83.

Finally, although the binding given to a book was a matter for the individual purchaser, I cannot resist showing (if only in black and white) what at least one contemporary owner of Herringman's folio considered appropriate dress for such a distinguished edition (Plate 97): a sumptuous binding of fine red morocco, with elaborate tooling in gilt, and painted floral onlays—a volume later in the library of Augustus Frederick, Duke of Sussex (1773–1843), and now in the Huntington.[68]

With its frontispiece and the prominence given on the title-page to her two tragedies, Herringman's edition was, in effect, elevating Orinda to the ranks of the major English *dramatists*. His was a folio edition which, tacitly, not only bore comparison with his 1664 folio of Thomas Killigrew's plays, but also set her in the mainstream tradition of Shakespeare's works in 1623, of Ben Jonson's works in 1640, and of Moseley's great edition of Beaumont and Fletcher in 1647.

Honouring her in this way, the edition effectively did for Katherine Philips what she could never do for herself in her own lifetime. It brought her works once and for all into the public domain; it established her as 'the matchless Orinda'—that epithet would now be applied to her for evermore[69]—and it put the seal on her posthumous fame[70]—

---

[68] The contemporary London binding is possibly by Richard Balley and comprises panelled red morocco, with an elaborately tooled centre panel made up of small floral and leaf tools, with mosaic tulip tool etc., the spine gilt, and gilt edges. The volume was in Evans's sale of the *Bibliotheca Sussexiana*, part V (April–May 1845), lot 930, sold to Pickering; and was later in the Robert Hoe sale at Anderson Auction Co., New York, part I: *L to Z* (May 1911), lot 2608. Since writing this, a further, even more resplendently bound copy of the 1667 folio has come to light in a fine sale catalogue of *Bookbindings in the British Isles . . . part I* published by Maggs Bros Ltd., London (catalogue No. 1212, summer 1996), item 46 (for £18,500). Illustrated in colour in the catalogue, the volume, once owned by Violet Trefusis (1894–1972), appeared earlier in the G. Michelmore & Co. catalogue *Two hundred extraordinarily important books* (*c*.1930), item 120 (with a folding plate), and was sold at Sotheby's, 9 April 1935, lot 383 (for £20). The panelled red morocco binding is elaborately tooled, partly on dark blue and light brown onlays, with a central pointed panel of a triple fillet enclosing a large central lozenge decorated with massed volutes including an eagle's head, corner-pieces with floral volutes and lozenge, and intervening spaces with flowers, pyramids of semi-circles, fronds and large tulips, the spine gilt, and gilt edges.

To these indications of a contemporary readership which included landed gentry and aristocrats we can add early inscriptions found in other copies of Herringman's folio, such as certain of those mentioned in Hageman and Sununu, ' "More copies of it abroad" ', 168 n. 37, as well as the Gell family of Hopton Hall, Derbyshire (Plate 95 above). Notable copies of the 1669 edition include one belonging to the Cotterell family (at least to Sir Charles's great-great-grandson) in the Folger Shakespeare Library (P 2034). Another in Marsh's Library, Dublin (G3.7.49), is inscribed by one 'B. Boyle', evidently a member of Lord Orrery's family: in its table of contents each of the poems relating to one of the Boyles is marked with an arrow. A copy of the 1669 edition associated with the family of Margaret Cavendish is recorded as item 656 in the catalogue of the sale by Nathaniel Noel, *Bibliotheca nobilissimi principis Johannis Ducis de Novo-Castro, &c.*, on 17 March 1718/19.

[69] The first reference I can find to 'matchless' is in the dedication of the 'Rosania MS' (to her 'matchless pen'). The most common epithet applied to her otherwise seems to be 'incomparable': see, for instance, Crooke's advertisements for *Pompey* cited earlier; the title-page of the 1664 *Poems*; and Dering's personal tribute to her on her death (*Index*, ii/2. 139). The word 'matchless', incidentally, could also mean 'unmarried'; though strictly inappropriate to Mrs Philips, it may conceivably have retained some of this sense in relation to her perceived sexual virtue.

[70] The cult of Orinda does effectively date from 1667, and few contributions to women's literature in Britain can ever have had so far-ranging an influence before modern times. For the post-1667 influence of Katherine Philips on women writers, see, *inter alia*, the account in Marilyn L. Williamson, *Raising their voices: British women writers, 1650–1750* (Detroit, 1990), 64–133. In the most extreme instance—in Jane Barker's novel *The lining of the patch-work screen* (London, 1726)—Orinda is depicted (pp. 174–7) as almost literally in a state of apotheosis, as the heroine, Galecia (or Galesia), dreams of her at her 'Annual Coronation' on Parnassus, 'seated on a Throne, as Queen of Female Writers, with a Golden Pen in her Hand for a Scepter, a Crown of Laurel on her Head', and regaled by singing bards, 'a Choir of pretty Creatures in form of Grasshoppers', nightingales, fairies, and other votaries.

PLATE 97: Sumptuous contemporary binding on a copy of Herringman's folio edition of Katherine Philips's *Poems*, 1667 (Huntington Library RB 144857)

all, we may reasonably be sure, under the approving auspices of the friends and 'Society' who had 'protected' her during her lifetime.[71]

It was evidently as a result of the impact of this edition that her third apotheosis of sorts came about: in her third medium, the *theatre*, and at nothing less than the English Court itself.

We can establish, in brief, that the impetus came from a group of amateur theatrical

---

[71] For some account of the tradition whereby books at this time could be treated as living things, as a resurrection from the dead, not only to defy time and mortality and to offer consolation, but also to establish a community of allegiance with like-minded readers, see Warren Chernaik, 'Books as memorials: The politics of consolation', *YES* 21 (1991), 207–17.

players centred on the King's illegitimate son, the 18-year-old Duke of Monmouth, and his 16-year-old wife Anne, Duchess of Monmouth.[72] Following the scheduling of their first new venture, in Dryden's *The Indian Emperour* (eventually presented on 13 January 1667/8),[73] what more suitable heroic tragedy to present before the Court than one by the currently fashionable Mrs Philips[74]—one, indeed, completely fresh and unperformed? There in the new folio edition was her second translation from Pierre Corneille—the tragedy *Horace*. The only problem: it was unfinished—lacking the final act or so.

Here enter the prematurely ageing poet Sir John Denham (1615–69). It was Denham who was persuaded to complete *Horace*—not so much, I think, by his current publisher, Herringman,[75] as by the young Duchess of Monmouth, who we know was on very friendly terms with him at this time.[76] That his translation was completed with a stage production in mind is evident, since his rendition of the remaining part of the play reduces Corneille's original by 25 per cent: from 458 lines to 346—just the kind of reduction we would expect if the play as a whole were being cut to manageable proportions for an actual performance.

Now enter one further major player in this little drama—none other than the King's principal mistress, the formidable Barbara Villiers, Lady Castlemaine. Now 26 years old, Lady Castlemaine (1641–1709) was not noted for her diffidence in matters of public representation. In Plate 98 we see her in one of Lely's great portraits, now at

[72] For references to the two Monmouths' patronage of a licensed troupe of actors and personal involvement in Court masques and theatricals in the 1660s (at least until the Duchess's accident on 8 May 1668, which left her lame), see, *inter alia*, Pepys, vi. 29 (a masquerade in 1665 featuring both Monmouths and Castlemaine); Allardyce Nicoll, *Restoration drama* (Cambridge, 1923; 4th edn., reprinted 1977), 314, 358; and Kenneth M. Cameron, 'The Monmouth and Portsmouth troupes', *TN* 17 (1962–3), 89–94. The lady in waiting Margaret Blagge recorded in her diary: 'go not to the Duchess of Monmouth above once a week, except when we dress to rehearse'; cited in Boswell, 130. An incidental connection between Monmouth and Katherine Philips is the versions of poems by her which he later copied in his pocketbook (now BL Egerton MS 1527): see Elizabeth H. Hageman and Andrea Sununu, 'New manuscript texts of Katherine Philips, the "matchless Orinda" ', *EMS* 4 (1993), 174–219 (pp. 209–14).

[73] Dryden published *The Indian Emperour* some months earlier with a fulsome dedication to the Duchess of Monmouth (dated 12 October 1667) in which he stresses her 'beauty', as well as her 'goodness', 'Virtue', and 'Honour' at Court. Pepys reports on 14 January 1667/8 that in the Court performance the day before, the Duchess was one of only two competent performers—who 'did do most extraordinary well' (Pepys, ix. 23).

[74] In the context of the Herringman folio, one wonders too whether an anonymous and lost play called *The poetess*, presented by the King's Company before the King himself on 7 October 1667, had anything to do with Orinda: see *The London stage 1660–1800*, part 1: *1660–1700*, ed. William Van Lennep (Carbondale, Ill., 1965), 119. The alternative is that it related, perhaps satirically, to the Duchess of Newcastle who made a memorable visit to London in the spring of that year—a suggestion made in Judith Milhous and Robert D. Hume, 'Lost English plays, 1660–1700', *HLB* 25 (1977), 5–33 (p. 15).

[75] By August 1667 Herringman was preparing for publication Denham's collected works, which were eventually entered in the Stationers' Register on 9 February 1667/8: see Brendan O Hehir, *Harmony from discords: A life of Sir John Denham* (Berkeley, 1968), 234–5. O Hehir suggests (pp. 235, 239) that Herringman persuaded Denham to finish off *Horace* so that a complete text could appear in his next edition of Philips's works (and see also Thomas, iii. 247–8). The second edition of Herringman's folio did not appear until 1669, however, and even then its general title-page made no mention of Denham's contribution.

[76] On 26 September 1667 Lord Lisle told Sir William Temple: 'Poor Sir John Denham is fallen to the ladies also. He is at many of the meetings at dinners, talks more than ever he did, and is extremely pleased with those that seem willing to hear him; and from that obligation exceedingly praises the Duchess of Monmouth and my Lady Cavendish' [i.e. Mary Butler, Lady Cavendish (1646–1710)], adding: 'if he had not the name of being mad, I believe in most companies he would be thought wittier than ever he was': *The works of Sir William Temple, Bart.*, 4 vols. (London, 1814), i. 459; cited in O Hehir, *Harmony from discords*, 242. The Lady Cavendish mentioned here was the second daughter of the Duke of Ormonde, Lord Lieutenant of Ireland, and was Katherine Philips's 'Polycrite'. One wonders whether she too contributed to the decision to stage *Horace*.

PLATE 98: Sir Peter Lely's portrait of Lady Castlemaine as the goddess Minerva (Collection of Her Majesty the Queen, Hampton Court)

Hampton Court.[77] Whereas Margaret Cavendish had herself represented under the auspices of Minerva, goddess of wisdom, the liberal arts, and heroic virtue (Plate 96), Castlemaine allows herself to be portrayed, characteristically, as the goddess herself, Minerva being traditionally the only goddess equal to Zeus (or Jupiter), her attributes—at least as seen in the Renaissance period—including her power wisely and

---

[77] A colour reproduction of this painting was used for the cover of the female verse anthology *Kissing the rod* (1988).

intelligently to guide authority to enlightened policy.[78] Through her privileged status and her power, Castlemaine could effectively appropriate the symbols of what Margaret Cavendish herself called 'Amazonian Government'.[79]

This Castlemaine also did, on the present occasion, by allying with her friend the Duchess of Monmouth,[80] by adopting, like her, one of the two leading female roles in *Horace*, by acting (so far as we know, for the very first time),[81] and by using this as an opportunity to reassert her authority before the whole Court.[82]

We know the cast for the performance since two manuscript cast-lists for it can now be identified—both inscribed in copies of the 1667 Herringman folio. One, written in a hand that can be identified as that of John Egerton, second Earl of Bridgewater (1622–89), is at Harvard (Plate 99);[83] the other, in an unidentified hand, is at Trinity College Dublin (Plate 100). Between them, these cast-lists give us a clear enough idea of most of the main players, although the few discrepancies between them (in the key role of Horace himself, as well as in the parts of Curtius and Valerius) are a salutary reminder to theatre historians that records of this kind, perhaps jotted down from imperfect memory or hearsay, cannot unquestionably be relied upon in every detail.

The parts may be seen to have been played by a group of young male and female courtiers predominantly within the Monmouth faction, or who had links of friendship (or more) with Lady Castlemaine. Captain Charles O'Brien (as either Curtius or Valerius, knights on opposite factions, both in love with the Camilla of Lady Castlemaine) was son of the Earl of Inchiquin and an officer in the King's Life Guard of Horse under Monmouth's command; he was serving in Monmouth's entourage in France but

---

[78] Sometimes erroneously described as representing Bellona, goddess of war (whose traditional depiction, with a whip, torch in hand, and dishevelled hair, is quite different), Lely's painting clearly represents Minerva, complete with her traditional helmet, plume, spear, and shield bearing the head of Medusa. For the Renaissance symbolism of Minerva, see Parry, 'Cavendish memorials', 275–87.

[79] Margaret Cavendish, 'To all writing ladies', in *Poems and fancies* (London, 1653); facsimile edition by Scolar Press (Menston, 1972), after p. 160 (sig. Aa^{r-v}).

[80] Castlemaine was on friendly terms with the young Duchess, as witnessed, for instance, by the incident in June 1667 when she and the King were 'all mad in hunting of a poor moth' at the Duchess of Monmouth's (Pepys, ix. 282; and see also ix. 469); moreover, her friendship with the young Duke of Monmouth is supposed to have alarmed the King into hurrying preparations for his wedding in order to withdraw him from her attractions. For general biographical accounts of Castlemaine, see, *inter alia*, G. Steinman Steinman, *A memoir of Barbara Duchess of Cleveland* (privately circulated, 1871), Philip W. Sergeant, *My Lady Castlemaine* (London, 1912), Margaret Gilmour, *The great lady* (London, 1944), Allen Andrews, *The royal whore* (London, 1971), and Elizabeth Hamilton, *The illustrious lady* (London, 1980); also, for lively comment on the power she exerted over Pepys, E. Pearlman, 'Pepys and Lady Castlemaine', *Restoration*, 7 (1983), 43–53, and related correspondence in vol. 9 (1985), 31–8.

[81] In this connection, one might wonder whether it was a coincidence that Lady Castlemaine was involved about this time (see Pepys, ix. 156) in a liaison with the greatest actor of his day, Charles Hart (a former keeper of Nell Gwyn), who, among other favours, might well have given her some tuition in acting, or at least in the art of declamation.

[82] Castlemaine had been Charles II's *maîtresse en titre* for seven years, having borne him five children—five at any rate that he acknowledged. Despite occasional gossip reported by Pepys that she was still as powerful at Court as ever she was (e.g. Pepys, ix. 27), there were also reports that the King was growing weary of her ('and would give anything to remove her; but he is so weak in his passion that he dare not do it': Pepys, viii. 432). Her position was not so secure that it could not benefit from a little positive reinforcement.

[83] This Bridgewater was brother of Alice, Countess of Carbery (1619–89), to whom one of Philips's poems is addressed (Thomas, i. 84–5, and see Hageman and Sununu, 'New manuscript texts', 180–3); both had performed as children in the John Milton–Henry Lawes masque of *Comus*. This cast-list was first cited in *LS* i. 128.

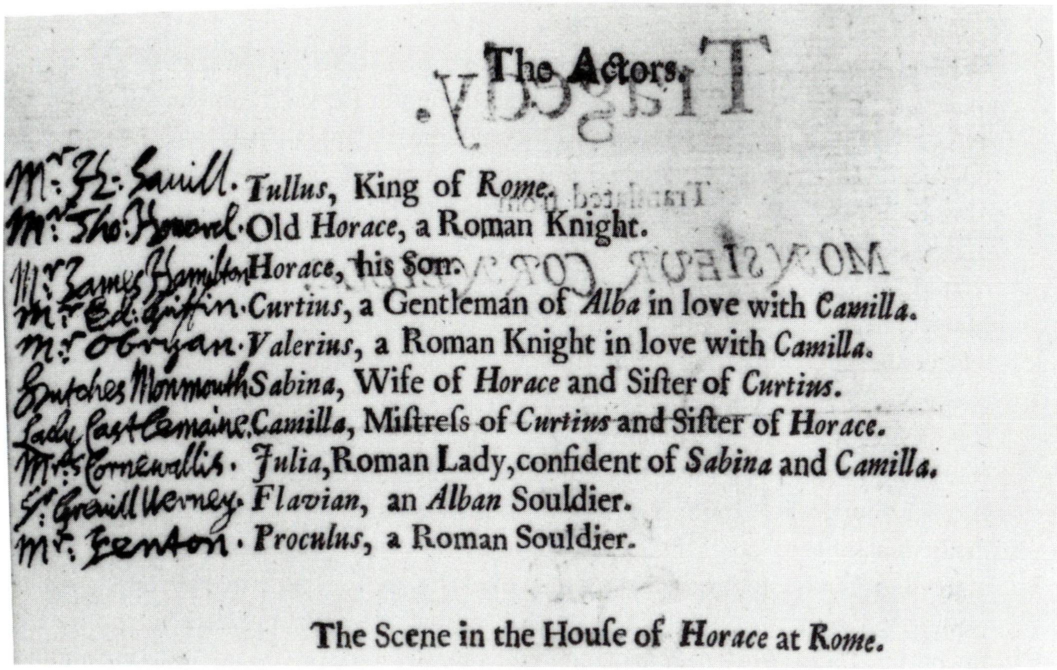

The Actors.

Mr H. Savill. Tullus, King of Rome.
Mr Tho. Howard. Old Horace, a Roman Knight.
Mr Barney Hamilton Horace, his Son.
Mr Ed. Griffin. Curtius, a Gentleman of Alba in love with Camilla.
Mr O'Bryan. Valerius, a Roman Knight in love with Camilla.
Dutches Monmouth Sabina, Wife of Horace and Sister of Curtius.
Lady Castlemaine. Camilla, Mistress of Curtius and Sister of Horace.
Mrs Cornewallis. Julia, Roman Lady, confident of Sabina and Camilla.
Sr Grevill Verney. Flavian, an Alban Souldier.
Mr Fenton. Proculus, a Roman Souldier.

The Scene in the House of Horace at Rome.

PLATE 99: Cast-list of *Horace* in a copy of Katherine Philips's *Poems*, 1667 (Harvard, Houghton Library fEC65.P5397.667p)

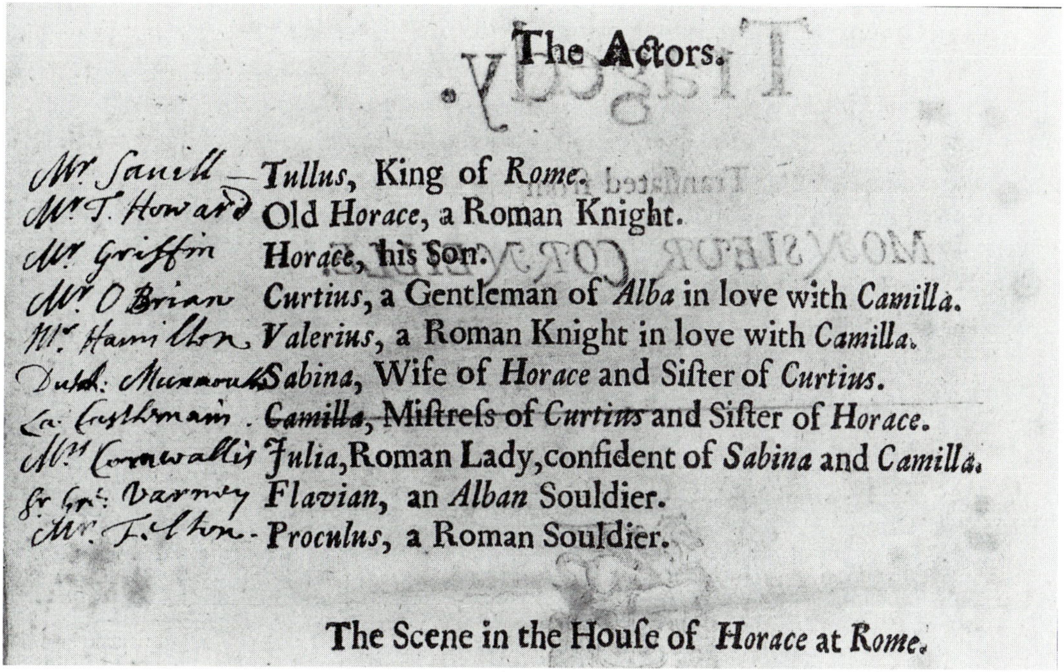

The Actors.

Mr Savill — Tullus, King of Rome.
Mr T. Howard Old Horace, a Roman Knight.
Mr Griffin Horace, his Son.
Mr O'Brian Curtius, a Gentleman of Alba in love with Camilla.
Mr Hamilton Valerius, a Roman Knight in love with Camilla.
Dutch: Monmouth Sabina, Wife of Horace and Sister of Curtius.
La: Castlemain Camilla, Mistress of Curtius and Sister of Horace.
Mrs Cornwallis Julia, Roman Lady, confident of Sabina and Camilla.
Sr Gr: Varney Flavian, an Alban Souldier.
Mr Felton Proculus, a Roman Souldier.

The Scene in the House of Horace at Rome.

PLATE 100: Cast-list of *Horace* in a copy of Katherine Philips's *Poems*, 1667 (Trinity College Dublin, Old Library V.ee.4, sig. Aaaa[v])

two weeks before the present performance, and he had also taken part in *The Indian Emperour* in the previous month, where, according to Pepys, 'he spoke and did well; but, above all things, did dance most incomparably'.[84] Mrs Cornwallis (who played Julia, confidante of both Sabina and Camilla) was a lady in waiting of the Queen Mother's household, and she too had acted well in *The Indian Emperour*.[85] Two others were the Earl of Carlisle's brother Thomas Howard (as the stern Old Horace), who was related to Lady Castlemaine through his marriage to the Duke of Buckingham's sister, Mary Villiers,[86] and Sir Greville Verney (as the soldier Flavius), both of whom had also recently been members of Monmouth's entourage in France.[87] The soldier and Groom of the King's Bedchamber James Hamilton (as either the young Horace or Valerius) had connections with Castlemaine in so far as he was earlier reported to have been enamoured of her.[88] Of the three remaining young courtiers, Henry Savile (as Tullus, King of Rome) was rumoured to be one of Castlemaine's old flames; he was Groom of the Bedchamber to James, Duke of York, and would later succeed Hamilton as Groom of the Bedchamber to the King; he would himself dabble in verse in due course; and he would later be remembered as the rakish crony and correspondent of the Earl of Rochester.[89] Edward Griffin (as either the young Horace or Curtius) was yet another Groom of the Bedchamber to the Duke of York and was, by all accounts, a familiar 'court coxcomb' and gambling and horse-racing companion of the King.[90] And Thomas Felton (as the Roman soldier Proculus) was an allegedly handsome man and also a Groom of the King's Bedchamber.[91]

With this assembly of noble young courtiers, *Horace* was presented before 'the whole Court' at Whitehall on the evening of Shrove Tuesday (traditionally a carnival day), 4 February 1667/8.[92] 'None but the Nobility [was] admitted to see it,' says one source[93]— and we know that these included both the King and Queen, as well as the disapproving diarist John Evelyn and the somewhat more approving Swedish Ambassador, Count Dohna, who observed 'the greatest pleasure and contentment' with which the performance was attended.[94] The assembled courtiers and dignitaries would also, presumably,

---

[84] Pepys, viii. 489; ix. 23–4; CSPD, 1667–8, pp. 178 *et passim*.   [85] Pepys, ix. 23.

[86] Anthony Hamilton, *Memoirs of the Comte de Gramont*, ed. Cyril Hughes Hartmann (New York, 1930), 348–9.

[87] CSPD, 1667–8, pp. 167, 178.

[88] Pepys, v. 21; *Memoirs of Gramont*, 347; *The Rochester–Savile letters 1671–1680*, ed. John Harold Wilson (Columbus, Oh., 1941), *passim*.

[89] For Henry Savile (1642–87), see, *inter alia*, *DNB*; *Rochester–Savile letters*; and various references in Pepys.

[90] *POAS*, i. 367.   [91] Wilson, *Court satires*, 238.

[92] Accounts of the performance cited here are found in the following sources: (i) John Starkey in one of his MS newsletters sent to Sir Willoughby Aston, Bt. (BL Add. MS 36916, f. 62r); cited in *LS* i. 129; (ii) John Evelyn's entry for 4 February 1667/8 in his autograph *Kalendarium* (now in the BL): see Evelyn, iii. 505; cited in *LS* i. 129; (iii) Official letter dated 8 February 1667/8 in the letterbook of the Swedish Embassy in London under Field-Marshal Christopher Delphicus von Dohna, Count von Dohna (1628–68) (BL Sloane MS 1974, f. 8v); cited in Ethel Seaton, *Literary relations of England and Scandinavia in the seventeenth century* (Oxford, 1935), 37–8; recorded in *LS* i. 129; English translation supplied by courtesy of Candy Winberg; (iv) Entry by Thomas Rugge in his autograph *Mercurius politicus redivivus*, vol. ii (BL Add. MS 10117, f. 218v); and (v) Lorenzo Magalotti's list of 'Poeti famosi in Inghilterra', printed in Crinò (ed.), *I letterati*, 14, 20.

[93] J. Starkey, BL Add. MS 36916, f. 62r.   [94] Count von Dohna, BL Sloane MS 1974, f. 8v.

have included Katherine Philips's old friend Sir Charles Cotterell (1612?–1702), who was still officiating at Court as the Master of Ceremonies, with his newly appointed assistant Peter du Moulin. One extant record of a tradesman's bill gives us the tiniest glimpse of the characteristic preparations made: 6 shillings 'ffor Twelue [extra] Latten' [yellow metal] Candlestickes for the Theater att Whitehall on Shrouetewsday att night'.[95] And we know also that the performance was interlarded with dances—"twixt each act a Masque & *Antique*: [was] daunced'[96]—a feature that would explain why the performance was described in certain chronicles as 'a great Mask'.[97]

The play was introduced by a striking Prologue, a manuscript copy of which is to be found at Trinity College, Dublin (Plate 101).[98] The Prologue was evidently spoken by a man (though not the Duke of Monmouth, since he had been sent on a mission to France at this time).[99] Its whole thrust was to prepare the way for the entrance of the women: indeed, to stress, in gallant vein, the whole importance of women—not least, Orinda herself, whose 'noble muse' brought Corneille's play 'to Brittain'

> And foreign verse our English accents taught.

Now, he implies, the present women will make *Horace* even better:

> And by our Ladyes he mounts higher yet.[100]

If the audience had any doubt about the ladies' power, it would have been dispelled when the Duchess of Monmouth immediately entered in the role of Sabina, and even more so when she was joined in the second scene by Lady Castlemaine, as her sister-in-sorrow, Camilla. Their impact was perhaps not so much because of their acting—though the lines did give Castlemaine opportunity to declaim, Minerva-like, suitably lofty sentiments about the Divinity which shone through in Kings[101]—but because of

[95] PRO LC 9/271, f. 67r; also cited in Boswell, 159–60. [96] Evelyn, iii. 505. [97] Rugge, *Mercurius*, vol. ii.

[98] One other text of the Prologue is known, headed 'Prologue to *Horace*, spoken by the *Dutchess of Munmouth*, at Court', in *Covent Garden drollery* (London, 1672); ed. Montague Summers (London, 1927), 62–3, and ed. G. Thorn-Drury (London, 1928), 80–1. This Prologue is also quoted elsewhere, notably in Gerard Langbaine, *An account of the English dramatick poets* (Oxford, 1691), 404–5, and in Thomas Pope Blount, *De re poetica* (London, 1694), 168. It is printed in Thomas, iii. 121–2.

[99] CSPD, 1667–8, pp. 171, 272. There is some confusion in reports on the speaker of this Prologue. Langbaine (*Account*, 404–5) refers to '*Horace* . . . acted at Court, by Persons of Quality; the Duke of *Monmouth* speaking the Prologue', an account repeated as item 276 in the *H* section in *Biographia dramatica; or, A companion to the playhouse* by David Erskine Baker, continued by Isaac Reed and Stephen Jones, 3 vols. (London, 1812), ii. 310. In fact, Monmouth set sail for Dieppe on 16 January and did not return to England until 21 March 1667/8. Mention of the Duchess of Monmouth in the 1672 printing is almost equally unlikely for the reasons here given, and evidently arises from the persistent association of this performance with the Monmouth group.

[100] The only interesting variants between the MS and 1672 printed texts are the changes in line 15 from 'Orinda's noble muse' (MS) to 'Orinda's matchless muse' (1672)—and cf. n. 69 above—and in line 28 from 'Our Basilisks could shoot them from the Stage' (MS) to 'Our Basilisks, could shout 'em from the Stage!' (1672).

[101] For instance:

> For the same Gods guided our Princes choice,
> Nor speak they often in the Peoples voice;
> Their Counsail shines not in a vulgar brest;
> But Kings that represent them, know it best.
> In whose supream authoritie, we see
> A secret Ray of their Divinity.
> (III. iii. 11–16: Thomas, iii. 158.)

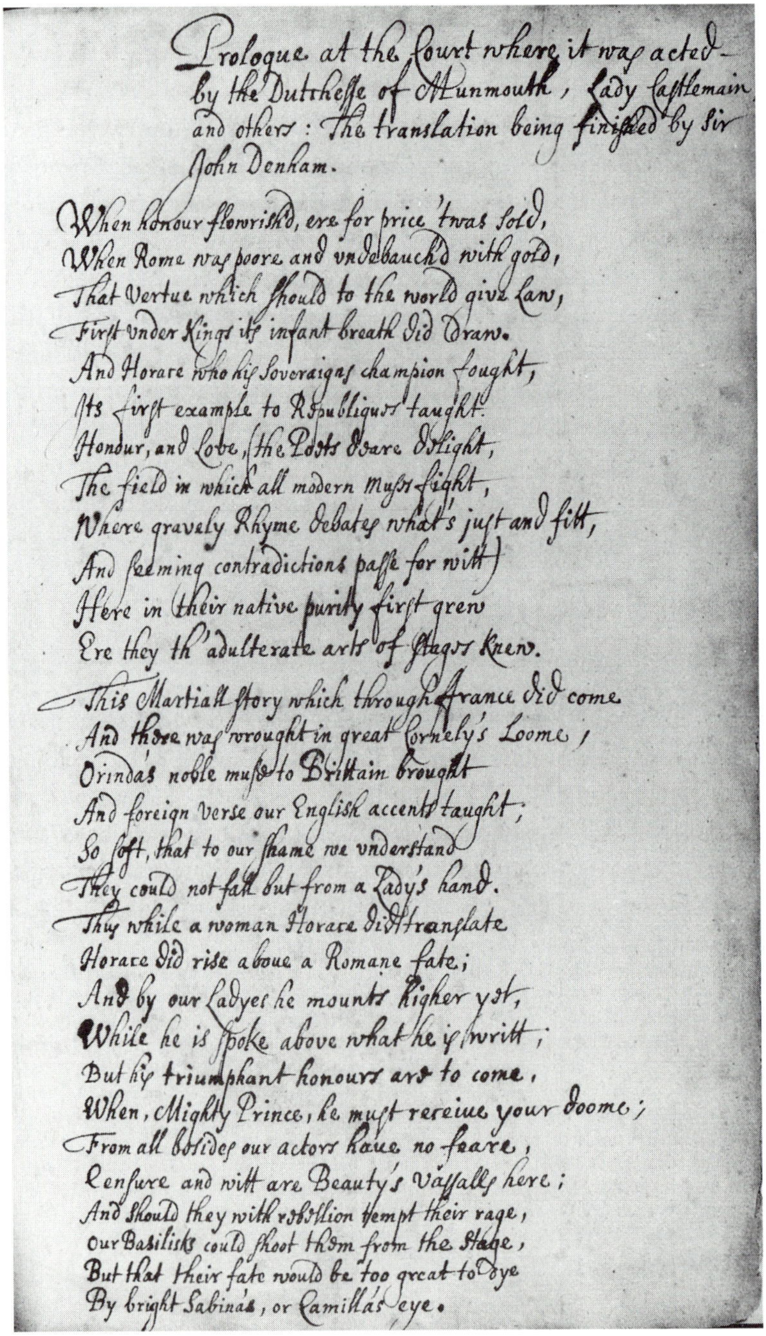

Prologue at the court where it was acted
by the Dutchesse of Munmouth, Lady Castlemain
and others: The translation being finished by Sir
John Denham.

When honour flowrish'd, ere for price 'twas sold,
When Rome was poore and undebauch'd with gold,
That Vertue which should to the world give law,
First under Kings its infant breath did draw.
And Horace who his Soveraigns champion fought,
Its first example to Republiques taught.
Honour, and Love, the Poets deare delight,
The field in which all modern Muses fight,
Where gravely Rhyme debates what's just and fitt,
And seeming contradictions passe for witt)
Here in their native purity first grew
Ere they th'adulterate arts of stages knew.

This Martiall story which through France did come,
And there was wrought in great Cornely's Loome;
Orinda's noble muse to Brittain brought
And foreign verse our English accents taught;
So soft, that to our shame we understand
They could not fall but from a Lady's hand.
Thus while a woman Horace did translate
Horace did rise above a Romane fate;
And by our Ladyes he mounts higher yet,
While he is spoke above what he is writt;
But his triumphant honours are to come,
When, Mighty Prince, he must receive your doome;
From all besides our actors have no feare,
Censure and witt are Beauty's vassalls here;
And should they with rebellion tempt their rage,
Our Basilisks could shoot them from the stage,
But that their fate would be too great to dye
By bright Sabina's, or Camilla's eye.

PLATE 101: Prologue to *Horace* in a copy of Katherine Philips's *Poems*, 1667 (Trinity College Dublin, Old Library V.ee.4, after p. 112 at end)

their astonishing appearance, Castlemaine's above all. The scandalized John Evelyn records: 'The excessive galantry of the Ladies was infinite'—meaning the display of *jewellery* they were wearing. 'Those especialy on that < > Castlemaine', he says—he leaves a blank before 'Castlemaine', meaning, perhaps, 'that unspeakable', but much more likely 'that whore', a word he cannot bring himself to write: 'those especially' on her were 'esteemed at 40000 pounds & more: & far out shining the Queene &c.'[102] Other accounts of Castlemaine's jewellery and attire are even more extravagant. She 'Apeared in a dress of dimonds & pretious stones', wrote one chronicler;[103] and in a satire a few weeks later, addressed to her as patroness of the London whores and brothels, she is represented as saying: 'Splendidly did we appear upon the Theatre at Whitehall being *to amazement* wonderfully deck'd with Jewels and Diamonds, which the (abhorred and to be undone) Subjects of this Kingdom have payed for'.[104] It is even reported that she was 'adornd with Jewells to the Value of 200000ll. the Crowne Jewels being taken from the tower for her'.[105] The Crown Jewels? The very symbols of monarchal power itself? Even Charles II, who did not scruple to subject Queen Catherine to the indignity of his Court mistresses, might have hesitated to allow one of them to proclaim quite so ostentatiously that his women really did rule at Whitehall! Nevertheless, these very exaggerations of report may be symptomatic of what a stir the spectacle did in fact make.[106]

Nor can one resist adding a coda to this account. For, besides all else, Castlemaine was motivated by jealousy and a spirit of revenge. At the Court performance of *The Indian Emperour* a month earlier, on 14 January, the audience included the King's recently acquired mistress, the actress Moll Davies, to whom, according to Pepys, he had presented 'a ring of £700, which she shews to every body, and owns that the King did give it her'. The King gazed on her during the performance, he says, and Lady Castlemaine was

---

[102] Evelyn, iii. 505.   [103] Rugge, *Mercurius*, vol. ii.

[104] *The gracious answer of the most illustrious lady of pleasure, the Countess of Castlem[aine] to the poor whores petition*, a printed broadside satire in the persona of Lady Castlemaine allegedly 'Given at our Closet in Kingstreet Westminster, Die Veneris April 24, 1668' [Wing G1472; BL pressmark: C.45.k.4 (5)]; reprinted in Steinman, *Memoir*, 104–11. This satire was a response to the serious apprentice riots of Easter 1668, for which see Tim Harris, 'The Bawdy House Riots of 1668', *HJ* 29 (1986), 537–56.

[105] J. Starkey, BL Add. MS 36916, f. 62r.

[106] We might concede the possibility that the King gave or lent Castlemaine some jewellery out of the Jewel House (though there are no surviving records for this period to corroborate this). We know that his gifts for theatrical purposes could be quite spectacular on occasions, such as in October 1661 when he gave his Coronation suit—a fairly resonant symbol of regal power—to Thomas Betterton to use at the new playhouse in Lincoln's Inn Fields: see John Downes, *Roscius Anglicanus* (London, 1708), 21. He was also remarkably generous to Lady Castlemaine on other occasions, such as on 29 August 1667 when he ordered 5,600 ounces of silver plate borrowed by her from the Jewel House to be new made in accordance with her instructions and delivered to her as a free gift of the King: CSPD, 1667, p. 425. While it is most unlikely that Castlemaine would have been given any of the actual regalia (crown, orb, sceptre, staff, or sword of state), she might just conceivably have been allowed to wear jewels taken *out* of the Crown. Nevertheless, the reports of this are probably as exaggerated as the figures of £200,000 or even £40,000 mentioned by Rugge and Evelyn; for the cost of the entire new set of Crown Jewels made by Sir Robert Vyner in 1661 was only £21,978 9s. 11d. (or possibly even no more than £12,050 3s. 5d.): see relevant accounts in Sir George Younghusband, *The Crown Jewels of England* (London, 1919), Lord Twining, *A history of the Crown Jewels of Europe* (London, 1960), 150–2, and Martin Holmes and H. D. W. Sitwell, *The English Regalia* (London, 1972). Besides all this, it seems unthinkable that Castlemaine would not have had her portrait painted wearing this attire to commemorate this remarkable distinction had it occurred, and none of her many extant portraits shows such features.

'melancholy and out of humour, all the play, not smiling once'.[107] So her 'excessive gallantry' in *Horace* was in part a flamboyant response—a characteristic gesture of 'one-upmanship'—to the £700 ring which her rival had displayed to all the Court!

So followed the enactment of a potentially powerful drama[108] in which two families are compelled to fight each other despite various members on both sides having conflicting interests of love and honour. After the young Horace (either Hamilton or Griffin) has been heroically upbraided by his wife Sabina (the Duchess of Monmouth) for killing both her brother Curtius (either Griffin or O'Brien) and his own sister Camilla (Lady Castlemaine)—a speech which elicits Horace's declaration on the strange 'Empire' which such 'weak assailants' as 'Women' should have over 'Man's Soul'[109]— King Tullus (Savile) steps forward to resolve a totally insoluble human dilemma as only a sanctioned monarch can. Responding to Valerius' appeal for justice ('since the powers above does Kings intrust, | To distribute below what's fit and just'),[110] Tullus imposes a general reconciliation and, in conclusion, signals the restoration of order and harmony by calling for a 'dance'.

He then speaks the Epilogue: one which reinforces the whole impetus of the Prologue *and* of the performance just witnessed. I have found this in two manuscript texts—again, both written in copies of the 1667 Herringman folio: one in the Victoria and Albert Museum (Plate 102); the other once again at Trinity College, Dublin (Plate 103).[111] Savile as Tullus steps forward, to lay down, as it were, his assumed crown before the real Crown present in the audience, and declares:

> Our Author's credit, and Translator's fame
> Have soar'd above the reach of any blame.
> Our beauteous Ladyes though in meaner dresse,
> What e're they do can neuer want successe.
> We onely doubt, and begg your gracious doome,
> For Six poor Subjects, and one King of Rome;
> If any else dare say we acted ill,
> Our Ladyes take our part, and they can Kill.[112]

---

[107] Pepys, ix. 24. A somewhat amusing perspective on the scale of the King's present is provided by Pepys's rather glum reckoning a month later that a valentine ring for his cousin was likely to cost him £4 or £5 (Pepys, ix. 67–8).

[108] No one who saw Sydnee Blake's production of Corneille's *Horace* in a new blank-verse translation by Alan Brownjohn at the Lyric Theatre Studio, Hammersmith, between 2 and 19 October 1996, will have any doubt about the extraordinary power which Corneille's tragedy *can* exert. How this, for the most part, softly spoken, relatively realistic, unadorned, and intense representation of Corneille's tightly constructed tragedy would compare with the Baroque, rhetorical presentation of 1668 one can only imagine!

[109] Thomas, iii. 250 (Denham's translation).   [110] Ibid. 253.

[111] The Dyce text was recorded in my *Index*, ii/2. 138. It was printed in Thomas, iii. 91, where it is mistakenly relegated to *Pompey*, a confusion which the discovery of the Dublin text helps to clear up. The only substantive variant in the two texts occurs in line 4, where the Dublin MS says 'As ample pardon' instead of the Dyce MS's 'As ample freedome'.

[112] This Epilogue slightly echoes the Epilogue to Dryden's *The Indian Emperour*, published in October 1667. Cf. the last four lines:
> Last, for the Ladies, 'tis *Apollo's* will,
> They should have pow'r to save, but not to kill:
> For Love and He long since have thought it fit
> Wit live by Beauty, Beauty raign by Wit.

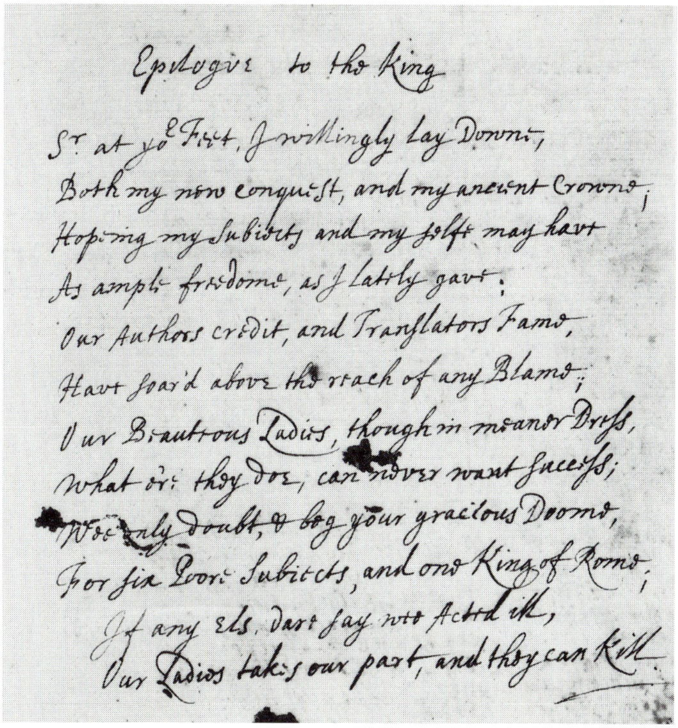

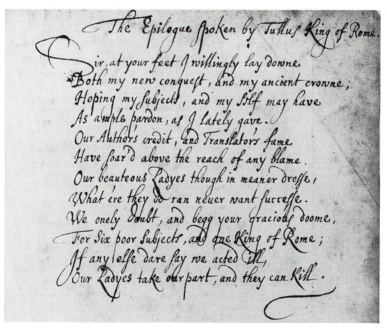

PLATE 102: Epilogue to *Horace* in a copy of Katherine Philips's *Poems*, 1667 (Victoria & Albert Museum Dyce Catalogue No. 7416)

PLATE 103: Epilogue to *Horace* in a copy of Katherine Philips's *Poems*, 1667 (Trinity College Dublin, Old Library V.ee.4, after p. 112 at end)

Within less than twelve months, Katherine Philips's *Horace* had made its final descent into a fully public sphere—from the Royal Court to the London playhouse. The King's Company presented it at the Theatre Royal in Bridges Street on at least six occasions, between 16 January and 15 February 1668/9—two of them attended again by the King, once with the Queen.[113] Mary Evelyn could report that the play 'takes'—meaning, 'is successful'—but, as she says herself, it was presented 'with a farce and dances betweene every Act, composed by [John] Lacy and played by him and Nell'.[114]

Pepys, of course, is more to the point:

[Tuesday the 19th] . . . and so to the King's House to see *Horace*; this the third day of its acting—a silly Tragedy; but Lacy hath made a farce of several dances, between each act, one. But his words are but silly, and invention not extraordinary as to the dances; only some Dutchmen come out of the mouth and tail of a Hamburgh sow. Thence, not much pleased with the play.[115]

So had it, then, come to this? From a serious, lofty, neo-classical tragedy by Corneille, transformed into English verse with scrupulous attention to accuracy of interpretation by Katherine Philips in the last year of her life—completed by Sir John Denham in, as it happens, virtually the last year of *his* life[116]—to, finally, a truncated production, enlivened for London audiences by the relief of dancers coming out of the head and backside of a pig—and now in the hands of the King's new mistress—the 'popular', Protestant, Cockney one: Nell Gwyn? It would seem, indeed, that Katherine Philips had made an accurate prediction, in January 1663/4, when she had seen the consequences of the unauthorized printing of her works—which condemned her 'unfortunate person . . . to play the Mountebank, and dance upon the Ropes to entertain all the rabble'.[117] This was the ultimate, maybe inevitable, fate of an author who surrendered control of her texts: who did become *public*.

No, this was not Orinda's apotheosis on the stage. But perhaps that Court performance a year earlier *was*.

There is some irony in that Lady Castlemaine should be the subject of one of Katherine Philips's last known letters—written on 22 January 1663/4 to Dorothy Osborne. Reflecting on the power-struggle at Court between Castlemaine and her current rival, Frances Stuart, Philips comments, with sententious irony, on Castlemaine's recent conversion to Roman Catholicism—'a religion', she says, which provides 'Ladys of her Morallity' with 'soe many shorter ways to heaven then repentance'.[118] Censure, yes,

---

[113] *LS* i. 153–6. Writing to her uncle Herbert Aston on 16 January [1668/9], Elizabeth Cottington described it as 'a new play, which was never acted but by the lady Castlemaine' (BL Add. MS 36452, f. 83r; cited in *Kissing the rod*, 233).

[114] Mary Evelyn to James Tyrrell, 10 [or possibly 20] February 1668/9 (in two letterbooks: BL uncatalogued Evelyn Papers 9 and a 'Mrs E' folder of fragile material).

[115] Pepys, ix. 420.

[116] Denham died in March 1668/9. One of the overseers of his will was his good friend the Royalist propagandist Sir John Berkenhead (1617–89), Katherine Philips's 'Cratander'.

[117] Thomas, ii. 129.   [118] Ibid. 141.

and in a sense it cuts to the essence of Castlemaine and her public representations—she who had the sanctioned power to bypass normal morality and, in effect, appropriate to herself 'virtues' she never had; she with the heroic energy and wisdom of Minerva (never having been near either a battlefield or a Council of State); she with the chastity and philanthropy of St Barbara and St Catherine, not to mention the Madonna (other roles she adopted, or accepted, on canvas).

Yet, even so, how could Castlemaine—the star of the Court; the most powerful *woman* there—more powerful than the Queen (whose 'galantry' she symptomatically outshone);[119] more powerful than the patroness Katherine Philips had sought, the Duchess of York;[120] Castlemaine, a woman who, both by physical, sexual attraction and by aristocratic status, as well as by her concomitant right to public representation, personified everything that the plain, bourgeois Katherine Philips was debarred from—how could Castlemaine *not* have exercised some measure of fascination on a woman of so aspiring, so politically conscious a disposition as Philips, however much she disapproved of her morally?

True, on that Shrove Tuesday evening of 1668, Castlemaine *had* in some measure appropriated a work by Orinda for her own political purposes. True, high art had, in some degree, been vulgarized—even prostituted, perhaps. The 'virtuous' Mrs Philips, as Evelyn implied, fully recognizing the irony of the situation—'virtuous' in the moral sense—was in the hands of the arch royal courtesan herself,[121]—who was unashamedly free to flaunt *her* 'virtues', her power or *virtù*, in public, just as she pleased.

But if Katherine Philips's ghost was present on that occasion—as it surveyed the whole English Court gathered to see *her* play; as it heard *her* lines, or most of them, delivered by some of the most glittering stars of that firmament; as it saw *her* drama reach the ultimate audience to which she could ever have aspired in her lifetime: on the stage at Whitehall, where she was openly proclaimed to be a 'noble', famous writer, whose very authorship was invoked to lend distinction to the performance—as her ghost experienced all this, one cannot help suspecting that its reactions would not have been wholly negative. Whatever other sensations it might have felt, there would, surely, have been no little sense of pride, of vindication, and, yes . . . perhaps even of triumph.

[119] Evelyn, iii. 505.

[120] Ironically enough, Anne Hyde had also converted to Catholicism. Her father, the Earl of Clarendon, to whom Lady Castlemaine had proved an implacable enemy, had been dismissed from his office as Lord Chancellor on 30 August 1667.

[121] Evelyn, iii. 505.

APPENDIX I

Seventeenth-century characters of clerks and scriveners

This is a selection of notable 'characters' and other treatments of clerks and scriveners of various kinds that I have come across, arranged chronologically according to publication or approximate transcription date (though the date of composition may be considerably earlier in some cases). The selection excludes a multiplicity of passing allusions to scribes which can be found in many other poems, plays, and prose works, as well as many related 'characters' (of lawyers, attorneys, moneylenders, brokers, 'extortioners', 'pettifoggers', and so on). In the case of some particularly lengthy works, relevant extracts only are reproduced.

1. Thomas Dekker

THE BELL-MANS second Nights walke
[A description of the Hall where matters are tried in Hell]

... The causes decided here are many; the Clients that complained many; the Councellors (that plead till they be hoarse,) many; the Attorneys (that runne vp and downe,) infinite: the Clarkes of the Court, not to be numbred. All these haue their hands full; day and night are they so plagued with the bawling of Clients, that they neuer can rest.

The Inck where-with they write, is the bloud of Coniurers: they haue no Paper, but all things are ingrossed in Parchment, and that Parchment is made of Scriueners Skinnes flead off, after they haue beene punished for Forgerie: their Standishes[1] are the Sculs of Usurers: their Pennes, the bones of vnconscionable Brokers, and hard-hearted Creditors, that haue made Dyce of other mens bones, or else of periured Executors and blind Ouer-seers, that haue eaten vp Widdowes and Orphanes to the bare bones: and those Pennes are made of purpose without Nebs, because they may cast Inck but slowly, in mockery of those, who in their life time were slowe in yeelding drops of pitty ...

[Extract. By Thomas Dekker (1572?–1632). From chapter 2 of his *Lanthorne and candle-light. or The bellmans second nights walke* (London, 1608), sig. Cᵛ. Reprinted from the 2nd edn. (1609) in *The non-dramatic works of Thomas Dekker*, ed. Alexander B. Grosart, 4 vols. (for private circulation, 1885), iii. 171–303 (pp. 205, 207–8). Forms chapter I in a slightly emended version in *English villanies* (London, 1632).]

---

[1] Standishes] inkstands or inkwells.

2. Thomas Dekker

The Gull-groper

This *Gul-groper* is commonly an old Mony-monger, who hauing trauaild through all the follyes of the world in his youth, knowes them well, and shunnes them in his age . . . If my yong Estrich gape to swallow downe this mettall (& for the most part they are very greedy, hauing such prouander set before them) then is the gold powred on the board, a Bond is made for repaiment, at the next quarter day when *Exhibition* is sent in, and because it is all gold, and cost so much the changing, The Scriuener (who is a whelpe of the old Mastiues owne breeding) knows what words will bite, which thus he fastens vpon him, and in this Nette the Gull is sure to be taken (howsoeuer:) for if he fall to play againe, & loose, the hoary Goat-bearded Satyre that stands at his elbow, laughes in his sleeue . . .

[Extract. By Thomas Dekker. From chapter 3 of his *Lanthorne and candle-light* (1608), sigs. D2ᵛ–3ʳ. Grosart edn., iii. 222–3; *English villanies* (1632), ch. II.]

3. Thomas Ravenscroft(?)

The Scriueners seruants Song of Holborne

MY master is so wise, so wise, that hee's procceded wittall,[2]
my Mistris is a foole, a foole, and yet tis the most get-all.
Let the Vsurer cram him in interest that excell,
their pits enough to damme him before he goes to hell.
In Holborne some: In Fleetestreete some:
where eare he come, there some, there some,
Where eare he come,
where eare he come,
theirs some, theirs some.

[Complete text. Author uncertain; musical setting by Thomas Ravenscroft (1592?–1635?). From his *Melismata: Mvsicall phansies. fitting the covrt, citie, and covntrey hvmovrs to 3, 4, and 5. voyces* (London, 1611), among 'Citie conceites', No. 12, sigs. D3ᵛ–4ʳ.]

4. John Stephens

A Lawyers Clarke

Is his Masters right hand, except hee writes with his left:[3] or the second dresser of Sheep-skinnes: one that can extract more from the parchment, then the Husband-man from the Fleece. He is a weake Grammarian; for hee beginnes to peirce, before he can construe well: witnesse the Chamber-maid. Neither can you discommend him: for his best education hath beene at a dull

---

[2] wittall] wittol: a man who is aware of and complaisant about the infidelity of his wife; a contented cuckold (*OED*).
[3] *with his left*] i.e. left-handed, characterized by underhand dealings (*OED*).

Writing-schoole. hee doth gladly imitate Gentlemen in their garments, they allure the Wenches, and may (perhaps) provoke his Mistresse: but then hee must bee a Customer to Cookes shoppes, and low Ordinaries,[4] or visite the Broaker, to be-speake Silke stockings; without which hee thinkes *Gentry* doth much degenerate: presuming on *which*, and his plausible discourse, he dares attempt a mistresse: but if hee chooses worthily, hee feeles himselfe worthily contemned, because hee woes with bawdery in text; and with Iests, or speeches stolne from Playes, or from the common-helping *Arcadia*. Hee may bee reasonably commaunded by his maister in attendance: but if he rides with a Cloake-bagge, he thinkes himselfe disgraced behinde his backe. Howsoever, he is otherwise a peaceable companion: for as hee continually makes agreement, to himselfe sits quietly, by his owne Embleme of meeknesse, the sheeps-skinne; except the itch troubles him. You can make no question that he is not ignorant to dispatch readily; for he hath his businesse at his fingers end. Hee may pretend *Schollership*, but all *that* is nothing to a Iugglers, who exceeds in the slight of hand; which is the Art of both. Hee trembles therefore alike with all *Handicrafts*, (though he be most valorous) to thinke he should dare stocke in't the court: for vpon his Palmes and Fingers depend his *In-comes*. Hee is no vaine Disputant; his knowledge is positiue ingrossed, and so vpon record. *Selfe-conceit* in labours, hee refuses: for hee labours about nothing which is not iustifiable by *Presidents*; either of *West*,[5] his master, or a teacher. His Poetry is meere naturall, if he hath any; that costs him no labour: in carriage, and the rest, hee barely imitates; that labour is worth nothing. Hee is not ashamed of what he doth: for he regards not to haue a finger, but a whole hand in the businesse. To which purpose you may see his name subscribed in Court, after *sealed* and *delivered*. Hee doth relye vpon his masters practise, large indentures, and a deske to write vpon. *Westminster* likewise doth not altogether not concerne him: hee hath a motion *thither*, and a motion *there*: thither hee moues by way of iniunction from his Master: there he moues in the common place of breake-fasts, for reliefe of his stomacke; and if hee can match his breake fast and dinner without grudging of his stomacke, hee hath his desire. Hee is a follower: for he weares a livery; but no seruant, for hee payes his owne wages. Serving himselfe, he serues God by occasion: for whilst hee loues his gaine, and serues his desire of getting, hee hates idlenesse. If his master thriues, hee cannot doe amisse; for hee leades the way, and still rides before: but if hee incline to the consumption of state, hee needes a master that can thriue in that practise also, to recover him. Hee is the Sophister, or Solliciter to an Atturney; and from himselfe hee proceeds to an Atturney: that is his commencemente.

[Complete text. By John Stephens (*fl*.1611–17). From his *Satyrical essayes characters and others, or accurate and quick descriptions, fitted to the life of their subiects* (London, 1615), 275–9 [Murphy, 28–29 (a)].]

5. John Stephens

A crafty Scriuener

Is the curse of mans crafty dealing, a curious workeman, and may be free of the Locke-smithes,[6] for full of Instruments hee is, and Engines: and makes Manacles for any mans wearing aboue Twenty One. His first ambition commonly is to ioyne forces, and make vp his defects of policy, and custome by

---

[4] Ordinaries] eating-houses or taverns.

[5] *West*] *Symbolaeographia, which may be termed the art, description, or image of instruments, covenants, contracts, &c., or the notarie or scriuenor* (London, 1590) by William West (*fl*.1568–94), a standard legal textbook which went through many editions.

[6] *free of the Locke-smithes*] a freeman (having served his apprenticeship) in the guild of locksmiths.

partaking in anothers proiects: then doth hee readily aspire to frequented places, a conuenient shop, the notice of his neighbours, and to engrosse credit, or some text Widdow, by the *nouerint* of his Grogren Gowne:[7] A common strumpet neuer fawned so much on yong heire, as hee with flattery obserues the Vsurer, and with nice dutifull care to preserue him, makes his rotten hide, the chief Indentures that containe his Title. Obligations be his best prayers; for hee cannot tie God to performe conditions, or put in suertyship: his friendship hath a *Counter mand* of being too honest; which hee will obey, rather then not saue by the bargaine. Hee is the safest man from danger in the pedigree of rapines; for first, the gallant liues by sale and Country Tenants; the Cittizen by the Gallant; the Scriuener and the deuill vpon both, or all: So neither liues by losse with the Gallant, nor vpon trust, with the Citizen: his condemnation is a knot of *Seales* and their *Impression*: the first discouer to him a conformed vnity; yet none hath more hand in the procuring of variance. The last discouers a tractable nature, which *giues* and *takes* impression. Of the first (that is to giue) he knowes no meaning but when he giues the print of his fist, that it may sticke by elder brothers a whole age. Of the last (that is to take impression) hee knowes none but a wrong meaning: for the best seale that imprints loue in him, is onely the Kings picture; and that loue continues no longer then he beholds it. His quils and instruments betoken peace: you cannot therefore expect more valour in him, then to win ground by the aduantage of weake Prodigals, and such as runne away from thriftinesse: they be most importunate with him: with them hee preuailes most: to them he sets his extortious nature at the highest value, because they be most willing to make it their peny-worth. His memory is his owne; another cannot safely trust it in reckoning the day of payment: for he reckons what he can saue, by renewing the hazard of a second forfeit, not your losse by the first: and so he ouer-reaches you, by ouer-reaching the time, when you trust his memory: which (like an old ridden Iade) lookes not to the Iourneies end but to the baiting place, though he goes further then the iournies end: If you trust him therefore you may feele the forfeite, and pay largely for an acquittance. His learning iumps iust with, or fals sometimes short of an Atturnies; being onely able to repeate the *afore-said* form to thousand purposes: So all his mistery is indeed nothing to encrease his *Art*, but his *Policy*, or plaine knauery: And that, being serued in, to the worlds banquet, represents a large foxes head, and a little Sheepe-skinne in diuers dishes. It is the totall of his Creed, that nothing should bee iustified, or called lawful, which hath not hand and Seale: that makes him exercise *Hand* and *Seale*, as the warrant for deuises of his *head* and *Soule*. He neuer rayses the spirit of a *Prodigall* by charmes, but he together rayses the spirit of mammon a Citizen, and then this potent coniurer binds them both fast in a *Quadrangle*. Hee will seeme to know the Statute and common Law; but the construction failes commonly (for he looks to his owne aduantage) except the Law hath practised vpon his hearing, to teach the comment when he mistakes the Law. Hauing at length beene a long Auditor to the sweete lecture of Vsury, hee loues the matter so well, that he becomes proficient, graduate, and professour in the Science but after generall profession hee approaches quickely to his center (from whence he sprung) *Nothing*.

[Complete text. By John Stephens. From his *Satyrical essayes characters and others* (1615), 284–91.]

---

[7] the *nouerint* of his Grogren Gowne] the advertising or showiness (*noverint* = 'let all men know') of his grogram gown (a gown made of a course fabric of silk mixed with mohair or wool).

6. Anonymous

A Puny-clarke

He is tane from *Grammar-schoole* halfe codled, and can hardly shake off his dreames of breeching in a twelue-month. Hee is a Farmers sonne, and his Fathers vtmost ambition is to make him an *Atturney*. He doth itch towards a Poet, and greases his breches extreamely with feeding without a napkin. He studies false dice to cheate Costermongers, & is most chargeable to the butler of some *Inne of Chancery*, for pissing in their Greene-pots.[8] Hee eates Ginger bread at a Play-house; and is so saucy, that he venters fairely for a broken pate, at the banketing house, and hath it. He would neuer come to haue any wit, but for a long *vacation*, for that makes him bethinke him how hee shall shift another day. He praies hotely against fasting; and so hee may sup well on Friday nights, he cares not though his master be a Puritan. He practises to make the words in his *Declaration* spread, as a Sewer doth the dishes at a Niggards Table; a Clarke of a swooping *Dash*, is as commendable as a Flanders horse of a large taile. Though you be neuer so much delai'd, you must not call his Master knaue; that makes him go beyond himselfe, and write a challenge in Court hand; for it may be his own another day. These are some certaine of his *liberall faculties*: but in the Terme time, his *Clog* is a *Buckrom bag*. Lastly, which is great pitty, hee neuer comes to his full growth, with bearing on his sholder the sinfull burden of his Master at seuerall Courts in *Westminster*.

[Complete text. From *New and choise characters, of seuerall authors: Together with that exquisite and unmatcht poeme, The wife, written by Syr Thomas Ouerburie* (London, 1615), sig. K2ʳ⁻ᵛ [Murphy, 17–19 (e)]. Edited (from the 'ninth impression' of *Sʳ Thomas Ouerbury his wife*, 1616) in *The miscellaneous works in prose and verse of Sir Thomas Overbury, Knt. now first collected*, ed. Edward F. Rimbault, LL D. (London, 1890), 113–14.]

7. Anonymous

A Diuellish Vsurer

. . . Hee can be no mans friend; for all men he hath most interest in, he vndo's: and a double-dealer he is certainely; for by his good will hee euer takes the forfaite. He puts his money to the vnnaturall Act of generation; and his Scriuener is the superuisor Bawd to't. Good Deedes he loues none, but Seal'd and Deliuered . . . He hates all but Law-Latine; yet thinkes hee might be drawne to loue a Scholler, could he reduce the yeere to a shorter compasse, that his vse-money might come in the faster . . . Grauitie he pretends in all things, but in his priuate Whore; for he will not in a hundreth pound take one light six-pence . . . The Table he keepes is able to starue twenty tall men; his seruants haue not their liuing, but their dying from him; and that's of Hunger. A spare Dyet hee commends in all men, but himselfe . . .

[Extracts. From *New and choise characters, of seuerall authors* (1615), sigs. L5ᵛ–6ᵛ. Complete text edited (from the 1616 'ninth impression') in Rimbault edn., 133–5; Murphy, *Cabinet*, 107–9. Adaptations of

---

[8] Greene-pots] green-glazed earthenware was commonly used in the Inns of Court and Chancery: see L. G. Matthews and H. J. M. Green, 'Post-medieval pottery of the Inns of Court', *Post-Medieval Archaeology*, 3 (1969), 1–17.

this character were later published, as 'Vn vsurier' (in French), in James Dymocke, *Le vice ridicule et la vertu louée* (Louvain, 1671), 248–52 [Murphy, 78–83], and, as 'A covetous griping usurer and extortioner', in Anon., *The character of a Whig, under several denominations* (London, 1700), 113–15 [Murphy, 92–3].]

8. Anonymous

A Creditour

. . . He is the bloud hound of the law, and hunts counter very swiftly and with great iudgement . . . He is a lawyers moyle and the onely Beast vpon which he ambles so often to Westminster and a lawyer is his God Almighty in him onely he trusts, to him he flyes in all his troubles . . . A Scriuener is his farrier and helps to recouer all his diseased and maymed obligations . . . He is a knaue trap-baited with parchment and wax, the fearefull myce he catches are debtors, with whom scratching Atturneyes like cats play a good while and then mouze them, The belly is an vnsatiable creditour but man worse.

[Extracts, from *S*ⁱ*ʳ Thomas Ouerbury his wife*, 'ninth impression' (London, 1616), sigs. R4ᵛ–6ᵛ [Murphy, 20–1]. Complete text in Rimbault edn., 160–2.]

9. John Heath

A broking Scriuener is a Barbersurgian.

Who in his Apprenticehood being brought vp to the Art of *Polling*,⁹ is now made free of the *Shauers*.¹⁰ He hath his Shop fully furnisht with most rare and cunning *Instruments*. His chiefe customers consists of Vsurers and mad-men, which mad-men he so hampers, keeping them *fast bound*, that in six Moneths many of them recouer their wits againe. He begins to haue some practise in Phisicke; for, [i]f any young Gentleman be troubled with a *loosenesse*, he can giue him a *bynding potion*: and againe, if he be bound, he can minister vnto him a *purging pill*, that shall fetch an extraordinarie quantitie of *yellow stuffe* from him. He neuer mist of his cunning but once, when looking into the Market-place through a *window*, he lost one of his eares, and neuer since could be cured.

[Complete text. By John Heath (*fl. c.*1585–1619). From *The hovse of correction: or, Certayne satyricall epigrams, written by I.H. Gent. together with a few characters* (London, 1619), sig. D3ᵛ [Murphy, 124].]

10. John Heath

On a Scriuener.

I Told a Scriuener of his Briberie,
His Broking, Forging, Cheating, Knauery,

⁹ *Polling*] meaning extortion and plundering and also hair-cutting.
¹⁰ made free of the *Shauers*] made free of the guild of barbers or surgeons (with a pun on 'shavers', meaning swindlers).

He sayd, he heard me not; so't may appeare,
How could he heare, that had no Eares to heare?

[Complete text. By John Heath. From his *The hovse of correction* (1619), sig. C4ʳ.]

11. Robert Hayman

A Scriuener on a Trotter

Scriueners get most by riding trotting horses,
Copper-Ars, and Gall,[11] for Inke towards their losses.

[Complete text. By Robert Hayman (*c*.1579–1631?). From R.H., *Qvodlibets, lately come over from New Britaniola, Old Newfovndland* (London, 1628), book I, No. 58, p. 9.]

12. Anonymous

A Charector of a London Scriuenor

A London Scriuenoʳ is the deerest childe of his Mother Mony, yet spurious and dares not acknowledge his father Mouʳ: Dyablo. The Corruption of many conduceth to his generation, & like to a Phoenix he is raised out of the ashes of others: He is Pandor to his Parents & discouers theyre shame for there is no match that hee makes for them that muste not Bee knowne vnto all men. Hee is brought vp after the nobliest way at his languages and weapons & can wᵗʰ a goose quill giue the best swordman a *Venny* & a foyle too. And though a gouneman he is noe great Scholler yet trades much in Lattine. Hee is a Good Text man & conuersant in scripture & proues the lawfullnes of his profession from Gods own wordes *crescite & multiplicamini*[12] wᶜʰ he applyes to Myneralls and his owne conscience. He likes the Lawe better then the Gospell for howeuer his quallityes bee his conditions are good in Lawe, though they may suffer some question in equity. Hee approues (as the Text of moste comforte in the Gospell) the Parrable of the Tal-lents, his Relligion serues hym to expounde that place [of *deleted*] according to the Annalogie of his owne ffaithe and [conscience *deleted*] charity. Hee likes not the euangellicall counsell: Owe nothinge to any man but Brotherly loue for that holdes noe correspondency Wᵗʰ his profession. He is an excellent Mecannick and can wᵗʰ a parchments Chaine binde the strongest man & his Heyres too. He can compas more Lande wᵗʰ halfe a Shipskin then Dydo got for hyr Byrsa of Hyarbas.[13] His Wife was the Daughter of som ritch Vseror whom hyr ffather['s] good husbandry had kept longe vnmarried that he mighte by that match rather hope for propogation of his mony then any issue of hyr body howeuer beegotten. But if a more curious peece she was then caste

---

[11] Copper-Ars, and Gall] copperas, protosulphates of copper, iron, or zinc used in the manufacture of ink, as is gall, a substance from trees; both terms subject to puns here (gall also meaning bile or an essentially bitter substance).

[12] *crescite & multiplicamini*] Be fruitful and multiply (Genesis 2: 28).

[13] He can compas more Lande wᵗʰ halfe a Shipskin then Dydo got for hyr Byrsa of Hyarbas] Queen Dido purchased from local inhabitants on the African coast as much land as could be covered by a bull's hide, cut into thongs; upon this she built the citadel of Byrsa, centre of her new city of Carthage. Iarbus was the King of Mauritania who threatened to wage war on Carthage.

uppon hym by some ritch Batchelo[r] to saue the charges of Midwiues Nurses and Education, and his mony is his stocke of credit in the Towne. His Wife to ad perfection to hyr husbands Profession putts all to vse too and hyr Husband is noe loser by it: And thus in his Shopp w[ch] is the Gentlemans house of Correction for this tyme ile leaue hym expectinge more the reapeale of the laste Acte of Parlyament for theyre reformation then his owne saluation.

[Complete text from BL Add. MS 25303, ff. 183v–184r, a miscellany possibly compiled by a member of one of the Inns of Court and perhaps originally presented to Thomas Darcy, Viscount Colchester (*c.*1565–1640); *c.*1620s–1630s.]

13. Francis Lenton

A Lawyers Clarke,

Is a spruce youth somewhat aboue the degree of a Scriuener, much conuersant amongst sheets & skins, Subiects he works vpon much, & is a kind of a Iugler, who by slight of hand, will suddenly make a cleanly conueyance of your estate, that you shall not afterwards need to study how you may prodigally spend it; and he will so contriue it by president, that he will make you an example whilest you liue. Hee is one who will doe more with a gray Goose wing, than euer *Robin Hood* could doe, and is very dangerous, if once hee puts his hand to't. Foure pence a sheet hath furnisht him with a new Suit, and he sometimes executes the place of a Gentleman-vsher vpon his Mistris. Hee is a man generally of no solidity, except by his much costiuenes with contunuall sitting, yet a man of great study, insomuch it hath so stupified him, that he lookes for his pen when it stickes in's eare. Littleton[14] is too obscure for his capacity, and not one amongst forty of them can reade Law French. He is commonly a good fellow, and loues to gaine no more than hee meanes to spend. Hee hath a peece of *Iudas* his office, (the Carriage of the Bagge,) which were it ful of Peeces, as it is of Papers, hee might chance to shew his Master a tricke for't. Hee aspiers sometimes to his Masters daughter, but being stau'd off there, hee choppes vpon the Chambermaid, and there stickes fast. He hath lookt for preferment till age hath dimm'd his eyesight, and is now enduouring to goe Clarke of a Band in the next voluntary Voyage; which if hee speed, the Leagre so belouzeth him,[15] that hee returneth with much Humility, and poorely prostrates himselfe for a halfe-penny a sheet. He is a meere Clarke without any other quality, and hath seldome any commendation, but hee writes a faire hand.

[Complete text. By Francis Lenton (*fl.*1620s–1640s). From F. L. Gent., *Characterismi: or, Lentons leasvres. expressed in essayes and characters, neuer before written on* (London, 1631), No. 13, sigs. [C7[v]–9[r]] [Murphy, 48–9].]

---

[14] Littleton] The *Tenures* of Sir Thomas Littleton (1422–81), a standard legal textbook which, with various commentaries, went through many editions from the late 15th century onwards.

[15] the Leagre so belouzeth him] the leaguer (military camp or siege, with a possible pun on 'ledger') so bellows (blows or blasts) him.

14. Wye Saltonstall

A Lawyers Clearke

His father thought it too chargable to keepe him at Schoole til he could read *Harry Stottle*, and therefore preferd him to a man of Law. His maister is his genius, and dictates to him before he sets pen to paper. If he be to make a Bond or Bill, for feare of writing false Latin, he abbreviates the ending and termination of his word with a dash, and so leaves it doubtfull. He sits nigh the dore to give accesse to strangers, and at their going forth gives them a legge in expectation. His master is a cunning jugler of lands and knowes how to convay them underhand, hee onely coppyes them over againe, and lookes for a fee for expedition. His utmost knowledge is the names of the Courts and their severall offices, and begins after a while like a Pie that has his tongue slit, to chatter out some tearmes of Law, with more audacity than knowledge. At a new play hee'le be sure to be seene in the threepeny Roome, and buyes his pippins before he goes in, because hee can have more for mony. When hee heares some stale jest (which he best apprehends) he fils the house with an ignorant laughter. He weares cutfingerd dogskin gloves, for his ease, or the desire of bribes makes his hands grow itchy. In the vacation his master goes into the countrey to keepe Courts, and then hee's tide to a Cloakebagge and rides after him. He cals himselfe the hand of the Law, and commends the wisedome thereof, in having so many words goe to a bargaine, for that both lengthens them, and makes his fees the larger. Hee would faine read *Littleton*[16] if he might have a comment on him, otherwise hee's too obscure, and dotes much on *Wests* Symboliography[17] for teaching him the forme of an acquittance. In his freshmanship he hunts after cheape venerye, and is in debt to the Cooke, for Eele pyes on fasting dayes, and friday nights. The corruption of him is a weake Atturney, then he trafiques with countrymens businesses, and brings them downe a bill of charges, worse than a Taylers for a suite in the last fashion, and here we leave him, for now hee's at the highest.

[Complete text. By Wye Saltonstall (*fl.*1630–40). From his *Picturae loquentes. or Pictures drawne forth in characters* (London, 1631), No. 11, sigs. D2ᵛ–3ᵛ [Murphy, 50 (a)]. Edited from 2nd edn. (1635) in Murphy, *Cabinet*, 223–4.]

15. Wye Saltonstall

A Scrivener

Is a Christian Canniball that devoures men alive. He sits behinde a deske like a Spider in a Cobweb to watch what flies will fall into his net. He abuses money by using it, and so contrary to the nature thereof puts it to generation, while like a common whore, hee lets her out to trading. He lookes so thinne that a man may picke a good stomacke out of his face, and he wishes his belly were a lether bagge that so being once full it might never be empty. He will lend money upon good security, and then you must pay for procuring and ensealing of writings, and the utmost extremity is his friendship. Besides this he is so impudent in his Art of undoing others, that hee begins with *Noverint universi*, let all men know it. He is a Scribe by profession, for he devoures widdowes houses,[18] and a Pharisee in his religion, for though he doe no good, yet he loves good

---

[16]   *Littleton*] see n. 14 above.   [17]   *Wests* Symboliography] see n. 5 above.
[18]   he devoures widdowes houses] Matthew 23: 14, etc.: see n. 26 below.

deedes in Parchment. Hee has no signe but a few tottering Labells, which are hang'd there to shew their masters desert. Country fellowes admire him, and his pen is better to him than their Plough; while the parchment is the soyle, money is the seede, and usury the harvest which he reapes, and brings dry into his Coffer which is his Barne. He workes upon the occasions of other men, and his Bonds are like flyes in winter, which lye dead for a time, but afterward recover life, and contrary to other things, they have most force when they are ready to expire. He is no scholler yet is a great writer, and is never confuted, but in the Chancery or Star-chamber and there his fallacies are discern'd, and he punished. He will feede you with hope of money till your necessity is growne so urgent, that you are willing to yeeld to any conditions, and then he will worke you like waxe, and make you buy your owne undoing. He has blanckes ready to insert names, and in drawing of writings hee will leave out some materiall clause, that so it may occasion a suite in Law. Discord is his delight, and hee cares for no musicke but telling of money. He loves Almanackes because they shew him the day of the moneth, and the yeare of our Lord, and he is alwayes in the future tense, hoping for time to come. To conclude his life is so blacke that no Inke can paint it forth, he is one of the Devils engines to ruine others, he is a paper worme, or a racke for honest men, and his *Vltimum vale*[19] is a deceitfull breaking.

[Complete text. By Wye Saltonstall. From his *Picturae loquentes*, 2nd edn. (London, 1635), No. 33, sigs. G6ᵛ–8ᵛ [Murphy, 50–51 (b)]. Edited in Murphy, *Cabinet*, 220–2.]

16. Anonymous

On a Scriuener

Here to a period is the Scriuener come
This is his last sheet; his full point this tombe
Of all aspersions I excuse him not,
'Tis plain hee liu'd not without many a blot.
Yet hee no ill example shew'd to any;   5
But rather gaue good coppies vnto many.
Hee in good letters hath been allway bred,
And hath writ more then many men haue read.
Hee rulers had at his commaund; by law
Allthough hee could not hang, yet he could draw.   10
Hee farre more bondmen had, or made then any:
A dash alone of his pen ruin'd many;
That not without good reason wee may call
His letters (great or little) capitall.
Yet is the scruener's fate as sure as iust: 15
When hee hath all don, then hee falls to dust.

[Complete text from Bodleian Library MS Eng. poet. f. 27, p. 196, a miscellany, *c*.1630s. Other slightly variant versions are in Corpus Christi College, Oxford, MS 328, f. 58r; Dr Williams Library MSS 28.49, p. [2 rev.]; and *Witt's recreations* (London, 1640), Epitaph No. 36; reprinted in *Facetiae*, ed. Thomas Park and Edward Dubois (1817), new edn. by J. C. Hotten, 2 vols. (London, 1874), ii. 270 (No. 175).]

---

[19] *Vltimum vale*] 'last farewell'.

17. Anonymous

The pens prosopopeia to the Scrivener

Thinke who when you cut the quill,
Wounded was yet did no ill;
When you mend me, thinke you must
Mend your selfe, else you're unjust
When you dip my nib in Inke,   5
Thinke on him that gall did drinke,
When the Inke sheds from your pen,
Thinke who shed his blood for men;
When you write, but thinke on this,
And you ne're shall write amisse.   10

[Complete text from *Witt's recreations* (London, 1640), No. 463; also reprinted in *Facetiae* (1874), ii. 26–7 (No. 56).]

18. Anonymous

On a Scrivener

May all men by these presents testifie
A lurching[20] Scrivener here fast bound doth lie.

[Complete text from *Witt's recreations*, 2nd edn. (London, 1641), Epitaph 30; also reprinted in *Facetiae* (1874), ii. 236 (Epitaph 49).]

19. Thomas Jordan

A Usurer

Be it known to all men by these Presents, that   1
This great Extorter, was a spurious Brat . . .
. . . Him and a Conjurer, Sathan doth fool   65
Alike, they both are practiz'd in one School:
The sweet Sin makes his Intellect so dim,
He thinks he hath the Devil, when he hath Him;
The Scrivener, and the Broker, are his two
Assisting Suffragans, that must undo   70
The sliding Knots, of such mens Fortunes which
Contemn the paltry Pride of being Rich . . .

[Extracts (lines 1–2, 65–72 out of 80 lines). By Thomas Jordan (*c*.1620–85?). From T. J., *Pictures of passions, fancies, & affections. Poetically deciphered in variety of characters* (London, 1641), sigs. D1ᵛ–2ᵛ [Murphy, 53].]

---

²⁰ lurching] 'characterized by forestalling others at meals, gluttonous . . . pilfering' (*OED*).

20. **Samuel Butler**

A Scrivener

Is a writer of great authority, and one whose works are for the most part authentic; for if he be discover'd to have committed a fault he expiates the offence with his ears, as *Caligula* made the bad writers of his time do theirs with their tongues. He dashes the latter end of *Latin* words always, and the middle of *English*. He puts out other mens money & his own to nurse together, takes brokage for both, and if either miscarry knows how to secure his own, and with *Solomon's* harlot to lay claim to the live child. If he be dextrous at *Short-hand*, his pen is like the tongue of a ready speaker, as *David's* tongue was of a ready writer. He is the usurer's pimp, that *procures* statute, bond, and mortgage to satisfy his insatiable desire of getting. One of his chiefest talents is to discover exactly and readily how able any man is to be trusted, and upon a good occasion to help him pass muster with the usurer for a valuable share in the purchase, and to cast up suddenly, according to the desperation of the debt, what is justly due for procuring, as the present rates go. He has a table of use upon use in his memory, and can tell readily what a penny let out in the *Conqueror's* time would amount to this present year. He is very skilful at his weapon, and has most certain & excellent guards against the sword of Justice; and knows how to defend his money & his ears against all penalties of the law, in despight of all it can do or say to the contrary. When he deals with a small usurer, whose custom he does not greatly care for, he will let his money lye dead in his hands, until he admits of such security, as he can be best paid to approve of. His employments should be virtuous, for they lye between two contrary vices, Avarice & prodigality, both which he serves in their several ways, until the lean one has devour'd the fat, and he had his share of both. He stretches parchment with his tongue, as shoemakers do leather with their teeth, and multiplies words to no purpose, but to increase the bulk of the instrument; this he calls drawing, that is drawing it out at length.

[Complete text. By Samuel Butler (1612–80). From the transcript belonging to Robert Thyer (1709–81) of Butler's lost autograph MS, in BL Add. MS 32626, f. 138r; also edited in Butler's *Characters and passages from note-books*, ed. A. R. Waller (Cambridge, 1908), 256.]

21. **Jeremiah Wells**

A London Scrivener

Is a Creature begot by a *Pen*, and hatcht up in an *Ink-pot*. Lesser stuff serves to *his* production, then to a *Country Pedler's*: the wing of a Goose sets up forty of them. His *Gown* is curs'd to a perpetual *Autumn*, hence 'tis ever bare, and has as little *woo'l* upon it, as if at next remove it were to be made *Parchment*; his *Ears* hang on like rotten fruit, the least unkind blast of a Passenger blows them off; his Ink is *Poyson* had it neither *Gall* nor *Copprice*;[21] he looks like the *by-blow* of a *Country Attorny*, from whom he differs as a *Botcher* does from a *Taylor*. The *Attorny* may have the honour to go to Hell on *horse-back*, while the base knave fairly *foots* it after him. With Relation to the *Common-wealth* he is a *necessary Evil*, without whom men would grow *honest* and *friends*, and then the *Body Politick* must needs fall, being no longer compounded of different *Elements* and

[21] *Gall* nor *Copprice*] see n. 11 above.

Humours. Better *Schollers* there are many, but few greater *Writers*: and those that have cursed the Invention of the *Press* for *others* sakes, may more justly do the same to that of the *Pen* for *his*. I should guess his Trade of very great *Antiquity*, since *I* read *God* made *Indentures* of *Covenant* with *Adam*,[22] but that we know *Adam* had no *money*, and the *Scrivener* would not do it *Gratis*. Beside, had *God* made *Scriveners*, he would never have pronounced of the seven days work, that all was *good*. Had *Scriveners* bin in the *old World*, it had saved the *Deluge*, and accursed Mankind had destroyed one another. A *surreptitious* race of men, not of *Gods Creation*, but born (like *Vermin*) out of the *corruption* of several *Ages*, (or like some *Africk* Monsters) the *Amphibious* product of a *Heterogenous* Copulation: for when Persons of *different Interests* and *humours* met together in a Contract, this *Jarring Conjunction* begat *Scriveners*, who at first (*Viper-like*) devoured their *Parents*, and have ever since (like a *Wolf* in the side) gnaw'd their *Livelyhood* out of the *bowells* of those they hang upon. Methinks they should be banished all well governed *Kingdoms*; or at least (like *Jews* in *Italy*) wear a mark of *distinction* about them, like persons that dwell in *Infected houses*, that endangered Passengers may see and avoid them. Where they once get in, they spread like the *Itch*, and become as universal as the *Sickness*; had a *Scrivener* bin among the *Israelites*, there needed no other punishment to have forced them out of *Egypt*: They themselves had bin the *greatest Plague*, and *Pharaoh* would have *fled*, not *pursued* them into the *bottom* of the *Sea*. A Generation of men able to *enter* into the *Devil*, the onely thing more unsatiate then *Hell*: some men pretend to *fear* and *honour* them, but 'tis as men Court their *Hangman*, for a more *favourable Execution*; or as the *Indians* Worship the *Devil* and the *Spaniard*, that they may do them the *less harm*. When he is *examining* an *Estate*, you would imagine him *casting* its *water* to find what disease it labours of, and to be sure (like a Knavish *Chirurgeon*) he will either *find* a Cure of it, or *make* one. Sometimes he plays the *Baud*, prostitutes the same *Title* to all commers, and (if you fee him soundly) will not stick to Mortgage the *same* Estate for you to *seven* several Persons: sometimes he *solders* a *crackt* Title, and passes it away for a pure *Maiden head*; if it be *weak*, he dares strengthen it by Forgery; and secure but his *Ears*, his *man* and *he* (two *Knights* o'th' *Post*) shall out-swear the *Devil*. If you would make a safe *Purchase*, you must spend half the value of your Land in *searching* the *Title*: then he tells you, your Estate is *secured*, that is the best part of it to *himself*. But all the flaws he finds in the Title, may be stopt up with money from the *adverse party*: if *both* fee him soundly, then, that he may deal equally between man and man, he makes them *alike miserable*, drawing the conveyances on either side so *weak*, and yet so *strong*, that *neither* party shall have the *advantage*; but *both* endeavouring to *recover* what *each* knows to be his *own*, and *he* to be *neithers*, they at last *waste* away their Estates (like a *Snow-ball*) with *handling* it, spend *double* the *purchase-money* to *secure* the *Land*, and the *Usurers* (to end the strife) *seize* on that which *each* of them have *Mortgaged*, and *neither* can *redeem*. Then the *Usurers* part stakes, and so *lim* and *canton* out a brave *Estate*, (like *Alexanders Empire*) into *petty Lordships*. If he deale in *mony*, his *Usurer* and *he*, are like the *Hunter* and his *Dog*, (or to speak in their own Phrase) they answer each other, as the *Counter-part* and *Original Indenture*: then (like the *Devil*) he walks up and down seeking whom he may devour;[23] does his best endeavour to make your poor, that you may be forc't for *supply* to *him*, who is the *last remedy*, and indeed worse then the *disease*. If you would *borrow*, he marches to your *Neighbours*, enquiring into your *Estate*, and smelling at your *Reputa-*

---

[22] *God* made *Indentures* of *Covenant* with *Adam*] This assertion would seem to have no biblical justification, God's first recorded covenant being with Noah after the Flood, signified by the rainbow (Genesis 9: 8–17). The writer is presumably taking liberties in order to set up his next point; and see also pp. 7–8 above.

[23] (like the *Devil*) he walks up and down seeking whom he may devour] 'your adversary the devil, as a roaring lion, walketh about, seeking whom he may devour': 1 Peter 5: 8.

tion, spoyling your *good name* to gain you *credit*. He is for maintaining *old Customes*, and (among the rest) for that of *ten* in the *hundred*, and what now a dayes *bate* the *Usurer*, you must *pay* the *Scrivener*. If his *Usurer* and *he* chance to start a *young Heir*, he is employed, like the *Hound*, to pursue the *Game*, which he never leaves till he hath given him a *Mortal gripe*: then like the *Lyon* and the *Jackall* they *divide* the *Prey*; the *Usurer gnaws off* all the *flesh*, and the *Scrivener picks the bones*. To strike the greater terrour into the *Novice*, he seats himself in all his *Formalities*, his furr'd *Cap* and *Gown*, his *Pen* to *one Ear*, (if *both* be not off for *Forgery*) in the mid'st of a company of *Writings*, the *Cases* of so many undone persons, a sight worse then the *Gallowes*, able to extort *Confession* without the help of a *Wrack*, composing his *Countenance* after the gravest Mode, *dreadfully ridiculous*, and most *Majestically simple*, when after a tedious *harangue* (like a *Dog* making a *circle* before he lies down) of the ill fortunes of those young men which fall into the hands of *Knavish* Scriveners, (where he reads him his own Doom in the *third* Person) and of *his happiness* in lighting on him (where to understand him rightly, he must read him *backwards*) telling him how desirous he is of his *prosperity*, seeing to *hang* upon him to *prevent* his *ruine*, (when 'tis as a *weight* hangs on a *Clock*, to drive him on *faster*; (or as an *Angler*, seeming to *draw away* the baite, that he may the more *greedily take it*) at last he falls upon that he hath most mind to, his *estate*: Desires him to deal plainly, and lay open his *case*, as a *sick man* does to his *Physitian*, that he may the better *Cure* him, whereas 'tis really like the *Baring* a man's breast to his *Enemy*, that he may the surer *wound* him: while my *Youngester*, not daring to do otherwise, deals (*God* knows) very *simply* and *honestly*: the *Scrivener* mean time, like an *Inquisitor*, stretching him upon the *Wrack*, writing down his *Confession*, out of all which he draws up a *Sentence*, miscalled a *Bond* or *Conveyance*: and when he hath wound him up to the *highest peg*, and perceives him pumpt quite *dry*, he lets him *down*, presents him a *paper*, makes him Sign and Seal the Warrant of his own *Execution*: and then by *Law Condemns* and *Executes* him. This unmerciful *Thief* robs the very *Beggar*, and sticks not to pick a *Courtiers* pocket, though he knows 'tis the *Kings mony*. He is so strict a Prosecuter of Justice, that he maintains it beyond the utmost *rigour*; stretches *Justice her self* upon the *wrack*, and upon an *hours failure*, seizes more then the *forfeiture*. He prays for *Non-performance* of the Condition, that he may take the Advantage of the *Penalty*: and exceeds so far in Cruelty, that cursed *Jew*, that he will have not the *flesh* alone, but the *blood* too.[24] When you have incurr'd a *forfeiture*, he tells you the *exactness* of the *Law*, and to be secure from the *Usurer*, you must compound with the *Scrivener*, and almost *pay* the *Penalty* to be *freed* from it. But when he has *Bound* you never so fast, for *mony*, he will *Release* you; teach you to *evade* the Articles himself *composed*, content so he may be a *Knave*, to prove no *Scrivener*. Thus he plays *fast* and *loose*, breaths *hot* and *cold*, and the same *Devil* that *binds* the Charms, *unties* them too. 'Tis a pretty sight to see them running about the *Exchange*, *smelling* at the *Merchants*, just like *Dogs*, *fawning* upon *some*, and *biting* others. If any be in his *Books*, he sticks to him like a *Remora*,[25] a sufficient *Lett* to his weightiest *affairs*; and while his *Vessel* suffers *Shipwrack abroad*, he himself splits on a more dangerous *Rock*, enchanted by these *Syrens at home*. A Plague worse then *Pirates*, *Shipwrack* it self cannot *save* you from them: your very *Convoyes* (your *sureties*) *protect* you not from them, but *secure* you the faster to them. No *mony*, which secures you from a *Theif*, will not save you from *him*: he is *one* misery after the very *last*, the cause of our *ruine* and the *effect* too: when all other misfortunes have *destroyed* us, he follows as a *reserve*, and after *Execution quarters* us. When all the *World* has *shaken*

[24] that cursed *Jew* . . . *blood* too] see Shakespeare's *The Merchant of Venice*.

[25] *Remora*] 'The sucking-fish . . . believed by the ancients to have the power of staying the course of any ship to which it attached itself' (*OED*).

you *off*, he *seizes* you; *Lice* and *Scriveners* stick fast unto you when you are *beggard*. If a man *wade* innocently into the *muddy streams* of *Suretyship*, he is suddenly seiz'd by these *Leeches*, which once *fastened*, will never leave sucking till he *faint*, or they *burst* and *die*. He has a great stroke at *killing* men; a miserable *comforter* of *languishing* patients; one of those *ill-bodeing* creatures that *haunt* houses against a *time* of *Death*; a *Devil* that comes to *torment* men *before* their *time*. While the *Divine prepares* you for *Death*; and the *Physitian hastens* it, he does *both*. Like the *Hangman*, he first *disrobes* you of your *outer garments*, and then *kills* you. That you may go to *Heaven* the *lighter*, he disburdens you of your *Earth*, your *Estate*, and then *perswades* you out of *despair* to *die*, having parted with all the *World*, and nothing now left you to forsake, but your *body*. For a good Fee, he will do a *friend* a *Courtesie*, and leave the intended *Heir* so disputable, that the *deceased Testator* may as soon interpret his own mind as the *Lawyer*: inserting such *equivocal* terms, as may be interpreted to be *any mans Will* more then the *Testators*; rendring the sense as *amphibious* as that of the *Oracles*; and indeed like the *last words* of *dying man*, *ambiguous* and *unintelligible*. If he *foist* in a good Legacy for *himself*, he knows 'tis *past discovery*; 'tis but *skipping* it in the *reading*, and the Will *sealed* up till the *Testators Death*, who can *betray* him? Thus he *Cheats* you *In the Name of God*, and says his prayers *backwards* indeed, *beginning* his *Rogueries* with an *Amen*: so that you sign a *blank* though it be full of *Writing*, and this your most *Voluntary* act is yet *against* your *Will*. He begins very *piously*, and bequeaths your first Legacy, your *Soul*, with a great deal of *Complement* to *God Almighty*; to whom he *commends* you with as much form of *expression* and abundance of *significant* words, as if he made *Indentures* with the *Almighty* to receive you, and would be sure he should find no *starting holes* to *evade* the *Articles*. And he makes your *Will* like a *Pharisees long prayer*, with a *house* at the *end* of it.[26] When he has done, he *turns* you over to the *Divine*, before whom he has commonly the honour to be *preferred*, and there he leaves you like a *Christmas box*, expecting no more out of you till you are *broke*. To conclude, like the *Mullet* his *blood* is *Ink*; 'tis the *skin* of a *Sheep*, not the *wooll* that *cloaths* him, and a *Goose quil*, not the *flesh*, that *feeds* him. 'Tis one of the last trades men can fly too, indeed the *very last*, being but a more *noble Theivery*, a *gentiler* way of *picking pockets*: a *ruined* Persons last *refuge*, where he *revenges* his *destruction* by *repaying* it: being himself *undone*, he strives to *ruine* others; and like a right *Devil*, draws as many as he can into that *hell* where himself ha's *perished*. But I have made a *Character* as long as an *Indenture*; I leave him with the *prayer of all good People*, that he may be *poyson'd with his own Ink*, *stab'd* with his *Penknife*, his *Ears* remaine in the *Pillory*, his *Nodle* set out at the *Shop-door* for a *Loggerhead*, and the *rest* of him hang'd up to *Eternity* in a *Label*; and since it is impossible he should get to *Heaven*, for *Hell's sake* may he *hang between*.

[Complete text. By Jeremiah (or Jeremia, Jeremias, or Jeremy) Wells (1646–79), Fellow of St John's College, Oxford. From his *The character of a London scrivener*, printed anonymously, with separate title-page, after Abraham Cowley's *Poems upon divers occasions* (London, 1667), 129–37 [Murphy, 145]. An adaptation and abridgement of this character was later published, as 'A wheedling cheating scrivener', in Anon., *The character of a Whig, under several denominations* (London, 1700), 115–21.]

---

[26] he makes your *Will* like a *Pharisees long prayer*, with a *house* at the *end* of it] 'Woe unto you, scribes and Pharisees, hypocrites! for ye devour widows' houses, and for a pretence make long prayer': Matthew 23: 14; and cf. Mark 38: 40 and Luke 20: 46–7.

22. Richard Head

The Scrivener

The *Scrivener* being already ingeniously dissected, in a *Character* not long since Printed,[27] I shall forbear Killing him again, but only give you a short Account of some remarkable Passages in his Life and Conversation.

Upon his first starting into the World, having but little moneys in his hands of his own, or others, being but a young man, and moneyed men fearful of trusting him, he is forced to employ what he hath by him to the best advantage; and like an honest man that intends to thrive in this World, though he be damn'd for it forever in the World to come, he first tries how widely his Conscience will stretch, and, if he finds it hide-bound, he will pinch it with his teeth, as a Shoomaker his leather, but that he will make it give way . . . If the Sum were any thing considerable, though he had the money by him, yet he would make use of his accustomed delays, though he knew the Borrower responsible, and would not part with a farthing, till he had made enquiry after that he knew as well as any man could tell him; and in the end must have *Procuration* for his own money, and if *Continuation* be required, he shall pay sauce for it. Though the Law allows but six *per Cent*.[28] yet he knows several ways to make forty, by making in the first place a *Bond* which shall be due to a Confident of his, a Prisoner in the *Kings Bench*, and recovering the penalty at *Common-Law*, leaves the poor Debtor to sue for relief in *Chancery* one that is a Prisoner . . . And lastly, (not to trouble you with more instances) by taking *Judgements*, or *Warrants of Attorney*, and for a little money sweep away three times the value in commodities, to the utter ruine of many Families. A *Mort-gage* is a sweet gain to him; what a fine Bill of Charges will he reckon . . . To be short, the *Tricks* and *Wheedles* of a *Scrivener* are so many, that they are innumerable. How many devices hath he in *Last Wills and Testaments*, not only altering the minde of the Testator, but many times making himself *Executor*? How many Knavish Partialities does he use in *Lease*? What Benefit does he not make by *Arbitrations*, by drawing up an *Award*, making it void or obliging to whom he pleases; by *Counter-Bonds* and *Letters of Attorney*, by putting in *his* use for *my* use? Lastly, consider his dexterity and ability in counterfeiting Bonds, by which and other indirect means he hath gotten a plentiful estate, to live pleasantly here, to be miserable hereafter.

[Extracts. By Richard Head (1637?–86?), author of *The English rogue* (1665). From chapter XIV in his *Proteus redivivus: or The art of wheedling, or insinuation* (London, 1675), 349–52 [Murphy, 147–8].][29]

---

[27] The *Scrivener* . . . in a *Character* not long since Printed] Presumably a reference to Jeremiah Wells's character (No. 21 above), which Head quotes at one point (*'seeking* (like the Devil) *whom he might devour'*: p. 287, and see n. 23 above).

[28] Though the Law allows but six *per Cent*] The interest rate was regulated by Usury Acts and had been officially 6% since 1651, a level reinforced by the Government during the Exchequer crisis in 1672, although in practice the various procuration, brokerage, and gratuity fees charged by scriveners could amount to a higher remuneration.

[29] Chapter IX of *Proteus redivivus* (pp. 273–92), headed 'The countrey-attorney, pettifogger, and other law hangers-on' (and partly derived from John Earles's *Microcosmographie*), recounts the similar ruses and cheats by which a 'Scriveners Clerk . . . having learned to engross an Indenture' rises to his master's position, thence to a 'pretended *Sollicitor*', and, by means of forgery, deceit, perjury, and false-swearing confederates, as well as several marriages to heiresses and wealthy widows, to riches, the pillory, and the gallows.

23. Robert Dixon

Canidia; or The witches. A rhapsody

[Part 2, Canto X, p. 49]

Clerks and Lawyers shall befriend 'um
With Writes and *Melius Inquirendum*.[30]
They'll dress up Lies in Pinkum prankum,
And th'Worlds Fools and Knaves shall thank 'um

[Part 2, Canto XI, p. 50]

A False Bond, or a forged Deed,
Shall make whole Families Bleed

[Part 2, Canto XV, p. 74]

There's a *Scrivener* in the Town,
No Gentleman, nor yet no Clown:
Partiperpale, up and down,
Betwixt the Cloak and the Gown.
No Lawyer, but a Law-Driver,
A vexatious Suit-Contriver,
Understands deep Points of Law,
In any Evidence to make a Flaw.
A cleanly Conveyancer of Lands,
Or Houses, into his own Hands.

Such an One has the unhappy Curse,
To be a Master of every Mans Purse.
To know every Mans Estate,
Be it early, be it late;
Be it in, or out of Date.
For a Mortgage, or a Sale
He's ready, he will ne're turn Tail.
Have you a Golden Mine lies by you,
This is the only Man to try you.
Intrust him with your Coyn, estsoon
He'l take his Interest by the *Moon*.
He regards not *Solar* years,
No more than Orphan, or Widows Tears.
Let him alone to tare and rack
The Cloaths from the Strangers Back.
Let him alone to make his Best,
And pop you off with Bare Interest

[Part 2, Canto XV, p. 75]

There's your Hand and Seal to show it,
But what's Interest, you shall never know it.

---

[30] *Melius Inquirendum*] 'the better must be sought out'.

For you, they shall take care to bestow it,
For fear you should overflow it

[Part 2, Canto XV, p. 76]
There's a prime Mortgage, there he lurches,
And turns it into a Purchase,
He's free to lend, and you to borrow,
You shall find it to your Sorrow,
For you shall be a Beggar to morrow,
He plunges you in Suits of Laws,
Tells you, Your Causes have no Flaws;
'Till you are left alone 'ith' Lurch,
With never a farthing in your Purse.

Let all your Deeds be at his Commands,
You never shall get 'um out of his hands

[Part 3, Canto IV, p. 19]
These Tricks a Witch understands
Better than Questions and Commands:
Better than forging Bills or Bonds,
Or putting Deeds in Scriveners hands

[Part 3, Canto IX, p. 56]
There comes a Lion,[31] my Heart pants,
Beware of false Bonds and Counterfeit Grants;
A cheating Scrivener never custom wants

[Part 3, Canto X, p. 70]
Call for a Scrivener, Set your Hands
And Seals, to convey all your Lands.
There's no Denial, it must be so,
If you come in to Cuckolds Row

[Part 3, Canto X, p. 77]
The Scrivener, Devil and his Dam,
'*Faciunt nos Longam Literam*[32]

[Part 5, Canto II, p. 26]
Master Scrivener, this is your drift,
To get all he has, and leave him to shift,
By this way you give Debtors a Lift

[Part 5, Canto IV, p. 42]
Unjust Stewards, Clerks and Scribes,
Drain poor Souls with Fees and Bribes

[Part 5, Canto IV, pp. 42–3]
The Divels will one day crack their Crowns,
Pickled Knaves, as e're wore Gowns.
That can do more mischief with the dash of a Pen,

[31] There comes a Lion] Cf. n. 23 above.   [32] *Faciunt nos* [i.e. *nobis*] *Longam Literam*] 'they make a long letter for us'.

Than a Thousand poor labouring men,
That steal a few Nail or Chips,
And suffer the Stocks or Whips.
Those that can *Scribere cum Dasho*,
Deserve the Halter more than the *Slasho*;
Wou'd the World were well rid of the ugly Trasho

[Extracts. By Robert Dixon (*fl.*1680s). From R: D:, *Canidia; or The witches. A rhapsody* (London, 1683).]

24. Anonymous

The Clubmen of the House of Commons 1694

The Scrivener Cuckold So proud he is grown
Of his Wealth and his plate, tho it was never known
That to such a Toadstool such favour was shown
                    Which [nobody can deny]

[Extract only (14th stanza: lines 53–6 out of 120 lines), satirizing the wealthy scrivener Sir Robert Clayton, MP (1629–1707). From BL Harley MS 7315, f. 238v. Complete text in *POAS*, v. 429–38.]

Manuscripts by the Feathery Scribe

This checklist, arranged alphabetically by geographical location, covers all examples of the Feathery Scribe's writing that I have come across hitherto. All texts listed here, as well as their titles or headings cited, are entirely in Feathery's hand unless otherwise stated. The titles are cited as accurately as is practicable, although, given the circumstances of their accumulation, in a variety of locations over a period of two decades, there will inevitably be occasional inconsistencies (unclear distinction between minuscule and majuscule lettering, for instance, or punctuation overlooked because of faded ink, etc.). To simplify matters I have also decided to make no attempt to reproduce the prolific diacritics found in these titles, the scribe's characteristic swirling tildes covering not only standard abbreviations (such as 'con' or 'Robte') but much other lettering besides. Although generally citing titles of each 'work', I have opted to summarize a few collections of multiple works, such as brief poems or letters.

Some standard printed sources are cited for identification purposes, although I have not attempted to track down all printings of every title (such as miscellaneous state papers or parliamentary speeches), nor to record other MS copies of each title (which are sometimes numerous) unless of special interest (such as authors' own manuscripts or manuscripts owned by Sir Robert Cotton).

Those 'works' which appear to correspond to items represented in the list of papers found in Ralph Starkey's study (see Appendix III below) are signalled accordingly ('Cf. Starkey No. 1', etc.). References to the catalogues of the public notary Humphrey Dyson (d. c.1632) are to his manuscript catalogues, including prices paid or charged, in All Souls College, Oxford, MS 117 (see Chapter 3 n. 35 above), and for references to Sir Richard Grosvenor's list of manuscript volumes, see Chapter 3 n. 46 above.

Three manuscripts discovered at copy-editing stage of this book have been added as Nos. 17A, 79A, and 110A, and cross-referenced accordingly. It is unlikely that they will be the last additional products of the Feathery Scribe to come to light.

Aberystwyth, National Library of Wales

1. Castell Gorfod MS 1

[Folio, 88 leaves; volume of state tracts; from the library of the 19th-century antiquary Joseph Joseph, FSA, of Brecon, enlarged by James Buckley of Castellgorfod, Breconshire. Watermark: pillars. See also p. 269 below.]

1.1. ff. 1r–5r: *A: Lre written by the Lordes: of the Councell, to kinge James, dated the < > daye of, < > Anno, < > Touchinge, meanes to aduaunce his Revenewes by vnusuall meanes, soe as the kinge will take the Acte vppon himselfe, and bee their Protection:*

[Probably dated early 1606. Cf. 53.12, 71, 82.4, and 83 below; Starkey No. 19.]

1.2. ff. 5r–6v: *Abatementes now in beinge: or to bee very shortlye, vppon the Marryage of the Ladye Elizabeth to the Counte Pallatyne of the*

Rhine, Anno..1613: and otherwise ffor the kings Beniffitt, by the Comissione^rs; of the Treasurye:

[Financial report by Henry Howard, Earl of Northampton (1540–1614), Commissioner of the Treasury, relating to the marriage of Princess Elizabeth (1596–1662) and Frederick V (1596–1632), Elector Palatine and later King of Bohemia, in March 1612/13. Northampton's autograph MS in BL Cotton MS Cleopatra F. VI, ff. 84r–85r; Cotton's other copy is MS Titus C. VII, f. 200r–v. Cf. 33.4, 53.14, 71, and 83 below; Starkey No. 25.]

1.3. ff. 6v–7r: *Sir Thomas Smyth One Off the Sheriffes of London, his Protestacon Touchinge his Speech, vsed to the Earle of Essex when hee ffledd into London, and other Accidente[s], Touchinge thesame Earle:*

[By Sir Thomas Smith (1558?–1625). Cf. 1.17, 82.5, and 109.12 below; Starkey No. 13.]

1.4. ff. 7v–18v: [*Letters by Sir Walter Ralegh*]

[Eight letters by Sir Walter Ralegh (1554–1618), to James I, Queen Anne, Lady Ralegh, Cecil, Carr, and others, chiefly 1603-7. Cf. 1.6, 23, 28, 35.3, 70, 108.6, 108.19 below.]

1.5. ff. 18v–19v: *The: Coppye Off a Lre written by· S^r: Robte Carre, Viscounte Rochester, and after Earle of Somersett, vnto the Lord Henry Howarde, Earle of Northampton, Anno, 1612: the viij^th of October:*

[By Robert Carr, Earl of Somerset (d. 1645), 8 October 1612. Cf. 35.4, 52, 92.11, and 108.9 below. This letter is mentioned as item 12 in one of Starkey's lists of MSS in BL Harley MS 537, f. 84r–v.]

1.6. ff. 19v–24r: [*Letters by Sir Walter Ralegh*]

[Two letters by Sir Walter Ralegh, to Cecil and James I. Cf. 1.4 above and 23, 28, 35.3, 70, 108.6, and 108.19 below.]

1.7. ff. 24v–32v: *The Three Greate Kingdoms of England, ffraunce, and Spayne, as they nowe stande, are to bee compared to the ellection of a Kinge of poland . . .*

[Dated 1623. Cf. 102 and 109 below. See Plate 29 above.]

1.8. ff. 32v–40v: *A Consideracon vppon the p^rsent Treatye of Marryage, Betwene England, and Spayne*

1.9. ff. 40v–44v: *A: Relation Off the proceedinges: against Ambassad^rs: whoe haue miscarryed themselves, and exceeded their comission in Actinge things against the State wherein they are imployed, out of the power of their Negotiacon written by S^r: Robte Cotton, the xxvij^th: of Aprill, 1624*

[By Sir Robert Cotton (1571–1631). *Cottoni posthuma*, No. 1. Cf. 17A.4, and 78 below; Starkey No. 43 n. 7.]

1.10. ff. 45r–49v: *A: Lre written by Inioza to kinge James, Touchinge the Duke of Bucke[s]: his Accons, and miscarryage in Spayne*

[By the Marquis St Germain Inijosa, Ambassador of Spain, 1623. Cf. 53 below; Starkey No. 42. A copy in Starkey's hand is BL Harley MS 304, ff. 42r–44v.]

1.11. ff. 49v–62v: *A: Lre written ffrom a ffrinde namelesse, to the Lower howse of Parliam^te*

[Anonymous 'Letter, touching the Inconveniences and Grievances of the State . . . called *A Speech without doors*', 1627: Rushworth, i. 489–98. Cf. 28, 40.1, 53, 61, 78.2, 83.3, 106.5, and 112 below; Starkey No. 64.]

1.12. ff. 63r–64v: *Questions Toucheinge: a Controversie of preceedencye, happened of late, Betwene two gentlemen:*

[Cf. 108.25 below.]

1.13. ff. 64v–65r: *Certayne Articles Off Comes Imperij, taken out of an Epistle of Counte Arundell:*

[By Thomas Howard, second Earl of Arundel (1585–1646). Cf. Starkey No. 6.]

1.14. ff. 65v–67r: *The Death Off Queene Elizabeth, wth hir declaracon of hir Successor:*

[Somers, i. 246–8. Cf. 82.9 and 83 below; Starkey No. 1.]

1.15. ff. 67r–72r: *Liddington the Secretarye of Scotland his Lre, to S^r: Willm Cecill, the Queene of Englandes Secretarye, Touchinge the Tytle of the Queene of Scotts, to the Crowne of England: i566*

[By William Maitland, Laird of Lethington (1528?–73), Scottish Secretary of State, 4 January 1566[/7]. Cotton's copy of this letter is BL Cotton MS Titus C. VII, ff. 105r–108r. Cf. 53.2 and 71 below; Starkey No. 14.]

1.16. ff. 72v–75r: *Henrye Cuffe Secretarye to the Earle of Essex his Lre, to M^r: Secretarye Cecill, declareinge the effect,: of the Instructions, fframed by the Earle of Essex, and delivered to the Ambassad^or of the kinge of Scottes, Touchinge his Tytle to the Crowne of England wch Lre, was written, after Cuffes Condempnacon:*

[By Henry Cuffe (1563–1601), 1601. Spedding, ix. 352–5. Cotton's copies are BL Cotton MSS Titus C. VII, ff. 58r–59r, and, in the hand of Henry Howard, Earl of Northampton, Vitellius C. XVII, ff. 363r–364r. Cf. 19, 53.1, 71, and 82.1 below; Starkey No. 12.]

1.17. ff. 75v–76r: *Sir Thomas Smyth one off the Sheriffs of London his Protestacon Touchinge his Speech vsed to the Earle of Essex, when hee ffledd into London and other Accidents Touchinge thesame Earle:*

[By Sir Thomas Smith (1558?–1625). Cf. 1.3 above and 82.5 and 109.12 below.]

1.18. f. 76r–v: *The Archduke Ernestus his Lre, to Queene Elizabeth, dated the xiiij: of October 1595:*

[By Ernest de Vasseur, Archduke of Austria and Governor of the Spanish Netherlands. Cf. 109.17 below; Starkey No. 10.]

1.19. ff. 76v–77r: *Queene Elizabeth hir: Lre to the Archduke Ernestus, in October 1595:*

[By Queen Elizabeth (1533–1603; reigned 1558–1603), 30 October 1595. Harrison, 230–1 (dated *c*.20 October 1594). Cotton's copy is BL Cotton MS Titus C. VII, ff. 38v–39r. Cf. 109.18 below; Starkey No. 10.]

1.20. ff. 77v–78v: *A: Lre ffrom Queene: Elizabeth, to the kinge of Scotts the iiij^th of Januarij, 1602: Written wth hir owne hand, Touchinge hir disswadeinge him to Receyve in his Countrye an Ambassador ffrom Spayne sheweinge hir groundes of vndertaken the Protection of the Lowe Countryes:*

[By Queen Elizabeth. Cf. 53.5 and 71 below; Starkey No. 17.]

1.21. ff. 79r–82r: *Queene Elizabethes Lre written to the kinge of Scotts dated the xi^o: of Maye, 1601: Touchinge Vallentyne Thomas, S^r: Willm Eve^rs, and Asheffeild, and an increase of 2000^li: Pencon, to make vpp the some of 5000^li: Pencon yearlye ffrom the Queene; to the kinge of Scotts:*

[By Queen Elizabeth. Cf. 71 below; Starkey No. 16.]

1.22. ff. 82r–83v: *The Ladye Elizabeth: hir graces Aunsweare the xxvj^th of Aprill, 1558: To S^r: Thomas Pope knight, beinge sent ffrom the Queenes Matie: to vnderstand, how hir grace lyked of the Motion of Marryage, made by the kinge ellect of Swethlandes Messenger:*

[Account by Sir Thomas Pope (1507?–59) of the answer by Princess, later Queen Elizabeth,

26 April 1558. Somers, i. 56–7. Cotton's copies are BL Cotton MSS Titus C. VII, ff. 42r–43r, and Vitellius C. XVI, ff. 334r–335v. Cf. 33, 53.4, and 109.10 below; Starkey No. 11.]

1.23. ff. 83v–84r: *Queene Elizabethes Lre to the Duke of Wirtenbergh, in Aunswere of his Offerr, to Assist hir, in the p'fferringe hir in Marryage, Dated the xxvij^th: of Januarij, 1563:*

[By Queen Elizabeth. Somers, i. 175. Cf. 53.9 and 109.11 below; Starkey No. 31.]

1.24. ff. 84r–86r: *The Examination Off: Sir Anthonye Browne, Touchinge the Ladye Maryes Submission, to kinge Henry the, 8: hir ffather:*

[Relating to the judge Sir Anthony Browne (1510?–67) in 1559-60. Cotton's copy is BL Cotton MS Titus C. VII, f. 187r–v. Cf. 71 below; Starkey No. 20.]

1.25. ff. 86r–87r: *Directions Off Queene Marye to hir Councell, Touchinge the Refforminge of the Church, to the Romane Religion, out of hir owne Originall:*

[By Queen Mary I (1516-58; reigned 1553-8). Cotton's copy is BL Cotton MS Titus C. VII, f. 120v. Cf. 53.3 and 71 below; Starkey No. 15.]

1.26. ff. 87v–88v: *The Coppye Off a Lre: written by the Lord Chauncello^r: Ellesme^r: to the kinge, desireinge to bee discharged of his offyce, thorough his inffirmetye, and weaknesse to supplye the same, Anno: 1612*

[By Sir Thomas Egerton, Baron Ellesmere and Viscount Brackley (1540?–1617), Lord Chancellor, 1612/13. *Cabala: sive Scrinia sacra* (London, 1663), 236; Somers, ii. 170–1. Cotton's copy is BL Cotton MS Titus C. VII, f. 29r–v. Cf. 13.8, 53.10, 82.3, and 83 below; Starkey No. 8.]

2. Wynnstay MS 44

[Folio, 107 leaves (206 pages); a single treatise; from the library of the William Watkins Wynn family of Wynnstay. Watermark: quatrefoils within circle.]

An: Arguement, vppon, the Question of Imposicions, devided, and digested into sundrye Chapt^rs By S^r: John Davyes, his Mat^ies; Attournye generall of Ireland, &c

[By Sir John Davies (1569–1626), 1610. Printed in London, 1656 [Wing D407]: cf. *Index*, i/1, DaJ 256–80; Baker, *CUL* 242. This treatise was cited in a parliamentary speech by Mr Creskeld (or Creshold) in the debates on Habeas Corpus and the Supply on 25 March 1628 (*Parliamentary history*, ii. 244–5). Cf. 18.2, 21, and 52 below. In two hands: Feathery responsible for title-page, ff. 2r–20v, ff. 53v (resuming at last two words of fifth line) to 71v, a one-line insertion on f. 104r, and foliation throughout; a second scribe responsible for ff. 21v–53v (most of first five lines) and 72r–105r.]

Cambridge, University Library

3. Add. MS 9276

[Folio, nearly 600 pages; composite volume of seventeen political tracts, including 'The Prayer used in the Kings Army after the Battaile of Kineton [Edgehill] 1642' added to a blank leaf (No. 2), and tracts by or attributed to Bacon (including, No. 1, his speech on the naturalization of the Scots: cf. 78.4 below), Ralegh, Wotton, and the Northumberland–Vere challenge (No. 10: cf. 11 below), in several scribal hands; stamped name on flyleaf of Sir Richard Betenson, Bt. (? the first Baronet, d. 1679; Betenson also owned Phillipps MS 2519 in University of London Library, MS 309, which is similarly associated with Feathery's scriptorium); Phillipps MS 2402; bookplate of Sir Thomas Brooke, FSA (1830–1908), of Armitage Bridge House, Huddersfield (cf. 9 below); later bookplate of Lord Fairfax of Cameron; Sotheby's, 14 December 1993 (Fairfax sale), Lot 30, and (with facsimile example in the catalogue) 13 December 1994, lot 538.]

3.1. No. 7: *An:; Aunswere, to, the, Coppye of a Rayleinge Invectyve (against, the Regyment of woemen in generall) wth Certayne Malliparte, exceptions, to, dyvers, and sundrye matters, of State, Wrytten, to Queene Elizabeth, By the Right honno^ble: Henrye Lord Howard, Late Earle, of Northampton:*

[By Henry Howard, Earl of Northampton: the dedication of his answer to John Knox's *First blast of the trumpet against the monstrous regiment of women* (1558); otherwise known as 'A Dutiful Defence of the Lawful Regiment of Women', 1570s. Cf. 17A and 30 below. Cotton's copy (presented to him by the author in 1613 and with Northampton's autograph annotations), evidently lent to Ralph Starkey before 23 April 1621, is BL Harley MS 6257. Starkey mentions this work as item 47 in his list of MSS in BL Harley MS 537, ff. 82r–83v, and its loan from Cotton is recorded in BL Harley MS 6018, f. 150r. Other presentation copies with the author's autograph additions are BL Add. MS 24652 (to a member of the Heneage family); Lansdowne MS 813 (to Sir George Carey); Bodleian Library MS Bodl. 903 (to [? Sir John] Stanhope); Harvard fMS 826 (to the Earl of Essex); Magdalene College, Cambridge, Pepys Library No. 2191 (to Lord Burghley, with Burghley's annotations); and University College London MS Ogden 16 (to [? William] Trumbull) [illustrated in Woudhuysen, plate II, after p. 272]. Title-page only in Feathery's hand; the text (117 pages) in another scribal hand (also responsible for a copy of the same dedication in BL Harley MS 7021, ff. 65r–122r); some notes on the final blank page in yet another hand [as in No. 2 of the MS, 1642] remarking on ways in which English queens furthered the causes of religion in England. See Plate 27 above.]

3.2. No. 12: *Obseruations Politticall: And,: Civill; Wrytten, by: S^r: ffrauncis Bacon: knight, &c*

[A series of essays here erroneously ascribed to Sir Francis Bacon, Viscount St Albans (1561–1626). Attributed to 'T: B:' in a formal presentation copy to Lord North, Treasurer, on 132 folio leaves in vellum gilt, once owned by the Earl of Bridgewater, now in the Huntington Library, EL 1174. Cf. Starkey No. 51 ('Diverse wrytings . . . of . . . Bacons'). Title-page and three-line heading of table of contents in Feathery's hand; the remaining two pages of table of contents and the ninety pages of text in another scribal hand (also responsible for copies of the same work in 17A.1 below, and in BL Harley MS 1853, ff. 39r–89v). See Plates 48, 49, and 50 above.]

3.3. No. 15: *A: Discours: Touchinge a Marryage, Betwene Prince Henrye of England, And, a Daughter of Savoye; Wrytten, by S^r: Walter Rawleighe, Kn^te: Beinge, thereto Comaunded: by thesame Prince; &c:*

[By Sir Walter Ralegh: cf. *Index*, i/2, RaW 621–47. Cotton's copy, in the hand of Ralph Starkey, is BL Cotton MS Vitellius C. XVI, ff. 529r–538r. This discourse is mentioned as item 1 in one of Starkey's lists of MSS in BL Harley MS 537, f. 84r. Cf. 27, 98, and 108.29 below. 37 pages. Facsimile of title-page in Sotheby's sale catalogue, 13 December 1994, lot 538 (p. 193). See Plate 28 above.]

4. MS Dd. 3. 86

[Folio, 438 pages; composite volume of tracts (including Cotton) in various hands; No. 2 (on Mary Queen of Scots, 1571) in the hand of Ralph Starkey; bookplate of John Moore (1646–1714), Bishop of Ely. Watermark in Feathery items: grapes.]

4.1. No. 5: *The: Arguem^te and Opinyon Concerninge the Case of Shipp: Monye of S^r; John, Brampston, Knight, Lord Cheiffe Justice of the Kinges Bench: in the Excheque^r: Chamber; the: 9th of Junij: Trin: 14: Caroli, 1638: Betwene the Kinges Attournye, Pe^te And John Hambden, Esquier, deffend^te*

[Arguments of Sir John Bramston (1577–1654) *pro* John Hampden (1594–1643): *State trials*, iii. 1243–51; cf. Baker, *CUL* 23–4. 16 leaves (32 pages).]

4.2. No. 6: *The: Case: Off Shipp: monye Mich: xiij: Caroli, Argued in the Exchequer Chamber, by M*^r^: *S*^te^: *Johns of Lincolnes Inne; S*^r^: *Edward Littleton his Ma*^ties^: *Solicitor, M*^r^: *Holborne of Lincolnes Inn, And S*^r^: *John Bancke[s], Knight, his Ma*^ties^: *Attournye generall vizt*

[Arguments of Oliver St John (1598?–1673), Sir Edward Littleton (1589–1645), Robert Holborne (d. 1647), and Sir John Bankes (1589–1644): *State trials*, iii. 855–1065. Cf. 5.1, 5.5, and 8 below. 33 leaves (65 pages).]

5. MS Dd. 9. 22

[Folio, 298 leaves; composite volume of speeches relating to Ship Money and legal materials; book-plate of George I. Cf. Baker, *CUL* 88–9.]

5.1. ff. 1r–10v: *The: Arguem*^te^: *Off: Sir: John Bancke[s], knight; his Ma*^ties:^ *Attournye Generall*

[Arguments of Sir John Bankes: *State trials*, iii. 1014–65. Cf. 4.2 above. Watermark: fleur-de-lis.]

5.2. ff. 11r–24v: *The: Arguem*^te^: *Off m*^r^: *Justice Barcklye The Tenth of ffebruarij: Concerninge Shipp: Monye; pro Rege:*

[Argument of Sir Robert Berkeley (1584–1656), Justice of the King's Bench: *State trials*, iii. 1087–125. Watermark: grapes.]

5.3. f. 27r: *The: Arguem*^te^: *Off M*^r^. *Barron Treave*^r^: *Pasch: xiiij: Caroli, Concerninge Shipp: Monye, Pro Rege:*

[Argument of Sir Thomas Trevor (1586–1656): *State trials*, iii. 1125–7. Watermark: grapes.]

5.4. ff. 119r–168v: *The argument of S*^r^ *John ffinch Lord cheife Justice of the Comon pleas in the exchequer chamber in the case concerneing shipp mony Termo. s*^ta^ *trin .14. Caroli 9. Junij .1638.*

[Argument of Sir John Finch (1584–1660): *State trials*, iii. 1216–43. Feathery responsible for ff. 147r–168v; another scribe for ff. 119r–146v. Watermark: grapes.]

5.5. ff. 169r–216r: *The Replye Off m*^r^: *Holborne of Lincolnes Inn, of Councell w*^th^ *M*^r^: *Hambden, to the Arrguem*^te^: *of S*^r^: *Edward Littleton knight, his Ma*^ties^: *Solicito*^r^: *generall, 2: Ocobris, xiij: Caroli, in Camera, Sccij*

[Argument of Robert Holborne (d. 1647): *State trials*, iii. 963–1014. Cf. 4.2 above. Watermark: fleur-de-lis.]

6. MS Ee. 2. 32

[Folio, 374 leaves (plus blanks); volume of tracts, including Cotton, Ralegh, Essex's Charge against Wimbledon and his answer (ff. 43r–73r: cf. Starkey No. 89), 'Advertisement of a loyal subject' (ff. 75r–78v: cf. 20.8 below), Eglisham's 'Forerunner of Revenge' (ff. 159r–182v: cf. Starkey No. 84), Cope's 'Apology for Cecil' (ff. 183r–195r: cf. 105.3 below), Townshend's Journal of Parliament 1597 (ff. 209r–237v: cf. 73 below), ' A Reconciliation' (ff. 239r–265v: cf. 34 below), Cotton's 'That the Kings of England . . .' (ff. 285r–302v: cf. Starkey No. 43 n. 7), and 'Oaths' (ff. 303r–371v: cf. 12 below); 1640 material added to f. 12r; in several scribal hands, with table of contents; bookplate of John Moore, Bishop of Ely. Watermark in Feathery items: pillars.]

6.1. ff. 1r–11v: *The manner Off the: sicknes, and death of Prince Henrye, Sonne to Kinge James, Anno, 1612*

[Part of a tract by Sir Charles Cornwallis (d. 1629), 1626. Printed as *The life and death of our late most incomparable and heroique Prince Henry, Prince of Wales, &c.* (London, 1641) [Wing C6329–30]; Somers, ii. 217–25 and 225–52; Thomas Baker's transcript of this MS printed in Francis Peck, *Desiderata curiosa*, 2 vols. (London, 1779), i. 199–205. Cotton's copy of part of the tract is BL Cotton MS Titus C. VII, ff. 62r–67r. Cf. 9, 18, 20, 35.2, 53, 67, and 83 below; Starkey No. 2.]

6.2. ff. 13r–41v: *A: Discourse Off the high Co^{rte}: of Parliam^{te}: And of the Aucthoritye of thesame, Collected out of the Comon Lawes of the Lande, and other good Auctho^{rs}:*

[By Ralph Starkey (d. 1628), [1620–5]. Printed anonymously as *The priviledge and practice of Parliament* (London, 1628) [STC 7749]. Cf. 44, 74, and 108 below. ff. 13r–30r in Feathery's hand; ff. 30v–41v in a second scribal hand.]

6.3. ff. 89r–91v: *Proposicons made by the Ambassado^{rs}: of the Kinge of ffraunce, to the Assemblye of the States generall; of the Vnited Provinces of the Lowe Countryes, vppon Presentacon of the Lres of his Matie: to the said Lordes the States, the xij^{o}: of december, 1618: Touchinge the poyntes noted in the Margent:*

[Cf. 53.6 and 109.19 below; Starkey No. 28.]

6.4. ff. 92r–95v: *The Antiquitye Vse and Privelidge of Cittyes, Burroughes, and Townes, Wrytten by M^{r}: ffrauncis Tate of the Middle Temple London:*

[By Francis Tate (1560–1616), beginning 'They that are conversant in Stories . . .', 9 February 1598. Gutch, i. 1–5. Cf. 83 and 109.20 below; Starkey No. 35.]

6.5. ff. 97r–98v: *Ordinarye Annuall Receipts of the Exchequer:* and *Ordinarye Annuall: Yssues of the Excheque^{r}:*

[Exchequer accounts. A scribal copy is in Cotton's collection of Exchequer papers: BL Cotton MS Cleopatra F. VI, ff. 102v–103r; another in Titus C. VII, ff. 201v–202r. Cf. 33.3, 53.13, 83, and 109.14 below; Starkey Nos. 26 and 27.]

6.6. ff. 99r–102v: *A: Lre wrytten by Sir: Phillipp: Sidnye, to his Brother Robte Sidnye, (nowe Lord Lisle) shewinge what Course was ffit ffor him to hould in his Travills:*

[By Sir Philip Sidney (1554–86). Somers, i. 494–6; Feuillerat, iii. 124–7; and cf. *Index*, i/2. 466. Cf. 20.2 and 53 below; Starkey No. 40.]

6.7. ff. 151r–158v: *The Politia Or Governm^{te}: of the Vnited Provinces:*

[By Sir Clement Edmondes (1564?–1622), Clerk of the Privy Council, 1615. Somers, iii. 630–5. Cotton's copy is BL Cotton MS Titus C. VII, ff. 34r–38r. Cf. 33, 83.2, and 109.15 below; Starkey No. 9.]

6.8. ff. 267r–284r: *A: Shorte veiw to bee: taken of greate Brittayne, and Spayne:*

[By Sir Francis Bacon, *c*.1619. Spedding, xiv. 22–8: cf. *Index*, i/1 BcF 281–2. Cf. 33.1 below.]

7. MS Ee. 4. 18

[Folio, 12 leaves (23 pages); a single tract; bookplate of John Moore, Bishop of Ely.]

A: Breiffe: Discours Concerninge: free: Trade:

[Headed on f. 2r: 'A:, Breiffe:, Discours: Concerninge ffree Trade, shewinge, the Convenyent Scituacon of this Island, wth the Inconveniencyes, by Incorporated Societyes, And the Benifitte[s] of Libertye; And free Tradeinge; The Presidente[s], ffor Straungers, Tradeing in Germany, The possibillitye, easelye to effect; the dyeinge; and dressinge of Cloth; The Inlarginge of Trades; by the Staple of Corne, And the Meanes, to Corect the Trade of ffisheinge, Breifflye Comprised, ffor the Benifitt of this kingdome.' Cf. 23.5 and 43 below.]

8. MS Mm. 6. 63

[Folio, 216 leaves (including blanks); composite volume of tracts, in various hands, including autograph drafts on Ship Money by Sir Edward Littleton, *Leicester's commonwealth* (ff. 155r–180v: cf. 84 below), and arguments on 'The Five Knights Case' (ff. 181r–204v: cf. Starkey No. 83); bookplate of John Moore, Bishop of Ely.]

No. 1: ff. 1r–52v: *The: Arguemᵗᵉ: Off Sir Edward: Littleton Knight, of the Inner Temple, made in the Excheque'ʳ: Chamber, pro Rege:*

[Argument of Sir Edward Littleton versus John Hampden, 1638: *State trials*, iii. 923–62; cf. Baker, *CUL* 513–14. Cf. 4.2 above. Incomplete at end. Watermark: elaborate fleur-de-lis.]

Cambridge, Massachusetts, Harvard University, Houghton Library

9. MS Eng 897

[Small quarto, 27 leaves (52 pages) plus 5 blanks; a single tract; bound in purple velvet; '1448' inside cover; bookplate of Sir Thomas Brooke of Armitage Bridge House (cf. 3 above); given to Harvard in 1926 in memory of Lionel de Jersey Harvard, killed in action 30 March 1918. Watermark: urn (D/IV).]

A discourse of the Lyfe of the most illustrious Prince Henrye, Late Prince of Wales, Wrytten Anno: 1626: by Sʳ: Charles Cornwallyes Knight, some=tymes Treasurer of his Highnes Howse:

[By Sir Charles Cornwallis. Cf. 6.1 above and 18, 20, 35.2, 53, 67, and 83 below.]

10. fMS Eng 1084

[Folio, 264 leaves (including some blanks); composite volume of tracts (including arguments on Ship Money) in five scribal hands; later Phillipps MS 10463; bookplate of Alfred Wynne Corrie, and owned before 1924 by William Appleton Coolidge; cf. Baker, *USA* ii. 221 (No. 938).]

ff. 1r–116r: *Camera, Stellata: Reportes Off the Starrchamber: Pasche: Primo: Caroli Regis:*

[Star Chamber cases, 1625–37. Cf. 29, 101, and 110A below; Starkey No. 80 (*ante* 1628). Feathery is responsible for the title-page, ff. 1r–23v, the catchword at the bottom of f. 30v, ff. 31r–32r, 35r–81r, and f. 83r (title-page only: 'An: Exacte Coppye Off the Censure passed, by the Lordes and others of his Maᵗⁱᵉˢ: most honnoᵇˡᵉ privye Councell, vppon the Lord Bᵖᵖ: of Lincolne, ii: Julij: 13: Caroli Regis, Anno Dni: 1637. In Camera Stellata:'). Watermark: pillars (IEAN).]

11. fMS Eng 1205

[Folio, 10 leaves (19 pages); a single tract; acquired 30 January 1947.]

The: Coppye:, Off; the, Challenge: sent, by the Earle of Northumberland, to Sʳ: ffrauncis Veere, And; Sʳ: ffrauncis his Aunswere; &c

[Challenge to a duel by Henry Percy, ninth Earl of Northumberland (1564–1632), 23/4 April 1602, and answer on 26 April by Sir Francis Vere (1560–1609). Somers, i. 487–92; Braunmuller, 122–9 (commentary, pp. 422–3). Cotton's copy of the Northumberland challenge alone, in Starkey's hand, is BL Cotton MS Titus C. IV, ff. 486r–488v (and the exchange recorded, against 'fo. 341' and 'fo. 342', in Starkey's list in BL Harley MS 537, f. 91r–v). Cf. 3 above and 23.4, 28, 41.9, and 105.4 below. A reader's clumsy underlinings of some lines and phrases on ff. [7r–10r]. Watermark: pillars.]

12. fMS Eng 1266, Volume I

[Folio, 317 leaves; volume of state tracts, by Ralegh, Cotton, Richard Corbett, Sir Kenelm Digby, and others, in various hands; once owned by Sir Richard Grosvenor (1585–1645) (*Liber 9* in his list of MS volumes, 18 February 1634/5); from the muniments of the Duke of Westminster, Eaton Hall, Cheshire, recorded in HMC, 3rd Report (1872), Appendix, 211–12 [MS 4]; Sotheby's, 19

July 1966, lot 486; microfilm in BL, RP 170; cf. Baker, *USA* ii. 224 (Nos. 947–50).]

ff. 274r–317v: *The Booke of Oathes Auncient and moderne*

[Compilation of various kinds of oaths used throughout the realm by public officers, merchants, etc., including the date 1625 on f. 275r; ff. 288r–v and 290r–293v excised; probably unfinished. Cf. No. 6 above; Starkey No. 62. Watermark: pillars.]

Cambridge, Massachusetts, Harvard University, Law School Library

13. MS 1034

[Folio, 570 numbered leaves (but some misnumbered), entirely in Feathery's hand; four-page index in a later hand (*c.*1839, referring to this volume 'in the possession of Mr. Rooke') and other material loosely inserted; name inscribed on first page: 'J Trevor', possibly a member of the Trevor family of Denbighshire, such as the politician Sir John Trevor (d. 1673) or his eponymous son (1626–72), Secretary of State, but most likely Sir John Trevor (1637–1717), Speaker of the House of Commons and Master of the Rolls; various underlinings in red pencil, and black and red ink, and copious annotations by readers commenting on clauses, etc., including a late 17th-century hand (possibly Trevor's) making remarks addressed to a Lord Chancellor: see pp. 98–99 above and Plate 57); acquired from Sweet & Maxwell on 14 February 1950 at the same time as MSS belonging to Thomas Powys (d. 1671), Sergeant at Law (including a companion volume not in Feathery's hand, MS 1035, and another copy of Lambarde's *Archeion*, MS 1036); cf. Baker, *USA* ii. 117–19 (No. 559). Watermark: pillars.]

Chauncerie

A huge legal compilation relating to the Court of Chancery and its history, assembled from a variety of sources from the thirteenth century to 1617, including accounts and expositions of the nature and authority of various offices (such as those of the Lord Chancellor and the Cursitors and Clerks of Chancery), legal opinions and arguments, cases (including Allen's and Richard Glanville's, the Earl of Oxford's, Lord Cromwell's, the Earl of Southampton's, and 'Cases of Conscience'), Acts of Council, Chancery ordinances, oaths, fees and charges, bills and proclamations, records from Chancery archives (from Henry III onwards), an account of patents of the Master of the Rolls (from Edward I onwards), historical tracts, and other records, precedents, and related materials, the authors and contributors including Cardinal Wolsey, Sir Nicholas Bacon, Sir John Puckering, John Croke (ff. 71r–74r: cf. 111.1 below), a Council letter concerning Sir Edward Coke (30 June 1616), and others; related in large part to the Chancery collection made for the Master of the Rolls and Lord Keeper, Sir Thomas Egerton, by his deputy William Lambarde (1536–1601), Master in Chancery, and continued by Egerton: see Paul L. Ward, 'William Lambarde's Collections on Chancery', *HLB* 7 (1953), 271–98, and Baker, *CUL* 265–75. A substantially similar collection owned by Cotton, and partly in Starkey's hand (on ff. 104r–115v, 295r–299r), is BL Add. MS 46410 (formerly Claudius B. VIII), ff. 3r–299r. Cf. 111 below; Starkey No. 81.

Inter alia the compilation includes the following tracts, speeches and letters:

13.1. ff. 1r–13r: *A Discours of the highe Co^{rte[s]}: of Justices in England, and especiallye of the Chauncery Co^{rte}: and of the Lord Chauncello^{r}: Wrytten by Willm Lambert, Armiger:*

[By William Lambarde, beginning 'That wch wee call Co^{rte[s]} in ffrenche is called (Curia) in Lattyne . . .', and dated from 'Ightam in Kent this viij^{th} of Marche: 1576[/7]', being an early draft for his *Archeion*. Full version printed in London, 1635 [STC 15143]: cf. Baker, *CUL* 265–7. Three copies owned by Cotton are BL Cotton MS Vespasian C. XIV, part II, ff. 54r–55v (fragment) and Add. MS 46410, ff. 3r–19r, 87r–94v. Cf. 111 below.]

13.2. ff. 77v–92r: *Some Noates and observa-cons vppon the Statute of Magna Carta, Chap: xxix^th, and other Statutes, Conscernenge the Proceedinges in the Chauncery, in Courses of Equetye, and Conscyence, Collected by the Lord Ellesme^r: ffor the Kengs Learned Counsells direction, the Moneth of September: 1615: Anno xiij^th Jacobi*

> [By Sir Thomas Egerton, Baron Ellesmere, 1615. Printed as *The priviledges and prerogatives of the high court of Chancery* (London, 1641) [Wing E540]; cf. Baker, *CUL* 269. Cf. 109 and 111.3 below.]

13.3. ff. 140v–146v: *A: Discours written by M^r: John Selden Student in the Middle Temple, London, and dedicated vnto S^r: ffrauncis Bacon knight, Lord Keeper of the greate Seale, of England, of the Auncyent, Mencon, Coniunction or division, of the Two, greate Offyces of State, the Chauncellorshipp, and Keeper of the greate Seale of England, in Anno: 1617*

> [By John Selden (1584–1654). Printed as *A brief discourse touching the office of Lord Chancellor of England* (London, 1671) [Wing S2420]; cf. Baker, *CUL* 266. Cf. 82.10 below; Starkey No. 37.]

13.4. ff. 147r–155v: *The: effect of that wch was spoken by the Lord Keeper S^r: ffrauncis Bacon Knight, Att the takeinge of his Place in the Chauncery, in Perfformance of the Chardge; his Matie: had given him, When hee receyved the greate Seale of England, the vij^o: of Maye 1617*

> [By Sir Francis Bacon. *Resuscitatio*, ed. William Rawley (London, 1657) [Wing B319], 79–86; Spedding, xiii. 182–93. Cf. 82.7 and 83 below.]

13.5. ff. 156r–174v: *Ordinaunces made by the Lorde Chauncello^r: S^r: ffrauncis Bacon, Lord Verulam, Viscounte, S^te: Albons, ffor the Better, and more Reguler Administracon of Justyce, in the Chauncerye, to bee duelye observed, saveinge the Prerogatyve of the Co^rte: And Publyshed in Open Co^rte: the xxiij^o: daye of Januarij 1618*

> [By Sir Francis Bacon: his *Ordinances in Chancery*. Printed in London, 1642 [Wing B316]; Spedding, vii. 755–74: cf. *Index*, i/1, BcF 234–53. Includes (ff. 172v–174v) 'Addiconall Rules': printed in *Orders of the high court of Chancery*, ed. G. W. Sanders (London, 1845), part i, 129–31. Cf. 111 below; Starkey No. 66.]

13.6. ff. 177v–180v: *The: Antiquitie of the Lord Chauncellor of Englandes Offyce, Collected by M^r. Tate, of the Middle Temple, London:*

> [By Francis Tate, beginning 'It: is most true wch Casciodorus in his Booke of Epistles sayth . . .'. Cf. 82.11 below.]

13.7. ff. 182v–186v: *The Oration of S^r: James Dyer Knight, Lord Cheeiffe Justyce of the Comon Pleas, and other of the Queenes Maties: Justices of hir Co^rte[s]: of Westm^r: By virtue of hir Maties: Lres of Privye Seale to them directed, Conscerninge the Jurisdiction, and Libertyes of the Countye Pallatyne of Chester, and the Aucthoretye of the Chambleyne, and his Offyce there:*

> [By Sir James Dyer (1512–82) and other judges, 2–10 February 1568/9. Cf. 109.4 below.]

13.8. ff. 187r–188v: *The Coppie of A Lre: wrytten by the Lorde Chauncello^r: Ellesme^r: to the Kinge desireinge to bee dischardged of his Offyce, thoroughe his inffirmetye, and weaknesse, to supplye the same, An^o: 1612*

> [By Sir Thomas Egerton, Baron Ellesmere. Cf. 1.26 above and 53.10, 82.3, and 83 below.]

13.9. ff. 190r–326v: *Causes in Chauncerie gathered by S^r; George Carye, one of the M^rs: of the Chauncerye, in An^o 1601: out of the Labo^rs: of M^r: Willm Lambert*

[By William Lambarde and Sir George Carew (d. 1612), Master in Chancery. Printed substantially in *Reports or causes in Chancery, collected by Sir George Cary . . . out of the labours of Mr William Lambert* (London, 1650) [Wing C555].]

13.10. ff. 490v–499r: *The Courte of Chauncerye*

[By Sir Robert Cotton (so attributed in BL Hargrave MS 227, ff. 3r–72r), beginning 'There is a Booke called the Myrror of Justices . . .'.]

14. MS 1054

[Folio, 262 leaves; composite volume of tracts on parliament, in various scribal hands; inscribed in Court hand by one 'M: Bayley' or 'W: Cauyley' (cf. 111 below); Phillipps MS 15141; acquired from James Tregaskis, 4 June 1902; cf. Baker, *USA* ii. 123–4 (No. 573). Watermark: pillars (VAD). Cf. Starkey No. 67.]

14.1. ff. [37r–39r]: *Off the Antiquetye Off Parleam*^te[s]:

[By Sir Robert Cotton, beginning 'The Auncyent and ffirst Parliam^te: that I haue read of . . .'. Printed (anonymously) in Sir John Dodderidge, *The several opinions of sundry learned antiquaries . . . touching . . . Parliament* (London, 1658) [Wing D1796], 40–7; Hearne, i. 293–5. Cf. 23 below.]

14.2. ff. [39r–41v]: *Off the Antiquetye off Parliam*^te[s]:

[By Arthur Agard (1540–1615), beginning 'That wch wee in Englishe call Parliam^te . . .'. Printed in Dodderidge, *The several opinions of sundry learned antiquaries . . . touching . . . Parliament* (1658), 48–58; Hearne, i. 295–8. Cf. 23 below.]

14.3. ff. [41v–44r]: *Temps Ed: le Conffessoris Summons doit eo :40: iours deuant le Session:*

[By Sir John Dodderidge (1555–1628), beginning 'The Sumons of the Cleargie, Archb^pps,

B^pps: . . .' . Printed in Dodderidge, *The several opinions of sundry learned antiquaries . . . touching . . . Parliament* (1658), 28–39; Hearne, i. 289–93. Cf. 23 below.]

14.4. ff. [44v–46v]: *The Antiquetye Off: Parliam*^te[s]:

[By William Camden (1551–1623), beginning 'That there were such lyke Assemblyes as Parliam^te[s] . . .'. Printed in Dodderidge, *The several opinions of sundry learned antiquaries . . . touching . . . Parliament* (1658), 74–85; Hearne, i. 303–6: cf. *Index*, i/1, CmW 72–88. Cf. 23 below.]

14.5. ff. [87r–225r]: *Modus tenendi Parliamentum in Apud Anglos Composed by Henry Elsinge Clerke of Parliaments*

[By Henry Elsynge (1598–1654), Clerk of the House of Commons. Printed as *The ancient method and manner of holding of Parliaments in England* (London, 1660) [Wing E645]. Feathery is responsible only for twenty-two lines on f. [112r], from mid-sentence at the top of the page to the first word of the penultimate line; all the rest of the text is in at least two other scribal hands. Watermark: pillars (RDP).]

Chicago, University Library

15. MS 847

[Folio, 28 leaves (55 pages); two tracts. Watermark: grapes.]

15.1. ff. [1r–21v]: *A: Collection Off Such thinges, As Robte Late Earle of Salisburye, thought ffitt, to offer vnto Kinge James his Ma*^tie. *Touching the necessitye, of callinge a Parliam*^te.

[Materials collected by Sir Robert Cecil, first Earl of Salisbury (1563?–1612), 1604. Cf. 54 and 93 below and also University of London MS 309, ff. 6r–8r.]

15.2. ff. [23r–28v]: *Certayne Replyes and: Obiections, Aunswered, by Willm Lord Burleigh, Att the Councell Table vizt: whether it maye stand wth good pollicye, ffor hir Matie to ioyne w^th: J J: in their Enterprise of: J:*

[By William Cecil, Lord Burghley (1520–98), Secretary of State, 25 February 1570/1 to 31 March 1571. Cf. 25 and 41.3 below.]

16. MS 878

[Folio, 176 leaves (plus three blanks); composite volume of state tracts principally by Cotton, the last three by Lord Burghley and Sir Robert Cecil (on 'The state of a secretaries place': cf. 77.3 and 78.8 below), in various scribal hands, one that of Ralph Starkey; readers' annotations include (f. 48r) a note in a treatise on France referring to 'the present designes of 1644'.]

ff. [114r–123r]: *A: Speech Deliuered by S^r: Robte Cotton, knight, and Barronett att the Councell Table the < > daye of September, 1626: Touchinge debaseinge of Coyne:*

[By Sir Robert Cotton, 2 September 1626. *Cottoni posthuma*, No. 12. Reader's corrections and marginal notes (including the finishing of a sentence on f. 119v). Cf. 23 below. Watermark: pillars (RDP). See Plate 54 above.]

Dublin, Trinity College

17. MS 588

[Folio, 232 leaves; composite volume of state tracts; purchased from a Mr Mercier, 1807; old pressmark E.3.25.]

ff. 2r–16r: *The: Coppye: Off: a; Letter: wrytten by S^r: Phillipp Sidnye to Queene Elizabeth. Touchinge her Marryage, wth Mownsieur &tc*

[By Sir Philip Sidney: cf. *Index*, i/2, SiP 198; Appendix IV below, No. 34. Cf. 18.1, 20.1, 41.10, 53, 57.4, 64, 78.7, 105.1, and 110 below; Starkey No. 39. Title-page inscribed 'N. 52' and

'AA. May. 7. 1691. New . . .'. Watermark: quatrefoils within circle. See Plate 73 above.]

17A. MS 731

[Folio, 586 leaves; volume of state tracts, including Northampton's Answer to Knox (ff. 1r–54r: cf. 3.1 above), Eglisham's 'The ffore Runner of Revenge' (ff. 285r–317r: cf. Starkey No. 84), Hyde's 'Disparitie betweene the Earle of Essex and . . . Buck[ingham]' (ff. 318r–336v: cf. 59 below), Fleetwood's account of Buckingham's Isle of Rhé expedition (ff. 361r–371v: cf. Starkey No. 56), and accounts of Bristol's answer in Parliament about the Spanish Match negotiations (ff. 272r–554v: cf. 46.4 below); in several scribal hands; bequeathed by Sir Jerome Alexander (c.1600–70), Justice of the Irish Common Pleas; old pressmark G. 4.9.]

17A.1. ff. 175r–220v: *Observations Polliticall and Civil*

[Cf. 3.2 above. Most of f. 183v until f. 220v in Feathery's hand; title-page and ff. 176r until near the end of the fifth line on f. 183v in the hand of another scribe. Watermark: quatrefoils within circle.]

17A.2. ff. 221r–268v: *ffragmenta Regalia Or: Observacons on the late Queene Elizabeth, hir tymes, and ffavorites*

[By Sir Robert Naunton (1563–1635). Printed in London, 1641 [Wing N249]; Somers, i. 251–83. Cf. 60 and 62 below. Title-page only in Feathery's hand; the text, on ff. 222r–268v, in another scribal hand. Watermark: pillars.]

17A.3. ff. 269r–284r: *The Arraignm^te: Off Marvin Lord Awdlye, Earle of Castlehaven, Att the kinge[s] Bench Barre, the :xxv: of Aprill, 1631*

[Account of the arraignment of Mervyn Touchet, second Earl of Castlehaven (1593–1631), convicted of sexual depravity on 25 April and executed on 14 May 1631. Printed as *The arraignment and conviction of Mervin Lord Avdley* (London, 1642[/3]) [Wing A3743]. Cf. 41 and 109 below. Watermark: pillars.]

17A.4. ff. 571r–577v: *A: Relacon:, Off: the: Proceedinges, against Ambassado^{rs}: whoe haue miscarryed themselves, and exceeded their Comission, in Actinge thinges against the State; wherein they are imployed, out of the power of their Negotiacon, Wrytten by S^r: Robte Cotton, Knight, and Barronett, xxvij^o: Aprill, 1624: By expresse: Comaund, ffrom the Duke: of Buckingham*

[By Sir Robert Cotton. Cf. 1.9 above and 78 below. Watermark: pillars.]

18. MS 732

[Folio, 385 leaves; composite volume of state tracts, by Ralegh, Tate (cf. 6.4 above), Cornwallis (cf. 6.1 above), and others; bequeathed after 1670 by Sir Jerome Alexander; old pressmark G.4.10.]

18.1. ff. 33r–45r: *The Coppye Off a Lre written by S^r: Phillipp: Sidnye to Queene Elizabeth, touchinge hir Marryage w^{th}: Mounsieur:*

[By Sir Philip Sidney: cf. *Index*, i/2, SiP 213; Appendix IV below, No. 35. Cf. 17 above and 20.1, 41.10, 53, 57.4, 64, 78.7, 105.1, and 110 below. Title-page and ff. 38r–45r in Feathery's hand; ff. 34r–37v in another scribal hand. Watermark: pillars. See Plates 70 and 72 above.]

18.2. ff. 284r–385v: *An; argum^t Vpon the Question of Impositions devided and digested into sundry chapters by Sr John Davyes knight his Ma^{ts} Attourney generall of Ireland*

[By Sir John Davies: cf. *Index*, i/1, DaJ 276. Cf. 2 above and 21 and 52 below. The title-page (f. 284r) and two-line heading on f. 285r in another scribal hand; the text on ff. 285r–385v in Feathery's hand, but for brief insertions in yet another hand on ff. 292v–293r and a correction on f. 294r.]

19. MS 734

[Folio, 390 leaves; volume of state tracts, including works by Bacon, Bodley, (his 'Life', ff. 241r–244r: cf. 82.8 below), Cuffe (ff. 259r–261v: cf. 1.16 above), James I (to Calvert: cf. 20.9 below), and Sir Henry Wallop (ff. 267r–268v: cf. 57.16 below), and the proceedings against Monson (cf. 23.6 below), in several scribal hands; bequeathed after 1670 by Sir Jerome Alexander; old pressmark G.4.12.]

19.1. ff. 1r–19r: *A: Brevyate: Concerninge the Memorable, States, and Condicons: of the Co^{rte[s]}: of Recordes, kepte in, and aboute the Cittyes of London, and Westminster, whatt Magistrates, Offyce^{rs}: and Manner of dealinge[s], att the Comon Lawes, of England, are vsed in everye thesame Co^{rte[s]}: &c*

[Anonymous treatise apparently written in 1588. Title-page only in Feathery's hand; the text (ff. 2r–19r) in another scribal hand. Watermark: pillars.]

19.2. ff. 39r–46v: *A: Treatise:, Off, Particuler Estates, Wrytten, by S^r: John Dodderidge knight*

[By Sir John Dodderidge. Watermark: pillars.]

19.3. ff. 47r–50r: *A: Relacon and, opinyon of M^r: Serieante[s] fleetwoodes, Concerninge the Originall of Co^{rte[s]}: &c*

[By William Fleetwood (1525?–94), Recorder of London. Cf. 23, 41.4, 106.6, and 109.2 below. Watermark: pillars.]

19.4. ff. 57r–116r: *Englandes: Epiniomis: Or: A Collection, out of the Authenticque historyans, And, a Comentarye of those Lawes, The Originall of manye of our Moderne, whereby the kingdome of England, hath been ffrom tyme; to tyme governed vnder both prophane; and Christian Princes, since the ffirst Inhabitante[s], To the end of kinge Johns Raigne wrytten: By: John Seldon: Esquyer &c*

[By John Selden. Printed in London, 1683 [Wing S2427]. Cf. 40.2 and 87 below. Feathery responsible for two title-pages (ff. 57r, 60r), the table of contents (ff. 58r–59v), the text on ff. 61r–85v, and the beginning of f. 86r (running head and 'Cap: 8: Henrye:'); another scribe for the rest of the text on ff. 86r–116r. Watermark: pillars.]

19.5. ff. 117r–184r: *A Late Enqurye by his Maties Commssioners after exactted fees and Innovated offices*

[Report dated 1623. Another scribe responsible for title-page and text on ff. 121r–160v and 175r–184r; Feathery for 'The: Table: Off,: the severall Heades wrytten in this Booke, vizt' (ff. 118r–120r) and the text on ff. 161r–174v. Watermark: quatrefoils within circle.]

19.6. ff. 185r–188v: *A: Coppye Off a Lre sent ffrom the greate Magull, to the kinge of greate Brittaine*

[By Jahangir (1569–1627), Emperor of Hindustan (reigned 1605–27). Cf. 72.9 below. Watermark: pillars.]

19.7. ff. 189r–190r: *A: Coppye Off the Councells Lres, to the Sheriffe, and the Justices of the Peace, in the Countye of South^{ton}*

[By the Queen's Privy Council, 19 October 1579. Watermark: pillars.]

19.8. ff. 191r–198r: *The Coppye Off a Letter written by M^r: Thomas Killegrewe, dated att Orleans, the, vij°: daye of december, newe stile, 1635*

[By Thomas Killigrew (1612–83), about the diabolical possession of nuns at Loudun, 1635. Printed from a MS at Magdalene College, Cambridge, Pepys Library No. 2099, in *European Magazine*, 43 (1803), 102–6; the events treated, with a bibliography, in Aldous Huxley, *The devils of Loudun* (London, 1952). Another MS

copy, possibly associated with Feathery's scriptorium, is Trinity College Dublin MS 532, ff. 99r–115r.]

20. MS 802

[Folio, 201 leaves; composite volume of state tracts, including the execution speech of William Parry (cf. 45.3 below), Cornwallis (cf. 6.1 above), Coke (cf. 53.18 below), and 'A Reconciliation' (cf 34 below); acquired before *c.*1670; old pressmark E.1.10. Watermark in Feathery items: pillars.]

20.1. ff. 1r–10v: *A Letter Written by Sir Phillipp Sidney vnto Queene Elizabeth touching her marriage with Monsuer:*

[By Sir Philip Sidney: cf. *Index*, i/2, SiP 214; Appendix IV below, No. 36. Cf. 17 and 18.1 above and 41.10, 53, 57.4, 64, 78.7, 105.1, and 110 below. Heading on f. 1r (and possibly the first word of the main text: 'Most') in another scribal hand; rest of the text on ff. 1r–10v in Feathery's hand.]

20.2. ff. 11r–14v: *A Leetter written by Sir Phillipp Sidney to a brother of his touching the direction of his Trauaile*

[By Sir Philip Sidney. Cf. 6.6 above and 53 below. Heading on f. 11r and first word of main text ('My') in another scribal hand; rest of the text on ff. 11r–14v in Feathery's hand until the very end, when the first scribe adds the subscription 'Your assured louing brother Phillipp Sidney' on f. 14v.]

20.3. ff. 53r–59r: *A: Breiffe Discours: of the Trayterous Attempts, and practizes, of the Earles of Northumb: and Westmorland, and other Trayto^{rs}: and Rebells, Assembled in the North pts of England, < > 1589*

[An anonymous account (here misdated) of the Northern Rebellion of 1569 led by Thomas Percy, seventh Earl of Northumberland (1528–72), and Charles Neville, sixth Earl of Westmorland (1543–1601).]

20.4. ff. 60r–62v: *The Hermitts Oration att Theobaldes, penned by S^r: Robte Cecill, Anno: 1594*

[By Sir Robert Cecil, later Earl of Salisbury. John Nichols, *The progresses and public processions of Queen Elizabeth*, 3 vols. (London, 1823), iii. 241–5. Cf. 35 and 92.10 below.]

20.5. ff. 63r–65r: *A: Lre written by Secretarye: Davison, beinge in disfavo^r: wth Queene Elizabeth, to the Earle of Essex:*

[By William Davison (1541?–1608), beginning 'My most honn^ble good Lord I might seeme wearisome . . .', 1596.]

20.6. ff. 72r–86v: *A: Relation Off the: Carriage of the Marryage, that should have made made [sic], Betwene the Prince of England, And the Infanta Maior of Spayne, And alsoe after wth the Younger Infanta: Written by S^r: Charles Cornewallis:*

[By Sir Charles Cornwallis. Gutch, i. 133–55; Somers, ii. 492–501. Cf. 35, 58, and 108.5 below; Starkey No. 53.]

20.7. ff. 130r–133v: *The Resolution of all the Judges vpon seuerall questions against Popish Recusants Trinity Terme 2° Caroli. Regis: 1626.*

[Cf. Starkey No. 38. ff. 130r–131v in another scribal hand; ff. 132r–133v in Feathery's hand.]

20.8. ff. 169r–173r: *Aduertisements Off a Loyall Sub^t: to his gratious Soveraigne, drawne ffrom Observacons, of the Peoples Speeches:*

[Written 1603–4; Somers, ii. 144–8; Braunmuller, 326–37 (commentary pp. 448–9). Cotton's copy is BL Cotton MS Faustina C. II, ff. 63r–64r. Cf. 6 above and 42, 71, 83.1, and 108.7 below.]

20.9. ff. 174r–175v: *A Letter written from Kinge James to Secretarie Calvert*

[By James I (1566–1625; reigned 1603–25), 16 December 1621. Cf. 19 above. f. 174r until halfway down f. 175r in another scribal hand; Feathery takes over in mid-sentence and finishes on f. 175v.]

20.10. ff. 176r–177r: *A Lre wrytten ffrom: kinge James, to the Speaker of the Comons Howse of Parliam^te:*

[By James I, 17 December 1621.]

21. MS 845

[Folio, two tracts and state letters bound together; the second from the library principally of James Ussher (1581–1656), Archbishop of Armagh (library shelfmark 'BBB.57'); old pressmark F.3.20.]

No. 2: *An Argument vpon The question of Impositions devided and digested into sundrye chapters by Sr John Dauis Knight his Ma^ts Attorney generall of IRELAND*

[By Sir John Davies: cf. *Index*, i/1, DaJ 277. Cf. 2 and 18.2 above and 52 below. 112 leaves (221 pages), and two blanks, foliated 113–14. Title-page and ff. 40r–63v, 66r–96v in another scribal hand; ff. 2r–39v, 64r–65v, 97r–112v in Feathery's hand, as well as foliation throughout. Watermark: quatrefoils within circle.]

22. MS 861

[Folio, 429 leaves (plus blanks); composite volume of state tracts, by Sir Robert Cecil (cf. 77.3 below), Ralegh, and others, and Essex's charge against Wimbledon (cf. Starkey No. 89); bequeathed after 1670 by Sir Jerome Alexander; old pressmark G.4.8. Watermark in Feathery items: pillars.]

22.1. ff. 8r–16v: *The: Charracter: Off: a: puritan:*

[Anonymous character, beginning 'Benevolent: Reader: ffor thie Mirth meerlye . . .'.]

22.2. ff. 306r–312v: *A: Shorte Discours, proveinge That princes extremityes haue been Beyound, the ease, of their Sub^{ts}: by Reason of Warres Wrytten. By, S^r: Robte, Cotton, knight, and Barronett, &c*

[By Sir Robert Cotton, beginning 'Haveinge: thus farre, wth as light a hand as I could drawe downe the many and mighty Burthens of the Comon Wealth . . .': being the second half of Cotton's 'Answer made by command of Prince Henry to certain propositions of war and peace'. Cf. 28 below, also 57.8, 80, and 85. Title-page (f. 306r) and heading and first word of the main text on f. 307r in Feathery's hand; rest of the text on ff. 307r–312v in another scribal hand.]

23. MS 862

[Folio, 381 leaves; volume of state tracts up to 1641, including letters by Ralegh (ff. 152r–161r), Fleetwood's 'Relation of Courts' (ff. 174r–175v: cf. 19.3 above), discourses on Parliament by Cotton, Agard, Dodderidge, and Camden (ff. 298r–303v, 306r–308r: cf. 14.1–4 above), and Cotton's speech on the debasing of coin (ff. 372r–381r: cf. 16 above), in several scribal hands; bequeathed after 1670 by Sir Jerome Alexander; old pressmark G.4.13.]

23.1. ff. 1r–7v: *A: Relation: Off: the Lowe Countryes, And ffirst; of the Archduke Albertus; &c*

[Anonymous tract, beginning 'The: said Countrye, was gyven, to his wyfe Isabell, daughter to Phillipp: the second . . .'. Cf. 26 below. Watermark: quatrefoils within circle.]

23.2. ff. 8r–26r: *A: Shorte: Discours: Concerninge: the ffirst devision, of: England As it is nowe generally named, into Shires, wth the Jurisdiction of B^{pps}: and Bishopprickes, And other thinges heerein Conteyned; &c:*

[By William Bird (1538?–1623). Cf. 55, 57.2, and 79A below. Title-page (f. 8r) only in Feathery's hand; text in two other scribal hands. Watermark: quatrefoils within circle.]

23.3. ff. 27r–126v: *A True Relation, as it was reported in Parliamente; of the whole important passages, of ye Prince his being in Spaine, with the treatie of the marriage, and the restitucon of the Pallatinate, with the speeches and passages in Parliam^t: taken, verbatim, out of the Record*

[Parliamentary debates concerning the abortive Spanish match, 1623. Feathery responsible for 'The: Table: Off, the: severall heades, Conteyned in this Booke; vizt' (ff. 28r–29r) and the text on ff. 30r–72v; another scribe for the title (f. 27r) and ff. 73r–126v. Watermark: quatrefoils within circle.]

23.4. ff. 127r–138v: *The: Coppye, Off: the Challendge sent by the Earle of Northumberland, to S^r: ffrauncis Veere; And, S^r: ffrauncis Veere his Aunswere, &c*

[By Henry Percy, Earl of Northumberland, and Sir Francis Vere. Cf. 3 and 11 above and 28, 41.9, and 105.4 below. Title-page (f. 127r) only in Feathery's hand; text (ff. 128r–138v) in another scribal hand. Watermark: quatrefoils within circle.]

23.5. ff. 139r–151v: *A Discours Concerninge ffree Tradeinge, wth the Inconveniencyes, by Incorporated Societyes, And, the Beniffitte[s] of Libtye, and ffree Tradeinge, &c*

[Cf. 7 above and 43 below. Watermark: quatrefoils within circle.]

23.6. ff. 176r–178v: *A; Relation:, Off,: the Manne^r: of the proceedinge, w^{th}: S^r: Thomas Mounson, vppon the Pleadinge of his Pardon, in the Co^{rte}: of the kinges Bench, the :xij: of ffebruarij .1616.*

[Account relating to the implication of Sir Thomas Monson (1564–1641) in the Overbury murder; cf. Baker, *CUL* 129–30. Cf. 19 above and 41.5 and 78.9 below. Heading only in Feathery's hand; the text in another scribal hand. Watermark: quatrefoils within circle.]

23.7. ff. 360r–365r: *A: Breiffe Discourse: proveinge that the Howse of Comons, haue equall power wth the Peeres, in poynte of Judicature: wrytten by Sir Rob^{te} Cotton to S^{r}: Edward Mountague, Anno: Dni: 1621:*

[By Sir Robert Cotton. Printed in [London?], 1640[/1] [STC 22165–6]; *Cottoni posthuma*, No. 14. Cf. 100 below. Watermark: pillars.]

Hamilton, Massachusetts, Robert S. Pirie

24. [No shelfmark]

[Folio, 40 leaves; composite volume of tracts; sold at Christie's, London, 12 June 1980 (Arthur A. Houghton, Jr sale), lot 482 (and plate 42 after p. 132); Christie's, New York, 18 November 1988 (John F. Fleming sale), lot 334.]

[No. 1]: *A: Discours: wrytten by: S^{r}: John Sucklinge knight, To the Earle of Dorsett:*

[By Sir John Suckling (1609-42): his 'An Account of Religion by Reason', written 1637, printed in *Fragmenta aurea* (London, 1646) [Wing S6126]: cf. *Index*, ii/2, SuJ 143; also University of London MS 309, ff. 290r–304r (SuJ 142). 15 leaves (29 pages). Chiefly in Feathery's hand; last two pages in another scribal hand. Reader's marginal annotations.]

London, Dr Peter Beal

25. MS 1

[Folio, 8 leaves (15 pages), now bound as a separate tract; inscriptions: 'Henry Vansie Salusbury Doctor's Commons Novr. 1824', 'J. Lee. Doctors Commons. January 1828' [i.e. presumably Dr John Lee, FRS (1783–1866) of Hartwell House, near Aylesbury, Buckinghamshire], and 'Mss of the late Sir Thomas Salusbury Judge of the Admiralty'; bookplate with motto 'Verum atque decens'; later in the library of William Amhurst

Tyssen-Amherst, first Baron Amherst of Hackney (1835–1909). Watermark: grapes on pedestal (IVG).]

Certayne Replyes and: Obiections, Aunswered, by Willm Lord Burleigh, Att the Councell: Table, videlt whether it maye stand with: good pollicye ffor hir Matie: to ioyne wth: J J: in their Enterprise of :#:

[By William Cecil, Lord Burghley. Cf. 15.2 above and 41.3 below. See Plate 34 above.]

26. MS 2

[Folio, 6 leaves (12 pages); a separate tract (disbound); acquired in 1983 from Philip Robinson. Watermark: quatrefoils within circle.]

A: Breiffe: Discours off: the Lowe Countryes, And, ffirst of the Lowe Countryes; of Albertus:

[Cf. 23.1 above. See Plates 25 and 26 above.]

London, British Library

27. Additional MS 4149

[Folio, 346 leaves; compilation of historical materials and some poems from *temp.* Edward IV to 1623, predominantly in the hand of Ralph Starkey, including Sir Thomas Smith's dialogue concerning the Queen's marrying 1560 (ff. 38r–87v: cf. 95.2 below), materials relating to the proposed Spanish match, 1623, including Prince Charles's letter to the Pope (ff. 282v–283v: cf. 53.16 below), and tracts (some concerning marriage) by Bacon, Cornwallis (ff. 132r–152v, 153r–158r: cf. 37.1 and 37.3 below), Ralegh (ff. 184r–192v, 193r–203v: cf. 108.28 below and 3.3 above), the Earl of Devonshire (ff. 306v–319v: cf. 35.12 below), and others; from the library of Sir Simonds D'Ewes; later owned by Dr Thomas Birch (1705–66).]

f. 183r–v: *The kinge of Denmarcke, to his Matie: the xiiij of Aug: 1606: ffrom Shipboarde Concerninge a Suppos'ed Scandall touching the Countesse of Nottingham*

[By Christian IV, King of Denmark (1577–1648), 1606.]

28. Additional MS 11308

[Folio, 200 leaves; composite volume of state tracts, including 'Tom Tell-Trothe' (ff. 2r–26v: cf. Starkey No. 63), the Northumberland–Vere challenge (ff. 86r–96v: cf. 11 above), letters by Ralegh (ff. 135r–142v), and Letter to Parliament (ff. 143r–163v: cf. 1.11 above), in various scribal hands; purchased from Rodd, 11 February 1838. Watermark: quatrefoils within circle.]

ff. 59r–77v: *An: Aunswere made: by Comaund of Prince Henrye, to Certayne Proposicons of Warre., and Peace, Wrytten, by S*: *Robte Cotton Knight, and Barronett. And p'sented to his Highnes, &*

[By Sir Robert Cotton, April 1609. Printed in London, 1655 [Wing C6477–8]. Cotton's own working copy is BL Cotton MS Cleopatra F. VI, ff. 1r–38r. Cf. 22.2 above and 57.8, 80, and 85 below.]

29. Additional MS 11764

[Folio, 260 leaves; volume of state papers, in various hands; purchased from A. Robertson, 3 April 1841.]

ff. 2r–30v: [*Reports of Several Cases in the Star Chamber in the Reign of King Charles the first*]

[Cf. 10 above, and 101, and 110A below. Title given in a table of contents on f. 1r in a later hand. ff. 2r–10r in another scribal hand; ff. 10v–30v in Feathery's hand, concluding cases for 7–15 February 1633/4. Watermark: grapes.]

30. Additional MS 12513

[Folio, 45 leaves (88 pages); a single tract; owned by Edward Umfreville (d. 1786) of the Inner Temple (and his note: 'a Coppy of a most excellent & well composed Treatise wrote in An°. 32°. Eliz:'); bookplate of the Strawberry Hill Library of Horace Walpole, fourth Earl of Orford (1717–97), and

part of lot 91 in the Strawberry Hill sale, 6th day, 30 April 1842. Watermark: elaborate urn.]

An: Aunswere:, To, the: Coppye of a Rayleinge Invectyve, (Against the Regym^te: of Woemen in generall) w^th: Certayne Malliparte dyceptions to dyvers and sundrye, matters of the State, Wrytten To Queene Elizabeth, By the Right honno^ble: Henrye Lord Howarde, Late Earle of North^ton

[By Henry Howard, Earl of Northampton. Cf. 3.1 and 17A above.]

31. Additional MS 18201

[Folio, 80 leaves; volume of state papers relating to the proposed Spanish match, 1622–3, in two scribal hands; Puttick & Simpson's, 3 July 1850, lot 58. Watermark: pillars.]

ff. 1r–28r: [*Letters on the Spanish Match*]

[Eight state letters by James I, Frederick, King of Bohemia, Philip IV, Count Olivares, Pope Gregory XV and Prince Charles (ff. 16v–20v: cf. 53.15–16 below), and Thomas Alured, concerning the proposed marriage of Prince Charles and the Spanish Infanta, 1622–3.]

32. Additional MS 35838

[Folio, 425 leaves; composite volume of 17th- and 18th-century papers of various size.]

ff. 53r–83v: [*Speeches by Sir Nicholas Bacon*]

[Portion of a folio MS collection of speeches by Sir Nicholas Bacon (1509–79), Lord Keeper, to Queen Elizabeth, the Privy Council, Parliament, etc., one (ff. 71r–76r) dated 1562, two (ff. 68r–76r) concerning the Queen's marriage and succession. Cf. 71 below. Incomplete; ff. 53r–67r in another scribal hand; ff. 68r–83v in Feathery's hand. Watermark: grapes.]

33. Additional MS 48062

[Folio, 430 leaves; composite volume of state tracts, including 'Tom Tell Troth' (ff. 245r–283v:

cf. 28 above), 'The Policia' (ff. 288r–296v: cf. 6.7 above), the exchange between Queen Elizabeth and Sir Thomas Pope (ff. 297r–298v: cf. 1.22 above), and tracts by Cornwallis (ff. 326r–367v: cf. 37.1 below) and Ralegh, in various hands; also including earlier items docketed by Robert Beale (1541–1601), Clerk of the Queen's Council; among the Yelverton Papers (MS 68) belonging to Sir Henry Yelverton (1566–1629), Justice of the Common Pleas, and his family. Watermark in Feathery items: pillars (RDP).]

33.1. ff. 300r–316r: *A: Shorte veiwe to bee: taken of greate Brittayne, and Spayne*

[By Sir Francis Bacon. Cf. 6.8 above.]

33.2. ff. 318r–321r: *Questions propounded by Queene Marye, and Aunswered by Hir Councell, Touchinge the Contynuance of a Treatye made by Hen: 8: wth the Empero^{r}: and Kinge of ffraunce, ffor Maintenance of a Quarrell, Betwene ffraunce, and Kinge Phillipp: of Spayne:*

[By Mary I (1516–58; reigned 1553–58) and her Privy Council. Cotton's copy is BL Cotton MS Titus C. VII, ff. 198r–199r. Cf. Starkey No. 24.]

33.3. ff. 321r–322v: *Ordinarye Annuall: Receipte[s] of Thexcheque^{r}:* and *Ordinarye Annuall: Issues of the Excheque^{r}:*

[Cf. 6.5 above and 53.13, 83, and 109.14 below.]

33.4. ff. 323r–324v: *Abatements now in beinge or to bee very shortlye, vppon the Marryage; of the Ladye Elizabeth to the Counte Pallatyne of the Rhine, Anno 1613; and otherwise ffor the kinge[s] Beniffitt, By the Comissione^{rs}: of the Treasurye:*

[By Henry Howard, Earl of Northampton. Cf. 1.2 above and 53.14, 71, and 83 below.]

34. Additional MS 48063

[Folio, 266 leaves; composite volume of state tracts, in various hands; among the Yelverton Papers (MS 69) belonging to Sir Henry Yelverton (1566–1629), Justice of the Common Pleas, and his family. Watermark: pillars.]

ff. 99r–117r: *A: Reconsiliacon made: Betwene the kinge, and his Sub^{te[s]}: Touchinge the demaund of his Right, in ould debte[s], and Landes, quiettlye enioyed tyme out of minde, &^{c}:*

[Cf. 6 and 20 above and 35 and 63 below; Starkey No. 45. ff. 99r–100r in Feathery's hand, a second scribe taking over two-thirds of the way down f. 100r until the end of f. 116v, with Feathery resuming in mid-sentence to conclude with the last page, f. 117r. Watermark: pillars.]

35. Additional MS 73087

[Folio, 229 leaves; volume of state letters, speeches, and tracts, including tracts by Cotton and Camden on the Lords Steward, Constable, and Marshal of England (ff. 97r–135v: cf. 88 below), Bacon, Cecil (including 'The Hermitts Oration', ff. 170v–174r: cf. 20.4 above), John Williams, Bishop of Lincoln (f. 174r–v: cf. 109.7 below), Cornwallis (ff. 178r–197r: cf. 20.6 above), and 'A Reconcilliation' (ff. 198r–219r: cf. 34 above), in two scribal hands; a poem by Ben Jonson ('On the right ho^{ble}: and virtuos Lord Weston Lo: Trer of England vppon the daye he was made Earle of Portland | To the enuios', beginning 'Looke vpp thou seede of enuye and still bringe' [*The Vnderwood* lxxiii: 17 February 1632/3]) added on f. 220r in a third scribal hand; signed on ff. [iii] and 219r by 'Ric: Tichbone' [probably Sir Richard Tichborne, second Baronet, MP (*c*.1578–1652): cf. 71 below]; briefly discussed in C. Deedes, 'Unpublished letters of Sir Walter Ralegh', *N&Q* 8th ser. 3 (24 June 1893), 481–2, and 4 (8 July–12 August 1893), 21–2, 63–4, 121–2; James Tregaskis, catalogue No. 1022 (1948), item 29; afterwards owned by Agnes Latham (1905–96), editor of Ralegh's *Poems* (1929). Watermark: pillars (RDP).]

35.1. ff. [iii^r–vi^v]: *A Table of all the seuerall Tractes and Treatices written in this Booke followinge vidlet*

[List of contents of the volume; the heading in the hand of the second scribe; the text entirely in Feathery's hand.]

35.2. ff. 1r–13r: *The Manner Off the Sicknes and death of Prince Henry Sonne to Kinge James Anno 1612*

[By Sir Charles Cornwallis. Cf. 6.1, 9, 18, and 20 above and 53, 67, and 83 below.]

35.3. ff. 13r–23r, 24v–34r: [*Letters by Sir Walter Ralegh*]

[Ten letters by Sir Walter Ralegh, to Lords Nottingham, Suffolk, Devonshire, Carr, Cecil, James I, Queen Anne, Sir Ralph Winwood, and Ralegh's wife, 1603–11? Cf. 1.4, 1.6, 23, and 28 above and 70, 108.6, and 108.19 below.]

35.4. ff. 23r–24v: *The Coppye Off a Lre Wrytten by S^r: Robte Carre, Viscounte Rochester, And after Earle of Somersett, vnto the Lord Henry Howard, Earle of Northampton, Anno, 1612: the, viij^th of October:*

[By Sir Robert Carr, Earl of Somerset. cf. 1.5 above and 52, 92.11 and 108.9 below.]

35.5. ff. 34r–37v: *Sir Walter Rawleighs Conffession:*

[Ralegh's speech on the scaffold, 29 October 1618: cf. *Index*, i/2, RaW 739–822. Cf. 108.14 below.]

35.6. f. 38r: *A: Lre wrytten by M^r: Anthonye Babbington, to Queene Elizabeth:*

[By Anthony Babington (1561–86), conspirator: his letter to the Queen pleading for mercy, 19 September 1586, the day before his execution. John Nichols, *The progresses and public pro-

cessions of Queen Elizabeth* (1823), ii. 482. Cf. 92.12 below.]

35.7. ff. 38v–43v: *The Combatt betwixt the Lord Bruce, and S^r: Edward Sackvill:*

[Letters between Edward Bruce, second Lord Bruce of Kinloss, and Sir Edward Sackville, afterwards fourth Earl of Dorset (1590–1652), preceding their duel near Bergen-op-Zoom in August 1613 at which Bruce was killed, the last letter by Sackville giving an account of it dated 8 September 1613. Cf. 41 below.]

35.8. ff. 44r–47v: *Instructions giuen to our Right Trustie, and welbeloved Councello^r the Lord of Buckhurst, and our servante Robte Beale; sent by vs to the Scottishe Queene: November, 1586*

[By Queen Elizabeth after the trial of Mary Queen of Scots.]

35.9. ff. 47v–48v: *The Coppye Off a Lre, sent ffrom Queene Elizabeth, to S^r: Amyas Pawlett, Guardyan of the Scottishe Queene, whoe was prysoner in ffotheringhaye Castell in Northampton shier:*

[By Queen Elizabeth to Sir Amias Paulet. Harrison, 180 (dated *c.*September 1580). Cf. 53 below.]

35.10. ff. 48v–53r: *A: Lre Sent by the Justice: Clearcke of Scotland, to S^r: Archibald Dowglas Ambassador of Scotland, Resident in England, in Aunsweare to a fformer Lre, sent vnto him, by thesaid Ambassado^r:*

[By Sir Lewis Ballenden, Lord Justice Clerk of Scotland, to Sir Archibald Douglas (? the eighth Earl of Angus, 1555–88), after the execution of Mary Queen of Scots, Holyrood House, 24 October (no year).]

35.11. ff. 53r–72r: [*Negotiations with France*]

[Twelve state letters and memoranda by Sir Francis Walsingham (1530?–90), Lord Burghley, and Robert Dudley, Earl of Leicester (1532?–88), together with Queen Elizabeth's instructions to Walsingham's deputy Henry Killigrew, 19 October to 31 December 1571. Cf. 43, and 49 below; Starkey Nos. 61, and 76.]

35.12. ff. 73r–96r: *A: Discourse wrytten by the Earle of Deuonshire in defence of the Marriage wth the Lady Penelope Rich 1606*

[By Charles Blount, eighth Lord Mountjoy and Earl of Devonshire (1563–1606). Cf. 27 above; Starkey No. 54. ff. 73r–84r in the hand of the second scribe; ff. 85r–96r in Feathery's hand.]

35.13. f. 135v: *The Jurisdiction of the Lord high Conestable and Mareshall of England*

[The beginning of a text, occupying three quarters of a page, in the hand of the second scribe; deleted, and Feathery has added at the bottom the catchwords 'S^r: ffrauncis' in anticipation of the heading 'Sir ffrancis Bacons charge att the Sessions of the verge' on f. 136r.]

36. Additional MS [uncatalogued, Evelyn Papers, in box 'Historical 1']

[Folio, 30 pages; a single tract; first page marked 'MS/(34)'; among the MSS of John Evelyn (1620–1706). Watermarks: chiefly pillars; one tipped-in bifolium (ff. [11–12]) with lions rampant flanking a shield.]

The Comons declaracon, and Impeachm^{te}: against the Duke of Buckinghm:/

[1625.]

37. Cotton MS Vespasian C. X

[Folio, 348 leaves; a transcript of the diplomatic letterbook of Sir Charles Cornwallis, as English Ambassador in Madrid, 1607–8, entirely in Feathery's hand (but for the foliation and binding signatures at the foot of various pages); docketed on a flyleaf in the hand of Cotton's librarian Richard James (d. 1638): 'Matters Touching Spayne. in ye yeare 1607'. Watermark: spread eagle. This MS (and 38 below) used as a source in Edmund Sawyer, *Memorials of affairs of state . . . collected (chiefly) from the original papers of the Rt. Hon. Sir Ralph Winwood*, 3 vols. (London, 1725); and see also Francis O. Edward, SJ, 'A letter book of the first Earl of Salisbury at Stonyhurst College, with special reference to the Spanish correspondence', *JSA* 4 (1972), 486–505.]

37.1. ff. 1r–35r: *Discourse of the State of Spayne, Wrytten by my Lo^d: aboute the Beginninge of this yeare 1607*

[By Sir Charles Cornwallis, beginning 'The kinge possesseth at this p^rsente Spayne entirelye . . .', 1607. Somers. iii. 304–15. Cf. 27 and 33 above.]

37.2. ff. 35r–180v, 189r–348r: [*Diplomatic correspondence of Sir Charles Cornwallis*]

[Series of *c*.105 letters, from 5 February 1606/7 to April 1608 (plus one of 7 November 1614), including *c*.83 by Cornwallis himself, 11 by Sir Robert Cecil, Earl of Salisbury, and others by the Earl of Northampton, James I, Lords Dunbar and Denny, the Privy Council, the Duke of Lerma, Secretary Prada, and some freed galley slaves.]

37.3. ff. 180v–188v: *A discourse wrytten by my Lo: to prove that a Coniunction, by Allyance of England, and Spayne, is the most honno^{ble}: and proffitablest Course, ffor both the Monarchies; especyallie ffor Spayne:*

[By Sir Charles Cornwallis, beginning 'The surest, most sollid, and honn^{ble}: meanes . . .', September 1607. Cf. 27 above.]

38. Cotton MS Vespasian C. XI

[Folio, 405 leaves; diplomatic correspondence of Sir Charles Cornwallis, English Ambassador in Madrid, 1608–9, with some subsequent letters to 1611, being a continuation of 37 above, the text entirely in Feathery's hand (but for the foliation and binding signatures at the foot of various pages); notes and docketing on flyleaves in the hands of Sir William Dugdale and Cotton's librarian, Richard James. Watermark: spread eagle. This MS used in Sawyer and cited in Edward: cf. 37 above.]

[*Diplomatic correspondence of Sir Charles Cornwallis*]

[Series of *c*.161 letters and 14 memorials and enclosures, from 2 April 1608 to 8 January 1610[/11], including *c*.127 by Cornwallis himself, 11 by Sir Robert Cecil, Earl of Salisbury, 5 by the Earl of Northampton, 5 by the Privy Council, 4 by King James, and others by Prince Henry, Philip III, Thomas Nevinson, Levinius Munck, and Francis Cottington. f. 2r–v is misbound at the beginning.]

39. Hargrave MS 165

[Folio, 167 leaves; volume of Chancery tracts, including one by John Selden, in various scribal hands; from the successive libraries of John Anstis (1669–1744), George Hardinge (1743–1816), and Francis Hargrave (1741?–1821).]

ff. 3r–153r: *Breviatte Out Off the Recordes in the Tower Conscerninge the Authoritye Off the Chauncerye: with Directions: howe to ffinde the Originalls*

[Readers' annotations. Watermark: pillars.]

40. Hargrave MS 225

[Folio, 337 leaves; volume of state tracts, in various scribal hands. Watermark in Feathery items: pillars.]

40.1. ff. 162r–179v: *The: Coppye Off: a: Letter wrytten to the Lower Howse of Parliam^te:*

Touchinge dyvers Inconveniencyes and greivaunces of the State, &^c

[Cf. 1.11 above and 53, 61, 78.2, 83.3, 106.5, and 112 below.]

40.2. ff. 180r–239r: *Englandes Epiniomis Or: A Collection, out of the Authenticque Historyans, And a Commentarye of those Lawes, The originall of manye of our Moderne; whereby the kingdome of England, hath been from tyme to tyme governed, vnder both prophane, and Christian Princes, since the ffirst Inhabitants, to the end of Kinge Johns Raigne, &^c: Wrytten: By: John: Seldon Esquy^re &^c*

[By John Selden. Cf. 19.4 above and 87 below. ff. 180r–212v, 220r–239r, and running heads throughout in Feathery's hand; ff. 213r–219r in another scribal hand.]

40.3. ff. 240r–248v: *An: Aunswere, to Certayne Arguem^ts: raysed ffrom supposed Antiquityes, and practise, by some Members, of the Lower Howse of Parliam^te: to prove, That Ecclesiasticall Lawes, ought to bee enacted by Temporall Men*

40.4. f. 249r–v: *The: wordes, wherewith: Henrye Earle of Oxfford, greate Chamberleyne of England is Charged in the Infformacon, of M^r: Attournye generall, in the Starrchamber*

[Arraignment of Henry de Vere, eighteenth Earl of Oxford (1598–1625), 1622. Cf. Starkey No. 65.]

41. Hargrave MS 226

[Folio, 313 leaves; volume of state tracts, speeches, and letters, dating up to 1631, including Fleetwood's account of Buckingham's Isle of Rhé expedition (ff. 216r–218r: cf. Starkey No. 56), the 'Combat' between Bruce and Sackville (ff. 245r–249v: cf. 35.7 above), the arraignment of Castlehaven (ff. 311r–313v: cf. 17A.3 above), and materials by Ralegh, Cotton, and Bristol; in various scribal hands; given to Francis Hargrave by George

Hardinge (inscription dated 16 July 1789). Water-mark in Feathery items: usually pillars (IEAN).]

41.1. ff. 2r–17v: *Sir: ffrauncis Bacon: his Speech, Att the Arraignem^{te}, of Rob^{te} Earle of Somersett*

[By Sir Francis Bacon, 25 May 1616. Printed in *Baconiana*, [ed. Tenison] (London, 1679) [Wing B269], 14–36; Spedding, xii. 307–20.]

41.2. ff. 104r–115r: *The humble Answere and advise of his Ma^{ts}: councell vppon certaine proposicons*

[Cf. 78.1 below. Entirely in another scribal hand until the very end, when Feathery adds the last one and a half lines on f. 115r.]

41.3. ff. 208r–215v: *Certayne: Replyes: and Obiections, Aunswered, by Willm Lord Burleigh, Att the Councell, Table, videlt/: whether, itt, maye, stande with good pollicye, ffor hir Matie: to ioyne wth JJ in their Enterpryse of J:*

[By William Cecil, Lord Burghley. Cf. 15.2 and 25 above.]

41.4. ff. 229r–231r: *The Relacon and, Opin-yon of Mr Serieant ffeetwoode, Concern-inge, the Originall, and begininge of Co^{rts}: in England, &^c*

[By William Fleetwood. Cf. 19.3 and 23 above and 106.6 and 109.2 below.]

41.5. ff. 231r–233v: *A: Relacon, off: the Man-ner of the proceedinge, wth S^r: Thomas Monnson, vppon the Pleadinge of his Pardon, in the Co^{rte}: of the Kinges Bench, the xij^o: of ffebruarij 1616*

[Cf. 19 and 23.6 above and 78.9 below.]

41.6. ff. 233v–235r: *The: Coppye, Off: a, Let-ter Wrytten ffrom the kinge of Morroco, to the kinge of England:*

[By the King of Morocco, 1637.]

41.7. f. 235r–v: *A: Letter, Sent, to, a, ffrinde w^{th}, a, Present*

[Anonymous, beginning 'Sir, Lowly fortune beggeth Acceptance . . .'.]

41.8. ff. 236r–243r: *The: Character Off the incomperable Ladye, the Countesse of Carlile; And the most excellent Lord, The Earle of Northumberland*

Anonymous accounts of:

  i. (ff. 237r–240v) Lucy Hay, Countess of Carlisle (1599–1660)

[Imperfect, lacking two leaves at the end.]

  ii. (ff. 241r–243r) her father, Henry Percy, ninth Earl of Northumberland (1564–1632), who was released from the Tower in 1621.

[Most of this character is printed in John W. Shirley, *Thomas Harriot: A biography* (Oxford, 1983), 207–8. Reader's markings. Watermark: grapes.]

41.9. ff. 250r–260r: *The: Coppye Off the Challendge, sent by the Earle of Northumberland to S^r: ffrauncis Veere; And S^r: ffrauncis Veeres Aunswere:*

[By Henry Percy, Earl of Northumberland, and Sir Francis Vere. Cf. 3, 11, 23.4, and 28 above and 105.4 below.]

41.10. ff. 270r–282v: *The: Coppye: Off: a: Letter: written by S^r: Phillipp: Sidnye, to Queene Elizabeth, Touchinge hir Marryage; wth Moun-sieur*

[By Sir Philip Sidney: cf. *Index*, i/2, SiP 193; Appendix IV below, No. 14. Cf. 17, 18.1, and 20.1 above and 53, 57.4, 64, 78.7, 105.1, and 110 below. Title-page (f. 270r) and ff. 273r–282v in Feathery's hand; ff. 271r–272v in another scribal hand. Reader's markings.]

42. Harley MS 35

[Folio, 522 leaves; composite volume of historical letters and tracts, in various hands, one that of Ralph Starkey, including his copy of 'Advertisement of a loyal subject' (ff. 460r–462v: cf. 20.8 above); from the library of Sir Simonds D'Ewes (1602–50): see Watson, 163.]

42.1. ff. 180r–327r: [*Historical Passages of Ireland both ancient and modern*]

[Collection of state letters and discourses relating to Ireland 1552–1611, by Thomas Cusacke, Chancellor of Ireland, the Archbishop of Armagh, the Privy Council, Sir Richard Bingham, William Wyse, Sir Robert Cecil, Justice Saxey, James I, and others. Title added in a modern hand.]

42.2. ff. 458r–459v: *S͏ʳ: John Cooke his speeche at the conference, Betwene the Lordis and Comons, aboute the Peticon to the kinge against Recusants xxviijᵗʰ: Martij: 1628:*

[By Sir John Coke (1563–1644), Secretary of State.]

43. Harley MS 36

[Folio, 396 leaves; volume of transcripts of state papers, including 'A Brief Discourse concerning Free Trade' (ff. 28r–41v: cf. 7 above), and Tourneur's 'Character of Robert Earl of Salisbury' ascribed to 'Guil: Tourneur' (ff. 394r–396v: cf. 77.2 and 108.8 below); chiefly in the hand of Ralph Starkey; from the library of Sir Simonds D'Ewes: see Watson, 288.]

ff. 104r–179v: *S͏ʳ: ffrauncis Walsingham Leidger Ambassador ffor Queene Elizabeth, his Negociacons wᵗʰ: the kinge of ffraunce Beginninge in Anᵒ: 1571: and Contynueinge there till: Anᵒ: 1572*

[Negotiations and correspondence of Sir Francis Walsingham with the King of France in 1571–2. Cf. 35.11 above and 49 below; Starkey No. 76.]

44. Harley MS 37

[Folio, 357 leaves; volume of state tracts and speeches, including Ralph Starkey's 'Discourse of the High Court of Parliament' (ff. 36r–60v: cf. 6.2 above) and Essex's charges against Wimbledon (ff. 88r–111v: cf. Starkey No. 89); parts of the compilation in the hand of Ralph Starkey; from the library of Sir Simonds D'Ewes: see Watson, 154, 159.]

44.1. ff. 204r–210v: *The Kinges Speech in the Vpper howse of Parliamᵗᵉ: the ffirst daye of the Apparaunce beinge the xvijᵗʰ: of Marche: Anᵒ: 1627*

[By Charles I (1600–49; reigned 1625–49): his speech in the House of Lords, 17 March 1627/8: Rushworth, i. 476–7.]

44.2. ff. 231r–246v: *The whole Coppies of the Presidents of Record menconed in the Argumᵗᵉ: deliued by M͏ʳ: John Seldon, Att the ffirst Conference wᵗʰ the Lordes toucheinge the Libtye of the Person of everye ffreeman, the ixᵗʰ of Aprill: 1628*

[By John Selden: Rushworth, i. 530–2. Cf. Starkey No. 83.]

44.3. ff. 247r–254v: *The Substance of the obiections made by m͏ʳ Atturney generall before a Comittie of bothe Howses, to the Argumente that was Made by the Howse of Comons at the first Conference wᵗʰ the Lordes, out of presidents of Recorde, and Resolucons of Judges in formere tymes touching the Libertie of the pson of euery freeman; And the Answers & replies then presentlie made by the Howse of Comons to those obiections by m͏ʳ Seldon the < > of Maye 1628*

[Arguments between Sir Robert Heath (1575–1649), Attorney-General, and John Selden: *State trials*, iii. 133–48, etc. Cf. Starkey No. 83. Almost entirely in the hand of Ralph Starkey; Feathery adds single-word corrections on ff. 247r and 249r; then, on f. 254v, after 1½ lines at the top of the page by Starkey, Feathery finishes the line and adds the last ten lines of text. See Plate 53 above.]

44.4. ff. 275r–276v: *Mr Mason of Lincolnes Inne his speache vppon the Bill p^r'sented to the Lower Howse toucheinge the Libtye of the Subiecte the < > daye of Maye: 1628*

[By Robert Mason (1571–1635): *Commons debates 1628*, iii. 540–1. Chiefly in the hand of Ralph Starkey; the title in the upper margin of f. 275r added by Feathery. See Plate 52 above.]

44.5. ff. 280r–283r: *Sr Henry Martynes Argumente deliuered at a Conference wth the Lordes, touchinge theire Addicon sent downe to the Comons vnder theire peticon of Right of the Subiecte the 23th: of May 1628*

[By Sir Henry Marten (1562?–1641), 23 May 1628: Rushworth, i. 579–84; *Commons debates 1628*, iii. 572–80. Chiefly in the hand of Ralph Starkey; a nine-word insertion in the margin of f. 281r and a six-line postscript on f. 283r added by Feathery.]

44.6. ff. 284r–301r: *The Speache of M^r: John Glanvile pronounced in a ffull Comittee of both Howses of Parliam^te the xxiij^th of Maye 1628; in the Paynted chambe^r at Westminister:*

[By Sir John Glanville (1586–1661), 23 May 1628: Rushworth, i. 568–79; *Commons debates 1628*, iii. 560–71. Twelve words after the word 'Parliam^te' in the title ('towchinge the Comons disallowance of the Addition to the peticon of Right') inserted by Ralph Starkey.]

45. Harley MS 39

[Folio, 432 leaves; volume of state tracts, letters and speeches, partly in the hand of Ralph Starkey; from the library of Sir Simonds D'Ewes: see Watson, 154–5, 239, 288; a note on f. 432v by Humfrey Wanley, 30 July 1714, recording Robert Harley's having lent this book eight or nine years earlier to Queen Anne and his extraction from it of some original royal letters. Watermark in Feathery items: pillars.]

45.1. ff. 291r–295r: *The Right Honno^ble: Tho: Viscount Brackley Lo: Chauncellor of England his Speeche: when Mountague the kinges Serieannte was made Cheefe Justice of the kinges Benche:*

[By Sir Thomas Egerton, Baron Ellesmere, Lord Chancellor, with the reply of Sir Henry Montagu (1563?–1642), 18 November 1616. Cotton's copy is BL Cotton MS Titus C. VII, ff. 45r–46v.]

45.2. f. 297r–v: *My Lo: Chauncellor Ellesmeere his Lre to the kinge ffor the Ressigneinge his Place: Anno: 1615*

[By Sir Thomas Egerton, Baron Ellesmere, 5 February 1615[/16]. Somers, ii. 170. Cotton's copy is BL Cotton MS Titus C. VII, f. 47r. Cf. 53.11 and 72.8 below.]

45.3. ff. 383r–386r: *The Sayeinges of Willm Parrye Doctor of the Ciuill Lawe, att his Execution in the Courte of the oulde Pallaise of Westminister ouer against the Starre chamber, the Second Daye of Marche, Anno: 1584:*

[Reported execution speech of William Parry, conspirator, 2 March 1584/5. Cf. 20 above.]

45.4. ff. 386v–392r: *The Manner and fforme of the Examinacon and Death of Willm Earle of Gowrye: Lo: Ruthen, and Dirletonn, and Greate Threasuror of Scotland: the Third Daye of Maye, after Eight Howers at Night 1544*

[Account of the trial and execution of William Ruthven, first Earl Gowrie (1541?–84), d. 2 May 1584.]

45.5. ff. 392v–403r: *The Arraignm^te: of S^r: John Parrott K^te: att Westminister the xxvij^o of Aprill: 1592: Anno: xxxiiij^o: of Queene Eliz:*

[Account of the arraignment for treason of Sir John Perrot (1527?–92), Lord Deputy of Ireland.]

45.6. ff. 403v–406v: *O: Royrke: his Attainder, att Westminister the seconde of August; the xxviij: of Eliz: 1586:*

[Account of the arraignment of the Irish chieftain Sir Brian-Na-Murtha-O'Rourke, who was tried and executed for treason in November 1591.]

45.7. ff. 407–409v: *A: true Coppie of M^r: Atturneye, and M^r: Serieaunte Hubberts: their opinyon Concerninge the Case of Alnage:*

[By Sir Edward Coke (1552–1634) and (Sir) Henry Hobart (d. 1625), Sergeant, later Chief Justice of the Common Pleas, 1603.]

45.8. ff. 410r–415r: *A Relation of soe muche as passed Betwene the Lordes of the Councell: and M^r: < > Corinton at the Councell: Table toucheinge his Refusall: to Contribute to the Lones he Beinge then Prissoner in the Gatehowse at Westm^r: in Aprill: 1627*

[Account relating to the politician William Coryton (d. 1651). Cf. 109.1 below; Starkey No. 59.]

46. Harley MS 160

[Folio, 234 leaves; composite volume of state tracts, much in the hand of Ralph Starkey; from the library of Sir Simonds D'Ewes: see Watson, 320.]

46.1. ff. 17r–18r: *The B^pp: of Lincolnes submisse Lre to the kings Mat^ie:*

[By John Williams (1582–1650), Bishop of Lincoln. *Cabala: sive Scrinia sacra* (London, 1654), 108. Watermark: rampant lion in crown.]

46.2. f. 20r: [*Letter by Lord Bristol*]

[Letter by John Digby, first Earl of Bristol (1580–1654), to Charles I, 12 January 1625/6. Cf. 71 below. Docketed by Ralph Starkey: 'The Kinge Answered this lre the 20th of february 1625'.]

46.3. f. 23r–v: *To The Right honno^ble. the Lo^s: of the Highe Howse of Parliam^te: The humble Peticon of John Earle of Bristoll*

[By John Digby, Earl of Bristol: Rushworth, i. 254–61. Cf. 92.3 below. Endorsed on f. 24v by Ralph Starkey: 'The Earle of Bristoles peticon to the Lordes of the vpper howse of Parliament presented to the Comytty of the same howse by the Countisse of Bristolle on Tusday the 18th of Aprill *1626* in the Afternoone'.]

46.4. ff. 25r–72r: *The Answere of John Earle of Bristoll to the Articles of severall Highe Treasons and other greate, and enormyous crymes offences, and Contempts, supposed, to be comytted by him, agaynst o^r: Late soveraigne Lord Kinge James, of Blessed Memorye deceased, and o^r: Soveraigne Lord the Kings Matie: that nowe is wherewth the said Earle is Chardged by his Maties: Attornye generall, on his Maties: behalfe, in the most highe, and honno^ble: Co^rte: of Parliam^te: before the Kinge, and the Lo^s: there:*

[By John Digby, Earl of Bristol, at his abortive trial, May–June 1626: Rushworth, i. 274–88. Cf. 17A above and 108.4 below. Watermark: urn.]

46.5. ff. 122r–124v: *The Remonstraunce of the Howse of Comons toutcheinge the causes of the greate greiveaunces of the Comon wealth, presented to his Matie: the < > daye of June 1628*

['The Commons Remonstrance against the Duke [of Buckingham]': Rushworth, i. 619–26. Cf. 47.11 below.]

46.6. f. 195r: *Iuramentu[m] Subclerici in officio Recordorum in Turre Londini*

[Formal oath, in English, of the Keeper of the Records in the Tower of London, comprising a heading and eleven lines cursorily written at the bottom half of a single page.]

47. Harley MS 161

[Folio, 256 leaves; composite volume of parliamentary speeches and materials up to 1628 (including letters by James I), some in the hand of Ralph Starkey; from the library of Sir Simonds D'Ewes: see Watson, 320.]

47.1. ff. 55r–56v: *The Three Subsidies, and three ffifteenes, graunted in parliam^te: ffor the Warres, and are thus certifyed by the severall. . . . . [sic] in their offices:*

[Annotated in Ralph Starkey's hand: 'The account of the Treasurers for the receipte of the .3. Subsedyes and .3. fyfteens . . . to the Comones house of parleament An° 1625'.]

47.2. ff. 65r–66v: *[Letters]*

[Letter by Edward, second Viscount Conway (1594–1655), to John Digby, Earl of Bristol, 24 March 1625/6, and Lord Bristol's reply, 30 March 1626. Cf. 71 below. Watermark: urn.]

47.3. ff. 81r–87r: *An explanacon from the kinge deliued by the Duke of Buck at a conference of both the houses in the paynted chamber the xxx^th of of [sic] March 1626*

[By Charles I and George Villiers, first Duke of Buckingham (1592–1628), 30 March 1625/6: Rushworth, i. 225–35. ff. 81r–84r in another scribal hand; ff. 85v–87r in Feathery's hand. Watermark: urn.]

47.4. ff. 139r–140r: *1626. A Speech intended to haue ben spoken this parleament*

[Anonymous and untitled speech beginning 'Mr Speaker, Althoughe the Constante wisdome of this Howse of Comons did well . . .'; docketed (f. 140v) as above in the hand of Ralph Starkey.]

47.5. f. 183r–v: *Quarto die Aprilis Anno Dni 1628*

[By Sir John Eliot, MP (1592–1632), his reply to the King's message to the Commons delivered by Sir John Coke, 4 April 1628: Rushworth, i. 524–5. In the hand of Ralph Starkey; a six-line endorsement in Feathery's hand written on the back (f. 183v, inverted).]

47.6. ff. 187r–195r: *M^r: Littletons Argum^te: Concerninge the personall Libtye of the Subiecte beffore the Lordes & Comons in the Painted Chamber And Reported the next daye in the higher Howse of Parliament by the Earle of Herteforde the 19. of Aprill 1628*

[By Sir Edward Littleton: *State trials*, iii. 85–94. Cf. Starkey No. 83. The heading partly comprised of corrections and interpolations in the hand of Ralph Starkey. See Plate 30 above.]

47.7. f. 196r: *A Message ffrom the kinge to the Lower Howse of Parliam^te Delivered by S^r. John Cooke the xij of Aprill: 1628:*

[By Charles I, 12 April 1628: Rushworth, i. 538–9. One page, trimmed to quarto-size, in a very cursive version of Feathery's hand; contemporary endorsement on fold.]

47.8. ff. 207r–208v: *Sr Edward Cookes Preamble wch he deliuered in the Painted Chamber in the presence of both houses when he presented the Peticon of Right of the Subiectes of England to the Lordes by Comaunde of the Comons of the Lower Howse the .8. of May .1628.*

[By Sir Edward Coke: Rushworth, i. 558–9. In the hand of Ralph Starkey, but with some corrections and interpolated words in Feathery's hand on ff. 207v–208r.]

47.9. ff. 212r–218v: *The obiections of the kinges Councell against the declaracon of the Comons: and the Answeres there vnto by m^r John Litleton the .16.th of May. 1628..*

[Heading and most of ff. 212r–214r in the hand

of Ralph Starkey; bottom of f. 214r and ff. 215r–218v in Feathery's hand. See Plate 51 above.]

47.10. ff. 225r–231r: *The Complaint of the Howse of Comons in Parliament against doctor Mainweringe, deliuered by m^r Pyme in the presence of both Howses the .31. of May .1628.*

[Delivered by John Pym: Rushworth, i. 593–604. ff. 225r to the beginning of line 17 on f. 227r and ff. 228r–231r in the hand of Ralph Starkey; a few words added by Feathery to the heading and on f. 226r, and all the text from the second word of line 17 on f. 227r until the end of that page is in his hand.]

47.11. ff. 237r–239r, 240r–242v: *The Remonstraunce of the House of Comons in Parliament toucheinge the daungerous Estate of the kingdome and the Greate greavaunce[s] of the Comon Wealth Presented to his Matie by the speaker in the Banquetinge House at Whithall the seventeenth daye of June 1628*

[Includes the King's answer on 17 June 1628. Cf. 46.5 above. In Ralph Starkey's hand, but with corrections in the heading and elsewhere on ff. 237r, 239r, 240v, 241r in Feathery's hand.]

47.12. f. 243r–v: *A Remonstrance voted to be deliuered to the kinge touching the subsedie of Tonnage and Poundage the same daye the Parliam^t ended beinge the .26. June .1628.*

[Parliamentary remonstrances: Rushworth, i. 628–30. In Ralph Starkey's hand, but with corrections of a few words in Feathery's hand.]

48. Harley MS 252

[Folio, 170 leaves; composite volume of state papers and tracts, partly in the hand of Ralph Starkey, one item in the hand of John Stow (1525?–1605); from the library of Sir Simonds D'Ewes: see Watson, 162, 322.]

ff. 15r–16v: [*State Tract*]

[Two-leaf fragment from a tract relating to state affairs from the Middle Ages to Henry VIII.]

49. Harley MS 260

[Folio, 451 leaves; volume of state papers, chiefly relating to negotiations for the proposed match between Queen Elizabeth and the Duc d'Alençon, between February 1570/1 and March 1572/3, in various scribal hands; from the library of Sir Simonds D'Ewes: see Watson, 110. Watermark: pillars.]

ff. 349r–362v: [*Negotiations with France*]

[Twelve letters by Walsingham, Sir Thomas Smith, Burghley, and Leicester, 17 October to 2 November 1572. Cf. 35.11 and 43 above. Twenty-eight pages in Feathery's hand, beginning in the middle of a letter by Walsingham and concluding in the middle of one by Leicester.]

50. Harley MS 293

[Folio, 242 leaves; composite volume of state papers, tracts, and poems; partly in the hand of Ralph Starkey (including a tract by Cotton: ff. 170r–178v); two items (ff. 32v, 44r–46v) in the hand of John Stow; from the library of Sir Simonds D'Ewes: see Watson, 141–2, 163, 324. Watermark in Feathery items: pillars.]

50.1. ff. 62r–70v: *Ordinaunces Toucheinge the Gouernm^{te}: of the Stewhoulders in Southwarcke vnder the Direction of the B:^{pp}: of: Winchester, instituted, in the Tyme of Henrye the Second:*

[Facsimile of f. 62r in E. J. Burford, *Bawds and lodgings: A history of the London Bankside brothels c.100–1675* (London, 1976), after p. 32.]

50.2. f. 70r–v: *A Cause in the Courte of Requestes ffor: the Buildinge of a Steeple, in the Church of Stopporte in Com Chester, staide by Prohibicon, out of the Kinges Benche:*

[A petition by John Brooke against Hugh Robothom.]

50.3. ff. 215r–216r: *A Proclamacon by the Kinges Maties: Comissioners: ffor the Hearinge, and, adiudginge of all: Claymes, and: Peticons of such as pretende, Right, to doe, anye: Seruyce at the Kinges, and: Queenes Maties: Coronacons:*

[Proclamation signed by Gilbert Talbot, seventh Earl of Shrewsbury (1553–1616), Henry Howard, Earl of Northampton, and John, Lord Lumley (1534?–1609), 13–14 July 1603. Watermark: pillars.]

51. Harley MS 298

[Folio, 174 leaves; composite volume of state tracts and papers, including Daniel's 'Breviary' (ff. 1–8v: cf. 95.1 below), letters by Bacon, and material relating to the marriage of Princess Elizabeth in 1612/13, incorporating material in the hands of Ralph Starkey, Sir Simonds D'Ewes, and William Dugdale: see Watson, 324. Watermark in Feathery items: pillars.]

51.1. ff. 18r–19v: [*Letter by Queen Elizabeth*]

[Portion of a letter by Queen Elizabeth, from Greenwich, 7 November 1579; lacking the beginning.]

51.2. ff. 20r–26v: *The Kinge of Scotts Proclamacon, made at Edinburghe the viij^{th}: Daye of Maye. 1570: {eiris. Confuteinge, and declareinge, the vaine vntrue, and Colorate pretensis of his Hines Rebellis Conspiratouris aganis his Matie: and Vsurparis of his Authoretye:*

[On behalf of the young James VI of Scotland (1566–1625) by Matthew Stewart, fourth or twelfth Earl of Lennox (1516–71), Lieutenant-General and afterwards Regent of Scotland (including tables of Scottish names: ff. 25v–26v).]

52. Harley MS 354

[Folio, 207 leaves; composite volume of tracts, including Cotton, the opening of Davies's 'Question concerning Impositions' (ff. 32r–33v: cf. 2 above), and Archbishop Abbot (cf. 108.16–17 and

109.6 below); partly in the hand of Ralph Starkey, including Cecil's 'State of a Secretary's Place' (cf. 77.3 below) and Carr's letter to Howard, 1612 (cf. 1.5 above); from the library of Simonds D'Ewes: see Watson, 238, 327.]

52.1. ff. 72r–73r: *The Empero^{rs}: Mandate, sent to ffranckfforde Marte, ffor confiscation of the B^{pp}: of Spallatoes Booke: in Anno 1617*

[By the Emperor Matthias (1557–1619), 1617. Watermark: pillars.]

52.2. ff. 148r–205r: [*The Journal of the Voyage & Enterprise upon Spaine, by the English & Dutch, under the command of S^r. Edward Cecyll, General by Sea & Land: from the 8th of Septemberr, 1625. to the 5th of December following, Wherein are sett down, all Instructions, warrants, Letters, &c.*]

[Journal of the *Swiftsure* covering the unsuccessful Cadiz expedition of 1625 commanded by Sir Edward Cecil, Viscount Wimbledon (1572–1638). Cf. Starkey No. 89. No title-page (title above given in printed catalogue of Harley MSS). Watermark: pillars, and armorial with crown and fleur-de-lis.]

52.3. ff. 206r–207v: *A Breife declaracon of the accompte of S^r: Thomas Middleto[n] K^t: and S^r: Edward Barkeham K^t: Aldermen of the Cittie of London, S^r: Paule Baynings. K^t: and Baron^t: [&c.]*

[Accounts of various London aldermen concerning the subsidies and fifteens from the time of the Act of Parliament for those subsidies until 30 June 1625. Docketed (f. 207v) by Ralph Starkey: 'A breefe declaracon -.of the Treasurors for the Recepte and disbursement of the .3. Subsedies and .3. fifteenes deliuered to the Comons howse of parleament An° 1625'. Watermark: armorial shield (R B).]

53. Harley MS 444

[Folio, 247 leaves; volume of state tracts and letters, including Queen Elizabeth to Sir Amias

Paulet (f. 1r–v: cf. 35.9 above), Sidney to Queen Elizabeth (ff. 3r–14r: cf. *Index*, i/2, SiP 194; 17 above, and Appendix IV below, No. 15) and to his brother (14r–17v: cf. 6.6 above), Cornwallis (ff. 57r–68v: cf. 6.1 above), Ralegh, Cotton, the Marquis Inijosa (ff. 73r–78v: cf. 1.10 above), the Letter to Parliament 1627 (ff. 162r–179v: cf. 1.11 above), Weldon (ff. 241r–245r: cf. 72.13 below), Lord Norris (ff. 245v–246v: cf. 71.4 below), and material relating to the 1623 Spanish match and the death of Buckingham in 1628; in various scribal hands, including Ralph Starkey (a tract on oaths: ff. 15r–92v); bought by Sir Robert Harley from the antiquary Peter Le Neve (1661–1729): see *Fontes Harleiani*, 219, 379. Watermark in Feathery items: pillars (RDP).]

53.1. ff. 18r–21r: *Henrye Cuffe Secretarye to the Earle of Essex his Lre, to M*ʳ*: Secretarye Cecill, declaringe the effect of the Instruccons, fframed by the Earle of Essex: and delivered to the Ambassador: of the kinge of Scotte[s], touchinge his Tytle, to the Crowne of England, w*ᶜʰ *Lre was wrytten after Cuffes Condempnacon*

[Cf. 1.16 and 19 above and 71 and 82.1 below.]

53.2. ff. 21r–27r: *Liddington the Secretarye of Scotland his Lre, to S*ʳ*: Willm Cecill, the Queene of Englandes Secretarye, Touchinge the Tytle of the Queene of Scotte[s], to the Crowne of England:*

[By William Maitland, Laird of Lethington. Cf. 1.15 above and 71 below.]

53.3. ff. 27r–28r: *Directions Off Queene Marye to hir Councell, Touchinge the Refforminge of the Church to the Romane Religion, out of hir owne Originall:*

[By Mary I. Cf. 1.25 above and 71 below.]

53.4. ff. 28r–29v: *The Ladye Elizabeth: hir graces Aunswere made att Hattfeild, the: 26: of Aprill, 1558: To S*ʳ*: Thomas Pope knight, beinge sent ffrom the Queenes Ma*ᵗⁱᵉ*: to vnderstand howe hir grace lyked of the Mocon of Marryage, made by the kinge Ellect of Swethlandes Messenger:*

[By Princess Elizabeth and Sir Thomas Pope. Cf. 1.22 and 33 above and 109.10 below.]

53.5. ff. 29v–31r: *A: Lre ffrom Queene Elizabeth, to the kinge of Scotte[s], dated the: 4*ᵗʰ*: of Januarij: 1602: wrytten, w*ᵗʰ *hir owne hand, Touchinge hir disswadeinge him, to Receyve in his Countrye an Ambassador ffrom Spayne, shewinge hir groundes of vndertakeinge the Protection of the Lowe Countryes:*

[By Queen Elizabeth. Cf. 1.20 above and 71 below.]

53.6. ff. 32v–34v: *Proposicons made by the Ambassado*ʳˢ*: of the Kinge of ffraunce, to the Assemblye of the States generall of the Vnyted Provinces of the Lowe Countryes, vppon, Presentacon of the Lres of his Ma*ᵗⁱᵉ*: to the said Lordes the States, The xij*°*: of December, 1618: Touchinge the pointes noted in the Margent:*

[Cf. 6.3 above and 109.19 below.]

53.7. ff. 34v–37v: *The Opinyon Off the: Auncyent Docto*ʳˢ*: of the Lawe, Whether it bee Lawffull ffor a Prince, Whose Sub*ᵗᵉ*: is wronged by a fforraigne Prince, to Lycence his Sub*ᵗᵉ*: to detayne the Bodye, and goodes of that Princes Sub*ᵗᵉ*: w*ᶜʰ *wrongeth:*

[Cotton's copy of this brief is BL Cotton MS Titus C. VII, ff. 27r–28r. Cf. 71.3 below; Starkey No. 30.]

53.8. ff. 37v–38r: *Whatt Privelidges an: Alyen hath vnder any other Prince, or State:*

[Cf. 109.21 below; Starkey No. 32.]

53.9. f. 38r–v: *Queene Elizabethes: Lre; to the Duke of Wirtenburghe, in Aunswere of his Oferr, to Assiste hir, in the p*ʳ*ferringe hir in Marryage, Dated the: xxvij*°*: of January: 1563:*

[By Queen Elizabeth. Cf. 1.23 above and 109.11 below.]

53.10. ff. 38v–40r: *The Coppye Off a Lre Wrytten by the Lord Chauncello*: *Ellesmee*: *to the Kinge, desireinge to bee discharged of his Offyce, throughe his inffirmety, and weaknes, to supplye thesame, Anno; 1612*

[By Sir Thomas Egerton, Baron Ellesmere. Cf. 1.26 and 13.8 above and 82.3 and 83 below.]

53.11. ff. 40v–41r: *Another Lre wrytten by: the Lord Chauncello*: *Egerton, to the Kinges Ma*^tie: *desireinge him to bee pleased to discharge him of his place:*

[By Sir Thomas Egerton, Baron Ellesmere. Cf. 45.2 above and 72.8 below.]

53.12. ff. 48r–52r: *A: Lre wrytten by the: Lordes of the Councell, to kinge James dated the < > of < > Anno, touchinge meanes to Advaunce the kinges Revenewes by vnusuall Meanes, soe as the kinge, will take the Acte vppon himselfe, and bee their Protection:*

[Cf. 1.1 above and 71, 82.4, and 83 below.]

53.13. ff. 52v–54r: *Ordinarye Annuall: Receipte[s] of The Exchequer:* and *Ordinarye Annuall Yssues: of The Exchequer:*

[Cf. 6.5 and 33.3 above and 83 and 109.14 below.]

53.14. ff. 54v–56r: *Abatements nowe in: beinge or to bee very shortlye; vppon the Marryage of the Ladye Elizabeth, to the Counte Pallatine of the Rhine, Anno, i613: And other Wise, ffor the Kinges Beniffitt by the Comissione*^rs: *of the Treasurye:*

[By Henry Howard, Earl of Northampton. Cf. 1.2 and 33.4 above and 71 and 83 below.]

53.15. ff. 69r–71r: *A: Lre ffrom the Pope to our Kinge, When hee was in Spayne ffor his Conversion*

[By Pope Gregory XV (1554–1623; pope 1621–3), to Prince Charles, 20 April 1623. *Cabala: sive Scrinia sacra* (1654), 212–14. Cf. 31 above.]

53.16. ff. 71v–72r: *The Aunswere Off the: Prince of England, to the Popes Lre, given att S*^te: *Peete*^rs: *the: xx*^th: *of Aprill, Anno 1623*

[By Prince Charles (afterwards Charles I). *Cabala: sive Scrinia sacra* (1654), 214–15; Rushworth, i. 82–3. Cf. 27 and 31 above.]

53.17. ff. 108r–115r: *A Councell of Warre: the xxvij*° *Nouembris 1587 An*° *Reginae Elizabeth*

[Fols. 108r–111v in another scribal hand; from the middle of a line in f. 111v until f. 115r in Feathery's hand. See Plate 45 above.]

53.18. ff. 185r–202r: *A: Treatise off Bayle: and Mainprize, Written att the Request of S*: *Willm Haydon, knight, by S*: *Edward Coke:*

[By Sir Edward Coke, *ante* 1594. Printed in London, 1635: cf. Baker, *CUL* 375. Cf. 20 above and 71 below; Starkey No. 44.]

54. Harley MS 737

[Folio, 455 leaves; composite volume of state tracts, including Cotton's 'That the Kings of England . . .' (ff. 151r–158v: cf. Starkey No. 43 n. 7), in various hands; from the library of Edward Stillingfleet (1635–99), Bishop of Worcester; bought by Sir Robert Harley in 1707: see *Fontes Harleiani*, 316, 385.]

ff. 33r–55r: *A: Collection of Such thinges, As Robte Late Earle: of Salisburye, thought ffitt to offerr, vnto kinge James his Ma*^tie: *Touchinge the necessitye of Callinge a Parliam*^te

[Cf. 15.1 above and 93 below. Title-page (f. 33r) and first line of heading on f. 34r in Feathery's hand; all the rest in another scribal hand. Watermark: grapes.]

55. Harley MS 738

[Folio, 346 leaves; composite volume of state tracts, in several hands; from the library of Bishop Stillingfleet; bought by Harley in 1707: see *Fontes Harleiani*, 316, 385.]

ff. 152r–168v: *A; Breiffe: Discours; Off: the ffirst devision of England, As it is nowe generallye named into Shires, wth the Originall, ffoundacon, And ffirst Beginege of all the Co^{rts}: of Justyce in England, wth the Jurisdictions, And Innuityes, of the Archb^{pps}: B^{pps}: And other Eccliall psons wth some other Remarckeable Passages of State: Wrytten by Willm Byrde, of Grayes Inne Esquyer*

[By William Bird Cf. 23.2 above, and 57.2 and 79A below. Watermark: quatrefoils within circle.]

56. Harley MS 837

[Folio, 96 leaves; composite volume of MSS; ff. 62r–78v comprising a single unit in Feathery's hand with the general heading (f. 62r): 'A: Booke:, Off, verses &c.'; from the library of Bishop Stillingfleet; bought by Harley in 1707: see *Fontes Harleiani*, 316, 386. Watermark: urn.]

56.1. ff. 63r–70v: *Coopers: Hill:* (beginning 'Sure: wee haue Poetts that did never dreame')

[By Sir John Denham (1615–69). Printed in London, 1642 [Wing D993]: cf. *Index*, ii/1, DeJ 11.]

56.2. ff. 71r–73v: *Newes, ffrom:, Pernassus* (beginning 'Appollo: ffor some private end')

56.3. ff. 74r–75r: *Off: Jacke, and, Tom:* (beginning 'Whatt: suddayne Chaunce, hath dark't of late')

[Poem about the Spanish match, 1623; Crum W705.]

56.4. ff. 75v–77v: *The: powtes:, Complaynte vppon draynnge of the ffennes, in Cambridgeshire, Elye; and Wisbiche* (beginning 'Come: Brothers of the Water')

56.5. ff. 77v–78v: *The: Comon,wealthe:, Off: Byrdes* (beginning 'Listen: gallantes, to my wordes')

[By James Shirley (1596–1666). Printed in his *Poems* (London, 1646): cf. *Index*, ii/2, ShJ 10.]

57. Harley MS 1323

[Folio, 285 leaves; composite volume of state tracts up to 1624, in various scribal hands.]

57.1. ff. 1r–12r: *Kinge: James, his Speeches: Concerninge the Affayers, and, State of the kingdome, ffor Supplye, in his Ingagem^{ts}: in Warres And, ffor the deffence of the kingdome, wth some other Remarckeable passages of State &^{c}:*

[Parliamentary speeches by and addressed to James I. Watermark: elaborate urn.]

57.2. ff. 13r–33r: *A: Breiffe: Discours: Concerninge, The ffirst devision of England, as it is nowe generallye named, into Shires, wth the Originall ffoundacon, and ffirst beginege of all the Co^{rts}. of Justice in England, wth the Jurisdictions, and Imunityes, of Archb^{pps}: B^{pps} And, other Eccliall psons, And, some other occurrences of State, Wrytten, by Willm Byrde, of Grayes Inne Esquyer*

[By William Bird. Cf. 23.2 and 55 above, and 79A below. Watermark: urn.]

57.3. ff. 34r–42r: *The: Coppye of a Lre, Wrytten, By Queene Anne Bullen, To kinge Hen: the, 8th: ffound amongst the Lord Cromwells Papers;*

ffol,——2 / A: Lre: ffounde, Amongst some Jesuites, Latelye taken, Att Clarckenwell, London, directed, to the ffather Rector, Att Bruxells, ffol,——4

i. (ff. 35r–36v) By Anne Boleyn (1507–36). Cf. 72.1 below.

ii. (ff. 37r–42r) An alleged Jesuit letter [March 1628]; but cf. the copy in BL Harley MS 286, ff. 298r–302r, where Sir Simonds D'Ewes has commented: 'This was a vaine invented Lre framed as was conceived by Sr John Maynard': i.e. Sir John Maynard (1592–1658). Another MS copy, possibly associated with Feathery's scriptorium, is Trinity College Dublin MS 532, ff. 242r–252r. Title-page inscribed 'John Jermy' or 'Jerney'. Watermark: elaborate urn.

57.4. ff. 43r–56v: *The: Coppye Off:, a; Letter Wrytten by S^r: phillipp: Sidnye, To: Queene Elizabeth, touchinge, hir Marryage, wth Mounsieur: &^c*

[By Sir Philip Sidney: cf. *Index*, i/2, SiP 195; Appendix IV below, No. 16. Cf. 17, 18.1, 20.1, 41.10, and 53 above, and 64, 78.7, 105.1, and 110 below. Watermark: elaborate urn. See Plates 74 and 75 above.]

57.5. ff. 68r–94r: *Obseruacons: Concerninge the Nobillitye of England, Auncyent, And Moderne &^c*

[Cf. 79 below; Starkey No. 36. Watermark: quatrefoils within circle.]

57.6. ff. 139r–143r: *A: Breiffe, discours: Or, a deffence, ffor the Alteracon of England, to the Name, of greate Brittayne*

[Watermark: urn.]

57.7. ff. 151r–183v: *A; Breiffe: Discours; Or: a,: True Relacon; of the Embassye of Marshall*

Bassomperie, Lord of Barre; Ambassado^r, extraordinarye ffrom his Christyan Matie: of ffraunce, vnto kinge Charles his Matie: of England, Concerninge the Breach of Certayne Contracts of the Treatyes, of Peace, and Amitye; The manner of the sendinge home of the Queenes Catholicque Offycers; and Ministers, The particuler Aunsweres of his Matie: therevnto, wth some Certayne occurrences Concerninge Rochell, and the Pallatynate; And dyvers other, most Remarckeable, and Important passages of State; Wrytten; by H: W: &^c

[Account concerning Charles I's expulsion of Henrietta Maria's French attendants on 31 July–10 August 1626 and Louis XIII's official complaint presented by François, Baron de Bassompierre (1579–1646), Marshal of France. Watermark: crozier armorial (PLAMY) akin to Heawood 1220.]

57.8. ff. 216r–234v: *Princes: Extremityes, Beyounde: the ease of their people By Reason of Warres &^c*

[By Sir Robert Cotton, the second half of his 'Answer made by command of Prince Henry to certain propositions of war and peace'. Cf. 28 above, also 22.2 above and 80 and 85 below. Title-page only in Feathery's hand; text (ff. 217r–234v) in another scribal hand.]

57.9. f. 240r: *The: Table:*

[A one-page table of contents, listing seven items, serving as a general title-page to the letters on ff. 241r–252r which, with f. 240, form a single unit.]

57.10. ff. 241r–246r: *The; Coppye:, Off,: a,: Letter, Off: Advyce; Wrytten by S^r: Thomas Egerton Lord keeper of the greate Seale of Engld To Rob^te: late Earle of Essex Earle Marshall of England, And, the Earle of Essex: his Aunsweare therevnto:*

i. (ff. 241r–243r) By Sir Thomas Egerton,

Baron Ellesmere, 1598. *Scrinia sacra* (London, 1654), 27–9; Braunmuller, 54–61 (commentary, p. 417). Cf. 72.2 below.

ii. (ff. 243v–246r), headed separately 'The Earle: Off: Essex his Aunswer', by Robert Devereux, second Earl of Essex (1566–1601), 1598. *Scrinia sacra* (1654), 29–31; Braunmuller, 60–9 (commentary, p. 418). Cf. 72.3 below.

57.11. ff. 246r–247v: *The:, Earle:, Off:, Essex, his Lre: To Queene Elizabeth:*

[By Robert Devereux, second Earl of Essex. *Scrinia sacra* (1654), 25–6.]

57.12. f. 247v: *The:, Earle:, Off,: Essex, his Lre To M^r: Secretarye Davison, Att; his Retourne ffrom Portugall:*

[By Robert Devereux, second Earl of Essex, 11 July 1583. *Scrinia sacra* (1654), 22.]

57.13. f. 248r–v: *Another Lre:, Off, his to M^r: Secretarye Davison; in Italye*

[By Robert Devereux, second Earl of Essex, 8 January 1595/6. *Scrinia sacra* (1654), 20–1, and, from this MS, in *Davison's Poetical rhapsody*, ed. A. H. Bullen, 2 vols. (London, 1890), i, pp. xlviii–l.]

57.14. f. 249r–v: *A: Petitionarye, Lre: ffrom John Lillye, To Queene Elizabeth:*

[By John Lyly (1554–1606). Petition, probably 1598: cf. *Index*, i/2. 319. Printed from this MS in *The complete works of John Lyly*, ed. R. Warwick Bond, 3 vols. (Oxford, 1902; reprinted 1967), i. 64–5.]

57.15. f. 250r–v: *Another:, Lre: to, Queene Eliza: = /beth: ffrom John: Lillye*

[By John Lyly; probably 1601: cf. *Index*, i/2. 319. Printed from this MS in Bond edn., i. 70–1.]

57.16. ff. 250v–252r: *The Coppye, off: a Lre wrytten by S^r: Henrye Wallop: To: Queene Elizabeth:*

[By Sir Henry Wallop (1540?–99), 11 or 12 August 1583. *Scrinia sacra* (1654), 19–20. Cf. 19 above. Watermark: urn.]

57.17. ff. 273r–277v: *A:, Coppye, Off:, the Memoryall: w^{ch}, the Ambassado^r: of the kinge of Greate Brittayne gave, his Matie: the, 29: of Julij: 1624*

[Letter from Madrid, 25 August 1624, 'Translated verbatim, out of the Spanishe Coppie; 1624'.]

58. Harley MS 2208

[Folio, 240 leaves; composite volume of tracts, including Cotton (1624); bought by Sir Robert Harley on 13 August 1724 from the bookseller Nathaniel Noel (*fl.*1681–*c*.1753): see *Fontes Harleiani*, 254–5, 404.]

ff. 211r–227v: *Sir Charles Cornewallis his Relacon of the Carryage of the Marryage, that should haue been betwene the Prince of England, and the Inffanta of Spayne:*

[By Sir Charles Cornwallis. Cf. 20.6 and 35 above and 108.5 below. Watermark: pillars (RDP).]

59. Harley MS 5111

[Folio, 122 leaves; composite volume of state tracts, including Felltham's 'Three monethes observation of the Lowe Countries' (ff. 1r–13r: cf. 103 below), in various hands.]

ff. 53r–72v: *The: Difference: and: disparitye, Betwene the Estates, and Condicons, of George Duke of Buckingham; and Rob^{te} Earle of Essex*

[By Edward Hyde, first Earl of Clarendon (1608–74). Printed in *Reliquiae Wottonianae* (London, 1651) [Wing W3648]: cf. *Index*, ii/1,

ClE 10–12. Cf. 17A above, and also University of London MS 309, ff. 184r–205r. Title-page only in Feathery's hand; text (ff. 54r–72v) in another scribal hand. Docketed '(5)' and '16 October 1725' (i.e. after Lord Oxford's library had been sent from Brampton Bryan to London in 1724). Watermark: pillars.]

60. Harley MS 5141

[Folio; three tracts in different hands bound together.]

ff. 46r–81r: [*Fragmenta regalia*]

[By Sir Robert Naunton Cf. 17A.2 above and 62 below. Seventy-one page fragment, comprising the concluding portion of the work, here beginning at the sixth character; given to Sir Robert Harley in 1719 by the antiquary John Anstis (1669–1744): see *Fontes Harleiani*, 51, 453. Watermark: grapes.]

61. Harley MS 6842

[Folio, 313 leaves; composite volume of state papers (including a second copy of the Letter to Parliament in another hand: ff. 179r–185v), in various scribal hands, including Ralph Starkey.]

ff. 159r–166v: *The: Coppye:, Off: a; Letter Wrytten to the Lower Howse of Parliam^te Touchinge dyvers Inconveniencyes, and greivaunces of the State, &c*

[Cf. 1.11, 40.1, and 53 above and 78.2, 83.3, 106.5, and 112 below. 15 pages; imperfect. Watermark: quatrefoils within circle.]

62. Lansdowne MS 254

[Folio, 500 leaves; volume of miscellaneous tracts, including Naunton's 'Fragmenta regalia' (ff. 225r–251r: cf. 17A.2 above), in various scribal hands; among collections of William Petty, Lord Shelburne and first Marquess of Lansdowne (1737–1805). Watermark: grapes on pedestal (IVG).]

ff. 98r–145v: *A: Treatise: Off the: Highe: Courte: Off Starrchamber:*

[First part of a treatise by William Hudson (d. 1635), of Grays Inn, written 1621. Printed in Francis Hargrave, *Collectanea juridica*, 2 vols. (London, 1791–2), ii. 1–240, from BL Harley MS 1226, a MS allegedly in the hand of the author's son, Christopher Hudson, given to John Finch 19 December 1635; cf. Baker, *CUL* 438–9. Watermark: grapes.]

63. Lansdowne MS 798

[Folio, 180 leaves; composite volume of tracts, including 'A Reconciliacon' (ff. 58r–69v: cf. 34 above), in various scribal hands; among collections of the first Marquess of Lansdowne. Watermark: urn.]

ff. 1r–57v: *The Aunswere to Sir: John Davyes his Booke Off Impositions*

[Anonymous answer to Davies's treatise (cf. 2 above), beginning 'It will not bee denied that the power of imposicon hath soe great a trust in it . . .'. The title-page only in Feathery's hand; all the text (ff. 2r–57v) in another scribal hand.]

64. Sloane MS 24

[Folio, 16 leaves (30 pages); a single tract; docketed (f. 1r) '(30)', and with shelfmarks: 'M.S. 27. 2140. | MA. A. 72. | 24'. Watermark: quatrefoils within circle.]

The: Coppye:, Off: a: Lre Wrytten; by S^r: Phillipp: Sidnye; to Queene Elizabeth, Touchinge; hir Marryage, wth Mounsieur: &c

[By Sir Philip Sidney: cf. *Index*, i/2, SiP 198; Appendix IV below, No. 19. Cf. 17, 18.1, 20.1, 41.10, 53, and 57.4 above and 78.7, 96.1, and 110 below.]

65. Sloane MS 755

[Folio, 31 folio leaves (61 pages); a single tract; shelfmarks on title-page: 'LXXX | 996' and 'MS. A. 39. | 755'. Watermark: urn.]

A: Breiffe:, Discours: Touching the Lowe Coun-tryes, The Kinge of Spayne, The kinge of Scotte[s], The ffrench kinge; And; Queene Eliza-beth, wth some other Remarckeable, passages of State, Wrytten; by S^r ffrauncis Bacon, knight; &c

[Anonymous tract, beginning 'Lodwick Sforza holding by Tyrannies usurpation the dukedom of Millayne . . .'; not recorded among Bacon's works.]

66. Sloane MS 1710

[Folio, 359 leaves; composite volume of state papers, including some Latin verse.]

ff. 226r–247r: *A Sumarye:, Off,:, all:, the Exactions, Imposicons, Taxes, and, Loanes, Exacted, Leavyed, Taken, and Sett, vppon the State; As well, by prerogatyve Power, As generall graunte, ffrom, Willm the Conquero^r: To kinge James, &c*

[Anonymous treatise, beginning 'And first to begin with William the Conqueror . . .'. Cf. the similar subject in 75 below. Feathery's foliation from 1 to 22; later foliation in red from 312 to 332 (333 deleted); docketed '59'. Watermarks: urn and quatrefoils within circle.]

67. Sloane MS 3104

[Folio, 17 leaves (33 pages); a single tract; dock-eted with shelfmark: 'MS. A. 637 | 3104'. Water-mark: pillars.]

The: manner: Off: the Sicknesse, and Death: of Henrye Prince of Wales, eldest Sonne, to kinge: James, Anno, Dni: 1612

[By Sir Charles Cornwallis. Cf. 6.1, 9, 18, 20, 35.2, and 53 above and 83 below. ff. 2r–14v until three-quarters of the way down f. 14v in another scribal hand; title-page and the rest of f. 14v (mid-sentence) until the end on f. 17v in Feathery's hand.]

68. Sloane MS 3105

[Folio, 8 leaves (14 pages); a single tract; docketed with shelfmark: 'MS. A. 638 | 3105'. Watermark: pillars.]

A: True: Relacon, Concerninge: Newe England, As it was presented to his Matie

[Anonymous survey of New England beginning 'ffor the perfect vnderstandinge the state of Newe, England, There are these thinges, deserve Consideracon . . .'.]

69. Sloane MS 3106

[Folio, 14 leaves (36 pages); a single tract; docketed with shelfmark: 'MS. A. 639 | 3106 | XXIIJ', numbered in pencil '10', and also dock-eted 'never Printed'. Watermark: pillars.]

The: Coppye Off: a: Letter: wrytten, by S^r: Raphe Wynwood, ffrom Venyce, to S^r: ffoulke Grevill:, in England, partlye, aboute the Jesuite, wth other Intervenyent Passages, Anno, Dni: 1606

[By Sir Ralph Winwood (1563?–1617), about the Gunpowder Plot. Title-page and ff. 11r–14r in Feathery's hand; ff. 2r–10v in another scribal hand.]

70. Sloane MS 3520

[Folio, 18 leaves (32 pages); a single unit; docketed with shelfmarks: 'MS. A. 778 |3520 | XXIID'. Watermark: pillars.]

Diuers Letters wrytten: by Sir Walter Rawleigh: &c

[Seven letters by Sir Walter Ralegh, chiefly to his wife, and also to James I, Sir Ralph Winwood, and Robert Carr, Earl of Somerset, 1603–17. Cf. 1.4, 1.6, 23, 28, and 35.3 above and 108.6 and 108.19 below; Starkey, No. 50. Title-page in Feathery's hand; text (ff. 2r–17r) in another scribal hand.]

71. Stowe MS 145

[Folio, 179 leaves; volume of state tracts and letters from 1536 to 1628, including the Privy Council (cf. 1.1 above), Cuffe (cf. 1.16 above), Lethington (cf. 1.15 above), 'Aduertismentes of a Loyall Subiect' (cf. 20.8 above), Archbishop Abbot (cf. 109.6 below), Queen Mary (cf. 1.25 above), Queen Elizabeth (cf. 1.20 and 1.21 above), Sir Anthony Browne (cf. 1.24 above), Northampton's Abatements (cf. 1.2 above), Sir Edward Coke (cf. 53.18 above), Sir Nicholas Bacon (on the Alençon marriage: perhaps Starkey No. 3, and cf. 32 above), the Earl of Bristol (cf. 46.2 and 47.2 above), and others, as well as letters relating to the Commissioners at Boulogne, 1600 (cf. 106.2 below), in two scribal hands; list of 'Some of the Contents' in a later cursive hand on ff. 5r–6r; signed on ff. 1r and 178r by 'Ric. Tichbone' [probably Sir Richard Tichborne, MP, second Baronet (*c.*1587–1652): cf. 35 above]; docketed with shelf-mark 'Press VI—Nº 31'. Watermark: pillars.]

71.1. ff. 1r–4v: *A Table of all the severall Tracts and Treatices Written in this Booke Followinge videlicet*

> [Heading in another scribal hand; text of the table in Feathery's hand. See Plate 47 above.]

71.2. ff. 148r–150r: *A: Lre Off the viscounte Cranbornes, wrytten to Sʳ: Thomas Parrye, Ambassadoʳ: wᵗʰ the kinge of ffraunce, dated the, 14: of Aprill, 1604: Touchinge the Misellection of Sʳ: ffrauncis Goodwyne, and the Trayterous Speeches, vsed by Mʳ: Henrye Connstable:*

> [By Sir Robert Cecil, Earl of Salisbury. Cf. Starkey No. 29. Feathery also adds the catchwords on f. 147v.]

71.3. ff. 150v–154r: *The Opinyon Off the Auncyent Doctoʳˢ: of the Lawe, Whether it bee Lawfull ffor a Prince whose Subᵗᵉ: is wronged by a fforraigne Prince, to Lycence his Subᵗᵉ: to detayne the Bodye, and goodes of that Princes Subᵗᵉ: wᶜʰ wrongeth:*

> [Cf. 53.7 above.]

71.4. ff. 154r–155r: *A: Coppye Off the Lre, wᶜʰ the Lord Norris Wrytt to the kings Maᵗⁱᵉ: after hee had slayne one of the Lord Willoughbyes servants; vppon a quarrell Raysed Betwene the two Lordes: Anno 1615*

> [By Francis Norris, Earl of Berkshire (1579–1623), 1615. *Scrinia sacra* (1654), 89–90. Cf. 53 above and 82.2 below; Starkey No. 34.]

72. Stowe MS 151

[Folio, 214 leaves; volume of state letters and tracts from 1536 to 1628, including Felltham's 'Three Months Observation of the Low Countries' (ff. 102r–112v: cf. 103 below), and Essex's charge against Wimbledon (ff. 113r–148v: cf. Starkey No. 89), in three scribal hands. Feathery is responsible for foliation throughout the volume. Watermark: pillars.]

72.1. ff. 1r–2v: *Queene Anne Bullins: Lre, to Kinge Henry the,: 8: ffounde amonge Cromwells Papers:*

> [By Anne Boleyn. Cf. 57.3 (i) above.]

72.2. ff. 2v–4v: *Sir Thomas Egerton Lord Keeper of the greate Seale of England his Lre of Advice, to Robte Earle of Essex: Earl Marshall of England:*

> [By Sir Thomas Egerton, Baron Ellesmere, 1598. Cf. 57.10 (i) above.]

72.3. ff. 4v–7r: *My Lord of Essex his Aunswere:*

> [By Robert Devereux, second Earl of Essex, 1598. Cf. 57.10 (ii) above.]

72.4. f. 7r–v: *The Coppye Off a Lre wrytten by Mounsʳ: Toirax: Captayne of the fforte, in the Isle of Rhee, to the Duke of Buckingham generall, ffor the kinge of England, Att the Seidge thereof, 1627:*

> [By Jean de St Bonnet, Seigneur de Toiras

(1585–1636), Governor of the Isle de Rhé, later Marshal of France.]

72.5. ff. 7v–8v: *To a Ladye in the Courte*

[Signed 'A: B:', i.e. anonymous.]

72.6. f. 9r–v: *To the Right Honno*ble*: my Lord, the Earle of Essex: Earle Marshall of England, And hir Ma*ties*: Leiutennante, of hir Kingdome of Ireland:*

[By Charles Blount, Lord Mountjoy and afterwards Earl of Devonshire, c.1600. *Scrinia sacra* (1654), 35–6.]

72.7. f. 10r: *A: Lre ffrom. A: B: to his wyfe*

72.8. ff. 10v–11r: *A: Lre wrytten by the Lord Chauncellor Egerton to the Kinges Ma*tie*: desireinge him to bee pleased to discharge him of his Place*

[By Sir Thomas Egerton, Baron Ellesmere. Cf. 45.2 and 53.11 above.]

72.9. ff. 11r–12r: *A: Coppye Off the: greate Magulls Lre, to kinge James of England, aboute Amitye, and ffrindshipp:*

[By Jahangir, Emperor of Hindustan. Cf. 19.6 above.]

72.10. ff. 12r–13v: *A: Lre to the Earl of Klanrickard:*

[By Christopher Blount, a newsletter chiefly about Continental affairs, 7 March 1624[/5].]

72.11. ff. 13v–16r: *The Coppye Off a Lre the xij°: of March, 1628: ffrom Duca de Rohan, to the kinge of England:*

[By Henri, Duc de Rohan (1579–1638), Huguenot leader. *Scrinia sacra* (1654), 208–10; Rushworth, ii/1. 4–5.]

72.12. ff. 16r–17v: *A: Lre Sent ffrom the Councell, to the Justices in the Countrye, Conscerninge the Assessem*te*: of the Subsedye:*

72.13. ff. 17v–23v: *A. Progresse into Scotland w*th* the varyetie of the Countrye or, Anonimos:*

[By Sir Anthony Weldon (d. 1649?), 20 June 1617. Printed as *A perfect description of the people and country of Scotland* (London, 1649) [Wing W1277]. Cf. 53 above.]

72.14. ff. 24r–37r, 38r–45r: [*Letters by Sir William Pelham*]

[Fifteen letters by Sir William Pelham (d. 1587), Lord Justice of Ireland (one with Thomas Butler, Earl of Ormonde), to the Privy Councils of London and Dublin, Lord Burghley, Francis Walsingham, Sir William Morgan, Queen Elizabeth, the Earl of Kildare, Sir John Fitzgarrett, Surlye Boye, the Earl of Ormonde, and the Attorney-General, with two letters to Pelham by Ormonde (ff. 38r–39v) and Sir Hugh O'Reilly (ff. 42v–43r).]

72.15. f. 46r: *My Lord Chauncellor Bacons Opinyon Touchinge the imployem*te* of M*r*: Suttons Charritye, deliuerd vnto kinge James*

[By Sir Francis Bacon, *c.* January 1611/12. *Resuscitatio* (1657), 265–70; Spedding, xi. 249–54, and cf. *Index*, i/1. 20. Cf. Starkey No. 88. Heading, the first 3½ lines, and all foliation in Feathery's hand; rest of the text (ff. 46r–53v) in another scribal hand.]

72.16. ff. 212r–214r: *The Table Off the Seuerall Lres, Tracts, and Treatiyes, Wrytten in this Booke, viz*t*.*

[Index to the volume.]

73. Stowe MS 362

[Folio, 280 leaves; volume of parliamentary journals for 1597 and 1601–1601/2, in three scribal hands; docketed with shelfmark 'Press V—Nº 50'. Watermark: pillars.]

ff. 56r–270v: *The Journall: or Abstracte of soe much as passed in the Lower Howse, Att the Parliam^te: houlden, att Westmin^r: the xxvij^th: daye of October, Beinge Simon, and Judes [daye deleted], Eve, in the: xliij^th: yeare of Queene Elizabeth, And in the yeare of our Lord god, 1601: wch Parliam^te: ended the: xix^th: daye of December ffollowinge: Collected: by M^r: Heyward Townesend, beinge Burgesse in the said Parliam^te: ffor B^pps: Castle in Shropshier: xxvij^o: Octobris:*

[Compiled by Hayward Townshend (1576/7–1603?): see A. F. Pollard, 'Hayward Townshend's journals. III', *BIHR* 14 (1936–7), 149-65. Printed in Hayward Townshend, *Historical collections* (London, 1680) [Wing T1991]. Cotton's incomplete copy is BL Cotton MS Titus F. II. Cf. 6 above and 90 below; Starkey No. 69. Written in three scribal hands, Feathery's share being from f. 56r until near the end of the seventh line on f. 124r, and ff. 181r–270v.]

London, Inner Temple Library

74. Petyt MS 538, Vol. 14

[Folio, 234 leaves; composite volume of tracts relating to Parliament; owned by William Petyt (1641?–1707), antiquary and Keeper of the Records in the Tower of London.]

ff. 88r–115v: *A: Discours; Off, the: Highe Co^rte: of Parliam^te: And of the Aucthoritye of thesame; Collected out of the Comon Lawes of this Land, And dyve^rs: other good Auctho^rs: &c:*

[By Ralph Starkey. Cf. 6.2 and 44 above, and 108 below. Watermark: pillars (VAD).]

London, Lambeth Palace

75. MS 806

[Small quarto; composite volume of tracts (now in two parts, the first part 249 leaves); from the library

of Thomas Tenison (1636–1715), Archbishop of Canterbury.]

Part I, No. 13 (ff. 211r–246v): *Noe: poast: ffrom Heauen nor yett from Hell; Butt; a True Relacon and Anymadversion Wrytten and sent as an Antidode, To all Vnbeleivinge Brownists Prophane Annabaptistes Scismatticall Monnsters and such lyke Incendiaryes of the State proveinge by historyes And apparentlye shewinge by Recorde and Examples That his Maties: Taxacons haue not been vnusuall; His Proceedings Illegall nor his Governm^te Tyrannicall, As haue been through Impious, and Imprudent Pamphletts by some of them malitiouslye Invented, diabollically printed, And, by a most Supstitious and vnheard of waye, Protected, divulged, and scattered Abroade*

[By George Ashley, with dedicatory epistle to Charles I, giving historical precedents relating to monarchs' taxation from William the Conqueror to Queen Elizabeth. Cf. the similar subject in 66 above.]

London, University College London

76. MS Ogden 17

[Folio, 31 leaves (61 pages); a single tract; incomplete; from the library of Charles Kay Ogden (1889–1957). Watermark: pillars.]

The: Intelligencer, Or: An: Advertisem^te: Wrytten, vnto a Secretarye of my Lord Treasuro^rs: of England, to an Englishe Intelligencer, As hee passed through Germanye into Italye, Concerninge another Booke, newlye Wrytten, in Lattyn; and published in dyve^rs: Languages and Countryes, against hir Maties late Proclamacon ffor searche, and Apprehension of Seminarye Preistes, and their Receyvo^rs: Alsoe: Off a Letter wrytten by the Lord Treasuro^r: in deffence of his Gentrye, And Nobillitye, Intercepted, Published, and Answered by the Papistes, Anno, Dni: 1592

[Addressed to Lord Burghley and including extracts from 'the Booke of John Philopatris [i.e. Robert Persons], against hir Maties: Proclamacon'.]

77. MS Ogden 36

[Folio; volume of four tracts; the first three in Feathery's hand; the fourth (by Sir Daniel Donne about the Essex/Frances Howard divorce) in another scribal hand; docketed with shelfmark 'Ms | N° | 262'; bookplates of 'Tho Mostyn 1744 N°.56': i.e. MS 262 in the library of the Mostyn family, baronets, of Mostyn Hall, near Holywell, Wales, recorded in HMC, 4th Report (1874), appendix, 361; from the library of C. K. Ogden. Watermark: pillars.]

77.1. No. 1: *The Histories of Actiones Done, in England aboute the Beginninge of the Raigne of kinge James, Written, and sett forthe by an unknowne Author Concerninge Essex, Carr: Northampton and Ouerburye:*

[Anonymous tract beginning 'Howsoever everye Kingdome and Comon Wealth maye be Both well and vprightlye governed . . .'. 64 folio leaves (128 pages).]

77.2. No. 2: *The character of Robart Earle of Salisburye Lord high Treasuror of England &c: Written by m^r: Serill Turneur, and Dedicated to the most vnderstandinge, and the most worthie Ladie, the Ladie Theodosia Cecill: Dated, an°:*

[Possibly by Cyril Tourneur (1575?–1626): cf. *Index*, i/2, ToC 6. Listed in Humphrey Dyson's catalogues (f. [147v], '1612', No. 13) at the price of 8*d*. Cf. 43 above and 108.8 below. 5 leaves (9 pages).]

77.3. No. 3: *The State of a Secretaries Place, and the perill: Written by Robte, Earle of Salesburye, an°:*

[By Sir Robert Cecil, Earl of Salisbury. Printed as *The state and dignitie of secretarie of estates place* (London, 1642) [Wing S387]. Listed in

Humphrey Dyson's catalogues (f. [147v], '1612', No. 12) at the price of 6*d*. Cf. 16, 22, and 52 above and 78.8 below. 2 leaves (4 pages), from part-way down f. [5r] until the bottom of f. [6v].]

London, University of London

78. MS 308

[Folio, 282 leaves; composite volume of state tracts relating to the period 1571–1641, including Cotton's 'Relation of proceedings against ambassadors who have miscarried themselves' (ff. 273r–281r: cf. 1.9 above), in six scribal hands; Phillipps MS 10464; later in the library of Sir Edwin Durning-Lawrence (1837–1914).]

78.1. ff. 30–52: *Consideracons vppon his Maties estate, by Robte late Earle of Salisburye, wth the proposicons made by his Matie: To the Lordes of his Councell, And the Councells humble Aunswere; and advise Therevnto:*

[By Sir Robert Cecil, Earl of Salisbury, James I, and his Privy Council. Cf. 41.2 above.]

78.2. ff. 55r–72v: *The: Coppye Off a Letter: written to the Lower House of Parliam^t Touchinge dyvers Inconveniencyes and greivaunces of State &c:*

[Cf. 1.11, 40.1, 53, and 61 above and 83.3, 106.5, and 112 below.]

78.3. ff. 95r–180r: *Divers: Speeches: in: Parliament: Anno: 1640:*

[Parliamentary speeches chiefly in November–December 1640, including those by Charles I, the Keeper of the Great Seal (Sir John Finch), John Pym, Harbottle Grimston, Sir Edward Dering, and Sir John Culpeper: *Parliamentary history*, ii. 528 *et seq*. Title-page only (f. 95r) in Feathery's hand; text (ff. 97r–180r) in another scribal hand.]

78.4. ff. 183r–202r: *A: Speeche: Deliuered by Sir ffrauncis Bacon, in the Lower House of Parliam^te: Quinto Jacobi, Concerninge the Article, of generall; Naturalizacon: of the Scottishe Nation:*

> [By Sir Francis Bacon, 17 February 1606/7. Printed in London, 1641 [Wing B326]; Spedding, x. 307–25. Cf. 3 above. Watermark: pillars.]

78.5. ff. 204r–206v: *Sir: ffrauncis: Seymors: Speeche:*

> [Speech by Sir Francis Seymour (1590?–1664), November 1640: *Parliamentary history*, ii. 666–7.]

78.6. ff. 212r–214r: *A Speech: in Parliament: by S^r: Beniamyn Rudyard, on the < > of Aprill, 1640*

> [Speech by Sir Benjamin Rudyerd (1572–1658), 18? April 1640: *Parliamentary history*, ii. 544–51.]

78.7. ff. 230r–243v: *The: Coppye: Off a Letter written by S^r: Phillipp: Sidnye, to Queene Elizabeth, Touchinge hir Marryage wth Mounsieur:*

> [By Sir Philip Sidney: cf. *Index*, i/2, SiP 209; Appendix IV below, No. 30. Cf. 14, 18.1, 20.1, 41.10, 53, 57.4, and 64 above and 105.1 and 110 below. Title-page (f. 230r) and ff. 238r–243v in Feathery's hand; ff. 230(*bis*)–237v in another scribal hand.]

78.8. ff. 251r–254r: *The: State Off a Secretaryes Place, and the Perill, wrytten, by the Right honno^ble: Robte: later Earle of Salisburye:*

> [By Robert Cecil, Earl of Salisbury. Cf. 16, 22, 52 and 77.3 above.]

78.9. ff. 254v–256v: *A: Relation Off the manner of the proceedinge, wth S^r: Thomas Mounson, uppon the pleadinge of his pardon, in the Co^rte: of the Kinges Bench, the xij°: of ffebruarij; 1616*

> [Cf. 19, 23.6, and 41.5 above.]

Los Angeles, William Andrews Clark Memorial Library

79. fB618M3 T784 [c.1630] Bound

[Folio; composite volume of three tracts, the first by William Bird ('A treatise concerning ye nobility according to ye lawes of England': cf. Starkey No. 48); the third by John Selden ('The priviledges of the Baronage of England': cf. Starkey No. 87); once owned by Sir Richard Grosvenor (1585–1645); *Liber 3* in his list of MS volumes, 18 February 1634/5; from the muniments of the Duke of Westminster, Eaton Hall, Cheshire, recorded in HMC, 3rd Report (1872), appendix, 213 [MS 14]; Sotheby's, 19 July 1966, lot 488; Hofmann & Freeman, catalogue No. 21 (January 1968), item 57A; cf. Baker, *USA* ii. 27 (Nos. 234–5).]

No. 2: *Observations Conscerninge the Nobillety of England, Auncyent, and Moderne:*

> [Cf. 57.5 above. 17 leaves (33 pages). Watermark: pillars (R G).]

New Haven, Yale University, Osborn Collection

79A. b 167

[Folio, 18 leaves; a single tract (disbound). Watermark: quatrefoils within circle.]

A: Treatise: Concerninge The ffirst division, of England, As it is nowe genallye devided into Shires, of the Jurisdictions, and Innuityes, of Archb^pps: B^pps: and other Ecclesiasticall psons, wth dyvers other occurrences &^c:

> [By William Bird. Cf. 23.2, 55, and 57.2 above.]

80. b 180

[Folio, 21 leaves (36 pages); a single tract (disbound); reader's corrections on ff. [13r] and [14r]; acquired in 1952 from W. H. Robinson. Watermark: quatrefoils within circle. On first blank

(f. [1v]), on different paper (with watermark of elaborate horn device), is a cropped annotation in Feathery's hand: 'Vppon this, Essex his arraignm^te: | And Mountgomery vppon the Navye | Royall I receyved, } v^s:', and '555' in pencil; f. [1r] with '3' at top edge; and on last blank (f. [20r]) is Feathery's cropped annotation: 'vppon this thinge: | And the'. See Plate 35 above.]

An: Aunswere, made: by Comaund of Prince Henrye, to Certayne Proposicons, of Warre; and peace, Wrytten: By: Sir: Rob:te: Cotton Knight; and Barronett, And presented to his highnesse &c

[By Sir Robert Cotton. Cf. 28 above, also 22.2 and 57.8 above and 85 below.]

81. fb 59

[Folio, 279 pages; composite volume of eight state tracts (including speeches by Bacon), in several scribal hands; once owned by Sir Richard Grosvenor (1585–1645); from the muniments of the Duke of Westminster, Eaton Hall, this and fb 60 below recorded in HMC, 3rd Report (1872), appendix, 213–14 [MSS 17 and 20]; Hofmann & Freeman, catalogue No. 21 (January 1968), item 1, volumes i and iii; microfilm in BL, RP 217. Watermark: grapes.]

[No. 1]: *An: Exposicon vppon: the Comission, ffor Justices of the Peace, wth a Collection of Cases in Highe Treason, Pettye Treason, Murder, Homicyde, ffelonye, &c: out of the Bodye of the Lawe*

[114 pages. Only the title-page and the word 'ffinis' at the end in Feathery's hand; all the rest in another scribal hand.]

82. fb 60

[Folio, 476 leaves; composite volume of 23 state tracts by Bacon and others, in several scribal hands; similar provenance to fb 59 above; *Liber 4* in Sir Richard Grosvenor's list of MS volumes, 18 February 1634/5; cf. Baker, *USA* ii. 339–41 (Nos. 1359–66). This volume (including Nos. 82.1–7, 82.9–10 below) was evidently the principal source for University of London MS 285, which was copied by 25 April 1637 at Sir Roger Mostyn's house from books of Sir Richard Grosvenor's son: see Chapter 2 n. 25 above. Watermark: pillars (VAD).]

82.1. ff. 389r–391v: *Henry Cuffe Secretarye to the Earle of Essex his Lre to M^r: Secretarye Cecill, Declareinge the effect of the Instruccons, fframed by the Earle of Essex, and deliued to the Ambassador of the Kinge of Scotte[s], Touchinge his Tytle to the Crowne of England, wch Lre was written after Cuffes Condempnacon*

[By Henry Cuffe, 1601. Cf. 1.16, 19, 53.1, and 71 above.]

82.2. f. 395r–v: *A: Coppie of the Lre w^ch: the Lord Norrys writt to the Kinge[s] Matie: after hee had slayne one of the Lord Willoughbies Servante[s] vppon a quarrell Raysed Betwene the two Lordes; Anno, 1615*

[By Francis Norris. Cf. 71.4 above.]

82.3. ff. 397r–398r: *The Coppie of a Lre: written by the Lord Chauncello^r: Ellesmer, to the Kinge, desireinge to bee discharged of his offyce, through his inffirmety, and weaknes, to supplye thesame, Anno, 1612*

[By Sir Thomas Egerton, Baron Ellesmere. Cf. 1.26, 13.8, and 53.10 above and 83 below.]

82.4. ff. 399r–403r: *A Lre written by the Lordes of the Councell to Kinge James, dated the < > of < > Anno; < > Touchinge Meanes to advaunce the Kinge[s] Revenewes, by vnusuall, meanes, soe as the Kinge will take the Acte vppon himselfe, and bee their protection:*

[Cf. 1.1, 53.12, and 71 above and 83 below.]

82.5. f. 437r–v: *Sir Thomas Smythe one of the Sherriffe[s] of London, his ptestacon Touchinge his Speech, vsed to the Earle of Essex, when hee fledd into London, and other Accidente[s] touchinge the same Earle:*

[By Sir Thomas Smith (1558?–1625). Cf. 1.3 and 1.17 above and 109.12 below.]

82.6. ff. 439r–445v: *An Admonition ffrom A: ffrinde namelesse, to S*: *Edward Cooke Knight, Lord Cheiffe Justice of the Kinge[s] Bench, after his degradacon in Anno, 1616*

[Cf. Starkey No. 46.]

82.7. ff. 448r–456r: *The effect Of that which was spoken by the Lord Keeper, S*: *ffrauncis Bacon, Knight, att the takeinge of his place in the Chauncerye, in Perfformaunce of the Chardge his Ma*tie: *had given him, when hee Receyved the greate Seale of England the, vij*o: *of Maij; 1617*

[By Sir Francis Bacon. Cf. 13.4 above and 83 below.]

82.8. ff. 463r–466r: *The lyfe Of Sir Thomas Bodlye, Written w*th *his owne hande:*

[By Sir Thomas Bodley (1545–1613), 1609. Printed in Oxford, 1647 [Wing B3392]. Cotton's copy of part of this life is BL Cotton MS Titus C. VII, ff. 173r–174v. Cf. 19 above; Starkey No. 18.]

82.9. ff. 467r–468v: *The Death of Queene Elizabeth, w*th *hir declaracon of hir Successor:*

[Cf. 1.14 above and 83 below.]

82.10. ff. 469r–474r: *A: Discourse written by M*r: *John Seldon, Student in the Inner Temple London, and Dedicated vnto S*r: *ffrauncis Bacon Knight, Lord Keeper of the great Seale of England, of the Auncyent Mencon, Coniunction, or Devision, of the Two great Offyces of State; The Chauncellorshipp: and Keeper of the greate Seale of England, in Anno, 1617*

[By John Selden. Cf. 13.3 above.]

82.11. ff. 474r–476v: *The Antiquetye of the Lord Chauncello*r: *of Englandes offyce Collected by M*r *Tate of the Middle Temple London*

[By Francis Tate. Cf. 13.6 above.]

83. Gordonstoun Box V.

[Folio, 85 leaves; volume of 'Historical and Political Tracts Reign of James I', including 'The death of Queene Elizabeth' (f. 1: cf. 1.14 above), Cornwallis's 'Death of Prince Henry' (ff. 3r–14v: cf. 6.1 above), a letter by the Privy Council (cf. 1.1 above), Annual Receipts (f. 36: cf. 6.5 above), Northampton's Abatements (f. 37: cf. 1.2 above), Tate's 'Antiquitie of Cities' (f. 39: cf. 6.4 above), Ellesmere's letter to the King 1612/13 (f. 43: cf. 1.26 above), and speeches by Bacon (ff. 47 *et seq.*: cf. 13.4 above, 108.10 below, etc.), in various scribal hands; among papers relating to the families of Gordon of Gordonstoun and Cumming of Allyr, Scotland; acquired from A. Rosenthal, February 1954; cf. Baker, *USA* ii. 348 (No. 1395).]

83.1. ff. 17r–20v: *Obseruacons off a Loyall Sub*te: *to his gratious Soveraigne, drawne ffrom Observacons of the peoples speeches*

[Cf. 6, 20.8, 42, and 71 above and 108.7 below. In the heading 'K. James' is inserted after 'Soveraigne' in another hand. Watermark: pillars (RDP).]

83.2. ff. 21r–29r: *The politia or Governm*te: *of the Vnited Provinces:*

[By Sir Clement Edmondes. Cf. 6.7 and 33 above and 109.15 below. Heading alone in Feathery's hand; text in one or two other scribal hands.]

83.3. ff. 71r–85v: *A: Lre wrytten ffrom a ffrinde namelesse to the Parliam*te:

[Cf. 1.11, 40.1, 53, 61, and 78.2 above and 106.5 and 112 below. At end of heading 'of K. Charles' inserted in another hand, and corrections on ff. 74v, 75v; docketed '24:D'.]

New York, Pierpont Morgan Library

84. [MS with MA 1475]

[Folio, 230 pages; a single tract; imperfect, missing text at beginning evidently supplied on first 16 pages, on a different stock of paper (urn watermark), in a non-professional hand, heavily corrected; pp. [17–230] (with contemporary pagination of 4–230) in Feathery's hand; reader's corrections and annotations; other annotations on pp. 10 and [231] possibly relating to scriptorium clients in London. Watermark: pillars (ALD).]

A Coppie of a letter written by a M^r. of arte of Cambridge to his freind in London concerning some talke passed of late between two worshipfullful [sic] grave men about the psent state & some proceedings of ye Ea: of Leic: & his freinds in Englande

> [Libelous tract often attributed to Robert Persons (1546–1610) or Thomas Morgan (1543–1606?), but perhaps by exiled Catholic courtiers in Paris, including Charles Arundell. Printed anonymously, as *The copie of a leter, wryten by a master of arte of Cambridge to his friend in London*, in [?Paris], 1584 [STC 5742.9]; prohibited; then again, as *Leycesters common-wealth*, in London, 1641 [Wing L968.9]; ed. D. C. Peck (Athens, Oh., 1985). A copy owned by Ralph Starkey is BL Harley MS 557. Cf. 8 above and Starkey No. 86. The MS concludes on pp. 228–30, from a different stock of paper, with 'A: Godlye and proffitable: Meditacon, taken out of the, xxth: Chapter of the Booke of Job:'; subscribed 'a.. 5.. 6'. See Plates 39 and 40 above.]

Northampton, Northamptonshire Record Office

85. FH 4155

[Folio, 36 leaves (71 pages), foliated 49–84; a single tract; among the papers of the Finch and Hatton families. Watermark: quatrefoils within circle.]

Princes: Extremityes Beyounde the ease of their people, By reason of Warres

> [By Sir Robert Cotton: the second half of his 'Answer made by command of Prince Henry to certain propositions of war and peace'. Cf. 22.2, 28, 57.8, and 80 above.]

Oxford, Bodleian Library

86. MS Carte 122

[Folio, 82 leaves; two separate tracts, in two scribal hands, bound together (with a Norwich vellum deed as f. i); from the library of John Carte (1686–1754).]

ff. ii–iii, 1r–59v: *A: Shorte Compendium of all the Offices, and Offyce^{rs}: their dutyes, and proceedinges, in the Excheque^r:*

> [By Thomas Fanshawe (1533–1601). Printed as *The practice of the Exchequer Court, with its severall offices and officers* (London, 1658). Cf. 111 below. Watermark: grapes.]

87. MS Dugdale 28

[Folio, 370 leaves; composite volume of historical and heraldic tracts, in various scribal hands; compiled, annotated, and copiously indexed in his own hand by Sir William Dugdale (1605–86), Garter King-of-Arms; the name 'Thomas Longman' inscribed on f. 8v.]

ff. 135r–184v: *Englands Epinomis: Or: A: Collection Out Off the: Authentique historians, And a Comentarye of those Lawes, (The Originalls of Manye of our Moderne) whereby the kingdome of England, hath been ffrom tyme to tyme governed under both Prophane, and Christian Princes, since the ffirst Inhabitants to the end of Kinge Johns Raigne:*

> [By John Selden. Cf. 19.4 and 40.2 above. Name of John Allanson inscribed three times

and also 'Lamberts Lawes'; readers' corrections and annotations, including numerous in Dugdale's hand. Watermark: grapes. See Plates 55 and 56 above.]

88. MS Eng. misc. c. 139

[Folio, 259 leaves; volume of antiquarian tracts relating to heraldic offices and procedures, comprising two independent units foliated as a single series; the first part (ff. 1r–29v), written in two hands, owned in 1612 and annotated by William and Henry Crispe (see Woudhuysen, 132); the second part (ff. 30r–246r), written in three scribal hands; docketed with shelfmarks 'MSS. Lib. 33', 'B 89 438', '7J2', and 'Her. 10'; sold at Sotheby's, 17 June 1904 ('Library of a Gentleman in the Country'), lot 89; P. J. and A. E. Dobell, catalogue No. 80 (1928), item 719; *SC* 43575. Watermark in Feathery item: grapes.]

ff. 30r–246r: *A: Discourse off the Antiquitye, and Offyce, of the Lord Steward, Constable and Earle Marshall of England*

[A series of papers, tracts, reports, warrants, letters patent, and other heraldic records relating to the history, ordinances, procedures, cases, and other matters concerning the offices of Lord High Constable, Lord Steward, and Earl Marshal of England, from *temp.* Henry II to James I, including tracts by Cotton (5: some printed in Hearne, vol. ii) and William Camden (ff. 48v–51r, 71r–77v: cf. *Index*, i/1, CmW 23, 35); with a general title-page and table of contents. Cf. 35 above; Starkey No. 79. Fols. 30r–119v, 132r–145v, 150v–161r, 165v–205r (to line 13, half-way down the page) in Feathery's hand. Watermark: grapes.]

89. MS Perrott 7

[Folio, 207 leaves; composite volume of tracts, in various scribal hands; presented to the Bodleian in 1727 by Thomas Perrott of St John's College, Oxford (*matric.* 15 February 1709/10, DCL 1721).]

ff. 157r–180v: *M*^r^: *Secretarye Cecill His Negotiacons in ffraunce:*

[Negotiations of Sir Robert Cecil from 31 January to 19 February 1597/8 (as per present incomplete form). 47 pages; imperfect. Watermark: grapes.]

90. MS Rawl A. 100

[Folio, 206 leaves (412 pages); a single work; once owned by Sir Robert Oxenbridge, MP (1595–1638), of Hurstbourne Priors, Hampshire; later by Thomas Tanner (1674–1735), Bishop of St Asaph; bought from John Jackson of Tottenham High Cross. For MSS of similar provenance, cf. 95, 96, 97, and 108 below. Watermarks: horn device and urn.]

The Jurnall or Abstract of somuche as passed in the Lower howse, at the parleament holden at westminster begininge y^e^ *xxvij day of october being Simon and Judes [day* deleted*] Euen in the .43. yeare of [our* deleted*] Queene Elizabeth And the yeare of our Lord, 1601. w*^ch^: *Parliament ended y*^e^ *xix*^th^: *day of December following: Collected by m*^r^ *Heyward Touneshend, being a burgess for Bishopes Castle, for the said Parliament*

[By Hayward Townshend. Cf. 3 and 73 above. The heading in the hand of Ralph Starkey. A marginal note on f. 156r (also in Feathery's hand): 'Ra: Starkey, seruinge as, a bacheler, to, the Lo: mayor: bestowed this, on him'.]

91. MS Rawl. A. 141

[Folio, 72 leaves; composite volume of state tracts, in various scribal hands; from the library of Richard Rawlinson (1690–1755).]

91.1. ff. 65r–70r: *A:, Breiffe: Discourse concerninge the Empero*^rs^: *Election, The, Netherlandes, And the Lowe Countryes greatnes, w*^th^ *some other Affay*^rs^*e of State; Wrytten, by S*^r^: *Henrye Wootton. Knight &c*

[By Sir Henry Wotton (1568–1639), beginning 'In: the tyme of Charles le Mayne, and ffor a tyme after, the Election of the Empero^r: . . .': cf. *Index*, i/2, WoH 258. Watermark: urn.]

91.2. ff. 71r–72v: *M^r: Pyms, Declaracon, Off; the distempers of the State, and kingdome*

[By John Pym (1584–1643), 1640, an anti-Catholic speech beginning 'The distempers of the kingdome, are; soe well knowne, they neede noe Repeticon . . .'. Watermark: horn armorial (GAVILARD).]

92. MS Rawl. D. 692

[Folio, 292 leaves; composite volume of MSS, in various hands; ff. 87r–111r an independent folio pamphlet of state letters and speeches in a slightly variant version of Feathery's hand; ff. 89–110 originally foliated 1–23; the name 'William Howard | i635.' inscribed on f. 88r [perhaps ? Lord William Howard (1563–1640) of Naworth]; the number '55' at the top of ff. 87r and 111v; in the library of John Murray in 1749; afterwards owned by Richard Rawlinson. Watermark in the Feathery section: pillars (VAD).]

92.1. f. 87r: *The Table of all the Lres Written in this booke following*

[The table of contents of the pamphlet, listing 11 items. A small cross added against the ninth and tenth items.]

92.2. ff. 89r–94r: *The lord Digbies lre to the king the 17th of August, 1626 Deliu^ed att Bagshott/:/*

[By John Digby, Earl of Bristol; dated at the end from the Tower, 16 August 1626.]

92.3. ff. 94v–95v: *To the right honable the Lords of the Higher Howse of Parliament/:/ The humble peticon of John Earle of Bristoll, p^rsented to the Comittee of the same howse, by the*

Countesse of Bristoll, on Tuesday the xviij^th of Aprill 1626 in the afternoone

[By John Digby, Earl of Bristol. Cf. 46.3 above.]

92.4. ff. 95v–97r: *Bristolls lre to the Lord keep/:/*

[By John Digby, Earl of Bristol; dated from Sherborne, 12 April 1626.]

92.5. ff. 97v–98r: *A lre from S^r ffrancis Bacon to the Judges/:/*

[By Sir Francis Bacon, about deferring the argument in the case of a commendam; dated 25 April 1616.]

92.6. ff. 98r–100r: *A lre written from king James to the Judges/:/*

[By James I, concerning the same case, 1616.]

92.7. ff. 100r–104r: *Kinge James his speach 8th of March 1623 touching the Pallatinate and other affaires/:/*

[By James I, 8 March 1623/4. Rushworth i. 129–31.]

92.8. f. 104r–v: *The humble peticon of the Lord Viscount ffaukland one of the Lordes of yor Maties: most honable Privie counsell/:/*

[A petition by Henry Cary, first Viscount Falkland (d. 1633), Lord Deputy of Ireland, for the release of his son Lucius from the Fleet Prison, c.27 January 1630. *Cabala: sive Scrinia sacra* (1663), 238.]

92.9. ff. 105r–106r: *The kings lre to the paliament vppon Monday the xx^th of March in the ffirst yeare of his Raigne/:/*

[By Charles I, 20 March 1625/6. Rushworth, i. 214–15.]

92.10. ff. 106r–109r: *The hermits oration att Theoblale* [sic], *1594 penned by S' Robert Cecill*

[By Sir Robert Cecil. Cf. 20.4 and 35 above.]

92.11. ff. 109r–110v: *The coppy of a lre written, by S' Robert Carr, viscount Rochester, and after Earle of Sommset vnto the Lord Henry Howard, Earle of Northampton An° 1612 the xiij^{th} of October/:/*

[By Sir Robert Carr, Earl of Somerset; dated at the end from Royston, 8 October 1612. Cf. 1.5, 35.4, and 52 above and 108.9 below.]

92.12. ff. 110v–111r: *A lre written from M' Anthony Babington to the Queene/:/*

[By Anthony Babington, conspirator, 19 September 1586. Printed from this MS in Nichols's *Progresses*, ii. 482: cf. 35.6 above.]

92.13. f. 111v: *'ffarewell ffond Love vnder whose Childish Whipp:'*

[By Henry King (1592-1669), Bishop of Chichester: his poem 'The Farwell'. Printed in his *Poems* (London, 1657): cf. *Index*, ii/1, KiH 361. Written by Feathery in his mature script on a blank page at the end of the pamphlet. See Plate 58 above.]

93. MS Rawl. D. 918

[Folio, 341 leaves; composite volume of 17th- and 18th-century tracts, letters, and documents chiefly relating to parliamentary affairs, the Army, Navy, Exchequer, and Excise; from the library of Richard Rawlinson.]

ff. 1r–6v: *A: Collection: Off Such: thinges, As, Robte late Earle of Salisburye, thought ffitt to offerr vnto his Matie: vppon the occasion of callinge a Parliam^{te}:*

[By Sir Robert Cecil, Earl of Salisbury, 1604. Cf. 15.1 and 54 above. 12 pages; imperfect. Watermark: grapes.]

94. MS Rawl. poet. 31

[Folio, 50 leaves (99 pages); docketed with shelfmark [?]'Ent.13.1'; from the library of Richard Rawlinson. Watermark: grapes.]

[*Poems*]

[A verse miscellany, comprising some 76 poems (by Sir John Harington, Sir Henry Wotton, Thomas Campion, Ben Jonson, John Donne, Edward Lord Herbert of Cherbury, Sir Robert Ayton, Sir John Roe, William Herbert, Earl of Pembroke, Sir Benjamin Rudyerd, Francis Beaumont, and others); later docketed incorrectly: 'Sir John Harringtons Poems Written in the Reign of Queen Elizabeth' and 'S' J.hn Har[r]ingtons Poems temp Eliz.'. See Plates 59 and 60 above.]

95. MS Tanner 84

[Folio, 334 leaves; volume of tracts, in various scribal hands; successively owned by Sir Robert Oxenbridge, MP (1595–1638), of Hurstbourne Priors, Hampshire; by William Sancroft (1617–93), Archbishop of Canterbury (with his autograph corrections on the list of contents); and by Thomas Tanner, Bishop of St Asaph; once bought from John Jackson of Tottenham High Cross; the last page inscribed in pencil: 'This MS. belongs to D' Tanner | Lent me Friday May 2^d 1729 | Tho Hearne' [i.e. Thomas Hearne (1678–1735)]. For MSS of similar provenance, cf. 90 above and 96, 97, and 108 below.]

95.1. ff. 243r–263r: *A Breuiarie, of the historie, of Englande, from William .1. intitled, the, Conqueror: Written, by S': Walter Ral,=eigh Knight:*

[By Samuel Daniel (1563–1619). Printed, ascribed to Sir Walter Ralegh, as *An introduction to a breviary of the history of England* (London, 1693): cf. *Index*, i/1, DaS 31. Cotton's copy, in the hand of Ralph Starkey, is BL Cotton MS Titus F. III, ff. 309r–323v. Cf. 51 above and 108.20 below.]

95.2. ff. 263r–334v: *A Dialogue, disputeinge, the conveniencye, of Queene, Elizabethes, marriage, Written, by S^r: Thomas Smyth, one of the Principall, Secretaries, to the saide, Queene, Elizab:*

> [By Sir Thomas Smith (1513–77). Cf. 27 above. This dialogue is mentioned in one of Francis Davison's lists of MSS in BL Harley MS 298, f. 160r, and as item 60 in one of Ralph Starkey's lists in Harley MS 537, ff. 82r–83v.]

96. MS Tanner 85

[Folio, 266 leaves (534 pages); volume of tracts, in two or three scribal hands; similar provenance as MS Tanner 84: cf. 90 and 95 above and 97 and 108 below. Watermark: fleur-de-lis.]

96.1. ff. 1r–6v: *A Discourse, of the lawfulnes of Combattes, to be performed, in the presence, of the Kinge, or ye Conestable, and, marshall, of, England &c: Written, by S^r: Robarte Cotton, Knight:*

> [By Sir Robert Cotton, 1609. *Cottoni posthuma*, No. 4. Cotton's copy is BL Cotton MS Titus C. I, ff. 164r–167r.]

96.2. ff. 7r–13v: *of the Antiquetie, vse and cerimonye of Lawfull, Combattes, in England:*

> [By Sir John Davies, 22 May 1601. Hearne, ii. 180–7: cf. *Index*, i/1, DaJ 247.]

96.3. ff. 13v–15v: *[of the Antiquetie, vse and cerimonye of Lawfull, Combattes, in England:]*

> [By Sir John Davies, 22 May 1601. Hearne, ii. 187–90: cf. *Index*, i/1, DaJ 253.]

96.4. ff. 16r–19v: *of the Antiquitie, Vse, and, Ceremony of Lawfull, Combattes, in England Written by m^r: James, Whitelocke of the . . . . .* [sic]

> [By Sir James Whitelocke (1570–1632), 22 May 1601. Hearne, ii. 190–4.]

96.5. ff. 20r–39r: *Duello Foil'd: The whole proceedinges, in the orderly Dissoluinge, of a designe for single, fight, Betwene, two Valiant, gentlemen by occasion, Whereof, the vnlawfulnes; and wickednes, of a Duello, is preparatorilye, Disputed, according, to the Rules, of honno^r: and Right Reason: Written, by y^e: Lo: Henry Howard, Earle of Northampton An^o:*

> [By Henry Howard, Earl of Northampton. Hearne, ii. 223–42 (where it is misattributed to Sir Edward Coke). Cotton's copy, with Northampton's autograph annotations, is BL Cotton MS Titus C. I, ff. 358r–366r (and another copy with Northampton's autograph annotations is BL Add. MS 25247, ff. 46r–59r); Northampton's autograph drafts and compilations relating to duels are elsewhere in Cotton MSS Titus C. I and C. IV, and a MS of his related treatise with autograph annotations is at Castle Howard.]

96.6. ff. 39v–41v: *A Discourse touchinge the vnlawfulnes of priuate Combates; Written by S^r: Edward Cooke, Lord, Chiefe Justice of England, at the, request of ye Lord, Henry Howard, Earle of Northehampton:*

> [By Sir Edward Coke, 3 October 1609. Gutch, i. 9–12.]

96.7. ff. 42r–47v: *Of, a Lie; how it maye, be satisfied; or, at least, how, it ought, to be, dealt in by an, Earle Marshall: as also: What Lawes, are necessary to be Established to preuent, the, many, Barbarous mischeifes, that Daylie, doe, happen, for defaulte, of some such, course to be taken:*

> [Gutch, i. 12–23.]

96.8. ff. 48r–50r: *The Antiquitie, Vse and Ceremonies of Lawfull: Combattes, in England, Written by m^r: Francis Tate of the middle Temple, London, the xiij^th: of ffebruary: an^o: 1600*

> [By Francis Tate, 1600. Gutch, i. 6–8.]

96.9. ff. 51r–59v: *The manner, and order, of Combattinge, w^{thin}: Listes, sett, downe, by Thomas Duke of Gloucester, Vncle, to Kinge, Richard the Second:*

[By Thomas of Woodstock, Duke of Gloucester (1355–97), and addressed to Richard II.]

96.10. ff. 60r–107v: [*The manner of the lady Katharine of Spain's departure from her parents, her passage into England, her reception there, and the death of Prince Arthur, an. 1501–2.*]

[Untitled series of accounts relating to Katherine of Arragon's marriage with Prince Arthur, elder brother of Henry VIII, in 1501–2. Watermark: fleur-de-lis.]

97. MS Tanner 108

[Folio, 181 leaves; volume of two tracts, entirely in Feathery's hand; similar provenance as MSS Tanner 84 and 85: cf. 90, 95, 96 above and 108 below.]

97.1. ff. 1r–51v: *A Discourse playnelie, proueinge, that, aswell: the sentence, of Death, Latelie, giuen, againste, that, vnfortunate, Ladie, Marie, Late, Queene, of Scottes: as, also, the, Execution, of thesame, Sentence, was, hon-no^{ble}: iuste, necessarie, and, Lawfull: An°; 1587; / 29 Eliz:*

[By George Puttenham (d. 1590). Printed in *Accounts and papers relating to Mary Queen of Scots*, ed. Allan J. Crosby and John Bruce, Camden Society 93 (1867), 67–134. Cotton's copy (bound with some material in Ralph Starkey's hand) is BL Cotton MS Caligula D. I, ff. 37r–84v. Humphrey Dyson's copy, priced at 10*s.*, is Bodleian Library MS Willis 58, ff. 136r–173r. Cf. also 108 below. For copies associated with Sidney's *Letter to the Queen*, see below, Appendix IV, Nos. 11, 20, 37; also *Index*, i/2, PtG 2–5. 'A declaratione justefyinge the Queenes proceedinges against the Queene of Scottes' is mentioned in one of Starkey's lists of MSS in BL Harley MS 292, f. 139v. See Plate 31 above.]

97.2. ff. 52r–181r: *The, Life, and, manner, of, Death: of, that moste, holie, Prelate, and, Constante, Martir, John: ffisher, Bishop of, Rochester, and, Cardinall: of the holie churche, of Rome:*

[Ascribed here, after a final epigram, to 'J. C.'. A version printed in Thomas Bayly, *The life & death of that renowned John Fisher, Bishop of Rochester* (London, 1655); ed. Philip Hughes, *Saint John Fisher: The earliest English life* (London, 1935). Full text printed from BL Harley MS 6382 in *The life of Fisher*, ed. Ronald Bayne, Early English Text Society, ES 117 (London, 1921). Reader's annotation at the end: 'afection is all, or at lest a uery great matter in such relations as his is [*deleted*] which doe'. Watermark: fleur-de-lis. See Plate 33 above.]

Oxford, Dr Bent E. Juel-Jensen

98. [No shelfmark]

[Folio, 32 pages; a single tract; sold by B. A. Seaby Ltd. at Sotheby's, 31 July 1962, lot 554. A reader's trefoil marks in the margin. Watermark: pillars.]

A: Discours: Touchinge: a: Marryage, Betwene Prince Henrye of England, and a daughter of Savoye; Written, by S^r: Walter Rawleighe knight, beinge therevnto Comaunded by thesaid Prince:/

[By Sir Walter Ralegh: cf. *Index*, i/2, RAW 639. Cf. 3.3 above and 108.29 below.]

Oxford, The Queen's College

99. MS 280

[Folio, 306 leaves; composite volume of MSS, owned by Thomas Barlow (1607–91), Bishop of Lincoln.]

ff. 185r–203r: *A: Speeche: Delyvered by Rob^te late Earle of Salisburye; Lord Treasuro^r: of England, by the kinges specyall Appoyntem^te: Touchinge the necessitye of callinge a Parliam^te: Anno: Dn°: 1609: Annoq Regni Re: Jacobi, etc: Septimo*

[By Sir Robert Cecil, Earl of Salisbury. Watermark: pillars.]

100. MS 449

[Folio, 341 leaves; composite volume of tracts; owned by Thomas Barlow, Bishop of Lincoln.]

ff. 158r–164r: *A: Breiffe: Discours: proveinge that the Howse of Comons, hath equall power wth the peeres, in poynte of Judicature*

[By Sir Robert Cotton. Cf. 23.7 above. Title-page docketed by Barlow: 'This was printed (but falsely) in 1640, but noe authors name to it.' Watermark: pillars (VA5).]

Philadelphia, The Free Library of Philadelphia

101. Carson MS LC 14:44

[Folio, 170 leaves (including 13 blanks); composite volume of legal and political tracts, in various scribal hands; cf. Baker, *USA* ii. 307–8 (Nos. 1247–50).]

ff. 58r–105v: *Reportes: off the Starr chamber: Pasche: Anno primo Caroli: Regis:*

[Star Chamber cases, 1625-7, headed (f. 59r) 'Camera: Stellata:'; separate title-page on f. 90r: 'Reportes Off the Starr chamber pasche: secundo Caroli:'. Cf. 10 and 29 above, and 110A below. Chiefly in Feathery's hand; ff. 99v–100v, 103r–105v in another scribal hand.]

Philadelphia, Rosenbach Museum

102. MS 239/4

[Folio, 517 leaves; composite volume of state tracts and letters, principally by Cotton, Bacon, and Ralegh; collected early in 1674 by one 'Jo: Witham'. See also p. 269 below.]

No. 5, ff. 1r–7v: *The three Greate Kingdomes of England, ffrance and Spayne as they nowe stand, are to bee compared to the elleccon of a kinge of Poland . . .*

[Cf. 1.7 above and 109 below. Watermark: pillars]

San Marino, California, Huntington Library

103. HM 1420

[Folio, 24 leaves (45 pages); a single tract; title-page inscribed 'This was written by M^r. Jo: Silden to Mr Farnaby the eminent schoolma^r'; docketed No. 2; this MS apparently referred to in a note pasted into Bodleian MS Rawl. D. 1361: 'In a ms. sent to the Bodleian on approval 22.vii.22 by E. Williams, 87 Newtown Rd, Hove, which contained 5 items in a hand of the earlier 17th cent., viz . . .' (and cf. 110 below). Watermark: grapes.]

Three weekes Observation, of the States Countrye, and especiallye Holland

[By Owen Felltham (1602?–68). Printed in London, 1648. See Kees Van Strien, 'Owen Felltham's *A brief character of the Low-Countries*: A survey of the texts', *EMS* 6 (1997), 132–74 (plate 5, p. 146). Cf. also 59 and 72 above.]

Stafford, William Salt Library

104. M 527

[*Indenture, witnessed by Izaak Walton, 1635*]

[Indenture, on a single membrane of vellum (*c*.442 × 524 mm), whereby Robert Tichborne and Thomas Grinsell of London, executors of the late Dame Margaret Temple, by virtue of her Will dated 12 May 1617, grant the Mayor and Burgesses of Stafford the right to dispose as they see fit of Dame Margaret's bequest (£30 with interest at the rate of 6% or more if possible) to the poor of Stafford; the text written almost entirely in Feathery's hand; signed as witnesses by Izaak Walton, Stephen Noell, Gabriel Reve, William Mille, and Thomas Steward, 30 June 1635: cf. *Index*, ii/2. 622 (No. iii). See Plates 36–8 above.]

Taunton, Somerset Record Office

105. DD/AH/51/1

[Folio, 200 leaves; composite volume of state tracts, in various scribal hands; from the family archives of Sir Alexander Acland-Hood, of St Audries, Somerset; recorded in HMC, 6th Report (1877), appendix, 350.]

105.1. No. 3 (ff. 48r–60v): *The Coppye: Off a Lre wrytten, by S^r: phillipp. Sidnye, to Queene Elizabeth, Touchinge the Marryage, wth Mounsieur, &c*

[By Sir Philip Sidney: cf. *Index*, i/2, SiP 211; Appendix IV below, No. 33. Cf. 17, 18.1, 20.1, 41.10, 53, 57.4, 64, and 78.7 above and 110 below. See Plates 76 and 77 above.]

105.2. No. 4 (ff. 62r–69r): *The: Coppye: Off. a: Lre: wrytten by S^r: Thomas Bodley, To, S^r: ffrauncis Bacon, whoe desired, his Opinyon; and Judgm^t: Touchinge; his, Cogita: et, Visa, And some other Bookes*

[By Sir Thomas Bodley, 19 February 1607[/8]. *Scrinia sacra* (1654), 74–9.]

105.3. No. 5 (ff. 70r–82r): *A Apopologye,* [sic] *ffor Robert late Earle of Salisbury Lord Treasur^er of England [&c]*

[By Sir Walter Cope (d. 1614), Chamberlain of the Exchequer, 1612. Gutch, i. 119–33; entitled in various MS copies 'Il di loda la sera'. Cited in Starkey's list of MSS in BL Harley MS 298, ff. 156v–157r. Listed in Humphrey Dyson's catalogues (f. [147v], '1612', No. 15) at the price of 2s. Cf. 6 above; Starkey No. 52; also University of London MS 309, ff. 275r–288v.]

105.4. No. 6 (ff. 84r–95r): *The Coppye Off the Challendge, sent by the Earle of Northumberland, to S^r: ffrauncis Veere, on S^te: Georges daye, the last yeare of Queene Eliz: Anno, 1602*

[By Henry Percy, Earl of Northumberland, and also incorporating (ff. 89r–95r) the 'Aunswere, to the Earle of North^b: Challendge' by Sir Francis Vere. Cf. 3, 11, 23.4, 28, and 41.9 above.]

106. DD/AH/51/2

[Folio, 235 leaves; composite volume of state tracts, in various scribal hands; similar Acland-Hood provenance as 105 above.]

106.1. No. 1 (ff. 1r–11r): *A Breiffe: Abstracte: of the Question of precedencye, Betwene England and Spayne, Collected: By S^r: Rote Cotton, knight, and Barronett, Att hir Maties Comandem^te*

[By Sir Robert Cotton. *Cottoni posthuma*, No. 5. Cotton's copy is BL Cotton MS Julius C. IX, ff. 107r–21r.]

106.2. No. 2 (ff. 13r–53v): *The Instructions with the most important passages, that past Betwene the Comissione^rs of the kinge of Spayne, the Archdukes of Burgundyes and the Queene of England in their Negotiacon Aboute the Treatye of Peace; in Anno Dni 1600. And in :42: yeare of hir Raigne*

[Relating to the Commissioners at Boulogne, 1600. Cf. 71 above; Starkey Nos. 21–3.]

106.3. No. 3 (ff. 55r–67v): *The Coppye off: a: Lre: wrytten: by Pope Paulus the iiij^th: To the Emperor ffardinand, kinge of the Romans, Touchinge the Alteracon of tymes, The Conffusion of Religion, The devision of kingdomes, and provinces, And dyvers other Affayers of State, &c.*

[By Pope Paul IV (1476–1559; pope 1555–9).]

106.4. No. 4 (ff. 69r–146v): *Sir: George Caryes Negotiacons in ffraunce:*

[Negotiations of Sir George Carew (d. 1612) in 1605–9. Cf. Starkey No. 77. Heading only in Feathery's hand; text in another scribal hand.]

106.5. No. 5 (ff. 147r–165r): *The: Coppye: Off: a: Letter Wrytten to the Lower Howse of Parliam^{te}: Touchinge, dyvers greivances, and Inconveniencyes of the State, &c.*

[Cf. 1.11, 40.1, 53, 61, 78.2, and 83.3 above, and 112 below.]

106.6. No. 7 (ff. 194r–201r): *Serieaunt fleetwodes Relacon, and opinyon of Co^{rte[s]}:*

[By William Fleetwood. Cf. 19.3, 23, and 41.4 above and 109.2 below. Only headings on ff. 194r and 196r in Feathery's hand; the text in another scribal hand.]

106.7. No. 8 (ff. 202r–231v): *Certayne: Speciall: Proiecte[s], ffor the discoverye of Abuses, and misdemeano^{rs}: in Offycers, Tradesmen, and Merchante[s], &^x will bringe inffinyte somes of Monye to his Maties: Coffers, And much satisfaction, and good, to the Comon Wealth:*

[By Sir Stephen Procter. ff. 202r–209v and bottom of f. 230v to f. 231v in Feathery's hand; ff. 210–230v in another scribal hand.]

107. DD/AH/51/4

[Folio, 147 leaves; composite volume of state tracts, in various scribal hands; similar Acland-Hood provenance as 105 and 106 above.]

No. 5: *The: humble: Peticon, Declaracon: and Recantacon off John Pym: Esquyer, &c.*

[By John Pym: his letter to James I, summarizing his speech in Parliament on 28 November 1621: cf. *Commons debates 1621*, ii. 461–4; Sir Edward Nicholas, *Proceedings and debates of the House of Commons in 1620 and 1621*, 2 vols. (Oxford, 1766), ii. 230–41; William W. MacDonald, *The making of an English revolutionary* (London, 1982), 50–4. 11 leaves.]

Washington, DC, Folger Shakespeare Library

108. MS G. b. 9

[Folio, 334 leaves; volume of state letters and tracts, including Ralph Starkey's 'Discourse of the High Court of Parliament' (ff. 311r–334v: cf. 6.2 above), in two scribal hands, chiefly Feathery's; a companion volume to MS G. b. 8 (370 leaves, folio, including, on ff. 127–79, Puttenham's *Discourse* on Mary Queen of Scots: cf. 97.1 above, in scribal hands including the second scribe in G. b. 9, but not Feathery); the two sold at Sotheby's, 4 July 1955 (André de Coppet sale), lot 950; formerly MS Add. 35; cf. 90, 95, 96, and 97 above. Watermarks: pillars and urn.]

108.1. ff. 1r–61v: *A Dialogue, Betwene, a Councelor, and, a Justice, of Peace, of the, Succese, of, Parleamentes, since the, Conqueste, to this Time, Written, in the, Tower: of London, by S^r: Walter, Rauleghe, and, Dedicated, to Kinge James, o^r: Soueraigne, Lorde, in, an^o: 1610.*

[By Sir Walter Ralegh. Printed as *The prerogative of Parliaments in England* ([London], 1628) [STC 20649]: cf. *Index*, i/2, RaW 588. A copy in Ralph Starkey's hand is Folger Shakespeare Library MS V. b. 276.]

108.2. ff. 62r–93v: *A, Relation, of the, Troubles, of Italye stirred, by those, Princes, after, the Death, of Pope Leo: the, X^{th}: for, freinge, of their, Estates, out of, the Power, of the, Church, wth the proceedinge of the Cardynalles, in the Conclave at the Ellection of Pope, Adryan the Vi^{th}. 1521.*

108.3. ff. 93v–95v: *Orders, made, by Thomas of Lancaster for the placeinge of Kinges, Heraldes and sargeants at Armes:*

[By Thomas, Duke of Clarence (1388?–1421), at the siege of Caen, 3 September 1417. A scribal copy of these orders endorsed by Ralph Starkey (and marked by him 'Entered') is in the Essex Record Office, Colchester, D/DRg 3/4, item 5.]

108.4. ff. 96r–119r: *The, Articles, and, answeres, therunto, Wheruppon the, Earle, of. Bristoll: was, charged, in, his, Negotianatinge, of the, Match, w^{th}: Spayne;*

[Cf. 46.4 above.]

108.5. ff. 119v–136r: *A. Relation, of the Carriage, of, the, marriages that should, haue bene, made, Betwene the Prynce of England, and the Infannta, Mayor, and also afterwarde wth the younger Infannta:*

[By Sir Charles Cornwallis. Cf. 20.6, 35, and 58 above.]

108.6. ff. 136v–140v: [*Letters by Sir Walter Ralegh*]

[Three letters by Sir Walter Ralegh: two to the King, one to his wife (1603); untitled. Cf. 1.4, 1.6, 23, 28, 35.3, and 70 above, and 108.19 below.]

108.7. ff. 141r–145r: *Aduertisments, of a Loiall: Subiect, to his Gratious, Soueraigne, drawne from, obseruacons, of, the, peoples, speeches, written by an unknowne, Author, in An°. 1603.*

[Cf. 6, 20.8, 42, 71, and 83.1 above.]

108.8. ff. 145v–149r: *The, character of Robart, Earle, of, Salesburye, Lord, high, Treasuror of England &c written by, m^r: William, Turnour, and, dedicated to the moste, vnderstandinge and the moste, worthie Ladye, the Ladye, Theodosia Cecyll: Dated, an°. :*

[Possibly by Cyril Tourneur. Cf. 43 and 77.2 above.]

108.9. ff. 149v–150v: *The Coppie, of a letter, written by S^r: Robart, Carr, visconnte Rochester, and, after Earle of Somersett; vnto, the Lord, Henery, Howarde, Earle, of Northampton, An°: 1612. y^e, 8. of, October:*

[By Sir Robert Carr, Earl of Somerset. Cf. 1.5, 35.4, 52, and 92.11 above.]

108.10. ff. 151r–153v: *The coppie of the speeche, Deliuered by S^r: ffrancis Bacon, Knight, Solicetor, generall: vnto y^e: Kinge at the Arraignem^te: of the Lord, Sanquer, in the Kinges Benche, at Westminster, for procuringe the Murther, of John, Turner, A master of Defence y^e: xxvij^th of June: 1612:*

[By Sir Francis Bacon, 27 June 1612. *Cabala: sive Scrinia sacra* (1663), 368–9; Spedding, xi. 291–3. Cf. 83 above. This speech is mentioned as item 7 in one of Ralph Starkey's lists of MSS in BL Harley MS 537, f. 84r–v.]

108.11. f. 154r–v: *A Peticon, of y^e, Barronets, to the, Kinges, Matie: vppon, a Controuersie of precedencye, betwene, y^e, yonger Sonnes, of Visconnts, and Barones and the, Baronetts. in Aprill, an°: 1612. and in the, 10. Yeare, of the Kinge:*

[This petition is mentioned as No. 10 in one of Ralph Starkey's lists of MSS in BL Harley MS 537, f. 84r–v.]

108.12. ff. 155r–156v: *A Peticon of the Barones, to the, Kinge, Vppon, a controuersie, of Precedencye, betwene, the Barronetts, and o^r sonnes, in April An°: 1612 and in the. 10th. yeare of the kinge:*

[This petition is mentioned as No. 11 in one of Ralph Starkey's lists of MSS in BL Harley MS 537, f. 84r–v.]

108.13. ff. 157r–160v: *The Kinges Maties: speeche, in Parleament, the. 1. of May, an°:*

1604. touchinge the, Vnion, of England, and, Scotlande:

[Letter by James I, delivered to Parliament by Sir Roger Aston, 1 May 1604: *Parliamentary history*, i. 1021–2.]

108.14. ff. 161r–170v: *S^r: Walter Raleigh, his, speeche Deliuered, at his Death, beinge, Beheaded in the Ould Pallace in Westminster the xxix^th: Daye of October, betwene the Howres, of viij. and ix°, of the Clocke, in the Morninge, these Lordes, Beinge present, An°.. 1618:*

[Ralegh's speech on the scaffold, 29 October 1618, including at the end (f. 170r–v) 'This Epitath ffollowinge was wrytten, by S^r: Walter; Raleigh the night before he dyed:' (beginning 'Even suche is Tyme, y^t takes in Truste') and the couplet 'S^r: Walter, Raleigh, on the snuffe, of a Candle, the night before he suffered death:' (beginning 'Cowardes [doe *added in another hand*] ffeare to dye, but Courage stoute'): cf. *Index*, i/2, RaW 780, 58, 313. Cf. 35.5 above.]

108.15. ff. 171r–172v: *The Protection made, by Robarte, Earle, of Salesburye, vnto, one of his, Servantes, wch stood in daunger of, Arrestinge, in the Tyme of the Parleament, An°. 1614:*

[Presumably relating to Robert Cecil, first Earl of Salisbury (1563?–1612) and misdated 26 March '1614'.]

108.16. ff. 172v–174r: *[Letter by Archbishop Abbot]*

[Letter by George Abbot (1562–1633), Archbishop of Canterbury, to John Williams, Bishop of Lincoln, including James I's letter on directions for preachers, 12–15 August 1622: see Welsby, 107. *Scrinia sacra* (1654), 183–6. Cf. 52 above. Space left in MS for heading.]

108.17. ff. 174r–176r: *Directions, from his Matie: Concerninge Preachers:*

[By James I, 4 August 1622. *Scrinia sacra* (1654), 187–8. Cf. 108.16 above.]

108.18. ff. 176r–179v: *The, Kinges, ma^tie: of Englandes, Lre, to the, Emperor: sheweinge, his, ill, Requitall, to surpryse, the Lower, Pallatinate, at suche Tyme, as he was Treatinge ffor him, wth the Prynces of the Vnyon, Toucheinge the Bohemyan Warres, Moveinge him to surrender the Pallatinate, vppon the Prynce; Pallatinates, disclayme, of the, kingdome, of Bohemia, otherwyse, fforces should be demed to Recover the same:*

[By James I to the Emperor Ferdinand II, 12 November 1621.]

108.19. ff. 179v–184r: *The Letter written by S^r: Walter Raleigh, to Queene, Anne the < >. of < >, . an°: 16.8.*

[Three letters by Sir Walter Ralegh: to Queen Anne, to Nottingham, Suffolk, Devonshire, and Cecil (13 August 1603), and to his wife (14 November 1617). Cf. 1.4, 1.6, 23, 28, 35.3, 70, and 108.6 above.]

108.20. ff. 185r–205r: *A: Breuiarye, of the, Historie, of, Englande, from William .1. intituled the, Conqueror, Written, by S^r: Walter Raleigh, Knighte:*

[By Samuel Daniel: cf. *Index*, i/1, DaS 36. Cf. 51 and 95.1 above. See Plate 32 above.]

108.21. ff. 205v–210r: *The, Bishope, of Lincolne, Lorde Keeper; of the, greate, Seale, of Englande his speeche, in the, Yeilde, Hall, of London for, the, Collectinge, of the, Subsedye the. < > Daye of August, An°: 1621*

[By John Williams, Bishop of Lincoln, 1621.]

108.22. ff. 210r–226r: *Certeyne, articles, or consideracons, touchinge the Vnion of the King-*

domes, of England, and, Scotland, collected, and Digested, for his Ma*ties*: Better seruice:

[By Sir Francis Bacon, 1604. *Resuscitatio* (1657), 206–20; Spedding, x. 218–34: cf. *Index*, i/1, BcF 116–20.]

108.23. ff. 226r–241v: *Confirmatio, Comit, Palatini, Cestriae:*

[A Royal Letters Patent by Queen Elizabeth, in Latin, concerning the County Palatinate of Chester, 28 November 1559.]

108.24. ff. 242r–253v: *That, the, Counties, of, Gloucester, Hereford, Salop, and, Wigorne, are, noe, parcell: of Wales, or of the, Marches, of Wales:*

108.25. ff. 254r–256r: *Questiones, touchinge, a Controuersie, of, Precedence, happened, of Late, betwene, two, gentlemen:*

[Cf. 1.12 above.]

108.26. ff. 256r–265r: *A, Discourse, Collected, out, of the, Comon Lawes. proueinge, that, the, oathe, Ex, officio, is and hath bene, practised, in the Eccleasiasticall Courtes:*

108.27. ff. 265v–282v: *The, Charter, of the Keepers of the Portes graunted, and, confirmed, by Kinge Edward, the fowerth the, xxiij*th *Daye of March, in the, V*th *yeare, of the, same, Kinge:*

[A Royal Letters Patent by Edward IV (1442–83; reigned 1461–70, 1471–83), 23 March 1464/5.]

108.28. ff. 283r–295r: *A. matche, propounded, by, y*e: *Sauoyan betwene, the, Ladie Elizabeth, and, the, Prince, of, Piemont:*

[By Sir Walter Ralegh: cf. *Index*, i/2, RaW 656. Cotton's copy, in the hand of Ralph Starkey, is

BL Cotton MS Vitellius C. XVI, ff. 395r–403v. Cf. 27 above.]

108.29. ff. 295v–309v: *A: Discourse, toucheinge, a marriage betwene, Prince Henery, of England, and, a, Dawghter of Sauoye:*

[By Sir Walter Ralegh: cf. *Index*, i/2, RaW 637. Cf. 3.3, 27, and 98 above.]

109. **MS V. b. 50**

[Folio, 762 numbered pages (but lacking pp. 345–56); large volume of state and antiquarian tracts and papers for the period *c.*1530–1631, including works by Cotton, Camden, and Ellesmere (on Magna Carta, pp. 101–34: cf. 13.2 above), 'The three great Kingdomes of England France and Spaine' (pp. 281–301: cf. 1.7 above), Starkey's 'Discourse of Parliament' (pp. 387–446: cf. 6.2 above), William Bird's 'A Treatise concerninge the Nobilitie according to the Lawes of England' (pp. 233–80, 555–762: cf. 79 above), the arraignment and execution speech of Castlehaven (pp. 519–47: cf. 17A.3 above), and materials relating to the proposed Spanish match of 1623 and other foreign marriages; predominantly in two scribal hands; later owned by W. T. Smedley (1851–1943?) (his MS 43); acquired by Henry Clay Folger (1857–1930) *c.*1924; cf. Baker, *USA* ii. 76–7 (No. 420). Watermark in Feathery items: pillars (RP).]

109.1. pp. 177–86: *The Passages att the: Councell Table, Betwene the: Councell, and Willm Corriton: Esquie*r: *aboute reffuseinge to paye the Loane:*

[Cf. 45.8 above.]

109.2. pp. 189–91: *Serieante ffleetwoodes: Relacon, and opinyon of Co*rte[s]:

[By William Fleetwood. Cf. 19.3, 23, 41.4, and 106.6 above.]

109.3. pp. 191–3: *A: Lre wrytten by my Lo: Keeper, S*r: *Nicholas Bacon, vnto the Lordes of*

the *Councell, Conscerninge ffrauncis Kempes Complainte against him, Conscerninge the Offyce of the Clearckeshipp: of the Haniperne, in Anno: 1504:*

[By Sir Nicholas Bacon, Lord Keeper, 14 January 1564/5 (dated '1504' in error).]

109.4. pp. 194–200: *The Oration Off Sir James Dyer knight, Lord Cheiffe Justice of the Comon Pleas, And other of the Queenes Maties: Justices of hir Co^rte[s]: of Westm^r: By virtue of hir Maties: Lres of Privye Seale, to them directed, Conscerninge the Jurisdiction, and Libtyes, of the Countye Pallatyne of Chester, and the Aucthoritye of the Chambleyne, and his Offyce there:*

[By Sir James Dyer and other judges, 2–10 February 1568/9. Cf. 13.7 above.]

109.5. p. 201: *The Coppye Off: Quee: Eliz: Lre:*

[By Queen Elizabeth, concerning the jurisdiction of the County Palatinate of Chester, 2 February 1568/9.]

109.6. pp. 205–7: *A: Lre wrytten by the Archb^pp: of Canterburye to kinge Iames, vppon the Princes goeinge into Spayne:*

[Attributed to George Abbot, Archbishop of Canterbury, but a forgery, 8 August 1623; circulation prohibited: see Welsby, 108–10. Cf. 52 and 71 above.]

109.7. pp. 207–8: *The Coppye Off my Lord Keepers Lre, to the Iudges, Touchinge Tolleracon of Religion.*

[By John Williams, Bishop of Lincoln, 2 August 1622. Cf. 35 above.]

109.8. pp. 209–10: *2:v°: Hen: 8: Peeter Pence paid to the Popes Chamber, shalbee paid noe more,*

[Petition to Henry VIII for the repeal of the annual tribute to the Pope (suppressed in 1534), beginning 'Most: humblye sheweth, that where as the kinges of this Realme Auncientlye in the heate of Religion . . .'.]

109.9. pp. 211–13: *The Effecte Off a Motion made vnto Queene Elizabeth, by a principall person of the States, Anno: 1595*

[Cf. 109.16 below.]

109.10. pp. 214–19: *The Ladye Elizabeth: hir graces Aunsweare made att Hattffeild, the: xxvj^th: of Aprill, 1558: to S^r: Thomas Pope knight, beinge sent ffrom the Queenes Matie: to vnderstand, howe hir grace lyked of the Mocon of Marryage, Made by the kinge ellect of Swethlandes Messenger:*

[By Princess Elizabeth and Sir Thomas Pope. Cf. 1.22, 33, and 53.4 above.]

109.11. p. 217: *Queene Elizabethes: Lre, to the Duke of Wirtenberg, in Aunsweare of his Offerr to Assiste hir, in the p̃fferringe hir in Marryage, dated the: xxvij°: of Januarij: 1563*

[By Queen Elizabeth. Cf. 1.23, and 53.9 above.]

109.12. pp. 218–19: *Sir Thomas Smyth: one of the Sheriffs of London, his Protestacon touchinge his Speech vsed to the Earle of Essex: when hee ffledd into London, and other Accidents Touchinge thesame Earle*

[By Sir Thomas Smith (1558?–1625). Cf. 1.3, 1.17, and 82.5 above.]

109.13. pp. 225–6: *Ces Sont Les Responsions [. . .] en la Religeon del Hospitall, de Sent John*

109.14. pp. 227–30: *Ordinarye Anuall Receiptes of the Exchequer:* and *Ordinarye Anual Yssues out of the Exchequer*

[Cf. 6.5, 33.3, 53.13, and 83 above.]

109.15. pp. 357–74: *The Politia or gouern-ment of the vnited Prouinces.*

[By Sir Clement Edmondes. Cf. 6.7, 33, and 83.2 above. Heading in another scribal hand; text entirely in Feathery's hand.]

109.16. pp. 487–9: *The Effect Off a motion, or Overture, made vnto Queene Elizabeth, A Prin-cipall Person of the States: Anno, 1595*

[Cf. 109.9 above.]

109.17. p. 490: *The Archduke Ernestus: his Lre; to Queene Elizabeth, dated the: 14ᵗʰ: of October, 1595:*

[By Ernest, Archduke of Austria. Cf. 1.18 above.]

109.18. pp. 490–3: *Queene Elizabethes: Lre, to the Archduke Ernestus in October: 1595*

[By Queen Elizabeth. Cf. 1.19 above.]

109.19. pp. 493–9: *Proposicons made by the Ambassadoʳ, of the kinge of ffraunce, to the Assemblye of the States generall of the Vnyted Provinces of the Lowe Countryes, vppon Presen-tacon of the lres, of his Maᵗⁱᵉ: to the said Lordes, the States the, xij°: of December 1618: Touchinge the Poynte[s] noated in the Margent:*

[Cf. 6.3 and 53.6 above.]

109.20. pp. 503–11: *The Antiquitye vse: and Priuelidge of Cittyes, Burroughes, and Townes written by Mʳ: ffrauncis Tate of the Middle Tem-ple London*

[By Francis Tate, 1598. Cf. 6.4 and 83 above.]

109.21. p. 512: *Whatt Priuelidge an Alyen; hath, vnder any other Prince, or State:*

[Cf. 53.8 above.]

110. MS X. d. 210

[Folio, 18 leaves (34 pages); a single tract (dis-bound); title-page and ending (middle of last line on f. 17v and f. 18r) in Feathery's hand; rest of main text in another scribal hand; reader's correc-tions and deletions; title docketed with No. 5; acquired by Henry Clay Folger from E. Williams of Hove, 1923 (cf. 103 above); formerly MS 1132.2. Watermarks: pillars (IEAN).]

The Coppye Off a Lre wrytten: by Sʳ. Phillipp: Sidnye: to Queene Elizabeth; Touchinge hir Marryage wᵗʰ Mounsieur:

[By Sir Philip Sidney: cf. *Index*, i/2, SiP 202; Appendix IV below, No. 23. Cf. 17, 18.1, 20.1, 41.10, 53, 57.4, 64, 78.7, and 105.1 above.]

110A. MS X. d. 337

[Folio, 24 leaves; a single tract; inscribed on the title-page '12: sheetes'; cf. Baker, *USA*, ii. 88 (No. 458). Watermark: grapes.]

Diuers Cases Speeches: and presidents in the high Courte Off Starrchamber:

[Star Chamber cases, 1601–30. Cf. 10, 29, and 101 above.]

Washington, DC, Library of Congress, Law Library

111. Law MS 14

[Folio, 216 leaves (plus blanks); legal compilation relating chiefly to the Court of Chancery, including an early draft for Lambarde's *Archeion* (ff. 1r–13r: cf. 13.1 above), Bacon's Orders in Chancery with 'Addiconall rules' (ff. 168r–187r: cf. 13.5 above), and Fanshawe's discourse on the Court of Ex-chequer (ff. 188r–216v: cf. 86 above); in three or four scribal hands; inscribed by one 'M: Bayley' (cf. 14 above); Phillipps MS 15142; bookplate of F. William Cock, MD (1858–1943); acquired 25

October 1944; cf. Baker, *USA*, ii. 52 (No. 340), and 13 above.]

111.1. ff. 80v–84r: *Ordinaunces Explayned by M^r: Crooke, vppon the estate of the Chauncerye Co^rte: in Anno: 1554*

[By John Croke (d. 1554), Master in Chancery. Sir Alexander Croke, *The genealogical history of the Croke Family, originally named Le Blount*, 2 vols. (Oxford, 1823), ii. 819–21. Cf. 13 above. Title on f. 80v and text from line 7 on f. 81v until the end on f. 84r in Feathery's hand; the text on ff. 80v to line 6 on f. 81v in another scribal hand. Watermark: pillars (VAD).]

111.2. ff. 95r–104r: *The Constitucons and Orders Renewed, and Established, in the Pryson of the ffleete, An^o: 1561*

[The six-line heading on f. 95r in Feathery's hand; the text in another scribal hand. Watermark: pillars (RDP).]

111.3. ff. 105r–112r: *Certayne notes and observacons vppon the Statute of Magna Carta.*

Chap: 29. and other Statutes concernenge the proceedinges in the Chauncery in Courses of equity & conscience Collected by the Lord Ellesme^re for the Kinges Learned Counselle[s] direccon, the moneth of september 1615. Anno 13°. Jacobi:

[By Sir Thomas Egerton, Baron Ellesmere. Cf. 13.2 and 109 above. First line only of the heading on f. 105r apparently in Feathery's hand; all the rest in another scribal hand. Watermark: pillars (VAD).]

Watlington, Shirburn Castle, The Earl of Macclesfield

112. [Shelf 7, no number]

[Folio, 32 pages; a single tract. Watermark: pillars.]

A: Lre written to the: Lower Howse of Parliam^te:

[Cf. 1.11, 40.1, 53, 61, 78.2, 83.3, and 106.5 above.]

Catalogue of papers in Ralph Starkey's study

This list of eighty-nine manuscript works evidently found in Ralph Starkey's study after his death in October 1628 is written in a professional Secretary hand on three folio pages among the Ellesmere Papers in the Huntington Library, San Marino, California (EL 8175), and is printed here by permission of the Huntington Library. It is endorsed, apparently by John Egerton, first Earl of Bridgewater (1579–1649), 'Catologue of Papers in Mr Starkys study'. Bridgewater had become a Privy Counsellor in July 1626 and, like Simonds D'Ewes, he may have had a personal interest in Starkey's collections.

Any apparent correspondence between titles recorded here and texts represented in manuscripts copied by, or associated with, the Feathery Scribe is noted in square brackets. References here ('[cf. Feathery No. 1]', etc.) are to itemized numbers in Appendix II above.

It may be noted that the first thirty titles correspond exactly (and in the same order) to tracts copied on ff. 1r–92v of Inner Temple Library Petyt MS 538, vol. 49 (as well as title No. 33 on f. 93r–v). This is a folio volume evidently produced in the Feathery scriptorium (even with pillars watermark), although not in Feathery's own hand, and is cited below as 'Petyt MS'. Titles Nos. 1–4 and 6 are also largely duplicated in Petyt MS 538, vol. 50 (on ff. 102r–123r), a composite volume including (on ff. 1r–38v) material in Starkey's hand. Other notable collections of tracts corresponding to Starkey's titles include the Castell Gorfod MS (Feathery No. 1.14–22, 25–6), corresponding in irregular order to Starkey Nos. 1, 8, 10–17, and, especially, Rosenbach MS 239/4, No. 11 (162 pages 'selected out of a Book in ye hands of Sir Robert Cotton Knight and Baronett': cf. Feathery No. 102), corresponding in almost identical order to Starkey Nos. 1, 3–30, 32–5.

A Cattaloague

1 The death of Queene Elizabeth wth her declaration of her Successor [cf. Feathery No. 1.14]
2 The manner of ye Death and sicknesse of Prince Henry Sonne of Kinge James [cf. Feathery No. 6.1]
3 A discourse of Queene Eliz: intended Marryage wth ye Duke of Anioue[1]
4 The Earle of Hertfords fine in ye Starre chamb^r[2]
5 The Cause of ye Censure in ye Starre chamber against John Hales[3]
6 Privelidges of ye Earles of ye Empire in Germany [cf. Feathery No. 1.13]
7 An answere to ye Kings lre: for Staye of Justice by all ye Judges[4]
8 A lre written by ye lord Chauncellor Ellesmer to ye Kinge desireing to be discharged of his office of Chauncellorshipp by reason of his infirmetyes [cf. Feathery No. 1.26]
9 The Politia, or gouvrnm^t: of ye vnited Provinces [cf. Feathery No. 6.7]

---

[1] Evidently the discourse of 1570 by Sir Nicholas Bacon (1509–79): cf. Petyt MS, ff. 14v–22v, and Feathery Nos. 32 and 71.
[2] Proceedings against Edward Seymour, Earl of Hertford (1539?–1621), who was fined a total of £15,000 on 5 February 1562/3 for secretly marrying Lady Katherine Grey: cf. Petyt MS, ff. 22v–23r.
[3] The writer and MP John Hales (d. 1571) supported the marriage of Lord Hertford (see above).
[4] 25 April 1616: cf. Petyt MS, ff. 23v–24v.

10   The Arche duke Ernestus his lre to Queene Elizabeth and yᵉ Queenes answere [cf. Feathery Nos. 1.18–19]

11   The Lady Eliz: Answere to Queene Mary, touching her inclinacon to yeild to yᵉ Motion of Marriage wᵗʰ yᵉ kinge of Sweethland [cf. Feathery No. 1.22]

12   Henry Cuffe his lre to Mʳ Secretary Cecill touchinge yᵉ Instruccons, wᵗʰ yᵉ Earle of Essex sent privately to yᵉ Kinge of Scotts, touchinge his Tytle to yᵉ Crowne of England [cf. Feathery No. 1.16]

13   Sʳ Thomas Smyth one of yᵉ Sheriffs of London, his ptestatione, touching his Speech to yᵉ Earle of Essex when he fledd: into London [cf. Feathery No. 1.3]

14   Liddington Secretary of Scotland his Lre sent to Sʳ Willm Cecill, Secretary to Q: Eliz: touching the Queene of Scotts title to England [cf. Feathery No. 1.15]

15   Direccons of Q: Mary to yᵉ Councell touchinge yᵉ Reforming of yᵉ Church to yᵉ Roman Religion [cf. Feathery No. 1.25]

16   Queene Eliz: lre written to yᵉ kinge of Scotts touching Valentyne Thomas, Sʳ Willm Evers, and Ashefeild, and an increase of 2000ˡⁱ, to make vpp yᵉ Some of 5000ˡⁱ: Pencon yearely to yᵉ Kinge of Scotts [cf. Feathery No. 1.21]

17   Queene Eliz: her lre to yᵉ Kinge of Scotts persuadinge him not to admitt into his Country an Ambassador out of Spayne [cf. Feathery No. 1.20]

18   The life of Sʳ: Tho: Bodlye, written by himself [cf. Feathery No. 82.8]

19   A lre written by yᵉ Lords of yᵉ Councell to kinge James, touching meenes to aduance yᵉ Kinges Revenewes, by vnvsuall Courses, for as yᵉ kinge will take yᵉ Acte vpon himselfe and ptecte them [cf. Feathery No. 1.1]

20   The examinacon of Sʳ: Anthony Browne touching yᵉ Lady Maryes submission to her father Kinge Henry yᵉ 8ᵗʰ [cf. Feathery No. 1.24]

21   Intelligence from yᵉ Comission at Bulloigne, touching yᵉ treatye of Peace, and pointe of Precedencye betweene England and Spaine [cf. Feathery No. 106.2]

22   The Councells answere to yᵉ Comission of Bulloigne touching yᵉ treaty of Peace; and Precedencye betweene England and Spaine [cf. Feathery No. 106.2]

23   The Coppy of a lre sent from yᵉ Councell of England to yᵉ Comission of Bulloigne, touching yᵉ treatye of Peace, and yᵉ pointe of Precedency betweene England and Spaine [cf. Feathery No. 106.2]

24   Questions expounded by Q: Mary and answered by her Councell, touching yᵉ continuance of a treatye made by Hen: 8º: wᵗʰ yᵉ Emperor, and Kinge of Fraunce, for mayntenance of a Quarrell between Fraunce and Spaine [cf. Feathery No. 33.2]

25   Abatements in pʳsent Conceyved to be made, for yᵉ Kings Benifitt, by yᵉ Commissioners of yᵉ Treasurye [cf. Feathery No. 1.2]

26   Ordinary Annuall Receipts in yᵉ Exchequer [cf. Feathery No. 6.5]

27   Ordinary Annuall Yssues in yᵉ Exchequer [cf. Feathery No. 6.5]

28   Proposicons made by yᵉ Ambassadoʳˢ of yᵉ French King to yᵉ States generall of yᵉ vnited provinces, touching change of gouʳnmᵗ: of Synod then called, and the Treason of Barnevelt, & his fellowe prisoⁿʳˢ [cf. Feathery No. 6.3]

29   The Viscounte Cranborn's Lre written to Sʳ Thomas Barry in Fraunce, touching yᵉ miselleccon of Sʳ: Francis Goodwyne, to be a Knᵗ: for yᵉ Parliament and the effect of yᵉ intercepted lres of Mʳ Hen: Connstable to yᵉ Slaunder of yᵉ State [cf. Feathery No. 71.2]

30   The Opinion of yᵉ Auncient doctoʳˢ of yᵉ Lawe, whether it be lawfull for a prince, whose

Sub^te: is wronged by another prince to Lycence him to detayne ye Bodye, and goodes of y^t princes Sub^te: [cf. Feathery No. 53.7]

31 Q: Eliz: lre to ye Duke of Wirtenburgh touching her Marryage [cf. Feathery No. 1.23]

32 The Privelidges of an Alyen, by ye Lawes of England [cf. Feathery No. 53.8]

33 Verses made by Kinge James, on ye Death of Queene Anne[5]

34 The Lord Norris his lre to Kinge James, when he had Slayne, one of ye Lord Willoughbie Men [cf. Feathery No. 71.4]

35 The Antiquety, and Privelidges, of Cytties, and Burroughes [cf. Feathery No. 6.4]

36 Obseruacons concerning ye Nobility of England aunccient, and moderne [cf. Feathery No. 57.5]

37 A discourse written by Mr John Selden of ye Inner Temple, and dedicated to Sr Fra: Bacon of ye auncient Mencon, Conivnction, and Devysion, of ye two greate offices of State, ye Chauncellorship, and keeper of ye greate Seale of England [cf. Feathery No. 13.3]

38 The Resolucon of all ye Judges touching Recusantes in Trinitye Terme secdo Carolij [cf. Feathery No. 20.7]

39 Alre written by Sr Phillipp Sydnye to Q: Eliz: touching her marrying wth Mowns^r [cf. Feathery No. 17]

40 Alre written by S^r: Phillipp Sydnye to his Brother concerning derections in Travayle [cf. Feathery No. 6.6]

41 The repressing of ye increase of Priests Jesuites, and Recusants, w^thout draweing of Recorde, written by Sr Robt Cotton[6]

42 A lre Wrytten by Inouza to King James touching ye Douke of Buck: miscarryage in Spaine [cf. Feathery No. 1.10]

43 The Spanishe Busse written by Sr Robt Cotton Kn^t: and Barronett[7]

44 A Treatize of Bayle, and Mainepryse [cf. Feathery No. 53.18]

45 A treatize intituled Rege in Consulto, or a Reconciliacon betweene ye Kinge and his Sub^tes: [cf. Feathery No. 34]

46 An admonition from a frend namelesse, to Sr Edward Cooke, after his degradacon [cf. Feathery No. 82.6]

47 Touching ye Comendacns at Whitehall

48 A Treatize concerning ye Nobility according to ye Lawes of England[8]

49 A lre written by King James touching ye Wardshipp of Children, in ye life time of their parents

50 Diverse Wryteings, and lres, of Sr Walter Rawleighes [cf. Feathery No. 70]

51 Diverse Wrytings, lres, and Speeches of Sr Frauncis Bacons [cf. Feathery No. 3.2 *et alia*]

---

[5] Verses supposedly by James I on the death of Queen Anne of Denmark, March 1618/19 (eight lines, beginning 'Thee to invite the great God sent his star'): cf. Petyt MS, f. 93r–v; also Crum T1631.

[6] Possibly the 'Discourse touching Popish Recusants, Jesuits and Seminaries' printed in *Cottoni posthuma* (1651), No. 7.

[7] The identification of this work is uncertain. It might, perhaps, be one of Cotton's tracts relating to the proposed, abortive, Spanish Match of 1623: either 'That the kings of England have been pleased usually to consult with their peeres in the great councell . . . of marriage, peace, and warre', written in 1621/2, or else 'A remonstrance of the treaties of amitie and marriage before time, and of late of the house of Austria and Spaine', written in early 1624, or, just conceivably, 'A relation of the proceedings against ambassadors who have miscaried themselves', written in April 1624 (*Cottoni posthuma*, Nos. 2, 6, and 1 respectively; also cf. Feathery Nos. 6, 54, 1.9, 17A.4, and 78).

[8] *A treatise concerning the nobility according to the laws of England* by William Bird; printed, as enlarged by Sir John Dodderidge, as *The magazine of honour; or, A treatise of . . . nobility* ([London], 1642) [Wing B2955]; cf. Baker, *CUL* 191–2. Cotton's MS copy is BL Cotton MS Julius C. VIII, ff. 2v–91v. Cf. Feathery Nos. 79 and 109.

52 Sʳ Walter Copes appollegie on yᵉ behalfe of Sʳ Robt Cecill [cf. Feathery No. 105.3]

53 A Relacon of yᵉ Carryage of yᵉ Marryage that should haue beene made betweene yᵉ Sonne of England, and yᵉ Infanta, Maior of Spaine, and after wᵗʰ the Younger Infanta, Written by Sʳ. Charles Cornewallis [cf. Feathery No. 20.6]

54 A Discourse Written by yᵉ Lord of Devonshire in deffence of yᵉ Marryage, wᵗʰ yᵉ Lady Penelope Riche Anº: 1606 [cf. Feathery No. 35.12]

55 A Colleccon of Nobility, houshould, Coʳᵗˢ of Recorde, Admiralty, Mynte, Armory, Castles, Bulwarkes, Townes of Warr[e,] Marinoʳˢ: forests, and Parkes of yᵉ Kings of England

56 The Proceedings of yᵉ Iile of Rhee⁹

57 Rochells estate when yᵉ French King entered

58 The manner of yᵉ ellection of yᵉ Duke of Bucks: to yᵉ Chauncellorship of Cambridge

59 Mʳ Corryton at yᵉ Councell Table, about nonpaymᵗ of Loanes [cf. Feathery No. 45.8]

60 The Peticon of yᵉ Scottish, & Irish Nobility

61 Articles betweene England and Fraunce, touchinge yᵉ Marryage [cf. Feathery No. 35.11]

62 A booke of all yᵉ Oathes, Auncient and Moderne [cf. Feathery No. 12]

63 Tome Tell troth ¹⁰

64 A lre written to yᵉ Parliamᵗ [cf. Feathery No. 1.11]

65 The Informacon against yᵉ gent in yᵉ Starre Chamber [cf. Feathery No. 40.4]

66 Bacons Orders in Chauncery [cf. Feathery No. 13.5]

67 The Antiquety of Parliamᵗˢ [cf. Feathery No. 14]

68 A Parliamᵗ houlden at Westmʳ in Edward yᵉ second his time

69 A Parliamᵗ houlden in yᵉ 43º of Quee: Eliz: [cf. Feathery No. 73]

70 A Parliamᵗ houlden in yᵉ 18º of K: James

71 Divʳˢ passages of A Parliamᵗ houlden in Anº: 1623

72 A Journall of a Parliamᵗ houlden in Anno 1625. et 1626:

73 A Journall of a Parliament houlden in Anno 1627: et 1628:

74 A Journall of yᵉ last Parliament

75 A booke intituled Modus tenendi Parliamentu written by Mʳ Elsinge [cf. Feathery No. 14.5]

76 Sʳ Fra: Walsinghams Negotiacons in Fraunce [cf. Feathery No. 35.11]

77 Sʳ Geo Caryes Negotiacons in Fraunce [cf. Feathery No. 106.4]

78 Sʳ Richard Westons Negotiacons wᵗʰ yᵉ Arche dutches at Bruxells¹¹

79 A greate vollume of Steward, Connstable, and Marshall of England [cf. Feathery No. 88]

80 A greate vollume of yᵉ pceedings in yᵉ Starre chambʳ [cf. Feathery No. 10]

81 A greate vollume of yᵉ pceedings in yᵉ Chauncery [cf. Feathery No. 13]

82 The Acts of Councell of Phillipp and Mary

---

⁹ An account of the Duke of Buckingham's unsuccessful expedition against the Isle de Rhé, near La Rochelle, in 1627: probably William Fleetwood's *An unhappy view of the whole behaviour of . . . Buckingham* (London, 1648) [Wing F1259; Somers, v. 398–403], which first circulated in manuscript: e.g. University of London MSS 308, ff. 260r–271v, and 309, ff. 163r–177v (both MSS associated with Feathery's scriptorium), and Magdalene College, Cambridge, Pepys Library No. 2099, ff. 26r–36v. Cf. Feathery Nos. 17A and 41.

¹⁰ Anonymous tract criticizing James I's lack of support for the Elector Palatine in Bohemia, 1621–2. Printed as *Tom-Tell-Troth, or A free discovrse* ([London], 1642) [Wing T1786]; Somers, ii. 469–92. Cf. Feathery No. 28.

¹¹ Report of a diplomatic mission to Brussels concerning the Palatinate by Sir Richard Weston, later first Earl of Portland (1577–1635), presented to the Privy Council on 27 September 1622. (Another copy is Inner Temple Library Petyt MS 538, vol. 48, item 3.)

83 The Habeas Corpus Booke[12]
84 The forerunner of revenge, written by M[r] doctor Eglisham[13]
85 The Lord Burleighes Comon Wealth, otherwyse called y[e] Cecillyan gouernment[14]
86 The Earle of Leicester[s] C[omo]n wealth [cf. Feathery No. 84]
87 The Privelidge of y[e] Barronage of England when they sitt in Parliament, collected by M[r] Seldon of y[e] Inner Temple[15]
88 Bacons opinion of Suttons Hospitall [cf. Feathery No. 72.15]
89 Essex and Nyne Collonells, against Wimbleton for Cales Voyage[16]

[12] Probably a volume (such as 'The Habeas Corpus' MS in the House of Lords Record Office, Braye MS 78) dealing with 'The Five Knights Case' of November 1627, when the legality of the imprisonment of various persons for refusing to lend money to the King was disputed by Selden and others (*State trials*, iii. 2–59). Alternatively the MS might extend to the ensuing parliamentary debates on Habeas Corpus and the Liberty of the Subject in March–May 1628 and afterwards (*State trials*, iii. 59–234; *Commons debates 1628*, ii. 332 *et seq.*), contributions to which included Feathery Nos. 44.2–6 and 47.6. These speeches were widely copied (cf. Baker, *CUL* 135) and printed as *A Conference desired by the Lords . . . concerning the rights and privileges of the subjects* (London, 1642) [Wing E2793]. A copy of 'the habea Corpus Case' is priced at 4s. in the price-list of parliamentary separates in Inner Temple Library Petyt MS 538, vol. 18, f. 46r.

[13] *Podromus vindictae*, an attack (in Latin) on the Duke of Buckingham by the Scottish royal physician George Eglisham (*fl.*1612–42), published in London, 1626; translated as *The forerunner of revenge* and printed in 'Franckfort' [i.e. the Netherlands?], 1626 [STC 7548]; London, 1642 [Wing E256]. A copy of the English version in Starkey's own hand is Folger Shakespeare Library MS X.d. 236. There are various other MS copies: e.g. University of London MS 309, ff. 103r–132v; BL Add. MSS 4106, ff. 149v–157r; 22591, ff. 31r–39v; Egerton MS 2026, ff. 51v–60v; Stowe MS 182, ff. 76r–84r, and Folger Shakespeare Library MS V. a. 470. Cf. Feathery Nos. 6 and 17A.

[14] The identification of this work is uncertain, but it might possibly be the Catholic 'libel' generally attributed to Richard Verstegan, *A declaration of the true causes of the great troubles, presupposed to be intended against England*, often called *Cecil's commonwealth*. This was published [in Antwerp], 1592 [STC 10005], and many MS copies were circulated over the years (for some, see *Index*, i/2. 366; also i/1. 36–7 for Bacon's retaliation).

[15] John Selden, *The privileges of the baronage of England*, written in 1621, printed in London, 1642 [Wing S2434]; cf. Baker, *CUL* 21; Feathery No. 79.

[16] The formal charges brought by the Vice-Admiral Robert Devereux, third Earl of Essex (1591–1646), against the Admiral Sir Edward Cecil, Viscount Wimbledon (1572–1638), following the disastrous Cadiz expedition of 1625. Printed, with Wimbledon's answer to the charges, in *The genuine works in verse and prose, of the Right Honourable George Granville, Lord Lansdowne*, 2 vols. (London, 1732), ii. 257–315. Cf. Feathery Nos. 6, 22, 44, and 72, and also 52.2.

Manuscript texts of Sidney's
Letter to Queen Elizabeth

The text of Sidney's *Letter* was subject, between *c*.1580 and *c*.1660, to a variety of treatments. It was, on occasions, very slightly expanded by interpolated additions; slightly curtailed by the omission of particular passages; rearranged into a different sequence of arguments; extensively adapted and paraphrased; abridged to a series of notes, extracts, or a résumé; and, in any event, subjected to editing by the scribes concerned, who supplied their own spelling, punctuation, paragraphing, and layout, as well as headings and, in certain cases (perhaps), valedictory subscriptions. While the history of transmission extends over a period of eighty years—and longer once printed editions begin to appear—it is not, perhaps, a continuous or consistent progression. In so far as the extant witnesses can be dated (which is not often, nor in any way is the evidence conclusive), copying would seem to have flourished in a series of stages: jumping from an initial circulation in the 1580s to some copying around the late 1590s (when the text was incorporated into formal compilations), to a limited phase of intermittent, disparate copying during the first two decades of the 17th century, and then to a great flurry of copying from around the mid-1620s to 1641, before a final, retrospective, antiquarian transcription in 1660.

While the schema, or stemma, of traditions (X1–3, Y1–3) suggested by the 1973 editors (see Plate 61 above) gives, as they admit, no more than 'a general picture of the relationship of the texts' and fails to 'take account of all stray agreements across the traditions', it will remain a provisionally useful guide to the pattern of transmission until such time as a thoroughly radical, comprehensive system of detailed collation of variants is established by a future editor.

The following list is substantially an amended, expanded, and updated version of that given in my *Index of English literary manuscripts*, volume i, part 2 (1980), 485–8: SiP 181–215. Sigla supplied in the 1973 edition by Duncan-Jones and Van Dorsten are cited for reference, as well as a few new sigla for manuscripts not recorded by them but which are cited in the amended stemma shown above (Figure 6).

Those manuscripts which are in any part written by the Feathery Scribe are already described in Appendix II above and are cross-referenced accordingly.

1. All Souls College, Oxford, MS 155, ff. 306r–312v.

Copy, headed in another hand 'Reasons offered agt Queen Elizabeths mariage wth ye Duke of Anjoy, Alanson; in a letter to her', on fourteen pages in a quarto volume of miscellaneous verse and prose transcribed from the Yelverton papers chiefly belonging to Sir Christopher Yelverton (1535?–1612), Sir Henry Yelverton (1566–1629), and their family; owned in 1679 by Narcissus Luttrell (1657–1732); *c*.1625–30s.

[*Index*, SiP 181. Tradition: predominantly *Y*. The text may possibly derive from Yelverton MS 49 (No. 12 below).]

2. Alnwick Castle, Muniments of the Duke of Northumberland, MS 525, pp. 55–61.

Copy in a single Secretary hand, untitled, on seven badly damaged pages, in a folio MS volume of prose works connected with the Court or state affairs; *c*.1590s?

[Reproduced in *Collotype facsimile & type transcript of an Elizabethan manuscript preserved at Alnwick Castle, Northumberland*, ed. Frank J. Burgoyne (London, 1904). *Index*, SiP 182. Siglum: *Nd*. Tradition: *Y3*.]

3. Bibliothèque Nationale, Paris, Cinq cents de Colbert n° 466, ff. 89r–95r.

Copy in a single Secretary hand, headed 'A discours of Syr Ph.S. to yᵉ Q. Mᵗʸ touching hir mariage wᵗʰ Monsʳ', on thirteen folio pages, docketed in a different hand 'Discours de Syr P.S. Sur le mariage de la Rᵉ. Elizab. auec Monsieur', in a composite volume of state documents generally appertaining to diplomatic relations between England and France; *c*.1580s.

[Printed in Feuillerat, iii. 51–60, 325–32. *Index*, SiP 184. Siglum: *BN*. Tradition: *X1*. See Plate 64 above.]

4. Bodleian Library MS Ashmole 800, ff. 1r–4r.

Copy in a single Secretary hand, headed 'Sʳ Phillip Sidney to hir Maᵗⁱᵉ', on seven closely-written folio pages, endorsed on f. 4v 'Sʳ Phillip Sidney to Quee Elizabeth Concning her Marriage wᵗʰ Mounser', in a composite volume of political papers and speeches (up to *c*.1640) in different hands (including the same hand as No. 27 below on ff. 46r–49r, a speech of 1637) collected by Elias Ashmole (1617–92); large urn watermark; early 17th century.

[*Index*, SiP 185. Siglum: *Ash*. Tradition: *X2*.]

5. Bodleian Library MS Douce 46, ff. 2r–15v.

Copy in a single predominently Secretary hand, originally untitled, with a title-page (f. 1r) added in a different hand: 'A Letter to Queen Elizabeth diswading her from marrying wᵗʰ. Monsieur written in the yeare 1581', on 28 octavo pages in a 164-page volume of tracts and sermons (up to *c*.1637, and including a copy of John Stubbs's *Gaping gulf*,

1579) in different hands; notes and accounts on f. 160r referring to Chancery Lane, Bishops Court, and Whites Alley; once owned by the bibliographer William Herbert (1711–95), whose signature is inside the cover, and then by Francis Douce (1757–1834); *SC* 21620; possibly end of 16th century–early 17th century.

[*Index*, SiP 186. Siglum: *D*. Tradition: *X1*.]

6. Bodleian Library MS Eng. hist. f. 8, ff. 91r–98r.

Copy in a single bold hand, headed 'A Letter written by Sʳ Phillip Sydny: unto Q ELIZabeth touching her mariage with Mounseiur', on fifteen pages in a 180-leaf octavo volume of tracts and papers relating to France; formerly Phillipps MS 11931; bookplate of Robert Steele, Wandsworth Common; sold at Sotheby's, 5 June 1899, lot 505; P. J. & A. E. Dobell's sale catalogue No. 73 (1928), item 455; *SC* 40353; early 17th century.

[*Index*, SiP 187. Tradition: predominantly *Y*.]

7. Bodleian Library MS Rawl. B. 151, ff. 3r–6r.

Text of a freely adapted paraphrase of the *Letter* in a single minuscule hand, headed 'The effect of a Discourse directed and delivered to Queen Elisabeth about her Mariage with Monsieur: *A°. 158i*: by Sʳ Philip Sidney' and ending ' . . . At your Majestys fete: Philip Sidney', on seven pages in a small quarto volume of transcripts of historical documents made by Robert Horn of Shropshire; 7 December 1618.

[*Index*, SiP 188. Siglum: *RB*. Tradition: *Y3*.]

8. Bradford Central Library Hopkinson MSS, Vol. 18, ff. 93r–99v.

Copy, headed 'To Queene Elizabeth about the mariage with monsier the Duke of Aniou' and signed at the end 'Ignoto', on fourteen pages in a 160-leaf folio volume of transcripts of state papers made by the Yorkshire antiquary John Hopkinson

(1610–80); formerly among MSS of Matthew Wilson at Eshton Hall, Yorkshire [recorded in HMC, 3rd Report (1872), appendix, 297]; 1660.

> [*Index*, SiP 189. Tradition: related to Nos. 9 and 31 below.]

9. British Library Add. MS 33271, ff. 32r–34r.

Copy in a single neat Secretary hand, untitled, on five pages (f. 33r–v misbound in reverse order), in a large double-folio compilation of state papers of *c*.1545–80 arranged according to subject, on vellum throughout, in a section under the classification 'Advice'; owned in 1702 by Richard Towneley, of Towneley Hall, near Burnley, Lancashire, and, before April 1887, by William Amhurst Tyssen-Amherst, first Baron Amherst of Hackney (1835–1909); *c*.1590s?

> [*Index*, SiP 190. Siglum: *A71*. Tradition: *XY*. It is textually related to Nos. 8 above and 31 below.]

10. British Library Add. MS 46366, ff. 100r–106r.

Copy in a single Secretary hand, untitled, on thirteen pages in a folio volume of miscellaneous tracts (up to *c*.1580) copied in two hands, owned by John Harington of Stepney (d. 1582) and then by his son Sir John Harington of Kelston (1560–1612); constituting volume i of the Harington Papers ('Prose nº. I', companion volume to 'Prose nº. II' [BL Add. MS 46367], 'Poetry I' [BL Egerton MS 2711], and 'Poetry II' [Arundel Castle]); urn watermark, with three rules above 'PO', otherwise similar to Briquet 12802 (Moscow 1594, but of type known in France from *c*.1549 onwards: cf. No. 18 below); *c*.1580.

> [*Index*, SiP 191. Tradition: predominantly *X*. See Plate 67 above.]

11. British Library Add. MS 48027, ff. 230r–235v.

Copy in a single neat Secretary hand, headed 'The copie of a Lre written to the Queen by Mr P.S.', this heading later extended in the hand of Robert Beale (1541–1601), Clerk of the Queen's Council, 'after wards called Sr Philipp Sidney, concrning the mareage wth Monsr d'Aniou', on twelve folio pages (with twelve blank pages: ff. 236r–241v), in a composite volume of state tracts and papers compiled by Beale, including John Stubbs's printed *Gaping gulf*, 1579 [ff. 152r–195v], and Lord Henry Howard's answer to it [ff. 197r–215r, probably in the same hand as Sidney's *Letter*], as well as a tract [ff. 37r–70v] docketed by Beale as being found in Howard's study and written 'by a fellowe that sumtimes was servant to a stationer [? Henry Cockyn: cf. *STC* iii. 42] dwelling at the Signe of the Olifant in Fletestreete', a tract relating to Mary Queen of Scots [ff. 380r–396v] docketed by Beale as 'written as I have heard by D[r John] Hamond at the req[ue]st of Sr Philipp Sedney', and George Puttenham's *Discourse* on Mary Queen of Scots [ff. 451r–476r: cf. Nos. 20 and 37 below]; among Beale papers descending to Sir Henry Yelverton (1566–1629), Justice of the Common Pleas, and his family (Yelverton MS 31) [first recorded in HMC, 2nd Report (1871), appendix, 41]; *c*.1580s.

> [*Index*, SiP 192. Tradition: *X*. See Plate 66 above.]

12. British Library Add. MS 48044, ff. 240r–246v.

Copy in a single Secretary hand, headed 'A letter Written to Queene Elizabeath against the Match wth: Monseieur', on fourteen folio pages, part of a single unit (ff. 215r–250v) of papers dating up to 1623, in a composite volume of state tracts among the papers of Sir Henry Yelverton (1566–1629), Justice of the Common Pleas, and his family (Yelverton MS 49); pillars watermark; *c*.1625–30s.

> [Cited in H. R. Woudhuysen, 'A crux in the text of Sidney's *A letter to Queen Elizabeth*', *N&Q* 229 (June 1984), 172–3. Tradition: predominantly *Y*. The text is related to the All Souls MS (No. 1 above), but not to the Beale MS (No. 11 above).]

13. British Library Cotton MS Caligula E. XII, part I, ff. 25r–31r.

Copy in the hand of Ralph Starkey (d. 1628), on thirteen badly damaged folio pages (part of a single section: ff. 17r–32v) and lacking any heading, in a composite volume of state tracts among the collections of Sir Robert Cotton (1571–1631); armorial watermark of Strasbourg lily with 'NCH' [of Nicolas Heusler: Basle, Geneva, Héricourt, 1585–1606] (Briquet 1347); *c.*1600s–1628.

[Cited in Woudhuysen, 'A crux in the text'. New siglum: *Cot.* Tradition: *XY.* See Plate 71 above.]

14. British Library Hargrave MS 226, ff. 270r–282v.

Copy partly in the hand of the Feathery Scribe; partly in the hand of another scribe (same as Nos. 23 and 30 below): see Appendix II above, No. 41.10.

[*Index*, SiP 193. Siglum: *H26.* Tradition: *Y2.*]

15. British Library Harley MS 444, ff. 2r–13r.

Copy in the hand of a professional scribe associated with the Feathery Scribe, headed 'A Letter written by S^r: Phillipp Sidney vnto Queene Elizabeth touching hir Marriage wth Mounseir', on twenty-three pages in a folio volume of transcripts of state papers; *c.*1625–30s.

[*Index*, SiP 194. Siglum: *H4.* Tradition: *XY.*]

16. British Library Harley MS 1323, ff. 43r–56v.

Copy in the hand of the Feathery Scribe: see Appendix II above, No. 57.4.

[*Index*, SiP 195. Siglum: *H23* and used as 1973 copy-text. Tradition: *Y1.* See Plates 74 and 75 above.]

17. British Library Harley MS 6845, ff. 199r–200v.

Copy of part of the letter in a single cursive Secretary hand which progressively degenerates, lacking the beginning and any heading, on two large folio leaves, with a later note in the gutter of f. 199r: 'Bought of H. W.' [similar inscriptions occur on ff. 12r and 13v (1581)]; in a 297-leaf composite volume of state papers; probably early 17th century.

[*Index*, SiP 196. Siglum: *H5* or *H45.* Tradition: *Y1*]

18. British Library Lansdowne MS 94, ff. 53r–56v.

Précis of the letter in a single cursive Secretary hand, originally untitled, on six folio pages (ff. 54r–56v), with blank wrappers (ff. 53r, 61v), docketed in another contemporary hand (f. 53r) '1579: Notes out of m^r Phillip Sidneys lre to ye Q. touching hir mariage wth. Monsieur', other inscriptions including '1579 | Bundle XII | Varia' (and scribbling in cipher on f. 53r in the same hand as the inscription on f. 61v: 'An^o. 1579 IV. LXXV. Articles propounded in behalf of ye Duke of Anjoy concerning marryinge wth ye Queen'), in a 196-leaf composite volume of state papers from the muniments of Sir William Cecil, Lord Burghley (1520–98); urn watermark similar to Briquet 12802 (Moscow 1594, but of type known in France from *c.*1549 onwards: cf. No. 10 above); *c.*1580.

[*Index*, SiP 197. Tradition: *X.* See Plate 69 above.]

19. British Library Sloane MS 24.

Copy in the hand of the Feathery Scribe: see Appendix II above, No. 64.

[*Index*, SiP 198. Siglum: *Slo.* Tradition: *Y1.*]

20. Cambridge University Library MS Kk. 1. 3(14), ff. 2v–6v.

Copy in a cursive, predominantly Secretary hand, untitled, on ten folio pages in a 38-leaf section in the same hand (including, [(13), ff. 1r–22r]

George Puttenham's *Discourse* on Mary Queen of Scots [cf. Nos. 11 above and 37 below]), in a composite volume of state tracts and other MSS; with a prayer added as a coda after the 'Finis' (f. 6v): 'God saue our gracious Queen Elizabeth; and so indue her wth his grace, and touch her heart wth the spirit of wisedome, that herein shee erre not, but maie doe onlie that, y^t maie make most for his glorie, best for her owne solace & comfort, and the good & quiet of our Land. Amen.'; possibly late 16th century–early 17th century.

[*Index*, SiP 199. Siglum: *Cm*. Tradition: *X2*.]

21. Cheshire Record Office DLT/B8, pp. 185–6.

Copy of the first twenty lines and then a series of condensed extracts from various parts of the *Letter* including the last few lines, in a cursive Secretary hand, headed 'Sr Phillip Sydney to her Matie: concerninge her Marriage wth Mounsieur', on two pages in a folio volume of transcripts of state letters and tracts once owned by the antiquary Sir Peter Leycester (1614–78) [recorded in HMC, 1st Report (1870), appendix, 47–8]; *c.*1625–30s.

[*Index*, SiP 200. Tradition: a sophisticated and emended text of uncertain derivation.]

22. Folger Shakespeare Library MS V. b. 151, ff. 57r–62v.

Copy in a neat, professional, predominantly Secretary hand, headed 'Sr Phillip Sidney his letter or Treatise to her Matie against Mounsiers Mariage', with the salutation ('Most ffeared & beloved, most sweete & Gratious Soveraigne') set apart and centred, on eleven folio pages, in a folio volume of transcripts of state papers and tracts predominantly in a single scribal hand; signature inside cover of 'H. Powle': i.e. Henry Powle (1630–92), Master of the Rolls, and his pressmark 'A.21.', as well as his partial contents list on f. 1r [his library and manuscript collection assembled with the help of John Bagford (1650–1716) and afterwards incorporated in the Lansdowne Manuscripts and elsewhere]; bookplate of Francis North, first Earl of Guilford (1704–90), of Wroxton Abbey; pur-

chased by Henry Clay Folger from the Arthur H. Clark Company, Cleveland (from their London warehouse), in August 1924; formerly MS 1291.3; *c.*1625–30s.

[*Index*, SiP 201. Tradition: predominantly *Y*.]

23. Folger Shakespeare Library MS X. d. 210.

Copy partly in the hand of the Feathery Scribe; partly in the hand of another scribe (same as Nos. 14 above and 30 below): see Appendix II above, No. 110.

[*Index*, SiP 202. Siglum: *Fol*. Tradition: *Y2*. See Plate 68 above.]

24. Huntington Library HM 102, ff. 1r–5v.

Copy in a single Secretary hand, headed 'S^r: Philip Sydney', on ten pages in an oblong quarto collection of state letters up to 1627; Phillipps MS 10665; *c.*1627–1630s.

[*Index*, SiP 203. Siglum: *Hn*. Tradition: *X2*.]

25. Inner Temple Library Petyt MS 538, vol. 51, ff. 110r–118v.

Copy in a single hand, headed 'A Coppie of A Letter written by Sr Phillipp Sydney vnto Queene Eliz: toucheing hir Marriage with Monsier' and with an extended valediction signed 'Phillipp Sydney', on eighteen pages in a composite folio volume of state papers; *c.*1625–30s.

[*Index*, SiP 204. Siglum: *Pet*. Tradition: *Y1–Y2*.]

26. Dr Bent E. Juel-Jensen, Oxford, [no shelf mark].

Copy in a Secretary hand, headed (with sidenote) 'Sr Philippe Sydneys Letter to the Q: concearning her mariage wth Mounsier' and the salutation ('Most feared & beloued sweete, and gracious

Souereigne') set apart and slightly engrossed, on twelve folio pages; in contemporary limp vellum and formerly bound with three other tracts dating up to 1626; William H. Robinson's sale catalogue No. 72 (1940), item 147; sold by Seven Gables Bookshop at Sotheby's, 10 April 1962, lot 467; *c.*1625–30s.

[*Index*, Sip 205. Siglum: *J*. Tradition: *Y*3.]

27. University of Kansas MS E205, vol. i, ff. 44r–59r.

Copy in a cursive professional hand which also occurs in No. 4 above and in volumes containing items written by the Feathery Scribe [including Nos. 16 above and 33 below, and Appendix II above, Nos. 50 and 62], the text set out with exceptional clarity, headed 'A Letter written by S^r. Philip Sidney to Queen Elizabeth touching her Marriage with Monsr. Duke of Aniow', and with the salutation ('Most feared and beloved, Most sweet and gratious Soveraigne') set out and centred; on thirty-one folio pages in a composite volume of state tracts belonging to the Mostyn family, Baronets, of Mostyn Hall, Flintshire [Mostyn MS 177, recorded in HMC, 4th Report (1874), appendix, 355; sold Sotheby's, 13 July 1920, lot 20]; *c.*1625–30s.

[*Index*, SiP 206. Tradition: a sophisticated and emended text, predominantly *Y*.]

28. University of Kansas MS 4A:1, pp. 38–48.

Copy in a single neat mixed hand, the order of some passages rearranged and the text occasionally abridged or slightly paraphrased, headed 'S^r: P: Sidnes ltre to the Queene agains^t the match with Mouncieur:', the salutation ('Most feared & beloved most sweet & gratious Queene') isolated and set out into the margin, signed at the end 'S^r: P: Sidney', on eleven folio pages in a 65-page volume of state letters and poems belonging to the Sotheby family of London and Ecton Hall, Northamptonshire; *c.*1625–30s.

[*Index*, SiP 207. Tradition: a sophisticated and

emended text incorporating readings of both *X* and *Y*; its ordering similar to No. 29 below.]

29. Leicestershire Record Office DG. 7/Lit.2, ff. 237r–241r.

Copy in a single mixed hand, the order of some passages rearranged and the text occasionally abridged or slightly paraphrased, headed 'Sr Phillip Sydney to her Matie Concerning Mounseur:', on nine folio pages, in a composite volume of MSS collected by William Parkhurst (*fl.*1604–67), erstwhile secretary of Sir Henry Wotton (1568–1639), among the muniments of the Finch family of Burley-on-the-Hill, Rutland [recorded in HMC, 7th Report (1879), appendix, 516]; *c.*1625–30s.

[*Index*, SiP 208. Tradition: a sophisticated and emended text incorporating readings of both *X* and *Y*; its ordering similar to No. 28 above.]

30. University of London MS 308, ff. 230r–243r.

Copy partly in the hand of the Feathery Scribe; partly in the hand of another scribe (same as Nos. 14 and 23 above): see Appendix II above, No. 78.7.

[*Index*, SiP 209. New siglum: *Lon.* Tradition: *Y*2.]

31. Meisei University, Tokyo, Japan, 'Crewe MS', pp. 1028–35.

Copy in a single Secretary hand, untitled and incomplete (skipping a leaf between pp. 1030 and 1031), on eight pages in a section of letters (pp. 877–1039) arranged according to subject, under the classification 'Aduise', in a 1039-page folio MS volume of transcripts of state letters and tracts; later in the library of C. K. Ogden (1889–1957) [sold at Sotheby's, 14 December 1976, lot 47]; *c.*1590s–1620s.

[*Index*, SiP 183 (formerly owned by Dr Peter Beal). Tradition: related to Nos. 8 and 9 above.]

32. Penshurst Place, Viscount De L'Isle, Sidney Papers B.

Copy; with brief valediction added: 'Your Majesties faythfull, humble, and obedient Subject, P. Sydney'; 17th century.

> [Printed in Arthur Collins, *Letters and memorials of state*, 2 vols. (London, 1746), i. 287–92. *Index*, SiP 210. Siglum: *Pen.* Tradition: *Y3.*]

33. Somerset Record Office DD/AH/51/1, ff. 48r–60v.

Copy in the hand of the Feathery Scribe: see Appendix II above, No. 105.1.

> [*Index*, SiP 211. New siglum: *Som.* Tradition: *Y1.* Cf. also No. 27 above. See Plates 76 and 77 above.]

34. Trinity College Dublin MS 588 (old pressmark E.3.25), ff. 2r–16r.

Copy in the hand of the Feathery Scribe: see Appendix II above, No. 17.

> [*Index*, SiP 212. Siglum: *T25.* Tradition: *Y1.* See Plate 73 above.]

35. Trinity College Dublin MS 732 (old pressmark G.4.10), ff. 33r–45r.

Copy partly in the hand of the Feathery Scribe: see Appendix II above, No. 18.1.

> [*Index*, SiP 213. Siglum: *TG10.* Tradition: *Y2.* See Plates 70 and 72 above.]

36. Trinity College Dublin MS 802 (old pressmark E.1.10), ff. 1r–10v.

Copy chiefly in the hand of the Feathery Scribe: see Appendix II above, No. 20.1.

> [*Index*, SiP 214. Siglum: *TE10.* Tradition: *XY.*]

37. Unlocated.

Copy 'in a very neat old Court Hand', headed 'A Letter written by Sir Phillip Sidney unto Queene Elizabeth touchinge hir Marriage with Mounseer', on 19 folio pages, following a 100-page copy in the same hand of George Puttenham's *Discourse* on Mary Queen of Scots (cf. Nos. 11 and 20 above); [Mostyn MS 261, recorded in HMC, 4th Report (1874), appendix, 361; Maggs catalogues No. 423 (1922), item 1127, and No. 550 (1931), item 987].

APPENDIX V

Katherine Philips's letter to Lady Fletcher

The text is printed here *verbatim et literatim* from the transcript which appears in a miscellany of Royalist verse, copied in a single hand in the mid-1650s, now at University College London, MS Ogden 42, p. 221. It is printed by permission of University College London.

The same[1]
To the noble Parthenia
The Lady ffletcher/[2]

Madam

    Ther were no excuse for such a presumption
as this from a person so vnworthy & so unknowne, were it
possible for me to be a stranger, where ever my dearest
Rosamia[3] hath an Interest. or for any one to want some
kind of worth where she will recom*m*end. All I can pretend   5
is a Sympathy with her noble Soule. & an admiration
of it. & both these speake me y^r servant, though at so
great a distance., ffor if I either love Rosamia, or honor
goodnesse (wch indeed is all one) I must be y^r votary,
who are Mistresse of a double happynesse. a freindship   10
from the paragon of the world, & a vertue to give
you title to it. Now since my devotion is as impossible
to be concealed as supprest. be pleased to accept an
Offering wch hath nothing can challenge so much as
a pardon, but the relegion that tenders it, & ye Subject.   15
for no language can be barbarous that speakes Rosamia
though the fancye that gave these lines a birth, is
really as barren as the Rocks & Mountaynes[4] it inhabitts.

Y^r most humble servant
Orinda

[1] The same] this epistle follows the poem (on pp. 217–20 of the MS) headed 'Orinda, To Parthenia. A shaddow of Rosamia' and signed 'Ka: Ph:'.

[2] Lady ffletcher] Elizabeth Hageman suggests that Lady Fletcher might be identified as either (i) Alice (d. early 1663/4), daughter of Hugh, Viscount Colerain, who on 27 February 1654/5 married Sir George Fletcher (*c.*1633–1700); or else (ii) Catherine, daughter of Sir George Dalton, wife of Sir Henry Fletcher who died fighting for the King in 1645, this Lady Fletcher later marrying (after 1655) Thomas Smith (1615–1702), who became Bishop of Carlisle.

[3] Rosamia] Rosania: i.e. Mary Aubrey (1631–1700), who married Sir William Montagu (1619?–1706). The spelling 'Rosamia' recalls the spelling 'Rosannia' which occurs repeatedly in the 1664 edition of *Poems by the Incomparable, Mrs. K.P.* and which is corrected to 'Rosania' in an inserted errata slip: '*For* Rosannia *read* Rosania *throughout*'.

[4] as barren as the Rocks & Mountaynes] i.e. the mountains of Wales, around Cardigan. Philips alludes to the Welsh mountains and their remoteness and barrenness in certain of her letters to Cotterell and Dorothy Osborne: see, for example, Thomas, ii. 88, 128, 138.

John Taylor's verse satire on Katherine Philips

The text is printed here *verbatim et literatim*, with no emendation of the ambiguous or erratic punctuation and spelling, from the transcript in University College London MS Ogden 42, pp. 225–6 (see Plates 78 and 79 above). It is printed by permission of University College London.

To M^{rs} K:P: from Mr J.T.

You dame of Corinth,[1] (save the shape.
        Com*m*itt no Rape.
Vpon the Muses be not bold.
        To make them scold,
Whose purer breasts, did never deigne   5
        To rage in vayne.[2]
But Bedlam ffuries, native hate.
        Only create,
The fetterd follies of thy Rhymes
        Like ill tun'd chymes.   10
The Jangling of bells backward rung
        So is thy tongue.
Snatcht from Vipers dryd' in Hell
        Alecto's[3] Cell
Ownes thee, the mistresse of her Schoole.   15
        Priapus[4] toole
Stole by Cherill[5] gave thee Lyfe
        On Priams wyfe.
But not while she was Hecuba,
        But turnd' to A.[6]   20

The following notes are based partly on information supplied by the *OED* and by the classical dictionaries of John Lempriere (1788), 3rd revised edn. by F. A. Wright and R. Willets (London 1984), and of Sir William Smith (1842), enlarged edn. revised by G. E. Marindin *et al.* (London, 1894), and *The Oxford Classical Dictionary*, 3rd edn., ed. Simon Hornblower and Antony Spawforth (Oxford, 1996).

[1] You dame of Corinth] i.e. 'You Corinthian woman': *Corinthian* meaning lascivious, whore-like. Taylor accuses Philips of being a prostitute except that ('save the shape') she does not have the figure for the job.

[2] To rage in vayne] a possible reflection on Philips' 'raging' against the 'libell' by J. Jones in her poems on the subject addressed to 'Lucasia' and, more especially, to her husband 'Antenor', as well as perhaps in her poem attacking Vavasor Powell (which started the controversy) (see Thomas, i. 69–70, 114–17).

[3] Alecto] Alecto, one of the furies, represented with a flaming torch, her head covered with serpents, and breathing vengeance, war and pestilence.

[4] Priapus] Priapus, son of Venus by Mercury or Adonis, a licentious god with a large penis.

[5] Cherill] i.e. presumably a 'churl' (cherelle, cherle, etc.: see *OED*): a lower-class man, husband, serf, peasant.

[6] Priams wyfe . . . Hecuba . . . turnd' to A] Hecuba, second wife of Priam, King of Troy, was noted for chastity and for being an inconsolable mother; after the fall of Troy, when pursued by Greek tormentors, she metamorphosed into a bitch who could only bark; thus 'turn'd to A' perhaps means 'turn'd to A [bitch]'. The implication is that Philips is the daughter of a bitch.

Some say you are Diana[7] fayre,

      And past compare.

I thinke so too; But only then.

      When Staggs & Men

Are made Identick by y[r] power.[8]   25

      Oft in an houre,

Save then with you, the Cyprian Queene.[9]

      Is often seene.

Not in her Glory, but the Nett.

      By Vulcan sett:[10]   30

That Sooty God,[11] had Eyes & Art.

      And playd his part.

But from Vulcan every day.

      Mars steales away.[12]

Yet I have seene him clad in Steele   35

      Which none did feele[13]

ffor which his noddle is prest downe

      With Lanthorne Crowne[14]

The Cause (Deare Mabb)[15] of y[r] desires

      To Regall fyres,   40

Your Sence in you, not reason move,[16]

      Monarchique Love.[17]

May you a second Sapho[18] prove

      To write in Love;

[7] Diana] Diana, goddess of hunting and patroness of chastity.

[8] When Staggs & Men . . . by y[r] power] when the huntsman Actaeon spied upon her bathing, Diana turned him into a stag, which was immediately torn to pieces by his hounds.

[9] the Cyprian Queene] Venus, goddess of beauty and of love, patroness of courtesans, who arose from the sea near Cyprus; she was forced by Jupiter to marry Vulcan.

[10] the Nett. By Vulcan sett] see n. 12 below.

[11] Vulcan . . . That Sooty God] the lame and ugly god Vulcan, who, generally sweaty and blackened with smoke, presided over fire and was patron of artists who worked iron and metal; cuckolded by Venus.

[12] But from Vulcan . . . Mars steales away] Mars, god of war, was Venus' lover. Apollo eventually informed her husband, Vulcan, who captured them with a net *in flagranti delicto* to the ridicule of the gods.

[13] him clad in Steele / Which none did feele] 'him' is ambiguous here, but the apparent implication is that one or other of Venus' partners is a soldier (in armour) who does not actually fight.

[14] his noddle . . . with Lanthorne Crowne] 'his' presumably refers here to the husband, Vulcan, who wears a crown shaped like a lantern and made of horn: i.e. a cuckold's crown. Ironically lanterns traditionally symbolised guiding lights: eg. Bacon spoke on 7 May 1617 of 'The Kings Chardge w[ch] is my Lanthorne'; Sir John Harington sent James I a lantern with accompanying verses to welcome him to his new kingdom in 1603; and in his eulogy 'Upon Mrs. K. Philips her Poems', Abraham Cowley declared:

    Orinda's inward Vertue is so bright,

    That, like a Lantern's fair enclosed light,

    It through the Paper shines where she doth write.

In her poem 'To Antenor' (l. 20), however, Philips describes her present wretched situation as 'this darke lanthorne's gall' (Thomas, i. 117).

[15] Mabb] Mab, a mop, a slattern, a woman of loose character; it also has the connotation of Queen Mab in Welsh mythology.

[16] Sence . . . not reason move] this may be an ironic echo of, and retort to, Philips' references to 'reason' in her poems on Vavasor Powell (l. 24) and to Lucasia (l. 2) (Thomas, i. 69, 114).

[17] The Cause . . . Monarchique Love] the insinuation here would seem to be that it is Philips' supposed adulterous tendencies which account for her Royalist sympathies.

[18] Sapho] Sappho, female Greek poet, author of love poetry; born *c.*600 BC on the island of Lesbos, whence the term 'Lesbian'. According to Ovid, she threw herself from a cliff because of unrequited love.

And if like her you doe not die   45
                              Then soone will I,
Iambick[19] you Lycambes ffate.[20]
                              To which no date,
Shall be, as long John Taylors stand
                              Poet at hand.   50
Or ffidlers, Tabrells,[21] Pastimes find
                              Or Cuckhold kind:

---

[19] Iambicke] iambic is a verse form using the iambus, a metrical foot consisting of a short followed by a long syllable; also a piece of invective or satirical verse; used here as a verb.

[20] Lycambes ffate] Lycambes renaged on his promise to marry his daughter, Neobule, to the poet Archilochus (a great developer of iambic verse, *fl. c.*650 BC). In revenge the poet wrote a series of satirical poems recounting in explicit detail the sexual experiences that he and others had enjoyed with both Neobule and her sister, in consequence of which Lycambes and his two daughters hanged themselves for shame. Thus Taylor is here threatening to satirise Philips (by exposing her supposed sexual misdemeanours) to the point of driving her to suicide.

[21] Tabrells] tabrels or timbrels, small drums held in the hand, like tambourines; suggestive of the traditional festivity accompanying the public exposure of whores.

Index of manuscripts cited

United Kingdom

ABERYSTWYTH

National Library of Wales

Castell Gorfod MS 1 65, 211–14, 269
NLW MS 775B 148, 163 n. 45
NLW MS 776B 168–73, 178 n. 69
Powis, 1959 deposit, Series II, Bundle XVI,
 No. 4 72 n. 12
Wynnstay MS 44 84 n. 25, 214

BRADFORD

Bradford Central Library

Hopkinson MSS, vol. 18 275–6

CAMBRIDGE

Cambridge University Library

Add. MS 9276 64, 65, 82, 84–6, 214–15
MS Dd. 3. 86 88 n. 28, 215–16
MS Dd. 6. 43 148 n. 6
MS Dd. 9. 22 79, 216
MS Ee. 2. 32 216–17
MS Ee. 4. 18 217
MS Ii. 5. 9 88 n. 28
MS Kk. 1. 3 128 n. 39, 277–8
MS Mm. 6. 63 218
Hengrave Hall MSS, 82 (4)–83 (1) 69 n. 12,
 71

Gonville and Caius College

MS 195 67 n. 6

Magdalene College, Pepys Library

No. 1774 69 n. 9
No. 2099 224, 272 n. 9
No. 2191 215

St John's College

MS L. 22 (James 374) 67 n. 6

CANTERBURY

Canterbury Cathedral

U210/2/2 38–57

CHESTER

Cheshire Record Office

DDX 255 88 n. 26
DLT/B8 124 n. 31, 278

CHICHESTER

West Sussex Record Office

Goodwood MS 1431/23, 29–30 30 n. 90

COLCHESTER

Essex Record Office

D/DRg 3/3 82 n. 22, 88 n. 28
D/DRg 3/4 89 n. 29, 263

IPSWICH

Suffolk Record Office

HA 93/2/3174 3 n. 8
HA 93/10/125 72 n. 14

LEICESTER

Leicestershire Record Office

DG. 7/Lit.2 279

LINCOLN

Lincolnshire Archives Office

Anc 15/B/4 29 n. 87

LONDON

The British Library

Additional MS 4106 273 n. 13
Additional MS 4149 88 n. 28, 227–8
Additional MS 4155 69 n. 10
Additional MS 10117 184 n. 92
Additional MS 11308 84 n. 25, 228
Additional MS 11764 228
Additional MS 12513 228
Additional MS 18201 228
Additional MS 18648 9 n. 43
Additional MS 20042 69 n. 9
Additional MS 22591 273 n. 13
Additional MS 24652 215
Additional MS 25247 258
Additional MS 25303 198–9
Additional MS 28758 155 n. 28
Additional MS 32626 203
Additional MS 33271 276
Additional MS 35838 228
Additional MS 36452 190 n. 113
Additional MS 36916 184 n. 92–3, 187 n. 105
Additional MS 39851 88 nn. 26 and 28
Additional MS 46366 122–5, 127, 129–30, 139 n. 53, 276
Additional MS 46367 276
Additional MS 46410 90 n. 36, 219
Additional MS 48027 4 n. 11, 119–22, 124–5, 127, 129–30, 276
Additional MS 48039 121 nn. 23–4
Additional MS 48044 129 n. 41, 276
Additional MS 48062 228–9
Additional MS 48063 229
Additional MS 48159 90 n. 33
Additional MS 48186 72 n. 12
Additional MS 72466 14 n. 65
Additional MS 73087 82 n. 23, 229–31
Additional [uncatalogued Evelyn MSS] 154 n. 19, 184 n. 92, 190 n. 114, 231
Arundel MS 22 69 n. 9
Cotton MS Caligula C. IX 90 n. 36
Cotton MS Caligula D. I 90 n. 36, 259

Cotton MS Caligula E. XII 90 n. 36, 133, 135, 277
Cotton MS Cleopatra E. IV 90 n. 36
Cotton MS Cleopatra F. I 90 n. 36
Cotton MS Cleopatra F. II 90 n. 36
Cotton MS Cleopatra F. VI 212, 217, 228
Cotton MS Faustina C. II 225
Cotton MS Faustina E. I 90 n. 36
Cotton MS Faustina E. VII 90 n. 36
Cotton MS Julius C. III 91 nn. 38–9
Cotton MS Julius C. VIII 271 n. 8
Cotton MS Julius C. IX 261
Cotton MS Otho E. VII 90 n. 36, 91 n. 37
Cotton MS Otho E. X 90 n. 36
Cotton MS Titus B. III 88 n. 26
Cotton MS Titus B. IV 90 n. 36
Cotton MS Titus B. V 90 n. 36
Cotton MS Titus B. XII 90 n. 36, 113, 115
Cotton MS Titus C. I 90 n. 36, 258
Cotton MS Titus C. IV 90 n. 36, 218, 258
Cotton MS Titus C. VII 212, 213, 214, 217, 229, 235, 240, 253
Cotton MS Titus F. I 90 n. 36
Cotton MS Titus F. II 249
Cotton MS Titus F. III 90 n. 36, 257
Cotton MS Titus F. IV 90 n. 36, 134 n. 50
Cotton MS Vespasian C. I 90 n. 36
Cotton MS Vespasian C. II 90 n. 36
Cotton MS Vespasian C. III 90 n. 36
Cotton MS Vespasian C. VII 90 n. 36
Cotton MS Vespasian C. VIII 90 n. 36
Cotton MS Vespasian C. X 91, 231
Cotton MS Vespasian C. XI 91, 232
Cotton MS Vespasian C. XII 90 n. 36
Cotton MS Vespasian C. XIII 90 n. 36
Cotton MS Vespasian C. XIV 90 n. 36, 219
Cotton MS Vitellius C. XVI 90 n. 36, 214, 215, 265
Cotton MS Vitellius C. XVII 213
Egerton MS 2026 273 n. 13
Egerton MS 2711 276
Egerton MS 2979 163 n. 45
Egerton MS 3330 99 n. 57
Egerton MS 3331 99 n. 57
Hargrave MS 165 232

Hargrave MS 225 232
Hargrave MS 226 18 n. 70, 136, 232–3, 277
Hargrave MS 227 221
Harley MS 35 234
Harley MS 36 234
Harley MS 37 90 n. 33, 93–5, 234–5
Harley MS 39 235–6
Harley MS 160 236
Harley MS 161 65–6, 86–8, 237–8
Harley MS 250 67 n. 6
Harley MS 252 238
Harley MS 260 79–82, 238
Harley MS 286 89, 243
Harley MS 292 92 n. 41, 259
Harley MS 293 134 n. 50, 238–9
Harley MS 298 92 n. 41, 239, 258, 261
Harley MS 304 212
Harley MS 306 88 n. 26, 92 n. 44
Harley MS 354 239
Harley MS 364 92 n. 44
Harley MS 444 79–80, 82 n. 23, 133, 239–41, 277
Harley MS 506 88 n. 26
Harley MS 537 88 n. 26, 92 n. 41, 212, 215, 218, 258, 263
Harley MS 557 254
Harley MS 558 90 n. 34
Harley MS 646 88 n. 27
Harley MS 737 241–2
Harley MS 738 242
Harley MS 837 104, 242
Harley MS 1226 245
Harley MS 1323 84 n. 25, 132, 140–3, 242–4, 277
Harley MS 1853 84 n. 25, 215
Harley MS 2012 88 n. 26
Harley MS 2208 244
Harley MS 4289 69 n. 11
Harley MS 5111 244–5
Harley MS 5141 245
Harley MS 6018 91 n. 38, 215
Harley MS 6257 215
Harley MS 6382 259
Harley MS 6842 245
Harley MS 6845 277

Harley MS 6846 91 n. 38
Harley MS 7021 84 n. 25, 215
Harley MS 7315 210
Harley MS 7650 3 n. 8
Lansdowne MS 94 125–6, 277
Lansdowne MS 163 88 nn. 26 and 28
Lansdowne MS 254 245
Lansdowne MS 798 245
Lansdowne MS 813 215
Lansdowne MS 1225 69 n. 9
Sloane MS 24 132, 245, 277
Sloane MS 755 245–6
Sloane MS 1710 246
Sloane MS 1974 184 nn. 92 and 94
Sloane MS 3104 246
Sloane MS 3105 246
Sloane MS 3106 246
Sloane MS 3520 246
Stowe MS 145 82–3, 247
Stowe MS 151 79, 81, 133 n. 48, 247–8
Stowe MS 182 273 n. 13
Stowe MS 362 248–9

Guildhall Library

MS 5370 65 n. 5

House of Lords Record Office

Braye MS 5 90 n. 33
Braye MS 78 273 n. 12
Historical Collections No. 53 94 n. 46
House of Commons Library MS 6 90 n. 33

Inner Temple Library

Misc. MS 199 89 n. 30
Petyt MS 538, vol. 14 249
Petyt MS 538, vol. 18 71 n. 12, 273 n. 12
Petyt MS 538, vol. 36 134 n. 50
Petyt MS 538, vol. 48 272 n. 11
Petyt MS 538, vol. 49 269, 271 n. 5
Petyt MS 538, vol. 50 88 n. 28, 269
Petyt MS 538, vol. 51 128 n. 37, 136–7, 278

Lambeth Palace

MS 806 77, 249

Public Record Office, Kew

LC 9/271 185 n. 95

SP 14/43/14 5 n. 14
SP 45/20 40 n. 25, 89 n. 29, 90 nn. 31–2, 91
    n. 40, 106 n. 66

University College London

MS Ogden 16 215
MS Ogden 17 249–50
MS Ogden 36 250
MS Ogden 42 148, 150, 152–3, 281, 282–4

University of London

MS 285 40 n. 25, 252
MS 308 124 n. 31, 136, 250–1, 272 n. 9, 279
MS 309 214, 221, 227, 245, 261, 272 n. 9,
    273 n. 13

Victoria & Albert Museum

Dyce Catalogue No. 7416;
    Pressmark D.23.A.33 Folio 188–9

Dr Williams Library

MSS 28.49 201

MAIDSTONE

Centre for Kentish Studies

U 1475 Z3 116 n. 18

NORTHAMPTON

Northamptonshire Record Office

FH 4155 254

NOTTINGHAM

University of Nottingham

Portland MS Pw V 424 25 n. 81

OXFORD

All Souls College

MS 117 72 n. 12, 90 n. 35, 211, 250, 261
MS 155 274, 276

Balliol College

MS 336 148–9 n. 9

Bodleian Library

MS Ashmole 800 275
MS Ashmole 840 88 n. 28
MS Aubrey 8 165 n. 49
MS Bodl. 903 215
MS Carte 122 254
MS Douce 46 275
MS Dugdale 28 96, 98, 99, 254–5
MS e. Mus. 131 32–3, 35–8, 40, 42–9, 52–5
MS Eng. hist. f. 8 129 n. 41, 275
MS Eng. misc. c. 139 107 n. 67, 255
MS Eng. poet. f. 27 201
MS Firth c. 16 77 n. 16
MS Perrott 4 88 n. 28
MS Perrott 7 255
MS Rawl A. 100 255
MS Rawl. A. 141 255–6
MS Rawl. B. 151 275
MS Rawl. D. 51 65 n. 5
MS Rawl. D. 692 95 n. 50, 99, 101, 104,
    256–7
MS Rawl. D. 918 257
MS Rawl. D. 1361 260
MS Rawl. poet. 31 102–4, 257
MS Tanner 72 88 n. 28
MS Tanner 84 257–8
MS Tanner 85 258–9
MS Tanner 103 88 n. 28
MS Tanner 108 66–8, 70, 259
MS Willis 58 69 n. 11, 134 n. 50, 259

Corpus Christi College

MS 328 201

The Queen's College

MS 280 259–60
MS 449 260

Worcester College

MSS 6.13 163 n. 45
MS 120: Plays 9, 19 163 n. 45

READING

Berkshire Record Office

D/EBtZ37 155 n. 28

RUTHIN

Denbighshire Record Office
DD/WY/2020 64 n. 4

STAFFORD

William Salt Library
M 527 72–4, 260–1

TAUNTON

Somerset Record Office
DD/AH/51/1 143–5, 261, 280
DD/AH/51/2 261–2
DD/AH/51/4 262

WHALLEY, LANCASHIRE

Stonyhurst College
MS A. V. 19 67 n. 6

Ireland

DUBLIN

Marsh's Library
G3.7.49 178 n. 68

Trinity College Dublin
MS 532 224, 243
MS 588 132, 138–9, 222, 280
MS 611 94 n. 46
MS 612 94 n. 46
MS 731 84 n. 25, 222–3
MS 732 82 n. 23, 133, 136–7, 223, 280
MS 734 223–4
MS 802 82 n. 23, 224–5, 280
MS 845 82 n. 23, 225
MS 861 225–6
MS 862 226–7
Old Library, V.ee.4 182–3, 185–6, 188–9

France

PARIS

Bibliothèque Nationale
Cinq cents de Colbert nº 466 113 n. 16,
    116–19, 122, 124–5, 127, 129–30, 275

Germany

REGENSBURG

Bischöfliches Zentralarchiv
BZA/Sch. F. XVII, Fasz. 4,
    No. 19 149 n. 10

Japan

TOKYO

Meisei University
Crewe MS 279

United States of America

AUSTIN, TEXAS

University of Texas at Austin
Pre-1700 MS 151 163 n. 45

CAMBRIDGE, MASSACHUSETTS

Harvard University, Houghton Library
fMS Eng 826 215
MS Eng 897 77, 218
fMS Eng 1084 218
fMS Eng 1205 18 n. 70, 218
fMS Eng 1266, vol. 1 218
fMS Eng 1266, vol. 2 94 n. 46
fEC65.P5397.667p 182–3
EC.D7187.644b (C) 34 n. 10

Harvard University, Law School Library
MS 1034 96, 98–100, 219–21
MS 1035 219

MS 1036 219
MS 1054 221

CHICAGO, ILLINOIS

University of Chicago Library
MS 847 221–2
MS 878 88 n. 28, 96–7, 222

LAWRENCE, KANSAS

*University of Kansas, Kenneth Spencer
    Research Library*
MS 4A:1 124 n. 32, 128 n. 39, 279
MS D 153 94 n. 46
MS E205 124 n. 32, 133 n. 50, 279

LOS ANGELES, CALIFORNIA

William Andrews Clark Memorial Library
fB618M3 T784 [*c.*1630] Bound 251

NEW HAVEN, CONNECTICUT

Yale University, Beinecke Library
Osborn Collection b 50 94 n. 46
Osborn Collection b 118 169 n. 59
Osborn Collection b 167 251
Osborn Collection b 180 69, 71, 251–2
Osborn Collection fb 59 252
Osborn Collection fb 60 252–3
Osborn Collection fb 178 94 n. 46
Osborn Collection Gordonstoun Box V 253

NEW YORK

Pierpont Morgan Library
MA 1475 113–14, 131
MS with MA 1475 74–7, 254

PHILADELPHIA, PENNSYLVANIA

The Free Library of Philadelphia
Carson MS LC 14:44 260

Rosenbach Museum
MS 239/4 260, 269

SAN MARINO, CALIFORNIA

The Huntington Library
EL 35.B.60 90 n. 34
EL 1174 215
EL 8175 94, 211, 269–73
HM 102 128 n. 37, 278
HM 1420 260

WASHINGTON, DC

The Folger Shakespeare Library
MS G. b. 8 262
MS G. b. 9 67, 69, 262–5
MS V. a. 470 273 n. 13
MS V. b. 50 82 n. 23, 265–7
MS V. b. 151 278
MS V. b. 184 88 n. 28
MS V. b. 276 88 n. 28, 262
MS X. d. 210 124, 136, 267, 278
MS X. d. 236 88 n. 28, 273 n. 13
MS X. d. 337 267
P 2034 178 n. 68

Library of Congress, Law Library
Law MS 14 267–8

Private owners in the United Kingdom and United States of America

*Alnwick Castle, Northumberland, The Duke of
    Northumberland*
MS 525 274–5

Arundel Castle, Sussex, The Duke of Norfolk
MSS (Special Press) 'Harrington MS. Temp.
    Eliz.' 276

Cambridge, Professor J. H. Baker
'Archeion' MS 16–18

Chatsworth House, Derbyshire, The Duke of Devonshire

Diary of Richard Boyle, Earl of Cork 160 n. 38

Eccleston, Cheshire, Eaton Estate Office, The Duke of Westminster

Miscellaneous 13 94 n. 46

Personal Papers 2/25 94 n. 46, 211, 251, 252

Personal Papers 2/26 94 n. 46

Hamilton, Massachusetts, Robert S. Pirie

Suckling MS 227

London, Dr Peter Beal

MS 1 67, 71, 227

MS 2 58–62, 227

Oxford, Dr Bent E. Juel-Jensen

Ralegh MS 259

Sidney MS 124 n. 31, 130 n. 42, 278–9

Penshurst Place, Kent, The Viscount De L'Isle

Sidney Papers B 280

Watlington, Oxfordshire, Shirburn Castle, The Earl of Macclesfield

MS [Shelf 7, no number] 268

Woburn Abbey, Bedfordshire, The Duke of Bedford

MSS HMC No. 26 57 n. 37

York, Castle Howard

Northampton MS 258

Private Collection

Derby MS 20–30

Bibliography

An act for turning the books of the law . . . into English, 22 November '1649' (London, [1650]).

ADAMS, SIMON, 'The papers of Robert Dudley, Earl of Leicester: II. The Atye–Cotton collection', *Archives*, 20/90 (October 1993), 131–44.

Anderson Auction Co. catalogue, New York, Robert Hoe sale, part I: L to Z (May 1911).

ANDREWS, ALLEN, *The royal whore* (London, 1971).

Anon., *The arraignment and conviction of Mervin Lord Avdley* (London, 1642[/3]).

Anon., *A brief discourse concerning printing and printers* (London, 1663).

Anon., *The character of a Whig* (London, 1700).

Anon., *The character of wit's squint-ey'd maid, pasquil-makers* (London, 1681).

Anon., *The compleat clark, and scriveners guide* (London, 1655).

Anon., *The copie of a leter, wryten by a master of arte of Cambrige to his friend in London* ([?Paris], 1584).

Anon., *The gracious answer of the most illustrious lady of pleasure, the Countess of Castlem[aine] to the poor whores petition* (London, 24 April 1668).

Anon., 'Letter of Mrs. Aphra Behn, the poetess, to Tonson, the bookseller', *GM* NS 5 (May 1836), 481–2.

Anon., *Leycesters common-wealth* (London, 1641).

Anon., *The Protestant cuckold: A new ballad. Being a full and perfect relation how B[enjamin] H[arris] the Protestant-news-forger, caught his beloved wife Ruth in ill circumstances* (London, 1681).

Anon., *Tom-Tell-Troth, or A free discovrse* ([London], 1642).

Anon., *The Wandering-Jew, telling fortvnes to English-men* (London, 1640).

Anon., *Will with a whisp to Robbin Goodfellow* (London, 1680).

AUBREY, JOHN, *Brief lives*, ed. Andrew Clark, 2 vols. (Oxford, 1898).

AUDIGUIER, VITAL D', *Love and valor or The diuers affections of Minerva*, trans. W.B. (London, 1638).

AUSTIN, SAMUEL, *Naps upon Parnassus* (London, 1658).

B., A., *Covent Garden drolery, or a colection . . . collected by R. B.* (London, 1672).

—— *Covent Garden Drollery*, ed. Montague Summers (London, 1927).

—— *Covent Garden Drollery*, ed. G. Thorn-Drury (London, 1928).

BACON, FRANCIS, *A speech . . . concerning the naturalization of the Scottish nation* (London, 1641).

—— *Ordinances in Chancery* (London, 1642).

—— *Resuscitatio, or, Bringing into publick light severall pieces of the works*, ed. William Rawley (London, 1657).

—— *Baconiana or, Certain remains of Sir Francis Bacon*, [ed. Thomas Tenison] (London, 1679).

—— *The works of Francis Bacon*, ed. James Spedding, Robert Leslie Ellis, and Douglas Denon Heath, 14 vols. (London, 1857–74).

BAKER, DAVID ERSKINE, *Biographia dramatica; or, A companion to the playhouse*, continued by Isaac Reed and Stephen Jones, 3 vols. (London, 1812).

BAKER, J. H., *English legal manuscripts in the United States of America: A descriptive list, part II: Early modern and modern periods (1558-1902)* (London, 1990).

—— with RINGROSE, J. S., *A catalogue of English legal manuscripts in Cambridge University Library* (Woodbridge, 1996).

BALD, R. C., *John Donne: A life* (Oxford, 1970).

BARKER, JANE, *Poeticall recreations* (London, 1688).

—— *The lining of the patch-work screen* (London, 1726).

BAYLY, THOMAS, *The life & death of that renowned John Fisher, Bishop of Rochester* (London, 1655).

BAYNE, RONALD (ed.), T*he life of Fisher*, Early English Text Society, ES 117 (London, 1921).

BEAL, PETER, *Index of English literary manuscripts*, vol. i: *1450–1625*, parts 1 and 2 (London, 1980); vol. ii: *1625–1700*, parts 1 (1987) and 2 (1993).

—— 'More Donne manuscripts', *JDJ* 6/2 (1987), 213–18.

—— ' "My books are the great joy of my life": Sir William Boothby, seventeenth-century bibliophile', *BC*, 46/3(Autumn 1997), 350–78.

BEARD, GEOFFREY, *The work of Grinling Gibbons* (London, 1989).

BEAUMONT, FRANCIS, and FLETCHER, JOHN, *Comedies and tragedies* (London, 1647).

[BELLARMINO, ROBERTO], *Jacob's ladder consisting of fifteene degrees or ascents to the knowledge of God*, ed. H.I[saacson?] (London, 1637).

BIDWELL, WILLIAM B., and JANSSON, MAIJA (eds.), *Proceedings in Parliament 1626*, 4 vols. (New Haven, 1991–6).

BIRD, WILLIAM, enlarged by DODDERIDGE, Sir JOHN, *The magazine of honour; or, A treatise of . . . nobility* ([London], 1642).

BLOUNT, THOMAS, *Glossographia* (London, 1656).

BLOUNT, THOMAS POPE, *De re poetica* (London, 1694).

Bodleian Library, *A summary catalogue of western manuscripts in the Bodleian Library at Oxford*, ed. F. Madan, H. H. E. Craster, N. Denholm-Young, R. W. Hunt, and P. D. Record, 7 vols. (Oxford, 1895–1953).

—— *Summary catalogue of post-medieval western manuscripts in the Bodleian Library Oxford*, ed. Mary Clapinson and T. D. Rogers, 3 vols. (Oxford, 1991).

BODLEY, Sir THOMAS, *The life of Sir Thomas Bodley written by himself* (Oxford, 1647).

BORGES, J. L., 'The *Biathanatos*', in *Other inquisitions 1937–1952*, trans. Ruth L. C. Simms (London, 1973), 89–92.

BOSWELL, ELEANORE, *The Restoration court stage (1660–1702)* (London, 1932; reprinted 1966).

BRAUNMULLER, A. R., *A seventeenth-century letter-book: A facsimile edition of Folger MS. V.a.321* (Newark, NJ, 1983).

BRIQUET, C. M., *Les filigranes*: The New Briquet. Jubilee edition. General Editor J. S. G. Simmons. A facsimile of the 1907 edition with supplementary material contributed by a number of scholars, ed. Allan Stevenson, 4 vols. (Amsterdam, 1968).

British Library, *The British Library catalogue of Additions to the Manuscripts: The Yelverton Manuscripts*, 2 vols. (London, 1994).

—— *A catalogue of the Harleian collection of manuscripts . . . in the British Museum* [begun by H. Wanley, successively continued by D. Casley, W. Hocker, and C. Morton, with index by T. Astle, 2 vols., 1759–63; revised by R. Nares, S. Shaw, and F. Douce, with indexes by T. H. Horne], 4 vols. (London, 1808–12).

British Library, *A catalogue of the Lansdowne Manuscripts in the British Museum*, [ed. Sir Henry Ellis and Francis Douce] (London, 1819).

BROOKS, C. W., HELMHOLZ, R. H., and STEIN, P. G., *Notaries public in England since the Reformation* (London, 1991).

BULLEN, A. H. (ed.), *Davison's Poetical rhapsody*, 2 vols. (London, 1890).

BURFORD, E. J., *Bawds and lodgings: A history of the London Bankside brothels c.100–1675* (London, 1976).

BURGOYNE, FRANK J. (ed.), *Collotype facsimile & type transcript of an Elizabethan manuscript preserved at Alnwick Castle, Northumberland* (London, 1904).

BUTLER, SAMUEL, *Characters and passages from note-books*, ed. A. R. Waller (Cambridge, 1908).

Cabala: sive Scrinia sacra. Mysteries of state & government (London, 1654).

—— (London, 1663).

Calendar of State Papers, Domestic series, of the reign of Charles II. 1667 (1866).

—— Domestic series, November 1667 to September 1668 (1893).

—— relating to Ireland, 1660–1662 (1905).

—— relating to Ireland, 1663–1665 (1907).

CAMERON, KENNETH M., 'The Monmouth and Portsmouth troupes', *TN* 17 (1962–3), 89–94.

CAMERON, WILLIAM J. (ed.), *Poems on affairs of state*, volume v (New Haven, 1971).

CAPP, BERNARD, *The world of John Taylor the water poet 1578–1653* (Oxford, 1994).

CAREW, Sir GEORGE, *Reports or causes in Chancery, collected by Sir George Cary . . . out of the labours of Mr William Lambert* (London, 1650).

CAREW, RICHARD, *The survey of Cornwall* (London, 1602); revised edn., with the life of the author [by Pierre Des Maizeaux] (London, 1723).

CARLETON, MARY, *The case of Madam Mary Carleton* (London, 1663).

CARTWRIGHT, WILLIAM, *Comedies tragi-comedies, with other poems, by Mᵣ William Cartwright* (London, 1651).

CAVENDISH, MARGARET, Duchess of Newcastle, *Philosophicall fancies* (London, 1653).

—— *Poems and fancies* (London, 1653); facsimile edition (Menston, 1972).

—— *The world's olio* (London, 1655).

—— *Natures pictvres drawn by fancies pencil to the life* (London, 1656).

—— *Plays, never before printed* (London, 1668).

CAVENDISH, WILLIAM, Duke of Newcastle, *The country captain* (The Hague, 1649).

CECIL, Sir ROBERT, Earl of Salisbury, *The state and dignitie of secretarie of estates place* (London, 1642).

CHAMBERLAIN, JOHN, *The letters of John Chamberlain*, ed. Norman Egbert McClure, 2 vols. (Philadelphia, 1939).

CHARTIER, ROGER, *The order of books* (Stanford, Calif., 1994).

CHAUCER, GEOFFREY, *The works of Geoffrey Chaucer*, ed. F. N. Robinson, 2nd edn. (Boston, 1961).

CHERNAIK, WARREN, 'Books as memorials: The politics of consolation', *YES* 21 (1991), 207–17.

—— *Sexual freedom in Restoration literature* (Cambridge, 1995).

Christies' catalogues, 12 June 1980; 18 November 1988 (New York).

CHURCHILL, W. A., *Watermarks in paper in Holland, England, France, etc. in the XVII and XVIII centuries and their interconnection* (Amsterdam, 1935).

CLEVELAND, JOHN, *The character of a London-diurnall* (London, 1647).

CLIONAS, [Letter to Mr Urban on Hubert's poem on Edward II], *GM* 94/2 (July 1824), 19–22.

Cobbett's complete collection of state trials, [compiled by T. B. Howell and T. J. Howell], 33 vols. [and general index by David Jardine] (London, 1809–28).

COLEMAN, D. C., 'London scriveners and the estate market in the later seventeenth century', *Economic History Review*, 2nd ser. 4 (1951–2), 221–30.

COLLINS, ARTHUR, *Letters and memorials of state*, 2 vols. (London, 1746).

—— *Historical collections of the noble families of Cavendishe, Holles, Vere, Hartley, and Ogle* (London, 1752).

COLLINSON, PATRICK, 'The Elizabethan exclusion crisis and the Elizabethan polity', *PBA* 84 (Oxford, 1994), 51–92.

A Conference desired by the Lords . . . concerning the rights and privileges of the subjects (London, 1642).

CORNWALLIS, Sir CHARLES, *The life and death of our late most incomparable and heroique Prince Henry, Prince of Wales, &c.* (London, 1641).

COTTON, Sir ROBERT, *An answer made by command of Prince Henry* (London, 1655).

CRINÒ, ANNA MARIO (ed.), *I letterati della restaurazione nell' relazione magalottiana del 1668* (Florence, 1956).

CROFT, PAULINE, 'Annual Parliaments and the Long Parliament', *BIHR* 59 (1986), 155–71.

CROKE, Sir ALEXANDER, *The genealogical history of the Croke family, originally named Le Blount*, 2 vols. (Oxford, 1823).

CROSBY, ALLAN J., and BRUCE, JOHN (eds.), *Accounts and papers relating to Mary Queen of Scots*, Camden Society 93 (1867).

CRUM, MARGARET (ed.), *First-line index of English poetry 1500–1800 in manuscripts of the Bodleian Library Oxford*, 2 vols. (Oxford, 1969).

CUST, RICHARD, and LAKE, PETER G., 'Sir Richard Grosvenor and the rhetoric of magistracy', *BIHR* 54/129 (May 1981), 40–53.

DALE, T. C., *The inhabitants of London in 1638*, Society of Genealogists (London, 1931).

DAVIES, Sir JOHN, *The question concerning impositions* (London, 1656).

DEEDES, C., 'Unpublished letters of Sir Walter Ralegh', *N&Q* 8th ser. 3 (24 June 1893), 481–2; 4 (8 July–12 August 1893), 21–2, 63–4, 121–2.

DEKKER, THOMAS, *The non-dramatic works of Thomas Dekker*, ed. Alexander B. Grosart, 4 vols. (for private circulation, 1885).

—— *English villanies* (London, 1632).

—— *Lanthorne and candle-light. or The bell-mans second nights walke* (London, 1608); and 2nd edn. (London, 1609).

DENHAM, Sir JOHN, *Coopers hill* (London, 1642).

D'EWES, Sir SIMONDS, *The autobiography and correspondence of Sir Simonds D'Ewes, Bart.*, ed. James Orchard Halliwell, 2 vols. (London, 1845).

DIXON, ROBERT, *Canidia; or The witches. A rhapsody* (London, 1683).

DOBELL, P. J. and A. E., catalogues Nos. 73 and 80 (1928).

DODDERIDGE, Sir JOHN (ed.), *The several opinions of sundry learned antiquaries . . . touching . . . Parliament* (London, 1658).

DONNE, JOHN, *Pseudo Martyr* (London, 1610).

—— *Biathanatos: A declaration of that paradoxe, or thesis, that selfe-homicide is not so naturally sinne, that it may never be otherwise* (London, [1647]).

—— *Letters to severall persons of honour* (London, 1651).

—— *The poems of John Donne*, ed. Herbert J. C. Grierson, 2 vols. (Oxford, 1912; reprinted 1968).

—— *Biathanatos: Reproduced from the first edition*, ed. J. William Hebel, The Facsimile Text Society (New York, 1930).

—— *Biathanatos*, A modern-spelling edition, with Introduction and Commentary, by Michael Rudick and M. Pabst Battin (New York, 1982).

—— *Biathanatos by John Donne*, ed. Ernest W. Sullivan II (Newark, NJ, 1984).

DOWNES, JOHN, *Roscius Anglicanus* (London, 1708).

DRAPER, PETER, *The house of Stanley* (Ormskirk, 1864).

DRYDEN, JOHN, *The Indian Emperour* (London, 1667).

—— *The Spanish fryar or, The double discovery* (London, 1681).

—— *Amphitryon; or, The two Socia's* (London, 1690).

DUNCAN-JONES, KATHERINE, *Sir Philip Sidney: Courtier poet* (New Haven, 1991).

DYMOCKE, JAMES, *Le vice ridicule et la vertu louée* (Louvain, 1671).

EARLE, PETER, *The making of the English middle classes: Business, society and family life in London, 1660–1730* (London, 1989).

EARLE[S], JOHN, *The autograph manuscript of Microcosmographie: A Scolar Press facsimile* (Leeds, 1966).

EDWARD, FRANCIS O., S J, 'A letter book of the first Earl of Salisbury at Stonyhurst College, with special reference to the Spanish correspondence', *JSA* 4 (1972), 486–505.

EDWARDS, EDWARD, *The life of Sir Walter Ralegh*, 2 vols. (London, 1868).

EGERTON, Sir THOMAS, Baron Ellesmere, *The priviledges and prerogatives of the high court of Chancery* (London, 1641).

EGLISHAM, GEORGE, *Podromus vindictae* (London, 1626); and translated as *The forerunner of revenge* ('Franckfort' [i.e. The Netherlands?], 1626); and new edn. (London, 1642).

ELIZABETH I, *The poems of Queen Elizabeth I*, ed. Leicester Bradner (Providence, RI, 1964).

ELSYNGE, HENRY, *The ancient method and manner of holding of Parliaments in England* (London, 1660).

Evans's catalogue *Bibliotheca Sussexiana*, part V (April–May 1845).

EVELYN, JOHN, *Memoirs, illustrative of the life and writings of John Evelyn*, ed. William Bray, 2 vols. (London, 1818).

—— *The diary of John Evelyn*, ed. E. S. De Beer, 6 vols. (Oxford, 1955).

EZELL, MARGARET J. M., *The patriarch's wife* (Chapel Hill, NC, 1987).

Facetiae. Musarum deliciae: or, The muses recreation, ed. Thomas Park and Edward Dubois, 2 vols. (London, 1817); new edn. by J. C. Hotten, 2 vols. (London, 1874).

FAGAN, LOUIS, *A descriptive catalogue of the engraved works of William Faithorne* (London, 1888).

FALKUS, CHRISTOPHER, *The life and times of Charles II* (London, 1972).

FANSHAWE, THOMAS, *The practice of the Exchequer Court, with its severall offices and officers* (London, 1658).

FAUST, JOAN, 'John Donne's verse letters to the Countess of Bedford: Mediators in a poet–patroness relationship', *JDJ* 12 (1993), 79–99.

FINLAY, MICHAEL, *Western writing implements in the age of the quill pen* (Carlisle, 1990).

FITZMAURICE, JAMES, 'Fancy and the family: Self-characterizations of Margaret Cavendish', *HLQ* 53 (1990), 199–209.

FLEETWOOD, WILLIAM, *An unhappy view of the whole behaviour of . . . Buckingham* (London, 1648).

FRASER, ANTONIA, *The weaker vessel* (New York, 1984).

FÜSSNER, F. SMITH, *The historical revolution: English historical thought 1580–1640* (New York, 1962; reprinted Westport, Conn., 1962), 92–106.

GAGEN, JEAN, 'Honor and fame in the works of the Duchess of Newcastle', *SP* 56 (1959), 519–38.

GAUDRIAULT, RAYMOND, *Filigranes et autres caractéristiques des papiers fabriqués en France aux XVIIᵉ et XVIIIᵉ siècles* (Paris, 1995).

GILMOUR, MARGARET, *The great lady* (London, 1944).

GOLDBERG, JONATHAN, *Writing matter: From the hands of the English Renaissance* (Stanford, Calif., 1990).

GRANT, DOUGLAS, *Margaret the first* (London, 1957).

GRANVILLE, GEORGE, Lord Lansdowne, *The genuine works in verse and prose, of the Right Honourable George Granville, Lord Lansdowne*, 2 vols. (London, 1732).

GREER, GERMAINE, *Slip-shod sibyls: Recognition, rejection and the woman poet* (London, 1995).

—— HASTINGS, SUSAN, MEDOFF, JESLYN, and SANSONE, MELINDA (eds.), *Kissing the rod: An anthology of seventeenth-century women's verse* (London, 1988).

GREG, W. W., *A companion to Arber* (Oxford, 1967).

GROSVENOR, Sir RICHARD, *The papers of Sir Richard Grosvenor, 1st Bart. (1585–1645)*, ed. Richard Cust, Record Society of Lancashire and Cheshire, vol. 134 (1996).

[GUTCH, JOHN (ed.)], *Collectanea curiosa; or Miscellaneous tracts, relating to the history and antiquities of England and Ireland [etc.]*, 2 vols. (Oxford, 1781).

GUTTERIDGE, H. C., 'The origin and historical development of the profession of notaries public in England', in *Cambridge legal essays written in honour of . . . Doctor Bond, Professor Buckland and Professor Kenny* (Cambridge, 1926), 123–37.

H., G., [Letter to the editor, on Thomas Killigrew's account of the devils of Loudun], *European Magazine*, 43 (February 1803), 102–6.

HABERMAS, JÜRGEN, *The structural transformation of the public sphere: An inquiry into a category of bourgeois society*, trans. Thomas Burger with the assistance of Frederick Lawrence (Cambridge, Mass., 1991).

HAGEMAN, ELIZABETH H., 'The "false printed" broadside of Katherine Philips's "To the Queens Majesty on her happy arrival" ', *Library*, 6th ser. 17/4 (December 1995), 321–6.

—— and SUNUNU, ANDREA, 'New manuscript texts of Katherine Philips, the "matchless Orinda" ', *EMS* 4 (1993), 174–219.

—— —— ' "More copies of it abroad than I could have imagin'd": Further manuscript texts of Katherine Philips, "the matchless Orinda" ', *EMS* 5 (1995), 127–69.

HALL, JOHN, *Jacobs ladder: or, The devout souls ascention to Heaven* (London, 1672).

HAMILTON, ANTHONY, *Memoirs of the Comte de Gramont*, ed. Cyril Hughes Hartmann (New York, 1930).

HAMILTON, ELIZABETH, *The illustrious lady* (London, 1980).

HAMMOND, PAUL, 'Censorship in the manuscript transmission of Restoration poetry', *E&S* NS 46 (1993), 39–62.

HARGRAVE, FRANCIS, *Collectanea juridica*, 2 vols. (London, 1791–2).

HARRIS, TIM, 'The Bawdy House Riots of 1668', *HJ* 29 (1986), 537–56.

HASLER, P. W. (ed.), *The House of Commons, 1558–1603* (in The History of Parliament series), vol. i (London, 1981).

HAYMAN, ROBERT, *Qvodlibets, lately come over from New Britaniola, Old Newfovndland* (London, 1628).

HEAD, RICHARD, *Proteus redivivus: or The art of wheedling, or insinuation* (London, 1675).

HEARNE, THOMAS (ed.), *A collection of curious discourses written by eminent antiquaries upon several heads in our English antiquities*, 2nd edn., 2 vols. (London, 1771).

HEATH, JOHN, *The hovse of correction: or, Certayne satyricall epigrams, written by I.H. Gent. together with a few characters* (London, 1619).

HEAWOOD, EDWARD, *Watermarks mainly of the 17th and 18th centuries* (Hilversum, 1950; reprinted 1969).

HEHIR, BRENDAN O, *Harmony from discords: A life of Sir John Denham* (Berkeley, Calif., 1968).

Historical Manuscripts Commission, *First report of the Royal Commission on Historical Manuscripts* (1870).

—— *Third report of the Royal Commission on Historical Manuscripts* (1872).

—— *Fourth report of the Royal Commission on Historical Manuscripts* (1874).

—— *Sixth report of the Royal Commission on Historical Manuscripts* (1877).

—— *Seventh report of the Royal Commission on Historical Manuscripts* (1879).

HOBBS, MARY, 'An edition of the Stoughton Manuscript . . . connected with Henry King . . . seen in relation to other contemporary poetry and song collections', Ph.D. thesis (University of London, 1973).

—— *Early seventeenth-century verse miscellany manuscripts* (Aldershot, 1992).

Hofmann & Freeman, catalogue No. 21 (January 1968).

HOLDSWORTH, Sir WILLIAM, *A history of English law*, 16 vols. (London, 1924).

HOLMES, MARTIN, and SITWELL, H. D. W., *The English regalia* (London, 1972).

HORNBLOWER, SIMON, and SPAWFORTH, ANTONY (eds.), *The Oxford classical dictionary*, 3rd edn. (Oxford, 1996).

HOWARD, WILLIAM, *Selections from the household books of the Lord William Howard of Naworth Castle*, Surtees Society 68 (1878).

HOWELL, JAMES (ed.), *Cottoni posthuma: Divers choice pieces of that renowned antiquary Sir Robert Cotton, knight and baronet* (London, 1651).

HUBERT, Sir FRANCIS, *The poems of Sir Francis Hubert*, ed. Bernard Mellor (Hong Kong, 1961).

HUGHES, PHILIP (ed.), *Saint John Fisher: The earliest English life* (London, 1935).

HUGHEY, RUTH, *John Harington of Stepney, Tudor gentleman: His life and works* (Columbus, Oh., 1971).

HUXLEY, ALDOUS, *The devils of Loudun* (London, 1952).

HYDE, RALPH, with FISHER, JOHN, and CLINE, ROGER, *The A to Z of Restoration London* (Lympne Castle, 1992).

JACKSON, WILLIAM A., 'Humphrey Dyson and his collections of Elizabethan proclamations', *HLB* 1 (1947), 76–89.

JAGER, ERIC, 'Did Eve invent writing? Script and the Fall in "The Adam Books" ', *SP* 93 (1996), 229–50.

JENKINS, R. T., *Orinda* (Caerdydd, Hughes a'i Fab, 1943).

JINNER, SARAH, *An almanack or prognostication for the year of our Lord 1658* (London, [1657/8]).

JOHNSON, ROBERT C., JANSSON COLE, MAIJA, KEELER, MARY FREAR, and BIDWELL, WILLIAM B. (eds.), *Commons debates 1628*, 6 vols. (New Haven, 1977–83) [last two volumes of the series retitled *Proceedings in Parliament 1628*].

JONES, KATHLEEN, *A glorious fame* (London, 1988).

JONES, NORMAN, *God and the moneylenders: Usury and law in early modern England* (Oxford, 1989).

JONSON, BEN, *The workes of Benjamin Jonson 1616*, facsimile edition by The Scolar Press (London, 1976).

——— *The workes of Benjamin Jonson the second [and third] volume* (London, 1640).

JORDAN, THOMAS, *Pictures of passions, fancies, & affections. Poetically deciphered in variety of characters* (London, 1641).

KEETON, G. W., *Lord Chancellor Jeffreys and the Stuart cause* (London, 1965).

KERRIDGE, ERIC, *Trade and banking in early modern England* (Manchester, 1988).

KILLIGREW, THOMAS, *Comedies and tragedies* (London, 1664).

KING, HENRY, *Poems* (London, 1657).

LAMBARDE, WILLIAM, *Archion* (London, 1635).

——— *Archeion*, 2nd edn. (London, 1635).

LANGBAINE, GERARD, *An account of the English dramatick poets* (Oxford, 1691).

LANGE, THOMAS, 'A rediscovered Esther Inglis calligraphic manuscript in the Huntington Library', *PBSA* 89 (1995), 339–42.

LAWES, HENRY, *Ayres and dialogues, the second book* (London, 1655).

LEMPRIERE, JOHN, *Bibliotheca classica; or, A classical dictionary* (Reading, 1788), 3rd revised edn. by F. A. Wright and R. Willets (London 1984).

LENTON, FRANCIS, *Characterismi: or, Lentons leasvres. Expressed in essayes and characters, neuer before written on* (London, 1631).

LILLYWHITE, BRYANT, *London signs: A reference book of London signs from earliest times to about the mid-nineteenth century* (London, 1972).

LINDENBAUM, PETER, 'Milton's contract', *Cardozo Arts & Entertainment Law Journal*, 10/2 (1992), 439–54.

——— 'The poet in the marketplace: Milton and Samuel Simmons', in P. G. Stanwood (ed.), *Of poetry and politics: New essays on Milton and his world* (Binghamton, NY, 1994), 249–62.

——— 'Authors and publishers in the late seventeenth century: New evidence on their relations', *Library*, 6th ser. 17/3 (September 1995), 250–69.

LORD, GEORGE DeF. (ed.), *Poems on affairs of state*, vol. i (New Haven, 1963).

LOSCOCCO, PAULA, ' "Manly sweetness": Katherine Philips among the neoclassicals', *HLQ* 56/3 (Summer 1993), 259–79.

LOVE, HAROLD, *Scribal publication in seventeenth-century England* (Oxford, 1993).

——— 'The Feathery Scribe', *TLS* 23 August 1996, p. 11.

LUND, ROGER D., '*Bibliotecha* [sic] and "the British dames": An early critique of the female wits of the Restoration', *Restoration*, 12 (1988), 96–105.

LYLY, JOHN, *The complete works of John Lyly*, ed. R. Warwick Bond, 3 vols. (Oxford, 1902; reprinted 1967).

LYNCH, KATHLEEN M., *Roger Boyle first Earl of Orrery* (Knoxville, Tenn., 1965).

MacDonald, William W., *The making of an English revolutionary* (London, 1982).

McKenzie, D. F., *Bibliography and the sociology of texts: The Panizzi Lectures 1985* (London, 1986).

—— 'Speech-manuscript-print', *LCUTA* 20 (1990), 87–109.

—— 'The London book trade in 1644', in John Horden (ed.), *Bibliographia* (Leeds, 1992), 131–51.

Maggs Bros., catalogues, No. 423 (1922); No. 550 (1931); No. 1212, *Bookbindings in the British Isles . . . part I* (summer 1996).

Manguel, Alberto, *A history of reading* (London, 1996).

Manley, Mrs [Delarivière], *The lost lover; or, The jealous husband* (London, 1696).

Marotti, Arthur F., *Manuscript, print, and the English Renaissance lyric* (Ithaca, NY, 1995).

Martin, Henri-Jean, *The history and power of writing* [1988], trans. Lydia G. Cochrane (Chicago, 1994).

Matthews, L. G., and Green, H. J. M., 'Post-medieval pottery of the Inns of Court', *Post-Medieval Archaeology*, 3 (1969), 1–17.

Melton, Frank T., *Sir Robert Clayton and the origins of English deposit banking, 1658–1685* (Cambridge, 1986).

Mengel, Elias F., Jr, (ed.), *Poems on affairs of state*, vol. ii (New Haven, 1965).

Mercurius Hibernicus No. 10, for 17–24 March 1662/3.

Mercurius Publicus for 25 June to 2 July 1663.

Michelmore, G., catalogue, *Two hundred extraordinarily important books* (*c*.1930).

Milhous, Judith, and Hume, Robert D., 'Lost English plays, 1660–1700', *HLB* 25 (1977), 5–33.

Miller, C. William, 'Henry Herringman, Restoration bookseller-publisher', *PBSA* 42 (1948), 292–306.

Moody, Ellen, 'Orinda, Rosania, Lucasia *et aliae* [*sic*]: Towards a new edition of the works of Katherine Philips', *PQ* 66 (1987), 325–54.

Morgan, Fidelis, *A woman of no character: An autobiography of Mrs Manley* (London, 1986).

Murphy, Gwendolen, *A bibliography of English character books 1608–1700* (Bibliographical Society, 1925).

—— *A cabinet of characters* (London, 1925).

Nashe, Thomas, *The works of Thomas Nashe*, ed. R. B. McKerrow, rev. F. P. Wilson, 5 vols. (Oxford, 1958–66).

Naunton, Sir Robert, *Fragmenta regalia* (London, 1641).

Nevinson, J. L., 'Lively drawings of a Suffolk scrivener', *Country Life Annual* (1964), 156–8.

[Newcomb, Revd Thomas], *Bibliotheca: A poem. Occasion'd by the sight of a modern library* (London, 1712).

Nicholas, Sir Edward, *Proceedings and debates of the House of Commons in 1620 and 1621*, 2 vols. (Oxford, 1766).

Nichols, John, *The progresses and public processions of Queen Elizabeth*, 4 vols. (London, 1788–1821); 2nd edn. 3 vols. (London, 1823).

Nicolas, Nicholas Harris, *Life of William Davison, secretary of state and privy counsellor to Queen Elizabeth* (London, 1823).

Nicoll, Allardyce, *Restoration drama* (Cambridge, 1923; 4th edn., reprinted 1977).

NIXON, HOWARD M., *Catalogue of the Pepys Library at Magdalene College Cambridge*, vol. vi: *Bindings* (Cambridge, 1984).

NOEL, NATHANIEL, catalogue, *Bibliotheca nobilissimi principis Johannis Ducis de Novo-Castro, &c.*, 17 March 1718/19.

NORTH, MARCY, 'Ignoto in the age of print: The manipulation of anonymity in early modern England', *SP* 91 (1994), 390–416.

NOTESTEIN, WALLACE, and RELF, FRANCES HELEN (eds.), *Commons debates for 1629*, (Minneapolis, 1921).

—— —— and SIMPSON, HARTLEY (eds.), *Commons debates 1621*, 7 vols. (New Haven, 1935).

O'DONNELL, MARY ANN, 'A verse miscellany of Aphra Behn: Bodleian Library MS Firth c.16', *EMS* 2 (1990), 189–227.

ONG, WALTER J., *Orality and literacy: The technologizing of the word* (1982; reprinted London, 1990).

OPIE, IONA and PETER (eds.), *The Oxford dictionary of nursery rhymes* (Oxford, 1951; reprinted 1983).

OSBORNE, DOROTHY, *Letters to Sir William Temple*, ed. Kenneth Parker (London, 1987).

OVERBURY, Sir THOMAS, *The miscellaneous works in prose and verse of Sir Thomas Overbury, Knt. now first collected*, ed. Edward F. Rimbault, LL D. (London, 1890).

—— *New and choise characters, of seueral authors: Together with that exquisite and unmatcht poeme, The wife, written by Syr Thomas Ouerburie* (London, 1615).

—— *Sr Thomas Ouerbury his wife* (London, 1616).

PAGE, WILLIAM (ed.), *The Victoria history of the county of Bedford*, vol. iii (London, 1912).

PARKER, WILLIAM RILEY, *Milton: A biography*, 2 vols. (Oxford, 1968).

The parliamentary history of England from the earliest period to the year 1803, vol. i: *1066–1625* (London, 1806) and vol. ii: *1625–1642* (London, 1807).

PARRY, GRAHAM, 'Cavendish memorials', *Seventeenth Century*, 9/2 (Autumn 1994), 275–87.

PATTERSON, ANNABEL, *Censorship and interpretation* (Madison, Wisc., 1984).

PEARLMAN, E., 'Pepys and Lady Castlemaine', *Restoration*, 7 (1983), 43–53, and related correspondence: 9 (1985), 31–8.

PECK, D. C. (ed.), *Leicester's commonwealth: The copy of a letter written by a Master of Art of Cambridge (1584) and related documents* (Athens, Oh., 1985).

PECK, FRANCIS, *Desiderata curiosa*, 2 vols. (London, 1779).

PEPYS, SAMUEL, *Letters and the second diary of Samuel Pepys*, ed. R. G. Howarth (London, 1932).

—— *The diary of Samuel Pepys*, ed. Robert Latham and William Matthews, 11 vols. (London, 1970–83).

PETRARCA, FRANCESCO, *Hülff Trost und Rath in allemanligen der Menschen* (Frankfurt, 1559).

PHILIPS, KATHERINE, *To the Queens Majesty on her happy arrival* (London, 1662).

—— *Pompey: A tragoedy* (Dublin, 1663).

—— *Poems by the incomparable, Mrs. K.P.* (London, 1664).

—— *Poems by the most deservedly admired Mrs. Katherine Philips the matchless Orinda* (London, 1667; reprinted London, 1669).

—— *The collected works of Katherine Philips the matchless Orinda*, ed. Patrick Thomas, Germaine Greer, and R. Little, 3 vols. (Stump Cross, 1990–3).

Philips, Katherine, *Poems (1667) by Katherine Philips*, A facsimile reproduction with an introduction by Travis Dupriest (Delmar, NY, 1992).

Phillips's catalogues, 11 November 1993; 8 September 1994.

Poems, by several persons (Dublin, 1663).

Pollard, A. F., 'Hayward Townshend's journals. III', *BIHR* 14 (1936–7), 149–65.

Pollard, A. W., and Redgrave, G. R., *A short-title catalogue of books printed in England, Scotland, & Ireland and of English books printed abroad 1475–1640*, first compiled by A. W. Pollard and G. R. Redgrave, 2nd edn. revised, begun by W. A. Jackson and F. S. Ferguson, completed by Katharine F. Pantzer, 3 vols. (London, 1976–91).

Pritchard, Allan, 'George Wither's quarrel with the Stationers: An anonymous reply to *The schollers purgatory*', *SB* 16 (1963), 27–42.

Proclamation for the suppressing of seditious and treasonable books and pamphlets, 31 October 1679.

Procter, Brian W., *Effigies poeticae, or the portraits of the British poets*, 2 vols. (London, 1824).

Puttick & Simpson's catalogue for 3 July 1850.

Ralegh, Sir Walter, *The prerogative of Parliaments in England* ([London], 1628).

—— [attrib.], *The cabinet-council: Containing the cheif arts of empire* (London, 1658).

—— [attrib.], *The arts of empire and mysteries of state* (London, 1692).

—— [attrib., but correctly Samuel Daniel], *An introduction to a breviary of the history of England* (London, 1693).

Ramsay, Nigel, 'Forgery and the rise of the London Scriveners' Company', in Robin Myers and Michael Harris (eds.), *Fakes and frauds* (Winchester, 1989), 99–108.

Ravenscroft, Thomas, *Melismata. Mvsicall phansies. fitting the covrt, citie, and covntrey hvmovrs to 3, 4, and 5. voyces* (London, 1611).

Raworth, Francis, *Jacobs ladder, or The protectorship of Sion* (London, 1655).

Reade, Aleyn Lyell, 'Michael Johnson and Lord Derby's library', *TLS* 27 July 1940, pp. 363, 365.

Richards, R. D., *The early history of banking in England* (London, 1929).

Rushworth, John, *Historical collections*, 7 vols. (London, 1659–1701).

Saltonstall, Wye, *Picturae loquentes. or Pictures drawne forth in characters* (London, 1631); 2nd edn. (London, 1635).

Sanders, G. W. (ed.), *Orders of the high court of Chancery and statutes of the realm relating to chancery*, vol. i, pts. 1, 2 (London, 1845).

Sant, Patricia M., and Brown, James N., 'Two unpublished poems by Katherine Philips', *ELR* 24 (1994), 211–25.

Sawyer, Edmund, *Memorials of affairs of state . . . collected (chiefly) from the original papers of the Rt. Hon. Sir Ralph Winwood*, 3 vols. (London, 1725).

Schofield, B., 'The Yelverton Manuscripts', *BMQ* 19 (1954), 3–9.

Scott-Elliot, A. H., and Yeo, Elspeth, 'Calligraphic manuscripts of Esther Inglis (1571–1624): A catalogue', *PBSA* 84 (1990), 11–86.

Scrinia Caeciliana: Mysteries of state & government . . . being a further additional supplement of the Cabala (London, 1663).

Scrinia sacra; secrets of empire . . . a supplement of the Cabala (London, 1654).

Seaton, Ethel, *Literary relations of England and Scandinavia in the seventeenth century* (Oxford, 1935).

Selden, John, *The priviledges of the baronage of England* (London, 1642).

—— *A brief discourse touching the office of Lord Chancellor of England* (London, 1671).

—— *England's epinomis* (London, 1683).

SELLIN, PAUL R., *So doth, so is religion: John Donne and diplomatic contexts in the Reformed Netherlands, 1619–1620* (Columbia, Mo., 1988).

SERGEANT, PHILIP W., *My Lady Castlemaine* (London, 1912).

SHAKESPEARE, WILLIAM, *Comedies, histories, & tragedies* (London, 1623).

SHARPE, KEVIN, *Sir Robert Cotton 1588-1631: History and politics in early modern England* (Oxford, 1979).

SHERMAN, SANDRA, 'Trembling texts: Margaret Cavendish and the dialectic of authorship', *ELR* 24 (1994), 184–210.

SHIFFLETT, ANDREW, ' "How many virtues must I hate?": Katherine Philips and the politics of clemency', *SP* 94 (1997), 103–35.

SHIRLEY, JAMES, *Poems* (London, 1646); Scolar Press Facsimile (Menston, 1970).

SHIRLEY, JOHN W., *Thomas Harriot: A biography* (Oxford, 1983).

SIDNEY, Sir PHILIP, *The prose works of Sir Philip Sidney*, ed. Albert Feuillerat, 4 vols. (Cambridge, 1912; reprinted 1968).

—— *The poems of Sir Philip Sidney*, ed. William A. Ringler, Jr (Oxford, 1962).

—— *The Countess of Pembroke's Arcadia (The Old Arcadia)*, ed. Jean Robertson (Oxford, 1973).

—— *Miscellaneous prose of Sir Philip Sidney*, ed. Katherine Duncan-Jones and Jan Van Dorsten (Oxford, 1973).

SIMPSON, EVELYN M., *A study of the prose works of John Donne* (Oxford, 1924; 2nd edn., 1948).

SMITH, HENRY, *Iacobs ladder, or The high way to Heaven* (London, 1595).

SMITH, Sir WILLIAM, *A classical dictionary of Greek and Roman biography, mythology and geography* [1842], revised edn. by G. E. Marindin *et al.* (London, 1894).

SOMERS, Lord, *A collection of scarce and valuable tracts, on the most interesting and entertaining subjects . . . particularly that of the late Lord Somers. The second edition revised . . . by Walter Scott*, 13 vols. (London, 1809–15).

Sotheby's catalogues, 5 June 1899; 17 June 1904; 13 July 1920; 9 April 1935; 4 July 1955; 31 July 1962; 19 July 1966; 20 February 1967; 14 December 1976; 6–7 December 1984; 22 November 1989; 15 December 1992; 14 December 1993; 19 July 1994; 13 December 1994; 15 May 1996; 16–17 December 1996.

SOUERS, PHILIP WEBSTER, *The matchless Orinda* (Cambridge, Mass., 1931).

SPELMAN, Sir HENRY, *Reliquiae Spelmannianae: The posthumous works of Sir Henry Spelman Kt.*, [ed. Edmund Gibson] (Oxford, 1698).

STANLEY, JAMES, Earl of Derby, *Private devotions and miscellanies of James seventh Earl of Derby, K.G.*, ed. Revd F. R. Raines, vol. i (Chetham Society 66, 1867).

STARKEY, RALPH, *The briefe contents of Ralph Starkye's bill, exhibited in Parliament* [London, 1628?].

—— *The priviledge and practice of Parliament* (London, 1628).

STEELE, R. L., 'Humphrey Dyson', *Library*, 3rd ser. 1 (1910), 144–51.

STEER, FRANCIS W. (ed.), *Scriveners' Company Common Paper 1357–1628* (London Record Society, 1968).

—— *A history of the Worshipful Company of Scriveners of London* (London, 1973).

STEINMAN, G. STEINMAN, *A memoir of Barbara Duchess of Cleveland* (privately circulated, 1871).

STEPHENS, JOHN, *Satyrical essayes characters and others, or Accurate and quick descriptions, fitted to the life of their subiects* (London, 1615).

STOW, JOHN, *A survey of London*, ed. Charles Lethbridge Kingsford, 2 vols. (Oxford, 1908).

Strawberry Hill sale catalogue, by George Robins, 25 April (and 23 following days) 1842.

STROUD, DOROTHY, 'Woburn Abbey, Bedfordshire: The last phase—I', *Country Life*, 8 July 1965.

STUBBS, JOHN, *The discouerie of a gaping gulf whereinto England is like to be swallowed by an other French mariage* (London, 1579).

—— *John Stubbs's Gaping gulf with letters and other relevant documents*, ed. Lloyd E. Berry (Charlottesville, Va., 1968).

STYLES, PHILIP, 'Politics and historical research in the early seventeenth century', in Levi Fox (ed.), *English historical scholarship in the sixteenth and seventeenth centuries* (London, 1956), 49–72.

SUCKLING, Sir JOHN, *Fragmenta aurea* (London, 1646).

SULLIVAN II, ERNEST W., 'The problem of text in Familiar Letters', *PBSA* 75 (1981), 115–126.

SUZUKI, MIHOKO, 'The case of Mary Carleton: Representing the female subject, 1663–73', *TSWL* 12/1 (Spring 1993), 61–83.

TAUBERT, SIGFRED, *Bibliopola . . . pictures and texts about the book trade*, 2 vols. (London, 1966).

TAYLOR, JEREMY, *Chrisis Teleiotike: A discourse of confirmation* (Dublin, 1663).

TAYLOR, JOHN, *A short relation of a long iourney made round or ovall by encompassing the Principalitie of Wales* [London, 1653].

TEMPLE, Sir WILLIAM, *The works of Sir William Temple, Bart.*, 4 vols. (London, 1814).

The thirtieth annual report of the Deputy Keeper of the Public Records (1869).

TINKER, NATHAN, 'John Grismond: Printer of the unauthorized edition of Katherine Philips's Poems (1664)', *ELN* 34/1 (September 1996), 30–5.

TITE, COLIN G. C., ' "Lost or stolen or strayed": A survey of manuscripts formerly in the Cotton Library', *BLJ* 18 (1992), 107–47.

—— *The manuscript library of Sir Robert Cotton: The Panizzi lectures 1993* (London, 1994).

TODD, JANET, *The secret life of Aphra Behn* (London, 1996).

TOWNSHEND, HAYWARD, *Historical collections* (London, 1680).

TREGASKIS, JAMES, catalogue No. 1022 (1948).

TRITHEMIUS, JOHANNES, *De laude scriptorum* (Mainz, 1494).

—— *In praise of scribes (De laude scriptorum)*, trans. Roland Behrendt, OSB, ed. Klaus Arnold (Lawrence, Kan., 1974).

—— *In praise of scribes (De laude scriptorum)*, trans. Elizabeth Bryson Bongie, ed. Michael S. Batts (Alcuin Society: Vancouver, 1977).

TWINING, Lord, *A history of the Crown Jewels of Europe* (London, 1960).

URRY, WILLIAM, *Christopher Marlowe and Canterbury* (London, 1988).

VAN LENNEP, WILLIAM (ed.), *The London stage 1660–1800*, part 1: *1660–1700* (Carbondale, Ill., 1965).

VAN NORDEN, LINDA, 'Sir Henry Spelman on the chronology of the Elizabethan College of Antiquaries', *HLQ* 13 (1949–50), 131–60.

VAN ORTROY, Fr, SJ (ed.), *Vie du bienheureux martyr Jean Fisher* (Brussels, 1893).

VAN STRIEN, KEES, 'Owen Felltham's *A brief character of the Low-Countries*: A survey of the texts', *EMS* 6 (1997), 132–74.

VANE, HENRY, *A pilgrimage into the land of promise, by the light of the vision of Jacobs ladder and faith* ([Holland], 1664).

VERSTEGAN, RICHARD, *A declaration of the true causes of the great troubles, presupposed to be intended against England* ([Antwerp], 1592).

VILLIERS, GEORGE, Duke of Buckingham, *Works*, 2 vols. (London, 1703).

VONNEGUT, KURT, *Palm Sunday* (New York, 1981).

WALL, JOHN, *Jacobs ladder or Christian advancement* (Oxford, 1626).

WARD, PAUL L., 'William Lambarde's Collections on Chancery', *HLB* 7 (1953), 271–98.

WATSON, ANDREW G., *The library of Sir Simonds D'Ewes* (London, 1966).

WELDON, Sir ANTHONY, *A perfect description of the people and country of Scotland* (London, 1649).

WELLS, JEREMIAH, *The character of a London scrivener*, printed with Abraham Cowley, *Poems upon divers occasions* (London, 1667).

WELSBY, PAUL A., *George Abbot: The unwanted archbishop 1562–1633* (London, 1962).

WERNHAM, R. B., 'The public records in the sixteenth and seventeenth centuries', in Levi Fox (ed.), *English historical scholarship in the sixteenth and seventeenth centuries* (London, 1956), 11–30.

WEST, WILLIAM, *Symbolaeographia, which may be termed the art, description, or image of instruments, covenants, contracts, &c., or the notarie or scriuenor* (London, 1590).

WILLIAMSON, MARILYN L., *Raising their voices: British women writers, 1650–1750* (Detroit, 1990).

WILSON, JOHN HAROLD (ed.), *The Rochester–Savile letters 1671–1680* (Columbus, Oh., 1941).

—— *Court satires of the Restoration* (Columbus, Oh., 1976).

WILSON, THOMAS, *Jacobs ladder, or A short treatise laying forth distinctly the seuerall degrees of Gods eternall purpose* (London, 1611).

WING, DONALD, *Short-title catalogue of books printed in England, Scotland, Ireland, Wales, and British America and of English books printed in other countries 1641–1700*, compiled by Donald Wing, 2nd edn. revised, 3 vols. (New York, 1982–94).

WINSTANLEY, GERRARD, *The law of freedom and other writings*, ed. Christopher Hill (Cambridge, 1983).

Witt's recreations (London, 1640), and 2nd edn. (London, 1641).

WOLLMAN, RICHARD B., 'The "press and the fire": Print and manuscript culture in Donne's circle', *SEL* 33 (1993), 85–97.

WORDEN, BLAIR, *The sound of virtue: Philip Sidney's Arcadia and Elizabethan politics* (New Haven, 1996).

WOTTON, Sir HENRY, *Reliquiae Wottonianae* (London, 1651).

WOUDHUYSEN, H. R., 'A crux in the text of Sidney's *A letter to Queen Elizabeth*', *N&Q* 229 (June 1984), 172–3.

—— *Sir Philip Sidney and the circulation of manuscripts 1558–1640* (Oxford, 1996).

WRIGHT, CYRIL ERNEST, 'The Elizabethan Society of Antiquaries and the formation of the Cottonian Library', in Francis Wormald and C. E. Wright (eds.), *The English library before 1700* (London 1958), 176–212.

—— *Fontes Harleiani* (London, 1972).

WRIGHT, R. W. M., *The pictorial history of Bath Abbey* (Stockport, 1962).

WYCHERLEY, WILLIAM, *The complete works of William Wycherley*, ed. Montague Summers, 4 vols. (London, 1924).

YOUNGHUSBAND, Sir GEORGE, *The Crown Jewels of England* (London, 1919).

General Index

Abbot, George, Archbishop 239, 247, 264, 266
Acland-Hood family 95, 261–2
Adrian VI, Pope 262
Agard, Arthur 90, 221, 226
Alençon, François, Duc d' ('Monsieur') 80,
    109–46 *passim*, 223, 224, 233, 238, 243, 245,
    247, 251, 261, 267, 269, 274–80
Alexander, Sir Jerome 95, 222, 223, 225, 226
Alured, Thomas 228
Amherst, William Amhurst-Tyssen-Amherst, first
    Baron 226, 276
Ancrum, Sir Robert Ker, Earl of 31, 32, 35, 37,
    54, 55
Anjou, François, Duc d' *see* Alençon, François,
    Duc d'
Anne, Queen 96, 235
Anne Boleyn, Queen 242–3, 249
Anne of Denmark, Queen 212, 230, 264, 271
Anstis, John 96, 232, 245
Archilochus 284 n. 20
Aristotle 53, 154
Armagh, Archbishop of 234
Arthur, Prince 259
Arundell, Charles 254
Arundel, Thomas Howard, second Earl of 107,
    213
Ashley, George 77, 249
Ashmole, Elias 175 n. 65, 275
Aston, Herbert 190 n. 113
Aston, Sir Roger 264
Atye, Sir Arthur 91 n. 39
Aubrey, John 165, 175 n. 64
Aubrey, Mary ('Rosania') 148, 168–73,
    175 n. 64, 178 n. 69, 281 n. 3
Audiguier, Vital d' 177 n. 67
Augustine, St 53
Augustus, Caesar 143
Ayton, Sir Robert 257

Babington, Anthony 230, 257
Bacon, Sir Francis, Viscount St Albans 18 n. 70,
    81, 82, 84–6, 92, 214, 215, 217, 220, 222, 223,
    227, 229, 231, 233, 239, 246, 248, 251, 252,
    253, 256, 260, 261, 263, 265, 267, 271, 272,
    273, 283 n. 14
Bacon, Sir Nicholas 91 n. 38, 219, 228, 247,
    265–6, 269
Bagford, John 278
Baker, Thomas 217
Ballenden, Sir Lewis 230
Balley, Richard 178 n. 68
Bankes, Sir John 216

Barker, Jane 178 n. 70
Barkham, Sir Edward 239
Barlow, Thomas, Bishop of Lincoln 95, 259, 260
Barnavelt, Sir John van Olden 270
Barneres, Robert 88 n. 26
Bassompierre, François, Baron de 243
Battin, M. Pabst 37–8, 46–7 n. 29, 51–2
Baynings, Sir Paul 239
Beale, Robert 4 n. 11, 119–21, 229, 230, 276
Beaumont, Francis 165, 178, 257
Bedford, Edward Russell, third Earl of 57
Bedford, Francis Russell, fourth Earl of 57
Bedford, John Russell, fourth Duke of 56
Bedford, Lucy, Countess of 57
Behn, Aphra 77 n. 16, 163, 174 n. 63
Bennet, Sir John 3 n. 8
Berkeley, Sir Robert 216
Berkenhead, Sir John ('Cratander') 190 n. 116
Betenson, Sir Richard 95, 214
Betterton, Thomas 187 n. 106
Bingham, Sir Richard 234
Birch, Thomas 227
Bird, William 105, 226, 242, 251, 265, 271
Blackett, Mrs 175 n. 64
Blount, Christopher 248
Bodley, Sir Thomas 223, 253, 261, 270
Bohun, Ralph 154 n. 19
Boleyn, Anne *see* Anne Boleyn
Boothby, Sir William 19 n. 72
Borges, Jorge Luis 32
Boye, Surlye 248
Boyle family 160–1, 178 n. 68
Bramston, Sir John 215–16
Bridgewater, John Egerton, first Earl of 215,
    269
Bridgewater, John Egerton, second Earl of 182
Bristol, George Digby, first Earl of 222, 232, 236,
    237, 247, 256, 263
Brooke, John 238
Brooke, Sir Thomas 214, 218
Browne, Sir Anthony 214, 247, 270
Bruce, Edward, second Lord 230, 232
Buckingham, George Villiers, first Duke of 106,
    212, 222, 231, 232, 236, 237, 240, 244, 247,
    271, 272, 273
Buckingham, George Villiers, second Duke of 20,
    29 n. 85 & n. 88, 184
Buckley, James 211
Burghley, William Cecil, Lord 4, 71, 109, 122,
    125–6, 213, 215, 222, 227, 231, 233, 238, 240,
    248, 250, 270, 273, 277
Butler, Samuel 203

Caesar, Sir Julius 88 n. 26
Calvert, George, first Lord Baltimore 90 n. 32, 223, 225
Camden, William 106, 221, 226, 229, 255, 265
Cameron, W. J. 45
Campion, Thomas 257
Capel, Revd. William 56
Carbery, Earl and Countess of 151 n. 15, 182 n. 83
Carew, Sir George 220–1, 262, 272
Carey, Sir George, second Baron Hunsdon 215
Carleton, Mary 177 n. 67
Carlisle, Lucy Hay, Countess of 233
Carr, Sir Robert, Earl of Somerset *see* Somerset, Earl of
Carte, John 254
Cartwright, William 153, 155–6, 164, 172
Castlehaven, Mervyn Touchet, second Earl of 222–3, 232, 265
Castlemaine, Barbara Villiers, Countess of (later Duchess of Cleveland) 175 n. 65, 180–4, 185, 187–8, 190–1
Catherine of Braganza, Queen 155, 158, 159, 187, 190, 191
Cavendish, Mary Butler, Lady ('Policrite') 151 n. 17, 180 n. 76
Cavendish, Margaret *see* Newcastle, Margaret Cavendish, Duchess of
Cavendish, William *see* Newcastle, William Cavendish, Duke of
Cecil, Sir Edward *see* Wimbledon, Viscount
Cecil, Sir Robert, first Earl of Salisbury 212, 216, 221, 222, 225, 229, 230, 231–2, 234, 239, 241, 247, 250, 251, 252, 255, 257, 259–60, 261, 263, 264, 270, 272
Cecil, Theodosia 250, 263
Chamberlain, John 5
Charles I 90 n. 33, 95, 105, 108, 134, 139, 226, 227, 228, 234, 236, 237, 238, 241, 243, 244, 247, 249, 253, 256, 263, 272
Charles II 20, 25, 164, 182 n. 82, 184, 187, 188, 190
Charles V 136, 143
Chaucer, Geoffrey 8, 165
Chernaik, Warren 163
Christian IV, King of Denmark 227–8
Clanricarde, Richard de Burgh, fourth Earl of 248
Clarence, Thomas, Duke of 262–3
Clarendon, Edward Hyde, first Earl of 10, 191 n. 120, 222, 244
Clarke, George 163 n. 45
Clarke, Sir William 163 n. 45
Clayton, Sir Robert 210
Clifton, Sir Gervase 34
Coats, John 88 n. 26
Cock, F. William 267
Cockyn, Henry 276

Coke, Sir Edward 5, 90 n. 32, 105, 219, 236, 237, 241, 247, 253, 258, 271
Coke, Sir John 234, 237
Colchester, Thomas Darcy, Viscount 199
Collins, Arthur 116 n. 18
Company of Scriveners 2–3 n. 7, 65
Constable, Henry 247, 270
Constable, Sir John 92
Conway, Sir Edward, first Viscount 34–5, 90 n. 32
Conway, Edward, second Viscount 237
Coolidge, William Appleton 218
Cope, Sir Walter 216, 261, 272
Corbett, Richard 218
Cork, Richard Boyle, Earl of 160
Corneille, Pierre 155, 180, 185, 188 n. 108, 190
Cornwallis, Mrs 184
Cornwallis, Sir Charles 77, 91, 105, 217, 218, 223, 224, 225, 227, 229, 230, 231–2, 240, 244, 246, 253, 263, 272
Corrie, Alfred Wynne 218
Coryton, William 236, 265, 272
Cotterell, Sir Charles 155 n. 29, 156, 159, 162, 164, 178 n. 68, 185, 281 n. 4
Cottington, Elizabeth 190 n. 113
Cottington, Francis 232
Cotton, Sir Robert 69, 71, 72 n. 12, 88 n. 26 & n. 27, 90–1, 92 nn. 41 and 44, 95, 96, 97, 105, 106, 133–4 n. 50, 211–68 *passim*, 269, 271, 277
Cowley, Abraham 150 n. 11, 159, 161, 165, 175, 283 n. 14
Cowper, Dame Sarah 30 n. 90
Crane, Ralph 58
Crew, Randolph 88 n. 26
Crispe, Henry and William 255
Croke, John 219, 268
Cromwell, Oliver 96
Cromwell, Thomas 242, 247
Crooke, John 155, 156, 159, 178 n. 69
Crown Jewels 187
Cuffe, Henry 213, 223, 240, 247, 252, 270
Culpeper, Sir John 250
Cumming family 253
Curll, Edmund 30
Cusacke, Thomas 234

Daniel, Samuel 69, 239, 257, 264
Davies, Sir John 214, 223, 225, 239, 245, 258
Davies, Moll 187
Davison, Christopher 92
Davison, Francis 91, 92, 258
Davison, William 4, 89, 91, 225, 244
Dekker, Thomas 192–3
Denham, Mr 88 n. 26
Denham, Sir John 104, 180, 186, 190, 242
Denny, Edward, Lord 231
Derby, James Stanley, tenth Earl of 21, 25

Derby, William Stanley, ninth Earl of 21, 24–5, 28–9
Dering, Sir Edward, first Baronet 250
Dering, Sir Edward, second Baronet 156, 159, 161, 163 n. 45, 178 n. 69
Devonshire, Charles Blount, Lord Mountjoy and Earl of 227, 230, 231, 248, 264, 272
D'Ewes, Sir Simonds 88, 89 n. 29, 227, 234, 235, 236, 237, 238, 239, 243
Dido, Queen 198 n. 13
Digby, Sir Kenelm 218
Dixon, Robert 208–10
Dodderidge, Sir John 106, 221, 223, 226, 271
Dohna, Count von 184
Doncaster, James Hay, first Viscount 37
Donne, Sir Daniel 250
Donne, John 6, 92, 103–4, 257; *Biathanatos* 31–57; *Pseudo-Martyr* 31, 48, 52
Donne, John, the Younger 34–5, 49, 52–4
Donne, Lucy 57
Dorchester, Sir Dudley Carleton, Viscount 90 n. 32
Dorset, Charles Sackville, sixth Earl of 25
Dorset, Sir Edward Sackville, fourth Earl of 230, 232
Dorset, Richard Sackville, third Earl of 72 n. 14
Dorset, Thomas Sackville, Lord Buckhurst and first Earl of 230
Douce, Francis 275
Douglas, Sir Archibald 230
Drury, Mr 88 n. 26
Dryden, John 8 n. 36, 20 n. 75, 149 n. 10, 165, 168 n. 56, 180, 188 n. 112
Dugdale, Sir William 96, 98, 232, 239, 254–5
Dunbar, Sir George Home, Earl of 231
Duncan-Jones, Katherine 109–46 *passim*
Duncombe, William 89
Dunton, John 30
Durning-Lawrence, Sir Edwin 250
Dyer, Sir James 220, 266
Dyson, Humphrey 69 n. 11, 72 n. 12, 90, 91 n. 39, 134 n. 50, 211, 250, 261

Earles, John 74, 106, 207 n. 29
Edmondes, Sir Clement 217, 253, 267
Edward I 219
Edward IV 227, 265
Edward VI 92 n. 41
Eglisham, George 216, 222, 273
Eleanor of Aquitaine, Queen 167 n. 53
Eliot, Sir John 237
Elizabeth I 4, 89, 90 n. 35, 91 n. 38, 92 n. 41, 106, 109–46 *passim*, 213–14, 222, 223, 224, 225, 228, 229, 230, 231, 233, 238, 239, 240, 241, 243, 244, 245, 246, 247, 248, 249, 251, 253, 255, 257, 258, 259, 265, 266, 267, 269, 270, 271, 274–80

Elizabeth, Queen of Bohemia 95, 211–12, 229, 241, 265
Ellesmere, Sir Thomas Egerton, Baron 90, 214, 219, 220, 235, 241, 243–4, 247, 252, 253, 265, 268, 269
Elsynge, Henry 221, 272
Ernest de Vasseur, Archduke 213, 267, 270
Essex, Robert Devereux, second Earl of 69, 106, 212, 215, 216, 222, 225, 240, 243–4, 247, 248, 252, 266, 270
Essex, Robert Devereux, third Earl of 225, 234, 247, 250, 273
Etherege, Sir George 149 n. 10
Evelyn, John 13, 96, 165, 184, 187, 191, 231
Evelyn, Mary 153–4, 190

Fairfax, Lord 214
Faithorne, William 175–6
Falkland, Henry Cary, first Viscount 256
Falkland, Lucius Cary, second Viscount 256
Fanshawe, Thomas 254, 267
Farnaby, Thomas 260
Feathery Scribe 58–108, 111, 132–46, 211–68, 269–73, 274, 277, 278, 279, 280
Felltham, Owen 244, 247, 260
Felton, Thomas 184
Ferdinand II, Emperor 264
Finch family 279
Finch, Sir John 216, 250
Finch-Hatton family 95, 254
Fisher, John, Bishop of Rochester 67, 70, 259
Fitzgarrett, Sir John 248
Fleetwood, William (Recorder of London) 223, 226, 233, 262, 265
Fleetwood, William 222, 272
Fleming, John F. 227
Fletcher, John 178
Fletcher, Lady ('Parthenia') 148, 150, 281
Flood, Sir Robert 3 n. 8, 71 n. 12
Folger, Henry Clay 265, 267, 278
Frederick V 212, 228, 229, 241, 264, 272
Frere, Daniel 15

Gardner, Dame Helen 32
Gell family 174, 178 n. 68
George I 96, 216
Gibbons, Grinling 165
Glanville, Sir John 235
Gloucester, Thomas of Woodstock, Duke of 259
Godolphin, William 148 n. 6
Goodwin, Sir Francis 247, 270
Goodyer, Sir Henry 34, 55, 57
Gordon family 95, 253
Gowrie, William Ruthven, first Earl 235
Greer, Germaine 162–5
Gregory XV, Pope 228, 241
Greville, Sir Fulke 246

Grey, Lady Katherine 269
Griffin, Edward 184, 188
Grimston, Harbottle 250
Grinsell, Thomas 72, 260
Grismond, John 161 n. 39
Grosvenor, Richard 40 n. 25, 252
Grosvenor, Sir Richard 94, 211, 218, 251, 252
Guilford, Francis North, first Earl of 278
Gwyn, Nell 182 n. 81, 190

Habermas, Jürgen 154
Hageman, Elizabeth 155, 281 n. 2
Hales, John 269
Hamilton, James 184, 188
Hamond, John 276
Hampden, John 215–16, 218
Hardinge, George 232–3
Hargrave, Francis 232
Harington, John 122–3, 125, 276
Harington, Sir John 122, 257, 276, 283 n. 14
Harley, Sir Robert, Earl of Oxford 88, 235, 240,
    241, 242, 244, 245
Hart, Charles 182 n. 81
Harvey, Mary, Lady Dering 159
Harvy, Sebastian 88 n. 26
Hatton, Sir Christopher 110
Hatton, Christopher, first Baron 96
Haydon, Sir William 241
Hayman, Robert 198
Head, Richard 207
Hearne, Thomas 257
Heath, John 197–8
Heath, Sir Robert 234
Heneage family 215
Henri III 109
Henri IV 96, 134
Henrietta Maria, Queen 134, 139, 243
Henry II 238
Henry III 219
Henry VIII 67, 229, 238, 242, 247, 266, 270
Henry, Prince 215, 216–17, 218, 226, 228, 230,
    232, 243, 246, 252, 253, 254, 265, 269
Herbert of Cherbury, Edward, Lord 32–5, 37, 40
    n. 25, 54, 55, 72 n. 12, 257
Herbert, William 275
Herringman, Henry 155, 156, 172–9, 180
Hertford, Edward Seymour, first Earl of 269
Hertford, William Seymour, second Earl of 237
Heusler, Nicolas 277
Hillel, Rabbi 45–6
Hobart, Sir Henry 236
Hodgson, Eleazor 92
Hoe, Robert 178 n. 68
Holborne, Sir Robert 216
Hopkinson, John 275
Horn, Robert 275
Hoskins, Sir John 175 n. 65

Houghton, Arthur A. 227
Howard, Frances 250
Howard, Henry, Earl of Northampton *see*
    Northampton, Henry Howard, Earl of
Howard, Thomas 184
Howard, William 95, 256
Howson, John, Bishop of Oxford 92
Hubert, Sir Francis 90 n. 34
Hudson, Christopher 245
Hudson, William 245
Hyde, Edward, Earl of Clarendon *see* Clarendon,
    Earl of

Iarbus, King 198 n. 13
Inglis, Esther 14 n. 65
Inglis, Sir Robert Harry 55–6
Inijosa, Marquis St Germain 212, 240
Ireland, William Henry 62–3

Jackson, John 255, 257
Jahangir, Emperor 224, 248
James I 3 n. 8, 92 n. 41, 105, 107, 128, 211–12,
    213, 221, 223, 225, 227, 228, 230, 231, 232,
    234, 239, 240, 241, 242, 246, 247, 248, 250,
    252, 253, 256, 263, 264, 268, 270, 271,
    283 n. 14
James, Richard 231, 232
James, Thomas 92 n. 44
Jeffreys, George, first Baron 98–100
Jeffreys, John 162, 164
Jinner, Sarah 151, 153, 155, 177 n. 67
John, King 254
Johnson, Michael 21 n. 79
Jones, J. 151, 282 n. 2
Jonson, Ben 9, 18 n. 70, 92, 104, 165, 175, 178,
    229, 257
Jordan, Thomas 202
Joseph, Joseph 211
Julian, Robert 20–30

Katherine of Arragon, Queen 259
Kildare, Gerald Fitzgerald, eleventh Earl of 248
Killigrew, Henry 231
Killigrew, Thomas 178, 224
King, Henry 99, 101, 104, 257
King, Oliver, Bishop of Bath and Wells 169 n. 58
Knollys, Lettice 110
Knox, John 215
Kytson, Lady Elizabeth 69 n. 12

Lacy, John 88 n. 26
Lacy, John (actor) 190
Lake, Sir Thomas 90 n. 32
Lambarde, William 15–18, 105, 219, 220–1, 267
Lancaster, Thomas of *see* Clarence, Thomas,
    Duke of
Langley, Thomas 130

Languet, Hubert 110, 111 n. 12, 119 n. 21
Lansdowne, William Petty, first Marquess of 245
Latham, Agnes 229
Laud, William, Archbishop 134
Lawes, Henry 155–7, 159, 182 n. 83
Lee, Dr John 227
Leicester, Robert Dudley, Earl of 64 n. 4,
    91 n. 39, 109–11, 113–14, 116, 118, 131, 132,
    231, 238, 273
Lely, Sir Peter 180–2
Le Neve, Peter 96, 240
Lennox, Ludovick Stuart, second Duke of
    92 n. 41
Lennox, Matthew Stewart, Earl of 239
Lenton, Francis 199
Leo X, Pope 262
Lerma, Francisco Gómez de Sandoval y Rojas,
    Duque de 231
L'Estrange, Roger 172 n. 61
Lethington, William Maitland, Laird of 213, 240,
    247, 270
Leycester, Sir Peter 278
Lindenbaum, Peter 163
Littleton, Sir Edward 66, 216, 218, 237
Littleton, Sir Thomas 199 n. 14, 200 n. 16
Louis XIII 243
Lucian 175 n. 65
Lumley, John, Lord 239
Luttrell, Narcissus 274
Lycambes 150–1, 284
Lyly, John 11 n. 61, 244

Magalotti, Lorenzo 175, 184 n. 92
Manley, Delarivière 147, 150, 165
Manwaring, Roger, Bishop of St Davids 238
Marriott, Richard 161–5, 172 n. 61
Marten, Sir Henry 105, 235
Mary I 92 n. 41, 214, 229, 240, 247, 270, 272
Mary II 30 n. 90
Mary Queen of Scots 4, 68, 89, 92 n. 41, 213,
    215, 230, 259, 262, 270, 276, 278, 280
Mason, Robert 93, 235
Matthias, Emperor 239
Maynard, Sir John 243
Maxwell, Anne 177 n. 66
Meautys, Thomas 92
Médicis, Catherine de 134
Médicis, Marie de 134
Medowes, James 88 n. 26
Middleton, Charles, second Earl of 149 n. 10
Middleton, Sir Thomas 239
Mildmay, Sir Walter 91 n. 38
Mille, William 261
Milton, John 11 n. 61, 163, 182 n. 83
Minerva 176–7, 181–2, 185, 191
Monmouth, Anne, Duchess of 180, 182, 185,
    186, 188

Monmouth, James Scott, Duke of 180, 182, 184,
    185
Monson, Sir Thomas 223, 226, 233, 251
Montagu, Sir Henry 235
Montagu, Sir William 168, 281 n. 3
Montgomery, John 69, 252
Moore, John, Bishop of Ely 96, 215, 216, 218
Mordaunt, Carey Frazier, Viscountess 30 n. 90
Morgan, Thomas 254
Morgan, Sir William 248
Morocco, King of 233
Morris, Revd. John 55–7
Morton, Sir Albertus 90 n. 32
Morton, Thomas 34 n. 13
Moseley, Humphrey 155–6, 172–3, 178
Mosley, Francis 88 n. 26
Mosley, Sir Nicholas 88 n. 26
Mostyn family 40 n. 25, 95, 250, 252, 279, 280
Moulin, Peter du 185
Munck, Levinius 232
Murray, John 256

Nashe, Thomas 11
Naunton, Sir Robert 90 n. 32, 222, 245
Nevinson, Thomas 232
Newcastle, Margaret Cavendish, Duchess of 151,
    153–4, 165–7, 176–7, 178 n. 68, 181, 182
Newcastle, William Cavendish, Duke of 3 n. 8,
    34, 154, 165–7
Newcomb, Revd. Thomas 151, 175 n. 64
New England 246
Noel, Nathaniel 244
Noell, Stephen 261
Norris, Francis, Earl of Berkshire 240, 247, 252,
    271
Northampton, Henry Howard, Earl of 64, 91 n. 38,
    95 n. 50, 111 n. 11, 121 n. 24, 212, 213, 215,
    222, 228, 229, 230, 231, 232, 239, 241, 247,
    250, 253, 257, 258, 263, 276
Northumberland, Henry Percy, ninth Earl of
    18 n. 70, 214, 218, 226, 228, 233, 261
Northumberland, Thomas Percy, seventh Earl of
    224
Nottingham, Charles Howard, first Earl of 230,
    264

O'Brien, Charles 182, 188
Ogden, Charles Kay 249, 250, 279
Ogilby, John 160
Olivares, Gaspar de Guzmán, El Conde-Duque de
    228
Ong, Walter 15
Ormonde, James Butler, Duke of 160, 169 n. 58,
    180 n. 76
Ormonde, Thomas Butler, Earl of 248
O'Reilly, Sir Hugh 248
O'Rourke, Sir Brian-Na-Murtha 236

Orrery, Roger Boyle, Earl of 159–61, 163 n. 45, 175, 178 n. 68
Osborne, Dorothy 151, 156 n. 32, 190, 281 n. 4
Overbury, Sir Thomas 196–7, 250
Owen, Anne, Viscountess Dungannon ('Lucasia') 169 n. 59, 282–4 n. 2 & n. 16
Oxenbridge, Sir Robert 94–5, 255, 257
Oxford, Henry de Vere, eighteenth Earl of 232
Oxford, Sir Robert Harley, Earl of *see* Harley, Sir Robert

Page, William 110
Parker (Macclesfield) family 95, 268
Parkhurst, William 279
Parry, Sir Thomas 247, 270
Parry, William 224, 235
Paul IV, Pope 261
Paulet, Sir Amias 230, 239–40
Pelham, Sir William 248
Pembroke, Henry Herbert, Earl of 109–10, 131 n. 45
Pembroke, William Herbert, Earl of 37, 257
Pepys, Samuel 21, 25, 172 n. 61, 182 nn. 80 and 82, 184, 187, 188 n. 107
Perrot, Sir John 235
Perrott, Thomas 255
Persons, Robert 250, 254
Petty family 95, 245
Petyt, William 96, 249
Pharisees 7, 45, 200, 206
Philip III 232
Philip IV 228
Philips, James ('Antenor') 163 n. 45, 282 n. 2, 283 n. 14
Philips, Katherine 147–91, 281, 282–4
Playford, John 155–6
Pope, Sir Thomas 213, 229, 240, 266
Popham, Sir John 71 n. 12
Portland, Sir Richard Weston, first Earl of 229, 272
Powell, Vavasor 282–4 nn. 2 and 16
Powle, Henry 278
Powys, Thomas 219
Poynter, Winifred 88 n. 26
Prada, Secretary 231
Prior, Matthew 165
Procter, Sir Stephen 262
Prynne, William 90 n. 32
Puckering, Sir John 219
Puttenham, George 68, 259, 262, 276, 278, 280
Pym, John 105, 238, 250, 256, 262

Ralegh, Lady 212, 230, 263, 264
Ralegh, Sir Walter 4–5, 18 n. 70, 82 n. 22, 90 n. 32, 105, 212, 214, 215, 216, 218, 223, 225, 227, 228, 229, 230, 232, 240, 246, 257, 259, 260, 262, 263, 264, 265, 271

Ravenscroft, Thomas 193
Rawlinson, Richard 255, 256, 257
Reve, Gabriel 261
Rich, Penelope 231, 272
Richard II 259
Robothom, Hugh 238
Rochester, John Wilmot, Earl of 21, 184
Rochester, Viscount *see* Somerset, Robert Carr, Earl of
Roe, Sir John 257
Rohan, Henri, Duc de 248
Roscommon, Wentworth Dillon, fourth Earl of 161, 175
Rudick, Michael 37–8, 46–7 n. 29, 51–2
Rudyerd, Sir Benjamin 251, 257

St Bartholomew's Day massacre 119 n. 21, 134
St Benet Sherehog 165
St Dunstan in the West 72, 104
St John, Oliver 216
Salisbury, Sir Robert Cecil, Earl of *see* Cecil, Sir Robert
Saltonstall, Wye 200–1
Sancroft, William, Archbishop 96, 257
Sanquhar, Robert Crichton, sixth Lord 263
Sappho 284 n. 18
Savile, Henry 148 n. 6, 184, 188
Saxey, Justice 234
Scarron, Paul 175 n. 65
Scriveners' Company *see* Company of Scriveners
Seile, Henry 16
Selden, John 89 n. 30, 90 n. 32, 96, 98–9, 105, 106 n. 65, 220, 223–4, 232, 234, 251, 253, 254, 260, 271, 272
Serarius, Nicolaus 45
Sextus Senensis 44, 45
Seymour, Sir Francis 251
Shakespeare, William 3–4, 40, 175, 178, 205 n. 24
Shapiro, I. A. 35
Shirley, James 242
Shrewsbury, Gilbert Talbot, seventh Earl of 239
Sidney, Sir Henry 113, 131 n. 45,
Sidney, Sir Philip 18 n. 70, 109–46, 149, 217, 222, 223, 224, 233, 240, 243, 245, 251, 261, 267, 271, 274–80
Sidney, Robert 113, 217, 224, 240, 271
Simier, Jean de 109, 110
Simpson, Evelyn M. 36
Smedley, W. T. 265
Smith, Thomas, Bishop of Carlisle 281 n. 2
Smith, Sir Thomas (Privy Counsellor) 227, 238, 258
Smith, Sir Thomas (Sheriff) 212, 213, 252–3, 266, 270
Somerset, Robert Carr, Earl of 212, 230, 233, 239, 246, 250, 257, 263

Somerton, John 30 n. 92
Sotheby family 279
Spelman, Sir Henry 107 n. 68
Spenser, Edmund 131 n. 45, 165
Stanesby, John *or* William 91 n. 38, 92
Stanhope, Sir John 215
Starkey, Elizabeth & James & Jane & John &
    Samuel & Thomas 88 n. 26
Starkey, Henry 88 n. 26
Starkey, Ralph 67 n. 6, 82 n. 22, 86–94, 104,
    133–5, 211–68 *passim*, 269–73, 277
Statham, William Thomas 40 n. 25
Steele, Robert 275
Stephens, John 193–5
Steward, Thomas 261
Stillingfleet, Edward, Bishop of Worcester 95–6,
    241, 242
Stow, John 67 n. 7, 238
Strange, Lord 5
Strangmant, James 88 n. 26
Stuart, Frances 190
Stubbs, John 110, 275, 276
Suckling, Sir John 227
Suffolk, Thomas Howard, first Earl of 230, 264
Sullivan, Ernest W. 35, 37, 44, 49, 52, 54
Sussex, Augustus Frederick, Duke of 178
Sussex, Thomas Radcliffe, third Earl of 109
Sweden, King of 213, 240, 266
Symcotts, George 72 n. 14

Tanner, Thomas, Bishop of St Asaph 96, 255, 257
Tate, Francis 106, 217, 220, 223, 253, 258, 267
Taylor, Jeremy 155 n. 29, 175 n. 65
Taylor, John 150–3, 282–4
Temple, Dame Margaret 72, 260
Temple, Sir William 180 n. 76
Tenison, Thomas, Archbishop 96, 249
Thomas, Valentine 213
Thyer, Robert 203
Thynne, Francis 88 n. 26
Tichborne, Sir Richard 95, 229, 247
Tichborne, Robert 72, 260
Toiras, Jean de St Bonnet, Seigneur de 247
Tonson, Jacob 163, 174 n. 63
Tourneur, Cyril 234, 250, 263
Towneley, Richard 276
Townshend, Hayward 216, 249, 255
Trefusis, Violet 178 n. 68
Trevor, Sir John 95, 98–100, 219
Trevor, Sir Thomas 216
Trithemius, Johannes 1–2, 5, 8, 15
Trumbull, William 215
Turner, John 263
Tyrrell, James ('Musidorus') 154 n. 19

Umfreville, Edward 228

Ussher, James, Archbishop 96, 225

Van Dorsten, Jan 109–46 *passim*
Vere, Sir Francis 18 n. 70, 214, 218, 226, 228,
    233, 261
Verney, Sir Greville 184
Verstegan, Richard 273
Vonnegut, Kurt 1–2, 5
Vyner, Sir Robert 187 n. 106

Waller, Edmund 151 n. 17
Wallop, Sir Henry 223, 244
Walpole, Horace, fourth Earl of Orford 228
Walsingham, Sir Francis 109, 111, 121, 132, 231,
    234, 238, 248
Walton, Izaak 72–4, 261
Wanley, Humfrey 80 n. 21, 235
Warcup, Lenthal 30 n. 92
Weldon, Sir Anthony 240, 248
Wells, Jeremiah 203–6, 207 n. 27
West, William 194 n. 5, 200 n. 17
Westminster, Duke of 251, 252
Westmorland, Charles Neville, sixth Earl of 224
Weston, Sir Richard *see* Portland, Earl of
Whitelocke, Sir James 258
William I 246, 249, 257, 264
Williams, E. 260, 267
Williams, John, Bishop of Lincoln 218, 229, 236,
    264, 266
Willoughby de Eresby, Robert Bertie, Lord 247,
    252, 271
Wilson, Matthew 276
Wilson, Dr Thomas 5
Wilson, Sir Thomas 40 n. 25, 89–90, 91 n. 40,
    106 n. 66
Wimbledon, Sir Edward Cecil, Viscount 216,
    225, 234, 239, 247, 273
Winstanley, Gerrard 3 n. 9
Winwood, Sir Ralph 230, 246
Witham, Jo. 260
Wolsey, Thomas, Cardinal 14 n. 65, 219
Wotton, Sir Henry 214, 255–6, 257, 279
Woudhuysen, Henry 128
Wright, John 90 n. 32
Württemberg, Duke of 214, 240, 266
Wycherley, William 149 n. 10
Wyn, William Watkins 214
Wynne, Owen 149 n. 10
Wyse, William 234

Yelverton, Sir Christopher 274
Yelverton, Sir Henry 229, 274, 276
York, Anne Hyde, Duchess of 164, 191
York, James, Duke of (James II) 184

Zouche, Edward, Lord 92